COMMON LAW LEGAL ENGLISH AND GRAMMAR

Lord Denning, an influential but controversial English judge, stated that 'Words are the lawyer's tools of trade'. This course book reflects that conviction as it focuses on words, the language of the law—legal terms, expressions and grammar—introduced systematically with relevant aspects of the law, and examined in context through analytical reading activities based on original legal texts selected for their interest and importance in different branches of the common law system. This book explores constitutional law, criminal law, tort and contract; yet includes international legal contexts, with a particular focus on human rights and European law.

The presentation of legal concepts and terminology in context in each chapter is graded so that the course progresses, building on the vocabulary and law encountered in earlier chapters. Each chapter, organised thematically, includes a series of activities—tasks—to complete, yet the book does not presuppose previous knowledge of legal English or of the common law: full answer keys and reflective commentary on both legal and linguistic aspects are given, and sections marked 'Advanced' offer especially challenging materials. Consolidation sections are designed to test students' global comprehension of the legal texts analysed, including precise usage of legal vocabulary in context, with solutions.

Common Law Legal English and Grammar is addressed to the non-native speaker of English, and in particular to intermediate to advanced students who are studying law, or academics with a professional interest in Anglo-American law. Practising lawyers will also find that the book offers valuable analysis of the language of legal documents.

Common Law
Legal English and Grammar

A Contextual Approach

Alison Riley
and
Patricia Sours

·HART·
PUBLISHING
OXFORD AND PORTLAND, OREGON
2014

Published in the United Kingdom by Hart Publishing Ltd
16C Worcester Place, Oxford, OX1 2JW
Telephone: +44 (0)1865 517530
Fax: +44 (0)1865 510710
E-mail: mail@hartpub.co.uk
Website: http://www.hartpub.co.uk

Published in North America (US and Canada) by
Hart Publishing
c/o International Specialized Book Services
920 NE 58th Avenue, Suite 300
Portland, OR 97213-3786
USA
Tel: +1 503 287 3093 or toll-free: (1) 800 944 6190
Fax: +1 503 280 8832
E-mail: orders@isbs.com
Website: http://www.isbs.com

Hart Publishing is an imprint of Bloomsbury Publishing plc.

British Library Cataloguing in Publication Data
Data Available

ISBN: 978-1-84946-576-2

Typeset by Compuscript Ltd, Shannon
Printed and bound in Great Britain by
CPI Group (UK) Ltd, Croydon CR0 4YY

To Catherine and Ken, Giovanni and Sara

Preface

This book aims to provide law students, legal academics and lawyers from overseas with a key to the English-speaking common law world. Designed as a university textbook in legal English, suitable for courses from intermediate to advanced level, you may also use this book to create a personal learning pathway in self-study mode, or for reading and consultation as a specialist linguistic and legal resource.

The essence of our approach in writing *Common Law Legal English and Grammar* has been to contextualise the study of legal English in a wide range of authentic legal contexts, enabling us to introduce, alongside the language of the law, branches of law such as tort, contract, constitutional and criminal law viewed from within the common law legal tradition, while also focusing on the international dimension where English is a major language of the law, from the United Nations to the Treaties of the European Union and a leading regional human rights system in the world such as the European Convention on Human Rights.

Naturally, in a work of this kind, we do not aim to provide complete coverage of one or other branches of the law but rather to introduce in tandem elements of the law with a structured course that emphasises the language of the law, including its linguistic and typographical features. Each Part of the book features three interacting elements: (i) Language and Law (A Riley), (ii) Legal Grammar and (iii) Consolidation (P Sours), where emphasis is on terminology—or rather the wider *vocabulary of the law*—which continues to be the essence of our approach, so that our readers will progressively build and consolidate their skills and knowledge as they move from chapter to chapter. By reading original legal texts selected for their interest and significance from the legal systems covered, consulting official websites, interacting and completing a wide range of language and legal *tasks*, continuous opportunities for consolidation and personalisation are given. Full keys to tasks and comment within the text support both teachers and students. Challenging new elements of law and language are gradually introduced at various levels of difficulty, with each of the six Parts based on a broad legal theme.

This book is based on our extensive experience teaching and designing courses for mixed-level classes with different areas of specialisation, at undergraduate and postgraduate level, in law faculties in Italy.[1] The success of our approach lies in the strong motivation for civil lawyers or others from a different legal tradition of

---

[1] A previous, Italian publication that provided the starting-point for this new, completely revised and expanded international edition, is available only in Italy, with Italian translations: *Legal English and the Common Law* by A Riley; *With Legal Grammar Handbook* by P Sours, Padua: Cedam, 2nd edn (2012).

learning not only to understand and use the English of the law, but also of gaining access to the texts, sources and legal methods of the common law.

We would like to thank our friend and mentor Peter Leyland for his encouragement and support in this project, literally from start to finish, including valuable criticism of the draft chapter on the UK Constitution: many thanks—all remaining inaccuracies are my own (AR). We are grateful to Richard Hart for embracing the novel idea of publishing a book that spans two fields, both law and language, not falling neatly into either one category or the other. Many thanks to Peter Wood of Withers LLP for permission to reproduce the commercial agreements used in this book. Alison would also like to thank Catherine and Elisabeth for their help in different ways. Lastly, warm and special thanks to friend and artist Putachad for creating the beautiful cover painting and, through sharing her interpretation, giving us a deeper insight into the meaning of the relation between law and language—the stuff of our work.

Alison Riley and Patricia Sours
November 2013

The author and publisher gratefully acknowledge the authors and publishers of extracted material which appears in this book, and in particular the following for permission to reprint extracts from the sources indicated:

Amnesty International: Amnesty International report: *Death Sentences and Executions* 2012 (2013) ACT/50/001/2013, London

BBC: 'Peers mount new bid to save hunts' and 'Pair guilty of hunting with dogs'

Crown Copyright for material from the following acts—Terrorism Act 2000; Scotland Act 1998; Hunting Act 2004; Theft Act 1968; Contracts (Rights of Third Parties) Act 1999; and Human Rights Act 1998. This material has been used under the Open Government Licence.

Crown Copyright for material from the following cases sourced from BAILII-*Apple Corps Ltd v Apple Computer Inc.*; *Donoghue v Stevenson*; *Douglas v Hello!*; *Letang v Cooper*; *Mainstream Properties Limited v Young*; *Miller v Jackson*; *Pepper v Hart*; *R v Hayter*; *R v Headteacher and Governors of Denbigh High School*; and *Samsung Electronics (UK) Limited v Apple Inc.* This parliamentary material is reproduced with the permission of the Controller of HMSO on behalf of Parliament

Crown Copyright: *Code for Crown Prosecutors*, 7th edn, January 2013

Council of Europe: European Convention on Human Rights

European Union: Directive 2002/58/EC of the European Parliament and of the Council of 12 July 2002 concerning the processing of personal data and the protection of privacy in the electronic communications sector; Treaty on the Functioning of the European Union consolidated version (Treaty of Rome) [2012] OJ C326/47 Arts 1-4; and Treaty on European Union consolidated version (Treaty of Maastricht) [2012] OJ C326/13 Consolidated Version of the Treaty on European Union [2010] OJ C83/01, Arts 1, 2 and 3(1), (2), (3)

House of Commons Library: Research Paper, 05/10 31 January 2005—*Criminal Law (Amendment) (Householder Protection) Bill*, Bill 20 of 2004–05. Parliamentary material is reproduced with the permission of the Controller of HMSO on behalf of Parliament

Little Brown Book Group/Nelson Rolihlahla Mandela: *Long Walk to Freedom*, London, 1994

Oxford University Press: Tom Bingham, *The Business of Judging. Selected Essays and Speeches 1985–1999*, Oxford, 2000; Ewan McKendrick, *Contract Law. Text, Cases, and Materials*, 5th edn, Oxford, 2012 and Steve Sheppard, *An Introduction to the Legal System of the United States*, 4th edn, Oxford, 2010

Peter Leyland: *The Constitution of the United Kingdom: A Contextual Analysis*, 2nd edn, Oxford, Hart Publishing, 2012

United Nations: Universal Declaration of Human Rights and the United Nations Security Council Resolution

Withers LLP: Agency Agreement; and Distribution Agreement

While every care has been taken to establish and acknowledge copyright, and to contact copyright owners, the publishers apologise for any accidental infringement and would be pleased to come to a suitable agreement with the rightful copyright owners in each case.

Table of Contents

Table of Cases

Table of Legislation and Other Legal Texts and Official Sources

Other Legal Texts and Official Sources

Part I

English in Legal Contexts in Common Law and International Perspectives

Chapter 1

LANGUAGE AND LAW

English Legal Contexts, Texts and Terminology

*English in legal contexts in international and national perspectives –
Vocabulary of the law – Introduction to English legal texts – English legal
texts in different legal contexts – Features of English legal
texts and language – Reflections on legal language*

To succeed in the profession of law, you must seek to cultivate command of
language. Words are the lawyer's tools of trade.

Lord Denning (1979), English judge and Master of the Rolls, 1899–1999

BEFORE WE BEGIN

Progressive, controversial, loved, criticised: Lord Denning was one of England's
most influential judges; as Master of the Rolls, he presided over the Civil Division
of the Court of Appeal in London during the twentieth century, and contributed
to the modernisation and development of the civil law in the United Kingdom,
reflecting the role of judges of the superior courts in *a common law legal system*. In
a common law system, *judicial precedent*—the law contained in decided cases—is
a *source* of law that must be followed, and judges have power to make law by
pronouncing new rules when deciding cases, if Parliament has not passed law on
the matter in dispute. This power is recognised as part of the *judicial function* in
a common law country.[1]

In his book *The Discipline of Law*,[2] quoted above, Lord Denning is addressing
young people as they prepare for a career in the law. He highlights the importance
of gaining great skill in the use of language. Words, not other implements, are the
lawyer's *tools of trade*. Is this emphasis on language and words applicable to your
legal system, too?

---

[1] See, e.g., EA Farnsworth (2010), *An Introduction to the Legal System of the United States*, 4th edn,
S Sheppard (ed), New York: Oxford University Press, pp 58–59, examined in 9.3.4 below, Task 6.
[2] A Denning (1979), *The Discipline of Law*, London: Butterworths.

When you first began to study law, even in your own language, what difficulties did you find in understanding university lectures and in using legal materials? Why was it hard to answer questions and express opinions?

Basic legal knowledge. The first challenge for a law student in any country of the world is to build a foundation of legal knowledge: the basics of the *legal system*; the role and powers of national and international *institutions*; the *sources* recognised by the courts as law (the *sources of law*); the *procedures* involved in resolving disputes and so on.

Technical language. As you gradually build this foundation of legal knowledge, you also familiarise yourself with the technical language of the law, by learning to understand and use *legal terminology*—a fundamental component of legal language and, indeed, of the law itself.

Conceptual thinking. It is essential to develop an ability to think in abstract concepts. *Legal concepts* are expressed in special ways; a concise definition may contain a complex set of rules, expressed in specialised terms. You need to recognise and adopt a lawyer's mode of thinking, basing your opinions on the knowledge and recognition of rules contained in valid sources, which you apply in a logical process to concrete cases, as you develop and present arguments using methods of *reasoning* accepted in your legal system.

As you study legal English, or indeed if you are studying law directly in the English language, you will confront similar difficulties. This book therefore aims to provide a foundation of legal knowledge, technical language and conceptual thinking typical of the common law world. We focus our attention on institutions, terminology and sources relevant in the English-speaking world and in international legal environments where English is used as a legal language. As you become familiar, in the chapters of this book, with aspects of English common law, or of international human rights law or of European Union law, by analysing and practising the specialised language of each legal order in context, you will gain competence and accuracy as your knowledge and awareness grow.

We sincerely hope that whatever your legal background, whether you are a first-year student or a university professor, you will find the process of studying *Common Law Legal English and Grammar* stimulating and rewarding.

1.1 Introduction to English in Legal Contexts in International and National Perspectives

All over the world today lawyers are using English in their professional lives. Courts and arbitrators in national and international legal contexts are pronouncing their decisions in English. International organisations such as the United Nations (UN) and Amnesty International, the leading non-governmental organisation in the field of human rights, are using English as a vital instrument to achieve their objectives.

In the corridors of the multilingual European Union (EU), English is frequently the language of communication, and it is one of the many languages of EU Treaties and other authentic legal texts. In international trade, English has become the *lingua franca* of modern times, permitting people and businesses around the world to interact successfully, frequently concluding contracts and resolving disputes in English even where their transaction has no link with an English-speaking country.

At international level, English is not the official language or the language of the law: no language has that status. But it is certainly a major language in legal contexts across the world today.

At national level, for historical and political reasons, many countries in different parts of the world have legal systems which operate in English. Frequently (but not always) such systems belong to *the common law family*. The common law is the body of legal rules established in decided cases (known as *precedents*), created and developed by the English superior courts over many centuries; a common law legal system is one based on this body of law. Members of the common law family share their origins with English law, with its principles, language and concepts; their common language—English—is a strong unifying factor.[3] Members of the common law family belong in all the continents of the world today, and most of these countries became fully independent from Britain long ago.[4] Even so, family unity in the common law world remains strong, as the following analysis from the perspective of civil lawyers (a *civil law system* is one based on Roman law) shows:

> [T]he whole law of these [common law] countries—not just the substantive law, but also the law of procedure, the courts system, the structure of legal professions, the whole style of legal thought and debate—is still strongly influenced by the legal ideas, institutions and methods of the Common Law.[5]

Legal systems operating in the English language may belong to an English-speaking country, such as the UK, the USA and Australia. In many countries, English is one of two or more official languages. For example, in Canada both English and French are official languages, enjoying 'equality of status and equal rights and privileges as to their use in all institutions of the Parliament and government of Canada'.[6]

---

[3] Despite George Bernard Shaw's famous view of England and America as 'two countries divided by a common language', attributed to Shaw, but not found in his published writings.

[4] At the time of British colonial expansion the common law was imported to North America, India, Australia, New Zealand, and many countries of Africa and south-east Asia. To view a map showing the distribution of different legal families in the world, consult Wikimedia Commons on the Internet.

[5] K Zweigert and H Kötz (1998), *An Introduction to Comparative Law*, 3rd edn (tr T Weir), Oxford: Clarendon Press, p 219.

[6] Canadian Charter of Rights and Freedoms (Part I of the Constitution Act 1982), s 16(1).

Not all countries where English is used as a legal language have common law legal systems. For example, in South Africa, which has a predominantly civil law system (based on Roman-Dutch law), the text of the Constitution was signed by Nelson Mandela on 16 December 1996, marking a new democratic era of equality after the long fight against the injustice and discrimination of the apartheid regime. English is just one of the 11 official languages, and the South African Constitution provides that all of these languages 'must enjoy parity of esteem and be treated equitably'[7] and may be used by the national government and provincial governments.[8]

The United Kingdom (UK) is a State composed of four countries, with three distinct legal systems: the English legal system (operating in England and Wales), the Northern Irish legal system and the Scottish legal system, a mixed system based partly on common law and partly on civil law, with canon law influences, too.[9] For this reason it is correct to distinguish clearly in legal language between the adjectives *English* and *British* in the UK context: we use *British* or *UK* when referring to the Constitution of the UK or to legislation, etc with national impact (e.g. the British/UK Government); we use *English* to refer to all aspects of the legal system operating in England and Wales (e.g. the English courts).

This chapter introduces you to the study of English legal language in international and national contexts, focusing on two essential aspects: terminology and texts.

We begin with ideas for building up a good legal vocabulary. A strong vocabulary focus is essential for you to understand legal English and express yourself in appropriate language. Effective dictionary use, the importance of context and your own personal terminology system are introduced (see 1.2).

This chapter also aims to present a panorama of legal text types found typically in the English language in various national and international contexts (at 1.3, 1.4), and to introduce you, as a foreign user of the language, to an effective approach to using original legal texts in English. In later chapters we shall examine in detail specific text types dealing with various branches of the law (criminal law, contract, etc). In this chapter you are invited to choose one or more texts from our wide selection for detailed personal study, according to your interest. In 1.5 below we consider the features and functions of legal texts, and investigate further the significant role of language in the law.

Lastly, we reflect on the peculiarities of legal language (see 1.6). Are legal texts really so hard to understand? Is their complexity justified, or does it simply preserve the legal profession's 'monopoly of explanation', as Kenny Hegland provocatively states: 'No doubt the social and economic position of lawyers is enhanced by

---

[7] Constitution of South Africa, Chapter 1, s 6(4).
[8] *Ibid*, s 6(3).
[9] For *Scots law*, see D Walker (1980), *The Oxford Companion to Law*, Oxford: Clarendon Press, p 1108 ff.

a system of complicated law.'[10] And on the subject of legal writing: 'Legal writing, it has been said, suffers from [only] two defects: style and content'.[11]

You are invited to consider and compare legal language in your system: does it also suffer from the same 'defects'?

1.2 The Vocabulary of the Law

1.2.1 Introduction to Terminology and Other Legal Vocabulary

Terminology is central to a course in legal English. Indeed, terminology is a fundamental component of the law itself.[12]

Law terms may be single words (like *courts, arbitrator, treaty*) or multi-word units (like *common law, equal rights, EU Treaties*) having specialised or technical meanings in the law. All examples are taken from 1.1 above. We can investigate the meaning of law terms using general dictionaries or, better, specialised law dictionaries or glossaries, discussed below.

Technical terminology is only part of the *vocabulary of the law*: in this chapter we have adopted this wider phrase to include not only strictly technical terms, but also the many other words, phrases and modes of expression that are typically found in legal discourse and may have special meanings or uses in legal contexts that are not found in general English. In addition to nouns (such as *dispute, constitution, privilege*), it is important to focus our attention on verbs, adjectives, adverbs and adverbial phrases (such as *conclude, equal, equitably, according to*). To research the vocabulary of the law, you will need to use a variety of reference works, introduced in 1.2.2 below.

Many activities (*Tasks*) in this book are designed to encourage you to improve and expand your knowledge of the vocabulary of the law as well as your lexical and linguistic skills. In this chapter we focus on discovering meaning and use with the support of appropriate dictionaries and resources (1.2.2); on examining legal vocabulary in use in a variety of original legal contexts (1.2.3, 1.2.4); and on creating your personal terminology system (1.2.5)—an effective method to build an individual collection of vocabulary of the law, thereby increasing your knowledge and ability to use legal language effectively.

---

[10] K Hegland (1983), *Introduction to the Study and Practice of Law*, St Paul, Minn: West Publishing Co, p 128.

[11] *Ibid*, p 122.

[12] This idea is explored fully in A Riley (1996) 30 *The Law Teacher* 68, 'The Meaning of Words in English Legal Texts: Mastering the Vocabulary of the Law—A Legal Task'.

1.2.2 Discovering Meaning and Dictionary Use

For a valid approach to discovering the meaning (or *use*) of terminology in legal contexts, examine the illustration below, using the term *will*; it is considered here only as a *noun* (not as a *verb*).

Definition of *will* from a general English monolingual learner's dictionary

Which meaning(s) could be relevant in a legal context?

> **will**[3] /wɪl/ *noun* **1** [C,U] the power of the mind to choose what to do; a feeling of strong determination: *Both her children have got very strong wills. . . .* **2** [sing] what sb wants to happen in a particular situation: *My mother doesn't want to sell the house and I don't want to go against her will.* **3** [C] a legal document in which you write down who should have your money and property after your death: *You really ought to make a will.* **4** –willed [in compounds] having the type of will mentioned: *a strong-willed/ weak-willed person.*[13]

Comment on a general English monolingual learner's dictionary

The *Oxford Wordpower Dictionary* is one example of an excellent monolingual learner's dictionary of English for intermediate to upper-intermediate learners of the language. The third meaning of *will* shown in the extract above is specifically legal—what is this type of document called in your language? The second meaning could also be relevant, e.g. the will of the parties to a contract.

In definition 3, we note one peculiarity for a lawyer: the reference to 'money and property'. Legally, these are not two distinct categories; in fact, money is simply one form of property, belonging in the class of *personal property* or *goods* (*moveable property*), as opposed to *real property* or *land* (*immoveable property*, including buildings, trees, lakes, etc).

The definitions of legal vocabulary in a good general English monolingual dictionary are simple and generally correct. They provide helpful grammatical information and examples so that we can observe correct *patterns* (structures) for using the word in complete sentences. We can also learn *collocations* (word partners that are typically found together), such as the verb + noun form in 3: *to make a will*. Phonetic script: /wɪl/ and the accompanying CD-Rom or online resources can teach you the correct pronunciation.

Using a dictionary, you could copy important information into your vocabulary notebook, as in the example below:

will [noun, Countable] pron: /wɪl/
Definition: A will is a legal document in which you write down who should have your

---

[13] *Oxford Wordpower Dictionary*, 4th edn (2012), Oxford: Oxford University Press, p 824.

money and property after your death. (Oxford Wordpower Dictionary)
*Example: You really ought to **make a will***
Collocation: to make a will
Translation (your language):..........................

These dictionaries contain all classes of words (verbs, adjectives, adverbs, etc), not just nouns. Depending on your language level, you could select an advanced level dictionary.[14]

Be aware that general dictionaries have some weak points for legal vocabulary research: they only contain commonly used words, so many law terms will not be found; you may find a common word, such as *land*, only in its general meaning (the solid part of the surface of the earth) but not in its legal meaning (the class of immoveable/real property); for complex terms, definitions may be too simple and therefore not entirely accurate. Often the wording of a legal term in a general dictionary is 'diluted', thus aiding comprehension but limiting the use of related words in a legal context.

In conclusion, we recommend that you use a general monolingual learner's dictionary of English for valuable support with vocabulary, collocations and grammar patterns. These reference works provide useful linguistic information and a good starting-point for more specific research using specialist dictionaries or resources.

Definition of will from a good specialised law dictionary

Compare this definition with the general dictionary definition above—what have you discovered?

> **will** *n.* A document by which a person (called the **testator**) appoints *executors to administer his estate after his death, and directs the manner in which it is to be distributed to the beneficiaries he specifies. To be valid, the will must comply with the formal requirements of the Wills Act 1837 (*see* EXECUTION OF WILL), the testator must have *testamentary capacity when the will is made, and he must make it of his own free wishes without any *undue influence. A will can be amended ...[15]

Comment on a specialised law dictionary

As the example shows, a good law dictionary is both a language resource and a legal resource. It explains a small aspect of the law and introduces related terminology (e.g. *the testator*) in the definition itself.

---

[14]   Such as the latest edition of *Macmillan English Dictionary for Advanced Learners*, available at <http://www.macmillandictionaries.com>; *Oxford Advanced Learner's Dictionary*, available at <http://www.oup.com/elt>; *Collins COBUILD Advanced Dictionary*, available at <http://www.cobuild.collins.co.uk>.
[15]   *A Dictionary of Law*, 7th edn (2009, updated reissue 2013), E Martin and J Law (eds), Oxford: Oxford University Press, p 590.

A *Dictionary of Law*, published by Oxford University Press, from which the extract above is taken, is an excellent example of a valid resource for legal terminology work. Only part of the full definition is reproduced here, since the dictionary provides more legal particulars about a valid will. The terms marked in **bold** or with an asterisk (*) are also defined in this dictionary. For the language of the law from the American perspective, the authoritative *Black's Law Dictionary*[16] is highly recommended.

One limit is that law dictionaries tend to focus mainly, or entirely, on nouns and noun forms, giving little or no attention to other parts of speech, such as verbs or adjectives. Another aspect is that it is more complicated to understand a specialised law dictionary than a general English dictionary.[17]

However, it is essential to use specialised works of reference for in-depth terminology work. Different law dictionaries have differing levels of technicality and difficulty, so search for one that is appropriate for you.

Task 1 Vocabulary in the law—meanings of words and dictionary use
— Examine the terms in the box below. Which words are familiar?
— Identify the nouns, verbs, adjectives. Do you know their legal meanings?
— Make a note of the words you know, writing a simple definition or a translation into your own language.
— Ask your teacher, or use dictionary resources such as a CD-Rom or website links for help with pronunciation.
— Use the dictionaries you have available to investigate legal meanings and discover unknown terms. Note down relevant definitions or other interesting information that you find.
— Discuss your work with other students. Which of these words can you link together in groups?

VOCABULARY OF THE LAW

party	rights	law	justice
guarantee	trust	freedom	liberty
be subjected to		be entitled to	presumed innocent
hearing	charge	offence	tribunal
guilty	trial	try will	determination

---

[16] *Black's Law Dictionary* by Henry Campbell Black, now in its 9th edn (2009), B Garner (ed), also available in a shorter, abridged edition, St Paul, Minn: West Publishing Co.
[17] Legal dictionaries are also available online with words that are embedded: clicking on the underlined word in the definition brings you to that word's meaning.

Comment

Did you know, or did you discover, the legal meanings of all 20 terms in Task 1? Many words in the vocabulary of the law are already part of our *general English* vocabulary. But in legal English they may have more specific, technical meanings, or even completely different meanings. We should always be aware of this possibility as we try to interpret a legal text.

Example: it's fun to go to a party! *But in legal language,* party *is a key noun with many uses, as explained in the Glossary of law terms at the end of this book—see below.*

> **Party**, *n.* **parties**, *n.pl.* A party is one of the sides taking part in a legal transaction, such as a contract (*a contracting party*) or a treaty (*a High Contracting Party*); each of the sides involved in a legal dispute is *a party to the case*; a person or entity outside a certain transaction is *a third party*; in politics and government, *a political party* is an organised group representing specific interests and policies, and seeking election.

As *party* illustrates, the meaning, or better, *use* of vocabulary in the law must be understood in relation to a specific context, explored below.

Refer to the Glossary to check your work in Task 1.

1.2.3 Examining Legal Vocabulary in Context

It is essential to develop the habit of focusing attentively on the use of legal vocabulary in the different legal contexts you meet. It is more interesting and productive to examine terminology in real legal contexts: you will expand your vocabulary, and also your legal knowledge. For example, a famous *Will*:[18]

> In the name of God, Amen. I, William Shakspeare, of Stratford-upon-Avon in the county of Warwick, Gent., in perfect health and memory (God be praised,) do make and ordain this my last will and testament, in manner and form following; that is to say: ... I give and bequeath unto my daughter Judith one hundred and fifty pounds of lawful English money ... I give and bequeath to Hamlet [Hamnet] Sadler twenty-six shillings eightpence, to buy him a ring; ...[19]

Comment

By examining vocabulary in authentic contexts like this, we can learn more about its meaning and appropriate use. Most of the language in Shakespeare's will, above, is still used in these legal documents today. For example: the pair of verbs,

---

[18] He would no doubt forgive the pun (play on words).

[19] From the original will in the office of the Prerogative Court of Canterbury in *The Works of William Shakspeare*, pp xiv–xv, London: Frederick Warne & Co; the volume has no date but a handwritten dedication dated 1899. The surname is usually spelt 'Shakespeare'.

'*I give and bequeath*' (*to bequeath* means specifically *to give personal property by will*). Observe also the classic phrase '*my last will and testament*' and observe the specific grammar pattern: *I give and bequeath to someone* (Judith) *something* (money). '*In perfect health and memory*' refers to the testator's mental health and therefore *capacity* to make a will.

The Internet is a convenient way to find original legal documents of interest. You can enrich your legal vocabulary by examining the content and language of even a short paragraph of text, as illustrated above. Many examples of original legal texts are provided in this book.

1.2.4 Vocabulary in Context: the Universal Declaration of Human Rights

The Universal Declaration of Human Rights (UDHR) was adopted and proclaimed by the General Assembly of the United Nations (UN) on 10 December 1948.[20] Did you know that every year on this date people celebrate International Human Rights Day all over the world?

What is the United Nations? What do you know about the UDHR? Visit the UN website <www.un.org> to discover more, before completing Task 2.

Task 2 Vocabulary focus in context—the UDHR
Examine extracts from the UDHR, below:

— First, read for global understanding: observe the organisation of elements in the text; what is the overall meaning and purpose of each part (preamble, proclamation, articles)?
— Then, read intensively to discover the meaning of the text in detail. Use a dictionary as needed.
— Find and highlight some vocabulary studied in Task 1 in the rich context of the UDHR: focus on both language and meaning. By observing their use in context, what can you discover about the words and phrases you have highlighted?
— Consider what you have learnt about the Universal Declaration.
— Visit the website of the United Nations to read the full text, composed of just 30 Articles, at <http://www.un.org/en/documents/udhr/>

PREAMBLE

Whereas recognition of the inherent dignity and of the equal and inalienable rights of all members of the human family is the foundation of freedom, justice and peace in the world, ...

---

[20] Universal Declaration of Human Rights (UDHR), adopted 10 December 1948, UNGA Res 217 A(III).

Now, Therefore THE GENERAL ASSEMBLY proclaims THIS UNIVERSAL DECLARATION OF HUMAN RIGHTS as a common standard of achievement for all peoples and all nations ...

Article 1.
All human beings are born free and equal in dignity and rights. They are endowed with reason and conscience and should act towards one another in a spirit of brotherhood.

Article 2.
Everyone is entitled to all the rights and freedoms set forth in this Declaration, without distinction of any kind, such as race, colour, sex, language, religion, political or other opinion, national or social origin, property, birth or other status. ...

Article 3.
Everyone has the right to life, liberty and security of person.

Article 4.
No one shall be held in slavery or servitude; slavery and the slave trade shall be prohibited in all their forms.

Article 5.
No one shall be subjected to torture or to cruel, inhuman or degrading treatment or punishment.

...

Article 10.
Everyone is entitled in full equality to a fair and public hearing by an independent and impartial tribunal, in the determination of his rights and obligations and of any criminal charge against him.

Article 11.
(1) Everyone charged with a penal offence has the right to be presumed innocent until proved guilty according to law in a public trial at which he has had all the guarantees necessary for his defence.

© United Nations

Key and commentary to Task 2—UDHR and vocabulary in context

Idealistic and eloquent, the UDHR has greatly inspired and contributed to the development of the international human rights movement that began after the First World War. It is a declaration, not a treaty; therefore, it is not a *legally binding* instrument: it does not have direct *legal force*, yet possesses great moral force.

The text is composed of: a *preamble* (a series of points explaining the background and purposes of the Declaration); the *proclamation*

('Now, Therefore THE GENERAL ASSEMBLY proclaims THIS UNIVERSAL DECLARATION OF HUMAN RIGHTS …'); followed by the main body of the document, consisting of *articles, each declaring the different rights and freedoms* stated ('*set forth*') in the Declaration. Its composition and language are similar to that of an international treaty. Articles 1 and 2 (the prohibitions on discrimination) are general in scope, while later articles declare specific rights (such as *the right to life, the right to a fair hearing*) and freedoms (such as *freedom from slavery, freedom from torture*).

You can observe the use of many basic *law terms* in the UDHR (such as *rights, justice, tribunal, trial*). By focusing on lexis (vocabulary) in such a rich, original context, we can expand our knowledge of words and phrases and learn to express legal themes and arguments in precise and appropriate English.

Focusing on vocabulary in context is extremely useful at different levels. Below, we consider:

a) meaning and use;
b) collocation; and
c) grammar patterns.

Many activities in this book will encourage you to focus on vocabulary in context.

Meaning and use. As in the example *party*, above, legal vocabulary may have different meanings depending on the context in which a term is used.

Example: guarantee. In Article 11 UDHR, and more generally in the fields of human rights and criminal law, the noun *guarantee* indicates a form of legal protection of a right, a *safeguard*. In Article 11 a person *accused of a crime* ('Everyone *charged with a penal offence*') has the right to enjoy 'all the *guarantees* necessary for his defence', such as the right to be informed of the accusations against him and sufficient time to prepare his defence. By contrast, the noun *guarantee* is commonly known in a commercial context, where it indicates a manufacturer's promise to repair, replace or compensate for defective goods (a *warranty*); in addition, a *guarantee* (also spelt *guaranty*) is a secondary agreement in which one person (the *guarantor*) assumes legal responsibility (*liability*) for the debt of another person if that person (the principal *debtor*) fails to pay or honour his or her obligation.

When interpreting a text, be sure to consider the precise meaning of words in the specific context.

Collocation. The term *collocation* indicates the way words naturally occur together in text.[21] We may think of collocations as words that are typically used in combination with each other, forming natural 'partnerships'.

---

[21] M Lewis (2000), 'Language in the lexical approach' in M Lewis (ed), *Teaching Collocation. Further Developments in the Lexical Approach*, Hove: Language Teaching Publications, pp 126–54, at p 132.

Example: innocent and the opposite, guilty, are two key adjectives in legal English. Notice the collocations we find by focusing on the language of Article 11 UDHR:

Innocent: presumed innocent (verb + adj) but also, *presumed innocent until proved guilty, the right to be presumed innocent* and the longer phrase *Everyone has the right to be presumed innocent.*

Guilty: *proved guilty* (verb + adj) but also, *presumed innocent until proved guilty, proved guilty according to law* and the longer phrase *Everyone has the right to be presumed innocent until proved guilty according to law*, expressing a human right, one of the principles of a *fair trial.*

By focusing our attention on collocations in legal language, we move from the level of the single word to possible or typical combinations of words and even entire phrases. By using this approach, we become aware of the way words are actually used in natural text, so developing our lexical skills and expanding our vocabulary. It is therefore essential to observe collocations as you work on a text and to record them systematically in your personal terminology system (1.2.5 below). This approach to vocabulary in context will also help you to memorise words in 'chunks' and could improve your ability to recall and use lexis, as native speakers do, in ready-made chunks, improving your fluency.[22]

Below are some different kinds of collocation with examples of the key legal noun *right*, from the UDHR, above:

adjective + **noun**	*human rights*
verb + **noun**	*Everyone has the right*
verb + adj + **noun**	*Everyone is entitled to all the rights*
noun/**noun** + *and* + **noun**/noun	*dignity and rights, rights and freedoms, rights and obligations*
noun + prep + noun	*the right to life*
noun + prep + poss adj + **noun**	*the determination of his rights*
noun + verb + adj	*the right to be presumed innocent*

Can you find further examples, with vocabulary of your choice, in the text?

Grammar patterns. On the relationship between grammar and lexis, linguist Dave Willis said, 'I used to think these were quite separate, that grammar was about sentences and lexis was about words'.[23] Instead, Willis points out that recent research is showing a closer link between vocabulary and grammar, as, 'in making sentences, we may start with the grammar, but the final shape of a sentence is determined by the words which make up the sentence'.[24] By focusing

---

[22] M Lewis (2002), *The Lexical Approach. The State of ELT and a Way Forward*, Boston, Mass: Thomson Heinle, p 121.

[23] D Willis (2003), *Rules, Patterns and Words: Grammar and Lexis in English Language Teaching*, Cambridge: Cambridge University Press, p 28.

[24] *Ibid.*

on the use of vocabulary in context, we may observe 'word patterns', or 'the grammar of words'.

Example: entitled
Pattern—*to be entitled to sth (something) = to have the right to sth*
Full example: *Everyone is entitled to all the rights and freedoms set forth in this Declaration, without distinction of any kind …* (Article 2 UDHR)

You will also find it helpful to consult a general monolingual learner's dictionary of English for the grammar of words. Again, it is useful to note such structural patterns in your personal terminology system (1.2.5 below), so that you can more easily use these words in well-structured sentences.
What grammatical relationships or structural patterns did you notice as you observed legal vocabulary in the UDHR in Task 2?

1.2.5 Create Your Personal Terminology System

Begin a systematic approach to legal vocabulary by starting your own *personal terminology system*—this is your personal collection of technical *law terms* and other *vocabulary of the law*, to build and expand during this course and as you continue your independent legal studies or research.

Make a habit of including collocations and grammar patterns you meet as you examine legal vocabulary in context; always provide definitions and full examples from original texts. Consult dictionaries as needed. As lawyers in training, always cite the source of your examples and definitions. This authenticates them, and the associations from your reading may help you to make better use of this vocabulary later.

Build your collection in a large notebook, on loose A4 sheets inserted in a ring file or folder, using a box of index cards, or on your personal computer or tablet.

Now is the best time to start this ongoing project! Follow the indications below, then begin by selecting a number of terms from Tasks 1 and 2, above.

You may choose one or more of the organising principles below, or adopt an individual approach that works for you:

— vocabulary organised alphabetically in an A–Z index;
— vocabulary organised thematically according to topics and branches of law, e.g. human rights, contract, courts and institutions, people, etc;
— vocabulary organised grammatically, e.g. verbs, nouns, adjectives.

Consider what has worked for you in the past, discuss your ideas with other students, be prepared to experiment and adapt.

Checklist for Your Personal Terminology System

For each term, include:

— grammatical category (noun, verb, etc)
— a definition (or a translation into your language if quick and appropriate)
— an example in context (copy a complete, meaningful sentence or paragraph of text)
— grammatical patterns you observe in texts or dictionaries
— collocations you observe in texts or dictionaries
— a translation where appropriate
— any other information that interests you.

Example for Your Personal Terminology System

Term: **trial** (*noun*)

Definition: **A trial** is the process of examining and deciding a civil or criminal case before a court, the judicial examination of a case to determine all questions of law or fact. (Glossary, *Common Law Legal English and Grammar*)

Example: Everyone charged with a penal offence has the right to be presumed innocent until proved guilty according to law in a public **trial** at which he has had all the guarantees necessary for his defence. (Art 11 para 1 UDHR)

Grammatical patterns: to be on trial for sth. *He was on trial for murder*

Collocations: fair trial, a public trial, to hold a trial

Translation into your language: ....

Other information: also, *hearing*—a fair and public hearing (Art 10 UDHR)

related verb: to try *She was tried for murder*

NB: *leave space to add further examples, collocations etc as you continue in your studies of legal English. State your sources.*

1.3 Introduction to English Legal Texts

The following pages contain a selection of 10 texts from different world contexts, including the USA, Britain, the European Union and international law. Each text concerns a legal theme, but not every one is a *legal text*. You will find many different *text types*,[25] such as an international *treaty*, a *judgment* (the decision of a court in a case) and a poem.

---

[25] *Text type* is used in this book for *genre*, adopting linguist John Swales' definition: examples of the same *genre* will share communicative purposes recognised by expert members of the parent discourse

The purpose of the activities in this section is to stimulate reflection about the specific characteristics of legal texts and to introduce you to different types of English legal text found in various national and international contexts.

Task 3 Global reading—identifying legal texts

For this activity, spend only a few minutes examining each of the 10 texts set out below. For each one, just answer the following three questions. This is a global reading activity. Do not try to understand the texts in detail at this stage. Do not try to translate them (not an effective strategy with complex legal texts).

1. Is it a legal text?
2. Can you identify the specific context, e.g. English law, EU law?
3. What different text types can you identify, e.g. a law, a treaty?

NOTE: *Check your answers to Task 3 in the Key provided in 1.3.1 below.*

Task 4 Examining a text in detail

Select one of the 10 texts presented in Task 3 above, for detailed individual study. If you are working in a group, each member selects a different text.

— Read your chosen text again to understand its global meaning more clearly. Observe the format of the text: how are the contents organised and arranged?
— Read the text in detail, aiming to understand the main points and important particulars. What is the meaning and legal effect of the text? Focus on the language used to achieve this.
— Find law terms of interest in the text and select some terms to research, adding them, with an example in context, to your personal terminology system.
— Consult 1.3.2 below to complete your preparation.
— In groups, explain your text and comment on its language with other members.

community, constituting the rationale for the genre, shaping the schematic structure of the discourse, and influencing choice of style and content. Examples of the genre will show similarities in style, content, structure and intended audience. J Swales (1990), *Genre Analysis*, Cambridge: Cambridge University Press, p 58.

Text 1

Terrorism Act 2000
Chapter 11

An Act to make provision about terrorism; and to make temporary provision for Northern Ireland about the prosecution and punishment of certain offences, the preservation of peace and the maintenance of order.

[20th July 2000]

BE IT ENACTED by the Queen's most Excellent Majesty, by and with the advice and consent of the Lords Spiritual and Temporal, and Commons, in this present Parliament assembled, and by the authority of the same, as follows:—

PART I
INTRODUCTORY

Terrorism: interpretation.

1.—(1) In this Act "terrorism" means the use or threat of action where—

    (a) the action falls within subsection (2),

    (b) the use or threat is designed to influence the government or an international governmental organisation or to intimidate the public or a section of the public, and

    (c) the use or threat is made for the purpose of advancing a political, religious, racial or ideological cause.

(2) Action falls within this subsection if it—

    (a) involves serious violence against a person,

    (b) involves serious damage to property,

    (c) endangers a person's life, other than that of the person committing the action,

    (d) creates a serious risk to the health or safety of the public or a section of the public, or

    (e) is designed seriously to interfere with or seriously to disrupt an electronic system.

(3) The use or threat of action falling within subsection (2) which involves the use of firearms or explosives is terrorism whether or not subsection (1)(b) is satisfied.

(4) In this section—

    (a) "action" includes action outside the United Kingdom,

    (b) a reference to any person or to property is a reference to any person or to property, wherever situated,

(c) a reference to the public includes a reference to the public of a country other than the United Kingdom, and

(d) "the government" means the government of the United Kingdom, or a Part of the United Kingdom or of a country other than the United Kingdom.

(5) In this Act a reference to action taken for the purposes of terrorism includes a reference to action taken for the benefit of a proscribed organisation.

The Terrorism Act 2000 is reproduced under the terms of
© Crown Copyright Policy Guidance issued by HMSO.

TEXT 2

I know not whether Laws be right,
Or whether Laws be wrong;
All that we know who lie in gaol [jail]
Is that the wall is strong;
And that each day is like a year,
A year whose days are long.

But this I know, that every Law
That men have made for Man,
Since first Man took his brother's life,
And the sad world began,
But straws the wheat and saves the chaff
With a most evil fan.

This too I know—and wise it were
If each could know the same—
That every prison that men build
Is built with bricks of shame,
And bound with bars lest Christ should see
How men their brothers maim.

With bars they blur the gracious moon,
And blind the goodly sun:
And they do well to hide their Hell,
For in it things are done
That Son of God nor son of Man
Ever should look upon!

TEXT 3

The GOVERNMENTS SIGNATORY HERETO, being members of the Council of Europe,

Considering the Universal Declaration of Human Rights proclaimed by the General Assembly of the United Nations on 10th December 1948;

Considering that this Declaration aims at securing the universal and effective recognition and observance of the Rights therein declared;

Considering that the aim of the Council of Europe is the achievement of greater unity between its members and that one of the methods by which that aim is to be pursued is the maintenance and further realisation of human rights and fundamental freedoms;

Reaffirming their profound belief in those fundamental freedoms which are the foundation of justice and peace in the world and are best maintained on the one hand by an effective political democracy and on the other by a common understanding and observance of the human rights upon which they depend;

Being resolved, as the governments of European countries which are like-minded and have a common heritage of political traditions, ideals, freedom and the rule of law, to take the first steps for the collective enforcement of certain of the rights stated in the Universal Declaration,

Have agreed as follows:

Article 1—Obligation to respect human rights

The High Contracting Parties shall secure to everyone within their jurisdiction the rights and freedoms defined in Section I of this Convention.

Section I—Rights and freedoms

Article 2—Right to life

1. Everyone's right to life shall be protected by law. No one shall be deprived of his life intentionally save in the execution of a sentence of a court following his conviction of a crime for which this penalty is provided by law.
2. Deprivation of life shall not be regarded as inflicted in contravention of this article when it results from the use of force which is no more than absolutely necessary:
    (a)   in defence of any person from unlawful violence;
    (b)   in order to effect a lawful arrest or to prevent the escape of a person lawfully detained;
    (c)   in action lawfully taken for the purpose of quelling a riot or insurrection.

© Source: <www.echr.coe.int>

TEXT 4

DATE   20[ ]
PARTIES
(1)   [   ] a company incorporated under the laws of England and Wales with
registered no. [ ] whose registered office is at
[   ] (the **'Principal'**); and
(2)   [   ] a company incorporated in [   ] with registered no. [   ] whose
registered office is at [   ] (the **'Agent'**).

RECITALS
The Principal manufactures and sells [*description of products*] and now wishes to appoint
the Agent as its exclusive agent for the promotion and sale of those products within the
Territory, as defined below.

OPERATIVE PROVISIONS [*selected clauses and subclauses*]
2.   **Appointment**

>   2.1.   The Principal hereby appoints the Agent as its sole agent to promote and sell
>   the Products in the Territory on the terms of this Agreement and the Agent
>   hereby accepts the appointment on those terms.

3.   **Agent's obligations**

>   The Agent undertakes and agrees with the Principal at all times during the term of
>   this Agreement:
>
>   ...
>
>   3.4.   To use its best endeavours to promote and sell the Products in the Territory
>   with all due care and diligence, to seek to improve the Principal's goodwill in
>   the Territory, and (but only on the Principal's standard terms and conditions
>   of sale unless specifically authorised otherwise by the Principal under clause 4)
>   without prior reference to the Principal to negotiate, conclude and enter into
>   contracts for the sale of the Products in the name of and on behalf of the
>   Principal.

23. **Governing law and jurisdiction**

>   This Agreement shall be governed by and construed in accordance with English
>   law and each party hereby irrevocably submits to the jurisdiction of the English
>   Courts.

As Witness the hands of the duly authorised representatives of the parties hereto the day
and year first above written.

[SIGNATURES]

Agency Agreement used courtesy of Withers LLP © Withers LLP

Text 5

United Nations

S/RES/1368 (2001)

Security Council

Distr.: General
12 September 2001

Resolution 1368 (2001)

**Adopted by the Security Council at its 4370th meeting,
on 12 September 2001**

The Security Council,

Reaffirming the principles and purposes of the Charter of the United Nations,

Determined to combat by all means threats to international peace and security caused by terrorist acts,

Recognizing the inherent right of individual or collective self-defence in accordance with the Charter,

1.   *Unequivocally condemns* in the strongest terms the horrifying terrorist attacks which took place on 11 September 2001 in New York, Washington, D.C. and Pennsylvania and *regards* such acts, like any act of international terrorism, as a threat to international peace and security;

2.   *Expresses* its deepest sympathy and condolences to the victims and their families and to the people and Government of the United States of America;

3.   *Calls* on all States to work together urgently to bring to justice the perpetrators, organizers and sponsors of these terrorist attacks and *stresses* that those responsible for aiding, supporting or harbouring the perpetrators, organizers and sponsors of these acts will be held accountable;

4.   *Calls also* on the international community to redouble their efforts to prevent and suppress terrorist acts including by increased cooperation and full implementation of the relevant international anti-terrorist conventions and Security Council resolutions, in particular resolution 1269 (1999) of 19 October 1999;

5.   *Expresses* its readiness to take all necessary steps to respond to the terrorist attacks of 11 September 2001, and to combat all forms of terrorism, in accordance with its responsibilities under the Charter of the United Nations;

6.   *Decides* to remain seized of the matter.

© Source: <www.un.org>

TEXT 6

DEATH SENTENCES AND EXECUTIONS 2012

Despite some negative developments, the use of the death penalty in 2012 overall confirmed the global trend towards abolition.

The USA was the only country in the Americas to have carried out executions in 2012. However, just nine states in the USA carried out executions in 2012, compared to 13 in 2011. Connecticut became the 17th abolitionist US state.

Despite setbacks in the Asia-Pacific region—including the resumption of executions in India and Pakistan—Viet Nam did not carry out death sentences and Singapore observed a moratorium on executions while considering amendments to its death penalty laws. In sub-Saharan Africa, further progress was visible. The government of Ghana plans to abolish the death penalty in the new Constitution. There are no more prisoners on death row in Sierra Leone.

Belarus continued to be the only country in Europe and central Asia to carry out executions. Legislation to remove the death penalty completely came into effect in Latvia in January, making it the 97th country abolitionist for all crimes worldwide.

In December the UN General Assembly adopted the fourth resolution on a moratorium on the use of the death penalty, with 111 Member States voting in favour.

This report analyzes some of the key developments in the application of the death penalty in 2012, presenting figures gathered by Amnesty International on the number of death sentences handed down and executions carried out during the year.

Amnesty International opposes the death penalty in all cases without exception, regardless of the nature or circumstances of the crime; guilt, innocence or other characteristics of the individual; or the method used by the state to carry out the execution.

Amnesty International (2013)
ACT/50/001/2013, London

TEXT 7

PREAMBLE

We the People of the United States, in Order to form a more perfect Union, establish Justice, insure domestic Tranquility, provide for the common defence, promote the general Welfare, and secure the Blessings of Liberty to ourselves and our Posterity, do ordain and establish this Constitution for the United States of America.

ARTICLE I

Section 1.   All legislative Powers herein granted shall be vested in a Congress of the United States, which shall consist of a Senate and House of Representatives.

Section 2.   [1] The House of Representatives shall be composed of Members chosen every second Year by the People of the several States, and the Electors in each State shall have the Qualifications requisite for Electors of the most numerous Branch of the State Legislature.

[2]   No Person shall be a Representative who shall not have attained to the Age of twenty five Years, and been seven Years a Citizen of the United States, and who shall not, when elected, be an Inhabitant of that State in which he shall be chosen.

[clauses [3] and [4] omitted]

[5]   The House of Representatives shall chuse their Speaker and other Officers; and shall have the sole Power of Impeachment.

Section 3.   [1] The Senate of the United States shall be composed of two Senators from each State, [chosen by the Legislature thereof,] for six Years; and each Senator shall have one Vote.

[clause 2 omitted]

[3]   No Person shall be a Senator who shall not have attained to the Age of thirty Years, and been nine Years a Citizen of the United States, and who shall not, when elected, be an Inhabitant of that State for which he shall be chosen.

[clauses [4] and [5] omitted]

[6]   The Senate shall have the sole Power to try all Impeachments. ... When the President of the United States is tried, the Chief Justice shall preside: And no Person shall be convicted without the Concurrence of two thirds of the Members present.

[7]   Judgment in Cases of Impeachment shall not extend further than to removal from Office, and disqualification to hold and enjoy any Office of honor, Trust or Profit under the United States: but the Party convicted shall nevertheless be liable and subject to Indictment, Trial, Judgment and Punishment, according to Law.

TEXT 8

Coroners Rules 1984

To: Ms ....
     street address
     Exeter

Summons to Juror

By virtue of a warrant of .... Dr ...... (*name*)...........................

one of her Majesty's Coroners for the .... District ....

of .... Exeter and Greater Devon ....

YOU ARE HEREBY SUMMONED to appear before her as a juror

on [*day of week*] .... the [*day/month/year*] .... at [*time*] ....

at (*state place*) .... County Hall, Topsham Road, Exeter ....

until you are no longer needed. The inquest is expected to last one day.

You must attend at the time and place shown above unless you are told by the officer
authorised by the Coroner that you need not do so.

Dated this .... day of .... [*month/year*] ....

[signature] .... [Coroner's Officer]
...

WARNING: YOU WILL BE LIABLE TO A FINE IF YOU:—
1.   Refuse to give the information necessary to decide if you are qualified to serve on a jury;
2.   Deliberately give false information or cause or permit false information to be given;
3.   Fail to attend for jury service or refuse without reasonable excuse to serve as a juror; or
4.   Serve on a jury knowing you are not qualified to do so.

Text 9

Judgment 26.11.92

HOUSE OF LORDS
PEPPER (HER MAJESTY'S INSPECTOR OF TAXES)
(RESPONDENT)
v.
HART
(APPELLANT)
AND NINE OTHER APPEALS
(CONSOLIDATED APPEALS)

Lord Chancellor
Lord Keith of Kinkel
Lord Bridge of Harwich
Lord Griffiths
Lord Ackner
Lord Oliver of Aylmerton
Lord Browne-Wilkinson

...

LORD GRIFFITHS. My Lords. I have long thought that the time had come to change the self-imposed judicial rule that forbade any reference to the legislative history of an enactment as an aid to its interpretation. The ever increasing volume of legislation must inevitably result in ambiguities of statutory language which are not perceived at the time the legislation is enacted. The object of the court in interpreting legislation is to give effect so far as the language permits to the intention of the legislature. If the language proves to be ambiguous I can see no sound reason not to consult Hansard to see if there is a clear statement of the meaning that the words were intended to carry. The days have long passed when the courts adopted a strict constructionist view of interpretation which required them to adopt the literal meaning of the language. The courts now adopt a purposive approach which seeks to give effect to the true purpose of legislation and are prepared to look at much extraneous material that bears upon the background against which the legislation was enacted. Why then cut ourselves off from the one source in which may be found an authoritative statement of the intention with which the legislation is placed before Parliament? ...

In my view this case provides a dramatic vindication of the decision to consult Hansard; had your Lordships not agreed to do so the result would have been to place a very heavy burden of taxation upon a large number of persons which Parliament never intended to impose.

I agree that this appeal should be allowed.

LORD ACKNER concurred with Lord Browne-Wilkinson.

...

TEXT 10

THE EUROPEAN PARLIAMENT AND THE COUNCIL OF THE EUROPEAN UNION,

Having regard to the Treaty establishing the European Community, and in particular Article 95 thereof,

Having regard to the proposal from the Commission(1), ...

Acting in accordance with the procedure laid down in Article 251 of the Treaty(3),

Whereas:

(1)   Directive 95/46/EC of the European Parliament and of the Council of 24 October 1995 on the protection of individuals with regard to the processing of personal data and on the free movement of such data requires Member States to ensure the rights and freedoms of natural persons with regard to the processing of personal data, and in particular their right to privacy, in order to ensure the free flow of personal data in the Community.

[recitals (2) to (49) omitted]

HAVE ADOPTED THIS DIRECTIVE:

Article 1 Scope and aim

1.   This Directive harmonises the provisions of the Member States required to ensure an equivalent level of protection of fundamental rights and freedoms, and in particular the right to privacy, with respect to the processing of personal data in the electronic communication sector and to ensure the free movement of such data and of electronic communication equipment and services in the Community.

[paragraphs 2 and 3 omitted]

Article 13 Unsolicited communications

1.   The use of automated calling systems without human intervention (automatic calling machines), facsimile machines (fax) or electronic mail for the purposes of direct marketing may only be allowed in respect of subscribers who have given their prior consent.
2.   Notwithstanding paragraph 1, where a natural or legal person obtains from its customers their electronic contact details for electronic mail, in the context of the sale of a product or a service, in accordance with Directive 95/46/EC, the same natural or legal person may use these electronic contact details for direct marketing of its own similar products or services provided that customers clearly and distinctly are given the opportunity to object, free of charge and in an easy manner, to such use of electronic contact details when they are collected and on the occasion of each message in case the customer has not initially refused such use.

[paragraphs 3–5 omitted] ...

1.3.1 Key to Task 3 Global Reading—Identifying Legal Texts

— TEXT 1 is a legal text. It is an example of legislation from a national legal setting: a UK law, called an Act of Parliament.
— TEXT 2 is not a legal text, but a work of literary expression: part of a poem by Oscar Wilde.
— TEXT 3 is an important type of international legal text. It is a treaty: the European Convention on Human Rights.
— TEXT 4 is a legal text in the field of private law. It is a legal document made by parties operating in different countries of the world: an international commercial contract.
— TEXT 5 is a legal text. It is the decision of an international organ: a United Nations Security Council resolution.
— TEXT 6 is not a legal text. It is the summary of an Amnesty International human rights report on the use of the death penalty in the world in 2012.
— TEXT 7 is a fundamental type of legal text within a national legal system: a constitution. It is the Constitution of the United States.
— TEXT 8 is a legal text. It is a legal document relating to a court proceeding in England and Wales.
— TEXT 9 is a legal text from a national legal setting. It is part of a judgment in an appeal case in the United Kingdom.
— TEXT 10 is a legal text from the European Union legal order. It is an EU directive, a type of legislative text.

1.3.2 Commentary on the Selection of 10 Text Types

> *The commentary below gives details of the legal context, text type and cultural and legal background for each of the 10 texts. It highlights some key linguistic features typical of the text type but does not examine closely the specific content of each text. Use the commentary relating to your chosen text in Task 4 to complete your preparation during this activity. After the group discussion, read the commentary for the remaining texts. Always refer to the example text itself as you read.*

Text 1 Legislation: Terrorism Act 2000

This is the first part of a UK *Act of Parliament*, also called *a law, a statute* or *an enactment. Legislation* is a primary *source of law*, creating legal obligations and effects that are generally applicable in *a jurisdiction*, in this case the United Kingdom.[26]

---

[26] However, note that in this particular law, under s 1(4)(a) 'action' includes action outside the United Kingdom, and the definition of terrorism is specifically not limited to things taking place in the UK or related to things in the UK (see s 1(4)).

The extract begins with *the short title* of the law ('Terrorism Act 2000'), used to cite the Act as a legal source. There follows the numerical reference in the statute book or UK collection of laws ('Chapter 11'), then *the long title*, which describes the purpose of this law ('An Act to make provision about terrorism ...'), followed by the date on which the Act received *Royal Assent* and became law.

The second paragraph contains *the enacting words* ('*Be it enacted ...*'), a standard formula declaring the Act to be a legal source deriving from the authority of the UK legislature, that is *the Queen in Parliament*, composed of the monarch, the House of Lords and the House of Commons, mentioned in turn.

The remaining text shows section 1 (s 1) of the Act. In the UK, Acts are arranged in *sections* (not articles) and sections may be grouped in *Parts*, here Part I. Section 1 is an *interpretation section*, frequently found at the beginning of a law to define key terms used in the text.[27] It is divided into five subsections, marked (1), (2) etc, each expressed in a single grammatical sentence; taken together, they provide a definition of *terrorism*, although the specific *offence* (crime) of terrorism is not created by the statute. Later legislation refers to this definition, which was expanded in 2006 to include cases where the use or threat of action is designed to influence not only *governments* but also *international governmental organisations*,[28] and extended to include the purpose of advancing a 'racial' cause in 2009.[29]

Little words like conjunctions may be vitally important in legal texts: notice that 'terrorism' as defined in the Act must include elements (a), (b) *and* (c) of section 1(1),[30] while the classes of 'action' that constitute terrorism under section 1(1)(a) are listed in paragraphs (a) to (e) of section 1(2) and are alternatives: only one element would be sufficient to constitute terrorism, as indicated by the conjunction *or* at the end of section 1(2)(d).

As the text signals, at the time of the Terrorism Act 2000, Northern Ireland was considered the main terrorist danger for the United Kingdom. Since the attacks of 11 September 2001 perpetrated in the United States and the rise of Islamist terrorism, the UK Parliament has *enacted* other laws providing powers to respond to the changing terrorist threat. Delicate issues are raised by the problem of reaching an acceptable balance between the human rights of individual suspects and the need to provide security and protection for the population and the State. These have resulted in controversial court cases[31] and repeated legislative intervention on terrorism.

---

[27] Also legal documents such as contracts may start with a *definitions clause*.
[28] By s 34 of the Terrorism Act 2006.
[29] By the Counter-Terrorism Act 2008, s 75(1)(2)(a).
[30] Although s 1(3) creates an exception where firearms or explosives are used.
[31] For example, the *Belmarsh Detainees* case: *A and Others v Secretary of State for the Home Department* [2004] UKHL 56, discussed in P Leyland (2012), *The Constitution of the United Kingdom. A Contextual Analysis*, 2nd edn, Oxford: Hart Publishing, pp 236–39.

United Kingdom Acts of Parliament may be accessed on the Internet, as may 'Explanatory Notes' to clarify meaning.[32] Legislation as a source of law is examined in depth in chapter three.

Text 2 A poem: *The Ballad of Reading Gaol*

These verses are from the much longer poem *The Ballad of Reading Gaol*,[33] written by a convicted prisoner—Oscar Wilde—to protest against the brutality of *imprisonment* as a form of punishment and against the infliction of the death penalty, which he witnessed while in jail. This text is set in the context of *crime and punishment*. However, although it speaks about legal themes and uses legal vocabulary, it is clearly not a legal text but a work of literary expression and protest. We may say that its *functions* are literary expression and protest. Its author was involved in the legal process but was not a legal expert; he poses questions to which a *system of criminal justice* should respond, about *punishment* and humane treatment of convicted criminals.

After Wilde's extraordinary success in the London theatre with *The Importance of Being Earnest* and *Lady Windermere's Fan*, he fell to disgrace through scandal and was condemned to two years' imprisonment with hard labour for indecency. The homosexual behaviour that led to his conviction in the Victorian era would not be criminal in England today, although it would still be punished severely in some countries of the world. On the contrary, in Europe, his right to express his sexual orientation would be protected by human rights law: see, for example, the prohibition of discrimination in the Charter of Fundamental Rights of the European Union (Charter of Nice), Article 21(1).[34] Wilde wrote *The Ballad of Reading Gaol* after his release from prison in 1897, and it was published in London under the name C.3.3. (Building C, Floor 3, Cell 3). His health suffered severely from the harsh prison regime and soon after, he died in France, in exile far from his family.

The concepts and language of criminal law, including punishment for crime, are examined in depth in chapter seven.

Text 3 An international treaty: European Convention on Human Rights

International *treaties* or *conventions* are a major source of international law; they are listed first in Article 38 of the Statute of the International Court of Justice

---

[32] <http://www.legislation.gov.uk>.

[33] Reading is a town in the south of England where Wilde was imprisoned. *Gaol* is another spelling for *jail* (prison).

[34] Charter of Fundamental Rights of the European Union (Charter of Nice) [2012] OJ C326/02.

(ICJ),[35] specifying the sources of international law applied by the ICJ, principal *judicial organ* of the United Nations. The term *treaty* may be defined as:

> an international agreement governed by international law and concluded in written form:
>
> (i)   between one or more States and one or more international organizations; or
> (ii)   between international organizations.[36]

Such an agreement may be embodied in one or more related instruments and be given any designation, such as *pact, convention, alliance, accord, charter.*

This particular example, the European Convention on Human Rights (ECHR) is an important regional instrument for the protection of human rights; its full name is the European Convention for the Protection of Human Rights and Fundamental Freedoms, and it was signed in Rome in 1950 under the auspices of the Council of Europe.[37] The authentic text of the ECHR is in both English and French. The original text has been amended by a series of *protocols.*[38]

The ECHR was inspired by the United Nations Universal Declaration of Human Rights, referred to here in the first *recital* of the *Preamble*—a series of listed points introduced by verbs, providing background information to the Convention and explaining its purposes: *Considering* ..., *Reaffirming* ..., *Being resolved* ... But unlike the Universal Declaration, the European Convention (as its name indicates) is a *legally binding agreement*, containing duties that *States Parties* to the Convention must respect. The first obligation assumed by the parties and imposed by Article 1 is to guarantee the rights and freedoms defined in the Convention to everyone within the States' *jurisdiction* (in international law, the territory over which a State has legal authority). The obligation is imposed in the language of the text by the typical use of the modal verb *shall* + infinitive ('*The High Contracting Parties* shall secure *to everyone within their jurisdiction the rights and freedoms* ...').

This extract includes:

— The parties and the expression of their agreement (*The GOVERNMENTS ... Have agreed as follows*). Observe how the basic Subject–Verb–Object sequence of the English sentence is interrupted by a long section of text (the preamble). This is a typical feature of legal English.
— The preamble (see above).

---

[35] The text of the Statute is available on the official website of the Court: <www.icj-cij.org>.

[36] Vienna Convention on the Law of Treaties between States and International Organizations or between International Organizations 1986, Art 2(1), adding 'international organizations' to the definition of 'treaty' provided by Art 2(1) of the Vienna Convention on the Law of Treaties of 1969.

[37] An association of European countries with 47 members today (see 5.2.1); all members of the EU are also members of the Council of Europe, but the two organisations are distinct.

[38] See 7.6.4 for Protocols 6 and 13, amending Art 2(1) in relation to the death penalty.

— From the body of the Convention text, Article 1 (Parties' obligation to observe the Convention) and Article 2 (the *right to life*, which must be protected by law but is subject to specified limitations).

The language of human rights is examined in depth with special reference to the protection of rights in the ECHR in chapter five; human rights in relation to criminal law and the death penalty are discussed in chapter seven.

Text 4 Legal document: a contract

A contract is a *legally binding agreement* between two or more *parties*. They may be *natural persons* (physical individuals) or, as in the text, *legal persons* (entities with *legal personality*). A valid contract may generally be oral or in writing, but it is common commercial practice to stipulate written contracts. In international transactions, the parties must choose the language in which to express their agreement. English is frequently chosen as a *lingua franca* between parties of different nationalities. This text was written by an English lawyer (a *solicitor*) and shows the following elements:

— The opening or *commencement* of the contract, giving the date of the agreement and details of the parties: the *Agent* and the *Principal*.
— The *recitals*, providing background information relevant to the agreement.
— Selected *operative provisions* from the body of the contract. Clause 2, 'Appointment': creates the agency relationship by agreement between the Principal and the Agent (*The Principal hereby appoints … And the Agent hereby accepts the appointment …*);
— Clause 3, '*Agent's obligations*': sets out the agent's principal duties under the contract (*The Agent undertakes and agrees …*). In sub-clause 3.4 we can see the nature of the agent's role: to promote and sell products, concluding contracts of sale with third parties *in the name of and on behalf of* the Principal.
— Clause 23, '*Governing law and jurisdiction*' defines two aspects: the *governing law*[39] identifies the legal system according to which the contract must be interpreted and applied ('English law'); *jurisdiction* indicates the *forum* competent to hear disputes, that is, the courts with authority to *adjudicate* in case of a dispute between the parties ('the English Courts').
— The conventional, one-line phrase, in archaic language, preceding the signatures of the parties' *duly authorised* representatives.

Observe the clearly structured format of the text. Each clause deals with one aspect of the agreement. Note the use of typographical devices to mark terms specially defined in the contract (e.g. *Principal, Products, Territory*). The language of contract law and of international commercial contracts is examined in depth in chapter eleven.

---

[39] Also called *applicable law* or *proper law*.

Text 5 Decision of an international organ: UN Security Council Resolution

This international legal text pronounces the Resolution of the United Nations
Security Council, made on 12 September 2001 in response to the 11 September
terrorist attacks on the United States.[40] A text of this kind is the result of *negotiation and agreement between the parties*, which produces legal effect.

Notice the structure and language of the text. A preamble composed of a series
of *recitals* ('*Reaffirming ... Determined ...*') is followed by a series of numbered
points, each beginning with a verb in the present simple tense ('*Expresses ... Calls
on ... Decides ...*') and specifying the steps that the Security Council *has resolved*
to take in response to the terrorist attacks.

We can see the reference in the recitals to the 'principles and purposes of the
Charter of the United Nations': the *purposes of the United Nations* are established in
Article 1 of the Charter, while its *principles* are stated in Article 2. Another relevant
source mentioned in the preamble to this Resolution is Article 51 of the Charter,
set out below, recognising '*the inherent right of individual or collective self-defence*'
of States:

> Nothing in the present Charter shall impair the inherent right of individual or collective
> self-defence if an armed attack occurs against a Member of the United Nations, until
> the Security Council has taken measures necessary to maintain international peace and
> security ...[41]

Article 51 does not limit ('*impair*') the right of States to respond to armed attack
in self-defence, either individually or collectively (by States belonging to an *alliance*, such as NATO). This right is 'inherent'—it is not *granted* by the Charter
but automatically *belongs to* every State under international law—and the right
can be exercised independently, *until* the Security Council has taken necessary
measures '*to maintain international peace and security*', reflecting the role of this
UN organ.

The final element of the resolution, point 6, indicates that the legal matter is not
closed with this resolution. In fact, the Security Council '*decides to remain seized of
the matter*', that is, to keep the issue open and subject to further decision-making
by the Council.

Security Council resolutions can be accessed freely on the United Nations
website.[42]

---

[40] United Nations Security Council Resolution S/RES/1368 (2001).
[41] United Nations Universal Declaration of Human Rights adopted and proclaimed by General
Assembly Resolution 217 A (III) of 10 December 1948.
[42] <www.un.org>.

Text 6 Summary of a Report

This summary introduces the findings of the Amnesty International Report *Death Sentences and Executions 2012*.[43] It is not a legal text—it does not create any legal effect—but it has a strong legal theme: the death penalty in law and practice in the world during the year 2012.

The purpose of the Report itself is to publish data and provide analysis of global developments in the application of the death penalty; Amnesty International's position of total opposition in all circumstances to the death penalty is stated clearly. The full document is available on the official website of this *international non-governmental human rights organisation*.[44]

The text opens with a one-sentence summary, announcing the overall 'global trend towards *abolition*'. In the following three paragraphs, specific areas of the world are reviewed. Trends are described and individual countries singled out for comment. Statistics are given, with details of specific State action: e.g. the '*moratorium on executions*' observed in Singapore (during a *moratorium*, condemned prisoners are not executed); the singular position of Belarus in Europe and Central Asia (the only country '*to carry out executions*').

The focus of the Report is on *State practice*, as well as relevant *legislation*: a careful distinction is made between cases where a judge *hands down* '*a death sentence*' and cases where an *execution is carried out*. Relevant legal bases include the adoption of a *resolution* by the *General Assembly of the United Nations*.

The Report is analytical, with data ('*figures*') gathered directly by Amnesty International: this groundwork is an important part of Amnesty International's role in promoting the *protection of human rights* wherever in the world they are violated. No country is free from criticism. In addition, Amnesty International works to defend rights through letter-writing campaigns supported by individual members, numbering more than three million people in over 150 countries, who campaign to end grave *abuses of human rights*, by raising public awareness and putting pressure on those responsible in governments across the world to respond.

Amnesty International was founded in 1961 by an English lawyer, Peter Benenson: he was outraged to discover that two Portuguese students had been imprisoned for raising their glasses in a toast '*to freedom*'; he published an article launching an 'Appeal for Amnesty 1961', the start of a worldwide campaign: 'His call to action resonated with the values and aspirations of people everywhere. This was the genesis of Amnesty International'.[45] Today, Amnesty International is organised in national sections; in line with its origins in Peter Benenson's actions, it continues to rely on support from committed individuals to perform its tasks, a

---

[43] *Death Sentences and Executions 2012* (2013) ACT/50/001/2013 (London: Amnesty International).

[44] <www.amnesty.org>.

[45] *The History of Amnesty International*, available at <www.amnesty.org>, visited 10 October 2013.

quality that helped earn it recognition in 1977 with the award of the Nobel Peace Prize, for 'the individual's deep and firmly rooted conviction that the ordinary man and woman is capable of making a meaningful contribution to peace'.[46]

Text 7 National constitutional law: Constitution of the United States

Written by *the framers* in 1787, the Constitution of the United States entered into force in 1789 after *ratification* by the participating States. The United States had existed as a Confederation for several years before adoption of this new *federal Constitution*, but this step was designed to form a stronger and 'more perfect Union', a nation created by the people, not existing by virtue of God or a king: '*We the people of the United States …*'

The extract shows the *Preamble*, expressing the dreams and hopes on which the Constitution is founded, and selected *sections* (§) and *clauses* of *Article I*, which establishes the *legislative branch* of the State and defines its composition and powers. Under Article I, § 1, 'All *legislative powers*' belong to (are '*vested in*') a *Congress*, composed of a *Senate* and *House of Representatives*.

In a country like the United States, where there is a *written Constitution* contained in a single legal text, *constitutional law* is concerned with the application of the Constitution and its authoritative interpretation by the Supreme Court.

Individual liberties are protected in the US Constitution by Article I, § 9 and by the first 10 *Amendments*, known collectively as the *Bill of Rights* and added in 1791.[47] The US Constitution is *entrenched*: under Article V, a special *legislative procedure* must be followed in order to make *amendments*. For example, in Article I, § 3, clause 1, the words in parentheses relating to how Senators are to be selected—'[chosen by the Legislature thereof]'—were later amended to read 'elected by the people thereof',[48] *thereof* meaning of that State.

It is interesting to note the enduring strength of a *written* Constitution and to consider how the meaning and effect of the term '*impeachment*' has evolved separately in British and American legal terminology. '*Impeachment*' in American law is defined as:

> A criminal proceeding against a public officer, before a *quasi* political court, instituted by a written accusation called 'articles of impeachment'; for example, a written accusation by the House of Representatives of the United States to the Senate of the United States against the President, Vice President, or an officer of the United States.[49]

---

[46] Presentation Speech by Aase Lionæs, Chairman of the Norwegian Nobel Committee, Oslo, 10 December 1977: The Nobel Peace Prize 1977—Presentation Speech, available at <www.nobelprize.org>, visited 9 October 2013.

[47] By contrast, for the *Bill of Rights* in the British Constitution (1689), see 3.1 and 3.2.4.

[48] XVIIth Amendment, § 1, 1913, also adding to Art I § 3, cl 1 the qualifications for electors, similar to those required in Art I § 2, cl 1 for the House of Representatives.

[49] H Black (1979), *Black's Law Dictionary*, 5th edn, St Paul, Minn: West Publishing Co, p 678.

We can find these elements by examining the constitutional text itself. By contrast, some English law dictionaries[50] do not cover this constitutional term, and the reason is to be found in *Osborn's Concise Law Dictionary*: 'A procedure by which a minister of the Crown may be tried in front of his peers in Parliament. Last used in the United Kingdom in 1805'.[51] The historic impeachment procedure involved an *accusation* by the House of Commons followed by *trial* in the House of Lords, and is paralleled in the American system; but in the UK, with its *unwritten Constitution*, impeachment is now considered *obsolete* because it has fallen into disuse.[52] The attempt by a group of British Members of Parliament (MPs) to *impeach* Tony Blair over the 'Conduct of the Prime Minister in relation to the war against Iraq'[53] failed when the motion was not given time by the Speaker of the House of Commons to permit debate. In modern times, different mechanisms have developed in the UK for the scrutiny of the executive.[54] By contrast, Article I of the Constitution of the United States not only provides for impeachment,[55] but also ensures *no immunity* from the ordinary criminal process, if the '*Party*'—even the President himself—is convicted in an impeachment proceeding.[56]

Constitutional law and language, with special reference to the unwritten British constitution, are examined in chapter three.

Text 8 A legal document in court proceedings: summons to juror

The text is a legal document relating to a type of proceeding called an *inquest*, conducted before the *coroner's court* of England and Wales. An *inquest* is 'a legal enquiry into the circumstances surrounding a person's death, where the person may have died a violent or unnatural death, or in certain other circumstances'.[57] A coroner is an *officer of the Crown*, who is medically or legally qualified and is responsible for *conducting inquests*, for which a *jury* may be required by law; in other cases, a coroner may decide to *summon a jury*, composed of from seven to 11 ordinary people. This document is a '*summons*'—an order to *appear before the court* at a particular time and place—to an individual who has been chosen at random from the adult population '*to serve* as a *juror*', that is, a member of a jury.

---

[50] For example, *A Dictionary of Law*, 7th edn (2009, updated reissue 2013), E Martin and J Law (eds), Oxford: Oxford University Press.

[51] *Osborn's Concise Law Dictionary*, 12th edn (2013), M Woodley (ed), London: Sweet & Maxwell, p 221.

[52] O Gay and N Davies (2011), House of Commons Library Standard Note, *Impeachment* SN/PC/02666.

[53] *Ibid*: Motion tabled in the House of Commons on 25 November 2004.

[54] *Ibid*, p 3; further, Prime Minister Gordon Brown established the Iraq Inquiry, which 'could be seen as a response to the group of MPs deciding to try and impeach the then Prime Minister' (p 6).

[55] Art I, § 2, cl 5 and § 3, cl 6.

[56] Art I, § 3, cl. 6.

[57] *Your Jury Service in the Coroner's Court* (2007). Leaflet produced by the UK Ministry of Justice: MoJ 11/07, p 3.

Procedure before the coroner's court is *governed by rules*, and this document—a *'Summons to Juror'*—refers to the 'Coroners Rules 1984' in its heading.

The document consists of a standard form, to be completed with specific details: the name and address of the person *summoned to serve on a jury*; the Coroner's name and district; specifications of when and where the addressee must *'appear'* before the Coroner; the date and signature of the *'Coroner's Officer'*—the official who assists coroners in their duties and usually acts as the *coroner's court official*.[58]

The role of the jury in an inquest is not to find anyone *guilty* or *not guilty*, as in a criminal case, but to record their *findings* (determination) 'of certain facts about the death', specifically: 'who the dead person was; and how, when and where that person came by his or her death'.[59] At the end of the proceeding, all jurors who agreed to the answers to the questions in the *verdict*, sign a form called the *Inquisition*, containing those answers.

We may classify this *Summons to Juror* as an official document, as opposed to a private legal document, such as a contract (Text 4 above) or will. It is typified by the standard form to be completed on an individual basis, with clear formatting and formal and technical language. It is legally valid and effective: in fact, the summons contains a *'warning'* to the addressee that he or she 'will *be liable to a fine*'—subject to payment of a money penalty—if he or she behaves in one of four ways listed, e.g. by failing to 'attend for *jury service*'. This summons was issued *'by virtue of a warrant'* of the Coroner—that is, on the basis of a written authority.

In chapter seven we consider the role of the English jury in criminal trials.

Text 9 A judgment: *Pepper v Hart*[60]

The text shows part of a *judgment* of the House of Lords, the historic supreme court of the United Kingdom,[61] which exercised the *judicial function* until 2009, when the new *Supreme Court of the United Kingdom* was established,[62] a body entirely independent of Parliament. Decisions of the House of Lords (and today, of the Supreme Court of the United Kingdom) are *precedents* that must be followed by all the other courts.

The case of *Pepper v Hart* created an important new principle in the field of *judicial interpretation* of legislation (*statutory interpretation*). It is a rare example of a case where the House of Lords changed its own previous precedent, using a power it had declared in 1966.[63] The question before the judges was whether it was

---

[58] *Ibid,* p 5.

[59] *Ibid,* pp 3–4.

[60] *Pepper v Hart* [1992] UKHL 3, [1993] AC 593.

[61] Except for Scottish criminal appeals; the judicial function was exercised by the Appellate Committee of the House of Lords.

[62] Under s 23(1) of the Constitutional Reform Act 2005.

[63] House of Lords 1966 Practice Statement of 26 July 1966, [1966] 3 All ER 77.

permissible to refer to reports of Parliamentary debates (published in *Hansard*) as an aid to *interpretation of a statute*; it was decided to change a long-established precedent and permit reference to such debates, in certain circumstances.

This extract contains part of the opinion of Lord Griffiths, one of the seven *Law Lords* who heard the case. In the opening sentence of his individual opinion, Lord Griffiths states his position in favour of the change. Notice that the judgment is not *collegiate* (expressed as a single judgment for the whole court) but individual and personal in style ('I have long thought ...'). This judgment was not unanimous but was decided by a majority of the panel of seven judges listed in the text.

A judgment produces legal effects directly *in the individual dispute* and, in the case of an appeal judgment of a superior English court, *in the development of legal rules contained in judicial precedent.*

We study the English judgment and the structure of the courts in depth in chapter nine of this book; we examine the style of judicial reasoning and the way legal rules develop in *a common law legal system.*

Text 10   European Union law: a directive

This text belongs in the context of EU law. It is part of an EU directive known as the *Directive on privacy and electronic communications*; its full title is 'Directive 2002/58/EC of the European Parliament and of the Council of 12 July 2002 concerning the processing of personal data and the protection of privacy in the electronic communications sector'.[64]

A directive is a type of legislative text. In the EU context, *treaties* are classified as *primary legislation*, while *legal acts of the Union*, such as *regulations* and *directives*, are classified as *secondary legislation*, enacted by the competent *EU institutions*.

In the case of a directive, Member States must pass national legislation to give effect to its provisions in *the national legal order*. This process is called *implementation* of a directive: all States must achieve the results set out in the directive, but the national authorities have a choice of *form and methods* for doing so,[65] allowing Member States to enact provisions in the way best suited to the national legal system.

The Directive on privacy and electronic communications was *implemented* in the United Kingdom by *statutory instrument*—a form of *delegated legislation* often used for this purpose.[66] Parliament may *delegate* legislative competence to another

---

[64] Directive on privacy and electronic communications [2002] OJ L201/37.

[65] Legal acts of the Union are set out in the TFEU: Treaty on the Functioning of the European Union consolidated version (Treaty of Rome) [2012] OJ C326/01, Art 288.

[66] The Privacy and Electronic Communications (EC Directive) Regulations 2003 (SI 2003/2426).

body or individual, in this case a Government minister, to enact provisions on a specific matter.

European Union law, including directives, can be accessed in English and all the other official languages in which authentic legal texts are produced, on the website of the European Union, *Europa*.[67] It is also possible to view bilingual displays of *parallel texts* online in the languages of your choice.

The language of the EU and its multilingual language policy are examined in chapter five, where we focus specifically on *the founding Treaties*, considered to be the constitution of the EU.

1.4   English Legal Texts in Different Legal Contexts

The selection of texts examined in Task 3 above illustrates the different legal contexts in the world today that provide a setting for a variety of legal texts in the English language.

1.4.1 Summary of Contexts and Text Types

Consult the following summary. As you work, think about the texts examined in 1.3 above, and decide which texts from the selection examined belong in which groups below.

Legal contexts for legal texts in English

— At national level: in *the English legal system* and other legal systems belonging to *the common law family*; in legal systems operating in the English language which are not common law systems or are *mixed systems.*
— At international level: in *the international legal order.*
— At regional level in Europe: in *the EU legal order.*
— In relation to any legal system in the world, when English is chosen by parties as an international *lingua franca*, e.g. in international commercial contracts or arbitration.

---

[67] <http://eur-lex.europa.eu>.

Primary legal texts typical of a common law legal system

— *Sources of law*: legislation (*statutes* and *delegated legislation*) and *judicial precedent* (*judgments*, published in the *law reports*); if there is a written constitution: *the Constitution*.
— *Legal documents* arising from individual legal acts and transactions: documents may be created by private individuals (e.g. *contracts, wills, articles of association*), or they may be issued in an institutional context (e.g. a *summons to juror*, an *arrest warrant*, a *divorce decree*).

We may classify these texts as 'primary legal texts' because they have the important characteristic of *producing legal effects*. We examine many such texts in this book.

Primary legal texts typical of the international and EU legal orders

— *Treaties*, e.g. the 1969 Vienna Convention on the Law of Treaties, the Geneva Conventions of 1949, the Treaty on European Union; certain *non-binding texts* such as the Universal Declaration of Human Rights are similar to this text type and may have indirect legal effect.
— In EU law: *secondary legislation* (*acts* created by the EU institutions, such as *regulations, directives*).
— *Resolutions* of decision-making bodies such as the UN Security Council, UN General Assembly or European Parliament;
— Texts in connection with *dispute resolution*, e.g. *judgments* of the ICJ and other international courts and tribunals, *arbitral awards*.

We examine various texts from the international and EU legal orders in this book.

Secondary legal texts: academic and professional literature

In addition to the primary texts listed above, there is a wide range of legal publications that we may describe as *academic and professional literature* and classify as 'secondary legal texts'. These texts do not produce legal effects, but like primary legal texts they are written by experts for experts (or trainees) and are essential to our knowledge and understanding of the law.

Secondary legal texts typical of a common law legal system are academic and professional literature used in connection with the study and practice of law and include the following (see 1.4.2 below for details of these text types):

— textbooks, cases and materials books
— law reviews
— dictionaries and other works of legal reference.

Secondary legal texts typical of the international and EU legal orders are similar to those found in the common law, but specialise, respectively, in international law (or a specialism such as international human rights law) or EU law.

1.4.2 Textbooks, Case Books and Law Reviews

Textbooks

A textbook presents and explains a whole branch or field of the law (e.g. criminal law, land law, EU law, human rights law). Written by an expert jurist, the textbook provides a coherent description of the law, and every comment is backed up by direct reference to the legal source, usually in footnotes (the section of a statute, the name of the case that is precedent for a rule etc). Textbooks are especially valuable in a common law legal system, where the law is not stated in general *codes* but is to be found in a number of sources, principally legislation and *case law* (precedent).

A textbook is usually several hundred pages long and provides an overview of the subject as well as detailed analysis and evaluations of developments in the law. If there is a branch of law in which you are especially interested, by using the index of the textbook you can easily find introductory pages, or a specific section or chapter of the book you would like to read. Textbook explanations are also excellent for finding definitions of legal terminology. We shall read some extracts from textbooks on contract law in chapter eleven.

Cases and materials books

Cases and materials books are edited collections of extracts from the most important precedents (*cases*) and other source materials (e.g. legislation) in a specific branch of the law, published in a single volume (e.g. cases and materials on constitutional law). The collection is compiled by an expert in the field, and the book may contain analytical comment in addition to the source materials themselves. These books are very convenient to use for students; however, they do not substitute for the *law reports*—published volumes containing complete texts of judgments that may be *cited* as the source of a legal rule in common law systems.[68]

Law reviews

Law reviews are important for the in-depth analysis and criticism of legal developments found in the leading articles, essential for academic study and research. They are published periodically and may be general, such as the *Law Quarterly Review* or the *Harvard Law Review*, or specialised, such as the *Criminal Law Review*, and national or international.

---

[68] See 9.3.1 for more on the law reports.

1.4.3 Reflections for You as a Language User: 'Legal Englishes'?

Given the different legal contexts in which English is used, can we consider legal English as a single variety of the language or should we talk about '*legal Englishes*', that is, different varieties of legal English, depending on the relevant legal context? It seems that different varieties of legal English exist, belonging to different legal settings as observed in this chapter: in the context of international law, EU law, English law, United States law and so on. Fortunately, as a general rule, English legal language examined in one setting is relevant and helpful in other contexts, too. As a foreign learner of legal English, simply be aware that variations may exist and use an appropriate range of reference works to support your studies. For instance, use an American law dictionary when reading a judgment of the US Supreme Court, the European Commission glossaries for an EU document, an English law dictionary for an English text.

At national level, there exists a basic similarity in legal English from different legal systems, which is extremely marked in the case of members of the common law family, given their shared legal and linguistic foundation. In time, local variations may have developed, for example in the meaning and use of terminology (e.g. *impeachment* in British and American constitutional law, 1.3 above), or to reflect different institutional arrangements (e.g. *Royal Assent* in the legislative procedure of the UK, a constitutional monarchy).

At international level, the language of public international law shares many of the terms and characteristics of the language of an internal legal system (e.g. the language of court procedure for the resolution of disputes). But there are important distinctions, too, both in text types and terminology. For example, the content and style of *judgments* differ; there are different sources of law; terminology may be used differently or exist specifically in the field of international law (e.g. *self-defence*, examined in international law in Text 5 above, exists with a related, but different, meaning in national criminal law.[69] For these reasons, we may regard the language of international law as a distinct variety of English legal language.

In Europe, the growth of the EU legal order has involved the creation and development of a specific variety of legal language, with its own terminology and text types, such as *directives* (Text 10 above). It also shares many terms and characteristics of both international and national legal language, and is based on treaties, a fundamental source (and text type) of international law. We examine the specific language of EU law in chapter five.

In conclusion, when using original legal materials, always start by identifying the specific legal context to which a text belongs, and bear this context in mind as you select and use appropriate reference sources to investigate the meaning of terminology in context.

---

[69] Self-defence in criminal law is examined in depth in 7.6.2 and 7.6.3.

1.4.4 Reflections for You as a Language User: Text Types

In this chapter, you have been introduced to various *text types* common in different national and international legal contexts in the world today. As for texts used in the legal system of your country, each English text type will have a specific format, features and functions that we can expect to find in other examples of the same text type. The same is true as regards international legal text types, where similar features will be found in the *parallel texts* that may exist in different languages (for example, an EU directive issued in the 24 official languages of the European Union). These features relate to the choice and organisation of content in the text; the style and formatting of the document; the choice of language and vocabulary used to express meaning in the text; as well as the functions and effect of the legal text itself.

These features may vary from one legal context to another: judgments of the UK Supreme Court and the US Supreme Court will have some different features and some common language, as will judgments of the Court of Justice of the European Union or of the European Court of Human Rights.

Attention to the features of specific text types that you meet, will enable you to approach other similar texts of the same type more quickly and effectively. It is especially useful to develop this strategy as a foreign user of English legal texts, since authentic legal materials certainly present a challenge, both linguistically and conceptually.

1.5 Features of English Legal Texts and Language—Advanced

In 1.3 above you examined a mixed selection of texts on legal themes and distinguished the legal from the non-legal texts. Even without an initial definition of 'legal text', as a lawyer or law student, your classification was probably accurate, as we hope you confirmed when checking in the Key.

Reflect on how you performed that activity. What elements helped you distinguish between legal and non-legal texts? Did your familiarity with legal texts in your own language assist you? What criteria did you adopt in identifying a text as legal or non-legal?

1.5.1 Text Types across Different Legal Orders

A statute, a judgment, a summons, a contract and a treaty are different types of legal text, which we may find in different legal orders. A treaty in international law, such as the Treaty of Rome, differs from an instrument of private law such as a written contract, even though both texts are based on agreement and create legal rights and duties for the parties. We may expect that written contracts from different legal systems, particularly in the common law world and in the globalised sphere of international commercial transactions, will be generally similar, although some aspects of language and content, including terminology, may differ from one context to another.

Again, if we examine a specific text type such as a judgment in different legal orders, we may find both similarities and differences in aspects such as content, text organisation, linguistic and judicial style, and even functions. For example, the judgment of an English superior court is noticeably different from the judgment of the ECJ, and performs slightly different functions within the legal system,[70] although both texts have the principal function of determining the legal dispute before the court.

Legislation, too, being an expression of national sovereignty, may vary from one legal system to another, although we can expect to find certain similarities in the texts of all legislation, including EU acts such as regulations or directives.

1.5.2 The Function of Legal Texts: Producing Legal Effects

We may distinguish in different ways between the texts mentioned in 1.5.1, above. However, they are all undoubtedly *legal texts*. They share the defining characteristic of primary legal texts: *they produce legal effect*. We would suggest that the purpose or *function* of this primary class of legal text is, precisely, to produce legal effect: to *create, impose, define, modify, enforce,* or *extinguish* legal rights and obligations.

That is why legal texts are instruments of such paramount importance: they produce legal effects and regulate significant aspects of people's lives, such as their property rights, business affairs and even family relationships. The characterising role of language in such texts is to perform legal actions; we say that it is *performative*. In fact, in legal texts we can find certain linguistic forms not found in other types of English text, that are typically used in legal language to obtain this performative function. For example, in texts such as laws, treaties and contracts, we frequently meet verb forms using the modal verb 'shall'. It is not used with future reference as in general English, but produces the legal effect of imposing an obligation or granting a power.

Observe these examples from the texts examined in 1.3 above:

— *In a treaty:* 'Everyone's right to life shall be protected by law.' From Article 2(1) ECHR. The use of *shall be protected* imposes the obligation on the States Parties legally to protect everyone's right to life.
— *In a legislative text:* 'The House of Representatives ... shall have the sole power of impeachment.' From Article I, § 2, cl 5 of the Constitution of

---

[70] Given the operation of judicial precedent as a primary source of English law and the various types of action that fall within the jurisdiction of the ECJ, examined in 5.2.4 below.

the United States. By these words, the power of impeachment under the Constitution is granted exclusively to the House of Representatives.
— *In a contract:* 'In his relations with the Agent the Principal shall act dutifully and in good faith.' The use of *shall act* in this clause imposes a legal duty on the Principal to act according to the specified standard.

1.5.3 Not Just Documents: the Role of Language in Law

A legal text may be the expression of individual choice (e.g. *a will*), or agreement in personal or business relations (e.g. *a contract, articles of association*, etc); it may be the expression of the will or decision of a body which, in a jurisdiction, has power to take measures affecting people's lives (the decree or judgment of a court, the enactment of a legislature). In these examples, the legal text represents more than just documentary evidence: it *embodies* the choice, agreement, decision or enactment. In other words, that choice, agreement, etc is *given effect* through the language used in the legal text itself. As a result, legal texts and the language used in such texts to create legal effects are crucially important.

What, for example, is the effect of the following clause in a contract?

> The Principal hereby appoints the Agent as its agent for the promotion of the Products in the Territory, and the Agent hereby agrees to act in that capacity, subject to the terms and conditions of this Agreement.

This clause, at the beginning of a commercial contract, has the effect of *creating the relationship* of Principal–Agent between the parties ('*The Principal hereby appoints the Agent ... the Agent hereby agrees to act in that capacity*'). The clause defines the scope of the agency relationship: it concerns the promotion of certain products in a certain geographical area (terms such as '*Products*' and '*Territory*', marked by initial capital (or 'upper-case') letters, are defined precisely in a previous clause of the contract). The clause also stipulates that the agency relationship is legally regulated by ('*subject to*') the contractual terms ('*terms and conditions*') contained in the contract ('*Agreement*') itself.

The example shows how even a single, short sentence from a legal text can produce a quantity of legal effect, significant for the people affected by it—in this case, the parties to the contract.

It is not surprising, then, that lawyers—and perhaps this is especially true in the common law world—are traditionally so attentive to language in the law. As we saw at the beginning of this chapter, Lord Denning, a prominent English judge, in advising young lawyers, focused on the importance of words—the lawyer's 'tools of trade':

> When you are called upon to address a judge, it is your words which count most. It is by them that you will hope to persuade the judge of the rightness of your cause. When you have to interpret a section in a Statute or a paragraph in a Regulation, you have to

study the very words. You have to discover the meaning by analysing the words—one by one—to the very last syllable. When you have to draw up a will or a contract, you have to choose your words well. You have to look into the future—envisage all the contingencies that may come to pass—and then use words to provide for them. On the words you use, your client's future may depend.[71]

We can note the power of language in the law: it is not purely expressive (as in literature) or descriptive (as in science and many other disciplines); language in a legal text does not simply *describe* phenomena which exist independently of the linguistic formulae in which they are expressed. Instead, legal principles are *embodied* in words, and this special relationship between language and law is particularly evident in certain types of legal text, notably legislation. In the words of the great English jurist Sir John Salmond:

> The very words in which it is expressed—the *litera scripta*—constitute a part of the law itself. Legal authority is possessed by the letter no less than by the spirit of the enactment ...[72]

Linguist John Swales, in a comparative study of the function and language forms of definitions in science and law, identifies a species of definition peculiar to legal texts: the definitions are, in effect, the law itself. This class of definition is authoritative and cannot be expressed in different words but must be learnt 'by heart and verbatim by all students'.[73] Is the same true for the legal language of your country?

Again, as section 1 of the Terrorism Act 2000 shows, a UK statute is a complex compendium of precise and detailed rules intended to cover every possible combination of future circumstances. This, together with the traditional literal approach of the English courts to *statutory interpretation*, gives particular weight to the exact choice of words in UK legislation.[74] It is true that British judges increasingly adopt the '*purposive approach*' in interpreting legislation, as Lord Griffiths explained in his judgment in *Pepper v Hart* (Text 9 above). But the decision of an English superior court as to the meaning of statutory words carries special legal weight, because the *doctrine of binding precedent* applies: that is to say, in a later similar case, the courts must *follow precedent*, by applying the same interpretation already given in the precedent. Where the later court is inferior in authority or (generally speaking) of the same level, we say that the precedent is *binding* (it *must* be followed); but even where the later court is superior in authority, the precedent will be *persuasive* (strongly influential). The doctrine of precedent is examined in depth in 9.3 and 9.6 below.

[71] Denning, above n 2, p 5.

[72] J Salmond (1947), *Jurisprudence*, 10th edn by G Williams, London: Sweet & Maxwell, p 169.

[73] J Swales (1981), 'Definitions in science and law—evidence for subject-specific course components' (1981) 81(3) *Fachsprache* 106.

[74] Riley, above n 12, p 69.

1.5.4 Written and Oral Language in the Law

In this book our attention is focused on written legal texts and language. Lord Denning, in the quotation set out in 1.5.3 above, pointed out the importance of both oral and written language for the aspiring lawyer.

In the courtroom, oral language is a vital instrument for the lawyer to persuade the judge to decide in favour of the party he or she represents. In the Anglo-American legal system with its *adversarial* form of trial, the oral proceedings in court are at the centre of the judicial process, in both criminal and civil cases.

> The Anglo-American civil trial provides the ideal forum for raising problems in this discursive manner. Throughout its history it has been strongly marked by the requirements of *trial by jury*, although today it is only in the United States that the jury has any practical importance in private law. The proceedings take place in a single session, spread over several days if necessary, and all the facts, as well as questions of law, are orally presented there and then by the litigants and discussed in an open and discursive manner, with the judge taking part.[75]

Written documents certainly have a role during the preparatory phase. For example, in a civil case, before the all-important *day in court*, a series of written documents initiate and support the oral proceeding, with each party *serving* a formal written *statement of case*[76] on the other. However, even the judgment of the court will be pronounced orally in almost all cases (except for the Supreme Court) and only subsequently written down word for word, for publication in the law reports. In fact, the availability of the final written text of the judgment in published form is necessary to the operation of judicial precedent as a source of law in the common law system: indeed, for hundreds of years accurate written reports of judgments have been published, providing a record of judicial pronouncements.[77]

We must observe that written texts are generally more important than spoken language in the law. An authoritative written text is often the final legal result obtained after a process of negotiation (as of a contract or treaty) or debate (as of a law enacted by Parliament), or of oral proceedings as described above (the published text of a judgment).

In conclusion, oral language is clearly a natural and integral part of legal activity and interaction, and a lawyer's choice of words is fundamental in legal situations such as the courtroom. However, written texts, importantly, provide a fixed and permanent record of legal acts and events, and for certain texts, such as a statute or a contract, are the direct source of legal obligation.

---

[75] Zweigert and Kötz, above n 5, p 263. The adversarial system of trial is examined in 7.3 below.

[76] *Statements of case* (previously called *pleadings*) include claim forms (the document initiating civil action), particulars of claims, defences, counterclaims and replies to defences. They must include a statement of truth and contain only material facts and allegations the party intends to prove at trial, not legal argument: *A Dictionary of Law*, above n 15, p 525.

[77] Discussed further in 9.3.1 below.

1.6   Reflections on Legal Language—Advanced

Task 5 Opinions on legal English

Examine the evaluations of legal English given in the extracts below and consider how they relate to the features of legal language and texts you have observed in this chapter. Consider the following questions:

— Why is it desirable to simplify legal language as much as possible?
— How do some writers justify the complexity of legal English?
— Which opinions do you particularly agree or disagree with ?
— In your view, which perspectives apply equally to the legal language of your country?

Discuss your answers and exchange views.

A   To speak of legal language as communicating meaning is in itself rather misleading. Of all uses of language it is perhaps the least communicative, in that it is designed not so much to enlighten language-users at large as to allow one expert to register information for scrutiny by another. ... It is a form of language which is about as far removed as possible from informal spontaneous conversation. ... The reliance on forms which were established in the past and the reluctance to take risks by adopting new and untested modes of expression contribute to the extreme linguistic conservatism of legal English.[78]

B   Legal gobbledygook is under increasing attack. Lawyer prose is described as 'wordy, unclear, pompous and dull'. Books and articles suggest that lawyers can and should write 'Plain English'. In government there are efforts to require that statutes and regulations be written in language which the average citizen can understand. ...

Yet the movements towards simplified legal codes have failed to produce laws 'understandable by all'. Indeed, it is quite common to hear lawyers say 'I don't know what that statute means because it hasn't been interpreted.' Why the failure? A very important question for you as a member of the profession.

No doubt the social and economic position of lawyers is enhanced by a system of complicated law. Have lawyers torpedoed the efforts to simplify, jealous of their 'monopoly of explanation'? Or does the fault lie with the suspicion that simple words and sentences cannot capture all the nuances that make rules just?[79]

---

[78] D Crystal and D Davy (1969), *Investigating English Style*, Harlow: Longman, pp 193–94.
[79] K Hegland (1983), *Introduction to the Study and Practice of Law*, St Paul, Minn: West Publishing Co, pp 127–28.

C   It is a well-established dictum that ignorance of the law is not a valid excuse, if we wish to defend ourselves against a charge of wrongdoing. But knowledge presupposes comprehension. It is this simple fact which has made people feel they have a right to demand clarity from those who draft statutes, and the many kinds of publication (leaflets, notices, official letters, application forms) which stem from them.

Considerable progress has now been made in raising public awareness of these issues, thanks largely to the work of the Plain English Campaign. Many complex legal documents have been rendered into a more accessible English ...[80]

D   *The text below reproduces and comments on the* caution, *that is the official police warning that must be given to a person suspected of a crime before questioning, or on arrest. Can you understand it? Can ordinary English people understand it? What are the implications for language use in legal settings?*

'You do not have to say anything. But it may harm your defence if you do not mention when questioned something which you later rely on in court. Anything you do say may be given in evidence' (Code C, para 10.4). ... A team of psychologists read the new caution to 109 ordinary people. On average about half thought it made sense but only one in four actually understood the first part which tells the individual of his right to remain silent; one in eight understood the second element which warns that exercise of the right may harm one's defence later; and one in three understood the third part, which says that anything said may be used in evidence. They concluded that the length and complexity of the new formula 'ensures that it is beyond the ability of most people in the street to absorb, let alone comprehend' [research reference given].[81]

Ideas for Further Reading

Bingham, Tom (2000), *The Business of Judging. Selected Essays and Speeches 1985–1999*, Oxford: Oxford University Press. From 'Part IX Miscellaneous', Paper 3: 'The Future of the Common Law' (pp 375–89). Senior Law Lord, Lord Bingham surveys its historical development and considers future prospects for the common law. Fascinating reading, advanced level.

Crystal, David (1995), *The Cambridge Encyclopedia of the English Language*, Cambridge: Cambridge University Press. From Chapter 21, 'Social Variation: Legal English' (pp 374–76) and 'Plain English' (p 377). Illustrated with many

---

[80] D Crystal (1995), *The Cambridge Encyclopedia of the English Language*, Cambridge: Cambridge University Press, p 376.

[81] M Zander (1999), *Cases and Materials on the English Legal System*, 8th edn, London: Butterworths, p 129.

examples, renowned linguist David Crystal discusses the history, functions and complexity of legal English, and considers both the need to simplify legal language and the problems involved. Also, for linguists, Crystal, David, and Davy, Derek (1969), *Investigating English Style*, Harlow: Longman, Chapter 8, 'The Language of Legal Documents', pp 193–217.

Denning, A (1979), *The Discipline of Law*, London: Butterworths. Recommended for all readers: Chapter 1, 'Command of language' (pp 5–8). Written by an eminent judge, renowned for his role in the development of English civil law in the twentieth century, this paperback provides a fascinating, personal view of the judge's role in ensuring that principles of law respond to the developing needs of modern society. In 'Part One: The Construction of Documents' (pp 3–57), Lord Denning explores the difficulty of interpreting legal texts, illustrated by analysis of problems in significant cases in which he was judge. Should rigid legal rules or justice prevail in interpretation? For advanced readers, according to interest: Chapter 2, 'The interpretation of statutes' (pp 9–22); Chapter 3, 'The interpretation of wills and other unilateral documents' (pp 23–31); Chapter 4, 'The construction of contracts' and Chapter 5, 'Looking for help' (pp 32–57).

Fletcher, George P, and Sheppard, Steve (2005), *American Law in a Global Context*, New York: Oxford University Press. Chapter 3, 'The Language of Law. Common and Civil' (pp 54–74) looks at the importance of language in relation to the law itself. There is interesting discussion from a comparative angle of how the single English word 'law' corresponds to two Continental law terms (e.g. French *loi/droit*); for an in-depth study and comparison of self-defence in national and international law, see Chapter 29, 'Self-Defense: Domestic and International' (pp 568–90).

Riley, Alison (1996) 30 *The Law Teacher*, 'The Meaning of Words in English Legal Texts: Mastering the Vocabulary of the Law—A Legal Task' 68–83. Considers the special importance of words in the English legal system, analysing the classes and features of legal vocabulary and the contextual factors that accompany specific legal meanings. Advanced reading, of particular interest to teachers of legal English.

Chapter 2

LEGAL GRAMMAR

Text Layout and Use of Formal Terminology

Historical background – Text-mapping devices – Capitalisation – Punctuation –
Lexical variation – All-inclusiveness

The minute you read something that you can't understand, you can almost be
sure that it was drawn up by a lawyer.

Will Rogers, American entertainer, 1879–1935

Legal documents today are still greatly influenced by traditions established in the
past. Visual coherence of legal texts through the use of text-mapping devices, use
of punctuation (or the lack of it) and capitalisation, is essential to understanding the logical progression of their content. This chapter provides an overview of
these features.

2.1 Historical Background

Legal documents were originally written on wide pieces of parchment.[1] It was not
uncommon for a single sentence to extend from margin to margin without any
spacing or indentation. It has been suggested that this unbroken format was used
not only to avoid fraudulent deletions or additions, but also for economic use
of the parchment.[2] Another characteristic of legal texts is the words themselves,
which are notoriously difficult for the non-specialist. Frequent use of archaic
English, mixed with Latin and French legal terminology, distinguishes it from
Standard English, as does its extreme conservatism and formality, not to mention

---

[1] Parchment = paper-like quality made from the skin of a sheep or a goat.
[2] D Crystal and D Davy (1969), 'The Language of Legal Documents', *Investigating English Style*,
Harlow: Longman, p 197.

its 'tortuous syntax'.[3] Punctuation is another peculiarity: practically non-existent in early legal texts, even today, limiting punctuation to a minimum is the norm.

Yet this complexity of language which is characteristic of legal discourse is, at the present time, undergoing some significant changes: drafters are being requested, and indeed required in some jurisdictions, to make legal texts comprehensible to the non-specialist. In the 1970s, a movement called the Plain Language Movement grew in response to what is often called 'legalese'—the complicated language of legal documents—and it has had a consequential impact on the writing of documents in many countries, including those of the European Union. Various reforms have been proposed, such as: reducing the use of archaic and Latin expressions; restrictive use or total elimination of 'shall'; and even eliminating nominalisations which typically characterise legal texts.[4] However, progress is slow.

> [T]he main test can only come with time as the texts are subjected to the scrutiny of legal experts, for the final word must surely lie with the lawyers and judges who will be required to interpret the wording of the laws.[5]

2.2 Textual-mapping Devices

Today legal documents continue to be lengthy, yet through textual-mapping devices (use of space, sections and subsections) or capitalisation for typographical emphasis on words (type size, italics or bold), texts are more visually comprehensible for cross-referencing and for the logical progression of content and meaning.

Task 1 Read, scan and observe—textual-mapping devices
Scan Text 1 (an Act), Text 5 (a resolution), and Text 4 (a contract) in chapter one. Observe the following graphic devices in these prescriptive[6] texts:

— spacing
— sections
— use of bold
— font (type size and style)
— italics or capitalisation.

Highlight the script changes (the use of bold, capital letters, or the italics). Can you think of some reasons why drafters of these documents chose to alter the script?

---

[3] VK Bhatia (1993), 'Legal Discourse in Professional Settings', *Analyzing Genre*, London: Longman, p 101.

[4] C Williams (2007), *Tradition and Change in Legal English: Verbal Constructions in Prescriptive Texts*, Bern: Peter Lang. See ch 6 in this book for a comprehensive, up-to-date description of the Plain Language Movement.

[5] *Ibid*, p 193.

[6] Prescriptive texts impose an obligation or confer a right, such as treaties, constitutions, resolutions, contracts and legislative Acts.

2.3 CAPITALISATION

The criteria for deciding to use capitalisation or script changes (such as italics or capitals (upper case characters)) are not always clear. Crystal and Davy[7] have suggested some possible reasons: to dignify an item, for emphasis, for job titles and institutions, and to highlight specific words which are defined in the legal document.

2.3.1 Initial Capitalisation

Capitalisation of the first letter (other than proper names) is used for emphasis and is described as 'dignifying' a lexical item.[8] In the 'enacting words' of a UK Act of Parliament (e.g. the Terrorism Act 2000—see 1.3, Text 1), the letter 'B' is larger than the rest and in bold, while 'it' and 'enacted' are capitalised (upper case). This technique adds visual emphasis and further underlines the importance of the clause.

B<small>E IT</small> E<small>NACTED</small> by the Queen's most Excellent Majesty, by and with the advice and consent of the Lords Spiritual and Temporal, and Commons, in this present Parliament assembled, and by the authority of the same, as follows: ...[9]

Observe these recitals taken from preambles. The first letter is capitalised for emphasis even though it is not the beginning of the grammatical sentence:

Recognizing the urgent need for the universal application to women of the rights and principles with regard to equality, security, liberty, integrity and dignity of all human beings ...[10]

Whereas the people of New South Wales, Victoria, South Australia, Queensland, and Tasmania, humbly relying on the blessing of Almighty God, ...[11]

Reaffirming its commitment to strive for the promotion and protection of the rights of the child in all avenues of life ...[12]

---

[7] Crystal and Davy, above n 2.

[8] *Ibid*, p 199.

[9] Terrorism Act 2000, c 11.

[10] Declaration on the Elimination of Violence against Women (plenary meeting 20 December 1993) UNGA Res 48/104.

[11] Commonwealth of Australia Constitution Act 1900.

[12] Optional Protocol to the Convention on the Rights of the Child on the sale of children, child prostitution and child pornography (adopted 25 May 2000, entered into force 18 January 2002) UNGA Res 54/263, Preamble.

2.3.2 Emphasis within the Clause

It is not only the first word that is capitalised. Those that the draftsman considers important for a specific context are also capitalised:

> We the People of the United States, in Order to form a more perfect Union, establish Justice, insure domestic Tranquility, provide for the common defence, promote the general Welfare, and secure the Blessings of Liberty to ourselves and our Posterity, do ordain and establish this Constitution for the United States of America.[13]

2.3.3 Job Titles and Institutions

Job titles and institutions are capitalised. These rules conform to standard rules for capitalisation:

> The Secretary of State may by order make such transitional provision about the entitlement of holders of hereditary peerages to vote at elections to the House of Commons or the European Parliament as he considers appropriate.[14]

2.3.4 Specific Words

Script changes may occur in certain words. These include capitalisation (some or all the letters of a word), type size and style, and use of italics. Crystal and Davy[15] have grouped these changes into categories: proper names, personalia,[16] specific words defined in the document and organisational parts of the document.

Capitalisation may vary: all the letters may be in upper case, all in italics, or just the first letter capitalised and the rest in italics. The following examples were taken from a treaty:

— Proper names (standard capitalisation rules), e.g. Secretary-General of the United Nations, General Assembly of the United Nations;

— Personalia, e.g. HIGH CONTRACTING PARTIES, States Parties, States Members;

— Words that are given precise definitions in the document itself, e.g. the word *Committee* was specifically defined in this treaty:

> 1. There shall be established a Committee against Torture (hereinafter referred to as the Committee).[17]

— Organisation references, e.g. PART I, GENERAL PROVISIONS, *Article 1, Article 2, Section.*

---

[13] United States Constitution (adopted 1787, entered into force in 1789), Preamble.
[14] House of Lords Act 1999, s 5(3).
[15] Crystal and Davy, above n 2.
[16] Personalia (plural) refer to other similar references which are associated with that word.
[17] Convention against Torture and Other Cruel, Inhuman or Degrading Treatment or Punishment (adopted 10 December 1984, entered into force 26 June 1987) UNGA Res 39/46 Part II, art 17(1).

2.4 Punctuation

The absence of punctuation in legal documents has been widely debated over the years. As mentioned in 2.1 above, early legal documents consisted of uninterrupted text to avoid forgeries. Mellinkoff[18] adds an interesting historical dimension to the evolution of punctuation by suggesting that it was originally introduced in the eighteenth century in oral readings as a prosaic device to indicate the point at which the speaker should pause. Crystal and Davy[19] question the idea that earlier legal documents were 'punctuationless', stating that this was a later development. Nevertheless, while there is still distrust in the excessive use of punctuation, it is generally accepted as a guide to grammatical structure and coherence.

Task 2 Read, scan and observe—punctuation for coherence
This task draws your attention to the use of punctuation as a structural and cohesive device in legal documents. Scan Text 5 (a resolution), in chapter one:

— How many sentences are there in this extract?
— Which punctuation device—the comma [,], the full stop or period [.], the colon [:], or the semicolon [;]—is used the most?

Punctuation will be discussed further in chapter four.

2.5 Lexical Variation

2.5.1 Archaic Words and Phrases

Archaic words and phrases are often used, reflecting tradition and formality, with a distinct preference for the use of the suffix *–eth*, such as in *witnesseth*.[20] Instead of writing out the phrase in full, such as 'this document witnesseth that …', the single word *witnesseth* is often in bold and with a different or larger script style, and as such it assumes the quality of an imperative. Commonly placed at the beginning of contracts (although sometimes at the end) and affidavits, it is rarely used in contemporary English texts.[21] Other *–eth* examples include: *sayeth* (*saith*) and *deposeth*.

> **WITNESSETH** that in consideration of the promises and the agreement herein contained and intending to be legally bound hereby …

---

[18] Cited in Crystal and Davy, above n 2, p 200.
[19] *Ibid.*
[20] Witnesseth typically appears at the beginning of contracts and affidavits.
[21] 'Up to the 17th century, the suffix *–eth* was merely an alternate third person singular inflection for an English verb…', for example: he *calleth* instead of he calls (present-tense indicative). However, it still occasionally can be found in legal texts. See BA Garner (1995), *A Dictionary of Modern Legal Usage*, 2nd edn, New York: Oxford University Press, p 329.

Some archaic words still in use today include: hereto, hereon, hereunder, hereby, herein, hereinbefore, thereof, whereof, whereas, witnesseth, aforesaid, hereinbefore, hath been and duly made, e.g.:[22]

> *Whereas* the people of New South Wales, Victoria, South Australia, Queensland, and Tasmania, humbly relying on the blessing of Almighty God, have agreed to unite in one indissoluble Federal Commonwealth under the Crown of the United Kingdom of Great Britain and Ireland, and under the Constitution *hereby* established: …[23]

> Neither slavery nor involuntary servitude, except as a punishment for crime *whereof* the party shall have been *duly* convicted, shall exist within the United States, or any place subject to their jurisdiction.[24]

2.5.2 Law French and Law Latin

Over the centuries, legal terminology has acquired words derived from both French and Latin because of their shared linguistic history and the common law system.[25] Apart from being considered prestigious and dignified, many of these words and phrases are the technical language of law. Some Law French words include: *estoppel, fee, appeal, indictment, quash* and *acquis communautaire* (a contemporary French expression specific to EU law), e.g.:

The entire body of European Union laws is known as the *acquis communautaire.*

Observe the following:

> The Union shall be served by a single institutional framework which shall ensure the consistency and the continuity of the activities carried out in order to attain its objectives while respecting and building upon the 'acquis communautaire'.[26]

> The Divisional Court allowed the appeals and *quashed* the convictions.[27]

Some Law Latin terms include: *obiter dictum,*[28] *jus commune, amicus curiae, certiorari, habeas corpus, subpoena, prima facie, ratio decidendi, nolle prosequi, res judicata, bona fide, ex post facto*. For example:

> The privilege of the Writ of *Habeas Corpus* shall not be suspended, unless when in Cases of Rebellion or Invasion the public Safety may require it. No Bill of Attainder or *ex post facto* Law shall be passed.[29]

---

[22] See Table 2.1 at the end of this chapter for the interpretations of some of these words.

[23] Commonwealth of Australia Constitution Act 1900, recital in Preamble.

[24] United States Constitution, amend XIII, § 1 (proposed 31 January 1865, ratified 6 December 1865), Slavery Abolished.

[25] See Williams, above n 4, p 30, for a more in-depth account.

[26] Consolidated Version of the Treaty on European Union [2002] OJ C325/10, Art 3.

[27] *Director of Public Prosecutions v Jones and Another* [1999] UKHL 5.

[28] The plural form of *obiter dictum* is *obiter dicta.*

[29] US Constitution, Art I § 9, Limits on Congress.

2.5.3 Variation in Pronunciation

The pronunciation of Law Latin and Law French can vary from country to country. Check a legal dictionary for the correct pronunciation and word stress.

> **Task 3 Scan Text 4 (a contract)—archaic, Law Latin and Law French terms**
> Scan Text 4 in chapter one and write any archaic, Law Latin or Law French terms that were cited earlier in the spaces below. Are there any words that are frequently repeated? If you are unfamiliar with the meanings of the words, consult Table 2.1 at the end of this chapter. Observe these terms in other legal texts.
>
> ....
>
> ....
>
> ....
>
> ....
>
> ....

2.6 ALL-INCLUSIVENESS

Bhatia[30] says that legal writing tends to be 'all-inclusive' in order to maximise understanding and exactness of reference. Crystal and Davy[31] confirm this when they state that 'the lexical item is solemnly repeated' to avoid any possible ambiguities or misinterpretation. As a result, legal texts have acquired some rather unusual characteristics which in another genre would be considered unacceptable: repetition of words and expressions and syntactic structures, rare use of pronouns for anaphoric reference,[32] amplification of synonyms, and common use of double nouns or adjectives with the conjunction *and* to render words all-inclusive.

2.6.1 Frequent Repetition of Lexical Items, Expressions and Syntactic Structures

Repetition of a noun instead of substitution with pronouns such as *she, he, it* or *they* is particularly common. Observe the repetition of 'European Parliament'

---

[30] Bhatia, above n 3, p 102.
[31] Crystal and Davy, above n 2, p 202.
[32] An anaphoric reference identifies what has been referred to previously in a text.

in the following extract, instead of substituting it with a pronoun for anaphoric reference:

> The Presidency shall consult the *European Parliament* on the main aspects and the basic choices of the common foreign and security policy and shall ensure that the views of the *European Parliament* are duly taken into consideration. The *European Parliament* shall be kept regularly informed by the Presidency and the Commission of the development of the Union's foreign and security policy. The *European Parliament* may ask questions of the Council or make recommendations to it.[33]

Frequent repetition of expressions include: *in accordance with, in respect of, pursuant to, in pursuance of, implementation of, measures adopted by, deliver opinions at, ensure that the, be composed of, for the purpose of, by virtue of.*

Recurrent use of syntactic organisation is also common. For example, recitals found in the preambles to treaties inevitably use non-finite *–ed* participle phrases and non-finite *–ing* forms,[34] such as:

> DETERMINED to lay the foundations of an ever closer union among the peoples of Europe,

> RESOLVED to ensure the economic and social progress of their countries by common action to eliminate the barriers which divide Europe,

> AFFIRMING as the essential objective of their efforts the constant improvement of the living and working conditions of their peoples,

> RECOGNIZING that the removal of existing obstacles calls for concerted action in order to guarantee steady expansion, balanced trade and fair competition,

> ...[35]

2.6.2 Doubling or Tripling Words and Synonym Strings

For exactness of reference, words are often doubled or tripled in order to become more all-inclusive. George P Krapp says that doubling was abundantly present also in Old English and is certainly not a new phenomenon, while Garner suggests that writers in the Early Renaissance often paired words together for etymological reasons, for example *goods and chattels* (both indicating moveable property) which have survived in legal language from Old English and Old French respectively.[36]

---

[33] Treaty on European Union [Maastricht1992] OJ C191/01, Art J(7).

[34] Non-finite verbs such as *resolved* or *affirming* in preambles lack tense and mood. For example, we have no idea of when this statement was made. A finite verb will provide the tense, the participants and the number of participants.

[35] The recitals were taken from the Preamble to the Consolidated Version of the Treaty Establishing the European Community [2002] OJ C325.

[36] GP Krapp (1962), *A Comprehensive Guide to Good English*, New York: Ungar, as cited in Garner, above n 21, p 292.

The following lists cite just a few common legal doublets and triplets in legal texts (note that that these words are *synonyms* and have similar meanings):

— Doublets: *act* and *deed*; *authorise* and *direct*; *authorise* and *empower*; *by* and *through*; *bind* and *obligate*; *execute* and *perform*; *force* and *effect*; *keep* and *maintain*; *legal* and *valid*; *null* and *void*; *power* and *authority*; *terms* and *conditions*; *uphold* and *support*; *will* and *testament*.

— Triplets: *cancel, annul* and *set aside*; *form, manner* and *method*; *pay, satisfy* and *discharge*; *promise, agree* and *covenant*; *right, title* and *interest*; *way, shape* and *form*.

2.6.3 Compound Subjects/Objects/Adjectives/Verbs

Words or phrases that have some semantic relationship (some shared meaning in a specific context) are often expanded further through the use of the conjunctions *and* or *or* (but are not synonyms). They are sometimes referred to as binomial or multinomial expressions. Once again, this is a strategy typical of legal texts in order to extend a wider frame of reference. Some examples include:

advice and consent; capital and earnings; signed and delivered; capital and payments; Cases and Codes; the circumstances and the manner; in whole or in part; establish and maintain; claims and liabilities; small and medium-sized undertakings; ratifications deposited and accessions notified; common foreign and security policy; protecting works and other subject-matter; under or in accordance with.

KEY AND COMMENTARY

> **Key**
>
> **Task 1   Read, scan and observe—textual-mapping devices**
> The drafters of these documents chose to alter the text for many reasons: to dignify an item, for emphasis, for job titles and institutions, and for specific words that are defined in the legal document.
>
> **Task 2   Read, scan and observe—punctuation for coherence**
>
> — There is *one* sentence.
> — Frequency of punctuation: comma (11), semicolon (5), full stop or period (1), colon (0).
>
> **Task 3   Scan Text 4 (a contract)—archaic, Law Latin and Law French terms**
>
> — Archaic, Law Latin and Law French terms: hereto, hereby, duly
> — The modal auxiliary *shall* is frequently repeated.

Commentary

Drafters of legal documents use distinct text-mapping devices so that the reader is able to follow without much difficulty the progression of content in these typically wordy documents. As you have noticed, spacing is important, as is the use of script changes for emphasis, capitalisation for stressing the importance of certain lexical terms, and organisational lettering or numbering for systematic sequencing of amendments or provisions (for example in a treaty or an Act). The sentences are generally long and complex, yet thanks to the graphological support of textual mapping, any section of the document becomes 'readable' without having to refer back to the beginning of the document. Drafters of legal documents aim for exactness of reference and all-inclusiveness so that every possible contingency is unambiguous. Achieving this is not always such an easy task.

Table 2.1: Legal jargon table with definitions

Legal jargon	Part of speech	Meaning
aforementioned, said, aforesaid	adjective	the exact same one mentioned above (an anaphoric referent)
duly, duly made	adverb	properly
hereafter	adverb	from this point onwards; henceforth
hereby	adverb	by these very words
herein	adverb	in this document, or section, or matter
hereinafter	adverb	later in the document
hereof	adverb	of this section, of this provision
hereto	adverb	to this document
heretofore	adverb	before now, up to now
hereunder	adverb	in accordance with this document, later in this document
herewith	adverb	with or in this document
therein	adverb	in that place and time
thereof	adverb	of that, it or them
thereto/thereunto	adverb	to that or them
theretofore	adverb	up to that time
thereupon	adverb	without delay; promptly
whereas	conjunction	given the fact that; while
whereof	relative pronoun	of what, of which
whilst (BrE)	conjunction	while, although, whereas
witnesseth	imperative or present tense (third person singular)	'This document witnesses that ...' *Witnesseth* usually appears in all capitals (upper case), or is otherwise distinguished from other words typographically (for example, in italics). It may also occur at the end of a document.

CONSOLIDATION PART I – LANGUAGE FOCUS TASKS

Task A – Which One Word or Phrase is Out of Context?

0	recital	article	preamble	statute
1	enactment	judgment	code	legislation
2	ratify	adopt	enact	sign
3	charter	treaty	pact	declaration
4	a resolution	an Act	long title	short title
5	Maastricht	Rome	Lisbon	Frankfurt
6	arrest warrant	divorce decree	delegated legislation	affidavit
7	constitutional convention	Royal Prerogative	Royal Assent	judicial precedent
8	legal codes	*ratio decidendi*	*stare decisis*	binding precedent
9	House of Lords	House of Commons	Lords Spiritual	Lords Temporal
10	Scotland Act 1998	constitutional reform	devolution	common law
11	18 years old	minor	age of majority	adult
12	US Constitution	UN Security Council Resolution	The Ballad of Reading Gaol	Terrorism Act 2000

Task B – Match the Terms with the Definition[1]

recitals	legally binding	declaration
jurisdiction	High Contracting Parties	treaty
protocols	preamble	ratify
binding precedent	Royal Prerogative	*ratio decidendi*
constitutional convention	*stare decisis*	affidavit

1	....	nations (States) that are party to an agreement
2	....	an obligation not imposed in the British constitution by law or by judicial precedent but by usage
3	....	to confirm or approve of an agreement officially so that it becomes valid
4	....	a judicial decision which future courts must follow when deciding on similar cases
5	....	treaties may often be amended with these additions
6	....	in international law, it is the territory over which a State has legal authority
7	....	an introductory statement (to a treaty, a constitution or other legal instrument, which explains the document's basis and objective)
8	....	a series of listed points providing background information and explaining a document's purpose
9	....	an official statement that is not legally binding

[1] Task B references used to create definitions: BA Garner (1995), *A Dictionary of Modern Legal Usage*, 2nd edn, Oxford: Oxford University Press; *Black's Law Dictionary, Pocket Edition* (1996), BA Garner (ed), Eagan, Minn: West Publishing Co; *Oxford Dictionary of Law* (2009), J Law and E Martin (eds), 7th edn, Oxford: Oxford University Press.

10	....	a Latin phrase meaning: 'stand by the decision'—refers to the obligation of courts to honour past precedents
11	....	rights and powers belonging to the British King or Queen
12	....	a Latin phrase meaning 'the reason for the decision'—the principle or rule of law on which a judicial decision is founded
13	....	convention, a pact, an accord, an alliance, charter
14	....	having legal effect
15	....	a written statement of facts sworn before an authorised officer

Task C – Word Formation

a) Fill in the spaces below [...] with the appropriate word form.

Words that are not necessarily used in a legal context, or a variant no longer in use, have not been included in the table. The [x] in the table indicates that the form does not exist or that it is uncommon in a legal context. If necessary, read chapter 10 before doing this task or consult a dictionary.

	verb	**noun** (concept)	**noun** (person)	**adjective**
1	to oblige/ .... (2)	obligation	x	obligatory obligated
2	to legislate	legislation	legislator/ legislature	....
3	to judge/to judicialize (AmE)	judgment	judge/ .... (2)	judicial
4	to litigate	....	litigant litigator	litigatory/litigable litigational/ litigated litigious
5	....	approbation approval	x	approved approving

6	to ratify	....	x	ratified
7	....	prohibition	x	prohibitory/ prohibited
8	to enact	....	x	enacting/enacted

b)   Using the table above, insert the appropriate word in the spaces below: verb, noun (concept), noun (person) or adjective:

9   The right of .... review is one of the powers of the US Supreme Court.

10   In cases where .... exists to govern an issue in a dispute, that is the source of law which courts must use to resolve the dispute.

11   Lord Bingham's opinion is considered to be the leading .... in the case.

12   In the Terrorism Act 2000, the second paragraph contains the .... words 'Be it enacted', a standard formula declaring the Act to be a legal source.

13   Should the wearing of the burqa be .... in public schools?

14   A settlement was reached after more than five years of .... on behalf of the residents.

15   The parliaments of Australia and Indonesia have not yet .... the treaty.

Task D – Prefixes and Suffixes

Fill in the missing suffixes or prefixes to the following terms. Identify the appropriate word form.

The [x] indicates that the form does not exist or that it is uncommon in a legal context.

	Prefixes	*adjective*	*noun concept*
0	contested	uncontested	x
1	legal		x
2	compatible		
3	accessible		
4	direct		x
5	lawful		x

	Suffixes		
0	constitution	constitutional	constitutionality
6	implement		
7	sovereign	x	
8	limit		
9	parliament		x
10	violate		

TASK E – COLLOCATION

Match the words 1–10 with the appropriate words a–j, and write the matching identifiers in the first column of the table. Think about the meaning of each term or phrase.

...1d...	1	The Queen	a	binding agreement
......	2	trial	b	decrees
......	3	statutory	c	self-defence
......	4	hereby	d	in Parliament
......	5	divorce	e	legal effect
......	6	legally	f	legislation
......	7	collective	g	by jury
......	8	reach	h	interpretation
......	9	secondary	i	appoints
......	10	producing	j	a verdict

Part II

The Language of a Legal System and the British Constitution

Chapter 3

LANGUAGE AND LAW

Sources of Law and the Constitution of the UK

Introduction to the sources of law – The British constitutional monarchy – Consulting legislation: UK constitutional reform – Parliament: the House of Lords and the House of Commons – Law, the legislature and the courts – Constitutional legislation and EU law in the national system

Whereas the Lords Spiritual and Temporal and Commons assembled at Westminster, lawfully, … being now assembled in a full and free representative of this nation … do in the first place (as their ancestors in like case have usually done) for the vindicating and asserting their ancient rights and liberties declare:

That the pretended power of suspending the laws or the execution of laws by regal authority without consent of Parliament is illegal;

That the pretended power of dispensing with laws or the execution of laws by regal authority, as it hath been assumed and exercised of late, is illegal; …

That the freedom of speech and debates or proceedings in Parliament ought not to be impeached or questioned in any court or place out of Parliament; …

And that for redress of all grievances, and for the amending, strengthening and preserving of the laws, Parliaments ought to be held frequently.

Bill of Rights 1689

3.1 INTRODUCTION TO THE SOURCES OF LAW

3.1.1 Introduction

Laws, courts and the constitution are at the heart of a legal system. In this chapter, we study the foundations of a legal system and its language in the context of English law and the British Constitution.

The English legal system has two principal sources of law: legislation and judicial precedent. In this chapter, we answer questions such as: What is the nature of each source? What is the relationship between them? What language do we use to talk about them? One of the key distinctions between the common law and civil law legal families is the different system of sources. We examine the role of legislation in a common law system, highlighting the different functions of Parliament and the courts. The use of judicial precedent as a source of law is introduced, a theme explored further in chapter nine.

It is well known that the United Kingdom does not have a *written constitution*. In chapter one we examined part of the Constitution of the United States of America. No equivalent constitutional text exists in the UK, even though many constitutions in the world today have been shaped by the Westminster[1] model of government. So, is it true to say that Britain has a constitution? Naturally, the answer is yes: a State's constitution is the system of rules defining the composition, powers and relations of the *State organs* (the *legislature*, *executive* and *judiciary*); it also regulates relations between the State and individuals, and defines the scope and limits of State powers to interfere with personal freedom.

The UK has a constitution, but it is not embodied in a single written text: it is *unwritten*. Professor Leyland explains that '[i]n modern times there has been no single domestic event that has required a comprehensive revision of the UK constitution and so the United Kingdom has no constitutional text with this special status'.[2] The constitution derives instead from a variety of sources, including legislation, judicial precedent and a particular constitutional source, called *convention*. We examine examples of these sources in this chapter.

The British Constitution has 'evolved in phases reflecting the political, social, and economic experiences of many centuries'.[3] The historic Bill of Rights, cited above, is one constitutional source. The *rights and liberties* it asserted in 1689 were already defined as '*ancient* rights and liberties'. The Bill of Rights marked a shift in the balance of power between King and Parliament. From that time on, the supremacy of Parliament was not open to question: it stated that it is '*illegal*' for the monarch, using '*regal* authority' to suspend laws '*without consent of Parliament*'. Significantly, it followed a dramatic period in English history: civil war, revolution, the legal execution of a King[4] and an interlude of republican government.[5] England had four separate constitutions between 1649 and 1659,[6] then a chaotic period leading up to the restoration of the monarchy in 1660.[7]

The Constitution of the United Kingdom is still evolving today. During the period of Labour Government from 1997, important constitutional reforms were introduced by statute, and further significant reforms have been made more recently by the

---

[1] Since the time of King Canute (1016–35) Westminster has been the seat of government in England (and later, of the United Kingdom). The name *Westminster* is sometimes used as a synonym for *government* or *parliament*. The Palace of Westminster, originally a royal residence, houses the two chambers of Parliament: the House of Lords and the House of Commons.

[2] P Leyland (2012), *The Constitution of the United Kingdom. A Contextual Analysis*, 2nd edn, Oxford: Hart Publishing, p 14.

[3] Ibid.

[4] Charles I.

[5] From 1649 to 1660.

[6] K Morgan (1984), *The Oxford Illustrated History of Britain*, Oxford: Oxford University Press, p 325.

[7] Charles II.

Conservative-Liberal Democrat Coalition Government.[8] We examine some constitutional reforms in 3.2 and 3.3 below,[9] while also focusing on two principal actors in the Constitution: the *monarch* and the *Prime Minister*. The relative powers of the two Houses of Parliament are viewed in the context of a controversial Act (see 3.4).

In the Advanced section of this chapter, we consider the relative roles in the Constitution of the legislature and the judiciary, and the importance of statute as a constitutional source; we also consult some legislation in the fields of contract and criminal law (at 3.5). To conclude, the doctrine of *parliamentary sovereignty* is discussed, in the light of the impact of EU law in the national system (see 3.6).

3.1.2 Terminology Focus: Laws and Legislation, Courts and Cases

Task 1 Word associations
— Which of the following terms do you associate with Laws and Legislation (L), or with the Courts and Cases (C), or both (LC)?
— Use the Glossary or a dictionary to check your ideas and note any useful information: a good definition, a collocation, word families.
— As you study this chapter, observe the use of these terms and select examples and definitions to expand your personal terminology system.[10]
— Consider appropriate translations for these terms.

Act	(L)	*an Act of Parliament; Scotland Act 1998*
Approval	(L)	*Parliament's approval of a law; to approve a law*
A Bill	(L)	*a proposal of law; a Bill becomes an Act*
A claim	(C)	*a civil claim; a claimant makes a claim*
A judge	(C)	
A judgment		
A precedent		
A (legal) rule		
A sentence of imprisonment		
A verdict of not guilty		
Case law		
Law reform		
Statute law		
The Act provides that …		
The defendant		
The judiciary		
The jury		

---

[8] From May 2010.
[9] While the Human Rights Act 1998 is examined in 5.4.
[10] Introduced in 1.2.5 above.

The legislature
To enact law

Check your answers in the Key at the end of this chapter.

3.1.3 Translating Legal Terminology

Translating legal terminology into your own language can be a useful aid to grasping English legal terms and increasing your knowledge of specialised vocabulary. But legal translation is not an easy task: we strongly advise you not to use phrase by phrase translation as a method for understanding English legal texts. The techniques practised in this book, including global reading followed by reading for detail and searching for legal content, are more effective approaches; building your knowledge of text types and legal background is also essential.

When you choose to translate terminology, your task is to look for an *equivalent* term—if it exists—in the other legal system and language. This is a comparative legal task which requires you to compare two different legal cultures. We must be sensitive to how terminology expresses the particular categories, concepts, institutions, methods and procedures of a certain legal system. Where the two systems belong to two different *legal families*, differences may be marked.

Example: Act. Consider the function of an Act in the UK legal system.[11] *What source of law is comparable in your system? What terminology is used for that source?*

The term(s) you choose as translations for *Act* should be equivalent in the different legal systems, even though the system of sources, and also legislative *procedures*, may be different in the UK and your country.

To take another example: *rule* or *legal rule* is a basic law term. It may be associated with both legislation and with cases (solution LC in Task 1): in fact, in a common law system, *rules* may derive from either *statute law* or *judicial precedent*. In legal English, the term *rule* is used more frequently than *norm*, a term found more often in international law and in philosophical discussions of general legal theory. Does the legal language of your system possess one or two terms for *rule* and *norm*? If more than one, are the terms used distinctly?

Sometimes we may be satisfied with our translation even if the terms are not precisely equivalent in the two legal systems we are comparing. For example, we should be aware that the *legal rule* contained in a common law *precedent* is closely linked to *the facts of the case*.[12] By contrast, the rule contained in a *civil law code* is not linked to a particular dispute but is a generalised, abstract norm. Subtle distinctions such as these are inevitable when we translate terminology between different legal systems and families.

---

[11] Discussed in 1.3 above, Text 1.
[12] This is explored in 9.3.3.

> NOTE: *When translating, remember to use your legal knowledge about both legal systems to arrive at suitable solutions; use specialised works of reference, such as law dictionaries in each language. Do not accept general bilingual dictionary translations without critical reflection.*

A technique that is especially useful for translating institutional terminology—where it is appropriate to do so—is to use a 'transparent translation': the meaning of the term should be evident in the other language, because similar vocabulary is used, even if no corresponding institution exists in that system, or even if the institutional language of that system is distinct. From the 'transparent' words chosen in the translation, an expert in the subject should understand the meaning.

Example: *Court of Cassation* (not an English institution) to translate *Cour de cassation* (French).[13]

Could you suggest translations into your language for the following terms from chapter one? Royal Assent, jury, Senator

Lastly, we must accept that some English law terms do not have a true equivalent in the language of the civil law and vice versa. A well-known example is the term *trust*: the trust was developed by the English Court of Chancery as part of *Equity*, a system of rules and principles created to supplement the common law where this had become too rigid to provide justice in individual cases.

A *trust* is a complex type of property arrangement where, for example, the interests of a weak *beneficiary*—such as a child—can be protected, since the *trust property* is transferred from the original owner (the *settlor*) to one or more legal owners (the *trustees*), who hold the property *on trust* and must administer it, in accordance with the terms of the trust, for the benefit of the *beneficiaries*. The trust has a wide variety of applications; one contemporary example is the creation of a *statutory trust* (one created by statute law) to protect the clients of a bank from losing their money in the case of the firm's insolvency.[14] The trust, as such, is a term untranslatable into many languages, since it has no direct conceptual equivalent in the civil law;[15] it may, however, be possible to compare civil law solutions.[16]

> NOTE: *With these ideas in mind, critically assess your translations of the terms in Task 1 above. As you continue to read this chapter, consider possible translations of key terminology, where this is helpful to you.*

---

[13] Translation taken from the European Union IATE (InterActive Terminology for Europe) multilingual database, which can be freely consulted online: <http://iate.europa.eu>.

[14] These rules, contained in ch 7 of the *Client Assets Sourcebook*, known as 'CASS 7' (issued by the Financial Services Authority for the safeguarding and distribution of client money in implementation of the Markets in Financial Instruments Directive 2004/39/EC), are explained by Lord Hope in his judgment in *In the matter of Lehman Brothers International (Europe) (In Administration)*; *In the matter of the Insolvency Act 1986* [2012] UKSC 6.

[15] F de Franchis (1984), *Dizionario giuridico, Vol 1 Inglese-italiano*, Milan: Giuffré, p 1477.

[16] *Ibid*, pp 1477–87.

3.1.4 Legislation and Judicial Precedent

English law has two principal sources: legislation and judicial precedent. What is the nature of each source? What is the relationship between them? What language is used to talk about these different sources of law? In Task 2 below, some language and basic facts are introduced. You will observe that it is appropriate to use distinct terminology and other legal vocabulary for the two sources.

Task 2 Introducing legislation and judicial precedent

Examine the following table, which introduces some terminology and key aspects of legislation and judicial precedent. Try to understand the main distinctions and observe the specific language used for each source.

As you work, insert these missing terms in suitable positions in the text: *common law – legislative – the law reports – case law – enactments – secondary legislation – ratio decidendi – to follow precedent – statutes.*

LEGISLATION	JUDICIAL PRECEDENT
Definition Law or laws enacted by the legislative organ (the *legislature*) following a recognised procedure. Also called: *Acts of Parliament,* _____ , *laws* or _____. Collective terms: *legislation, statute law, enacted law.* **Example** *The European Communities Act 1972* gave effect in the national legal system to Britain's obligations as a Member State of the European Communities–today, the European Union. *By virtue of this Act,* EU law is also a source of English law and *prevails over national law* in cases of conflict.[17]	**Definition** The body of legal rules established in decided cases, created and developed by the English superior courts. Also called: *judicial decision, precedent,* _____, _____. Precedents may also be called *authorities.* Singular: a precedent, an authority. The principles of the common law are found in *judgments* of the superior courts, published in the volumes of _____. **Example** *Carlill v Carbolic Smoke Ball Co* [1893] 1 QB 256 is *a precedent* in the English law of contract: *it established the principle* of unilateral contracts, namely, that an offer made to the public in general may form the basis of a contract and that the offer is accepted by an individual who performs the conditions (forming a binding contract).[18]

---

[17] For more on this subject, see 3.6.2 below.

[18] The judgment in this case is analysed for the foreign reader in A Riley (1991), *English for Law,* Harlow: Pearson Education Limited, pp 116–32.

Further information *Delegated legislation* (also called _____) may be enacted by other persons or bodies under authority delegated by Parliament. E.g. Directive 2002/58/EC *was* *implemented* in UK law by the Privacy and Electronic Communications (EC Directive) Regulations 2003, a *statutory* *instrument* made by the designated government minister.	**Further information** The part of a judgment which is *binding* and operates as precedent is only the _____. That is, the reason or principle upon which the judges' decision on *the issue* (the question before the court) was based.[19]
Operation as a source of law In cases where legislation exists *to* *govern* a legal question in a *dispute*, that is the source of law which the courts must *apply*. Legislation *has priority over* judicial precedent: it must be applied even if there is a conflicting precedent. **The role of the courts** The courts *interpret* the provisions of the law by examining the _____ text to find *the* *intention of Parliament*, a process called *statutory interpretation*. The job of the courts is to apply the law to the specific facts of the individual dispute.	**Operation as a source of law** In cases where no legislation exists *to govern an issue in a dispute*, precedent is the source of law that the courts use to resolve it, *creating, developing* and *applying* principles on a case-by-case basis. According to the *doctrine* *of binding precedent*, courts deciding later, similar cases *must* apply the same principles established in precedent. We say that the courts *are bound* _____. The doctrine of binding precedent is also known by the Latin term *stare decisis*. The system operates within the strict framework of the *hierarchy of the* *courts*.[20]
The doctrine of binding precedent also applies to *statutory interpretation*. Therefore, where the courts have interpreted a legislative provision in a specific way in relation to certain facts in a previous case, the same interpretation must be given by courts in *later similar cases*, always subject to the *hierarchy of the courts*.	

Check your answers in the Key at the end of this chapter.

---

[19] For more on the *ratio decidendi*, see 9.3.3 and 9.6.2 below.
[20] Examined in 9.3.3 below.

SECTION ONE

3.2 Introduction to the British Constitutional Monarchy

3.2.1 Legislation and the Legislature: the Queen in Parliament

Legislation is *enacted law*: it is formally enacted by the *legislature*—the State organ with legislative power—according to a procedure recognised as valid for producing law within the legal system. Enacted law is also called *written law*. Legislation is commonly referred to in Britain as *statute law*. The *legislature* may also be called *the legislator* or *law-maker*.[21]

By contrast, judicial precedent is *unwritten law*: it is pronounced by the judges when deciding cases, but is not formally *enacted* by the legislature. We refer to it as *judge-made law*, or frequently as *common law* or *case law*.

Even in the common law system, judges are not *legislators* and distinct terminology is used; but we sometimes use the term *judicial law-making* to refer to the judges' creative role in developing legal principles. They do not have general legislative power but only power to determine the legal questions that come before the court in the course of disputes.

The legislature is one of the three main *powers* or *State organs*, together with the *executive* and the *judiciary* (the collective term for all judges). The legislature may be defined as 'the body having primary power to make written law'.[22] Notice, below, the two meanings of the term *legislation*:

> **Legislation** *n* **1.** The whole or any part of a country's written law. In the UK the term is normally confined to Acts of Parliament, but in its broadest sense it also includes law made under powers conferred by Act of Parliament ... **2.** The process of making written law.[23]

Acts of Parliament are classified as *primary legislation*: they are enacted directly by the legislature itself. And normally when we refer to *legislation* we mean, precisely, an Act or Acts of Parliament. But the legislature may also *delegate legislative power* to another body or individual, such as a government minister. When that body exercises the power granted to it by Parliament, the provisions it enacts are not primary but *subordinate legislation*, also called *secondary* or *delegated legislation*.[24]

In the UK Constitution the legal name for the legislature is *the Queen in Parliament*.[25] It is composed of the monarch (the Queen or King, the *Sovereign*),

---

[21] *Legislator* is a personalised form, less commonly used.
[22] *A Dictionary of Law*, 7th edn (2009, updated reissue 2013), E Martin and J Law (eds), Oxford: Oxford University Press, p 322.
[23] *Ibid.*
[24] E.g. the *statutory instrument* used to implement the EU Directive examined in ch 1, Text 10.
[25] The King in Parliament when the monarch is a king.

the House of Lords and the House of Commons. These three components are all mentioned in the *enacting words*, that is, the formula that introduces the main body of an Act of Parliament, giving it the *force of law*.

The enacting words

> BE IT ENACTED by the Queen's most Excellent Majesty, by and with the advice and consent of the Lords Spiritual and Temporal, and Commons, in this present Parliament assembled, and by the authority of the same, as follows:–

The enacting words refer first to the Queen, then to the House of Lords with its two classes of *peers* (the Lords Spiritual and the Lords Temporal)[26] and lastly to the House of Commons.

But which of these three elements is the most important component of the legislature today? In a modern democracy, it is naturally the body that *represents* the people: the House of Commons—the *representative body*—whose members are elected by *direct universal adult suffrage*.[27] The UK is not an *absolute monarchy* but has evolved over the centuries from a *ruling monarchy*, where a monarch governs the country in person, to a *constitutional monarchy*: this means that the powers of the monarch are constitutionally limited. In addition, the House of Commons today has supremacy over the House of Lords, a body that is still *unelected* and therefore *not* representative, although some reforms have been made and there are further proposals for *reform*.[28]

3.2.2 The Prime Minister

The leader of the *government* is the Prime Minister (PM), who is always a Member of the House of Commons. In the absence of a written constitution, the office of Prime Minister is not defined by statute but originated through practice from the early eighteenth century: the Prime Minister emerged as a leading political figure among the King's small group of ministers; he had to have the confidence of both the King and Parliament.[29]

Today it is a recognised rule of the constitution based on practice that the Prime Minister is the leader of the *political party* with a majority of *seats* in the House of Commons: this is a *constitutional convention*—an obligation imposed not by a statute or by the common law but by usage. A *convention* is a recognised

---

[26] The Lords Temporal are the life peers and 92 hereditary peers remaining after the House of Lords Act 1999 (3.4.1 below); the Lords Spiritual are the Archbishops and certain bishops of the Church of England. The British monarch is the temporal head of the Church of England, while its spiritual head is the Archbishop of Canterbury.

[27] For women's suffrage, see 3.6.1 below.

[28] See 3.4.1 below.

[29] Leyland, above n 2, p 158.

political practice considered *binding* by all the actors in the British Constitution. *By convention*, the Prime Minister chooses the government ministers, and invites the most important ministers to form a *Cabinet*, over which the Prime Minister presides; Cabinet meetings are held in the Prime Minister's Office and official London home, 10 Downing Street, in Whitehall.

Task 3 Reading and reflection—the Prime Minister

What is the importance of the Prime Minister in the UK Constitution today? Read Peter Leyland's analysis, below, for general understanding. Then read the text in detail to answer the following questions. Focus on both language and meaning.

1. What is the role of the Prime Minister in the Constitution?
2. What are the chief responsibilities of the Prime Minister?
3. What impact do different personal styles have on the post of PM?
4. What are the PM's powers in relation to government ministers?
5. What functions does the PM perform at international level?
6. Why do you think it is apt to call some Prime Ministers elected monarchs?

> In terms of the exercise of constitutional power, it is helpful to view the UK political system as hierarchical, with the Prime Minister, and the Office at 10 Downing Street, at the apex of a triangle. At the next level we find the Cabinet Office, the departments of state, and then junior ministers responsible for particular policy domains. ...

> Not only does the holder of prime ministerial office head the government, represent the nation, and lead the largest political party, but the Prime Minister is responsible for taking many decisions that determine domestic policy and the conduct of foreign affairs and for making an enormous range of appointments (in many cases these are rubber-stamped by the monarch).

> While it is widely recognised that a UK Prime Minister has wide-ranging powers at his or her disposal, it is also clear that there is considerable scope to pursue a personal style of leadership. Some Prime Ministers, for example, John Major, favoured a more collegiate approach (a style referred to as *primus inter pares*) while others such as Margaret Thatcher and Tony Blair mould the office around their own personality, and they have become known for a more presidential style of leadership (virtually an *elected monarch*) ...

> In the contemporary constitution it is the support of Parliament, or more precisely the elected House of Commons, that is crucial. After a general election the leader of the political party with a majority in the House of Commons will be called upon by the sovereign to form a government, and he or she will automatically become Prime Minister. ... Once confirmed in office by the monarch, a Prime Minister is responsible for forming the government. The only limits on the selections dictated by convention are that all ministers must

be members of Parliament and that the Prime Minister and the Chancellor of the Exchequer must be members of the House of Commons. ... A Prime Minister can also dismiss ministers and reconstitute the government at any time by reshuffling the pack. ... Many of the powers that the Prime Minister now enjoys are prerogative powers which were formerly the personal prerogatives of the Sovereign. ...

As head of the government, the Prime Minister represents the nation on the international stage and at EU summits. In this capacity the UK Prime Minister often takes a leading role, together with the Foreign Office, when entering into treaty negotiations with other nations.

(Extracts from P Leyland (2012), *The Constitution of the United Kingdom. A Contextual Analysis*, 2nd edn, Oxford: Hart Publishing, pp 158–60) © Peter Leyland 2012

Key and commentary to Task 3 Reading and reflection—the Prime Minister

1. The PM—the '*holder of prime ministerial office*'—is the most important political figure in the Constitution, 'at the apex' (the top) of a *hierarchical* political system; he or she is the *head of the government* (or, *he or she heads* the government).

2. The PM is responsible for the government of the country and has '*wide-ranging powers*': to decide *home* affairs ('*domestic* policy') and '*foreign affairs*'; he or she also makes many '*appointments*', having the right to select individuals for public positions; and these are formally but automatically approved by the Queen (they are 'rubber-stamped by the monarch').

3. The 'personal style of *leadership*' has a great impact on the post: one PM may act as '*primus inter pares*' (*first among equals*) in the Cabinet of ministers over which he or she presides; but another personality may adopt a 'more *presidential* style of leadership', as Margaret Thatcher and Tony Blair notably did.

4. The PM is entirely responsible for *forming the government*. He or she has a virtually free choice in selecting the ministers: *by convention* they must be members of the House of Lords or the House of Commons, while the Chancellor of the Exchequer (the government's chief financial minister), must, like the PM, be an elected Member of the House of Commons. But the PM also has power to vary the composition of the government by *dismissing ministers* and substituting them at his or her pleasure: this is known as a *Cabinet reshuffle*—'reshuffling the pack' is a metaphor from a game of cards. The power of the PM to select all the ministers will be limited when, as at the time of writing, there is a *coalition agreement*.[30]

---

[30] Since some senior ministers will be chosen by the other coalition party, currently the Liberal Democrats, whose leader, Nick Clegg, is Deputy Prime Minister.

5. The PM '*represents the nation*' as head of the government 'on the international stage' in general and also within the EU. '*EU summits*' are regular high-level meetings of the Heads of State or Government in a body officially called the *European Council*, which decides major directions in EU policy.[31] The PM is also actively involved in international '*treaty negotiations*', an example of a *prerogative* that previously belonged to the Sovereign and is now exercised by the PM.

6. A monarch is more elevated than a mere 'first among equals'; the British PM is an *elected* Member of Parliament, but if he or she adopts a very dominant style of leadership, with less '*collegiate*' *decision-making*, an '*elected monarch*' seems a very apt description; all the more so given that the PM today exercises many prerogative powers previously exercised in person by the King or Queen.

Comment

Peter Leyland's analysis, examined in Task 3 above, shows what a crucially important figure the British Prime Minister is in the modern Constitution. He or she is not quite a President yet exercises extensive *executive powers* as head of the government. Many of these powers were exercised as *prerogatives* directly by the ruling monarch in the past. But the Prime Minister is not *Head of State*—that is the Queen's supreme position. Further, the Prime Minister must be 'confirmed in office' (*appointed*) by the Queen, even though a convention determines the identity of who shall be Prime Minister after a general election: he or she is the leader of the political party with a majority of seats in the House of Commons.[32] This convention is so strong, that if a Prime Minister loses the party leadership during a *term* of government, he or she must resign and the new party leader will be appointed Prime Minister:[33] 'The source of the Prime Minister's political authority derives from his or her place as party leader.'[34] Note that the Prime Minister is not directly elected but must win a seat in Parliament by being elected as Member of Parliament for a constituency, in addition to being leader of the majority party.

It is interesting to note that at EU summit meetings of *Heads of State or Government*, under the terms of the Treaty on European Union, it must be the

---

[31] Treaty on European Union consolidated version (Treaty of Maastricht) [2012] OJ C326/01, provides in Art 10(2): 'Member States are represented in the European Council by their Heads of State or Government and in the Council by their governments, themselves democratically accountable either to their national Parliaments, or to their citizens.'

[32] Where there is no clear majority there is a 'hung Parliament'. See Leyland, above n 2, p 37 for analysis of changing practice in the flexible British Constitution.

[33] As happened in 1990 when Margaret Thatcher was followed by John Major (Conservative PMs) and in 2007 when Tony Blair was followed by Gordon Brown (Labour PMs).

[34] Leyland, above n 2, p 162.

Prime Minister and not the Queen who represents the UK: the relevant Treaty provision stipulates that the representative for each Member State must be 'democratically accountable either to their national Parliaments, or to their citizens'.[35] The Queen would not, therefore, qualify. By contrast, the Prime Minister is *accountable* to Parliament and must *respond* for his or her own actions and those of the government, justifying political choices before Parliament: it is the role of Parliament, and especially of the organised Opposition, to *scrutinise* the work of the government.

3.2.3 The House of Commons

Each seat in the House of Commons is held by one *elected politician* called a *Member of Parliament* (MP). A single MP is the only representative of voters in each geographical voting area, called a *constituency*. There are currently 650 MPs in the House of Commons, representing the people of England (52 million), Northern Ireland (1.8 million), Scotland (5 million) and Wales (3.5 million).[36] With an electoral system most commonly described in racing terminology—*first past the post*—it is the candidate who obtains the highest number of votes in that constituency who is elected to Parliament. All votes for the other candidates are lost, since there is currently no form of *proportional representation* in UK general elections: so, votes for a candidate who comes second or third are not redistributed. This system has favoured the development of only two big parties at any one time, nationally,[37] although parties with strong support concentrated in a specific region can also be successful, as they are able to win seats by coming first in many constituencies in the area where they are popular.[38] One advantage of this electoral system is that extremist parties do not gain sufficient votes to obtain representation in Parliament. But the system is very disadvantageous for a party that often comes second to one of the two biggest parties in different constituencies.[39] In May 2011 a UK referendum was held on electoral reform for the House of Commons, but 67.9 per cent of voters opposed changing the voting system to AV (Alternative Vote).[40]

In order to *fulfil* its function as the nation's *executive*, the government must be able to *implement its policies* (such as *foreign policy, monetary policy*). It does this by

---

[35] Treaty on European Union consolidated version (Treaty of Maastricht) [2012] OJ C326/01, Art 10(2).

[36] Population statistics from Leyland, above n 2, p 306.

[37] The Conservative Party (also known as the Tories) and the Labour Party have dominated British politics since the end of the Second World War; before that time, the Tories and Liberals (previously called Whigs).

[38] Such as the Scottish National Party in Scotland.

[39] As for the Liberal Democrats: a Lib-Dem candidate may be second to Labour in one constituency and second to the Conservatives in another, thus gaining many votes but no seats in Parliament.

[40] See House of Commons Library Research Paper 11/44, *Alternative Vote Referendum 2011*.

proposing legislation to Parliament for enactment.[41] A Bill can be *introduced* first in the House of Commons or first in the House of Lords, completing the entire legislative procedure in both Houses before it receives Royal Assent and becomes an Act.[42] However, if the House of Commons does not approve a Bill proposed by the government as part of its legislative programme, a political crisis will follow, and if the government loses *a vote of confidence* in the House of Commons, the Prime Minister must offer his or her *resignation* to the Sovereign.

Under the Parliament Act 1911, the *maximum* life of a Parliament was set at five years, but by convention, the Prime Minister had an important political power: to decide when *to call a general election* during that five-year period, by advising the monarch *to dissolve Parliament*. Under the Conservative-Liberal Democrat Coalition Government formed in May 2010, the convention was modified, in effect depriving the Prime Minister of this power to determine the time of elections. The Fixed-term Parliaments Act 2011 sets the date of the next general election (*polling day*) as 7 May 2015; the reform also provides generally for fixed-term Parliaments of five years (section 1); some exceptions are possible under section 2. If the Government is *defeated* in a vote of no confidence, a general election will follow. Under section 3 of the Act, the Queen loses her *prerogative power* to dissolve Parliament; *dissolution* of Parliament will now take place automatically under the provisions of the Act. Although this Act apparently determines the precise date of future elections, we should remember that Parliament has the power to repeal it any time, or to amend it, for example by reducing the fixed term of a Parliament from five to four years.

In your opinion, what is the political impact of this reform?

3.2.4 Constitutional Monarchy

The UK is a constitutional monarchy where 'the Queen reigns but does not rule'.[43] This means that the Sovereign holds the position of King or Queen (the Queen *reigns*), but he or she does not govern (*rule*) the country: that is the role of the government, led by the Prime Minister and effected through legislation approved by Parliament. The official website of the British monarchy explains this *form of State*:

> Constitutional monarchy is a form of government in which a king or queen acts as Head of State, while the ability to make and pass legislation resides with an elected Parliament.

---

[41] Here 'enactment' means the act of passing law.
[42] In 3.4.2 below an unusual exception is discussed.
[43] A comment made by 19th-century constitutional writer Walter Bagehot about Queen Victoria: Leyland, above n 2, p 88.

The Sovereign governs according to the constitution—that is, according to rules, rather than according to his or her own free will.[44]

The Bill of Rights 1689 (cited at the beginning of this chapter) shows one critical point in history when power moved away from the King to Parliament, but the whole process lasted hundreds of years. The Bill of Rights declared that it was *illegal* for the monarch unilaterally to exercise certain powers over laws:

That the pretended power of suspending the laws or the execution of laws by regal authority without consent of Parliament is *illegal*;

That the pretended power of dispensing with laws or the execution of laws by regal authority, as it hath [has] been assumed and exercised of late, is *illegal*; ...

The Bill abolished the powers—used by the King and recognised by the courts—of suspending laws (except where authorised by Parliament), or of exempting particular persons from the application of penal laws (*the dispensing power*).[45]

Just 40 years earlier, in 1649, Charles I had been tried for his life.[46] Accused of treason, he based his defence on *the divine right of kings*, claiming that the King was *not subject to the law*. His defence failed and he was executed at Whitehall. Even the King or Queen is subject to the law and must act 'according to rules', not 'according to his or her own free will', as the royal website affirms.

Next, we read Peter Leyland's analysis of the role of the monarch in the Constitution today. The author points out that the *terminology* of British government is 'misleading'—in other words, it does not create an accurate picture of reality.

Examine the passages below and underline examples of 'misleading' terminology. Find information in the text to support the central statement: '[The Queen] performs an important constitutional role but is, in fact, left with very little real political power.'

The path to constitutional monarchy has involved both the deliberate curtailment of royal power and its gradual erosion. *The terminology is somewhat misleading.* The government is still described as Her Majesty's government, central government acts in the name of the Crown, and the courts are presided over by Her Majesty's judges, but in modern times the monarch, although head of state, has a greatly subordinate constitutional role to Parliament, the government and the courts. This is now accepted by reigning monarchs without question. ...

[T]he evolution from a ruling monarchy to a constitutional monarchy took many hundreds of years.

Moreover, the link with the past has special significance because, for a nation which has not experienced a recent political revolution, the monarchy represents tradition and continuity. The Queen, as a symbol of national identity, can be said to personify

---

[44] <http://www.royal.gov.uk>, accessed 22 January 2008.

[45] D Walker (1980), *The Oxford Companion to Law*, Oxford: Clarendon Press, pp 364 and 529.

[46] 'Tried for his life' indicates that, if condemned, he would receive the death penalty.

the state. *She performs an important constitutional role but is, in fact, left with very little real political power.* It is a convention of the highest constitutional importance that the monarch always follows the advice of her ministers. Many of the most far-reaching powers which formerly were exercised by the monarch, mainly prerogative powers, are now in the hands of the Prime Minister and the government. Although these powers are exercised by the government, they are still performed in the name of the monarch. (emphasis added)[47]

Comment: constitutional monarchy

It has been a long 'path to constitutional monarchy', involving a combination of deliberate restriction ('*curtailment*') and gradual loss ('*erosion*') of royal power. Using terminology such as 'Her Majesty's Government' or 'Her Majesty's judges', or government acts performed 'in the name of the Crown' or 'in the name of the monarch' is *misleading*, as the monarch today is without question in a 'greatly subordinate constitutional role to Parliament, the government and the courts' (see Leyland, above).

As the above passage emphasises, the Queen does not exercise real power, because *by convention* she *must* act on the advice of her ministers. However, as Head of State, the Queen is an important *symbol* of national identity, who is considered to 'personify the state'. In the UK, one does not refer to 'the State' as an entity responsible for the workings of government, but to 'the Crown' or 'the Government'.

An essential step performed by the Crown is the Royal Assent, the final step in the legislative process, which transforms a proposal of law into a law: the *Bill* becomes an *Act*. An Act *comes into force* on the day of Royal Assent, except where the legislative text specifies a different date. However, the monarch's Royal Assent to Bills approved by Parliament is not a personal political act; it is a formality, reflecting her symbolic role as *Head of State* in the Constitution today.

Why can the monarch not refuse to give the Royal Assent?

It has long been established that the royal assent to Bills that have completed their passage through the House of Commons and the House of Lords is never refused by the reigning monarch. To do so would undermine the capacity of a representative Parliament to pass legislation.[48]

The Royal Assent is part of *the Royal Prerogative*: that is, the various rights and powers that the king or queen still has at a particular point in history. *Prerogative powers* are of great importance, as we have seen in the extracts above; they include

---

[47] Leyland, above n 2, extracts from pp 87–89.
[48] *Ibid*, p 36.

matters of national security, defence and treaty-making power. But 'the prerogative is now in the hands of the Prime Minister, ministers, or officials' and for this
reason, the Queen 'has a major presence in many areas but exercises only limited
power'.[49] The Queen maintains a special relationship with the Prime Minister;
frequent *audiences* are held and as *constitutional monarch* she retains 'the right
to be consulted, the right to encourage, the right to warn'.[50] In other words, the
Queen may express her views, but the Prime Minister, as political leader, will take
the decisions.

British government policies and proposed reforms are announced to Parliament
in the *Queen's Speech*, or *Speech from the Throne*, at the beginning of each parliamentary session. The speech illustrates the relationship between the British
monarchy and government today: while the Queen announces the government
programme and refers to '*My Government*', the speech is prepared by the political
leader: the Prime Minister.

Consult the following extract from the first Queen's Speech of Gordon Brown's pre-
miership.[51] What reform did the Queen announce in response to the urgent questions
of climate change and protection of the environment?

> My Lords and Members of the House of Commons
> My Government will take forward policies to respond to the rising
> aspirations of the people of the United Kingdom; to ensure security for
> all; and to entrust more power to Parliament and the people. ...
> My Government is committed to protecting the environment and to tackling climate
> change, both at home and abroad.
> A Bill will be brought forward to make the United Kingdom the first
> country in the world to introduce a legally binding framework to reduce
> carbon dioxide emissions. ...[52]

A *legally binding* framework is one which *must* be observed by law. Once the Bill
is approved and becomes an Act, it is a law operating in the national (or *domestic*)
legal system: the British courts must *enforce* it (apply it and give it legal effect).

Queen Elizabeth II celebrated 60 years of her *reign* with her Diamond Jubilee in
2012; she will soon become the *longest reigning monarch* ever.[53] Her extensive experience of matters of state has included relationships with 12 Prime Ministers during

---

[49] *Ibid*, p 90.

[50] The royal website <http://www.royal.gov.uk> on the page 'The Queen in Parliament' gives this
classic formula stated by W Bagehot in *The English Constitution* 1867.

[51] Period as premier (Prime Minister); Gordon Brown followed Tony Blair in 2007.

[52] Queen's Speech, 6 November 2007. The Climate Change Bill 2007–08 was introduced to provide
for both environmental aspects stated in the Queen's Speech. The Bill received Royal Assent on 26
November 2008 and became the Climate Change Act 2008.

[53] Her great-great-grandmother, Queen Victoria, reigned for 63 years and 216 days from 1837–
1901, so the Queen will have to reign until 10 September 2015 to reign longer: see <http//: www.
britroyals.com>.

that period, ranging from Sir Winston Churchill in the post-War years, to Tony Blair, Gordon Brown and David Cameron so far in the twenty-first century.

Task 4 Consultation and discussion—the Prime Minister and the Queen
Choose one of the options below to learn more about the Prime Minister and the Queen in the British system of government, according to your interests. Share your work with other members of the class and critically discuss the British system, comparing elements from other constitutions that you know.

1. Visit the Number 10 website <*http://www.number10.gov.uk*> and discover information about the office of UK Prime Minister, and how government works, including introductions to the system of government, policies, and interesting topics and profiles of notable Prime Ministers of the past. You may also access a variety of resources, including video, podcast and audio.
2. To discover more about the British monarchy and the role of Queen Elizabeth II, consult the official website <*http://www.royal.gov.uk*>, where you can learn about the role of the monarchy, investigating topics such as the Queen and the law, Queen and government, the Queen as fount of justice.
3. Watch the film *The Queen* (2006) by Stephen Frears, set in the early days of Tony Blair's premiership in 1997 and focusing especially on the week after Princess Diana's death. Why did that personal tragedy develop into a crisis for the British monarchy? Consider the respective roles played by the Queen and the Prime Minister, explored in this interesting film.

3.3 Consulting Legislation: UK Constitutional Reform

The period of Labour Government with Tony Blair as Prime Minister from 1997 to 2007, was marked by major constitutional reform. At the *State opening of Parliament* in May 1997, Queen Elizabeth II declared:

> A bill will be introduced to incorporate into United Kingdom law the main provisions of the European Convention on Human Rights.[54]

And another important *constitutional reform* was announced:

> Decentralisation is essential to my government's vision of a modern nation. Legislation will be introduced to allow the people of Scotland and Wales to vote in referendums on my government's proposals for a devolved Scottish Parliament and

---

[54] This reform is examined in 5.4 below.

the establishment of a Welsh Assembly. If these proposals are approved in the referendums, my government will bring forward legislation to implement them. (May 1997, Queen's Speech)

As declared, *referendums* were held and *decentralisation* was approved by the people of Scotland and Wales. Then, as announced in the Queen's Speech, *devolution* of power away from *central government* in London was introduced by legislation: the Scotland Act 1998, Government of Wales Act 1998 and Northern Ireland Act 1998. These are examples of statutes that change the Constitution: they are part of British constitutional law, recognised as *common law 'constitutional statutes'*.[55] In the following section we examine some provisions of the Scotland Act 1998.

Referendums[56] are not a regular feature of the British Constitution. There are no basic rules to determine when a referendum should be held, as in some written constitutions. Instead, the Government may decide *to hold a referendum* if it considers it is politically convenient to reach a decision only on the basis of popular support: for example, the referendum held in May 2011 on electoral reform.[57] On important EU matters, however, the European Union Act 2011 introduced a new requirement in the UK *to hold a popular referendum*, in addition to passing an Act of Parliament, to validate the adoption of changes in EU law that would *transfer powers or competences* to the EU.[58]

3.3.1 The Scotland Act 1998—Devolution

Having examined the Terrorism Act 2000 in chapter one (Text 1), you are familiar with an Act of the UK Parliament as a text type and also with some aspects of legislative texts in English. In the next task, we examine an important constitutional statute: the Scotland Act 1998, part of the *devolution legislation*.

Task 5 Global reading—Scotland Act 1998
For this first task, do not try to understand the Act in detail. Observe the extracts from the Scotland Act 1998 below, and identify the various elements and the purpose of this law:

1. The short title (what is the name of this law?)
2. The long title (what is the purpose of this law?)
3. Some sections of the Act (identify the subject of each section)
4. An appendix to the Act.

---

[55] Discussed in 3.6.2 below.
[56] Or *referenda* (pl).
[57] See 3.2.3.
[58] For further discussion, see 3.6.2.

Scotland Act 1998

1998 CHAPTER 46

An Act to provide for the establishment of a Scottish Parliament and Administration and other changes in the government of Scotland; to provide for changes in the constitution and functions of certain public authorities; to provide for the variation of the basic rate of income tax in relation to income of Scottish taxpayers in accordance with a resolution of the Scottish Parliament; to amend the law about parliamentary constituencies in Scotland; and for connected purposes.

[19th November 1998]

Be it enacted by the Queen's most Excellent Majesty, by and with the advice and consent of the Lords Spiritual and Temporal, and Commons, in this present Parliament assembled, and by the authority of the same, as follows:—

Part I The Scottish Parliament

The Scottish Parliament

1   The Scottish Parliament

(1) There shall be a Scottish Parliament.

...

Legislation

28   Acts of the Scottish Parliament

(1) Subject to section 29, the Parliament may make laws, to be known as Acts of the Scottish Parliament.

(2) Proposed Acts of the Scottish Parliament shall be known as Bills; and a Bill shall become an Act of the Scottish Parliament when it has been passed by the Parliament and has received Royal Assent.

...

(7) This section does not affect the power of the Parliament of the United Kingdom to make laws for Scotland.

29   Legislative competence

(1) An Act of the Scottish Parliament is not law so far as any provision of the Act is outside the legislative competence of the Parliament.

(2) A provision is outside that competence so far as any of the following paragraphs apply—

    (a) it would form part of the law of a country or territory other than Scotland, or confer or remove functions exercisable otherwise than in or as regards Scotland,

(b) it relates to reserved matters,

...

(d) it is incompatible with any of the Convention rights or with EU law,[59]

...

Part II The Scottish Administration

Ministers and their staff

44 The Scottish Executive

(1) There shall be a Scottish Executive whose members shall be—
   (a) the First Minister,
   (b) such Ministers as the First Minister may appoint under section 47, and
   (c) the Lord Advocate and the Solicitor General for Scotland.
(2) The members of the Scottish Executive are referred to collectively as the Scottish Ministers.

   ...

SCHEDULE 5 Reserved matters
Part I General reservations

The Constitution

1   The following aspects of the constitution are reserved matters, that is—
   (a) the Crown, including succession to the Crown and a regency,
   (b) the Union of the Kingdoms of Scotland and England,
   (c) the Parliament of the United Kingdom,

   ...

Foreign affairs etc.

7(1) International relations, including relations with territories outside the United Kingdom, the European Union[60] (and their institutions) and other international organisations, regulation of international trade, and international development assistance and co-operation are reserved matters.

   ...

© Crown Copyright 1998

The Scotland Act 1998 is reproduced under the terms of Crown Copyright Policy Guidance issued by HMSO

---

[59] In the original text, *Community law:* words substituted (22 April 2011) by the Treaty of Lisbon (Changes in Terminology) Order 2011 (SI 2011/1043), Arts 3, 6.
[60] As n 59 above.

Key and commentary to Task 5 Global reading—Scotland Act 1998

1. The *Scotland Act 1998* is the short title of the Act, used to identify it as a legal source. The Act may also be identified by its year and chapter number—'1998 CHAPTER 46'—indicating that it was the 46th Act given Royal Assent in the year 1998.

2. The first paragraph of text is the *long title* of the Act. It begins typically '*An Act to provide for* the establishment of a Scottish Parliament ... ; *to provide for* changes in the constitution ...'. 'To provide for' means *to govern by law, to regulate by legislation*. The use of the infinitive with 'to' in the long title expresses purpose (*to provide* for ... *to amend* the law ...). Each phrase lists one or more purposes of the Act, principal among them 'the *establishment* of a Scottish Parliament and Administration'. The grammatical subject of each verb (*An Act*) is used only once, at the beginning of this long sentence, with its repeating structure. *To establish* means to create, *institute* or *found* an institution or organisation. One purpose of the Act is '*to amend the law* about parliamentary *constituencies* in Scotland'. The choice of verb specifies that this part of the Act involves modifying (*amending*) past law.

3. The Act begins with section 1, concerning the Scottish Parliament. In section 1(1) the Scottish Parliament is created: '*There shall be* a Scottish Parliament.' The legal effect of the proclamation is expressed using the modal verb *shall*, typical of legislative language, as well as contracts and treaties. Similarly, in section 44(1), the Scottish Executive is *established*. Section 28 concerns Acts of the Scottish Parliament and section 29 concerns the legislative competence of the Parliament.

4. Schedule 5 is an appendix to the Act concerning '*Reserved matters*'. These are first mentioned in section 29(1)(b), therefore they relate to *legislative competence*. The text gives extracts from two *paragraphs* of Schedule 5, concerning the constitution (paragraph 1) and foreign affairs, etc (paragraph 2). A *schedule* is an *appendix* or *annex* to an Act or other legal text, giving details not included in the main body of the text.

Comment

Clearly, the Act is a constitutional reform of great significance for the United Kingdom, and especially for the people of Scotland. We can observe the textual organisation and language of a typical Act of Parliament: all UK laws, even constitutional statutes, are enacted in the ordinary way.

The Scotland Act 1998 provides for devolution to Scotland, creating a Scottish Parliament (section 1) and Executive, known as the *Scottish Ministers* and headed by the *First Minister* (section 44). As the names suggest, these organs have *wide legislative and governmental powers* at Scottish level. The name *Scottish Government* is now used for the executive branch of government in Scotland.

The modern Scottish Parliament was established in 1999 in the capital of Scotland, Edinburgh. The historic Scottish Parliament, and also the English Parliament, had been *abolished* by statute almost 300 years earlier after the political unification of Scotland with England; a single Parliament for Great Britain was established in London, at Westminster,[61] which co-exists today with the Scottish Parliament at Holyrood, in Edinburgh.

Task 6 Reading for detail—Scotland Act 1998

Examine the provisions of the Scotland Act 1998 in detail to discover more about the Scottish model for devolution.

Answer the following questions. Focus your attention on both meaning and language:

1. What power is granted to the Scottish Parliament by section 28(1)?
2. According to section 28(2), what is the legislative procedure for Scottish Acts?
3. Can the UK Parliament continue to legislate for Scotland?
4. What limits are placed by section 29 on the Scottish Parliament's powers?
5. Identify some important reserved matters in Schedule 5.

Key and commentary to Task 6 Reading for detail—Scotland Act 1998

1. Under section 28(1) the Scottish Parliament has *legislative power*, or *capacity*, indicated by the use of the modal verb *may* ('the Parliament *may make laws*'). This legislative power is not absolute, it is '*Subject to* section 29': that is, section 29 *places limits on* or *has priority over* section 28(1). The legal name of the laws is decided: '*to be known as* Acts of the Scottish Parliament', while proposals of law 'shall be known as *Bills*' under section 28(2).

2. Under section 28(2) a Scottish Bill must be approved ('*passed*') by the Scottish Parliament *and* receive the Royal Assent before it becomes an Act. This final step is significant: it emphasises that Scotland remains part of the United Kingdom, with the monarch as Head of State and part of the Scottish legislature, as for the Westminster Parliament.

3. Yes, the UK Parliament can continue to legislate for Scotland; according to section 28(7), the power of the UK Parliament is not changed (*affected*).

4. Section 29 places a series of limits on the legislative power of the Scottish Parliament. Under section 29(1), an Act is invalidated ('*not law*') with respect to any provision ('in so far as') that exceeds the legislative

---

[61] The Treaty of Union of 1707 between England and Scotland unified the two countries. The Acts of Union of 1706 and 1707, leading to the single Parliament, are referred to in s 37 of the Scotland Act 1998.

competence of the Parliament. Section 29(2) defines in the list of paragraphs ((a), (b), (c), etc) the situations where a provision is, precisely, *'outside the legislative competence'*. Paragraph (a) limits the competence to Scottish law and territory and related functions; paragraph (b) places a limit on 'reserved matters' (typically for a legal text we need to refer to another part of the text for details, see Schedule 5 and question 5 below); paragraph (c) imposes a limit in relation to Britain's obligations under European Convention on Human Rights law (*Convention rights*, protected at national level via the Human Rights Act 1998) and under EU law.

5. *Reserved matters*, outside the legislative competence of the Scottish Parliament, are specified in Schedule 5 to the Act. They include: in paragraph 1, 'aspects of the constitution', listed in a series of sub-paragraphs and including the British monarchy, the Union between Scotland and England, and the UK Parliament; paragraph 7 reserves international relations, including relations with EU institutions, in addition to international trade. This last limit on the legislative powers of the Scottish Parliament does not include the *observance* and *implementation* of international obligations.[62] These may originate under EU law or the European Convention on Human Rights, effective in the legal systems of the United Kingdom *by virtue of* national Acts of Parliament.[63]

Comment

We can see from the *devolution legislation* examined above that the Scottish Parliament enjoys wide legislative powers over Scottish matters. Further, more competences and greater powers to raise revenue through taxation (listed in the long title as one of the purposes of the 1998 Act) have subsequently been granted to reflect changing conditions.[64] However, Scotland remains constitutionally part of the United Kingdom with the British monarch as Head of State. The Scottish Parliament cannot pass a *valid law* declaring Scottish independence: any such law would have to be enacted by the Westminster Parliament which, as was noted above, retains sovereignty.

At the time of writing, with the Scottish National Party in power in Edinburgh, and on the basis of a political agreement between the UK Prime Minister David Cameron and the Scottish First Minister Alex Salmond,[65] the issue of independence is on the political agenda both at Scottish level and nationally in the UK.

---

[62] According to the Scotland Act 1998, Sch 5, para 7(2).
[63] Respectively, the European Communities Act 1972 and the Human Rights Act 1998.
[64] Leyland, above n 2, p 305: under the Scotland Act 2012.
[65] The so-called 'Edinburgh Agreement' between the UK Government and the Scottish Government on a referendum on independence for Scotland, Edinburgh, 15 October 2012.

On 18 September 2014 the people of Scotland are to vote[66] in a referendum on independence: the result is non-binding, but could potentially be the first step in the direction of a newly independent Scotland. This would have to be the result of a political negotiation, which could take place if the referendum result is in favour of independence.

The single question voters are to answer is the following: 'Should Scotland be an independent country? Yes/No'.

NOTE: *Visit the official websites of the Scottish Government and the UK Government for further documentation, updates and political discussion:* <http://www.scotland.gov.uk> *and* < http://www.gov.uk>.

3.4 PARLIAMENT: THE HOUSE OF LORDS AND THE HOUSE OF COMMONS

3.4.1 The House of Lords and the House of Commons

The Queen in Parliament is composed of the monarch, the House of Lords and the House of Commons. In the *enacting words* that follow the short and long titles of a UK statute, the House of Lords is mentioned after the Queen and before the House of Commons:

> BE IT ENACTED by the Queen's most Excellent Majesty, by and with the advice and consent of the Lords Spiritual and Temporal, and Commons, in this present Parliament assembled, and by the authority of the same, as follows:—

The House of Lords is sometimes referred to as the *Upper House* or *Upper Chamber*, while the House of Commons is the *Lower House*. However, the *elected* House of Commons is more powerful than the *unelected* House of Lords. In fact, in some circumstances a Bill may become an Act even without the *approval* of the House of Lords. This is possible under two Acts of Parliament that reduced the power of the Lords: the Parliament Acts 1911 and 1949.

For a long historical period up to 2009, the House of Lords had two *functions*:

a) *legislative*, as a chamber of a *bicameral* Parliament; and
b) *judicial*, as the highest court in the hierarchy of courts in the United Kingdom.

The *judicial function* was not performed by the whole House but by a group of the most senior judges: the *Lords of Appeal in Ordinary*, or *Law Lords*, members of the *Appellate Committee of the House of Lords*; technically, judgments of the

---

[66] The Scottish Parliamentary franchise enables British, Irish, qualifying Commonwealth citizens and EU citizens resident in Scotland to vote, and under the Edinburgh Agreement 2012, above n 65, the same principle should be applied for the independence referendum as for other Scottish elections.

Appellate Committee were adopted by the whole House. Today, the House of Lords still exercises its *legislative function* as the Upper Chamber of Parliament, but it no longer acts as a court. The judicial function of the House of Lords was transferred to a new court, completely independent of Parliament, which began work in October 2009: the *Supreme Court of the United Kingdom*.[67] See 9.3 and 9.6 below for further discussion of the jurisdiction and hierarchy of the English courts and the impact of this reform.

Reform of the House of Lords as *a legislative chamber* has long been the subject of debate. The obvious issue that demands a fresh constitutional solution is this: although the UK is a *parliamentary democracy*, the Upper Chamber of Parliament is *not democratically elected*. Its *temporal* members have either *inherited the right* to sit as members of the legislature (the *hereditary peers*), or they have been appointed by the monarch for life, as a result of political recommendation (the *life peers*). The Lords Spiritual are the Archbishops and certain bishops of the Church of England. The first stage of reform took place in 1999, with the *abolition* of most *hereditary peers* from the legislative chamber. By virtue of sections 1 and 2 of the House of Lords Act 1999, only 92 *hereditary peers* remain in the House.

In 2007, a Government *White Paper* on House of Lords Reform[68] was presented to Parliament by Jack Straw, then leader of the House of Commons and member of the Cabinet with responsibility for reform of the House of Lords. *White papers* are documents that, by *royal command*, the Government presents to Parliament for discussion. This one contains fascinating discussion of the role of a second chamber in *bicameral Parliaments*, as well as a detailed description of the history and role of the House of Lords and a survey of different options for reform. The Commons and Lords, however, have not been able to agree on the best model: would it be better for the House of Lords to be *fully elected*? Or *fully appointed*? Or to have a proportion of *elected members* and a proportion of *appointed members*? And if so, in what proportions? Further proposals have since been debated. There is opposition in the House of Lords itself to becoming an entirely *elected second chamber*; an elected chamber would have a strong claim to *legitimacy* and this could create a risk of competition with the Commons.[69] A recent House of Lords Library Note reviewing the attitudes of the public, has concluded that constitutional reform is not viewed as a priority by most people in the country, not surprising at a time of economic crisis, while there is 'contradictory evidence in how people view reform of the House, with some value placed on the independence offered by a House composed of appointed members, with value also placed on the democratic legitimacy conferred by elections if the House were to be reformed in this way'.[70] When it became clear that the House of Lords Reform

---

[67]   Constitutional Reform Act 2005, s 23.
[68]   *The House of Lords: Reform*, CM 7027, available online at <http://www.official-documents.gov.uk>.
[69]   Leyland, above n 2, p 133.
[70]   I Cruse (26 July 2012), 'Public Attitudes Towards the House of Lords and House of Lords Reform', *House of Lords Library Note*, LLN 2012/028.

Bill 2012–13, introduced into the House of Commons by the Deputy Prime Minister, was not fully supported by the Government, Mr Clegg announced that legislation for a step-by-step reform of the House of Lords, converting it into a smaller and mainly elected body, had been dropped.[71]

As regards the legislative powers of the House of Lords today, for most legislation the House of Lords has *a delaying power*, that is, power to delay a Bill passed by the Commons for maximum one year. After that period, if the House of Lords still refuses to approve the provisions of the Bill without *amendments*, the Bill can receive Royal Assent and become an Act directly (see 3.4.2 below).

The Lords only rarely uses its delaying power to block legislation: this is not surprising, since it constitutes a challenge to the House of Commons—the *elected, representative body*—and therefore to the democratic process. For the same reason, according to a constitutional convention known as the 'Salisbury Convention', the House of Lords will not use its delaying power to block a Bill that is introduced to implement a *commitment* (a promise, an *undertaking*) made by the party in government in its *election manifesto*.[72] Financial measures, called *money bills*, being essential to the Government's implementation of its policies, cannot be delayed by the House of Lords.

3.4.2 Case Study: A Controversial Law—the Hunting Ban

The law examined in Task 7 below and the resulting case in Task 8 show the problems that may arise when a controversial statute is enacted.

Task 7 Case study—a controversial law
At the beginning of the twenty-first century, many people on both sides of the debate felt very strongly about the Hunting Bill, a proposal to ban (prohibit) some traditional forms of hunting in England and Wales. While considered cruel by many citizens and actively opposed by animal rights activists, others defended the assumed right to hunt in the traditional way.

Read the news extract below and answer the following questions. Refer to a general English dictionary as needed:

1. What form of hunting was involved?
2. What was the position of the House of Lords?
3. What constitutional problem arose?
4. From the context, what do you suppose the verb 'to override' means?

---

[71] The House of Lords Reform Bill, introduced into the House of Commons on 27 June 2012, its withdrawal announced on 6 August 2012, at <http://www.parliament.uk>; see 'House of Lords Reform Bill 2012–13: decision not to proceed', SN/PC/06405, 25 September 2012, House of Commons Library; the Bill was discussed in detail in Research Paper 12/37, House of Lords Reform Bill 2012–13, 4 July 2012.

[72] P Leyland (2012). *The Constitution of the United Kingdom*, above n 2, p 139.

BBC NEWS[73]
Peers mount new bid to save hunts

MPs and peers are on a collision course over fox-hunting in England and Wales after the House of Lords voted for licensed hunts instead of a full ban …

In the long-running and fierce public debate on the issue, the House of Lords has blocked previous attempts to outlaw hunting with dogs.

If they reject the same bill proposing an outright ban again, the Parliament Act could be used to override Lords opposition.

© BBC © Source: http://news.bbc.co.uk

Key and commentary to Task 7 Case study—a controversial law
1. Fox-hunting is specifically mentioned in line 1: for sport, a group of riders with hounds (dogs) search for a fox in the countryside to chase and kill; if caught, the fox is killed by the hounds, not directly by the hunters. The proposed law would cover 'hunting with dogs', which is broader than fox-hunting.
2. The BBC reports that the House of Lords voted against the Bill proposing a complete ban (a full or outright ban) on hunting. But it voted in favour of licensed hunts, instead: that is, hunts would be permitted, but only with a licence (an authority) to hunt.
3. The Lords wanted to amend the Bill that had been approved by the Commons. As they had already blocked this Bill before (the House of Lords had used its delaying power), a fresh refusal to accept 'an outright ban' (a direct ban) would lead to a 'collision' with the House of Commons. If the House of Lords were to reject the Bill again, it could be necessary to use the Parliament Act[74] to pass the law, ignoring the opposition of the Lords ('to override Lords opposition').
4. To override means to use superior authority to reverse or cancel a decision: in this case, the superior authority of the House of Commons.

To find out whether the Lords approved the Hunting Act 2004, read the enacting words of the statute, below. Observe the date of Royal Assent.

---

[73] 'Peers mount new bid to save hunts', *BBC news*, 26 October 2004: http://news.bbc.co.uk.
[74] The journalist's reference is to the Parliament Acts 1911 and 1949, discussed below.

Hunting Act 2004

2004 CHAPTER 37

An Act to make provision about hunting wild mammals with dogs; to prohibit hare coursing; and for connected purposes.

[18th November 2004]

Be it enacted by The Queen's most Excellent Majesty, by and with the advice and consent of the Commons in this present Parliament assembled, in accordance with the provisions of the Parliament Acts 1911 and 1949, and by the authority of the same, as follows:—

The enacting words of the Hunting Act 2004 show that the House of Lords did not approve the Bill. Therefore, *the Parliament Acts 1911 and 1949 were invoked* and the Bill became law without the approval of the Upper Chamber. Note that a year before, the House of Lords had used its delaying power to block the Bill for a one-year period.

Sections 1 to 4 of the Hunting Act 2004 are reproduced below. What offences are created in these sections of the Act? What exemptions or defences are permitted?

Part 1 Offences

1 Hunting wild mammals with dogs

A person commits an offence if he hunts a wild mammal with a dog, unless his hunting is exempt.

2 Exempt hunting

(1)   Hunting is exempt if it is within a class specified in Schedule 1.

(2)   The Secretary of State may by order amend Schedule 1 so as to vary a class of exempt hunting.

3 Hunting: assistance

(1)   A person commits an offence if he knowingly permits land which belongs to him to be entered or used in the course of the commission of an offence under section 1.

(2)   A person commits an offence if he knowingly permits a dog which belongs to him to be used in the course of the commission of an offence under section 1.

4 Hunting: defence

It is a defence for a person charged with an offence under section 1 in respect of hunting to show that he reasonably believed that the hunting was exempt.

© Crown Copyright
Source: http://www.legislation.gov.uk

Comment: Hunting Act 2004

From 18 February 2005, it became an offence, under section 1 of the Hunting Act 2004, to hunt a wild mammal with a dog in England and Wales. This section creates a crime (*'A person commits an offence if ...'*). Fox-hunting is the obvious example, but the ban includes hunting other wild animals in the class of mammals, such as deer. Birds are not protected, as they are not mammals; further, the Act only prohibits hunting with one or more dogs.

Under section 3 of the Act, other offences are created: by section 3(1), the owner of land must not *'knowingly permit'* hunters to enter or use his land for *illegal hunting* under section 1; according to section 3(2), the owner of a dog must not knowingly permit the animal to be used for illegal hunting. In both of these crimes, note the *conduct element* (the actions) and the *mental element* (the state of mind), which for both offences is *'knowingly'* (with knowledge, consciously). These two elements of a crime, known by the Latin terms *actus reus* and *mens rea*, are examined in 7.4 below.

Section 2(1) permits *exemptions* for hunting 'within a class specified in Schedule 1' to the Act; under section 2(2) the government minister (*Secretary of State*) has power to change the 'classes of *exempt hunting*' listed in the Schedule. If hunting is *exempt*, it is not subject to section 1, therefore not an offence.

As for *defences*, under section 4, a hunter accused of committing a crime ('*charged with an offence*') under section 1 *has a defence* if he can '*show* that he *reasonably believed* the hunting was exempt': if so, he will be found *not guilty* in a criminal trial. However, he must 'show' (*prove*) that:

a)   he believed his hunting was exempt from the ban; and
b)   his belief was reasonable.

The first test is subjective (he *believed*: his state of mind), while the second test is objective: was it *reasonable* for him to hold that belief?

Disappointed hunters reacted to the Hunting Act 2004 with a campaign of *civil disobedience*, with many continuing to hunt all over the country. In addition, hunters mounted a *legal challenge* to the *validity* of the Act, in a case which went on appeal to the House of Lords (exercising its judicial function), but were not successful:[75] the Hunting Act remained in force.

In Task 8 below we examine a news report of one case brought against hunters under the Hunting Act 2004.

---

[75] *Jackson v Attorney General* [2005] UKHL 56. Available at <http://www.bailii.org>. This case is of great constitutional interest: see P Leyland and G Anthony (2009), *Textbook on Administrative Law*, 6th edn, Oxford: Oxford University Press, p 21.

Task 8 Reading a news report: the hunting ban—a case study
Examine the news report below to understand the facts of the case. Then
read the text in detail. Focus on both meaning and language.

— What were the consequences for the two men?
— Can you link the elements of this case to the relevant sections of the
  Hunting Act 2004, examined above?

BBC NEWS[76]	LANGUAGE FOCUS
Pair guilty of hunting with dogs	
Two men have been found guilty of illegally hunting deer with hounds. ...	*Guilty of doing sth*
	Legal/ illegal – illegally
Both men had denied contravening the Hunting Act, which came into force in February 2005.	*To deny doing sth*
	To contravene an Act
The LACS [League Against Cruel Sports] said it launched the prosecution because no attempt was made to shoot the deer humanely or call off the hounds during the hunt.	*To come into force*
	The prosecution
Spokesman Douglas Batchelor said: 'Justice has prevailed today in what was a clear-cut case of blatant law-breaking by hunters who believe themselves to be above the law.'	*Justice has prevailed*
	To break the law: law-breaking (n)
	To be above the law
Down, 44, of Bagborough, Somerset, and Pillivant, 36, of Willand, Devon, had argued throughout the trial that they had been hunting the deer within the law.	*To be/do sth within the law*
District Judge David Parsons said their argument was 'disingenuous' and fined both men £500 and ordered them to pay £1,000 each as a contribution towards costs.	*To fine someone (a sum of money). To order someone to pay costs*
He said: 'Neither defendant has established on the balance of probability that he reasonably believed the hunting was exempt.'	*Did the defendants reasonably believe the hunting was exempt?*
Robbie Marsland, UK director of the International Fund for Animal Welfare (IFAW), welcomed the decision.	
He said: 'This is the second time that the league has taken and won a private prosecution and IFAW congratulates them for that.	*A private prosecution*
'In the light of this ruling it is very difficult to see how anyone could go out stag hunting in the belief that they are acting lawfully.'	*Ruling: decision, judgment*
	To act lawfully or
07/06/2007	*unlawfully.*

© *BBC*
Source: http://news.bbc.co.uk

[76] 'Pair guilty of hunting with dogs', *BBC News*, 7 June 2007, at <http://news.bbc.co.uk>.

Key and commentary on Task 8 Reading a news report: the hunting ban—a case study

The BBC news report states that two men were *convicted* (*'found guilty'*) of 'illegally hunting deer with hounds'. They *committed an offence* under section 1 of the Hunting Act 2004, which provides that it is illegal to hunt 'wild mammals' with dogs—they were hunting *'illegally'* (adverb).

The accused men (the *defendants*) had declared that they were *not guilty* (*they 'denied contravening'* the Act). But they were *convicted* because at the trial they did not prove (*establish*) that they *'reasonably believed* the hunting was *exempt'*: so, their defence under section 4 of the Act failed because both the criminal conduct and the required mental element were present.

The consequence was that each man had to pay a fine of £500 (they were *'fined'*) plus £1,000 as a contribution towards the costs of the action.

The criminal proceeding (*prosecution*) was promoted by a private entity, the LACS. This is an unusual procedure, as prosecutions are generally conducted by the *Crown Prosecution Service* (CPS), a public body.[77] Commentators interviewed by the media underline the importance of *prosecuting* hunters who deliberately and obviously *break the law*, as in this case ('a case of *blatant law-breaking'*).

The following year, one newspaper reported: 'Traditional Boxing Day hunt meetings took place as usual, in spite of the three-year-old ban on hunting with hounds.'[78] 'Boxing Day' is 26 December, the day after Christmas Day and a traditional day for hunting for some classes of English society. On Boxing Day 2012, BBC News reported on television that over 300 hunts had taken place across the country that day.

For detailed reports of continued activity by hunters *in breach of the law*, and updates regarding possible legislative reform, visit the website of the organisation POWA (Protect Our Wild Animals) at <http:// www.powa.org.uk>. Hunting was banned by the 2004 Act during a period of Labour Government; however, the Act may soon be repealed. The Coalition agreement between the Conservatives and Liberal-Democrats, who formed a Government in May 2010, includes 'a promise for *a free vote* in the House of Commons on the repeal of the Hunting Act 2004': if the vote is in favour of repealing the Act, a Bill will be introduced in both Houses of Parliament for approval.[79]

What is your response to the case reported above and the range of issues it raises? Discuss your views and the wider legal and social implications of a law, such as the Hunting Act, that so strongly divides public opinion.

[77] The Crown Prosecution Service is examined in 7.2.1.
[78] 'The hunt goes on—as law fails to keep up', 4 January 2008, *Guardian Weekly*.
[79] See <https://www.gov.uk/government/policies>, 30 October 2013.

SECTION TWO

3.5 Law, the Legislature and the Courts—Advanced

3.5.1 The Relative Roles of Legislation and Judicial Precedent

Legislation, or *statute law*, is the first of the two primary sources of English law. It is first in two senses. First, legislation *has priority over* judicial precedent: in case of conflict, *the provisions of a statute* must be applied by the courts. Secondly, more of our law derives from legislation than from judicial precedent today. This is quite a recent development, in contrast with the tradition of the common law.

What reasons are there for the change? Read the explanation below:

> Until fairly recently, lawyers tended to think of the common law as the main part of our legal system. The reality today is quite different. When one considers disputes before tribunals, lower courts, the High Court, the Court of Appeal, and the House of Lords, the interpretation and application of legal texts is the dominant source of law of our time. Owing particularly to the flood of legislation to give effect to the requirements of the social welfare state, and the European dimension, the preponderance of enacted law over common law is increasing year by year.[80]

Two major reasons given by Lord Steyn are the need for legislation to regulate *the welfare State* (e.g. laws on education, social security, pensions) and the need for legislation *to fulfil the obligations* of European Union membership (e.g. giving effect to the Treaties in the national system, *implementing directives*).

As we can see, even if the UK legislature has not enacted *codes* as in civil law countries, legislation is extremely important today in the common law system. There is much legislation in nearly every *branch of the law*: criminal law, contract, company law, labour law and so on. Zweigert and Kötz note the increasing tendency in the common law 'to use legislation in order to unify, rationalize, and simplify the law'.[81]

However, it is the common law—judicial precedent—that provides the basic framework and principle of the legal system. As one commentator explains:

> [N]early every branch of the common law is now heavily affected by statute. But statute is not 'code'. In particular, whereas the code represents the 'default' principle in civil law systems, common law principle is the 'default' rule in common law jurisdictions. So statutes in common law systems are not regarded as a source of principle upon which flesh is put by interstitial case law development. Indeed statute is widely thought to be irrelevant to the development of the common law.[82]

---

[80] J Steyn, '*Pepper v Hart*; A Re-examination' (2001) 21(1) *OJLS* 59.
[81] K Zweigert and H Kötz (1998), *An Introduction to Comparative Law*, 3rd edn (tr T Weir), Oxford: Clarendon Press, p 271.
[82] J Beatson 'The Role of Statute in the Development of Common Law Doctrine' (2001) 117 *LQR* 247.

Like the 'default' setting on a computer, which automatically operates where no other choice is specifically adopted, 'common law principle' automatically operates as the source of law the courts use and develop to resolve disputes in the absence of legislation. On the other hand, where legislation exists to govern an issue in a dispute, that is the source of law that the courts must use to resolve the case. Remember, also, that where the courts have interpreted a legislative provision in a specific way in relation to certain facts in a previous case, the same interpretation must be given by courts *in later similar cases*, according to the doctrine of binding precedent.

Judicial precedent as a source of law is examined in depth in chapter nine.

3.5.2 The Different Roles of the Legislature and the Courts

The function of the legislature is *to enact law*. The function of the courts is *to interpret and apply the law* to individual cases which come before them for decision.

In the case of *Blackburn v Attorney-General*,[83] Lord Justice Salmon explains the roles of the legislature and the courts with regard to legislation:

> As to Parliament, in the present state of the law, it can enact, amend and repeal any legislation it pleases. The sole power of the courts is to decide and enforce what is the law and not what it should be—now, or in the future.[84]

Notice the collocation of legal verbs and nouns in this extract: Parliament *enacts*, *amends* and *repeals* (*abrogates*) law, while the courts *decide* what is the law and *enforce* it.

In *Blackburn v Attorney-General*, an ordinary citizen, Mr Blackburn, *took proceedings against* the Government in an attempt to prevent Britain from joining the (then) European Communities.[85] At that time, Britain was negotiating entry to the European Communities, but no treaty had yet been signed. The Attorney-General (AG) is the principal law officer of the Crown, who is the chief legal adviser of the Government and leader of the English Bar; he or she may represent the Crown in litigation. Each of the three Court of Appeal judges clarified the powers of the British State organs. In the words of Lord Justice Stamp:

> I agree that the appeal should be dismissed: but I should express no view whatsoever upon the legal implications of this country becoming a party to the Treaty of Rome. … I think he [Mr Blackburn] confused the division of the powers of the Crown, Parliament and the courts. The Crown enters into treaties; Parliament enacts laws; and

---

[83] *Blackburn v Attorney-General* [1971] EWCA Civ 7, [1971] 2 All ER 1380.

[84] Salmon LJ in *Blackburn v Attorney-General* [1971] 2 All ER 1380, 1383.

[85] In particular, the European Economic Community (EEC), established by the first Treaty of Rome, signed in 1957; today, the term 'European Union' has superseded 'European Community' or European Communities': see 5.3.1 below.

it is the duty of this court in proper cases to interpret those laws when made; but it is no part of this court's function or duty to make declarations in general terms regarding the powers of Parliament, more particularly where the circumstances in which the court is asked to intervene are purely hypothetical.[86]

Central to the dispute in *Blackburn v Attorney-General* was the fundamental principle of the British Constitution: the *doctrine of parliamentary sovereignty*. According to this doctrine, Parliament can make any law it pleases at any time and no Parliament can *bind*[87] another: this means that at any time, today's Parliament cannot restrict the legislative powers of future Parliaments. This is true even of constitutional statutes:

> [A]ll laws may be repealed by the ordinary legislature, even the conditions under which the English and Scottish Parliaments agreed to merge themselves in the Parliament of Great Britain.[88]

The function of the courts, when deciding a case which is covered by legislation, is *to interpret* the provisions of the Act by examining the language of the statute to find the intention of Parliament (a process called *statutory interpretation*) and to apply the law to the specific facts of the individual dispute.

In reality, cases often involve a combination of aspects covered by legislation and other aspects depending on common law rules and principles. Even where a case is covered entirely by legislation, lawyers must always refer to previous judgments *to argue their case*.[89] This is because not only the principles of the common law, but also the judicial interpretation of statutes are subject to the *doctrine of binding precedent*. Thus, once a particular interpretation of the words of a statute has been adopted in relation to particular circumstances by a superior court, the same interpretation must be given *in later, similar cases*, having regard to the position of the earlier and the later court in *the hierarchy of the courts*.[90]

3.5.3 Parliament's Role as Legislator: Examples in Criminal Law and Contract Law

Parliament is sovereign: it can in legal theory enact any law it wants. More and more legislation—both *primary* and *secondary*—is enacted every year. However, the *legal rules* in many areas of the law are still to be found in judicial precedent; it is important to remember that the common law system is not *codified*.

---

[86] Stamp LJ in *Blackburn v Attorney-General*, above n 83, p 1383.

[87] In this phrase 'bind' means to impose an obligatory limit.

[88] The words of renowned jurist Professor Maitland, *Constitutional History of England* (1908) at p 332, cited by Lord Denning in *Blackburn v Attorney-General*, above n 83, p 1382.

[89] To support their case by legal argument.

[90] For the hierarchy of the English courts, see 9.3 below.

In what circumstances does Parliament typically legislate? Some examples are discussed below:
Parliament may legislate to establish new law in an area that demands legislative attention, such as terrorism, as we observed when examining UK terrorism legislation.[91] A different example in the field of private law is the enactment of the Civil Partnership Act 2004, which created a new legal relationship for same-sex couples, followed by the Marriage (Same Sex Couples) Act 2013, in response to the changing needs of society.

Parliament may legislate in order to change pre-existing law—which may consist of legislation or precedent—by introducing new legal rules:

— If the *rules* Parliament wishes to change are contained in legislation, it may specifically *amend* or *repeal* the earlier enactment or part of it by express words. In any case, according to the *doctrine of implied repeal*, a later law *has priority over* an earlier one if there is any *inconsistency* (conflict) between them. By implication the later law *repeals the conflicting provision* enacted earlier. There are some limits on this doctrine, discussed in 3.6.2 below.

— If, instead, the *rules* Parliament wishes to change are contained in precedent, Parliament may enact a law, *establishing a new rule* for the future, since legislation *has priority over* judicial precedent as a source of law. An example is the Contracts (Rights of Third Parties) Act 1999, examined in Task 10 below.

In some cases, Parliament legislates in order *to revise* the law by improving and clarifying it, for example bringing together and redefining in legislative form an area of the common law. The principles that previously derived from precedents may be integrated with new rules and of course may be modified, depending on *the will of the legislator*. An important example of such *revision* of pre-existing law took place in 1968; for the first time in English law, an important sector of the criminal law was regulated by statute: *theft*, the crime of *stealing*. The long title of the Theft Act 1968 begins:

> An Act to revise the law of England and Wales as to theft and similar or associated offences …

Offences are *crimes* and '[t]he modern tendency is to refer to crimes as offences'.[92] This development in the use of terminology could reflect the trend in our sources, moving from judicial precedent to legislation. The definition of *theft* and its component parts in section 1 of the Theft Act 1968 (see Task 9 below) largely put into legislative form the principles of the common law. In interpreting a statute like this, the courts have regard to the precedents that inspired the Act; previous

---

[91] Text 1 and relative comment in 1.3 above.
[92] *A Dictionary of Law*, above n 20, p 378.

statutes may be relevant,[93] and also, since *Pepper v Hart*,[94] the courts may consider parliamentary debate during the passage of the Bill.

Task 9   Consulting legislation—Criminal law
— What is the definition of 'theft' in your legal system? What is its legal source?
— Consult the Theft Act 1968, below, to understand the elements of theft in English law. Is it comparable with theft in your system?
— What factors do you need to take into account?
— In English law, what distinguishes 'robbery' from 'theft'?

THEFT ACT 1968

1968 CHAPTER 60

An Act to revise the law of England and Wales as to theft and similar or associated offences, and in connection therewith to make provision as to criminal proceedings by one party to a marriage against the other ...

[26th July 1968]

Be it enacted ...

1.—(1)   A person is guilty of theft if he dishonestly appropriates property belonging to another with the intention of permanently depriving the other of it; and 'thief' and 'steal' shall be construed[95] accordingly.

(2)   It is immaterial whether the appropriation is made with a view to gain, or is made for the thief's own benefit.

...

7.   A person guilty of theft shall on conviction on indictment be liable to imprisonment for a term not exceeding ten years.

8.—(1)   A person is guilty of robbery if he steals, and immediately before or at the time of doing so, and in order to do so, he uses force on any person or puts or seeks to put any person in fear of being then and there subjected to force.

(2)   A person guilty of robbery, or of an assault with intent to rob, shall on conviction on indictment be liable to imprisonment for life.

© Crown Copyright
The Theft Act 1968 is reproduced under the terms of Crown Copyright
Policy Guidance issued by HMSO

---

[93] The Larceny Act 1916.
[94] *Pepper v Hart* [1992] UKHL 3, [1993] AC 593, examined in 1.3 above, Text 9.
[95] *To construe* = to interpret a legal document such as a statute, will, etc. Noun: *construction*.

Key and commentary to Task 9 Consulting legislation—criminal law
Each term in the definition of *theft* in section 1(1) of the Theft Act 1968 is itself defined in the next five sections of the Act: 'dishonestly' (section 2), 'appropriates' (section 3), 'property' (section 4) and so on. A series of related crimes is defined and *governed by* the Act: *theft* (sections 1–7), *robbery* (section 8), *burglary* (section 9) and so on. You may refer to the text of the Act to understand the nature of the various offences and the penalty provided by law.[96] For example, *robbery* carries a punishment of *life imprisonment*: under section 8(2), 'A person convicted of robbery ... *shall be liable* ... to imprisonment for life'. A person who *steals* is called a *thief*; a person who *robs* is a *robber*.
Robbery involves *stealing* (defined in section 1 of the Act), but it is made especially serious by the extra element of using force on a person or putting a person *in fear of force.*

Is there an equivalent offence to robbery in your legal system?

Task 10 Consulting legislation—contract law
In this Task, you will read an extract from an important statute on contract law enacted in 1999, passed in order to change an old common law doctrine. Before the Act, according to the traditional common law doctrine of *privity of contract*, only the parties to a contract could enforce the contract in court proceedings; a third party—anyone who is not a party to the contract—had no such right.

— Consult section 1 of the Act, below, to discover how the 1999 Act changed the law with regard to third parties in England, Wales and Northern Ireland. Compare the pre-existing common law doctrine with the new statutory rule.
— What is the position of third parties today?
— What limits apply to the rights of third parties?

CONTRACTS (RIGHTS OF THIRD PARTIES) ACT 1999

1999 CHAPTER 31

An Act to make provision for the enforcement of contractual terms by third parties.

Be it enacted by the Queen's most Excellent Majesty, by and with the advice and consent of the Lords Spiritual and Temporal, and Commons,

---

[96] Search for the Act by its short title at <http://www.legislation.gov.uk>.

in this present Parliament assembled, and by the authority of the same, as follows:—

1. Right of third party to enforce contractual term

(1) Subject to the provisions of this Act, a person who is not a party to a contract (a 'third party') may in his own right enforce a term of the contract if—

   (a) the contract expressly provides that he may, or
   (b) subject to subsection (2), the term purports to confer a benefit on him.

(2) Subsection (1)(b) does not apply if on a proper construction of the contract it appears that the parties did not intend the term to be enforceable by the third party.

(3) The third party must be expressly identified in the contract by name, as a member of a class or as answering a particular description but need not be in existence when the contract is entered into.

(4) This section does not confer a right on a third party to enforce a term of a contract otherwise than subject to and in accordance with any other relevant terms of the contract.

(5) For the purpose of exercising his right to enforce a term of the contract, there shall be available to the third party any remedy that would have been available to him in an action for breach of contract if he had been a party to the contract (and the rules relating to damages, injunctions, specific performance and other relief shall apply accordingly).

...

Key and commentary to Task 10 Consulting legislation—contract law

The 1999 Act reforms the old common law rule of *privity of contract*. Section 1 gives effect to this main purpose of the Act. Under the Act, it is now possible for *a third party* 'in his own right' (that is, directly and independently) to *enforce a term* of the contract.

This rule applies within the limits specified in the Act (*'Subject to the provisions of this Act'*). There is a two-part test for the circumstances in which a third party may enforce a term of the contract under section 1(1):

(a) if the contract *expressly* gives this right to the third party, or (b) if the contract *purports to confer a benefit* on the third party (ie this appears from the meaning or substance of the contract). But section 1(2) places a condition on this last possibility: it does not apply if, on a true construction (interpretation) of the contract, the parties *did not intend* the third party to have a right to enforce it.

Under section 1(4), the third party's right to enforcement is *subject to and in accordance with* the terms of the contract: for example, the contracting parties may set a condition that the third party can enforce the right by *arbitration* but not *litigation*.[97]

Under section 1(3), the third party must be identifiable, but may come into existence in the future: this would cover an unborn child or a future *spouse*,[98] or *a company* not yet *incorporated*.

Section 1(5) provides details of *enforcement*: a third party has the right to all the *remedies* that a contracting party could *claim* in *an action for breach of contract* (a party is *in breach* if it does not fulfil its side of the contract). This means that the third party can *seek a remedy*[99] from a court, such as *damages* (money compensation, the basic *common law remedy* for breach of contract); or the *equitable remedies* of *specific performance* (an order to perform the terms of a contract) or *an injunction* (an order to do or not to do a particular act).[100]

Clearly, the Contracts (Rights of Third Parties) Act 1999 has completely transformed the legal position of interested third parties to a contract under English (and Northern Irish) law.

3.6 Constitutional Legislation and EU Law in the National System—Advanced

3.6.1 Legislation as a Source of Constitutional Law

Legislation is the most important *source of constitutional law* in the United Kingdom legal system today. Periodically, in the past and in modern times, Parliament has legislated on *constitutional matters* to change or adapt the Constitution. Acts of Parliament regulate key aspects such as the *succession to the*

---

[97] This example is given in the 'Explanatory Notes', designed to explain the meaning and effect of UK legislation: they are a helpful aid to understanding the text of the Act. Both Acts and Explanatory Notes may be consulted at <http://www.legislation.gov.uk>, by searching for the Act by its short title.

[98] A spouse is a husband or wife.

[99] To seek a remedy = to request a remedy.

[100] See 9.2.6 below for more on common law or equitable remedies.

throne, electoral rights and the supremacy of the House of Commons over the House of Lords. As we have seen above, a major period of constitutional reform began with Tony Blair's premiership in 1997: *devolution* was introduced for Scotland, Wales and Northern Ireland; some reforms were made to the House of Lords and the historic Lord Chancellor's office; the Supreme Court of the United Kingdom was established; and Convention rights were guaranteed for the first time by the national courts.[101]

Parliament may enact *constitutional reforms* in response to changes in social or institutional needs. For example, during the First World War, 1914–18, women in Britain took on a new social and economic role. By January 1918, almost five million women were in employment, in factories and performing clerical and administrative work previously done only by men.[102] The suffragettes and suffragists, who had fought dramatically for women's *suffrage* (the right to vote) in the pre-war years, had suspended their militancy in 1914. But thanks to the status women acquired as citizens during the War, *they were granted the franchise* (the right to vote, *suffrage*) by law in 1918. A historian explains:

> It was hardly possible to argue now that women were incapable of exercising the rights
> of citizenship to the full; in the 1918 Representation of the People Act, therefore,
> women thirty and over were given the vote. A long, bitter saga of persecution and
> prejudice ended ...[103]

The same Act *extended the franchise* to all men over 21, so British women had not yet gained equality; but in 1928 women were given *equal voting rights* with men; they immediately became the majority of *the electorate* (the body of people with the right to vote). Later in the twentieth century, in response to further social change, the voting age was reduced to 18 for everybody by the Representation of the People Act 1969. And in the same period, the Family Law Reform Act 1968 reduced the *age of majority* from 21 to 18: that is, the full age when a person can exercise full *legal capacity* and is no longer a *minor* but an *adult.*

When Parliament enacts a constitutional law, like those mentioned above, there is no special *procedure, parliamentary majority,* text type or language. All UK laws are enacted following the ordinary procedure and—on the basis of *Parliamentary sovereignty*—may be amended or repealed at any time. Even constitutional laws are not *entrenched*: that is, they are not protected by a *special legislative procedure.* However, as a matter of political realism, it is hard to imagine that Parliament could ever repeal certain laws, such as those granting the vote to women. In the words of Lord Denning:

> We have all been brought up to believe that, in legal theory, one Parliament cannot
> bind another and that no Act is irreversible. But legal theory does not always march

---

[101] Constitutional statutes referred to in this period include the Scotland Act 1998, Government of Wales Acts 1998 and 2006, Northern Ireland Act 1998, Human Rights Act 1998, House of Lords Act 1999, Constitutional Reform Act 2005.

[102] Morgan, above n 6, p 529.

[103] *Ibid*, p 530.

alongside political reality. … Take the Acts which have granted independence to the Dominions and territories overseas. Can anyone imagine that Parliament could or would reverse those laws and take away their independence? Most clearly not. Freedom once given cannot be taken away. Legal theory must give way to practical politics.[104]

3.6.2 Parliamentary Sovereignty and the Supremacy of EU Law

In a relatively recent development, a new category of legislation described as *common law 'constitutional statutes'* was recognised by the courts in the case of *Thoburn v Sunderland City Council*.[105] These are particularly significant constitutional statutes. *Thoburn* arose out of a dispute concerning EU obligations in the national legal system. It is also known as *the Metric Martyrs case*, since it involved *an appeal* by various British traders *against* their *criminal conviction* for selling fruit, fish and vegetables in traditional imperial measures (pounds and ounces) instead of metric measures (kilos and grams); this was a *requirement* of EU law, implemented at national level by subordinate legislation.

Since the UK Constitution is not entrenched, even constitutional statutes *may be repealed* in the ordinary way by the use of *express words* in a later law, which indicate Parliament's intention to repeal the earlier statute (known as *express repeal*). However, in the opinion of Lord Justice Laws in *Thoburn*, *common law 'constitutional statutes'* are not subject to another general rule of interpretation, according to which, if a later statute is incompatible with an earlier one, the later law has priority and *implicitly* repeals any earlier conflicting provisions (known as *the doctrine of implied repeal*).[106] Lord Justice Laws's statements in *Thoburn* on implied repeal, pronounced *obiter*,[107] are controversial;[108] however, his definition of *constitutional statutes* is very useful and he listed some *common law constitutional statutes*, including the European Communities Act 1972 and the *devolution legislation* examined earlier in this chapter. But the list is not definitive. In effect, Leyland and Anthony point out that this development is part of an increasing 'assertion of judicial authority' and 'places the courts in an even more influential position, as it is they—through the use of the common law—who become responsible for identifying constitutional statutes'.[109]

What is the essence of Lord Justice Laws's definition, given below?

> In my opinion a constitutional statute is one which (a) conditions the legal relationship between the citizen and the state, in some general or overarching manner, or

---

[104] *Blackburn v Attorney-General*, above n 83, p 1382.

[105] *Thoburn v Sunderland City Council* [2002] EWHC 195 (Admin), [2003] QB 151.

[106] *Ibid*, [63].

[107] *Obiter* (Latin, adverb) means 'by the way'; *obiter dicta* are not part of binding precedent, therefore not part of the *ratio decidendi* of a judgment; for more on this point, see 9.3.3 below.

[108] Leyland, above n 2, pp 55–56.

[109] Leyland and Anthony, above n 75, p 28.

(b) enlarges or diminishes the scope of what we would now regard as fundamental rights ... The special status of constitutional statutes follows the special status of constitutional rights. Examples are the Magna Carta, the Bill of Rights 1689, the Act of Union, the Reform Acts which distributed and enlarged the franchise, the [Human Rights Act 1998], the Scotland Act 1998 and the Government of Wales Act 1998. The [European Communities Act 1972] clearly belongs in this family. It incorporated the whole corpus of substantive Community rights and obligations, and gave overriding domestic effect to the judicial and administrative machinery of Community law.[110]

The essence of a constitutional statute is that it affects ('*conditions*') the fundamental rights of the individual, and its special status depends on the 'special status' of such constitutional rights.

The *doctrine of implied repeal*, introduced above, is an aspect of Parliamentary sovereignty, the basic doctrine of the UK Constitution. Lord Justice Laws describes 'the rule that Parliament cannot bind its successors' as 'the engine of the doctrine of implied repeal'.[111] In relation to the EU dimension of the debate, has Parliamentary sovereignty been limited by the EU Treaties?

Examine Trevor Hartley's explanation, below, remembering that 'Community Treaties' are today called EU Treaties:

> The basic principle of the UK constitution is the sovereignty of Parliament. There are no legal limits to the power of Parliament to pass any law it wants, except that it cannot validly restrict its own future powers. From a practical point of view, there are all sorts of limits to Parliament's powers. That is accepted. But there are no *legal* limits. There are no limits that a UK court would recognize. As we saw in *Salomon v Customs and Excise*[112] ... the power of Parliament 'extends to breaking treaties'. Therefore the existence of the Community Treaties does not limit the sovereignty of Parliament.[113]

The British Parliament, according to the basic principle of UK constitutional law, *cannot* limit its own future powers: *one Parliament cannot bind another*. To give effect to the obligations of European Community membership as from 1 January 1973, Parliament passed the European Communities Act 1972. Since that time, British courts have recognised *the supremacy of EU law* in cases of conflict with *domestic law*. But that supremacy is given by *national law*: by the European Communities Act 1972, accompanied by a new approach to judicial interpretation.

As Lord Denning explained, in the first dispute where *an inconsistency* (a conflict) arose between English law, in the form of an Act of Parliament, and EC law

---

[110] *Thoburn v Sunderland City Council*, above n 105, [62].
[111] *Ibid*, [58].
[112] *Salomon v Commissioners of Customs and Excise* [1967] 2 QB 116 (CA).
[113] T Hartley (2004), *European Union Law in a Global Context. Text, Cases and Materials*, Cambridge: Cambridge University Press, p 160.

(Article 119 of the Treaty of Rome on equal pay for equal work, now Article 157 TFEU):[114]

> Community law is now part of our law; and, whenever there is any inconsistency, Community law has priority ... It is part of our law which overrides any other part which is inconsistent with it.[115]

The British courts, by giving priority to EU law, are interpreting the true intention of Parliament: that is, to observe its EU obligations.

This principle was made clear by the House of Lords in the important case of *Factortame (No 2)*.[116] Even *primary legislation* (Acts of Parliament) enacted *after* the European Communities Act 1972 and where the clear words of the Act are inconsistent with EU rights, will not be applied by the British courts. Lord Bridge of Harwich explains the legal basis for this:

> If the supremacy within the European Community of Community law over the national law of member states was not always inherent in the EEC Treaty (Cmnd 5179-II) it was certainly well established in the jurisprudence of the European Court of Justice long before the United Kingdom joined the Community. Thus, whatever limitation of its sovereignty Parliament accepted when it enacted the European Communities Act 1972 was entirely voluntary. Under the terms of the Act of 1972 it has always been clear that it was the duty of a United Kingdom court, when delivering final judgment, to override any rule of national law found to be in conflict with any directly enforceable rule of Community law.[117]

The House of Lords explained that at the time of British *accession* to the European Community, the Court of Justice had already established in its *case law* ('*jurisprudence*') the principle of supremacy of Community law over the national law of *Member States*. Parliament had therefore shown its intention to accept that principle by passing the 1972 Act.

However, if Parliament at any time states clearly and expressly in the text of a statute that it intends to legislate in a manner *inconsistent* with its EU obligations, the English courts recognise that it will be their duty to apply that legislation: the UK Act of Parliament will prevail over EU law.[118] If this happens, the UK will be *in breach* of its international treaty obligations, with all the consequences that may follow. To conclude, Hartley underlines that

> the effect of Community law in the legal systems of the Member States ultimately depends on Member-State law, not Community law. ... The sovereignty (ultimate

---

[114] Treaty on the Functioning of the European Union consolidated version [2012] OJ C326/01, Art 157.

[115] *Macarthys Ltd v Smith* case C-129/79 [1980] EWCA Civ 7, [1981] 1 All ER 111. Consult A Riley (1991), *English for Law*, Harlow: Pearson Education Ltd, pp 90–99, for comment and exercises on the language and content of the Court of Appeal judgment in *Macarthys Ltd v Smith*.

[116] *R v Secretary of State for Transport, ex parte Factortame Ltd (No 2)* [1990] UKHL 13.

[117] *Ibid*, Lord Bridge of Harwich, para 4.

[118] Lord Denning in *Macarthys Ltd v Smith* [1979] 3 All ER 325, 329.

authority) of the Member States remains intact. This is why the Community is still an international organization (albeit with supranational powers), not a federal State.[119]

The constitutional position described above appears to have been strengthened by an important statute: the European Union Act 2011. Part 1 of the Act ('Restrictions on Treaties and Decisions relating to EU') introduces three types of control before the UK Government can *ratify* or *approve* a treaty or decision amending the Treaty on European Union (TEU) or the Treaty on the Functioning of the European Union (TFEU), or for the approval of certain other decisions. The three forms of control are:

— primary legislation and a referendum
— primary legislation
— *approval of a motion without amendment* in both Houses of Parliament.[120]

The provisions of the Act are designed to *prevent* any further *transfer of sovereignty* or powers from the UK to the EU: the *referendum lock* will ensure that certain proposed future treaties, or amendments to the treaties that transferred areas of power or competences, would be subject to popular approval; in fact the validity of the legislation is subject to prior approval in the referendum. Through approval in such referendums, any greater participation of the UK in deeper European integration would be *endorsed* by democratic support.

Part 3 of the European Union Act 2011 expressly provides that *directly applicable* or *directly effective EU law* takes effect in the UK national legal order only by virtue of the European Communities Act 1972 or by virtue of any other Act of Parliament:

18 Status of EU law dependent on continuing statutory basis

Directly applicable or directly effective EU law (that is, the rights, powers, liabilities, obligations, restrictions, remedies and procedures referred to in section 2(1) of the European Communities Act 1972) falls to be recognised and available in law in the United Kingdom only by virtue of that Act or where it is required to be recognised and available in law by virtue of any other Act.

This provision explicitly reinforces the *statutory basis* of the effectiveness of EU law in the UK legal order.[121] It seems that British Parliamentary sovereignty remains intact. However, the Act is the subject of interesting constitutional debate and it is still early to assess its impact.

---

[119] Hartley, above n 113, p 164.

[120] For this information, the text of the European Union Act 2011 and Explanatory Notes to the Act and its Commencement Orders have been used, available on <http://www.legislation.gov.uk>.

[121] In any case, a national law is necessary because the UK legal system is *dualist*: see 5.4.2.

Task 12 Discussion and comparison—the supremacy of EU law
You will be able to complete this Task if your country is one of the 28 Member States of the European Union.

Research your answers to the following questions in the legal system of your country, then discuss your ideas and compare the British approach, outlined above:

1.   What legal mechanisms are used to give effect to EU law in the legal system of your country? Consider the Treaties and EU acts (e.g. regulations).
2.   Is the principle of supremacy of EU law observed at national level? What is its legal status?
3.   What constitutional issues are raised where EU law and domestic law are inconsistent (e.g. sovereignty)?
4.   Research any significant case law involving your country, in which there has been a conflict between national law and EU law.

Use your knowledge and research to discuss and compare the different approaches in the national legal systems to the implementation of EU law and to the principle of supremacy of EU law.

Do you think the EU will ever become a federal state? Or will it remain an international organisation 'with supranational powers' (Hartley, above)?

Key to Task 1

Laws and Legislation: a legal rule, law reform, statute law, the Act provides that, the legislature, to enact law.
Cases and Courts: a judgment, a precedent, a legal rule, a sentence of imprisonment (imposed by the judge), a verdict of not guilty, case law, the defendant, the judiciary, the jury.

Key to Task 2

Legislation: statutes/enactments, secondary legislation, legislative.
Judicial Precedent: case law/common law, the law reports, *ratio decidendi*, to follow precedent.

Ideas for Further Reading

Bingham, Tom (2010), *The Rule of Law*, London: Penguin Books. Chapter 2, 'Some History', discusses significant historical steps leading towards the present-day conception of the rule of law. Ranging from Magna Carta to the Universal Declaration of Human Rights, with interesting episodes in British and American legal history (pp 10–33).

Brazier, Rodney (1999), 'The Constitution of the United Kingdom' in 58(1) *Cambridge Law Journal* 96, investigates the devolution legislation and its constitutional impact in depth (advanced level reading).

Farnsworth, E Allan (2010), *An Introduction to the Legal System of the United States*, 4th edn (ed Sheppard, Steve), New York: Oxford University Press. With historical analysis and clear discussion of the sources and techniques of the US legal system. Recommended for all. Chapter 1, 'Historical Background' (pp 3–16); Chapter 6, 'The Legislative System' (pp 69–80); Chapter 7, 'Statutes' (pp 81–90).

Hartley, Trevor C (2004), *European Union Law in a Global Context Text, Cases and Materials*, Cambridge: Cambridge University Press. Advanced level reading for in-depth analysis of the EU Treaties in the UK legal system covering the European Communities Act 1972 and the supremacy of EU law and Parliamentary sovereignty (pp 160–65). The author examines EU law in its international context, making it accessible also to readers from outside the EU legal order.

Leyland, Peter (2012), *Constitution of the United Kingdom. A Contextual Analysis*, 2nd edn, Oxford: Hart Publishing. Highly recommended reading, this clear description of the UK Constitution enables law students and scholars from different legal backgrounds to understand the key principles of the UK Constitution, set in their historical context; at the same time, the author assesses and criticises the strengths and weaknesses of the system, evaluating the scope and impact of reforms and discussing future prospects. In particular, Chapter 1, 'UK Constitution: Context and History' (pp 1–24); Chapter 2, 'The Sources of the Constitution' (pp 25–43); Chapter 4, 'The Crown and the Constitution' (pp 87–105); from Chapter 5, 'Parliament' (pp 107–40); from Chapter 6, 'Government and Executive' (pp 157–64); from Chapter 8, 'Devolution, Regional Government and Local Government' (pp 243–53).

Chapter 4

LEGAL GRAMMAR

Punctuation

*The apostrophe – The comma – The semicolon – The colon – Parentheses –
The dash – The hyphen – Square brackets – Ellipses*

*Judges and jurists have written more nonsense about punctuation than any other
facet of the language.*

Bryan A Garner, author and editor of legal dictionaries, 1995

Punctuation serves as a guide to the grammatical structure and meaning of the
lengthy passages that characterise legal texts. The syntactic structure of legal texts
has been described as 'tortuous'[1] because of the complexity of its clauses and
phrases. However, punctuation and the textual-mapping devices used by drafters
provide visual and syntactic coherence. In fact, Crystal and Davy[2] describe how
whole sections of a legal document appear as 'self-contained units which convey
all the sense that has to be conveyed at any particular point and do not need to
be linked closely either to what follows or what has gone before'. In this chapter,
standard punctuation usage will be reviewed within the context of some of these
'self-contained units'.

Task 1 Read, scan, and observe—the comma and the apostrophe
Read the following text of a judgment. Highlight the comma [,] and the
possessive apostrophe ['']. Can you remember the rules for their usage?

> The type of discrimination referred to in paragraph (a) of that subsection
> is generally called 'direct' discrimination. When the present proceedings
> began in the county court, direct discrimination was alleged, but the learned

[1] VK Bhatia (1993), 'Legal Discourse in Professional Settings', *Analyzing Genre*, London: Longman,
p 101.
[2] D Crystal and D Davy (1969), 'The Language of Legal Documents', *Investigating English Style*,
Harlow: Longman, p 201.

judge held that there had been no direct discrimination, and his judgment on that point was not challenged in the Court of Appeal or before your Lordships' House. The appellant's case in this House was based entirely on 'indirect' discrimination, that is, discrimination contrary to paragraph (b) of subsection 1(1). When the proceedings began the appellants claimed damages, but that claim was not pursued before this House. Having regard to section 57(3) of the 1976 Act, it would have been unlikely to succeed. They now seek only a declaration that there has been unlawful discrimination against them contrary to the Act.[3]

4.1 THE APOSTROPHE

The apostrophe ['] has different functions: in contractions, such as *aren't* instead of *are not*; for possessives, such as *William's* sister (the sister of William); and in possessive plurals, such as the *judges' opinion* when there is more than one judge.

4.1.1 Contractions

Contractions mark where the letters in the word are omitted, such as:

cannot – *can't*, would – *wouldn't*, he is – *he's*, he has – *he's*, I would – *I'd*, I had – *I'd*, they are – *they're*. Note the irregular form: will not – *won't*.

NOTE: *Because contractions convey an informal tone, they are generally avoided in legal documents. This is true for any formal writing where a personal register[4] is not appropriate.*

4.1.2 Singular Possessive

An apostrophe signals possession or ownership. For the singular possessive, the general rule is to add ['s] after all singular possessives, e.g.:

The appellant's case, Lord Mansfield's speech, Divisional Court's judgments, Microsoft's market shares, Lord Esher's judgment, the EU's annual budget, etc.

---

[3] *Mandla (Sewa Singh) v Dowell Lee* [1982] UKHL 7.
[4] D Crystal defines *register* as a variety of language that is defined 'according to its use in social situations'. *Dictionary of Linguistics and Phonetics* (1992), Oxford: Blackwell, p 295.

If the word ends with an [s], you still use the ['s], e.g.: *the witness's testimony, Judge James's opinion, Congress's decision, etc.* Exceptions to this rule include:

a)   biblical and classical references, such as: *Jesus' suffering, Aristophanes' plays* and *Achilles' heel,* etc;
b)   a business named in a plural form, e.g.: *General Motors* becomes *General Motors'* to indicate the possessive;
c)   a business with a single name that exists in a possessive form, e.g.: *McDonald's* (restaurant) would remain in the possessive form *McDonald's.*

NOTE: When is the possessive not used? For example, when using possessives for nouns that are inanimate objects, the possessive ['s] is discouraged in Standard English grammar books. Instead, it is suggested to use 'of' rather than the ['s], e.g.: the *top of the table, not* the *table's top.* However, it is not unusual to find examples of its use as a possessive in legal texts, e.g.: the Covenant's guarantees, the Directive's provisions.

Citing a complete specific reference is generally preferred because it is less ambiguous, e.g.: Article 11 of the Convention *not* the Convention's article, *or* Article 98(1) of the Regulation, *not* the Regulation's article.

4.1.3 Plural Possessive

To form the possessive of a plural noun that ends in an [s], add an apostrophe ['].
If the plural ends in another letter, use ['s], e.g.:

your Lordships' House (from the court case)
the defendants' convictions (more than one defendant)
the witnesses' testimony (more than one witness)
your Honours' original order (more than one judge)
women's rights (plural of woman)
children's right to play (plural of child)

Is the ownership joint or individual? For joint ownership, form the possessive with the last owner listed, e.g.:

David and John's brother was found guilty.
(same brother, a brother of both David and John)

For individual ownership, use the possessive form for each owner listed, e.g.:

David's and John's brothers were found guilty.
(different brothers, the brother of David and the brother of John)

4.2 THE COMMA

The comma is used in the widest variety of circumstances, yet in legal discourse its exclusion or inclusion can 'cause more mischief in the law than all the other punctuation marks combined'.[5] For example, Garner[6] cites a case[7] in which the dissenting judge stated that 'men's lives may depend upon a comma'.

Misuse of the comma can cause ambiguity or misunderstanding regarding the intended meaning of a legal text, or, as cited above, it can have a critical impact in a court case. Understanding the rules of commas in legal English can help you to understand the interconnection of elements in a text. Some of these rules will be discussed in this section.

4.2.1 Commas in Salutations, Closures and Dates

Comma rules vary in salutations and closures (letter-writing). American (AmE) and British (BrE) English generally use commas to mark the end of a salutation or of a closure (notice the full stop after Ms. which is AmE usage), e.g.:

Dear Ms. Gray,
Sincerely yours,

However, you may find examples in BrE letter-writing where they are not used, e.g.:

Dear Ms Padden
Yours sincerely

In a House of Lords opinion in an appeal judgment (until 2009 when the Supreme Court took over), the salutation commonly appeared as follows:

My Lords,

I have had the advantage of reading in draft the speech of my noble and learned friend Lord Rodger of Earlsferry. I agree with ...[8]

When dates are mentioned in a legal text, the comma is omitted, e.g.:

In December 1984 the General Assembly ...
18 December 1984 the General Assembly ...
18th December 1984 the General Assembly ...

---

[5] RC Wydick (1998), *Plain English for Lawyers*, 4th edn, Durham, NC: Carolina Academic Press, p 90.
[6] BA Garner (1995), *A Dictionary of Modern Legal Usage*, 2nd edn, New York: Oxford University Press, p 713.
[7] *US v Palmer* 16 US 3 Wheat 636 (1818).
[8] *Beggs v Scottish Ministers* (Scotland) [2007] UKHL 3.

Observe how the commas are omitted in this treaty and court case:

> Recalling article 3 of the Universal Declaration of Human Rights, adopted on 10 December 1948, and article 6 of the International Covenant on Civil and Political Rights, adopted on 16 December 1966 ...[9]

> In July 1978 the first appellant wished to enter his son as a pupil at Park Grove School, and he brought the boy to an interview with the respondent.[10]

4.2.2 Commas Separating Items in a Series

Commas are used to separate three or more words, phrases or clauses written in a series. A distinction can be made between what is often called the 'Oxford' comma and the 'plain' comma for words in a series:

plain: a, b, c and d.
Oxford: a, b, c, and d.

The so-called Oxford comma claims to be less ambiguous, e.g.:

George, Sam, Mary, and John were summoned to court.

Four different human entities—George as an individual, Sam as an individual, Mary as an individual, and John as an individual—were summoned to court, whereas,

George, Sam, Mary and John were summoned to court.

allows for the possibility that George as an individual and Sam as an individual were summoned to court, while Mary and John *as a couple* were summoned to court.

Whether to include or not the 'series' comma (the last comma in the series) is still debated, and differences in its usage are observable in legal texts. However, if the last common is eliminated, it should not be ambiguous.

Please note that Hart publications uses plain commas, not 'Oxford commas', except where a clausal comma is called for or where 'and' precedes a combination at the end of a sentence as illustrated above.

---

[9] Second Optional Protocol to the International Covenant on Civil and Political Rights 1989, aiming at the abolition of the death penalty (adopted and proclaimed 15 December 1989) UNGA Res 44/128, recital.

[10] *Mandla (Sewa Singh) v Dowell Lee*, above n 3.

Task 2 Read, scan and observe—comma variation
Highlight the series commas in the following documents. Observe the omission or addition of the comma before *and* (the last word) in a series.

1. Justice Kennedy, with whom Justice Souter, Justice Ginsburg, and Justice Breyer join as to Parts I and II, concurring in part.[11] (USA)
2. In 1978 the school had about 300 pupils (about 75% boys and 25% girls) of whom over 200 were English, five were Sikhs, 34 Hindus, 16 Persians, six Negroes, seven Chinese and 15 from European countries.[12] (UK)
3. THE COURT OF FIRST INSTANCE (Grand Chamber) hereby: Orders Microsoft to bear its own costs … incurred by the Commission in connection with the intervention of The Computing Technology Industry Association, Association for Competitive Technology, TeamSystem, Mamut, DMDsecure.com, MPS Broadband, Pace Micro Technology, Quantel, Tandberg Television and Exor; …[13]

Have you noted any differences in how the series comma is used in these texts? Is any ambiguity created by not using the last comma in a series?

4.2.3 Commas Join Independent Clauses

An independent clause is a complete thought and can stand on its own. To join two independent clauses (two complete thoughts) use coordinating conjunctions *and, but, for, or, nor, so* and *yet*. Remember that your choice of *which* conjunction to use in a clause affects its meaning (see 6.2.1). Insert different conjunctions in the brackets [ ] in the sentence below. Have the meanings changed?

The jury had mixed feelings about the defendant's testimony, [ ] *they couldn't agree that he was guilty of negligence.*

4.2.4 Introductory Words or Phrases are Followed by a Comma

Common introductory phrases that should be followed by a comma include: participial, verbless phrases and infinitive phrases:

Having driven while intoxicated, he could not expect a reduced sentence. (participial)

---

[11] *Hamdan v Rumsfield* (Case No 05-184) 415 F 3d 33, reversed and remanded.
[12] *Mandla (Sewa Singh) v Dowell Lee*, above n 3.
[13] *Microsoft Corp v Commission of the European Communities* [2007] ECR Page II-03601, in Judgment of the Court of First Instance (Grand Chamber), Case No: T-201/04.

Although an excellent law student, he was having problems passing the Bar.[14] (verbless)

To win the case, more witnesses were needed to testify on her behalf. (infinitive)

Single words or short phrases which link the meaning of a new sentence to the preceding text may be additive (*moreover, in addition, furthermore, likewise [similar to]*), contrastive (*however, nevertheless, in contrast, on the other hand*) or consequential (*as a result, therefore, thus, consequently*). They are followed by a comma, e.g.:

> *However,* this point did not arise in the questions stated for the opinion of the Divisional Court ...[15]

> *Likewise,* prisoners of war must at all times be protected, particularly against acts of violence or intimidation and against insults and public curiosity.[16]

4.2.5 Commas to Indicate Parenthetical Statements

Commas are used to frame clauses, phrases and words that are parenthetical. Parenthetical statements are extra comments by the author, which add more information to the sentence. They can be a *word, phrase* or *clause* and, depending on their position in the sentence, are framed with commas, e.g.:

— *Clause*: 'This Convention, *of which the Chinese, English, French, Russian and Spanish texts are equally authentic,* shall be deposited in the archives of the United Nations.'[17]
   (This is a non-restrictive relative clause.)
— *Phrase*: 'Highways are, *no doubt,* dedicated prima facie for the purpose of passage ...'[18]
   (This phrase is added for emphasis and comments on the 'truth value' of the sentence.)
— *Word*: 'The defendant's activities, *however,* fell outside "an ordinary and reasonable user of the highway" and so amounted to a trespass.'[19]
   (The word 'however' links the meaning of the sentence to what went before.)

---

[14] In the USA, to practise law you must pass the Bar exam. It is one of several steps needed for being licensed to practise law.

[15] *Director of Public Prosecutions v Jones and Another* [1999] UKHL 5.

[16] Geneva Convention relative to the Treatment of Prisoners of War (adopted 12 August 1949, entered into force 21 October 1950) 75 UNTS 135, Art 13.

[17] International Convention on the Elimination of All Forms of Racial Discrimination (adopted 21 December1965, entered into force 4 January1969) 660 UNTS 195, Art 25(1).

[18] *DPP v Jones,* above n 15.

[19] *Ibid.*

4.2.6 Non-restrictive and Restrictive Elements

A non-restrictive element modifies or adds extra information to the sentence. The non-restrictive elements are framed by commas, e.g.:

(f) The action of a State in allowing its territory, *which it has placed at the disposal of another State,* to be used by that other State for perpetrating an act of aggression against a third State; …[20]

In contrast, a restrictive clause *defines or limits* what precedes it and is not framed with commas, e.g.:

All the cases which were decided at a later date will not be taken into consideration.

The judge who presided over the hearing is unavailable for comment.

and from a judgment:

A person who takes part in an assembly which he knows is prohibited by an order under section 14A is guilty of an offence.[21]

The clause *who takes part in an assembly which he knows is prohibited by an order under section 14A* is restrictive and not framed by commas because it states the specific condition that is needed to be guilty of the offence.

4.2.7 A Dependent Clause (Subordinate Clause) and the Main Clause

If the dependent clause introduces the sentence, a comma separates the dependent clause from the main clause:

When the present proceedings began in the county court, direct discrimination was alleged …[22]

4.2.8 Commas Separate Two or More Coordinate Adjectives

Use commas to separate two or more coordinate adjectives that describe the same noun. Coordinate adjectives are adjectives with equal ('co'-ordinate) status in describing the noun; neither adjective is considered subordinate to the other.

To determine their status, reverse the order of the adjectives or add *and*. If the meaning is changed, a comma may be added between the final adjective and the noun itself.

---

[20] Definition of Aggression (adopted without a vote on 14 December 1974) UNGA Res 3314 (XXIX), Art 3(f).

[21] Trespassory Assemblies Act of 1986, s 14B(2).

[22] *Mandla (Sewa Singh) v Dowell Lee,* above n 3.

Observe the different order of this sentence where the two adjectives have equal status and the meaning is the same for each variation:

[T]he purpose of Rule 11 as a whole is to bring home to the individual signer his personal, non-delegable responsibility.[23]

[T]he purpose of Rule 11 as a whole is to bring home to the individual signer his non-delegable, personal responsibility.

[T]he purpose of Rule 11 as a whole is to bring home to the individual signer his non-delegable and personal responsibility.

[T]he purpose of Rule 11 as a whole is to bring home to the individual signer his personal and non-delegable responsibility.[24]

4.2.9 Commas to Contrast

Use a comma to separate contrasted coordinate elements. The comma is placed near the end of a sentence, e.g.:

But the group was in the nature of an assembly, not a procession.[25]

4.2.10 Use of the Comma in Quotations

In standard rules of grammar, a comma is inserted between the main discourse and a quotation, such as:

The verdict was read without emotion, 'Guilty'.

However in legal texts, the colon is often used instead of a comma to introduce a lengthy quotation, such as in this judgment, e.g.:

In the judgments in Harrison v Duke of Rutland the words of Crompton J in Regina v Pratt 4 E & B 860 were quoted:

'I take it to be clear law that, if a man uses the land over which there is a right of way for any purpose, lawful or unlawful, other than that of passing and repassing, he is a trespasser.'[26]

---

[23] [T] indicates that in the original version the 't' was not capitalised (lower case).
[24] *Pavelic & LeFlore v Marvel Entertainment Group*, 493 US 120, 110 S Ct 456, 107 LEd2d 438 (1989).
[25] *DPP v Jones*, above n 15.
[26] *Ibid.*

4.3 THE SEMICOLON

A semicolon connects clauses of similar importance, and as a result, it is also one of the punctuation marks most frequently used in legal documents. Instead of creating new sentences, drafters of legal texts create long sentences with multiple clauses or phrases, punctuated with semicolons that are proportionately spaced for legibility and coherence (see Text 5 in chapter one or any other legal texts in this book).

4.3.1 A Semicolon for Items in a Series

When the items in a series are closely related, a semicolon is often preferred instead of forming a new sentence. In this example taken from a Convention, the phrase 'the following acts' signals that a list will follow (a colon is used to introduce the list) and then the items are divided into subparagraphs separated by semicolons:[27]

> To this end the following acts are and shall remain prohibited at any time and in any place whatsoever with respect to the above-mentioned persons:
> (a) Violence to life and person, in particular murder of all kinds, mutilation, cruel treatment and torture;
> (b) Taking of hostages;
> (c) Outrages upon personal dignity, in particular, humiliating and degrading treatment;
> (d) The passing of sentences and the carrying out of executions without previous judgment pronounced by a regularly constituted court affording all the judicial guarantees which are recognized as indispensable by civilized peoples.[28]

However, subsections with spacing are not always preferred, as in this example that describes the Scotland Act 1998:

> An Act to provide for the establishment of a Scottish Parliament and Administration and other changes in the government of Scotland; to provide for changes in the constitution and functions of certain public authorities; to provide for the variation of the basic rate of income tax in relation to income of Scottish taxpayers in accordance with a resolution of the Scottish Parliament; to amend the law about parliamentary constituencies in Scotland; and for connected purposes.

Quite frequently, the semicolon separates items in a complicated series, e.g.:

> [T]he Community Courts can carry out only a limited review of such assessments (Case C-269/90 Technische Universität München [1991] ECR I-5469, paragraph 13;

---

[27] See Terrorism Act 2000 in ch 1 of this book.
[28] Geneva Convention relative to the Treatment of Prisoners of War, above n 16.

Joined Cases C-204/00 P, C-205/00 P, C-211/00 P, C-213/00 P, C-217/00 P and C-219/00 P Aalborg Portland and Others v Commission [2004] ECR I-123, paragraph 279; and ...[29]

4.3.2 Semicolons and Independent Clauses

Use a semicolon to join two closely related independent clauses without a conjunction (see 4.2.3), e.g.:

> The Court of Criminal Appeals functions as the military's intermediate appeals court; it is established by the Judge Advocate General for each Armed Service and composed of appellate military judges.[30]

> Everyone has the right to freedom of thought, conscience and religion; this right includes freedom to change his religion or belief and freedom, either alone or in community with others and in public or private, ...[31]

A semicolon separates independent clauses with transitional word(s) or expressions such as *therefore, furthermore, that is, thus, such as, for example.* The semicolon is placed before the transitional word and is followed by a comma, e.g.:

We insisted on a hearing; however, the request was refused.

The court ordered a preliminary injunction; therefore, the plaintiff was protected from any harm before the court had a chance to decide the case.

Once again, the choice of the transitional expression is dependent on its semantic relationship with the clause that precedes it (*exemplification, cause/effect, consequence, contrast, addition, and the like*). This will be described further in the other chapters.

4.4 THE COLON

4.4.1 Introduces a List of Items, a Summary or Further Elaboration, or for Emphasis

The colon [:] commonly lists single items, e.g.:

The following persons were chosen from a jury list to serve as jurors: Heflin, Vieille and Rapp.

---

[29] *Microsoft v Commission*, above n 13, para 85.
[30] *Hamden v Rumsfeld*, above n 11.
[31] European Convention on Human Rights 1950, Art 9(1).

summarises, e.g.:

There are two main classes of homicide: murder and manslaughter.[32]

or introduces a group of items, such as in this directive which also uses spacing and sectioning to facilitate comprehension:

Member States shall provide adequate legal protection against the manufacture, import, distribution, sale, rental, advertisement for sale or rental, or possession for commercial purposes of devices, products or components or the provision of services which:
(a) are promoted, advertised or marketed for the purpose of circumvention of, or
(b) have only a limited commercially significant purpose or use other than to circumvent, or
(c) are primarily designed, produced, adapted or performed for the purpose of enabling or facilitating the circumvention of,
any effective technological measure.[33]

The colon provides a link between what was stated in the first part of a clause or phrase to the second part, and it is often used to highlight or explain further an important point, e.g.:

Provided an assembly is reasonable and non-obstructive, taking into account its size, duration and the nature of the highway on which it takes place, it is irrelevant whether it is premeditated or spontaneous: what matters is its objective nature.[34]

First of all, for the purpose of its assessment, there is no need for Microsoft to have already acquired a dominant position on the relevant secondary market by means of its abusive conduct: what matters is that there is a risk of elimination of competition on that market.[35]

Punctuation can be a very effective tool in persuasive legal writing such as in this example:

The defendant's motivation was obvious: revenge.

4.4.2 The Colon Introduces a Long Quotation

Colons are often used in legal texts to introduce a long quotation, e.g.:

Wills J said, at p 197:
'The only "dedication" in the legal sense that we are aware of is that of a public right of passage, of which the legal description is a "right for all Her Majesty's subjects at all seasons of the year freely and at their will to pass and repass without let or hindrance".'[36]

---

[32] Avoid using a colon after a verb or preposition that introduces a list, e.g.: *Two classes of homicide are: murder and manslaughter.* (This is incorrect.)
[33] Directive on the harmonisation of certain aspects of copyright and related rights in the information society [2001] OJ LI67/29, Art 6(2).
[34] *DPP v Jones,* above n 15.
[35] *Microsoft v Commission*, above n 13, para 475.
[36] *DPP v Jones,* above n 15.

4.5 Parentheses (AmE) Brackets (BrE)

— label items in texts, such as 'paragraph (a)', 'section (c)'
— introduce shorthand expressions, e.g. '(EU)' or
— provide a definition of a term used from that point on in the text, such as: 'Race Relations Act ("the 1976 Act")'.

They are also used to avoid ambiguities through brief explanations, e.g.:

> Neither as a group nor as individuals were any of those twenty, and in particular, of course, the Appellants (whom it must always be remembered we have to consider individually as distinct both from the group and each other) being destructive, violent, disorderly, threatening a breach of the peace or, on the evidence, doing anything other than reasonably using the highway.[37]

> The constitution of the United States was expressly based on separation of powers—the executive (President), the legislature (Senate/House of Representatives) and the judiciary (Supreme Court) are discrete bodies.[38]

4.6 The Dash

The dash signals an abrupt break, yet it can be distinguished from the comma (which tends to be neutral) or the parentheses (usually subordinate).[39] The dash is often used for emphasis, such as in a parenthetical phrase, or for inserting a further explanation or afterthought.

There are two types which can be distinguished by their length: one is short (the en-dash or en-rule) and the other is long (the em-dash or em-rule). The en-dash [–] is wider than the hyphen [-] and narrower than the em dash [—].

The longer em-dash[40] interrupts the structure of the sentence and can be used to set off a parenthetical phrase (without spaces), e.g.:

The judge—overcome with anger—abruptly adjourned the court.

> If this be the correct principle—and, so far as we are aware, it has never been laid down in terms—there seems to be no reason why it should not apply equally to the Divisional Court of the Queen's Bench.[41]

---

[37] *Ibid.*

[38] F Russell and C Locke (1993), *English Law and Language*, Hemel Hempstead; Prentice Hall International (UK) Ltd, p 28.

[39] Wydick , above n 5, p 98.

[40] The longer dash [—] is not commonly found on the keyboard, but it can be inserted from the Toolbar in Word as a symbol.

[41] KA Carleton (1964), *Law in the Making*, 7th edn, Oxford: Clarendon Press, p 240.

However, rules vary regarding on whether the dash should be long (without spaces) [—], or short [–] (with a space before and after the dash). Observe this example:

> France and Greenpeace agreed on 19 December 1985 to negotiate damages – France having admitted legal liability on 10 December.[42]

Garner says[43] that these longer dashes are 'the second most underused mark of punctuation in legal texts (*periods* being the most underused)'. In this remark he is not inferring that the em-dash should not be used, but further explains that it provides a break from excessive use of commas and can be useful in legal discourse.

Nonetheless, modern typographers and publishers increasingly use the en-dash (spaced) instead of the em-dash, especially because of its ease to use on the keyboard.

Probably the most familiar usage of the short en-dash [–] is when it is used as an equivalent of *to* (indicating a range of pages or period of time); however, it is used without spaces, e.g.:

2005[–]2008, pages 55[–]60

> In legal texts, the short dash is also used as an organisational device, e.g.:

Community action shall aim to:
– facilitate adaptation to industrial changes, in particular through vocational training and retraining;
– improve initial and continuing vocational training in order to facilitate vocational integration and reintegration into the labour market; ...[44]

4.7 THE HYPHEN

The use or non-use of a hyphen [-] in words is best determined by checking a dictionary, as its usage changes over time. Just a few of the rules will be mentioned here.

A hyphen is used when two or more words function together to modify a noun, e.g.:

self-governing colony, English-speaking countries, above-mentioned persons, open-ended inter-sessional working groups, multi-racial society, child-rearing responsibilities, judge-made presumption, first-instance hearing, common-law rule [*common law rule*]

---

[42] M Pugh (1987), 'Legal Aspects of the Rainbow Warrior Affair', (1991) 36 *ICLQ*, 655 as cited in A Riley (1991), *English for Law*, Harlow: Pearson Education Limited, p 178.

[43] Garner, above n 6, p 715.

[44] Treaty Establishing the European Community [Treaty of Rome 1957], Art 127(2).

However, when the words function as a noun phrase, no hyphen is used, e.g.:

> The constitutional principles, rules and practices of the United Kingdom have never been codified, they derive from *statute law*, from *common law*, and from conventions of the constitution ...[45]

Hyphens are used when it is essential to avoid ambiguity, e.g.:

pre-litigation, pre-enforcement, post-sentencing

If two or more phrasal adjectives share a common element (usually the last word), the shared element is used only once, while the first element is followed by a hyphen, e.g.:

Long- and short-term interest rates

general- or public-interest law

For compound numbers or fractions, a hyphen is used, e.g.:

ninety-nine, one-fourth, two hundred thirty-three [AmE], *two hundred and thirty-three* [BrE]

Foreign words (such as words of Latin origin) are not hyphenated, e.g.: *bona fide purchaser, ex post facto.*

4.8 Square Brackets

Inserting brackets [ ] can provide extra information for clarity or to avoid ambiguity, e.g.:

> On that last point, Microsoft observes that, at recital 669 to the contested decision, the Commission states that 'Novell's "clientless" work group server operating systems cannot use the full capabilities of the Windows client PCs and work group servers in the same way that [Windows] work group server operating systems can'.[46]

or they can signal an adjustment or change from the original version of a text that is being cited. For example, in this original quotation from the US Constitution, Amendment VI, the 'I' is capitalised (upper case), while in the newly written sentence the 'i' (lower case) is used.

Original quotation:

> In all criminal prosecutions, the accused shall enjoy the right to a speedy and public trial, by an impartial jury of the State and district wherein the crime shall have been committed ...

---

[45] KR Simmons (1976), *International Encyclopedia of Comparative Law: National Report—the UK*, cited in Riley, above n 42, p 36.
[46] *Microsoft v Commission*, above n 13, para 126.

This sentence was written with Amendment VI incorporated into it:

> The sixth amendment states that '[i]n all criminal prosecutions, the accused shall enjoy the right to a speedy and public trial, by an impartial jury of the State and district wherein the crime shall have been committed ...'.

4.9 ELLIPSES

Writers of legal documents use an ellipsis (a series of three period-dots) to indicate an omission of a quotation from an original text. Rules for usage of the ellipsis vary greatly between BrE and AmE, particularly in regard to spacing between the three consecutive dots and the use of a full stop/period after the ellipsis. These two variations will be compared for clarity.

An ellipsis may appear as three consecutive dots *with a space between them* and on each side (AmE) [. . .][47] or as three consecutive dots *with no spaces between them* and a space on each side [...] (BrE). The British version can be easily inserted (in Microsoft Word) by clicking 'Insert–Symbol–Ellipsis' (or 'Special Character' if 'Ellipsis' is not available).

Observe the omissions in this treaty:

Original extract from the Treaty Establishing the European Community

> The Commission shall report to the Council before 31 December 1988 and again before 31 December 1990 on the progress made towards achieving the internal market within the time limit fixed in Article 8a. The Council, acting by a qualified majority on a proposal from the Commission, shall determine the guidelines and conditions necessary to ensure balanced progress in all the sectors concerned.[48]

In the following example, the words enclosed by commas in the middle of the second sentence of the preceding extract have been omitted and replaced with an ellipsis. Observe the spacing between the dots:

> The Commission shall report to the Council before 31 December 1988 and again before 31 December 1990 on the progress made towards achieving the internal market within the time limit fixed in Article 8a. The Council . . . shall determine the guidelines and conditions necessary to ensure balanced progress in all the sectors concerned.

> The Commission shall report to the Council before 31 December 1988 and again before 31 December 1990 on the progress made towards achieving the internal market within the time limit fixed in Article 8a. The Council ... shall determine the guidelines and conditions necessary to ensure balanced progress in all the sectors concerned.

---

[47] See BA Garner (2001), *Legal Writing in Plain English*, Chicago, Ill: The University of Chicago Press, pp 158–59; and BA Garner (2009), Garner's Modern American Usage, 3rd edn, New York: Oxford University Press.

[48] Treaty Establishing the European Community, above n 44, Art 7(b).

There are also marked differences in BrE and AmE rules as regards the use or non-use of a full stop/period when the omission occurs between sentences or when the ellipsis ends the sentence.

American usage: When an ellipsis is placed *at the end of a sentence* to indicate omission of material (because the sentence continues), insert a space after the last word, then add the three consecutive ellipsis dots (with spaces between them) and a period/full stop (which marks the end of the sentence although it is typographically identical).

Observe the following extracts taken from the same treaty:

> The Council, acting by a qualified majority on a proposal from the Commission, shall determine the guidelines and conditions necessary to ensure balanced progress . . . .

British usage: Using the three-dot ellipsis (no spaces between them) indicates that the sentence(s) omission continues indefinitely, e.g.:

> The Council, acting by a qualified majority on a proposal from the Commission, shall determine the guidelines and conditions necessary to ensure balanced progress ...

Another rule that contrasts the two ellipsis punctuation styles is the use/non-use of the fourth full stop/period between sentences. In AmE, if the omission is made *after a completed sentence* (with a full stop) and the omission continues into the sentence(s) that follows, place a dot at the end of the completed sentence, then a space, followed by the three-dot ellipsis and a space before the continued quotation. In BrE, this distinction is not made.

This paragraph is an extract taken from the Treaty of Lisbon:[49]

> In its relations with the wider world, the Union shall uphold and promote its values and interests and contribute to the protection of its citizens. It shall contribute to peace, security, the sustainable development of the Earth, solidarity and mutual respect among peoples, free and fair trade, eradication of poverty and the protection of human rights, in particular the rights of the child, as well as to the strict observance and the development of international law, including respect for the principles of the United Nations Charter.

Observe the omissions in the treaty:

> In its relations with the wider world, the Union shall uphold and promote its values and interests and contribute to the protection of its citizens. . . . in particular the rights of the child, as well as to the strict observance and the development of international law, including respect for the principles of the United Nations Charter.

As you have observed, the first sentence was completed with a full stop, signaling the end of the sentence. But it has also been understood that with the ellipsis that followed, more words/sentences have been omitted.

---

[49] Treaty of Lisbon [2007] OJ C306/1, Art 2(5).

If just an ellipsis is inserted, it would indicate that sentences were omitted before the completion of the first sentence and continued until the end of the paragraph as in these examples:

> In its relations with the wider world, the Union shall uphold and promote its values and interests and contribute to the protection . . . including respect for the principles of the United Nations Charter.

> In its relations with the wider world, the Union shall uphold and promote its values and interests and contribute to the protection ... including respect for the principles of the United Nations Charter.

A final rule regards when entire paragraphs are omitted (for example selected articles of a treaty or sections of an Act): place the ellipsis[50] on a separate line (with spaces between the paragraphs). This informs the reader visually of the missing text(s). In AmE the ellipsis is centered, while in BrE it is on the left. In this example, taken from the Bill of Rights (the first 10 Amendments) of the United States Constitution, Articles III, IV and V have been omitted:

ARTICLE I

Congress shall make no law respecting an establishment of religion, or prohibiting the free exercise thereof; ... or the right of the people to peaceably assemble, and to petition the government for a redress of grievances.

ARTICLE II

A well-regulated Militia, being necessary to the security of a free State, the right of the people to keep and bear Arms, shall not be infringed.

...

ARTICLE VI

In all criminal prosecutions, the accused shall enjoy the right to a speedy and public trial, by an impartial jury of the State ... and to have the Assistance of Counsel for his defence.

These stylistic variations reflect different punctuation rules for the ellipsis. Certainly the British usage is easier and the insertion of the ellipsis a matter of using the toolbar in Microsoft Word. In this coursebook the British usage has been implemented.

Task 3 Read, scan and observe—the ellipses and brackets
Using the legal documents in this book or in other legal texts, observe the use of ellipses and brackets. How are they different from the rules indicated above?

---

[50] In some punctuation rules, four dots [. . . .] on a separate line are indicated for lengthy omitted material instead of three.

KEY AND COMMENTARY

Key

Task 1 Comma and apostrophe

The comma:

<u>When the present proceedings began in the county court,</u> (dependent clause, see 6.4.1 below) direct discrimination was alleged,

<u>but</u> the learned judge held that there had been no direct discrimination, <u>and</u> his judgment on that point was not challenged in the Court of Appeal or before your Lordships' House. (coordinating conjunctions, see 6.2.1)

The appellant's case in this House was based entirely on 'indirect' discrimination, <u>that is,</u> ... (parenthetical phrase, see 4.2.5)

When the proceedings began the appellants claimed damages, <u>but</u> that claim was not pursued before this House. (coordinating conjunction, see 6.2.1)

<u>Having regard to section 57(3) of the 1976 Act,</u> it would have been unlikely to succeed. (non-finite verb phrase, see 6.7.2)

The possessive apostrophe [']:

singular possessive: appellant's case

plural possessive: Lordships' House

Task 2 Comma variation

The UK (2.) and the EU (3.) have omitted the addition of a comma before the last word in a series, while the USA (1.) has included the comma. While the UK text 'seven Chinese and 15 from European countries' is not ambiguous for obvious reasons, in the EU text it is not clear if 'Tandberg Television and Exor' is one or two entities. Inclusion of the last comma in a series might be favoured over exclusion of the comma in order to avoid ambiguity.

Task 3 The ellipses and brackets

Because there are many different referencing methods/styles, punctuation may vary from publisher to publisher and from university to university, especially for ellipses and brackets. *Advice*: Follow the guidelines given in your particular academic setting or as requested by a publisher and be consistent in their usage.

Commentary

Thanks to textual-mapping and punctuation devices, the meaning of the 'self-contained' units in the lengthy passages of legal documents is more easily conveyed. As has been mentioned before, precision and clarity are essential to legal texts, and textual-mapping and punctuation facilitate this requirement. Although most legal texts conform to Standard English punctuation usage, rules do vary, as observed with the ellipsis. However one characteristic remains universal: punctuation is kept to a strict minimum.

CONSOLIDATION PART II – LANGUAGE FOCUS TASKS

Task A – Which One Word or Phrase is Out of Context?

0	reserved matters	no limitations of legislative competence	outside the legislative competence	restrictions of legislative competence
1	judge-made law	unwritten law	written law	common law
2	primary legislation	subordinate legislation	secondary legislation	delegated legislation
3	House of Commons	elected body	Lower House	Upper House
4	outlaw	override	approve	block
5	referendum	bill	statute	proposal

Task B – Match the Terms with the Definitions[1]

come into force	invoke	crime	exempt
fine	override	contravene	outlaw

[1] Task B references used to create definitions: BA Garner (1995), *A Dictionary of Modern Legal Usage*, 2nd edn, Oxford: Oxford University Press; *Black's Law Dictionary, Pocket edition* (1996), BA Garner (ed), Eagan, Minn: West Publishing Co; *Oxford Dictionary of Law* (2009), J Law and E Martin (eds), 7th edn, Oxford: Oxford University Press.

1	....	to be free or to release from a duty or liability to comply
2	....	to become legally effective (of an Act, a treaty, etc)
3	....	to cite as legally binding
4	....	to prohibit, to ban
5	....	offence (BrE) or offense (AmE)
6	....	to violate, to come into conflict with
7	....	a sum of money to pay as a penalty
8	....	to use official authority to ignore or change a decision that was made

Task C – Word Formation

a)   Fill in the spaces below [...] with the appropriate word form.

Words that are not necessarily used in a legal context, or a variant no longer in use, have not been included in the table. The [x] in the table indicates that the form does not exist or that it is uncommon in a legal context. If necessary, read chapter 10 before doing this task or consult a dictionary.

	verb	noun (concept)	noun (person)	adjective
1	to establish	....	x	established
2	to constitute	constitution/ constitutionality (*allowed by the constitution*)	x	....
3	....	amendment	x	amending
4	to regulate	regulation	regulator	regulative/ regulated/ regulable [AmE]/ (4) ....
5	to govern	government	governor	governing/ .... (2)
6	....	impeachment	x	impeachable
7	to implement	....	implementor or implementer [AmE]	implementing/ implemented

b) Using the table above, insert the appropriate word in the spaces below: verb, noun (concept), noun (person) or adjective:

8   The authorities have failed so far to ....…......... a law allowing unrestricted immigration.

9   One purpose of the Act is to ....…........... the law about parliamentary constituencies.

10 The Scottish Parliament has wide .... powers.

11 .... are the most direct form of EU law – as soon as they are passed, they have binding legal force throughout every Member State.

12 The UK today is a ....…..........monarchy.

13 The Scotland Act provided for the ....of a Scottish Parliament and Administration.

14 The court has to decide if the crime committed was an ....….... offense, which then could possibly result in removing the public official from office. [context: USA]

Task D – Prefixes and Suffixes

Fill in the missing suffixes or prefixes to the following terms. Identify the appropriate word form.

The [x] indicates that the form does not exist or that it is uncommon in a legal context.

	Prefixes	adjective	noun concept
1	centralisation		
2	equity	x	
3	obedience	x	
4	elected		x
5	section	x	
	Suffixes		
6	delegate	(2)	(1)
7	imprison		
8	intent		
9	liable	x	
10	appoint		

Task E – Collocation

Match the words 1–5 with the appropriate words a–e, and write the matching identifiers in the first column of the table. Think about the meaning of each term or phrase.

...1d...	1	legislative	a	to the throne
......	2	constitutional	b	legislation
......	3	succession	c	rule
......	4	Parliamentary	d	procedure
......	5	primary	e	sovereignty
......	6	equitable	f	party
......	7	legal	g	with
......	8	contracting	h	reforms
......	9	appeal	i	remedy
......	10	in accordance	j	against a conviction

Task F – Comprehension: True (T) or False (F)?

According to the Scotland Act 1998 ...

–	1	A Bill that is approved must receive the Royal Assent before it becomes an Act.
–	2	A Bill is a legislative proposal offered for debate before enactment.
–	3	Scotland still remains part of the United Kingdom with the Prime Minister as Head of State and part of the legislature.
–	4	The UK Parliament can continue to legislate for Scotland.
–	5	The power of the UK Parliament has been changed by the Scotland Act 1998.
–	6	The Scottish Parliament may make laws.
–	7	The Scottish Parliament can make a law outside the territory of Scotland.
–	8	Scotland has the legislative competence to regulate its own international trade with other countries.

Part III

International Treaties, Human Rights and European Integration

Chapter 5

LANGUAGE AND LAW

Treaties and Human Rights in the European Dimension

Introduction to European integration – Language choices in international legal contexts – Consulting treaty law: the European Union – Language of human rights and the European Convention on Human Rights – ECHR in the UK Constitution – Freedom of religion case study

A day will come when all the nations of this continent, without losing their distinct qualities or their glorious individuality, will fuse together in a higher unity and form the European brotherhood. A day will come when the only battlefield will be the marketplace for competing ideas. A day will come when bullets and bombs will be replaced by votes.

Victor Hugo, 1849

Victor Hugo spoke those prophetic words in 1849, but it took more than a century for his utopian predictions to start coming true. During that time, two world wars and countless other conflicts on European soil caused millions of deaths and there were times when all hope seemed lost. Today, the first decade of the 21st century offers brighter prospects, but it also brings Europe new difficulties and challenges.[1]

Pascal Fontaine, 2006

5.1 INTRODUCTION TO EUROPEAN INTEGRATION

5.1.1 Introduction

Victor Hugo's words, cited above, were truly prophetic. They seem to look forward to the European Union (EU) as it is today: founded on the European Community with its single market, based on competition and with citizens exercising the democratic right to vote for a European Parliament in Strasbourg.

---

[1] Both quotations are taken from P Fontaine (2006), *Europe in 12 lessons*, Luxembourg: Office for Official Publications of the European Communities, ch 12.

But, as Pascal Fontaine underlines, 100 years went by before these 'utopian predictions' began to come true, a period marked by terrible conflict in Europe, spreading to the whole world in two devastating World Wars. And how many centuries of battles had there been before the time of Victor Hugo? Wars between countries that today form a legal and economic Union of nearly 30 states and over 500 million citizens.

Peace in Europe has been the greatest achievement of *European integration*. This process began step by step after the end of the Second World War, with just a few founder members. Today it continues in an ongoing process 'of creating an ever closer union among the peoples of Europe', as proclaimed in the *Treaty on European Union*.[2] The EU was awarded the Nobel Peace Prize for 2012 in recognition of its 'most important result: the successful struggle for peace and reconciliation and for democracy and human rights. The stabilizing part played by the EU has helped to transform most of Europe from a continent of war to a continent of peace.'[3] And this remains true even in a time of economic crisis and social unrest like the present.

Belgium, France, Germany, Italy, Luxembourg and the Netherlands were the original six founders of the three *European Communities*, later known as the *European Community*, that were at the origin of the *European Union*, itself established in 1992. In post-war Europe, production of coal and steel—the materials of war—was the first to be regulated by treaty, with the creation of the *European Coal and Steel Community* (ECSC),[4] designed 'to create interdependence in coal and steel so that one country could no longer mobilise its armed forces without others knowing', helping to increase trust and reduce tension after the Second World War.[5]

The foundations of the EU are closely interconnected with the principles of another post-war agreement which has contributed to lasting peace in Europe and the promotion of justice: the European Convention for the Protection of Human Rights and Fundamental Freedoms (also known by the shorter name European Convention on Human Rights or ECHR) was signed by the original 10 Members of the *Council of Europe* in Rome in 1950. Although they remain distinct organisations, there are close connections between the Council of Europe and the EU today; all the Members of the EU are also Members of the Council of Europe, and not only every EU Member State but also the EU itself are *Parties* to the ECHR today.

---

[2] Treaty on European Union, consolidated version (Treaty of Maastricht, TEU) [2012] OJ C326/13, Art 1.

[3] Norwegian Nobel Committee Announcement: The Nobel Peace Prize for 2012, Oslo, 12 October 2012, available at <http://nobelpeaceprize.org>.

[4] The Treaty of Paris establishing the ECSC entered into force on 23 July 1952 and expired after 50 years on 23 July 2002: Treaty establishing the European Steel and Coal Community, signed in Paris, 18 April 1951, 11951K/TXT, at <http://eur-lex.europa.eu>.

[5] Information from the official website of the European Union at <http://www.europa.eu>.

Observe the shared values of the ECHR and the EU, in the treaty texts below:

European Convention on Human Rights[6]
Preamble
Reaffirming their profound belief in those fundamental freedoms which are the foundation of justice and peace in the world and are best maintained on the one hand by an effective political democracy and on the other by a common understanding and observance of the human rights upon which they depend ...

Treaty on European Union[7]
Article 2
The Union is founded on the values of respect for human dignity, freedom, democracy, equality, the rule of law and respect for human rights, including the rights of persons belonging to minorities. These values are common to the Member States in a society in which pluralism, non-discrimination, tolerance, justice, solidarity and equality between women and men prevail.

The *fundamental rights* protected by the ECHR have legal force in EU law as 'general principles of the Union's law'.[8]

In Section One of this chapter, we consider the importance of language choices in international legal settings: in the broader perspective of treaty law, and in specific organisations such as the United Nations and the Council of Europe; we explore multilingualism in the EU, and also consider the significance of language in relation to rights (see 5.2). We consult treaty law, with language and comprehension Tasks based on the EU Treaties, and we discover the rights of EU citizens (at 5.3).

In Section Two of this chapter, we examine the language of human rights in the context of the ECHR, and consider the problem of the enforcement of those rights before the national courts in the British legal system (see 5.4). By virtue of the Human Rights Act 1998, the ECHR today 'can be regarded as amounting to a constitutional charter of rights'.[9] We read the main sections of the Act to understand its mechanisms and impact in the UK Constitution (5.4). To conclude, we examine a controversial English case involving freedom of religion.[10] The freedom to manifest religion is protected by Article 9 ECHR, but in certain circumstances limitations may be justified, and in a multicultural society, such as Britain, not only strong beliefs, but also complex realities are at play. The chapter concludes with significant judicial reflections on this theme (see 5.5).

---

[6] Convention for the Protection of Human Rights and Fundamental Freedoms ETS No 005, Rome, 4 November 1950 (European Convention on Human Rights, ECHR).

[7] TEU [2012] OJ C326/13, above n 2, Art 2.

[8] *Ibid*, Art 6(3).

[9] P Leyland (2012), *The Constitution of the United Kingdom. A Contextual Analysis*, 2nd edn, Oxford: Hart Publishing, pp 29–30.

[10] *R (on the application of SB) v The Headteacher and Governors of Denbigh High School* [2005] EWCA Civ 199, [2006] UKHL15.

5.1.2 Terminology Focus—Legal Abbreviations

'European Union' is abbreviated to 'EU'. Abbreviations are typical of legal language, since they permit brief but precise identification of an institution, legal source or other entity. We have already met many abbreviations in this book and it is useful to include these in your personal terminology system. Those shown in the Task below are all commonly used in the contexts of the EU or the ECHR.

Task 1 In brief—European abbreviations
Using the clues in the third column of the table below, complete the table with the following abbreviations and their full English names, and also provide the corresponding abbreviations in your language, if applicable. Remember that even if you live outside Europe, your language may be an official language of the EU (e.g. Spanish, Portuguese, French).

Pay attention to the correct use of capital (upper-case) letters in the English names! The letters of the abbreviations will generally be capitals, for correct spelling; in speaking, each letter is pronounced individually. As you work, consider what you know about the scope and purpose of each treaty, entity or institution.

ABBREVIATIONS: TFEU—EEC—TEU—ECJ—MEP—CFSP—EESC—ECHR—ECB—EMU

FULL NAMES

Member of the European Parliament
Common Foreign and Security Policy
Economic and Monetary Union
European Economic and Social Committee
European Convention on Human Rights

European Central Bank
Treaty on European Union
European Economic Community
European Court of Justice
Treaty on the Functioning of the European Union

EN	FULL ENGLISH NAME	CLUES	YOUR LANGUAGE
1 MEP	Member of the European Parliament	Elected representative of the European people in the Strasbourg Parliament	
2		The Treaty of Lisbon gave the Treaty of Rome this new name, describing its modern function.	
3		Based in Frankfurt, this financial institution manages the euro and EU monetary policy	

(Continued)

EN	FULL ENGLISH NAME	CLUES	YOUR LANGUAGE
4		Established by the first Treaty of Rome, the economic aims of this Community were based on the creation of a common market	
5		This principle was formalised in the Maastricht Treaty, but national policy divisions between Member States concerning security and international relations make progress hard	
6		It involves close coordination of economic policies and the introduction of a single currency: the euro	
7		Inspired by the UDHR, this binding human rights instrument was signed in 1950 by Members of the Council of Europe	
8		The judicial organ of the European Union ensures observance of EU law and its uniform interpretation in the Member States	
9		A non-political consultative body that represents economic and social interest groups in civil society in the EU	
10		Also known as the Treaty of Maastricht, it marked a fundamental new stage in European integration	

To check your answers to Task 1: consult the EU official website at <http://europa.eu>, a vast multilingual resource containing both information for the general public and legal sources and informative documents. You can enter the website in any one of the 24 official languages and change language during consultation (useful for checking your comprehension or terminology across two European languages). As a starting point for this activity, go to the home page in English and enter 'How the EU works'. The website also contains many valuable glossaries that you may use.

SECTION ONE

5.2 Language Choices in International Legal Contexts

5.2.1 Treaty Law

In different international legal contexts, the parties involved—States or other subjects with *international legal personality*—must make choices about the language or languages they wish to use in their legal cooperation.

Treaty law is a major source of international law: this collective term indicates the legally binding obligations *mutually agreed* in treaties. When the parties agree on the text of a treaty, they may choose a single language or prefer to adopt the treaty text in two or more languages, deciding that each language text is equally authentic. An *authentic text* is not merely official but is a legally valid text: the language of this text will be interpreted and applied by a court or other body with jurisdiction, in case of dispute. For example, it is possible to consult a Portuguese translation of the *Charter of the United Nations*, but this is not an authentic Charter text.[11] The Vienna Convention on the Law of Treaties of 1969 *lays down*[12] rules on the interpretation of treaties authenticated in two or more languages, for example 'the terms of the treaty are presumed to have the same meaning in each authentic text'.[13]

Parties must make further choices to decide which language or languages to use in the work of an international body or court (for example, the UN Security Council, the European Court of Human Rights, the EU Commission), including the various legal and official documents these bodies produce.

Different solutions have been adopted by the members of the United Nations, the Council of Europe and the EU.

Do you know which languages are used in any of these contexts?

To give an idea of the importance of treaty law as an international source, the United Nations Headquarters Final Report on the 2013 'Treaty Event' gives these statistics:

> During the 2013 Treaty Event, fifty-nine (59) **States** undertook one hundred and thirteen (113) **treaty actions**. Nine (9) States participated at the level of **Head of State**, seven (7) States participated at the level of **Head of Government**, thirty-five (35) States participated at the **ministerial level**, and eight (8) States participated at the level of **Permanent Representative**.

---

[11] See 5.2.3 below.
[12] To lay down: to provide, to establish by law, treaty or judicial decision.
[13] Vienna Convention on the Law of Treaties 1969, Art 33(3).

There were a total of sixty (60) signatures, twenty-nine (29) ratifications, twelve (12) accessions, four (4) instruments of consents to be bound, four (4) acceptances, three (3) provisional applications, and one (1) declaration.[14]

The '*treaty actions*' concerned matters ranging from *commodities* (the *accession* of Ecuador to the International Cocoa Agreement, 2010)[15] to human rights (*signature* by Angola and *ratification* by Guinea-Bissau to the Convention against Torture and Other Cruel, Inhuman or Degrading Treatment or Punishment).[16] Issues such as health, education, the arms trade, child pornography, the environment, the use of weapons and the protection of migrant workers were all the subject of treaty actions listed in the Report.

5.2.2 The Council of Europe

The Council of Europe was *founded* in 1949 by a group of 10 countries: Belgium, Denmark, France, Ireland, Italy, Luxembourg, the Netherlands, Norway, Sweden and the United Kingdom. Today it has 47 Members (many more than the EU), giving it a genuine pan-European dimension.[17] It aims to protect *human rights*, *pluralist democracy* and *the rule of law*.

Examine the first article of the founding statute of the Council of Europe, below. What are the areas of its activity?

How does the Council of Europe achieve its aims?

Statute of the Council of Europe[18]
Article 1

a. The aim of the Council of Europe is to achieve a greater unity between its members for the purpose of safeguarding and realising the ideals and principles which are their common heritage and facilitating their economic and social progress.
b. This aim shall be pursued through the organs of the Council by discussion of questions of common concern and by agreements and common action in economic, social, cultural, scientific, legal and administrative matters and in the maintenance and further realisation of human rights and fundamental freedoms.
c. ...
d. Matters relating to national defence do not fall within the scope of the Council of Europe.

---

[14] Final Report, 'Treaty Event 2013: Towards Universal Participation and Implementation' (24–26 September and 30 September–1 October 2013, United Nations Headquarters), New York: United Nations Headquarters.

[15] International Cocoa Agreement, 2010, Geneva, 25 June 2010.

[16] Convention against Torture and Other Cruel, Inhuman or Degrading Treatment or Punishment, New York, 10 December 1984.

[17] For a detailed profile, consult the Council of Europe website at <http://www.coe.int>.

[18] Statute of the Council of Europe, signed in London 5 May 1949, CETS No 001.

Many areas of Council of Europe activity are mentioned, but *national defence* is specifically excluded. The Council achieves its aims through discussion, agreement and common action.

A fundamental achievement was the signing of the European Convention on Human Rights in Rome, in 1950. The Convention was inspired by the United Nations Universal Declaration of Human Rights of 1948(see 1.2.4 above); being a convention, the ECHR is *a legally binding instrument*, while the UDHR, being a declaration, has only indirect legal effect. The Convention is central to the legal protection of individual human rights in the Member States of the Council of Europe. It *came into force* in accordance with its final article, below.

After signing the Convention, what final legal step must States take? What are the languages of the ECHR?

Article 59 ECHR[19]

1. This Convention shall be open to the signature of the members of the Council of Europe. It shall be ratified. Ratifications shall be deposited with the Secretary General of the Council of Europe.
2. The present Convention shall come into force after the deposit of ten instruments of ratification.

...

Done at Rome this 4th day of November 1950, in English and French, both texts being equally authentic, in a single copy which shall remain deposited in the archives of the Council of Europe. The Secretary General shall transmit certified copies to each of the signatories.

After signing the Convention, written in two authentic texts in English and French, parties must *ratify* it. *Ratification* is a step by which the international obligation is assumed, in accordance with the national constitutional procedures of each State. Under Article 59, '*instruments of ratification*' must be deposited with the Secretary General of the Council of Europe, and, under paragraph 2, the Convention would come into force after the deposit of 10 such instruments. This in fact took three years: in September 1953, the Convention *entered into force*.

The Council of Europe has two official languages, which are also the languages of the Convention text and of the European Court of Human Rights: English and French. It also has three working languages: German, Italian and Russian.

---

[19] Convention for the Protection of Human Rights and Fundamental Freedoms (ECHR), above n 4. The full text is available on the official Council of Europe website at <http://www.coe.int>.

To imagine the variety of different languages in use at national level among the 47 Member States of the Council of Europe, look at the English names of these countries in the box below:

Albania, Andorra, Armenia, Austria, Azerbaijan, Belgium, Bosnia and Herzegovina, Bulgaria, Croatia, Cyprus, Czech Republic, Denmark, Estonia, Finland, France, Georgia, Germany, Greece, Hungary, Iceland, Ireland, Italy, Latvia, Liechtenstein, Lithuania, Luxembourg, 'The former Yugoslav Republic of Macedonia', Malta, Moldova, Monaco, Montenegro, Netherlands, Norway, Poland, Portugal, Romania, Russian Federation, San Marino, Serbia, Slovakia, Slovenia, Spain, Sweden, Switzerland, Turkey, Ukraine, United Kingdom.[20]

Task 2 Consulting treaty law—language and human rights

It is interesting to note that language use is a significant factor not only in relation to *procedural matters*, but also in relation to *substantive rights*.

Language is mentioned in the text of the ECHR, both in relation to non-discrimination (Article 14) and in relation to the right to liberty and security (Article 5) and the right to a fair trial (Article 6).

Examine the extracts from these Articles of the ECHR below, to understand their specific impact:

European Convention on Human Rights[21]
Article 5—Right to liberty and security
2. Everyone who is arrested shall be informed promptly, in a **language** which he understands, of the reasons for his arrest and of any charge[22] against him.

Article 6—Right to a fair trial
3. Everyone charged with a criminal offence has the following minimum rights:
    (a) to be informed promptly, in a **language** which he understands and in detail, of the nature and cause of the accusation against him;
    ...
    (e) to have the free assistance of an interpreter if he cannot understand or speak the **language** used in court.

Article 14—Prohibition of discrimination
The enjoyment of the rights and freedoms set forth in this Convention shall be secured without discrimination on any ground such as sex, race, colour, **language**, religion, political or other opinion, national or social origin, association with a national minority, property, birth or other status. (bold emphasis added)

---

[20] From the website of the Council of Europe, Venice Commission (the European Commission for Democracy through Law) at <http://www.venice.coe.int>.
[21] ECHR, above n 4, Arts 5(2), 6(3)(a) and (e), 14.
[22] A *charge* is a formal criminal accusation; to *charge* = to accuse formally of a crime.

Commentary to Task 2 Consulting treaty law—language and human rights

Article 5(2) protects a person at the time of arrest: he must be told quickly and without delay ('promptly') of the reasons for the arrest, and of any criminal accusations ('charges') against him, in a language he understands.

Article 6(3) protects a person from the time of *incrimination* and during trial: he must be told promptly and in detail about the nature and cause of the accusation against him, in a language he understands (subparagraph (a)); and he has a right to free interpretation in court if needed (subparagraph (e)).

Article 14 prohibits discrimination *on any ground* (for any basis or reason); the list of *grounds* is for example only ('such as …') and includes *discrimination on the ground of* language.

5.2.3 The United Nations

The *Charter of the United Nations* was established as a consequence of the United Nations Conference on International Organization held at San Francisco, and was signed on 26 June 1945 as the Second World War came to a close. Some aims of the new universal *international organisation* were to prevent future war, to maintain international peace and security, to develop friendly relations among nations and to promote respect for human rights. The *Purposes and Principles of the UN* may be examined in full in Articles 1 and 2 of the Charter text, while Article 7 sets out its principal organs, including the General Assembly and the Security Council.[23]

The Charter was *drafted* in five languages. To *draft*, or to *draw up*, means to write an official text such as a treaty, law or legal document.

Which are the languages and what are the effects of Article 111 below?

Charter of the United Nations[24]

Article 111

The present Charter, of which the Chinese, French, Russian, English, and Spanish texts are equally authentic, shall remain deposited in the archives of the Government of the United States of America. Duly certified copies thereof shall be transmitted by that Government to the Governments of the other signatory States.

Article 111 provides that the Charter texts are '*equally authentic*' in the five languages specified, and the texts must remain deposited in the US Government '*archives*'. It imposes a duty on the US Government to transmit '*duly certified*'[25] copies of the text ('*thereof*') to the Governments of the other '*signatory States*' (the States that have signed the Charter).

---

[23] The Charter text may be consulted on the official UN website at <http://www.un.org>.

[24] Charter of the United Nations, signed in San Francisco, 26 June 1945.

[25] The adverb *duly* and the related adjective *due* mean *as required*.

Today, with the addition of Arabic, the UN uses six official languages in its *intergovernmental meetings* and documents, and the *Secretariat* uses two working languages: English and French; simultaneous interpretation is provided into the other official languages of the body concerned at formal meetings.[26]

The International Court of Justice

The principal *judicial organ* of the UN is the *International Court of Justice* (ICJ), which has its seat in the Netherlands at The Hague (Den Haag). The *Statute* of the International Court of Justice is *annexed to* the UN Charter and forms an integral part of it. In Article 39, the Statute *lays down* the official languages of the Court, giving the parties to a case different options.

What are the official languages and what are the rules concerning the language of the authoritative text of the judgment?

Statute of the International Court of Justice[27]
Article 39

1. The official languages of the Court shall be French and English. If the parties agree that the case shall be conducted in French, the judgment shall be delivered in French. If the parties agree that the case shall be conducted in English, the judgment shall be delivered in English.
2. In the absence of an agreement as to which language shall be employed, each party may, in the pleadings, use the language which it prefers; the decision of the Court shall be given in French and English. In this case the Court shall at the same time determine which of the two texts shall be considered as authoritative.
3. The Court shall, at the request of any party, authorize a language other than French or English to be used by that party.

Under paragraph 1, French and English are both official languages of the Court, and the parties may agree to conduct a case in either language; *judgment* is then '*delivered*' (pronounced) in that language. If there is no agreement ('in the absence of agreement') it is possible for each party to use the language it prefers ('each party *may ...*') in *the pleadings*.[28] Judgment is then pronounced in both languages and the Court *determines* (decides) which is the *authoritative* text. Under paragraph 3, the Court must ('*shall*', not '*may*') authorise the use of another language ('*other than*' = not French or English) by a party, on request.

Aware of the language problem, the UN decided to operate in a limited number of key languages.

---

[26] Information from the UN website at <http://www.un.org>.
[27] Statute of the International Court of Justice, annexed to the Charter of the United Nations, signed in San Francisco, 26 June 1945.
[28] The term *pleadings* in international proceedings refers to both oral and written representations made to the court by each party.

Do you agree with the following justification for its restricted choice?

> An international organization must have effective ways to overcome language barriers
> to avoid becoming a Tower of Babel. Since almost every country in the world is repre-
> sented at the United Nations, it is not an exaggeration to say that the United Nations
> is a microcosm of the world.[29]

The biblical image of a 'Tower of Babel' suggests that if many different languages
were used, communication would be extremely difficult, if not impossible. From
its original 51 Members in 1945, the UN grew to 193 Members in 2011.[30]

5.2.4 The European Union and Multilingualism

In contrast with the UN, the EU is periodically accused in the media of being,
precisely, a 'Tower of Babel', criticised for the expense and bureaucracy involved
in its multilingual operations. Are such criticisms valid, or is the EU's policy of
multilingualism justified by the scope and nature of the Union itself? We examine
these alternative views below.

The Treaties

First, what does multilingualism in the EU context involve? The language of each
Member State has equal status as an official language of the European Union.
The primary legal texts of EU law are the *Treaties*, drawn up in all the official
languages, with each version being equally authentic. The only exception to this
was the ECSC Treaty, signed in Paris in 1951. It was drafted in a single text in
French, generally regarded as the authentic version and later translated into the
other languages. But when, in 1957, the same six *founder members* of the European
Communities signed the *Treaties of Rome*, establishing the EEC[31] and Euratom,[32]
they adopted, instead, a *multilingual* approach.

The EEC Treaty (*Treaty of Rome*) was drawn up by the six founder members in
a single original in the Dutch, French, German and Italian languages, all four texts
being equally authentic.[33]

As enlargement of the European Community began in the 1970s, with the
accession of Denmark, Ireland and the United Kingdom, more versions of the

---

[29] Information from the UN website at <http://www.un.org>.

[30] *Ibid.*

[31] Treaty establishing the European Economic Community, signed in Rome, 25 March 1957,
11957E/TXT, at <http://eur-lex.europa.eu>.

[32] Treaty establishing the European Atomic Energy Community, signed in Rome, 25 March 1957,
11957A/TXT, at <http://eur-lex.europa.eu>.

[33] Treaty establishing the European Economic Community, above n 31, Art 248.

Treaty in the new languages were added, and these, too, were given the status of authentic texts.

Each enlargement of the European Community—and of the EU since its creation in 1992—has brought together populations with different cultures, traditions and languages within a single economic and legal framework. Today, the EU has over 500 million *citizens*, from 28 different nations. This diversity may be seen as a problem—how can we all agree and communicate?—or as a challenge—how can we operate together in practical terms while giving value to our rich multilingual heritage?

There are currently 28 *Member States* and 24 official languages.[34] As more *candidate countries* join, new languages will be added, since each country decides, when joining the EU, which of its national languages it wishes to be used at EU level. The complete list of EU official languages is then agreed by all the *EU governments*.

Consult the article from the Treaty of Lisbon below, which came into force in 2009. Can you match the 23 languages to the corresponding 27 Member States? Can you locate these European States on a map? (Remember that the missing 28th Member State is Croatia, bringing the Croatian language into the EU in 2013.)

Treaty of Lisbon[35]
Article 7
This Treaty, referred to as the Treaty of Lisbon, drawn up in a single original in the Bulgarian, Czech, Danish, Dutch, English, Estonian, Finnish, French, German, Greek, Hungarian, Irish, Italian, Latvian, Lithuanian, Maltese, Polish, Portuguese, Romanian, Slovak, Slovenian, Spanish and Swedish languages, the texts in each of these languages being equally authentic, shall be deposited in the archives of the Government of the Italian Republic, which will transmit a certified copy to each of the governments of the other signatory States.

NOTE: *To check your knowledge, visit the Europa website at <http://www.europa.eu>.*

Founding treaties and accession treaties

The Treaty of Rome is one of the *founding treaties* of the EU; such treaties are also called *constitutive treaties* because they may be regarded as the *constitution* of the Community and the Union. They *set up* (establish, found) the various organs

---

[34] As from 1 July 2013, with the accession of Croatia.
[35] Treaty of Lisbon amending the Treaty on European Union and the Treaty establishing the European Community, signed at Lisbon, 13 December 2007, [2007] OJ C306/01.

of the Union and *grant* them their *powers*, delineating the areas of exclusive and shared competence between the Union and Member States.[36] They also contain provisions of *substantive law*, which would not normally be found in a constitution, for example the rules on *competition* in Chapter 1 of Title VII TFEU.

The *Accession Treaties* are another important class of treaty in the EU legal context. In international law, a *treaty of accession* is the type of agreement by which a State can become a party to a pre-existing treaty. In the EU context, the accession treaties provide the legal mechanism for enlargement, each time a new member *accedes to* (joins) the existing Community and Union. These treaties set out the principles for membership of the new States and regulate ratification.

While the Treaties are *primary law* in the EU legal system, *European Union acts*, such as *regulations* and *directives* are *secondary legislation*, published in all the working languages.[37] All language versions are equally authentic.

Task 3 Personal knowledge and research—European integration
Try to fill in the blanks using your own knowledge to complete the brief summary below of European integration from its origins to the present day.

The Six
The six States that began the process of European integration were the founder members of the three European Communities back in the 1950s: Italy, ... , ...….. , ...….. , ...…..
and the Netherlands. These six States were the original signatories in 1951 to the Treaty of Paris, establishing the European Coal and Steel Community, and subsequently on 25 March 1957 to the first Treaty of Rome, establishing the European Economic Community, and the second Treaty of Rome, founding the European Atomic Energy Community (Euratom).

The Nine
From 1 January 1973, with the first enlargement of the European Communities, three new States became Members, signing and ratifying the Treaty of Accession: .... , ... , and .... At this time, English, Irish and Danish became official languages. Norway also signed the Treaty of Accession, but did not become a Member as it failed to ratify the Treaty when 53 per cent of the population voted against EC membership in a referendum.

---

[36] See, e.g., Arts 3 and 4 in Task 5 below.
[37] All the official languages except Irish are classified as 'working languages'.

The Twelve

During the 1980s EC membership continued to grow, with the accession of .... in 1981, followed by .... and Portugal in 1986. In 1990, the size and population of the EC expanded further, with the incorporation of the East German *Bundesländer* thanks to the reunification of Germany. A major milestone was marked by the Twelve in 1992, with the signing of the Treaty on European Union in the Dutch town of Maastricht.

The Fifteen

During the 1990s, three more European States joined the European Union: ...., ... and .... in 1995. Many other countries, mainly from Eastern Europe, made applications and began long preparations to join. Candidate countries must first meet the *Copenhagen criteria*, including stable institutions guaranteeing democracy, the rule of law, and human rights, as well as a functioning market economy and the ability to implement all the obligations of EU membership in their national systems.

The Twenty-Five (2004)

The Twenty-Seven (2007)

The Twenty-Eight (2013)

Candidate countries and/or new Members (present day)

Check and complete your work by referring to the Europa website at <http://www.europa.eu>. Start, for example, with 'How the EU works'.

Investigate the 'Copenhagen criteria' and the conditions for accession of new countries. Can you see how the EU contributes to building peace and democracy in Europe? Focus on the stories of specific Member States.

Discuss what you have learnt with other members of the class.

The European Court of Justice

In proceedings before the *European Court of Justice*[38] in Luxembourg, any one of the official languages of the Member States may be designated as the 'language

---

[38] The Court of Justice of the European Communities was renamed under Art 2(2) of the Treaty of Lisbon: it is now called the 'Court of Justice of the European Union', and comprises the 'Court of Justice' (the superior court), the 'General Court' (previously the 'Court of First Instance', created in 1988) and the Civil Service Tribunal, created in 2004.

of the case', depending on the *parties to the action*. The case is conducted in this language with simultaneous interpretation of *oral proceedings* into other languages, as required. *Judgments* of the Court are issued in all official EU languages, but the judges traditionally speak French during *deliberations* (discussions leading to the decision), where interpreters may not be present. The style of judgments has also been strongly influenced by the Continental French model. In *direct actions* the language of the case is the language used in the *application*, while in *references for a preliminary ruling* the language of the case is the language of the national court. In this type of proceeding, a national court requests an *authoritative pronounce-ment* from the European Court about the interpretation or validity of a provision of EU law.[39] Note that terms like 'preliminary ruling' and 'direct action' have been specially coined (created) to reflect the distinctive procedures of EU law,[40] while terms such as 'judgment', 'application' and 'oral proceedings' are shared with the language of other legal contexts, both national and international.

Task 4 Consultation and discussion—multilingualism

The most widely spoken first language in the EU is German, with about 90 million native speakers. French, English and Italian are the mother tongues of about 60 million EU citizens each. But the most widely used language in the EU is English, since more people speak it as their first foreign language and young people increasingly choose to learn English, which seems to be emerging as a lingua franca in the EU.[41]

— Can you think of any reasons in favour of adopting a single, main language within the EU? Would you choose English or another language?
— Is there a risk of hegemony (dominance) of English in the EU?[42]
— From the discussion on the EU in the section above, what reasons can you see for maintaining EU multilingualism?

Discuss your ideas with a partner, then compare your views with the justifications of multilingualism given below in a European Commission publication:

Extracts from *Many tongues, one family*
The reasons why the European Union needs [24] official languages are not hard to find: they are democracy, transparency and the right to know.

---

[39] Treaty on the Functioning of the European Union consolidated version (TFEU, Treaty of Rome) [2012] OJ C326/47, Art 267.
[40] For more on the procedure and jurisdiction of the Court of Justice of the European Union, consult <http://curia.europa.eu.>.
[41] From *Many tongues, one family* (2004), Luxembourg: Office for Official Publications of the European Communities, p 5.
[42] Note for language teachers: for a critical appraisal of English as an international language, includ-ing its pedagogic implications for teachers aware of the risk of cultural hegemonism, see A Pennycook (1994), *The Cultural Politics of English as an International Language*, Harlow: Pearson Education Ltd.

EU legislation applies throughout the EU, and therefore to all its citizens. New legislation must be published and made available to them in their own language. As in any democracy, each citizen has a fundamental right to know why a particular item of legislation is being adopted and what it requires him or her to do.

It is also a basic tenet of the European Union that all its citizens and their elected representatives must have the same right of access to the EU and be able to communicate with its institutions and authorities in their national language. There cannot be double standards, say, between big and small countries or between those with well-known and lesser-known languages.[43]

Multilingualism—conclusions

The EU is not just another international organisation. By the instrument of the international treaty, the Member States have created a new legal order.[44] It has its roots in international law, but at the same time it penetrates the national legal systems and has become part of national law, in many areas previously reserved for national decision alone. It possesses institutions with legislative, executive and judicial functions, including a Parliament *directly elected by EU citizens*. In the Member States, both national institutions, such as the courts, and individual citizens are directly affected by EU law.

Like the European Commission, we believe that multilingualism is essential to the functions, legitimacy and efficacy of the Union. If we compare multinational bodies such as the UN or NATO, which have many members, they do not have a comparable *law-making function* or the *direct involvement of citizens*, which are central features of the EU. Binding legal texts such as the Treaties, EU acts (secondary EU legislation including regulations and directives) and judgments of the *Court of Justice* must be effective and accessible on an equal basis to the peoples of Europe in their own language.

On the other hand, for day-to-day activities different strategies are necessary, especially since the 2004 enlargement, when the number of languages suddenly rose from 11 to 20.

The Commission uses three working languages (English, French and German). *Draft policy papers* and *draft legislation* are produced only in these three languages, and are translated into all the official languages only at the final stages.[45] A 'Practical Guide' issued by the *European Parliament*, the *Council* and the

---

[43] From *Many tongues, one family*, above n 41, p 17.

[44] As the Court of Justice explained in Case 26/62 *NV Algemeine Transport- en Expeditie Onderneming van Gend & Loos v Netherlands Inland Revenue Administration* [1963] ECR 1.

[45] *Many tongues, one family*, above n 41, p 19.

Commission, is available for persons involved in the drafting of EU legislation.[46] Its first General Principle is that EU legislative acts 'shall be drafted clearly, simply and precisely'. One reason for this is the equality of citizens before the law: the law must be comprehensible and accessible to all. Article 1.2.1 of the Guide underlines that this principle is especially important in respect of EU legislative acts, 'which must fit into a system which is not only complex, but also multicultural and multilingual'. Like the Plain English Movement, the Guide advocates the use of plain language. Clarity is more important than style, repetition better than variety:

> 1.4.1. The author should attempt to reduce the legislative intention to simple terms, in order to be able to express it simply. In so far as possible, everyday language should be used. Where necessary, clarity of expression should take precedence over felicity of style. For example, the use of synonyms and different expressions to convey the same idea should be avoided.[47]

The European Parliament has developed a system of 'pivot' languages. These languages are English, French, German, Italian, Polish and Spanish, and a document presented in another language, for example Greek or Danish, is first translated into the pivot languages, then retranslated into the remaining languages. This reduces the number of bilateral combinations needed, for example from Maltese to Portuguese. With 25 Members and 20 languages by 2004, the EU already had 380 bilateral combinations.[48]

To learn more about languages in the EU, consult the Europa website.[49] There are challenging career opportunities for lawyer-linguists, selected by public competition.

5.2.5 Parallel Legal Texts as a Language Resource—the Treaty of Rome

One of the benefits of EU multilingualism is the fact that we can use authentic parallel texts, such as the Treaties,[50] to discover equivalent terms and expressions in different languages, an excellent resource for vocabulary expansion in the wide range of areas where the EU operates today.

You can compile personal vocabulary selections by consulting parallel texts on a theme of interest. For example, see Articles 136–138 TFEU for provisions specific to Member States whose currency is the euro.

---

[46] 'Joint Practical Guide. Guide of the European Parliament, the Council and the Commission for persons involved in the drafting of legislation within the Community institutions', Brussels, 16 March 2000, last updated April 2009, available at <http://eur-lex.europa.eu/en/techleg/index.htm>.

[47] *Ibid.*

[48] Data from *Many tongues, one family*, above n 41, p 19.

[49] The Europa Languages homepage offers many resources at <http://europa.eu/languages>.

[50] Available at <http://europa.eu/eu-law/treaties>.

Task 5 Parallel texts as a language resource—the Treaty of Rome

The phrases in the table below all appear in the first articles of the Treaty on the Functioning of the European Union (TFEU),[51] in which the areas of shared and exclusive competence of the Union and of the Member States are defined. The parallel English and French text is reproduced in Table 5.1 below.

— Read the text to understand its content.
— Examine the dual text, focusing on equivalent expression.
— Use the table below to note down terms and phrases that correspond in the two languages. Consult the Treaty on the Europa website to continue this activity; if you prefer, you may select different languages.

Article	English Version	French Version
1(1)	the functioning of the Union	le fonctionnement de l'Union
1(1)	the arrangements for exercising its competences	
1(2)		les traités sur lesquels est fondée l'Union
1(2)	'the Treaties'	
3(1)(a)		l'union douanière
3(1)(b)	the establishing of (the) competition rules (necessary)	
3(1)(c)		– la politique monétaire – la monnaie
4(2)		Les compétences partagées
4(2)(a)	internal market	
4(2)	*You select terms and phrases*	
4(2)		
Other Articles	*Consult the Treaty online*	

---

[51] Treaty on the Functioning of the European Union consolidated version (Treaty of Rome) [2012] OJ C326/47, extracts from Arts 1–4, see Table 5.1 below.

Table 5.1: Extracts from Articles 1–4 TFEU—parallel English and French

TREATY ON THE FUNCTIONING OF THE EUROPEAN UNION (CONSOLIDATED VERSION)	TRAITÉ SUR LE FONCTIONNEMENT DE L'UNION EUROPÉENNE (VERSION CONSOLIDÉE)
Article 1	*Article premier*
1. This Treaty organises the functioning of the Union and determines the areas of, delimitation of, and arrangements for exercising its competences. 2. This Treaty and the Treaty on European Union constitute the Treaties on which the Union is founded. These two Treaties, which have the same legal value, shall be referred to as 'the Treaties'.	1. Le présent traité organise le fonctionnement de l'Union et détermine les domaines, la délimitation et les modalités d'exercice de ses compétences. 2. Le présent traité et le traité sur l'Union européenne constituent les traités sur lesquels est fondée l'Union. Ces deux traités, qui ont la même valeur juridique, sont désignés par les mots «les traités».
Article 3	*Article 3*
1. The Union shall have exclusive competence in the following areas: (a) customs union; (b) the establishing of the competition rules necessary for the functioning of the internal market; (c) monetary policy for the Member States whose currency is the euro; …	1. L'Union dispose d'une compétence exclusive dans les domaines suivants: a) l'union douanière; b) l'établissement des règles de concurrence nécessaires au fonctionnement du marché intérieur; c) la politique monétaire pour les États membres dont la monnaie est l'euro; …
Article 4	*Article 4*
… 2. Shared competence between the Union and the Member States applies in the following principal areas: (a) internal market; (b) social policy, for the aspects defined in this Treaty; (c) economic, social and territorial cohesion; (d) agriculture and fisheries, excluding the conservation of marine biological resources; (e) environment; …	… 2. Les compétences partagées entre l'Union et les États membres s'appliquent aux principaux domaines suivants: a) le marché intérieur; b) la politique sociale, pour les aspects définis dans le présent traité; c) la cohésion économique, sociale et territoriale; d) l'agriculture et la pêche, à l'exclusion de la conservation des ressources biologiques de la mer; e) l'environnement; …

5.3 Consulting Treaty Law: The European Union

5.3.1 The Treaty on European Union

The Treaty on European Union (TEU), known as the Treaty of Maastricht, was signed on 7 February 1992 in the Dutch town; it established the EU in its first article.

What was the relation between the newly created European Union and the pre-existing European Communities?

> **Treaty on European Union**[52]
> *Article 1*
> By this Treaty, the HIGH CONTRACTING PARTIES establish among themselves a EUROPEAN UNION, hereinafter called 'the Union'.
>
> This Treaty marks a new stage in the process of creating an ever closer union among the peoples of Europe, in which decisions are taken as openly as possible and as closely as possible to the citizen.
>
> The Union shall be founded on the European Communities, supplemented by the policies and forms of cooperation established by this Treaty ...

The EU was '*founded on* the European Communities', which were the *first pillar of Maastricht* also called the *Community pillar*. But the TEU also introduced new '*policies and forms of cooperation*' in its second and third pillars, notably the development of the *common foreign and security policy*, and *police and judicial cooperation in criminal matters*. The EEC was renamed the EC by the TEU and continued in existence until 2009.

The Treaty of Lisbon, signed by EU leaders on 13 December 2007, introduced major amendments to both the EC and the EU Treaties. After some delays in the *ratification* process, it entered into force two years later, in December 2009. Under Article 2, it renamed the EC Treaty, which became the *Treaty on the Functioning of the European Union* (TFEU), and replaced the words 'Community' and 'European Community' or 'Communities' with the terms 'Union' and 'European Union'.[53] We can see the terminology of EU law rapidly evolving as the process of European integration moves forward.

In particular, Article 1 TEU as amended by the Treaty of Lisbon, shown below, re-established the EU legal order as follows.

Examine and compare the third paragraph of the amended article, below, with the third paragraph set out above. What changes have been introduced?

---

[52] Treaty on European Union consolidated version (Treaty of Maastricht) [2006] OJ C321/E, predating changes made by the Treaty of Lisbon.
[53] With a very few exceptions.

Treaty on European Union[54]
Article 1, 3rd paragraph

The Union shall be founded on the present Treaty and on the Treaty on the Functioning of the European Union (hereinafter referred to as 'the Treaties'). Those two Treaties shall have the same legal value. The Union shall replace and succeed the European Community.

The Union is now founded on both the TEU (the Treaty of Maastricht) and the TFEU (the Treaty of Rome), which have equal *'legal value'*; and the European Union replaces and *succeeds* the European Community (which therefore no longer exists as an independent entity).

5.3.2 Citizenship of the European Union

One important aim of the TEU was to introduce a new legal status for citizens of the Member States: *citizenship of the European Union.*[55]

What are the aims of EU citizenship? For some ideas, examine Article 3, below.

Treaty on European Union[56]
Article 3

1. The Union's aim is to promote peace, its values and the well-being of its peoples.[57]
2. The Union shall offer its citizens an area of freedom, security and justice without internal frontiers, in which the free movement of persons is ensured in conjunction with appropriate measures with respect to external border controls, asylum, immigration and the prevention and combating of crime.

    ...

5. In its relations with the wider world, the Union shall uphold and promote its values and interests and contribute to the protection of its citizens. ...

> NOTE: *For further ideas, consult the full text of Article 3 TEU. To expand your vocabulary, you may also choose to consult the parallel text in your language.*

Like national citizenship at State level, citizenship at EU level involves rights and duties, which are *laid down* in the Treaties.

Are you an EU citizen? Do you know your rights and duties? Reflect, and discuss what you know before consulting the Treaty text in the Task below.

---

[54] Treaty on European Union consolidated version (Treaty of Maastricht) [2012] OJ C326/13 (the version used in this book unless specified otherwise), Art 1, 3rd para.

[55] Citizenship = the status of being a citizen.

[56] Treaty on European Union consolidated version (Treaty of Maastricht) [2012] OJ C326/13, Art 3(1), (2) and (5).

[57] The values of the EU are listed in Art 2 TEU: refer to the Treaty text or see 5.1 above.

Task 6 Understanding treaty law—EU citizenship

Examine the Treaty provisions in detail to check or discover the rights of EU citizens. Answer the following questions, focusing your attention on both meaning and language:

1. What form of discrimination is prohibited by Article 18 TFEU?
2. What are the effects of Article 20?
3. Who is an EU citizen and what is the relation with national citizenship?
4. Examine rights (a) to (d) listed in Article 20(2). Are these the only rights citizens have? Are these rights absolute?
5. Which of the rights listed in Article 20(2) are more precisely regulated by Articles 21 and 22, respectively?
6. What right is *enshrined* (protected) in Article 21?
7. What different legislative powers are granted to the EU institutions by Article 21(2) and (3), and for what purposes?
8. What are the four democratic rights granted in Article 22?
9. Are the rights in Article 22(1) and (2) *absolute* or *qualified*? ('Qualified rights' permit limitations, 'absolute rights' do not.)
10. How can EU citizens communicate with and complain to EU bodies?

You may refer to a parallel Treaty text in another language before checking your answers in the Key below.

TREATY ON THE FUNCTIONING OF THE EUROPEAN UNION[58]
(CONSOLIDATED VERSION)

PART TWO
NON-DISCRIMINATION AND CITIZENSHIP OF THE UNION

Article 18
Within the scope of application of the Treaties, and without prejudice to any special provisions contained therein, any discrimination on grounds of nationality shall be prohibited.
The European Parliament and the Council, acting in accordance with the ordinary legislative procedure, may adopt rules designed to prohibit such discrimination.

Article 20
1. Citizenship of the Union is hereby established. Every person holding the nationality of a Member State shall be a citizen of the Union. Citizenship of the Union shall be additional to and not replace national citizenship.

---

[58] Treaty on the Functioning of the European Union consolidated version (Treaty of Rome) [2012] OJ C326/47.

2. Citizens of the Union shall enjoy the rights and be subject to the duties provided for in the Treaties. They shall have, inter alia:

(a) the right to move and reside freely within the territory of the Member States;

(b) the right to vote and to stand as candidates in elections to the European Parliament and in municipal elections in their Member State of residence, under the same conditions as nationals of that State;

(c) the right to enjoy, in the territory of a third country in which the Member State of which they are nationals is not represented, the protection of the diplomatic and consular authorities of any Member State on the same conditions as the nationals of that State;

(d) the right to petition the European Parliament, to apply to the European Ombudsman, and to address the institutions and advisory bodies of the Union in any of the Treaty languages and to obtain a reply in the same language.

These rights shall be exercised in accordance with the conditions and limits defined by the Treaties and by the measures adopted thereunder.

Article 21

1. Every citizen of the Union shall have the right to move and reside freely within the territory of the Member States, subject to the limitations and conditions laid down in the Treaties and by the measures adopted to give them effect.

2. If action by the Union should prove necessary to attain this objective and the Treaties have not provided the necessary powers, the European Parliament and the Council, acting in accordance with the ordinary legislative procedure, may adopt provisions with a view to facilitating the exercise of the rights referred to in paragraph 1.

3. For the same purposes as those referred to in paragraph 1 and if the Treaties have not provided the necessary powers, the Council, acting in accordance with a special legislative procedure, may adopt measures concerning social security or social protection. The Council shall act unanimously after consulting the European Parliament.

Article 22

1. Every citizen of the Union residing in a Member State of which he is not a national shall have the right to vote and to stand as a candidate at municipal elections in the Member State in which he resides, under the same conditions as nationals of that State. This right shall be exercised subject to detailed arrangements adopted by the Council, acting unanimously in accordance with a special legislative procedure and after

consulting the European Parliament; these arrangements may provide for derogations where warranted by problems specific to a Member State.

2. Without prejudice to Article 223(1) and to the provisions adopted for its implementation, every citizen of the Union residing in a Member State of which he is not a national shall have the right to vote and to stand as a candidate in elections to the European Parliament in the Member State in which he resides, under the same conditions as nationals of that State. This right shall be exercised subject to detailed arrangements adopted by the Council, acting unanimously in accordance with a special legislative procedure and after consulting the European Parliament; these arrangements may provide for derogations where warranted by problems specific to a Member State.

Key and commentary to Task 6 Understanding treaty law—EU citizenship

1. Article 18 TFEU prohibits discrimination on the basis (*grounds*) of nationality. The prohibition has effect in the ambit of EU law ('within the scope of application of the Treaties') and does not limit any special provisions in the Treaties ('without prejudice to ... therein'). Paragraph 2 confers legislative powers on the European Parliament and the Council.

2. Article 20 first creates the status of EU citizenship, then defines in paragraph (1) *who* qualifies as a citizen of the EU, and the relation between EU and national citizenship. Article 20(2) grants rights to the citizens and imposes duties on them: 'Citizens ... *shall enjoy the rights* and *be subject to the duties* provided for in the Treaties'.

3. All citizens of EU Member States are citizens of the EU: 'Every person *holding the nationality* of a Member State ...'. EU citizenship is in addition to national citizenship: it does not replace it.

4. The various rights listed in Article 20(2) are not the only rights EU citizens enjoy: this is indicated by the Latin phrase '*inter alia*' (among other things). The rights are not absolute: the final phrase shows that *conditions and limits* may be defined by the Treaties and by *measures adopted* under them ('*thereunder*'), such as regulations and directives.

5. The right to move and reside freely in Article 20(2)(a) is regulated in more detail by Article 21; the democratic rights in Article 20(2)(b) are

governed by Article 22(1) for municipal elections, and Article 22(2) for European Parliament elections.

6. Article 21 enshrines the freedom to move and take up residence anywhere in the territory of the Union. The right is not absolute, but '*subject to* the limitations and conditions laid down ...' in the Treaty or in certain other measures.

7. Article 21(2) gives the Parliament and Council power to legislate (they 'may adopt provisions'), using the *ordinary legislative procedure* with the aim of facilitating citizens' right to move and reside freely within the EU, but only if this action is necessary and the Treaties have not given the necessary powers. Article 21(3), instead, gives the Council of the EU power to adopt measures using a *special legislative procedure* in the field of social security or social protection.[59]

8. Article 22 is important for those Europeans who choose to live in another Member State: it preserves their electoral rights to the European Parliament and grants them electoral rights at municipal elections in the country where they reside. Article 22(1) grants the right to vote and also to *stand as a candidate* in local government elections ('*municipal elections*') in the country of residence. Article 22(2) grants the same two rights in elections to the European Parliament. Paragraph (2) begins '*Without prejudice to* Article 223(1) ...' This phrase fixes the priority between the two provisions: Article 223(1), which regulates elections to the European Parliament, has priority: it is not affected by Article 22(2).

9. In both cases, the rights are qualified: 'This right shall be exercised *subject to* detailed arrangements adopted by the Council ...; these arrangements *may provide for derogations where warranted*' (restrictions where these are justified) by specific problems.

10. Article 20(2)(d) gives citizens a direct right to communicate with the EU bodies and a means to resolve specific problems. The *Ombudsman* is appointed by the European Parliament to receive *complaints of maladministration* from citizens, but also from any other natural or legal person residing in a Member State. According to Article 227, the same persons, individually or in groups, *have the right to petition the European Parliament* about any matter in the ambit of the EU, of direct concern to them. Article 20 also ensures that the language of communication with EU institutions and bodies is chosen by the citizen.[60]

Comment—EU citizenship

Citizens are clearly an increasingly central priority of the EU. The first article of the founding Treaty talks of 'an ever closer union among the *peoples*[61] of Europe,

---

[59] Consult the Europa website to learn more about the different legislative procedures.

[60] For more detailed provisions, consult Arts 24, 227, 228 TFEU.

[61] Used as a countable noun, *a people* means the population of a particular place or country; here, plural, the *peoples* of Europe. Cf *people*—the irregular plural of 'person'; in legal English *persons* is usually preferred as the plural of *person*, e.g. *legal persons*.

in which decisions are taken … as closely as possible to *the citizen*'. We have seen that one of the primary objectives of the TEU is the introduction of citizenship to strengthen citizens' rights and ensure greater protection, both within the Union and in *third countries* (non-EU States). The Treaty Articles examined in Task 6 above established citizenship and the special rights attached to it; some of these were added at a later date when the Treaty of Amsterdam came into force in 1999. Citizens' rights and opportunities have continued to grow following the Treaty of Lisbon. For example, the *Citizens' Initiative* offers the chance for citizens from different Member States to join forces and take the initiative in advancing a request for a *legislative proposal* from the European Commission.

Examine the Treaty Article below. How is the Citizens' Initiative designed to work?

Treaty on European Union[62]
Article 11

4. Not less than one million citizens who are nationals of a significant number of Member States may take the initiative of inviting the European Commission, within the framework of its powers, to submit any appropriate proposal on matters where citizens consider that a legal act of the Union is required for the purpose of implementing the Treaties.

On a matter that concerns them, at least one million EU citizens from several different European States ('a significant number') must together invite the European Commission to propose legislation (to the EU legislative organs). As always, 'legal acts of the Union' can only be used to implement the Treaties. The Europa website provides practical assistance to people wishing to organise a Citizens' Initiative and explains that a *citizens' committee* composed of at least seven citizens resident in at least seven States has one year to collect certified 'statements of support', after which the Commission has three months to decide how to act.[63]

Lastly, it is important to underline that all EU citizens *enjoy equal rights*: Article 18 TFEU prohibits any discrimination on the basis of nationality between EU citizens, and many other Treaty Articles specifically guarantee equality, using the phrase 'under the same conditions as nationals of that State', as in many Articles we have examined in this section. Freedom of movement in Article 21 creates an exciting opportunity for citizens' mobility; not just for tourism, training or studies and not just for work (a freedom established in 1958 with the original Treaty of Rome), but a free choice, in principle, of where to live in the Union.

However, European citizens' rights may be subject to limits: Article 21 TFEU is not designed to permit EU citizens to take up residence in another Member State purely for the purpose of obtaining social security benefits: this is an area where enormous disparity between Member States continues to exist.[64]

---

[62] TEU [2012] OJ C326/13.

[63] The European Commission part of the Europa website at <http://ec.europa.eu>.

[64] For an interesting analysis, see MJ Elsmore and P Starup (2007), 'Union Citizenship—Background, Jurisprudence, and Perspective: The Past, Present, and Future of Law and Policy' 26 *Yearbook of European Union Law* 57.

Task 7 Consultation and research—the European Union

Using the resources of the Europa website, research an aspect of the EU in depth. As you work, focus on language and terminology as well as content and meaning. Take notes and prepare to make a brief, documented, presentation of your chosen topic. Some examples are suggested below:

1. Investigate one of the institutions or bodies of the EU: e.g. the European Parliament, the European Council, the Council of the European Union, the European Commission, the Ombudsman, the Court of Justice. Discover the composition, functions, powers and activities of the body concerned, and research a recent event or case, to illustrate that body's work.

2. Discover what contribution EU law is making in an area that concerns you: e.g. employment and social affairs, economic and monetary affairs, foreign and security policy, development and humanitarian aid, environment and energy. What provisions have already been adopted in that field in EU law? And what are the policies and plans of the EU for the future?

SECTION TWO

5.4 THE EUROPEAN CONVENTION ON HUMAN RIGHTS

5.4.1 The Language of Human Rights and the ECHR

The European Convention for the Protection of Human Rights and Fundamental Freedoms (European Convention on Human Rights or ECHR) was drawn up by the Council of Europe in 1950.[65] The ECHR, as declared in its Preamble, drew inspiration from the United Nations Universal Declaration of Human Rights of 1948 (UDHR).[66] The ECHR is an important *regional instrument for the protection of fundamental rights* and the most advanced international system for the legal enforcement of human rights in the world.

Do you live in one of the 47 Member States of the Council of Europe? Can you name some of the rights protected in the Convention?[67]

Print or download a copy of the ECHR to consult for the following Tasks.[68]

Task 8 Expressing human rights
First, consult the Articles of the UDHR examined in chapter one, Task 2. Highlight the different phrases used to express rights. Look for both positive forms (e.g. 'Everyone has the right to life ...'—Article 3) and negative forms (e.g. 'No one shall be held in slavery ...'—Article 4).

Next, examine the table below and observe more ways of expressing rights, both positive, and negative.

Finally, consult the text of the ECHR, particularly 'Section 1—Rights and Freedoms', Articles 2–18, and Protocols 1 and 13.

In addition to the rights in the table below, what other important rights and freedoms are protected in the Convention? Use Article headings (e.g. 'Article 14—Prohibition of discrimination') and read selectively, according to your interest, focusing on both meaning and language.

Select items from the Convention text and expand the table with other phrases used to express rights and freedoms.

[65] Convention for the Protection of Human Rights and Fundamental Freedoms, ETS No 005, open for signature in Rome, 4 November 1950, entry into force 3 September 1953.
[66] Universal Declaration of Human Rights (adopted 10 December 1948), UNGA Res 217 A(III) (UDHR).
[67] Arts 2 and 3 were examined in 1.3 above, Text 3.
[68] The Convention text and Protocols can be downloaded from the Council of Europe website, Treaty Office at <http://conventions.coe.int>.

WAYS OF EXPRESSING RIGHTS	
ECHR text: ways to *grant* rights and *prohibit* violations (creating legal effect in a *binding* text)	**Comment—*speaking about* rights: ways to *describe* rights and prohibitions**
'Everyone's right to life *shall be protected by law.'* Article 2(1)	Article 2 ECHR *enshrines the right to* life.
'No one shall be subjected to torture or to inhuman or degrading treatment or punishment.' Article 3	Torture *is prohibited* by Article 3. Article 3 *guarantees freedom from* inhuman punishment.
'No one shall be held in slavery or servitude.' Article 4(1)	Article 4 *prohibits* slavery and servitude.
'Everyone has the right to liberty and security of person.' Article 5(1)	Article 5 *protects the right to* liberty and security. *Everyone has the right to …*
'In the determination of his civil rights and obligations or of any criminal charge against him, *everyone is entitled to* a fair and public hearing …' Article 6(1)	*The right to* a fair trial *is guaranteed by* Article 6. *Everyone is entitled to* a fair trial under Article 6.
'Everyone has the right to freedom of thought, conscience and religion; …' Article 9(1)	Article 9 *safeguards freedom of* thought, conscience and religion.
Continue with further examples	*Continue with further examples*

Compare your examples with other members of the class and discuss the importance of various Convention rights. You may contribute to the discussion by reporting on a recent human rights issue covered in the media, a relevant court case, or a report or an appeal by a human rights organisation.[69] Comment on the issue or case, bearing in mind the rights listed in instruments such as the UDHR or ECHR: which rights do you think are relevant?

---

[69] As well as traditional news reports, you could visit the UN or Council of Europe websites, or the website of a human rights organisation such as Amnesty International, to gather information.

5.4.2 The UK and the Convention before the Human Rights Act 1998

The United Kingdom was one of the original signatories to the European Convention on Human Rights. In fact, British lawyers helped *to draft the Convention* and the UK ratified it, *in conformity with* Article 59, in 1951. As a Party to the ECHR, the UK was bound to observe its provisions as part of its obligations under international law, as soon as the Convention itself came into force on 3 September 1953.[70]

However, the UK Parliament did not immediately enact legislation to *incorporate* the Convention, that is, to *transpose* it into British law. This step was taken only in 1998, with the enactment of the Human Rights Act 1998.

To understand the implications of this, compare the British position when it joined the European Communities by ratifying the Treaty of Accession in 1972. The UK Parliament immediately enacted a statute: the European Communities Act 1972. This statute gave effect in the national legal system to the obligations of EC membership: Community law became part of national law by virtue of this Act, and from the date of UK membership (1 January 1973) it could be enforced directly before the national courts.[71]

The ECHR, on the other hand, could not be directly enforced before British courts until the year 2000, when the Human Rights Act 1998 came into effect.

The reason for this is that the British legal system is strictly *dualist*: in *dualism*, national law and international law are considered to be two separate systems operating in different fields; by contrast, in a *monist* system (noun, *monism*), national and international law are considered to form one legal structure and international law is supreme.

In the case of *Blackburn v Attorney-General*, Lord Denning explained the consequences of the British dualist approach for the courts:

> [The English courts] take no notice of treaties until they are embodied in laws enacted by Parliament, and then only to the extent that Parliament tells us.[72]

In other words, the British courts do not regard treaties as a direct source of legal obligation in the domestic system. A legislative enactment at national level is necessary *to incorporate the treaty* into the national legal system, and the courts will then apply the national law, giving effect to the treaty as enacted by Parliament ('only to the extent that Parliament tells us').

The result of the UK's failure to incorporate the ECHR was that for many years an individual victim who *alleged*[73] a violation of *Convention rights* (the rights protected in the ECHR) against the UK could *enforce* his or her rights only by *mak-*

---

[70] After the deposit of 10 instruments of ratification: Art 59 ECHR, considered in 5.2.2 above.

[71] See 3.6 above for further discussion of this point, including the supremacy of EU law in the British legal system.

[72] *Blackburn v Attorney-General* [1971] EWCA Civ 7, [1971] 2 All ER 1380, 1382.

[73] *To allege*—to state that certain facts are true, often indicating a crime. Noun, *allegation*.

ing an application directly to the *Convention bodies*: the European Commission of Human Rights and the European Court of Human Rights (ECtHR) in Strasbourg.[74] This was a long, expensive process, subject to certain limits, as provided in Article 35(1) ECHR below.

What are the effects of this Article?

European Convention on Human Rights[75]
Article 35—Admissibility criteria

1. The Court may only deal with the matter after all domestic remedies have been exhausted, according to the generally recognised rules of international law, and within a period of six months from the date on which the final decision was taken.

Under this Article, the power of the Court to '*deal with the matter*' (to examine the complaint) only comes into play after all '*domestic remedies*' (remedies available before the national courts) have been tried but have failed (they have been '*exhausted*'): this follows one of the '*generally recognised rules of international law*'. After *final judgment* before the national courts, a victim has a time limit of six months to apply to the Strasbourg Court; after that, the action is *time barred*.

UK violations

In the period up to 1998, the United Kingdom lost many cases before the European Court of Human Rights, leading to changes in *domestic law*. But this created tension and bad publicity for the UK Government, and embarrassment, usually for the Home Secretary, the Minister with responsibility for criminal justice, frequently responsible for procedures found by the Strasbourg Court to be *in violation of the Convention*. *Breaches* (violations) for which the United Kingdom was held responsible in this period included controversial matters such as *judicial corporal punishment, custodial sentences* to be served by young criminals, treatment of IRA prisoners and 'shoot to kill' operations by special security forces against suspected terrorists. Nationalist critics said that the UK should leave the European Convention on Human Rights, so as to avoid interference from Europe. By contrast, human rights supporters advocated a different legal solution to the problem, to give effective protection of ECHR rights at national level.

---

[74] Since the restructuring of the ECHR 'control machinery', only to the ECtHR, as the Commission was abolished: Protocol No 11 to the Convention for the Protection of Human Rights and Fundamental Freedoms, restructuring the control machinery established thereby, ETS No 155 (Strasbourg, 11 May 1994, entry into force 1 November 1998).
[75] ECHR, ETS No 005, Rome, 4 November 1950, Art 35(1).

5.4.3 The Human Rights Act 1998

A period of significant constitutional reform began in the UK in 1997, under Prime Minister Tony Blair.[76] At the State opening of Parliament just after the general election, Queen Elizabeth II announced:

May 1997, Queen's Speech

A bill will be introduced to incorporate into United Kingdom law the main provisions of the European Convention on Human Rights.

The Human Rights Bill received the Royal Assent in October 1998, but the Human Rights Act 1998 (HRA 1998) only came into force two years later. This preparatory period was necessary because of the complexity involved in adapting the approach of UK *public authorities* to the new legal regime. *Public authorities* include all branches of the public administration at local and national level, as well as bodies such as the police, prison service, schools and the courts themselves; Parliament, however, is excluded.[77]

Lord Bingham, pronouncing judgment in the House of Lords in a case heard under the HRA 1998, explained its purpose:

The purpose of the Human Rights Act 1998 was not to enlarge the rights or remedies of those in the United Kingdom whose Convention rights have been violated but to enable those rights and remedies to be asserted and enforced by the domestic courts of this country and not only by recourse to Strasbourg.[78]

The Human Rights Act 1998 has made it possible for a person whose Convention rights have been violated *to enforce those rights* directly before the national courts in the United Kingdom.

5.4.4 Consulting Legislation: the Human Rights Act 1998

What mechanisms are used by the Human Rights Act 1998 to *safeguard* (protect) individuals in the United Kingdom directly before the national courts from violations of their human rights? In Task 9 below we examine some of the main provisions of the Human Rights Act 1998.[79]

---

[76] Discussed in ch 3 above.

[77] Human Rights Act (HRA) 1998, s 6(3)(b).

[78] *R (on the application of Begum (by her litigation friend Rahman)) v Headteacher and Governors of Denbigh High School* [2007] 1 AC 100, [2006] UKHL 15 [29]. The *Denbigh High School case* is examined in 5.5 below.

[79] The full text of the Act can be consulted at <http://www.legislation.gov.uk>.

Task 9 Consulting legislation—the Human Rights Act 1998

First, read the section headings in the Act below, to identify the subject of each section (eg '1 The Convention Rights'). Then examine the following questions and read the relevant sections of the Act in detail to answer. Focus on both meaning and language:

1. What are 'the Convention rights'? Complete your answer by referring also to the text of the ECHR, or to Schedule 1 to the HRA 1998.
2. The fundamental provision of the HRA 1998 is section 6. What is its effect?
3. Under section 7 of the Act it is possible to enforce Convention rights directly before the courts in the UK. Who has the right to do so? Paragraphs (a) and (b) of section 7(1) provide two legal possibilities: what are they?
4. What remedies are available to a victim under section 8?
5. Under section 2, what is the significance for UK courts of the case law of the Convention bodies (principally the European Court of Human Rights)?
6. What new rule of statutory interpretation is introduced by section 3? Is it absolute? What classes of legislation are covered?

Human Rights Act 1998
1998 CHAPTER 42

An Act to give further effect to rights and freedoms guaranteed under the European Convention on Human Rights; to make provision with respect to holders of certain judicial offices who become judges of the European Court of Human Rights; and for connected purposes.

[9th November 1998]

Be it enacted by the Queen's most Excellent Majesty, by and with the advice and consent of the Lords Spiritual and Temporal, and Commons, in this present Parliament assembled, and by the authority of the same, as follows:—

1   The Convention Rights

(1) In this Act 'the Convention rights' means the rights and fundamental freedoms set out in—
   (a) Articles 2 to 12 and 14 of the Convention,
   (b) Articles 1 to 3 of the First Protocol, and
   (c) Article 1 of the Thirteenth Protocol,
   as read with Articles 16 to 18 of the Convention.

...

(3) The Articles are set out in Schedule 1.

...

2 Interpretation of Convention rights

(1) A court or tribunal determining a question which has arisen in connection with a Convention right must take into account any—

(a) judgment, decision, declaration or advisory opinion of the European Court of Human Rights,

...

whenever made or given, so far as, in the opinion of the court or tribunal, it is relevant to the proceedings in which that question has arisen.

...

3 Interpretation of legislation

(1) So far as it is possible to do so, primary legislation and subordinate legislation must be read and given effect in a way which is compatible with the Convention rights.

(2) This section—

(a) applies to primary legislation and subordinate legislation whenever enacted;

(b) does not affect the validity, continuing operation or enforcement of any incompatible primary legislation;

...

4 Declaration of incompatibility

...

(2) If the court is satisfied that the provision [of primary legislation] is incompatible with a Convention right, it may make a declaration of that incompatibility.

...

(6) A declaration under this section ('a declaration of incompatibility')—

(a) does not affect the validity, continuing operation or enforcement of the provision in respect of which it is given; and

(b) is not binding on the parties to the proceedings in which it is made.

...

6 Acts of public authorities

(1) It is unlawful for a public authority to act in a way which is incompatible with a Convention right.

...

(3) In this section "public authority" includes—

(a) a court or tribunal, and

(b) any person certain of whose functions are functions of a public nature, but does not include either House of Parliament or a person exercising functions in connection with proceedings in Parliament.

...

7 Proceedings

(1) A person who claims that a public authority has acted (or proposes to act) in a way which is made unlawful by section 6(1) may—

(a) bring proceedings against the authority under this Act in the appropriate court or tribunal, or

(b) rely on the Convention right or rights concerned in any legal proceedings, but only if he is (or would be) a victim of the unlawful act.

...

(7)   For the purposes of this section, a person is a victim of an unlawful act only if he would be a victim for the purposes of Article 34 of the Convention if proceedings were brought in the European Court of Human Rights in respect of that act.

(8)   Nothing in this Act creates a criminal offence.

...

8   Judicial remedies

(1)   In relation to any act (or proposed act) of a public authority which the court finds is (or would be) unlawful, it may grant such relief or remedy, or make such order, within its powers as it considers just and appropriate.

...

© Crown Copyright 1998
The Human Rights Act 1998 is reproduced under the terms of Crown Copyright Policy Guidance issued by HMSO

Key and commentary to Task 9 Consulting legislation—the Human Rights Act 1998

1.   The rights protected in the ECHR, in particular in Section One of that text, are now known as '*the Convention rights*', a term introduced by the Human Rights Act 1998 and defined in its section 1. You need to refer to the Convention text to check precisely which are the 'Convention rights'; they are also reproduced directly ('*set out*') in Schedule 1 to the Act itself. The Convention rights include: the right to life, the prohibition of torture and slavery, the right to liberty and security, the right to a fair trial, freedom of religion and expression, the prohibition of discrimination and of the death penalty.

2.   By section 6, the HRA 1998 *imposes a positive duty on public authorities to act in accordance with Convention rights*. They must not act *incompatibly* with a Convention right: it is '*unlawful*' to do so. *Unlawful* means *against the law*; it is the opposite of *lawful*. Sometimes, it is a synonym of *illegal* and means against the criminal law. In this sense, we find it in the names of certain criminal offences, such as *unlawful possession of drugs*. However, 'unlawful' does not necessarily mean *against the criminal law*. In fact, section 6 does not create a new criminal offence, a fact clearly stated in section 7(8) of the Act: 'Nothing in this Act creates a criminal offence.' We may contrast the language of section 6(1) of the HRA 1998 with the language of section 1 of the Hunting Act 2004,[80] which clearly creates a criminal offence: 'A person *commits an offence if* he hunts a wild mammal with a dog ...'

---

[80]   Examined in 3.4.2.

3. Only a *victim* of a violation (or a future victim where the public authority 'proposes to act') can enforce rights under the Act (we say, a victim has *standing*, or *locus standi*). This precludes groups, such as *human rights associations*, from using the Act to enforce rights in the collective interest. The victim may either: (a) take proceedings directly based on the HRA 1998 itself; or (b) in a case based on other legal grounds, such as common law rights, '*rely on*' the Convention rights, that is, use Convention rights in legal argument to support his or her case.

4. Under section 8 the court or tribunal has wide *discretionary powers*: '*It may grant such relief or remedy ... as it considers just and appropriate*'. Always '*within its powers*': the court cannot act *beyond* or *outside its powers (ultra vires)*. The terms '*relief*', '*remedy*' and '*redress*' are synonyms, typically *found in civil cases*.[81] A court may, for example, *award damages, quash* (annul) the unlawful decision, or order a public authority not to take a proposed action.

5. Section 2 defines the significance of the case law of the *Convention bodies*. Under this section, UK courts and tribunals 'must take into account' the case law and decisions of the European Court of Human Rights, the Commission and the Committee of Ministers, when 'determining a question which has arisen in connection with a Convention right'; this rule applies where, in the opinion of the UK court, the Strasbourg decision is relevant. The phrase 'must take into account' imposes a duty on the UK courts *to consider* the Strasbourg judgment or decision. But the UK court is not *bound* (obliged) *to follow* such a decision: in the language of the common law, the Strasbourg decision constitutes a *persuasive precedent*, not a *binding precedent*.

6. The new rule of statutory interpretation is not absolute: section 3(1) begins, 'So far as it is possible to do so'. The UK courts must *read* (interpret) and *give effect to* (apply) all UK legislation, both '*primary*' (Acts of Parliament) and '*subordinate*' (the various forms of delegated legislation) compatibly with Convention rights. Sections 3 and 4 are considered further below (see 5.4.5).

Comment

Under the Human Rights Act 1998, public authorities have a positive duty to act in a way which is compatible with Convention rights. The HRA 1998 does not impose criminal liability on public authorities, but may be invoked directly by a victim of a violation of a Convention right in order to safeguard his or her rights.

---

[81] *Remedy* (plural *remedies*) is the most commonly used; *relief* and *redress* are uncountable nouns: always used in the singular, no indefinite article.

If a victim takes proceedings (or alternatively, relies on the Act in proceedings) under section 7, and the court finds the public authority has acted (or proposes to act) incompatibly with Convention rights under section 6, the victim may have a remedy under section 8. This section grants wide discretionary powers to the court or tribunal to provide 'just and appropriate' relief.

Section 7 places a strict limit on the identity of the parties who may *invoke rights* under the Act; however, it is in line with Article 34 of the Convention itself, according to which:

> The Court may receive applications from any person, non-governmental organisation or group of individuals claiming to be the victim of a violation.[82]

Indeed, section 7(7) shows that this is the precise intention of the legislature.

A significant aspect of the Human Rights Act 1998 in relation to all UK legislation is found in section 3 of the Act. Even if this new rule of statutory interpretation is not absolute, it is without doubt a very important new standard of interpretation, applicable to both past and future UK legislation. Where this rule of interpretation in section 3 is not, however, sufficient to arrive at a compatible reading of the legislation, the courts may issue a 'declaration of incompatibility' under section 4 of the Act, discussed in 5.4.5 below.

As regards precedent, the UK courts are not strictly bound by the Strasbourg authorities, but the case law of the European Court of Human Rights will be strongly persuasive. The appeal to the House of Lords in the *Denbigh High School* case,[83] examined in 5.5.2 below, illustrates the careful attention paid by the British courts at the highest level to the case law of the European Court of Human Rights.

In the following section we examine further the constitutional implications of the Human Rights Act 1998.

5.4.5 Constitutional Questions Raised by the Human Rights Act 1998

We have seen how the Human Rights Act 1998 guarantees human rights directly before the British courts. This is considered such an important step that the rights *set out* in the Convention 'might now be regarded as being equivalent to a domestic bill of rights'.[84] We shall now consider the constitutional implications of the HRA 1998: has this Act changed the constitutional balance in the UK by altering the relative powers of State organs?

---

[82] ECHR ETS No 005 Art 34.
[83] *Denbigh High School* case [2007] 1 AC 100, [2006] UKHL 15.
[84] P Leyland (2012). *The Constitution of the United Kingdom*, above n 9, p 224.

Parliamentary sovereignty and the declaration of incompatibility

According to the basic principle of the British Constitution—*Parliamentary sovereignty*—the UK Parliament has unlimited legislative power.[85] There are no legal limits to its power to legislate in any way at any time (although there are political limits); further, the courts are bound to apply statute law, even if they think it is unjust. Has this constitutional balance of power between Parliament and the judiciary been affected by the Human Rights Act 1998?

To answer this question, we must examine section 4 of the HRA 1998, which determines the powers of British courts when they find that legislation is incompatible with Convention rights. This may happen in a case where the courts cannot *interpret* the legislation *compatibly* with Convention rights by using the *interpretative power* under section 3 (see 5.4.4 above) to 'transform it by stretching its meaning, where it is possible to do so, in order to achieve Convention compatibility'.[86]

Examine section 4 of the Human Rights Act 1998 carefully (see 5.4.4 above). What is a 'declaration of incompatibility'? What effect does such a declaration produce?

Under section 4 of the HRA 1998, the court has power to make a '*declaration of incompatibility*'. It *may* make a declaration if it '*is satisfied*' (decides) that a provision of primary legislation conflicts with a Convention right. The new law term 'declaration of incompatibility' is created in section 4(6), and paragraphs (a) and (b) specify two *non-effects* of a declaration:

a)   under section 4(6)(a) the *validity, operation* and *enforcement* of the incompatible provision are *not affected* (not changed), that is to say, the incompatible provision remains effective and in force;

b)   under paragraph (b) the declaration '*is not binding on the parties to the proceedings*' (the public authority and the victim). This means that also for the parties, the provision remains in force.

The legal effects of the judgment for the parties concerned are therefore limited to the wide powers of the court to grant the victim a remedy under section 8 (examined in the 'Key and commentary' to Task 9 above).

What is the reason for this solution? Are there any other consequences of a declaration of incompatibility? Constitutionalist Peter Leyland explains:

> It is stressed once again that the HRA 1998 seeks to prevent judicial supremacy from replacing Parliamentary supremacy. …
>
>   The courts are not given power to invalidate primary legislation. If they find it impossible to interpret legislation in a Convention-friendly way, they can issue a declaration of incompatibility under section 4. This does 'not affect the validity, continuing operation or enforcement' of the Act in question. The effect of a declaration

---

[85] You may refer to the discussion of this doctrine in 3.5.2, above.
[86] Leyland, above n 9, p 224.

of incompatibility is to refer the matter back to Parliament. The Act introduces a fast-track procedure for the purpose of amending any offending legislation (there have been examples of this procedure being used). After a declaration of incompatibility has been issued, section 6(2) stipulates that until such time as any offending legislation is amended it will not be unlawful for a public authority to act in a way which is incompatible with the Convention.[87]

If the courts had a general power to *invalidate* (*set aside, annul*) Acts of Parliament, '*judicial supremacy*' would replace '*Parliamentary supremacy*': in such a case, there would be the risk of serious conflict between the judiciary and Parliament. The Human Rights Act 1998, instead, preserves the pre-existing balance of power between the legislature and the judiciary: 'the effect of a declaration of incompatibility is *to refer the matter* back *to Parliament*'. The decision-making role of the executive is also preserved, since the decision to initiate change in the law is in the hands of government ministers. Legislation remains valid, until and unless it is changed directly by legislative enactment. A practical mechanism is introduced: a 'fast-track procedure' to facilitate rapid legislative change by 'amending any *offending legislation*'. This is called a *remedial order*; under the Act, a Minister of the Crown 'may *by order* make such amendments to the legislation as he considers necessary *to remove the incompatibility*'.[88]

Even if legislative change is not *mandatory*, 'there is clearly in some sense an expectation that remedial action will follow' a declaration, and a constitutional convention to this effect could develop.[89]

Leyland and Anthony stress that the role of the British courts in defending human rights has become much more prominent under the Human Rights Act 1998; even if the declaration of incompatibility does not *invalidate* incompatible legislation—and therefore sovereignty is preserved—it is 'intended to prompt Parliament to amend the offending legislation', and this may lead to great controversy where judges appear to invade 'the territory of political decision-making'.[90]

For an example of a case where a declaration of incompatibility was made, see the *Belmarsh Detainees* case,[91] concerning the rights of foreign terrorist suspects detained in a London prison. Parliament responded by changing the incompatible legislation.[92] However, it remains a problematic decision to define the appropriate powers for detaining terrorist suspects, compatibly with both their human rights and public security.

---

[87]   *Ibid*, 224–25.

[88]   HRA 1998, s 10(2).

[89]   G Marshall (1998), 'On Constitutional Theory' in B Markesinis (ed), *The Impact of the Human Rights Bill on English Law*, Oxford: Oxford University Press, ch 3, p 17.

[90]   P Leyland and G Anthony (2009), *Textbook on Administrative Law*, 6th edn, Oxford: Oxford University Press, p 21.

[91]   *A & Others v Secretary of State for the Home Department* [2004] UKHL 56 (*Belmarsh Detainees* case); see Leyland, above n 9, pp 236–39.

[92]   Provisions of the Anti-terrorism, Crime and Security Act 2001.

Fundamental law

Has the Act given the rights protected in the European Convention the status of *fundamental law?* Constitutionalist Ian Loveland, below, explains *entrenchment* and compares the British solution to that of other ECHR countries.

Examine the passage below. What is the major difference in approach?

> Although the passage of the Act marks a significant departure in the treatment of human rights issues, it does not at present endow the Convention's provisions with the status of 'fundamental law', as that term is understood in most other western constitutions. It does not try to safeguard Convention rights against amendment or repeal by simple legislative majorities. Entrenchment of human rights by requiring special procedures to alter them is widely established in western democracies. ... In the majority of its [ECHR] signatory states, its terms enjoy supra-legislative status, and may thus empower courts to invalidate incompatible national legislation (another characteristic of 'fundamental law'). The Human Rights Act makes no attempt to achieve similar results in the United Kingdom.[93]

We say that rights, constitutions or laws are *entrenched* when special procedures must be used to alter them. The Human Rights Act has not led to '*entrenchment*' of Convention rights in the UK legal system. The Act does not have a special legal status above other laws ('*supra-legislative status*'), as in many other European States, but can be amended or repealed by the ordinary legislative procedure, like all UK laws. However, as we saw in chapter three, the Human Rights Act 1998 belongs in the special category of *common law 'constitutional statutes'* as classified in the case of *Thoburn*,[94] and can therefore be repealed or amended only by express legislative provision.

Conclusion

In conclusion, we can observe that the Human Rights Act 1998 represents a significant new legal approach to the treatment of human rights issues in the UK, which has given UK courts a much more politically sensitive role. At the same time, it has preserved the constitutional balance between UK State organs and has not created fundamental law, or a supreme court with power to enforce constitutional rights by striking down incompatible legislation.

---

[93] I Loveland (1999), 'Incorporating the European Convention on Human Rights into UK Law' in *Parliamentary Affairs*, January 1999, p 115.

[94] *Thoburn v Sunderland City Council* [2002] EWHC 195 (Admin), [2003] QB 151; see 3.6.2 above.

5.5 Freedom of Religion: Advanced Case Study

The rights protected in the ECHR may be classified into different groups. *Absolute rights*, such as freedom from torture under Article 3, are not subject to any limitations; by contrast, *qualified rights* may be subject to certain limitations in defined circumstances. In the Convention text, the right may be protected in the first paragraph of the Article, and then *qualified* by introducing possible limits in its second paragraph. For example, the right to life is protected in Article 2(1) ECHR, while Article 2(2)(a) introduces a possible exception: necessary force can be used 'in defence of any person from unlawful violence'.[95]

Examine the two paragraphs of Article 8 below as an example of this mechanism. What two criteria are established that public authorities must observe? What are the 'protected interests' that may justify interference with the right to respect for private and family life?

European Convention on Human Rights[96]
Article 8—Right to respect for private and family life

1 Everyone has the right to respect for his private and family life, his home and his correspondence.
2 There shall be no interference by a public authority with the exercise of this right except such as is in accordance with the law and is necessary in a democratic society in the interests of national security, public safety or the economic well-being of the country, for the prevention of disorder or crime, for the protection of health or morals, or for the protection of the rights and freedoms of others.

You will note that public authorities can *interfere* with the exercise of the rights protected in Article 8(1) on the basis of two criteria:

a)   their interference must be '*in accordance with law*' (it must have a legal basis); and
b)   it must be '*necessary in a democratic society*'.

The *protected interests* listed in Article 8(2) range from 'national security', to 'the economic well-being of the country' and the '*protection of the rights and freedoms of others*'. Interference can only be justified on the grounds of one of these protected interests, and different Articles of the Convention may have different *protected interests*.

---

[95]   ECHR ETS No 005, Art 2, examined in 1.3 above, Text 3.
[96]   ECHR ETS No 005, Art 8.

Task 10   Consulting treaty law—European Convention on Human Rights
Consult the text of the European Convention on Human Rights, particularly 'Section 1—Rights and Freedoms', Articles 2–18.

Identify some 'absolute' and some 'qualified' rights. For qualified rights, examine the criteria that justify limitations and the list of protected interests. Focus on both language and meaning.

Read and consider the importance of Article 15 ('Derogation in time of emergency'). Which rights are *derogable* (derogation is permitted) and which are not? In case of *derogation*, the effect of a provision is suspended.

Discuss your observations and consider the choices made by the High Contracting Parties in the restrictions that may be imposed on the enjoyment of certain rights.

5.5.1   Freedom of Thought, Conscience and Religion: Article 9 ECHR

Article 9 ECHR protects *freedom of thought, conscience and religion.* Carefully examine the text of Article 9 below. Is freedom of religion an *absolute* or a *qualified* right? Among human rights, how important do you think the freedoms protected in Article 9 are? Is freedom of religion a *derogable* or an *inderogable* right? Refer to Article 15 ECHR for your answer.

Article 9—Freedom of thought, conscience and religion
1. Everyone has the right to freedom of thought, conscience and religion; this right includes freedom to change his religion or belief and freedom, either alone or in community with others and in public or private, to manifest his religion or belief, in worship, teaching, practice and observance.
2. Freedom to manifest one's religion or beliefs shall be subject only to such limitations as are prescribed by law and are necessary in a democratic society in the interests of public safety, for the protection of public order, health or morals, or for the protection of the rights and freedoms of others.

The freedom to hold a religious belief is *absolute*; however, the freedom to *manifest* religion, for example by dress, hair style or other behaviour, is *qualified*. According to paragraph (2) of Article 9, it may be 'subject to ... limitations', provided they are both '*prescribed by law*' and 'necessary in a democratic society in the interests of public safety' or for other specific reasons, including *the protection of other people's rights and freedoms.* States may take measures derogating from their obligations under Article 9 '[in] time of war or other public emergency threatening the life of the nation', as provided in Article 15.

5.5.2 Freedom to Manifest Religion: the *Denbigh High School* case

In the *Denbigh High School* case[97] the English courts had to decide a difficult issue under the Human Rights Act 1998, concerning freedom to manifest religion. Had the Convention rights of a Muslim schoolgirl been *infringed* (violated) by her school when she was not allowed to attend school wearing a particular type of dress (a jilbab) not permitted by the school uniform policy?

The school offered different uniform options, carefully designed to suit the needs of Muslim, Hindu and Sikh female pupils, and the headteacher of the school, herself a Muslim, believed the uniform was significant in 'promoting a positive sense of communal identity' as well as playing 'an integral part in securing high and improving standards'.[98] However, the school argued that the limits it imposed on the girl's right to manifest her religious belief were justified by the European Convention itself.

Shabina Begum stayed away from school for two years, before entering another school locally where girls were permitted to wear the jilbab. She issued a claim for *judicial review*[99] of the school's action, asserting that she had been unlawfully excluded from the school, which had also violated her right to manifest religious belief under Article 9 ECHR. The opening paragraph of the House of Lords judgment, below, summarises the dispute.

Who won the case at first instance? Who won the first appeal?

LORD BINGHAM OF CORNHILL
My Lords,

1. The respondent, Shabina Begum, is now aged 17. She contends that the appellants, who are the head teacher and governors of Denbigh High School in Luton ('the school'), excluded her from that school, unjustifiably limited her right under article 9 of the European Convention on Human Rights to manifest her religion or beliefs and violated her right not to be denied education under article 2 of the First Protocol to the Convention. Bennett J, ruling on the respondent's application for judicial review at first instance, rejected all these contentions: [2004] EWHC 1389 (Admin); [2004] ELR 374. The Court of Appeal (Brooke, Mummery and Scott Baker LJJ), reversing the judge, accepted each of them: [2005] EWCA Civ 199; [2005] 1 WLR 3372. The Appellants, with support from the Secretary of State for Education and Skills as intervener, submit that the judge was right and the Court of Appeal wrong.[100]

At first instance, the case was heard by Mr Justice Bennett ('Bennett J') in the High Court; the judge '*rejected* all [the claimant's] *contentions*': therefore, the school

---

[97] *R (on the application of Begum (by her litigation friend Rahman)) v Headteacher and Governors of Denbigh High School* [2007] 1 AC 100, [2006] UKHL 15 (*Denbigh High School* case).
[98] *Ibid*, para 6, per Lord Bingham.
[99] *Judicial review of administrative action* is part of the *supervisory jurisdiction* of the Queen's Bench Division of the High Court. As a public authority, the school must respect Convention rights under s 6 of the HRA 1998, examined in 5.4.4 above.
[100] *Denbigh High School* case [2006] UKHL 15, para 1.

won the case and Shabina Begum's application was *dismissed*. Next, the Court of Appeal overturned ('*reversed*') the judge's decision in 'a landmark ruling' that Shabina said would 'give hope and strength to other Muslim women'.[101] A *ruling* is a decision on a point of law by a court (verb, to *rule*); in the media the noun *ruling* is often used as a synonym of *judgment*. The case then went on further appeal to the House of Lords *for final decision*, with the school as *appellant* and Shabina, defending the appeal, as *respondent*.

The paragraph above is the first of 99 in the full text of the judgment. In the Task below you will read some significant paragraphs from Lord Bingham's opinion; it is considered to be *the leading judgment* in the case (that is, the most important judgment for its enunciation of legal principle). It is the first of five opinions individually pronounced by each member of the court.[102]

Task 11   Reading comprehension—the *Denbigh High School* case
First, read the text of the Denbigh High School case on the following pages for general understanding, and try to understand two main aspects of the case, specified in questions 1. and 2. below.

Then, read the case in detail, paragraph by paragraph, to understand Lord Bingham's reasoning. How does he approach the question? What legal sources does he rely on? What are the grounds for his decision? You may read independently, or use questions 3. to 8. below as a framework for comprehension of the text.

1. What is the issue in this appeal (the specific legal question that the court must decide in order to resolve the dispute)? The issue is often indicated by the key word, *whether*, followed by its precise formulation, in a phrase such as: 'The *question/issue* before the court is *whether* …'. A case may have more than one issue for decision.
2. What is Lord Bingham's decision in the case? This is the decision of the court, since the other Law Lords expressed agreement in their opinions.
3. What is the importance of the right to freedom of religion (paragraph 20)?
4. Why is article 9 *engaged* (legally applicable) in this case (paragraph 21)?
5. Were the school rules 'prescribed by law', one of the requirements to justify a limitation (paragraph 26)?
6. What is the relevance of the ECtHR judgment in *Sahin* (paragraph 32)?
7. Why does Lord Bingham reject Shabina's criticisms of the school's uniform policy (paragraph 33)?
8. Was the school justified in limiting Shabina's Convention right to manifest her religion (paragraph 34)? On what grounds?

---

[101] 'Schoolgirl wins two-year battle to wear Islamic dress', *Guardian Weekly Newspaper*, 11–17 March 2005.
[102] The full text of the judgment can be consulted at <http://www.bailii.org>.

HOUSE OF LORDS
[2006] UKHL 15

R (on the application of Begum (by her litigation friend Rahman)) v Headteacher and Governors of Denbigh High School

LORD BINGHAM OF CORNHILL

My Lords,

[Paras 1–19: the facts of the case and its legal history are examined]

20. ... The fundamental importance of this right [freedom of religion] in a pluralistic, multi-cultural society was clearly explained by my noble and learned friend Lord Nicholls of Birkenhead in *R (Williamson) v Secretary of State for Education and Employment* [2005] UKHL 15, [2005] 2 AC 246, paras 15–19, and by the South African Constitutional Court in *Christian Education South Africa v Minister of Education* [2001] 1 LRC 441, para 36. This is not in doubt. As pointed out by my noble and learned friend in para 16 of the passage cited, article 9 protects both the right to hold a belief, which is absolute, and a right to manifest belief, which is qualified.

21. It is common ground in these proceedings that at all material times the respondent sincerely held the religious belief which she professed to hold. ... Thus it is accepted, obviously rightly, that article 9(1) is engaged or applicable. That in itself makes this a significant case, since any sincere religious belief must command respect, particularly when derived from an ancient and respected religion. The main questions for consideration are, accordingly, whether the respondent's freedom to manifest her belief by her dress was subject to limitation (or, as it has more often been called, interference) within the meaning of article 9(2) and, if so, whether such limitation or interference was justified under that provision.

[Paras 22–25: the question of interference is decided by examining the Strasbourg case law]

26. To be justified under article 9(2) a limitation or interference must be (a) prescribed by law and (b) necessary in a democratic society for a permissible purpose, that is, it must be directed to a legitimate purpose and must be proportionate in scope and effect. ... The school authorities had statutory authority to lay down rules on uniform, and those rules were very clearly communicated to those affected by them. It was not suggested that the rules were not made for the legitimate purpose of protecting the rights and freedoms of others. So the issue is whether the rules and the school's insistence on them were in all the circumstances proportionate. ...

...

32. It is therefore necessary to consider the proportionality of the school's interference with the respondent's right to manifest her religious belief by wearing the jilbab to the school. In doing so we have the valuable guidance of the Grand Chamber of the Strasbourg court in *Sahin*, above, paras 104–111. The court there recognises the high importance of the rights protected by article 9; the need in some situations to restrict freedom to manifest religious belief; the value of religious harmony and tolerance between opposing or competing groups and of pluralism and broadmindedness; the need for compromise and balance; the role of the state in deciding what is necessary to protect the rights and freedoms of others; the variation of practice and tradition among member states; and the permissibility in some contexts of restricting the wearing of religious dress.

33. The respondent criticised the school for permitting the headscarf while refusing to permit the jilbab, for refusing permission to wear the jilbab when some other schools permitted it and for adhering to their own view of what Islamic dress required. None of these criticisms can in my opinion be sustained. … Different schools have different uniform policies, no doubt influenced by the composition of their pupil bodies and a range of other matters. Each school has to decide what uniform, if any, will best serve its wider educational purposes. The school did not reject the respondent's request out of hand: it took advice, and was told that its existing policy conformed with the requirements of mainstream Muslim opinion.

34. On the agreed facts, the school was in my opinion fully justified in acting as it did. It had taken immense pains to devise a uniform policy which respected Muslim beliefs but did so in an inclusive, unthreatening and uncompetitive way. The rules laid down were as far from being mindless as uniform rules could ever be. The school had enjoyed a period of harmony and success to which the uniform policy was thought to contribute. On further enquiry it still appeared that the rules were acceptable to mainstream Muslim opinion. It was feared that acceding to the respondent's request would or might have significant adverse repercussions. It would in my opinion be irresponsible of any court, lacking the experience, background and detailed knowledge of the head teacher, staff and governors, to overrule their judgment on a matter as sensitive as this. The power of decision has been given to them for the compelling reason that they are best placed to exercise it, and I see no reason to disturb their decision. …

[In paras 35–39, Article 2 of the First Protocol is considered]

40. For these reasons, and those given by Lord Hoffmann, with which I agree, I would allow the appeal, set aside the order of the Court of Appeal, and restore the order of the judge. …

Key and commentary to Task 11 Reading comprehension—the *Denbigh High School* case

1. Two interrelated issues are formulated in paragraph 21: first, '*whether* the respondent's freedom to manifest her belief by her dress was *subject to limitation … within the meaning of article 9(2)*; if so, secondly, *whether* such *limitation was justified*'. This second issue concerning *justification* is refined, in paragraph 26, to the question of *proportionality* ('*So the issue is whether* the rules … were … *proportionate.*').

2. Lord Bingham is in favour of *allowing the appeal* (paragraph 40). He decides (paragraph 34) that 'the school *was justified in acting* as it did'. He finds that the response of the school was proportionate and he will not interfere with such a sensitive decision. Since the other law lords agreed with him, this is the House of Lords' decision in the case.

3. Freedom of religion is *a right of fundamental importance* in a pluralistic, multicultural society, such as Britain (paragraph 20).

4. Article 9 is *engaged* (legally applicable) because Shabina sincerely held the religious belief in question. This point is not disputed, it is accepted by both parties: '*It is common ground that …*' (paragraph 21).

5. The school rules (paragraph 26) are created under *statutory authority*: the school has power '*to lay down*' (create, establish) its own rules on uniform, under power delegated by Act of Parliament. This satisfies the first condition for a limitation (*interference*) under Article 9(2): to be justified, interference must be '*prescribed by law*'. The '*legitimate purpose*' of the school rules is also recognised in paragraph 26: 'for protection of the rights and freedoms of others'.

6. *Sahin*[103] (paragraph 32) is a precedent of the Strasbourg Court, which, under section 2 HRA 1998 (see 5.4.4 above), the House of Lords must take into account. It is persuasive authority for a series of propositions relevant in this appeal. In *Sahin*, the Court established that it is sometimes necessary to restrict freedom to manifest religious belief; many factors are relevant, including 'the value of religious harmony and tolerance between opposing or competing groups' and 'the role of the state in deciding what is necessary *to protect the rights and freedoms of others*'.[104] This last point, mentioned specifically in Article 9(2) as a ground for

---

[103] *Sahin v Turkey*, judgment of 10 November 2005 (App no 44774/98) [2005] ECHR 819, (2007) 44 EHRR 5.

[104] *Ibid*. The ECtHR held that there was no violation of Leyla Sahin's Convention rights when she was not admitted to university lectures and exams because she was wearing the Islamic headscarf. The university regulations banning the headscarf were 'not directed against the applicant's religious affiliation, but pursued, among other things, the legitimate aim of protecting order and the rights and freedoms of others and were manifestly intended to preserve the secular nature of educational institutions' (para 165). Under Art 2 of its Constitution, 'The Republic of Turkey is a democratic, secular (*laik*) and social State based on the rule of law …' (para 29 of the judgment).

justifying a limitation, is also significant in the *Denbigh High School* case (see question 8. below).

7. In paragraph 33, Lord Bingham rejects each of Shabina's criticisms of the Denbigh High School uniform policy. Each school has a different policy, it is therefore irrelevant that other schools permit the jilbab. Each school must decide what is best for its 'wider educational purposes' (not only academic purposes) in relation to its specific needs. The school did not merely 'adhere to their own view' of Islamic dress, as alleged by Shabina, but requested advice from informed Muslim opinion, both when designing the uniform options and as a result of Shabina's demand (paragraph 34).

8. The school was justified in limiting Shabina's right to manifest her religious belief (paragraph 34). First, it had taken great care to respect Muslim beliefs when formulating its uniform policy, which it had done in 'an inclusive, unthreatening and uncompetitive way'. Then, the limitation is justified under Article 9(2) ECHR by the legitimate aim of protecting the rights and freedoms of others. Lord Bingham refers to this need when he says: 'It was feared [by the school] that *acceding to the respondent's request*[105] would or might have significant adverse repercussions.' The jilbab was a more extreme manifestation of religious faith, not adopted by mainstream Muslims, and the House of Lords recognised a risk that other, moderate, girls would then be under pressure to wear it. Evidence to this effect was produced.[106]

Comment—the *Denbigh High School* case, the Human Rights Act 1998 and freedom of religion

The House of Lords judgment in the *Denbigh High School* case illustrates the approach of the UK courts to human rights issues under the Human Rights Act 1998. References to the Convention text and to the relevant case law of the Strasbourg Court are central to the Law Lords' reasoning and decision in the case, and the House of Lords applies the ECHR *principle of proportionality*, an important innovation for *judicial review* by the UK courts. The *proportionality principle* 'gives judges a more sensitive tool to consider whether the restriction of a right can be justified': the question is whether the means used to limit the right or freedom is 'no more than is necessary to accomplish the objective'.[107]

---

[105] To accede to a request = to grant a request, to accept it.
[106] Referred to in the opinion of Baroness Hale, *Denbigh High School* case, above n 97, para 98.
[107] P Leyland (2007), *The Constitution of the United Kingdom. A Contextual Analysis*, Oxford: Hart Publishing, p 181.

With specific regard to freedom of religion, protected by Article 9 ECHR, the *Denbigh High School* case highlights the fundamental importance of this right, which is engaged when a sincere religious belief is held. It also shows the complex issues involved both for public authorities, when taking administrative decisions (in this case, the school), and for courts, when deciding whether a limitation of the right to manifest religious belief is justified in a particular case.

Lord Bingham states that it is not part of the judicial function to decide whether particular forms of dress that manifest religious belief should or should not be permitted in British schools; he underlines that 'this case concerns a particular pupil and a particular school in a particular place at a particular time'.[108]

Under the Human Rights Act 1998, public authorities in the UK must act compatibly with Convention rights. Where a body, such as a school, limits the right to manifest religious belief when Article 9 is engaged, it cannot do so in an arbitrary way, but only on the basis of the criteria laid down in Article 9(2), justifying interference with the right. In case of a dispute, the role of the courts is to decide whether the public authority has limited the right in a way which is *proportionate* and lawful.

Baroness Hale of Richmond, the only female judge in the *Denbigh High School* appeal, explores the complex network of factors implicated in freedom to manifest religion, in her opinion in the case:[109]

> If a woman freely chooses to adopt a way of life for herself, it is not for others, including other women who have chosen differently, to criticise or prevent her. Judge Tulkens, in *Sahin v Turkey*, at p 46, draws the analogy with freedom of speech. The European Court of Human Rights has never accepted that interference with the right of freedom of expression is justified by the fact that the ideas expressed may offend someone. Likewise, the sight of a woman in full purdah[110] may offend some people, and especially those western feminists who believe that it is a symbol of her oppression, but that could not be a good reason for prohibiting her from wearing it.[111]

But in a democratic society that protects individual freedoms, based on the rule of law, the possibility must also be considered that the decision to wear the veil may be the result of pressure on a girl living in a situation of patriarchal family control. The *balance* becomes one of protecting *individual freedom and autonomy* but at the same time guaranteeing respect for *women's and girls' rights to equality and freedom*, particularly within public educational institutions. Baroness Hale considers the complex tasks of schools: to educate young people from 'many and diverse families and communities in this country' while helping pupils achieve their full potential and promoting 'the ability of people of diverse races, religions

---

[108] *Denbigh High School* case, above n 97, para 2.
[109] *Ibid*, Baroness Hale's opinion, paras 96–99.
[110] Women *in purdah* are hidden from public view by a veil or curtain. *Purdah* is practised in some Muslim and Hindu societies. Here, it refers to clothing.
[111] *Denbigh High School* case, above n 97, para 96.

and cultures to live together in harmony'.[112] A school uniform may play a role in creating a sense of cohesion and community:

> But it does more than that. Like it or not, this is a society committed, in principle and in law, to equal freedom for men and women to choose how they will lead their lives within the law. Young girls from ethnic, cultural or religious minorities growing up here face particularly difficult choices: how far to adopt or to distance themselves from the dominant culture. A good school will enable and support them. This particular school is a good school: that, it appears, is one reason why Shabina Begum wanted to stay there.[113]

Baroness Hale concludes that the Denbigh High School had responded thoughtfully and proportionately to the complexities of the situation.[114] It was therefore justified in limiting Shabina's right to manifest her religion.

Task 12 Discussion—freedom to manifest religion

— What is your response to the *Denbigh High School* case?
— Do you have strong views on freedom to manifest religion?
— What controversies have arisen in your country or in other countries of the world in recent years (for example, concerning the Muslim veil or the Christian cross, or other religious symbols)?
— What role can and should the law play in relation to the above questions?
— Investigate a recent case or legislative provision in a country of your choice. Prepare to present and discuss your findings and views, basing your comment also on relevant legal sources, including the ECHR or other human rights instruments.

Ideas for Further Reading

Bingham, Tom (2010), *The Rule of Law*, London: Penguin Books. In Chapter 7, 'Human Rights', senior Law Lord, Lord Bingham, discusses the protection of human rights as part of the concept of the rule of law; interestingly, he reviews each of the fundamental human rights following the framework provided by the ECHR (pp 66–84).

Fontaine, P (2010), *Europe in 12 lessons*, Luxembourg: Office for Official Publications of the European Union. Available at the Europa website <http://europa.eu>. Each short lesson explains clearly and concisely an aspect of

---

[112] *Ibid*, para 97.
[113] *Ibid*.
[114] *Ibid*, para 98.

European integration, such as: How does the Union work? A citizens' Europe. Freedom, security and justice. Where will the EU's boundaries be drawn? What future is there for the euro?

Leyland, Peter (2012), *The Constitution of the United Kingdom. A Contextual Analysis*, 2nd edn, Oxford: Hart Publishing. EU law and the ECHR as sources of British law are briefly introduced in Chapter 2, 'The Sources of the Constitution, Part I' (pp 28–30); the impact of the Human Rights Act 1998 in UK constitutional law (including significant case law such as the *Denbigh High School* case) is clearly explained and analysed in Chapter 7, 'The Constitutional Role of the Courts, Part III The Courts and the Human Rights Act 1998', pp 223–40.

Loveland, Ian (1999), 'Incorporating the European Convention on Human Rights into UK Law' in *Parliamentary Affairs*, January 1999, vol 52 (113–27). This law review article examines in depth the mechanisms and effects of the Act. Advanced level reading.

Marshall, Geoffrey (1998), 'On Constitutional Theory' in Markesinis, Basil S (ed), *The Impact of the Human Rights Bill on English Law (The Clifford Chance Lectures, Volume 3)*, Oxford: Oxford University Press, Chapter 3, pp 15–20. For discussion of the constitutional implications of the Human Rights Act 1998 as a Bill of Rights, written at the time of its enactment in 1998, this chapter examines the implications of the declaration of incompatibility, relations between the judiciary and Parliament, and rights and the State. Advanced level reading.

Riley, Alison (1991), *English for Law*, Harlow: Pearson Education Ltd. For comprehension with focus on law and legal language in judgments concerning the EU and ECHR legal contexts: in the case of *Macarthys Ltd v Smith*, Court of Appeal judgment with a reference for a preliminary ruling to the ECJ (Case C-129/79), pp 90–99; in the judgment of the ECtHR in *Tyrer v The United Kingdom* Series A no 26 (1978), pp 143–75.

Chapter 6

LEGAL GRAMMAR

Basic Sentence Structure

Subject and predicate – Independent clauses – Position of subject – Dependent clauses and phrases – Front structures in sentences – Structures to modify the subject: noun phrases – Structures inserted after the subject – Expanding the predicate: adding a verb – Expanding the object – Structures inserted at the end

[Common law and the civil code are different in two main aspects.] First the civil code prefers generality whereas the common law goes for particularity. And, second, the civil code draftsman is eager to be widely understood by the ordinary leadership, whereas the common law draftsman seems to be more worried about not being misunderstood by the specialist community.

Vijay K Bhatia, linguist, 1969

The aim of this chapter is to review some basic principles of grammar by focusing on the primary unit of meaning: the sentence. What are the constituents of a sentence, how are words put together to form sentences and what syntactic structures are used?

Legal texts have the notorious tendency to be long-winded,[1] that is, they have excessively long sentences combined with difficult syntactic organisation of complex prepositional phrases, adverbials and binomial expressions. It therefore makes sense to focus on the simpler constructions and then explore the more difficult forms characteristic of legal discourse. Familiarising yourself with these basic structures becomes a basis for interpreting them.

6.1 SUBJECT AND PREDICATE

So, what is a *simple* sentence and what makes a sentence *complex*?

---

[1] Long-winded means prolonging the length of discourse (written or spoken) for more than is necessary.

Task 1 Read, scan and observe—the sentence
Read the following extract adapted from the 'Introduction to the Legal System of the People's Republic of China'.[2] Scan the text and circle the subject (sometimes it might be more than one word) in each sentence. Underline the main verbs in each sentence and double underline the auxiliary verbs. Place a slash [/] between the subject and the rest of the sentence. The first sentence has been done for you as an example.

1. Overview of Chinese Legal System
The People's Republic of China (PRC)/was established on October 1st, 1959. In a mere span of 53 years, the Chinese legal system has experienced tumultuous changes. It was established, destroyed, re-established and gradually transformed along with the society's transition from a planned economy to a market economy.

Observations
In this task, we are examining the basic constituents of a sentence: the subject and predicate. In the first sentence,

The People's Republic of China (PRC) was established on October 1st, 1959.

we have a complete thought, consisting of one main clause, and it can be considered as grammatically complete. *The People's Republic of China* is the subject, *was established on October 1st, 1959* is the predicate. If we eliminate the subject and keep only the predicate:

was established on October 1st, 1959

we would naturally ask *what* was established? If we take out the predicate and just keep the subject:

The People's Republic of China (PRC)

we would ask ourselves: *So, what about it?* It is obvious that for a thought to be complete we need both of these basic constituents of a sentence: the subject and the predicate.

In the second sentence,

In a mere span of 53 years, the Chinese legal system has experienced tumultuous changes.

the Chinese legal system is the subject (a noun phrase), while *has experienced tumultuous changes* is the predicate. Yet unlike the first sentence, it is longer and has two elements: an introductory prepositional phrase (followed by a

---

[2] Zhao Yuhong and R Sharma (2003), 'Introduction to the Legal system of the People's Republic of China' in *Multilingual and Multicultural Contexts of Legislation: An International Perspective*, VK Bhatia, CN Candlin, J Engberg and A Trosberg (eds), Bern: Peter Lang, p 25.

comma) and a main clause. As you will have noticed, the prepositional phrase *In a mere span of 53 years* does not have the basic subject-predicate structure necessary to be considered a complete thought. It is found in the main clause that follows it, *the Chinese legal system has experienced tumultuous changes.*

In the last sentence,

It was established, destroyed, re-established and gradually transformed along with the society's transition from a planned economy to a market economy.

the subject *It* is anaphoric, that is, it makes a direct reference to the subject in the preceding sentence (*the Chinese legal system*). The predicate *was established, destroyed, re-established and gradually transformed along with the society's transition from a planned economy to a market economy* contains four verb phrases followed by prepositional phrases.

The sentences in this extract are not what grammarians describe as *complex.* They are a reasonable length and contain one main clause. A simple sentence becomes complex when one or more subordinating clauses are added. Legal texts typically contain multiple subordinate clauses.

NOTE: A verb phrase *consists of one or more words. For example, I* study *law, I* have studied *law, I* should have studied *law.*

A noun phrase *typically consists of more than one word:* The Italian legal system. *The words* The Italian legal *add more information to the word at its head,* system.

The subject-predicate structure is lacking in both verb phrases and noun phrases. The subject-predicate structure is characteristic of clauses. *Clauses will be explained in the next section and in chapter twelve.*

6.2 Grammar Review: The Independent Clause: Subject + Verb

The basic unit of meaning in a sentence is the *subject* (S) and its *predicate.* The *subject* is often a noun phrase. Noun phrases as subjects[3] are introduced by a determiner such as an article (*a, an, the*) or a demonstrative (*this, that, these, those*). Sometimes one or more adjectives are added, followed by a noun or a pronoun (*he, they,* etc).

determiner + adjective(s) + noun = noun phrase (as subject)

For example:

The negotiating parties must agree on all the essential terms of their bargain.

---

[3] Noun phrases may also be the object in a clause, an adverbial or complement in a prepositional phrase.

> *NOTE:* Determiners in legal texts, *such, said* and *aforesaid,* are often used in the pre-modifying position (before the head noun) for precision of reference:
>
> *Such* legal protection should respect proportionality and should not prohibit those devices or activities … to circumvent the technical protection.[4]
>
> The restrictions permitted under this Convention to the *said* rights and freedoms shall not be applied for any purpose other than those for which they have been prescribed.[5]
>
> The Trial of all Crimes, except in Cases of Impeachment, shall be by Jury; and *such* Trial shall be held in the State where the *said* Crimes shall have been committed …[6]

A *predicate* consists of a verb (V) and the sentence elements that follow it. A group of words which contain a subject and verb (S + V) and express a complete thought is called an independent clause (often referred to as the *main clause*). Every sentence must have at least one independent clause.

A *simple sentence* has one independent clause, while a *complex sentence* may have one or more clauses that are coordinated or subordinated. The difference between a coordinating clause and subordinating clause is discussed in sections 6.2.1 and 6.4.1 below.

6.2.1 Verb Phrases in Independent Clauses

For an independent clause to be complete, the verb may be one word (with the singular verb indicating the past or present tense) or more than one word, including its auxiliaries. These are called *verb phrases.*

Subject	Predicate	
	VERB PHRASE	REST OF PREDICATE
Article 5*(1)(f)*	permits	detention in connection with immigration, asylum and extradition orders.
Article 6*(2)*	enshrines	in the Convention the right to be presumed innocent.

---

[4] Directive on the harmonisation of certain aspects of copyright and related rights in the information society [2001] OJ LI67/29, recital 48.

[5] Human Rights Act 1998, Sch 1, Pt I, Rights and Freedoms, Art 18, 'Limitation on use of restriction on rights'.

[6] United States Constitution, Art III § 2.

A Court	may not substitute	its own reasoning for that of medical experts.
The Court	has reviewed	several cases claiming State violations of the right to privacy through criminalisation of homosexual activities.[7]

A sentence may have more than one independent clause, provided that it is connected with a coordinating conjunction (*and, but, for, nor, so, yet, or*). Coordinating conjunctions connect two independent clauses the content of which is *related* or *equally important*. Coordinating conjunctions are usually found in the middle of two independent clauses, and the comma is placed *after* the first independent clause (unless both clauses are short). See Table 6.1 below.

Table 6.1: Coordinating conjunctions

and	connects two similar ideas
but	contrast two ideas
so	cause/effect, 1 causes 2
for	'because', cause/effect, 2 causes 1
nor	connects two negative alternatives
or	connects two alternative ideas
yet	contrasts (as in *but*)

The defendant was afraid to take the witness stand, **so** *he invoked the Fifth Amendment.*[8]

He must either pay the fine, **or** *he will have to go to jail.*

The District Attorney was disbarred, **for** *he had committed perjury.*[9]

He was convicted of the crime, **yet** *he was released because of health reasons.*

The prisoners were **neither** *allowed to communicate with their lawyers,* **nor** *had the opportunity to contact their families.*[10]

Observe this example from a Convention which uses *but* to contrast two ideas:

It may therefore be subject to certain restrictions, **but** these shall only be such as are provided by law and are necessary: ...[11]

---

[7] Text adapted from D Gomien (2005), *Short Guide to the European Convention on Human Rights*, 3rd edn, Strasbourg: Cedex Council of Europe Publishing.

[8] In the US Constitution, the Fifth Amendment states that in a criminal case, a person is not obliged to be a witness against himself.

[9] Perjury—intentionally making false statements while under oath (a solemn pledge).

[10] Neither/nor is used when you are talking about *two* things and you are making a negative statement about both of them.

[11] International Covenant on Civil and Political Rights (adopted 16 December 1966, entered into force 23 March 1976), UNGA Res 2200A (XXI), Art 19(3).

6.3 Position of Subject

The subject is usually in the first position in a sentence, with the structure: **S** (subject) – **V** (verb) – **O** (object). If a clause or phrase precedes the subject, the comma is normally placed after the clause finishes and before the subject. For example:

> In a few cases, individuals have complained about the type of facilities in which they have been detained.[12]

Task 2 Noun phrase as subject of sentence
Underline the subject noun phrase in the following sentences:

1. Everyone has the right to freedom of expression.[13]
2. An Act of Congress or of a state legislature begins with a title ('An Act to …'), which sets forth the subject of the statute, followed by an enacting clause ('Be it enacted by …'), and sometimes by a preamble or purpose clause stating the reason or policy behind the enactment.[14]
3. The ultimate arbiter of constitutional disputes is, of course, the Supreme Court of the United States.[15]

6.3.1 Subject Omission

In English, unlike many languages, the subject cannot be omitted. Even if the subject is a pronoun—*I, you, he, she, it, we, they*—it must *not* be excluded in a sentence.

Comparative law is an interesting subject. It is an interesting subject. Is an interesting subject.

Do not repeat the subject in a sentence twice.

Comparative law it is an interesting subject.

6.4 Dependent Clauses and Phrases

6.4.1 Dependent Clause

A dependent clause has a subject and verb, yet it cannot exist on its own. To make sense, it needs the main independent clause. Dependent clauses (often called subordinating clauses) are joined to independent clauses by subordinating

---

[12] Gomien, above n 7, p 34, regarding ECHR Protocol No 4, Art 2.
[13] ECHR, Art 10(1).
[14] E Allan Farnsworth (1996), *An Introduction to the Legal System of the United States*, 3rd edn, New York: Oceana Publications, p 73.
[15] *Ibid*, p 61.

conjunctions which show a relationship (such as contrast or cause/effect) between the two clauses.[16] The dependent clause may be placed before or after the main independent clause. For example:

Because the defendant was intoxicated at the time of the accident, it was probable that the jury would find him guilty.

Underline the dependent clause in this example from a Convention:

> Although Article 6 applies to many disputes between the individual and a State, various immunities of States or State agents or employees may bar the courts from adjudicating such cases.[17]

6.4.2 Phrase

A phrase, such as a single word or words, lacks the subject-predicate structure typical of clauses. Underline the phrases in the examples below.

> Furthermore, no Member State shall impose on the products of other Member States any internal taxation of such a nature as to afford indirect protection to other products.[18]

> Nevertheless, any such personal effects required for use by the prisoners of war whilst in captivity shall be replaced at the expense of the Detaining Power.[19]

> In addition, prisoners of war who work shall receive appropriate clothing, wherever the nature of the work demands.[20]

6.5 FRONT STRUCTURES IN SENTENCES

Adding a word or words (phrases or clauses) at the beginning of a sentence provides more information about the subject of the sentence or the meaning of the sentence as a whole. These sentence-initial elements *precede* the subject of the independent clause. If the element contains more than a word, it is separated from the subject by a comma. For example:

Feeling exhausted after my exams, I went home to sleep.

Feeling exhausted after my exams (sentence-initial element), *I went home to sleep.* (independent clause)

---

[16] A table of common connectives and their functions is to be found at the end of this chapter – see Table 6.5.

[17] Gomien, above n 7, p 55, regarding ECHR Art 6, Right to a fair trial.

[18] Consolidated Version of the Treaty Establishing the European Community [2002] OJ C325/33, Art 90.

[19] Convention relative to the Treatment of Prisoners of War (adopted 12 August 1949, entered into force 21 October 1950) 75 UNTS 135, Art 68.

[20] *Ibid*, Art 27.

Table 6.2 below illustrates some common sentence-initial elements that are used to introduce a sentence.

Table 6.2: Sentence-initial elements

Front sentence-initial elements	Example
a adverb (time phrase)	*Yesterday*
b time prepositional phrase	*On 22 May 1995,*
c place prepositional phrase	*In Strasbourg,*
d descriptive phrase	*Unhappy with the verdict,*
e adverb	*Consequently,*
f prepositional phrase	*With respect to this rule,*
g *–ing* form phrase	*Reaffirming the principles of the treaty,*
h *–ed* participle phrase	*Convinced of his innocence,*
i infinitive phrase	*To achieve these objectives,*
j dependent clause (adverbial)	*Because it promotes peace,*
k verbless clause	*The case over [being over],*

Task 3 STOP and CHECK—front structures in sentences

Underline the sentence-initial elements using Table 6.2 and identify which structure is used in the space provided (**a**, **b**, **c**, etc from the table). The first one is done for you as an example:

h　0　*Supported on this point by the Council, the Commission contends that …*

–　1　*Right or wrong, the verdict was decided: 'Not guilty'.*

–　2　*To consider this issue, I must first turn to the principal authorities.*

–　3　*Because they failed to find enough incriminating evidence, the trial was adjourned.*

–　4　*On 24 March 2004, the Commission adopted Decision 2007/53/EC.*

–　5　*With reference to recital 783, the Commission submits that …*

–　6　*In Trafalgar Square, the protesters held a public meeting.*

6.6 STRUCTURES TO MODIFY THE SUBJECT: NOUN PHRASES

Nouns form patterns with other words to create *noun phrases*. Their main function is to add information to the main noun or subject. Different syntactic informational structures can be used to modify or identify a noun phrase.

Task 4 Read, scan, and observe—noun phrase that modifies the subject

The headword[21] of the noun phrase is in *italics* in the sentences below. Different syntactic structures may be used to modify the subject. These different forms are noted on the left. In the sentence examples on the right, scan and underline the word or words in the noun phrase *that modifies or modify the subject* (including the determiner *the*). Sentence (a) is an example.

Syntactic structures	Examples
adjective(s)	(a) <u>The twelve British</u> *jurors* heard of plans to target a shopping centre with a giant fertiliser bomb.
noun as adjective[22]	(b) The jury *summation* was long and complicated.
prepositional phrase	(c) The *jurors* in the year-long Old Bailey trial heard of plans to target a shopping centre with a giant fertiliser bomb.
–ing phrase	(d) The *juror* sitting in the front row heard of plans to target a shopping centre with a giant fertiliser bomb.
non-restrictive relative clause	(f) The *jurors*, who/that were chosen from a wide selection of British citizens, had heard of plans to target a shopping centre with a giant fertiliser bomb.[23]

6.7 STRUCTURES INSERTED AFTER THE SUBJECT

Additional words can be added after the subject of the sentence, giving extra information about the subject (something that the reader might be interested in, yet not essential to identifying the subject). This extra information is separated from the rest of the sentence by commas.

6.7.1 Noun Phrase (Appositive)

An appositive identifies the same person(s) or thing(s) but with different names or words. It has the same syntactic function since one can be easily substituted for

---

[21] The *headword* dictates subject/verb agreement and is one of the most important elements in complex noun phrases. The rest of the sentence outside the noun phrase derives its meaning from the headword. S Greenbaum and R Quirk (1990), *A Student's Grammar of the English Language*, Harlow: Longman.

[22] The transformation of a noun into an adjective is common in legal texts, eg, State action, litigation problems, land patent, jury nullification, etc.

[23] Text adapted from 'Five get life over UK bomb plot: Profiles of the Guilty', *BBC News* Website, 30 April 2007 see <http://news.bbc.co.uk/2/hi/uk_news/6195914.stm>.

the other without changing the meaning. Appositive noun phrases can be framed by commas, parentheses or a dash, such as:

The defendant, a colleague of mine, has been accused of murder.

A colleague of mine, the defendant, has been accused of murder.

The defendant (a colleague of mine) has been accused of murder.

A colleague of mine—the defendant—has been accused of murder.

6.7.2 Non-finite *–ed* Participle and Non-finite *–ing* Form

These non-finite verb forms lack explicit reference to person or time. We have no idea of the number person(s) or when the action happened. For example, the verbal construction does not have the *–s* form for the third person singular or any past form. Observe these two examples taken from the Preamble to a Convention. The *–ing* and *–ed* forms are inserted after the subject (*The General Assembly*), followed by a rather lengthy series of recitals and then the verb phrase (*solemnly proclaims*).

The General Assembly,

Recognizing that effective implementation of the Convention on the Elimination of All Forms of Discrimination against Women would contribute to the elimination of violence against women …

Concerned that violence against women is an obstacle to the achievement of equality, development and peace, as recognized in the Nairobi Forward-looking Strategies for the Advancement of Women, …

…

Solemnly proclaims the following Declaration on the Elimination of Violence against Women and urges that every effort be made so that it becomes generally known and respected: …[24]

…

According to Crystal and Davy,[25] legal language has a 'fondness'[26] for these non-finite forms, while Williams[27] provides a possible explanation for why present participles (such as *Recognizing, Affirming*, etc) are preferred: they 'enhance the idea of the law always speaking'.

---

[24] Declaration on the Elimination of Violence against Women (plenary meeting 20 December 1993) UNGA Res 48/04, recitals in Preamble.

[25] D Crystal and D Davy (1969), 'The Language of Legal Documents', *Investigating English Style*, Harlow: Longman, p 205.

[26] If you have a *fondness* for something, you usually like doing it.

[27] C Williams (2007), *Tradition and Change in Legal English: Verbal Constructions in Prescriptive Texts*, Bern: Peter Lang, p 163.

NOTE: It is characteristic of Preambles to rotate between using the non-finite *–ed* participles and the non-finite *–ing* forms. Scan the legal texts in this book. Can you find any other examples of these non-finite forms?

6.7.3 Dependent Clauses

Adjectival clauses (commonly called *relative clauses*) are introduced by relative pronouns (*who, whom, which, that*[28]) and follow the noun phrase. Relative clauses describe the noun phrase further by providing more information, e.g.:

Law students who graduate from universities in Germany cannot practise law in the USA.

The noun phrase *Law students* is followed by information given in the relative clause that imposes limitations or restrictions: *who graduate from universities in Germany.* Which students cannot practise law in the USA.? *Law students who graduate from universities in Germany.* This information is essential to our understanding of the sentence. This is called a restrictive clause. This is described further in 6.7.4 below.

6.7.4 Restrictive Clauses and Non-restrictive Clauses

The *restrictive* (also called *defining*) clause identifies a person or thing, e.g.:

My sister who lives in San Francisco is a lawyer.
(But I have more than one sister. The others do not live in San Francisco.)

The *non-restrictive* (also called a *non-defining*) clause contains words that add extra information but are not essential to identifying the subject, e.g.:

My brother, who lives in Boston, is a judge.
(I have one brother and I have added extra information about him.)

6.8 Expanding the Predicate: Adding a Verb

Another verb can also be added to expand the predicate.

> They shall furthermore be bound by the Convention in relation to the said Power, if the latter *accepts and applies* the provisions thereof.[29]

---

[28] The relative pronoun *who* describes people (used in the subject position); *whom* describes people (object position); *which* describes concepts and things (subject or object position); and *that* describes people, concepts and things (subject or object position).

[29] Convention relative to the Treatment of Prisoners of War, above n 19, Pt I, Art 2.

Prisoners of war shall be *released and repatriated* without delay after the cessation of active hostilities, …[30]

6.9 EXPANDING THE OBJECT

Noun phrases which are the object of the verb may also be expanded in various ways: by adding adjectives, appositives, descriptive phrases (with *–ing* or *–ed* forms) or adjective clauses. See Table 6.3 below.

Table 6.3: Structures: Noun phrases

Structure	Example
adjective(s)	The prosecutor cross-examined *the famous defendant.*
appositive noun phrase	The prosecutor cross-examined the defendant, *a well-known attorney.*
–ed participle	The prosecutor cross-examined the witness *dressed in a black suit.*[31]
–ing form	The prosecutor cross-examined the witness *taking the witness stand.*
relative clause	The prosecutor cross-examined the defendant *who had just taken the witness stand.*

6.10 STRUCTURES INSERTED AT THE END

To add more information at the end of a sentence, the structures are similar to those described earlier for inserting a word or words that modifies or modify the subject (see 6.6 above). Once again, the main function is to add more information about the sentence as a whole or, after a comma, more information about the subject. See Table 6.4 below.

Table 6.4: Structures inserted at end

Structure	Examples
point in time adverb	The defendant was acquitted of murder *yesterday.*
place adverb phrase	The defendant was found not guilty *at the Monterey Municipal Court.*
manner[32] adverb	The prosecuting lawyer responded to the verdict *unenthusiastically.*
cause/reason[33] non-finite *–ing* form	The jurors were thankful that the case was over, *hoping not be summoned again in the near future.*

(Continued)

---

[30] *Ibid*, Art 118.
[31] The function of the participle *–ed* (dressed) functions here as a substitute for the relative clause *that/who* was dressed.
[32] A 'manner' adverb describes the way something is done: 'How?'
[33] A 'cause/reason' adverb answers the question of 'why' something was done.

Structure	Examples
descriptive phrase	The wife of the defendant was silent, *visibly exhausted.*
cause/reason adverbial clause	The counsel for the defence was convinced that his client would be acquitted *because there had been insufficient evidence to convict.*
subjunctive	The judge ordered *that the defendant be released immediately.**

*NOTE: That clauses with an infinitive (without *to*) are often used in prescriptive legal texts for commands or strong suggestions. This structure is called the mandative subjunctive.

Examples of the mandative subjunctive: *The Commission ruled that the contended decision be upheld. The statute required that mens rea be established.*

KEY AND COMMENTARY

Key

Task 1 Read, scan and observe—the sentence

1. Overview of Chinese Legal System

The People's Republic of China (PRC)/ <u>was</u> established on October 1st, 1959. In a mere span of 53 years, the Chinese legal system/ <u>has</u> experienced tumultuous changes. It/<u>was</u> established, destroyed, re-established and gradually transformed along with the society's transition from a planned economy to a market economy.

Task 2 Noun phrase as subject of sentence (underlined)

1. <u>Everyone</u> has the right to freedom of expression.
2. <u>An Act of Congress or of a state legislature</u> begins with a title ('An Act to …'), which sets forth the subject of the statute, followed by an enacting clause ('Be it enacted by …'), and sometimes by a preamble or purpose clause stating the reason or policy behind the enactment.
3. <u>The ultimate arbiter</u> of constitutional disputes is, of course, the Supreme Court of the United States.

Task 3 STOP and CHECK—front structures in sentences

0	h
1	k
2	i
3	j
4	b
5	f
6	c

Task 4 Read, scan, and observe—noun phrase that modifies the subject

(a)   The twelve British *jurors*

(b)   The jury *summation* was long and complicated.

(c)   The *jurors* in the year-long Old Bailey trial

(d)   The *juror* sitting in the front row

(e)   The *jurors* who/that were chosen from a wide selection of British citizens

---

Commentary

Greenbaum[34] states that 'the most important part [from] the point of view of its presentation of a message in a sequence' is the first part of a clause or a sentence in English. Yet in a legal context, the rationale for placing words or clauses in a sentence-initial position (also called pre-positioning) can be critical in certain legal contexts. Bhatia[35] explains why pre-positioning is essential for legislation:

> The main motivation for the pre-positioning of the case description comes from the requirement that very few legislative statements are of universal application and it is obviously crucial for the writer to specify the kind of case description(s) to which the rule applies.

He goes on to explain how the legal subject is often delayed in order that qualification[36] insertions may be stated. Qualifications tend to restrict the legislative provisions to limited situations that are described in the subordinate clauses, which in legal texts are frequently adverbials.

Adverbial clauses that begin with expressions such as *whereas, herein contained, stated hereon, on the expiration of*, are quite common, as are adverbial clauses that state a condition and begin the sentence with *if* or *where*. For example:

Whereas the people of New South Wales, Victoria, ...

If any member of the Commission no longer fulfils the conditions required for the performance of his duties ...

Where, in pursuance of this Treaty, the Council acts on a proposal ...

---

[34] S Greenbaum, G Leech, R Quirk and J Svartvik (1972), *A Grammar of Contemporary English*, London: Longman, p 945.

[35] VK Bhatia (1983), *An Applied Discourse Analysis of English Legislative Writing*, Birmingham: University of Aston, p 110.

[36] Qualifications are the conditions that are required for something, in this case a provision.

Crystal and Davy[37] confirm this use of adverbials in both pre- and post-positions and explain why they are used:

> It is perhaps the frequency of these adverbial elements that is the most notable feature; but almost equal in importance is the variety of positions that they adopt. Legal draftsmen take full advantage of adverbial mobility; but always as a means of clarifying meaning and avoiding ambiguity ...

Adverbials will be discussed again in chapter twelve, as well as the frequent use of nominal expressions (noun phrases) which, in legal texts, are often placed in the post-modifying position. The main objective of this chapter was to familiarise you with the basic sentence structure so that you are able to recognise the different types of syntactic structure used to expand verbs and nouns in a sentence whose critical priority remains, as outlined in chapter six, exactness of reference and the quality of being all-inclusive.

Table 6.5: Connectives

Connectives Two closely related ideas in a sentence may be connected by transition words. The writer's decision to choose one transition over another is determined by what was written before and what they decide to say next. These are some common connectives used in legal texts:	
To introduce a contrast	*however, whereas*
To intensify a comment or agreement, showing strong conviction	*indeed*
To emphasise the most important point	*in fact*
To introduce a consequence or result	*consequently, accordingly*
Cause/Effect or Effect/Cause	*whereas, inasmuch as, so that, since, because*
To show unexpected result	*nevertheless*
To make a statement more emphatic	*above all*

---

[37] Crystal and Davy, above n 25, p 204.

CONSOLIDATION PART III – LANGUAGE FOCUS TASKS

TASK A – WHICH ONE WORD OR PHRASE IS OUT OF CONTEXT?

0	UN Charter	ECHR	TEU	UDHR
1	Human Rights Act 1998	Scotland Act 1998	European Convention on Human Rights	House of Lords Act 1999
2	United Nations	Court of Justice	International Court of Justice	Charter of the United Nations
3	relief	redress	remedy	breach
4	discharged	abolished	implemented	dissolved
5	violation	observance	infringement	breach
6	The Netherlands	Italy	France	Great Britain
7	Council of the European Union	Court of Justice	Court of Auditors	Council of Europe
8	International Court of Justice	French and English	Luxembourg	judicial organ

TASK B – MATCH THE TERMS WITH THE DEFINITIONS[1]

a fair trial	rule of law	enforce	qualified
authentic	absolute	derogation	infringe

---

[1] Task B references used to create definitions: BA Garner (1995), *A Dictionary of Modern Legal Usage*, 2nd edn, Oxford: Oxford University Press; *Black's Law Dictionary, Pocket Edition* (1996), BA Garner (ed), Eagan, Minn: West Publishing Co; *Oxford Dictionary of Law* (2009), J Law and E Martin (eds), 7th edn, Oxford: Oxford University Press.

1	....	to give legal effect to a law, a rule or obligation
2	....	to violate, to break a law or rule
3	....	rights that are not subject to any limitations
4	....	a just, impartial hearing in both criminal and civil proceedings
5	....	a fundamental principle or doctrine of governance in democratic societies that the law must be fair and just: everyone is equal before the law
6	....	rights that are subject to certain limitations in defined circumstances
7	....	restricting the authority or power of a law; the abrogation or repeal of a law
8	....	a text which is valid in a court of law for interpretation and application

TASK C – WORD FORMATION

a)   Fill in the spaces below […] with the appropriate word form.

Words that are not necessarily used in a legal context, or a variant no longer in use, have not been included in the table. The [x] in the table indicates that the form does not exist or that it is uncommon in a legal context. If necessary, read chapter 10 before doing this task or consult a dictionary.

	verb	**noun** (concept)	**noun** (person)	**adjective**
1	to derogate	derogation [*of/ in*] or derogation [*from*]	x	....
2	....	incorporation	x	incorporated
3	to accede	....	x	x
4	to deliberate	....	x	x
5	to draft	drafting / .... (2)	drafter/draftsman	x

6	to entrench	....	x	entrenched
7	....	validity/validation	x	valid/validated
8	to persuade	x	x	....

b)   Using the table above, insert the appropriate word in the spaces below: verb, noun (concept), noun (person) or adjective:

9   The United Kingdom was one of the original signatories to the ECHR but the UK Parliament did not immediately enact legislation to .... the Convention into British law.

10   We say that rights, constitutions or laws are .... when special procedures must be used to alter them.

11   A treaty of .... is a type of a agreement by which a State can become party to a pre-existing treaty.

12   Judgments of the European Court of Justice are issued in all official EU languages, but during ...., where interpreters are not present, the judges traditionally speak French.

13   In situations in which *stare decisis* does not apply, the precedents of other common law courts remain .... as authority.

14   Article 15 of the ECHR provides for .... in times of emergency.

TASK D – PREFIXES AND SUFFIXES

Fill in the missing suffixes or prefixes to the following terms. Identify the appropriate word form.

The [x] indicates that the form does not exist or that it is uncommon in a legal context.

	Prefixes	*adjective*	*noun concept*
1	effective		x
2	validity	x	
	Suffixes		
3	discriminate	x	
4	account		
5	interfere	x	
6	prohibit	(2)	(1)
7	controversy		controversy

TASK E – COLLOCATION

Match the words 1–10 with the appropriate words a–j, and write the matching identifiers in the first column of the table. Think about the meaning of each term or phrase.

...1d...	1	declaration	a	powers
......	2	persuasive	b	by law
......	3	to act	c	a right
......	4	remedial	d	of incompatibility
......	5	discretionary	e	protection
......	6	prescribed	f	authentic
......	7	to invoke	g	precedent
......	8	entitled to	h	in accordance with
......	9	equally	i	certified
......	10	duly	j	order

TASK F – COMPREHENSION: TRUE (T) OR FALSE (F)?

1	The Council of Europe	–	was established to prevent future war and to maintain international peace and security.
2		–	has 47 Member States.
3		–	has two official languages: English and French.
4		–	is another name for the Council of the European Union.
5	The ECHR	–	is a legally binding instrument.
6		–	comes into force only after it has been ratified and deposited with the Secretary General of the Council of Europe by all the signatories to the convention.
7		–	was inspired by the Universal Declaration of Human Rights of 1948.
8	Citizenship of the Union	–	An EU citizen can stand as a candidate in elections to the European Parliament in a Member State even if he/she no longer resides in his/her State of national citizenship.

9		–	When travelling in a country outside the EU, an EU citizen is entitled to protection from the consular authorities of any other country if his/her consulate is not represented.
10		–	EU citizens can choose where to live and work in the Union.
11	The Universal Declaration of Human Rights	–	is a legally binding document.
12		–	is an aspiration as opposed to a legal requirement.
13		–	set up standards and principles for interpretation of human rights.

Part IV

Concepts and Language of Criminal Law

Chapter 7

LANGUAGE AND LAW

Common Law Perspectives of Crime and Punishment

Introduction to criminal law and terminology – Criminal prosecution – Crown Prosecution Service – Nelson Mandela's long walk to freedom – Criminal trial and conviction – Adversarial trial – Actus reus and mens rea – Homicide: murder and manslaughter – Defences – Crime and punishment

Someone must have been spreading lies about Josef K for without having done anything wrong he was arrested one morning. …

'No,' said the man by the window, throwing the book on to a small table and rising to his feet. 'You are not permitted to leave. You've been arrested.'

'So it seems,' K said. 'But why?' he asked.

'We are not authorized to tell you. Go to your room and wait. Proceedings have been started and you will be told everything in due course. I'm even exceeding my instructions by talking to you so freely.' …

Who on earth were these men? What were they talking about? Of which authorities were they the representatives? After all, K lived in a legally constituted state, there was peace in the land, the rule of law was fully established. Who dared seize him in his own flat? …

'How on earth can I be under arrest? And especially like this?'

'Now you're at it again,' said the warder, dipping his slice of bread and butter into the honey-pot. 'We don't answer questions like that.'

'You'll have to answer them,' K told him. 'Here are my identity papers. Now show me yours, and first of all show me the warrant for my arrest.'

'Good God!' said the warder. 'Why can't you accept what's happened instead of trying to provoke us pointlessly? Especially as we are now probably the closest friends you've got in the world!'

From *The Trial* by Franz Kafka (1883–1924)

7.1 Introduction to Criminal Law

7.1.1 Introduction

The criminal law is a major form of social control; it differs from one society to another and, at least in part, changes over time. More than other branches of the law, criminal law depends on the views of the community, as interpreted by the legislature.[1]

Can you think of types of conduct that were *illegal* in the past but are *legal* today in your country? Or have certain types of conduct become illegal in modern times that were legal in the past, like fox-hunting in England (see 3.4.2)? What possible *reforms* to the criminal law are currently the subject of debate in your country or other parts of the world, and why?

Important functions of the criminal law are to prevent crime and deter criminal behaviour (*prevention and deterrence*), to maintain order and protect the public (*law and order, protection*), to punish and to reform offenders (*retribution and rehabilitation*). In the criminal process, the State prosecutes, convicts and punishes people for behaviour which is *against the law*. Criminal *conviction* not only carries a *sentence* that imposes a punishment, such as *imprisonment* or a *fine*, but also carries civil and social consequences, such as disqualification from public office, moral blame and social stigma, having a profound effect on individual offenders and their families and communities.

Franz Kafka's disturbing novel, *The Trial*, highlights the vital personal interests at stake for a person accused of committing a crime, and the vulnerability of the individual to abuse by the authorities. Even the *rule of law*, comprising the principle of *supremacy of law*—according to which, officials can only exercise powers on a legitimate basis—can only guarantee respect for human rights if the notion includes not only *equality before the law*, but also *substantive* and *procedural* rules based on principles of justice and fairness. Some of the rights denied to K in *The Trial* are the right to liberty and security of person, the right to a fair trial, including the *presumption of innocence*, and ultimately, the right to life.[2] Eventually, although he has not 'done anything wrong', even he himself believes he is *guilty*.

Investigating crime and gathering evidence, bringing charges against the accused, prosecuting and proving guilt are all steps in the criminal process, followed by conviction, sentencing and punishment. What are the roles of the police and judiciary, and what other bodies are involved? States find different solutions to these questions and in Section One of this chapter, the English system is introduced; we also read a first-hand account by Nelson Mandela of one prosecution against him and other ANC leaders during his *long walk to*

---

[1] D Walker (1980), *The Oxford Companion to Law*, Oxford: Clarendon Press, pp 316–17.
[2] Protected respectively in Arts 5, 6 and 2 of the European Convention on Human Rights.

freedom, raising the question whether a black man can get a *fair trial* in a white man's court (at 7.2). In 7.3 we focus on criminal trial and conviction; the Anglo-American adversarial trial is introduced and we consider the roles played by the judge and jury, but also by the parties and witnesses during the all-important *day in court*.

Section Two begins by exploring the use of Latin maxims in legal English, leading us to the key elements of a crime: *actus reus* and *mens rea* (7.4). The Advanced part of the chapter (7.5 and 7.6) continues with key terms and concepts of *homicide* and *defences*, illustrated by case studies. English and American law, while sharing the same basic principles and method of trial centred around the jury system, have developed different 'degrees' of homicide, with different punishments imposed by law; the *death penalty* is an issue on which Europe and America now stand divided. Where does a person's right to use force in *self-defence* end? At what point can a victim of crime become punishable as an *offender*? We review some cases that shocked public opinion in Britain, and examine a proposal for reform of English law showing the difficult balance a system of criminal justice must reach between the rights of *law-abiding citizens* and the rights of individuals who break the law.

7.1.2 Terminology Focus—The Terminology of Criminal and Civil Law

Distinct terminology is used in criminal law and civil law. Task 1 aims to build your awareness and vocabulary in these two major fields of the law.

Task 1 The terminology of criminal and civil law

The extracts below are taken from a variety of documents and concern either criminal or civil law matters in the English legal system. Examine each extract and decide whether it refers to criminal or civil law. Attention: one extract contains elements of both!

Underline vocabulary specific to each field and focus on both meaning and form. Use a dictionary to supplement your own observations and note any useful information: a good definition, a translation, a grammar pattern or collocation.

As you study chapters seven and nine, observe the use of these terms in different contexts, and select examples and definitions to expand your personal terminology system in the fields of criminal and civil law.

Examples in context	*Language of ...*
1. The role of the <u>Crown Prosecution Service</u> is <u>to prosecute</u> cases firmly, fairly and effectively when there is sufficient evidence to provide a realistic prospect of <u>conviction</u>.	*criminal law*
2. Every <u>claim form</u> must contain a concise statement of the nature of <u>the claim</u> (CPR, r 16.2(1)(a). ... [T]his will be a simple statement, such as: <u>The claimant's claim</u> is for <u>damages for personal injuries</u> and interest arising out of a collision caused by <u>the defendant's negligence</u> when driving a motor car along Oxford Street, London W1 on 1 July 2005.	*civil law*
3. A person convicted of an offence on indictment may appeal to the Court of Appeal against his conviction.	
4. In January 1996, the CPS decided that there was insufficient evidence to prosecute a man who had surprised a burglar in his kitchen. There had been a struggle and the burglar later died of his injuries.	
5. On at least 3 occasions per week since 1 March 2006, the defendants have unlawfully entered into the claimant's garden and remained there for periods of up to 2 hours, using the same for football practice. Despite being orally requested to leave the garden by the claimant on several occasions, the defendants have refused to do so, and the claimant fears that unless an injunction is granted restraining such acts of trespass, they will be frequently repeated.	
6. There are 43 police forces across England and Wales responsible for the investigation of crime, collection of evidence and the arrest or detention of suspected offenders.	
7. The claimants in this case seek damages against the defendant firm for alleged negligence in the course of giving advice. The claim is made both for breach of contract and for breach of a common law duty of care.	
8. The defendant was found guilty of conspiring to cause explosions likely to endanger life.	
9. Last week, the Metropolitan Police's mystery tour cost the force £80,000 and an apology. The Met paid the damages to 23 anti-monarchists who were arrested while having lunch in a pub on the Queen's golden jubilee. The 23 protesters each received £3,500 as the Met settled their lawsuit out of court. [adapted]	
10. In 1996 a farmer who shot a thief stealing from his car was acquitted on charges of causing grievous bodily harm. He told the court that he never intended to shoot the thief.	

Sources

1. and 6.	Official website of the Crown Prosecution Service: <http://www.cps.gov.uk>.
2.	*Blackstone's Civil Practice 2006*, Chapter 23 Claim Form (from Brief details of claim, 23.4, pp 284–85).
3.	Criminal Appeal Act 1968, section 1(1).
4. and 10.	House of Commons Research Paper: Criminal Law (Amendment) (Householder Protection) Bill, Bill 20 of 2004–05, B Illustrations, case d. Hugh Williamson (4.) and case l. Kenneth Hall (10.)
5.	*Blackstone's Civil Practice 2006*, Chapter 24 Particulars of Claim (from example 24.2, p 300).
6.	See 1. above.
7.	From the judgment of Richards J in *Wade & Another v Poppleton & Appleby* [2003] EWHC 3159 (Ch).
8.	BBC News, 'Five get life over UK bomb plot' of 30 April 2007: <http://www.news.bbc.co.uk>.
9.	*Guardian Weekly Newspaper*, article of 12–18 February 2004: 'Met pays out £80,000 after jubilee mystery bus tour'.
10.	See 4. above.

Key and Comment

Texts 1, 3, 4, 6, 8 and 10 relate to criminal law. Texts 2, 5 and 7 relate to civil law. The text relating to both civil and criminal aspects is number 9. The anti-monarchy protesters were *arrested* by Metropolitan Police on the day of the Queen's Golden Jubilee celebrations. They were taken to different police stations on London buses (hence the reference in the title of the newspaper article to the 'jubilee mystery bus tour'), but the police had no evidence to justify their arrest; in fact, at the time, the protesters were peacefully having lunch and a pint of beer in a pub, having exercised their right to *freedom of expression*. In civil proceedings, the 23 protesters later claimed damages, pre-sumably for the tort of *false imprisonment*.[3] The parties '*settled their lawsuit out of court*'.[4] The words *settle*, *lawsuit* and *damages* indicate civil action.

See below, for further indications and definitions.

---

[3] False imprisonment is a form of *trespass to the person* (discussed in 9.2.4), which is both a crime and a tort.

[4] *To settle* a lawsuit means to reach an agreement that brings an end to a legal dispute; related noun *settlement*.

Follow-up to Task 1: Terminology focus
The terms from Task 1 above belonging specifically to either criminal or civil proceedings, are reproduced in the box below with simple definitions.

Consult the box and examine the examples in Task 1 again, observing the use of these terms in context.

Consider: collocations (eg 3. *convict* – a person convicted of an offence); and structural and lexical patterns used with these words (eg 10. *acquit* – a farmer was acquitted on charges of causing grievous bodily harm). Select some terms to add to your personal terminology system.

CIVIL LAW TERMS	CRIMINAL LAW TERMS
Example 2. *Claim* – a request to a civil court *Claimant* – (also, *plaintiff*) the party who takes civil proceedings against the *defendant* *Claim form* – the document that institutes civil proceedings	**Example 3.** *Offence* – a crime *Indictment* – a formal accusation of a crime *Conviction* – determination of guilt by the court *To convict* – to find guilty of a crime
Example 5. *Claimant, defendant* – the two parties in a civil action *Trespass* – a category of civil wrong, a *tort* *To grant an injunction* – a civil remedy, a court order to do or not to do specified acts	**Example 4.** *The CPS – Crown Prosecution Service*, examined below (7.2) *To prosecute* – to take criminal proceedings against
Example 7. *Claimants, claim* – as above *To seek damages* – in civil proceedings, to request money compensation from the defendant *Negligence* – the principal category of *civil wrong*, a *tort* *Breach of contract* – where a party breaks its contractual obligations *Breach of a duty of care* – typical of actions in civil law, which imposes *a duty* not to injure others	**Example 6.** (almost all the vocabulary of the example indicates criminal law) *Police forces, investigation of crime* *Collection of evidence* – clearly by a public body in this context *Arrest or detention of suspected offenders – offenders* are persons who have commited an *offence*, ie criminals
Example 9. *To settle a lawsuit* – to reach an agreement between the parties bringing an end to civil litigation (*out of court* – the settlement is reached independently of the court, privately) *To pay damages* – a defendant who loses a civil case may be ordered to compensate the claimant with the money remedy of *damages*	**Example 8.** *The defendant was found guilty* – clearly a criminal defendant, indicated by *guilty* (although this is sometimes used in fact in civil cases, e.g. *guilty of negligence*) and the nature of the crime following. *Conspiring* to cause explosions – *To conspire*, noun *conspiracy*, when individuals plan to commit a crime together

(Continued)

CIVIL LAW TERMS	CRIMINAL LAW TERMS
NB Many law terms in the examples are found in both criminal and civil contexts, e.g.: appeal, evidence, court; but the specific reference may be different, according to the legal context, e.g.: Court of Appeal – Criminal or Civil Division? Also, a criminal or civil defendant?	**Example 10.** *To acquit* – to find a defendant not guilty *Grievous bodily harm* – serious physical injury, a constituent of certain violent crimes *Charges* – accusations of a crimes

SECTION ONE

7.2 CRIMINAL PROSECUTION

Prosecution or *prosecuting* means *taking criminal action* (also called *criminal proceedings*) against a person accused of committing a crime: the *defendant* or the *accused*.

In a criminal case, the person who conducts the prosecution is the *prosecutor* or *public prosecutor*; he or she is often referred to directly as *the prosecution*. The defendant, as represented by his or her *defence lawyer*, may be referred to in the context of a criminal proceeding as *the defence* (US *defense*).

The lawyers *acting for* the prosecution and the defence are generally referred to in the context of the trial as *counsel for the prosecution* or *counsel for the defence*, or simply *counsel*.

Prosecutions in the English legal system are generally in the name of *the Crown*, as the monarch personifies and represents the State.[5]

Cases are *cited* (referred to) by name, or name + full *citation* in the law reports, as used in this book; case names are written in *italics*.

We write: *R v Straw* (*R* = *Regina* or *Rex*, Latin for Queen or King, *v* = *versus*); we say: 'the Crown against Straw'. In academic literature, just '*Straw*' may be used. Cf in the US: *People v Straw*, reflecting the role of the American people in the US Constitution.[6] At state level: *State [e.g. California] v McDonough*.

Cf in civil cases, we write *Smith v Jones*; we say 'Smith and Jones' or 'Smith against Jones'.

7.2.1 The Crown Prosecution Service

In England and Wales, the *Crown Prosecution Service* (CPS) is the independent, public body that is responsible for prosecuting criminal cases investigated by the police. The CPS was introduced by statute in 1985[7] to separate the roles of *investigation of crime*—the task of the police—and its prosecution in criminal action.

The CPS *reviews* cases submitted by the police, and decides the *charges* (the specific criminal accusations), except in minor cases, where charges will be decided by the police. The CPS also prepares cases for court and *pursues* court proceedings (it *prosecutes*).

The *Code for Crown Prosecutors*, examined in Task 2 below, is 'a key document for the CPS', which provides guidance to prosecutors on the *general principles* they should apply when making decisions about prosecutions.[8] It is issued by the

---

[5] For discussion on the constitutional monarchy, see 3.2 above; occasionally, private prosecutions may be brought, as in the prosecution of the hunters examined in 3.4.2.

[6] Introduced in 1.3, Text 7 (text and comment).

[7] Prosecution of Offences Act 1985.

[8] From the official CPS website: <http://www.cps.gov.uk>.

Director of Public Prosecutions (DPP), head of the CPS, while the *Attorney-General* (AG), the principal law officer of the Crown, is responsible to Parliament for the Service.

In deciding whether to prosecute, Crown Prosecutors must evaluate two critical questions:

— Is there enough evidence against the suspect? *and*
— Is it in the public interest for the CPS to bring the case to court?

Task 2 Consulting a public document: the Code for Crown Prosecutors
Examine extracts from the Code below to learn about the work of the CPS. Focus on both meaning and language as you complete this task:

1. Identify and distinguish between the different people mentioned in sections 1.4 and 2.2 of the Code.
2. Select three important duties that prosecutors have under section 2.2 and 2.4 of the Code.
3. Consider the obligation on prosecutors in 2.6. To refresh your memory, you may refer to our work on the Human Rights Act 1998 in 5.4.4.
4. What is 'the evidential stage' and what must prosecutors do?
5. How are prosecutors to approach *'the public interest stage'*?

The Code for Crown Prosecutors[9]

Introduction

1.4   In this Code, the term 'suspect' is used to describe a person who is not yet the subject of formal criminal proceedings; the term 'defendant' is used to describe a person who has been charged or summonsed; and the term 'offender' is used to describe a person who has admitted his or her guilt to a police officer or other investigator or prosecutor, or who has been found guilty in a court of law.

General Principles

2.2   It is the duty of prosecutors to make sure that the right person is prosecuted for the right offence and to bring offenders to justice wherever possible. Casework decisions taken fairly, impartially and with integrity help to secure justice for victims, witnesses, defendants and the public. Prosecutors must ensure that the law is properly applied; that relevant evidence is put before the court; and that obligations of disclosure are complied with.

---

[9] Extracts from the Code for Crown Prosecutors, 7th edn, January 2013, available electronically on the website <http://www.cps.gov.uk>.

2.4   Prosecutors must be fair, independent and objective. They must not let any personal views about the ethnic or national origin, gender, disability, age, religion or belief, political views, sexual orientation, or gender identity of the suspect, victim or any witness influence their decisions. Neither must prosecutors be affected by improper or undue pressure from any source. Prosecutors must always act in the interests of justice and not solely for the purpose of obtaining a conviction.

2.6   Prosecutors must apply the principles of the European Convention on Human Rights, in accordance with the Human Rights Act 1998, at each stage of a case. ...

...

The Evidential Stage

4.4   Prosecutors must be satisfied that there is sufficient evidence to provide a realistic prospect of conviction against each suspect on each charge. They must consider what the defence case may be, and how it is likely to affect the prospects of conviction. A case which does not pass the evidential stage must not proceed, no matter how serious or sensitive it may be.

...

4.6   When deciding whether there is sufficient evidence to prosecute, prosecutors should ask themselves the following:
Can the evidence be used in court?

...

Is the evidence reliable?

...

Is the evidence credible?

...

The Public Interest Stage

4.7   In every case where there is sufficient evidence to justify a prosecution, prosecutors must go on to consider whether a prosecution is required in the public interest.

4.8   It has never been the rule that a prosecution will automatically take place once the evidential stage is met. A prosecution will usually take place unless the prosecutor is satisfied that there are public interest factors tending against prosecution which outweigh those tending in favour. In some cases the prosecutor may be satisfied that the public interest can be properly served by offering the offender the opportunity to have the matter dealt with by an out-of-court disposal rather than bringing a prosecution.

4.9   When deciding the public interest, prosecutors should consider each of the questions set out below in paragraphs 4.12 a) to g) so as to determine the relevant public interest factors tending for and against prosecution. ...

...

4.12   Prosecutors should consider each of the following questions:

a)   How serious is the offence committed? The more serious the offence, the more likely it is that a prosecution is required.

...

Key and commentary to Task 2 Consulting a public document: the Code for Crown Prosecutors

1.   The Code mentions many different figures involved in various ways in a criminal case. In section 1.4: the *suspect*, who may become the *defendant*, and if found guilty becomes the *offender*; a *police officer* (or other *investigator*), a *prosecutor*. A person who has been '*summonsed*' has received a *summons*: that is, a court order to appear at a magistrates' court at a particular time and place. In addition, section 2.2 mentions *victims* of crime, *witnesses* and *the public*.

2.   Many duties of prosecutors are set out in sections 2.2 and 2.4. Three very important ones are: the duty '*to bring offenders to justice*' (prosecuting 'the right person' for 'the right offence'); the duty '*to ensure that the law is properly applied*'; the duty always to '*act in the interests of justice*'—the aim of the prosecutor cannot be merely to obtain a conviction. Your selection may be different, e.g. prosecutors must operate without discrimination.

3.   As a public authority, the CPS is under a duty *to act compatibly with the Convention rights of a suspect/defendant*, as provided by section 6 of the Human Rights Act 1998 (examined in 5.4.4 above). If prosecutors fail to respect such rights (for example, the right to liberty and security in Article 5 ECHR; the right to a fair trial in Article 6 ECHR), this will be *unlawful* under section 6 of the 1998 Act and a victim of such a violation will have the right to a *judicial remedy*, as provided by sections 7 and 8 of the Act.

4. The *evidential stage* is the first of two stages in the decision to prosecute. Even if the case is very serious or sensitive, prosecutors should prosecute only if there is '*sufficient evidence to provide a realistic prospect of conviction*', a test they must apply to each suspect (if more than one) and in relation to each charge (where a person is suspected of more than one offence) (section 4.4). The Code gives further explanation of what this means in section 4.5 (text not reproduced above): there is *a realistic prospect of conviction* where 'an *objective, impartial and reasonable jury* or *bench of magistrates* or *judge hearing a case alone ... is more likely than not to convict the defendant* of the charge alleged'. The questions in section 4.6 are to help prosecutors reach this decision by assessing the *evidence*, which must be *admissible* in court, '*reliable*' and '*credible*'.

5. Prosecutors must consider the *public interest stage* only if the evidential test has been satisfied (section 4.7). Even then, prosecution is not automatic: the prosecutor must *balance*, or weigh, the *public interest factors* tending in favour of prosecution with those tending against prosecution (section 4.8). A list of questions is provided (sections 4.9, 4.12) to enable prosecutors to identify the relevant public interest factors they need to take into consideration, e.g. section 4.12, para a), the seriousness of the offence. These two stages together (evidential and public interest) are known as the *Full Code Test*.

Comment

Before the introduction of the CPS, the police were responsible for both the investigation and prosecution of crime in England and Wales, while in the modern system the CPS operates independently of the police, although they work in close cooperation. Prosecutors cannot direct the police or other investigators.[10] On the other hand, it is the CPS that has final responsibility for the decision whether or not to prosecute in a case.[11] *The judiciary* are not involved in the investigation of crime or in the decision to prosecute; once a case goes to trial, the judge enters the scene as an impartial arbiter in the adversarial system, while the case is prepared and presented by the respective parties, generally represented by their lawyers, who present argument and produce evidence with the aim of convincing the court in the oral proceedings. The adversarial system, operating in both criminal and civil proceedings, is examined in 7.3.1 below.

Compare and Discuss

— *Who is responsible for investigating and prosecuting crime in your country?*
— *What are the roles of the police, the judiciary and other State bodies involved in the criminal justice system?*

---

[10] Code for Crown Prosecutors, s 3.2.
[11] Code for Crown Prosecutors, s 3.6.

— *Are prosecutors under an obligation to prosecute when they have notice of a crime? Or do they exercise discretion according to rules, like the CPS?*
— *Compare and discuss the organisation of criminal prosecution in England and Wales, and in your country, evaluating the merits of each system.*

7.2.2 Nelson Mandela's Long Walk to Freedom

A statesman of world standing, former South African President Nelson Mandela has been described as 'one of the most courageous and best-loved men of all time'.[12] On 11 February 1990, after spending 27 years in prison for his political opinions and leadership in the fight against apartheid, Mandela was released at the age of 71 by President De Klerk. The two men were jointly awarded the Nobel Peace Prize in 1993, 'for their work for the peaceful termination of the apartheid regime, and for laying the foundations for a new democratic South Africa'.[13] After democratic elections, a new Constitution was established and Mandela became the first President.

Nelson Mandela began writing his autobiography *Long Walk to Freedom*[14] clandestinely in jail in 1974, resuming work on it after his release. Near the end of this long, inspiring story he describes what it felt like to vote for the very first time and to live in a free country:

> I voted on 27 April [1994] ... I chose to vote in Natal to show the people in that divided province that there was no danger in going to the polling stations. ... The images of South Africans going to the polls that day are burned in my memory. Great lines of patient people snaking through the dirt roads and streets of towns and cities; old women who had waited half a century to cast their first votes saying that they felt like human beings for the first time in their lives; white men and women saying they were proud to live in a free country at last.[15]

In Task 3 below, we read extracts relating to events of more than 30 years earlier: the Treason Trial. In a long, complex criminal proceeding, Nelson Mandela and other African National Congress (ANC) leaders were prosecuted: *treason* is the most serious crime of betraying one's country by attempting through actions to *overthrow the government*. On 29 March 1961, the day of the court's verdict had arrived.

---

[12] By British Prime Minister Gordon Brown on the occasion of the unveiling of a statue of Mandela opposite the Houses of Parliament in London, September 2007.

[13] 'The Nobel Peace Prize 1993—Presentation Speech', Nobelprize.org. Nobel Media AB 2013. Web. 23 Feb 2014, <http://www.nobelprize.org/nobel_prizes/peace/laureates/1993/presentation-speech.html>

[14] Published in 1994 by Little, Brown and Company, London. This extract: N Mandela (1994), *Long Walk to Freedom*, 1995 Abacus edn, London: Little, Brown and Company, pp 307–09.

[15] *Ibid*, pp 742–43.

Task 3 Reading comprehension: *Long Walk to Freedom*
Read the extract below for general understanding:

1. What was the court's verdict in the Treason Trial?
2. How does Mandela explain the verdict reached by the court?

Read the text in detail to understand the most important points. Focus on both language and meaning.

3. List the court's *findings of fact* (determinations) about the ANC.
4. What was the prosecution case against ANC leaders?
5. Specify some elements of *a fair trial* or *a fair hearing*. Could a black man get *a fair trial* in a white man's court?
6. Describe how Mandela's attitude towards the law changed during his career as a young lawyer.
7. Was South Africa a country where *the rule of law* was established?

'Silence in court!' the orderly yelled, and Judge Rumpff announced that the three-judge panel had reached a verdict. Silence now reigned. In his deep, even voice, Judge Rumpff reviewed the court's conclusions. Yes, the African National Congress had been working to replace the government with 'a radically and fundamentally different form of state'; yes, the African National Congress had used illegal means of protest during the Defiance Campaign; yes, certain ANC leaders had made speeches advocating violence; and yes, there was a strong left-wing tendency in the ANC that was revealed in its anti-imperialist, anti-West, pro-Soviet attitudes, but:

> On all the evidence presented to this court and on our finding of fact it is impossible for this court to come to the conclusion that the African National Congress had acquired or adopted a policy to overthrow the state by violence, that is, in the sense that the masses had to be prepared or conditioned to commit direct acts of violence against the state.

The court said the prosecution had failed to prove that the ANC was a communist organization or that the Freedom Charter envisioned a communist state. After speaking for forty minutes, Justice Rumpff said, 'The accused are accordingly found not guilty and are discharged.' ...

I did not regard the verdict as a vindication of the legal system or evidence that a black man could get a fair trial in a white man's court. It was the right verdict and a just one, but it was largely as a result of a superior defence team and the fair-mindedness of these particular judges.

The court system, however, was perhaps the only place in South Africa where an African could possibly receive a fair hearing and where the rule of law might still apply. This was particularly true in courts presided over by enlightened judges who had been appointed by the United Party. Many of these men still stood by the rule of law.

As a student, I had been taught that South Africa was a place where the rule of law was paramount and applied to all persons, regardless of their social status or official position. I sincerely believed this and planned my life based on that assumption. But my career as a lawyer removed the scales from my eyes. I saw that there was a wide difference between what I had been taught in the lecture room and what I learned in the courtroom. I went from having an idealistic view of the law as a sword of justice to a perception of the law as a tool used by the ruling class to shape society in a way favourable to itself. I never expected justice in court, however much I fought for it, and though I sometimes received it.

Extract from *Long Walk to Freedom* by Nelson Mandela,
published by Little Brown Book Group.
© 1994 Nelson Rolihlahla Mandela

Key and commentary to Task 3 Reading comprehension: *Long Walk to Freedom*

1. Mandela and the other defendants in the Treason Trial were '*found not guilty*' of the crimes accused and were '*discharged*' (released).
2. Mandela explains the verdict by giving credit to 'a superior *defence team*' and the fact that—at this stage in the apartheid regime—certain judges were still independent (having been '*appointed*' by a different *political party*) and supported ('stood by') *the rule of law*.
3. The *findings of fact* are listed in the first paragraph and in the passage quoted directly from *the court's judgment*: the ANC had been working to radically change the '*form of state*' in South Africa; it had used '*illegal means of protest*' during the Defiance Campaign; ANC leaders had supported violence in their speeches; politically, it was strongly '*left-wing*'; but it had not 'acquired or *adopted a policy to overthrow the state by violence*' in the sense specified (see below).
4. The *prosecution case* was that the ANC was a *communist organization*; that its *charter*, the Freedom Charter, aspired to a communist form of State; that the *policy* of the ANC was to overthrow the State by violence, by conditioning the masses *to commit direct acts of violence against the State*.
5. The *right to a fair trial* includes: the right to a public hearing by an *independent and impartial tribunal established by law*; the right to a *defence*, with adequate time and facilities for its preparation; the right to *call and examine witnesses*; the presumption of innocence.[16] Although this particular court gave a verdict that was '*right*' and '*just*' (for the reasons given in 2. above) Mandela makes it clear that the *system* as such did not guarantee *a fair hearing* for an African: it was *a white man's court*.

---

[16] Refer to Article 6 ECHR—'Right to a fair trial'—for further details of this principle in European human rights law.

6. As *a law student* at university, Mandela believed in the law as '*a sword of justice*'—his view was abstract and idealistic. But in the courtroom during his '*career as a lawyer*', he became cynical, realising that the '*ruling class*' (Government) used the law as a tool for its own political purposes.
7. According to *the rule of law* officials must exercise their powers on a legitimate basis: while it is true that the South African Government had enacted laws that were enforced by public officials such as the police and courts, the laws themselves were racist, discriminatory and repressive. Without *equality before the law*, and *substantive* and *procedural* rules based on principles of justice and fairness, the rule of law cannot be respected. Therefore, the answer is *no*: South Africa was not a country where the rule of law was established.

Comment

After the verdict in the Treason Trial, Mandela was released and went into hiding, living a *clandestine* life apart from his family. Because of the State's *repressive laws*, he and other ANC leaders had decided ultimately that their historic strategy of *non-violent opposition* to apartheid had failed. *Armed rebellion* was the only way for Africans in South Africa to demand their *human rights and civil liberties.* Mandela—a qualified lawyer—now found himself travelling under cover to other African countries to receive instruction in military training; on his return, he took part in *sabotage* operations.

After his recapture, a new trial commenced on 15 October 1962. Mandela entered court on the first day of the trial wearing traditional African dress—a Xhosa leopard-skin *kaross*—to 'emphasize the symbolism that I was a black African walking into a white man's court'.[17]

The prosecution called more than a hundred witnesses to prove that Mandela was *guilty of the charges against him*: he was accused of leaving the country *illegally* and *inciting* African workers *to strike* during a three-day stay-at-home protest in May 1961; Mandela knew that he was *technically guilty of both charges*.[18] He chose to *conduct his own defence*, because—as he explained to the court—'this case is a trial of the aspirations of the African people'; his intention was 'to put the state on trial':[19]

I then made application for the recusal[20] of the magistrate on the grounds that I did not consider myself morally bound to obey laws made by a Parliament in which I had no representation. Nor was it possible to receive a fair trial from a white judge:

'Why is it that in this courtroom I am facing a white magistrate, confronted by a white prosecutor, escorted by white orderlies? Can anybody seriously suggest that in this type of atmosphere the scales of justice are evenly balanced? ... [T]he

---

17 Mandela, above n 14, pp 384–85.
18 *Ibid*, pp 386–87.
19 *Ibid*.
20 Removal of the judge because of a suspicion that he is not impartial.

real purpose of this rigid colour bar is to ensure that the justice dispensed by the courts should conform to the policy of the country, however much that policy might be in conflict with the norms of justice accepted in judiciaries throughout the civilized world ... Your Worship, I hate racial discrimination most intensely and in all its manifestations. I have fought it all my life. I fight it now, and I will do so until the end of my days.'[21]

Consider and discuss the wider implications of what you have read.

7.3 CRIMINAL TRIAL AND CONVICTION

7.3.1 The Adversarial Trial

A typical feature of common law countries is the *adversarial system* of trial, in both criminal and civil cases. It contrasts with the *inquisitorial system*, typical in civil law countries.

What roles are played in each system by the lawyers, the judge and the parties? Michael Zander points out the distinctions, below. As you read, notice the language the author uses to indicate contrasts between two differing aspects.

> The common law method of trial is often described as 'adversary' or 'accusatorial'—as distinct from the continental 'inquisitorial' method. The essence of the distinction is that, whereas in the inquisitorial system the dominant role is played by the court, in the adversary system it is played by the parties. In the adversary system, the judge is supposed to remain a passive and mainly silent umpire, listening to the evidence produced by the two parties. The parties decide what witnesses to call and in what order, the parties examine and cross-examine the witnesses and, if both sides decide not to call a witness who has potentially relevant evidence, there is nothing the court will do about it. ...
>
> By contrast, in the inquisitorial system the judge calls the witnesses and examines them, while the parties or their lawyers play a supporting or subsidiary role.[22]

The adverbial phrases 'as distinct from' and 'by contrast', and the conjunctions 'whereas' and 'while' are all useful linguistic indicators of a contrast between two differing aspects.

We can see that in the adversarial system the *parties*—prosecution and defence in a criminal trial, claimant/plaintiff and defendant in a civil trial—conduct the proceedings proactively, while the judge is a passive arbiter, unlike the 'continental'[23] method where the judge (or 'court') plays the dominant role, calling and examining witnesses. The *witnesses* play a fundamental part in adversarial trials, since the dispute is resolved through the oral proceedings: *hearings* are held in court

---

[21] *Ibid*, p 386.
[22] M Zander (1999), *Cases and Materials on the English Legal System*, 8th edn, London: Butterworths, pp 312–13.
[23] 'Continental' refers to the mainland continent of Europe, home of the civil law system based on Roman law, as opposed to the British Isles, home of the common law system.

on consecutive days until the end of the trial is reached, and each party *pleads* or *argues its case*, presenting legal *argument* to the court, producing evidence and calling witnesses to examine. As in sporting competitions, the judge is an '*umpire*', presiding over the court and ensuring that the contest between the *opponents* is played out according to the rules.

The parties, the lawyers and the witnesses

The task of the *advocate*, a term used to designate the role played by a lawyer when representing a client in a proceeding before a court or other body, is to 'build a story', by presenting a version of the facts that the court will find most credible.[24] Addressing young English lawyers in training for professional exams to become *solicitors*, one branch of the English legal profession, authors Brayne and Grimes give the following outline of a court proceeding, which highlights the importance of the skill of *advocacy*:

> First the scene is set through the opening speech. … Secondly, facts are then adduced in the form of evidence, that is, testimony from witnesses, documentary evidence and real evidence. This provides a story presented from the point of view of one of the parties, be it the prosecution or defence or the plaintiff or defendant. The most important element of this is the examination-in-chief. This is the examination by the lawyer of their own witnesses. The third stage is the challenging of this evidence by the opposing side. This is conducted through cross-examination. The purpose here is to undermine, discredit and otherwise challenge the version of events that has been presented by the opponent. Finally, the fourth stage is to present arguments based on the evidence and the applicable law in the form of a closing address. The last word is usually left to the party defending the proceedings.[25]

The *witnesses* give oral evidence, called *testimony*, to the court, as they are first *examined* during '*examination-in-chief*' then *cross-examined* by counsel for the opposing party. '*Cross-examination*' can place a witness under great stress, especially if his or her honesty and *credibility* are challenged. In addition to testimony, '*documentary evidence*' may be produced before the court, and *real evidence*, such as a gun, clothes or other objects that tend to prove the facts, may be produced for close physical examination by the court. Today, some evidence may consist of video footage viewed on a large screen in the courtroom, where, for instance, a defendant may be seen running away from the scene of a crime.

Lawyers from civil law systems may be surprised to learn that in the adversarial trial the defendant himself may *testify*,[26] giving his first-hand account of the events and his state of mind as he is examined and cross-examined; but the defendant has the right to remain silent (the *right of silence*) if he chooses, and his

---

[24] H Brayne and R Grimes (1994), *Professional Skills for Lawyers. A Student's Guide*, London: Butterworths, pp 377 and 412.

[25] *Ibid*, p 412.

[26] F de Franchis (1984), *Dizionario giuridico. Vol 1 Inglese–Italiano*, Milan: Giuffrè Editore, p 1536.

lawyer may advise him against *taking the witness stand* in order to avoid aggressive cross-examination by counsel for the opposition.

In addition to *eye-witnesses* and others, including any *victims*, who have direct knowledge of the crime, police officers may be called to give evidence about the events surrounding *arrest*, for example, or to give facts about the *real evidence*, explaining each item as it is produced in court, including how and where it was found. *Expert witnesses*, such as *forensic scientists* or psychiatrists, may be called by each party to supply the court with essential expert knowledge and analysis; in cases involving the law of another legal system, a qualified foreign lawyer will act as an expert witness to tell the English court the relevant legal rules of his country.

The jury

In *jury trials*, the efforts of counsel for each party, described above, will be directed towards convincing the 12 members of the *jury* in one sense or another. Sometimes, juries are still used in civil cases, but in England that is the exception;[27] on the other hand, the role of the jury in serious criminal cases is central in the English legal system. The *members of the jury*, called *jurors*, are chosen at random from the adult population aged between 18 and 70 who are registered as voters.[28] There are very few limits, and no particular qualifications are required; a jury is a random selection of ordinary people—a *lay* body, one that is not legally qualified. If *summoned for jury service* one cannot refuse without valid justification, since it is a *civic duty*; on the other side, *trial by jury* is considered a right for a criminal defendant, in more serious cases.

Lord Bingham emphasises the primary importance of the *criminal jury* in the adversarial trial:

> I am anxious to stress the central and also the extraordinary role of this body, quite different from the lay judges seen in the German criminal courts or the jurors found in the French *cours d'assises*. Unqualified by legal knowledge or forensic experience, jurors are nonetheless entrusted, in any major trial, however momentous, with the sole decision on whether the case is established against the defendant or not. The judge will instruct the jury on the relevant law, but the jury may acquit in disregard of his direction with impunity. The judge must tell the jury that its task is to decide the disputed issues of fact, ignoring any views of his which they do not accept. Any decision by the jury to acquit is final, any decision to convict (after a properly conducted trial and a correct direction on the law) is exceedingly hard to challenge.

Inquisitorial systems may use 'lay judges' or 'jurors', as in Germany and France, but their role is more limited (for example, to assist the judges in their decision-making

---

[27] For example in *defamation cases*; juries sometimes award enormous sums of damages in such cases.
[28] Juries Act 1974, s 1.

process); the English criminal jury, instead, is alone responsible for deciding whether the defendant is guilty: 'jurors *are entrusted with the sole decision* on *whether the case is established* against the defendant'. Jurors have no legal knowledge or experience of courts of law (no *'forensic* experience'), however, the jury alone decides whether *to acquit* (they find the defendant not guilty) or *to convict* (a finding of guilty), a decision that is final in the case of *acquittal* and virtually final in the case of *conviction*: a convicted offender can only appeal (*'challenge'* the decision) if the trial has not been 'properly conducted' or if the judge has *misdirected* the jury in his *summing-up*.

A criminal trial before a judge and a jury in England and Wales is held in the Crown Court and is known as a *contested trial*.[29] *Contested* indicates that the defendant *contests* (challenges, rebuts) the accusations against him and *pleads not guilty*, that is, declares, on *indictment* (accusation) at the beginning of the trial that he has not committed one or more of the offences with which he is charged. Trial by jury in the Crown Court is known as *trial on indictment*, as opposed to *summary trial* in the magistrates' court, the lowest level of criminal jurisdiction in England and Wales.[30] In *uncontested* cases, on the other hand, there is no dispute as to guilt, because the defendant *admits the charges* and *pleads guilty*; or because the prosecution case is withdrawn before the full trial begins.

Read the passage below to find out if the jurors must be unanimous in their decision. Why is it possible for the judge to direct the jury to acquit the defendant, and in what circumstances?

> The essence of the jury trial in England and Wales, is the idea that twelve people are drawn at random and, without training, asked to assess the factual circumstances that surround a particular case. Their verdict of 'not guilty' or 'guilty', given if necessary on a majority basis of ten to two, is their view of the facts. The judge takes responsibility for the law, so that if the prosecution alleges a series of factual hypotheses which, in the view of the judge, are not sufficient to constitute legal proof of the crime concerned even if they are true, the judge will direct the jury to find the defendant not guilty.[31]

The authors point out that 'if necessary' a *majority verdict* can be returned, provided a minimum of 10 jurors are in agreement. The judge is *responsible for the law*, therefore he can *direct the jury to acquit* if the legal requirements for a particular crime are not present.

The role of the jury is to decide the factual circumstances of a case (*the facts*); this includes not only 'what happened' in physical terms, but also the defendant's *state of mind*.[32] At the end of the trial, having heard all the evidence, the jury retires to *deliberate* and *reach a verdict*: guilty or not guilty. The *deliberations of the jury* are strictly secret and can never be revealed or discussed.

---

[29] F Cownie, A Bradney and M Burton (2013), *English Legal System in Context*, 6th edn, Oxford: Oxford University Press, p 335.
[30] See 9.3.3 for details of the hierarchy and jurisdiction of the English courts.
[31] Cownie *et al*, above n 29, p 336.
[32] For more on mental states and crime, see 7.4 below.

The proportion of trials by jury in the English legal system is actually small, and is likely to diminish over time.[33] However, statute law can create new tasks for juries, as in the example below.

Consider the example below. What offence was created by the Act? What is the role of the jury? What penalties are provided for a guilty organisation?

Understanding the Corporate Manslaughter and Corporate Homicide Act 2007

The Act sets out a new offence for convicting an organisation where a gross failure in the way activities were managed or organised results in a person's death. ... In England and Wales and Northern Ireland, the new offence will be called corporate manslaughter. It will be called corporate homicide in Scotland. ...

Juries will consider how the fatal activity was managed or organised throughout the organisation, including any systems and processes for managing safety and how these were operated in practice. ...

An organisation guilty of the offence will be liable to an unlimited fine. The Act also provides for courts to impose a publicity order, requiring the organisation to publicise its conviction and fine.[34]

An organisation convicted of the new offence created by the Act ('*corporate homicide*' in Scotland, '*corporate manslaughter*' in the rest of the UK) may suffer an '*unlimited fine*'—a criminal *pecuniary penalty* with no maximum limit; it will also be obliged to publicise both its conviction and the fine. The task of the jury is clearly central to the purpose of the Act, which is to impose criminal liability on an organisation for deaths caused as a consequence of a 'gross failure in the way activities were managed or organised'. The jury will look at the way the organisation's system was managed and operated in practice to reach its conclusion as to guilt.

Why do you think a lay jury, as opposed to professional judges, could be particularly suitable for this type of decision-making?

The judge

The judge *presides over the trial*; he or she is responsible for *the law*. In trials without a jury, the judge pronounces judgment directly in open court at the end of the hearings, formulating a reasoned judgment from notes taken during the hearings. In the case of trial by jury, once counsel have completed their closing speeches, the judge *directs the jury*, in the form of a *summing-up*: the jurors listen to *directions* on how to arrive at their decision, such as what standards and criteria they must use. It is not the judge's function to indicate to the jury that the defendant is guilty or not: that decision is the prerogative of the jurors alone, and they have the right to ignore any opinion the judge may express.

---

[33] Cownie *et al*, above n 29, p 346.
[34] Ministry of Justice document, October 2007: 'Understanding the Corporate Manslaughter and Corporate Homicide Act 2007'.

Task 4   The role of the judge

In the extract below, one of England's most eminent judges, Lord Bingham, discusses the various functions of the judge during a criminal trial.

Read the text for general understanding, noticing any differences between the English system and the system in your country.

Then, read the text in more detail to answer the questions below, focusing on both language and meaning:

1. What is the profile of a typical English judge?
2. Why is it particularly appropriate in criminal trials to say that the judge 'presides over' the trial?
3. What are three important functions of the judge in a criminal trial?
4. Which duty of the judge does Lord Bingham consider most important of all?

He will until appointed to the judicial bench in middle age, have spent his career in private practice, almost certainly as an advocate. It is customary to speak of the judge presiding over the trial, and in the case of a criminal trial, the expression is particularly apt. For the judge takes (or should take) no part in the adversarial contest between prosecuting and defending counsel. He will have played no part at all in the investigation and preparation of the case until he receives the papers very shortly before the trial begins. He is above the battle. But this detachment from the fray does not mean that he has no important role to play. His function is threefold. First of all it is his duty to see that the trial is regularly conducted according to settled legal rules ... [for example] to rule whether the evidence is admissible or not. Secondly, and perhaps more importantly, the judge has many discretionary powers ... which he exercises in accordance with what justice seems to him to require, his overriding duty being to ensure a fair trial for the defendant. ... Thus where two or more defendants are accused jointly, the judge may order them to be tried separately if he thinks it may be unfairly prejudicial to one defendant to be tried at the same time as another. ... The judge's third important role is to direct and sum up the case to the jury. So far as the law is concerned, he will instruct the jury as simply and as accurately as he can on the principles of law applicable to the case. Thus he will, for example, tell the jury what mental intention must be proved before they can convict of murder, or what are the ingredients of theft. ... He must also instruct them, as a matter of law, that they must not convict the defendant unless they are all (or, after a long period of deliberation and a further judicial direction, by a majority of not less than 10–2) sure that he is guilty.[35]

© Lord Bingham of Cornhill 2000

---

[35] T Bingham (2000), *The Business of Judging. Selected Essays and Speeches 1985–1999*, Oxford: Oxford University Press, Part VIII Crime and Punishment, Paper 1, 'The English Criminal Trial: The Credits and the Debits', pp 256–58.

Key to Task 4 The role of the judge

1. The profile Lord Bingham describes is of a man, middle-aged to old, who became a judge (was *'appointed to the judicial bench'*) after a career as a *barrister*: barristers are members of the Bar, that is, the branch of the English legal profession particularly qualified and skilled as *'advocates'*. *The bench/Bench* is a term often used collectively for judges, or to indicate a court; it originally referred to the seat of the judges in the courtroom.

2. It is apt to say the judge 'presides over' the trial, since he is 'above the battle', having taken no part in the investigation or preparation of the case, and given the dominant role of the parties (represented by *'prosecuting and defending counsel'*) in court. Notice the language that highlights the *adversarial* nature of the trial: 'battle', also 'fray' (battle or fight).

3. For your answer, follow the clear textual markers: 'First of all …', 'Secondly …', 'The judge's third important role is to …'. The three important functions of a judge in a criminal trial are:

    a) to guarantee the legality of proceedings;
    b) to exercise his *'discretionary powers'* in accordance with the demands of justice;
    c) to give simple, accurate directions to the jury in his summing-up *'on the principles of law applicable to the case'*.

4. The judge's *'overriding duty'*, the most important one of all in the view of Lord Bingham, is *'to ensure a fair trial for the defendant'*.

Comment

Note that the text above does not consider the final role played by the judge in the criminal process: that of *sentencing the offender* to a suitable punishment for the crime he has committed—a *punishment to fit the crime*.

Senior judges typically come from a limited sector of English society (as do *barristers*); although the need for wider representation of women and different ethnic groups and social classes is recognised, it will take many years for any changes to filter through.[36] A smaller proportion of English judges are appointed from among members of the other branch of the legal profession: *solicitors*. Barristers' monopoly of advocacy in the superior courts ended with the Courts and Legal Services Act 1990, and solicitors may today acquire such *rights of audience*. Note that there is no separate *judicial* career path that a young person may take straight after gaining his or her legal qualifications.

The judge's crucial role in ensuring that a defendant is given a fair trial is also highlighted in the passage below from a judgment pronounced by Lord Phillips,

---

[36] This is discussed critically in Cownie *et al*, above n 29, ch 9 'Judges and judging', pp 155–68.

President of the Supreme Court of the United Kingdom, in one of the earliest judgments of that Court, *R v Horncastle*.[37]

What are the two objectives of a fair criminal trial? And which of the two must have priority? Consider the metaphor Lord Phillips uses to describe the role of the judge.

16. The English criminal process is adversarial. Its focal point is the trial, which is the judicial part of the process . ...

...

18. There are two principal objectives of a fair criminal trial. The first is that a defendant who is innocent should be acquitted. The second is that a defendant who is guilty should be convicted. The first objective is in the interests of the individual; the second is in the interests of the victim in particular and society in general. The two objectives are sometimes in tension and, where they are, the first carries more weight than the second.

19. English law has different kinds of rules that are designed to ensure a fair trial. Some relate to the procedure itself, such as the right of the defendant to be informed of the case against him ...

20. Other rules relate to the evidence that can be placed before the tribunal, be it magistrates or a jury, which is to rule on the defendant's guilt. These are rules of 'admissibility'. Jury trials are presided over by a judge who acts as gatekeeper as to what is and what is not permitted to be placed before the jury as evidence. This is an important safeguard for the defendant. ...[38]

An innocent defendant must be acquitted, but a guilty defendant must be convicted: not only criminal defendants, but also victims of crime and society in general have *interests* that require protection. Where the two interests clash, those of the individual defendant must have priority.

The metaphor of the judge as gatekeeper seems particularly apt to show the role of the judge in deciding which evidence should be put before the jury, and this is an essential '*safeguard for the defendant*'.

7.3.2 A Criminal Conviction—Case Study: *R v Hayter*

Task 5 Reading a criminal judgment—Case study: *R v Hayter*[39]
First, read the extracts from the criminal appeal judgment below, for general understanding. Search for basic facts about the case.
Then, read the text in detail to answer the following questions. Focus on both meaning and language, observing the use of criminal terminology in context:
1.   What are the facts in this criminal case, who are the three defendants and what did each of them do?

---

[37] *R v Horncastle* [2009] UKSC 14, on appeal from [2009] EWCA Crim 964.
[38] *Ibid* [16], [18]–[20].
[39] *R v Hayter* [2005] UKHL 6.

2. Were the defendants convicted?
3. What was the evidence against them?
4. Why did one defendant appeal?
5. In chronological order, which three courts examined this murder case? What is the important question of law before the House of Lords in this judgment?

HOUSE OF LORDS
[2005] UKHL 6
Regina v Hayter
(Appellant) (On Appeal from the Court of Appeal (Criminal Division))

LORD STEYN
My Lords,
...
2. On the present appeal a point of law of general public importance arises about the principle that the confession of a defendant is inadmissible in a joint criminal case against a co-defendant.

3. What the point is, and how it arises, is best introduced by a simplified description of the real case of murder which in June 2001 came for trial before Judge Hyam, the Recorder of London, and a jury. The trial took place at the Central Criminal Court. Three defendants were charged with murder. All three were indicted as principals. The prosecution case was as follows. The first defendant (Bristow) was a woman who wanted to arrange a contract killing of her husband. The evidence against her came from a number of sources and was cogent. The third accused (Ryan) was the killer who actually shot and killed the husband of the first defendant. The evidence against the killer was solely based on a confession which he had allegedly made to his girlfriend. The prosecution case was that the contract killing was arranged by the first defendant through the second accused (Hayter) who engaged and paid the killer. The judge invited the jury to consider in logical phases the cases against the alleged killer, then against the woman who allegedly procured the killing, and finally against the middleman. The judge directed the jury that only if they found both the actual gunman, and the woman who arranged the killing, guilty of murder, would it be open to them, taking into account those findings of guilt, together with other evidence against the middleman, to convict the middleman. The jury convicted all three defendants of murder.

4. The principal argument on behalf of the middleman was and is that the rule that an out of court confession by one defendant may not be used by the prosecution against a co-defendant has been breached by the way in which the judge directed the jury.
...

Key and comment to Task 5 Reading a criminal judgment—Case study: *R v Hayter*

1. The facts of the case are that a woman planned to murder her husband and arranged a '*contract killing*': she hired 'a middleman' (an intermediary) to arrange the killing, which was carried out by a third *co-defendant* in this trial: '*the third accused*'.

2. All three defendants were charged with murder. And the jury convicted all three defendants.

3. There was convincing evidence from different sources against the wife, 'the first defendant'; the evidence against the killer was only based on *a confession* to his girlfriend; the evidence against the middleman appears to depend on the conviction of the other two defendants. The judge directed the jury to take those findings of guilt into account, with other evidence, against the middleman.

4. The middleman appealed, on the grounds that his conviction depended on an 'out of court confession' by another defendant, breaking a legal rule.

5. First, the *trial* was held in the '*Central Criminal Court*'—that is, the principal Crown Court for central London, often referred to as the *Old Bailey*, from its address; next, Hayter's *appeal* against conviction was heard by the Court of Appeal (Criminal Division) but was clearly dismissed; his *final appeal* (this judgment) was to the House of Lords. The House of Lords must decide whether the rule mentioned in paragraph 4 of Lord Steyn's speech (above), had been broken by the judge in directing the jury as he did: in other words, had the judge *misdirected* the jury? It is interesting to note in this case the interaction between the judge and jury in a criminal trial, and the importance of the judge's directions to the jurors before they decide if the defendant is guilty or not guilty. (Hayter lost this appeal.)

SECTION TWO

7.4 The Elements of a Crime: *Actus Reus* and *Mens Rea*—Advanced

Below, we examine the two constituent elements of a crime, known as *actus reus* and *mens rea*. To learn more about these terms, we make a short digression and consider some Latin maxims still used in English legal language today.

7.4.1 Latin Maxims

A feature of legal language in both national and international contexts is the use of *maxims* or *proverbs of the law*, which condense broad legal principles into concise phrases. Often, such maxims are in Latin. If you are a Latin scholar, your knowledge of the language should indicate the meaning of the words, but that is only a starting point for comprehending the legal significance of the maxim:[40]

> False and misleading when literally read, these established formulae provide useful means for the expression of leading doctrines of the law in a form which is at the same time brief and intelligible. They constitute a species of legal shorthand, useful to the lawyer, but dangerous to anyone else; for they can be read only in the light of expert knowledge of that law of which they are the elliptical expression.[41]

As with all legal language, Sir John Salmond, above, underlines the importance of using one's expert knowledge for full understanding of legal expression.

Task 6 Latin maxims
Are Latin words and phrases used in the legal language of your country? Are you familiar with some of the Latin maxims given below? From your knowledge of Latin and of law, try to work out their meaning and assess their possible legal significance:

Actus non facit reum nisi mens sit rea   *Nullum crimen sine lege*

Volenti non fit injuria   *Nulla poena sine lege*

---

[40] A Riley 'The Meaning of Words in English Legal Texts: Mastering the Vocabulary of the Law—A Legal Task' (1996) 30 *The Law Teacher* p 68 at 74.
[41] G Williams (ed) (1947), *Salmond on Jurisprudence*, 10th edn, London: Sweet & Maxwell, p 498.

Nullum crimen sine lege/Nulla poena sine lege

These maxims express fundamental principles of criminal law, accepted in most countries of the world; also known as the *principle of non-retroactivity*. The first maxim states that there is *no crime without law*, or *except by law*. All crimes must be provided by law; and behaviour that is immoral, bad or antisocial is not criminal, unless it falls into a category of *crime* as defined and established by the law.[42] Further, crimes cannot be created with retroactive effect. Correspondingly, the second maxim states that there can be no punishment except in accordance with law.[43]

The same principles are enshrined in the European Convention on Human Rights; Article 7, entitled '*No punishment without law*', has this effect:

> Article 7(1) of the Convention protects an individual from being convicted for a criminal offence which did not exist in law at the time the act was committed. This reflects the principle that only the law can define a crime and prescribe a penalty (*nullum crimen, nulla poena sine lege*).[44]

However, Article 7(2) of the Convention introduces a limitation: an act or omission which, at the time when it was committed, was 'criminal according to the general principles of law recognised by civilised nations' is not subject to the prohibition in Article 7(1). This recalls the prosecution of war crimes at Nuremberg and Tokyo at the end of the Second World War.[45]

Volenti non fit injuria

This maxim is found in the context of civil law in common law jurisdictions: there may be no *injury* (*harm* or *damage*) to a willing person; to put it another way, if a person consents by accepting a risk, any harm he suffers cannot later be considered an *injury* for which civil damages can be claimed. In the law of torts, the rule expressed in this maxim may provide a defence to a claim for damages where the *injured party* voluntarily accepted the risk of harm; for example, by participating in a dangerous sport, such as a boxing match. But the application of the maxim is restricted to civil law—no person can license another to commit a crime. It is also restricted to willing acceptance (*volenti*) not mere knowledge of risk (*scienti*).[46]

Actus non facit reum nisi mens sit rea

Two Latin terms are still used in the common law today to designate the two constituent elements of a crime: *actus reus* and *mens rea*. *Actus reus* refers to the concrete elements of the crime—the behaviour and results which the particular

---

[42] Walker, above n 1, p 317.

[43] *Osborn's Concise Law Dictionary* (2013), 12th edn, M Woodley (ed), London: Sweet & Maxwell, p 297.

[44] D Gomien (2005), *Short Guide to the European Convention on Human Rights*, 3rd edn, Strasbourg: Cedex Council of Europe Publishing, p 69.

[45] *Ibid*, p 71.

[46] *Osborn's Concise Law Dictionary*, above n 43, at p 447.

offence requires. It may be defined as: 'A wrongful deed which renders the actor criminally liable if combined with mens rea'.[47] For example, for crimes of *homicide* the *actus reus* consists of unlawfully *causing the death* of another person. The adjective *liable* (noun, *liability*) means responsible in law, answerable.

The term *mens rea* (sometimes transposed into the English expression *guilty mind*) refers to the mental component of the crime: the state of mind of the defendant, which is a necessary *ingredient of the offence*. Professor Andrew Ashworth explains as follows:

> The essence of the principle of *mens rea* is that criminal liability should be imposed only on persons who are sufficiently aware of what they are doing, and of the consequences it may have, that they can fairly be said to have chosen the behaviour and its consequences.[48]

The specific *mens rea* for murder, called *malice aforethought*, is central to the definition of this crime; it includes two alternative forms of intention:

> **malice aforethought.** The element of *mens rea* in the crime of murder. It is satisfied by an intention to kill or an intention to commit grievous bodily harm (*Moloney* [1985] 1 AC 905).[49]

The specific intention required for murder is not necessarily to kill another person; it is sufficient to *intend to cause* really serious injury: *grievous bodily harm*.

Intention is one of the main forms of *mens rea*. It is not the same as *motive*, which refers to a person's reason for doing something; for example, emotions such as jealousy or hatred could be *motives for murder*, but they do not amount to *intention*. A person is assumed to intend the inevitable consequences of his act. Where the consequences are only probable, or natural, the jury must decide whether the defendant did in fact intend the consequences. Note that the meaning of *intention, recklessness* and so on, and the tests and parameters for determining whether a defendant had a particular state of mind, have been developed by the courts. Professor Ashworth underlines that 'the courts do not adhere to a single definition of intention'[50] and explains the reason for this: the judiciary 'see the need to preserve an element of flexibility'.[51]

Recklessness is another form of *mens rea*: less than *intention* and more than *negligence*.[52] *Recklessness* means taking an unjustifiable risk, but the defendant must also *foresee* the risk of his actions, and proceed in any case, not caring about the consequences.

---

[47] H Black (1979), *Black's Law Dictionary*, 5th edn, St Paul, Minn: West Publishing Co, p 34.

[48] A Ashworth (2009), *Principles of Criminal Law*, 6th edn, Oxford: Oxford University Press, pp 154–55.

[49] *Osborn's Concise Law Dictionary*, above n 43, p 270.

[50] Ashworth, above n 48, p 175.

[51] *Ibid*, p 174.

[52] *Negligence* in criminal law has its ordinary meaning of carelessness; cf the specific *tort of negligence* in civil law, discussed in 9.2.4.

The term *malice* indicates evil motive or ill-will and is the *mens rea* for some *non-fatal offences against the person*, which must be committed *maliciously*; in English civil law, malice is a constituent of certain torts (*civil wrongs*), such as *defamation*.

Many minor *statutory offences*—that is, crimes created by statute as opposed to judicial precedent—require no specific *mens rea*: 'the mere intent to do the act forbidden by the statute is sufficient'.[53] But the main body of criminal law, including most serious crimes, is of common law derivation and *mens rea* is a necessary element in more serious crimes. This requirement is linked to the notion of *culpability*: a person should be punished for breaking the law where he is *to blame* (*culpable*) for his behaviour; conversely, if a person has behaved in an innocent way, not intending to do wrong, this should be *a defence* against a serious *criminal charge*.[54]

In a criminal proceeding, it is the duty of the prosecution *to prove* the *guilt* of the accused, including the necessary *mens rea* for the crime: We say that the *onus of proof*, or *burden of proof*, is *on the prosecution*.

As for the meaning of the Latin maxim *actus non facit reum nisi mens sit rea*, Lord Hailsham, the Lord Chancellor, explained that the law term *actus reus*, considered above, is not quite accurate:

> [The term *actus reus*] derives, I believe, from a mistranslation of the Latin aphorism *Actus non facit reum nisi mens sit rea*. Properly translated, this means 'an act does not make a *man* guilty of a crime unless his mind be also guilty.' It is thus not the *actus* which is *reus*, but the man and his mind respectively. Before the understanding of the Latin tongue has wholly died out of these islands, it is as well to record this as it has frequently led to confusion.[55]

It is not the *act* that is guilty, but the *mind* of the person who commits it.

For more about the different states of mind required for various crimes, consult a textbook on criminal law. See Ideas for Further Reading at the end of this chapter.

7.5 Homicide—Advanced

7.5.1 Introducing Key Terms and Concepts

It is not necessarily *unlawful* to kill another person. *Homicide* may be lawful or unlawful, and the law of homicide punishes *unlawful killing*.

---

[53] *Osborn's Concise Law Dictionary*, above n 43, p 277.
[54] P Leyland (2004), Lecture at the University of Ferrara Law Faculty: *Evolving concepts of moral blameworthiness in English criminal law*.
[55] *Haughton v Smith* [1973] UKHL 4, [1975] AC 476 (HL).

As an example of *lawful killing*, death may be caused accidentally, without intention or fault, or may be justified by a lawful excuse such as *self-defence* (US *self-defense*). For example, in the case below, the *coroner*, after investigating the death of an intruder in the home killed by an elderly, blind man, Mr O'Connor, decided:

> I believe Mr O'Connor acted within reasonable grounds to protect himself and his wife and therefore record a verdict that Lee Ross Kelso was lawfully killed.[56]

In a proceeding of this type, known as an *inquest*, the coroner *conducts an investigation* into the cause of a death suspected of being violent or unnatural, or when a *post-mortem examination* (or *autopsy*) is held. An inquest is distinct from any criminal proceedings that may be brought against a person accused of *unlawfully* causing a victim's death.

Task 7   Dictionary research—key terms in homicide

Use your law dictionary to investigate the meaning of the following terms of central importance for the most serious chapter of the criminal law: offences resulting in the death of another person:
homicide – murder – manslaughter – self-defence –
diminished responsibility – provocation – suicide pact
Compare your findings and reflect on possible translations into your own language. Remember to search for equivalent concepts in the two legal systems. What difficulties do you find?

As you study the following pages, compare your own dictionary research in the task above, with the definitions and comment provided below.[57]

7.5.2   Homicide: Murder and Manslaughter

The two main classes of homicide are murder and manslaughter. *Manslaughter*, in turn, has two categories: *voluntary* and *involuntary manslaughter*.

Examine the traditional definition of homicide given by Chief Justice Coke:[58]

> **homicide.** Coke CJ defined homicide as:
> 'when a man of sound memory and of the age of discretion, unlawfully killeth within any county of the realm any reasonable creature *in rerum naturae* under the king's

---

[56] House of Commons Research Paper: Criminal Law (Amendment) (Householder Protection) Bill, Bill 20 of 2004–05, B Illustrations, case 'p.', *O'Connor.*

[57] For more in-depth investigation of concepts and law in this section, you are recommended to consult a textbook on criminal law; see Further Reading at the end of this chapter.

[58] Sir Edward Coke (1552–1634) wrote the first modern 'textbook' on the common law—Coke's *Institutes* is a legal encyclopaedia of enormous influence in the development of modern English law.

peace with malice aforethought, either expressed by the party or implied by law so as the party wounded or hurt, etc., die of the wound or hurt, etc., within a year and a day after the same.'

That definition remains valid for murder today, save that the Law Reform (Year and a Day Rule) Act 1996 abolished the requirement for the death to occur within that period. If it occurs more than three years later the consent of the Attorney-General is necessary for a prosecution. Murder is punishable with a mandatory sentence of life imprisonment.

...

Manslaughter has two categories: voluntary manslaughter is murder reduced to man-slaughter by reason of an extenuating circumstance such as loss of self control *(q.v.)* or diminished responsibility *(q.v.)*; involuntary manslaughter is an unlawful killing without malice aforethought. Manslaughter is punishable by a maximum sentence of life imprisonment.[59]

Chief Justice Coke's definition of *homicide* today corresponds to the most serious crime: *murder*. We learn from *Osborn's Concise Law Dictionary* that the definition of 'murder' was changed by statute as recently as 1996 with the abolition of the 'year and a day rule'; this reflects advances in the field of medical science, since it is now possible for victims to be kept alive for years after they have suffered injury.[60]

Now examine the definition of *murder* in the same dictionary:

murder. The crime of unlawful killing during the Queen's Peace with malice afore-thought *(q.v.)*; as where the accused causes death by an unlawful act with the intention to cause death or grievous bodily harm *(R v Moloney* [1985] AC 905). The burden of proving malice aforethought rests upon the prosecution *(Woolmington v DPP* [1935] AC 462). [...] The partial defence of provocation *(q.v.)*, diminished responsibility *(q.v.)* and killing in pursuance of a suicide pact *(q.v.)* reduce murder liability to volun-tary manslaughter. A person who killed but lacked the mens rea for murder when he did so may be found guilty of manslaughter, provided he killed as part of an unlawful and dangerous act or with gross negligence or recklessness. See MANSLAUGHTER.[61]

Note how the dictionary definition refers to judicial precedents as sources for the law of murder: there is no statutory definition. Murder and manslaughter are closely connected. If a person kills without the *mens rea* for murder *(malice aforethought*, examined in 7.4.1 above), he may still be guilty of involuntary man-slaughter. But even if he killed with malice aforethought, liability will be reduced from murder to *voluntary manslaughter* if he succeeds in one of the three *partial defences* mentioned in the definition above: provocation (now 'loss of control'), diminished responsibility and killing in pursuance of a suicide pact (see 7.6.1 below). The judge will then have discretion to impose the maximum penalty of life imprisonment or a lighter *prison sentence*, as appropriate.

---

[59] *Osborn's Concise Law Dictionary*, above n 43, p 216.
[60] Ashworth, above n 48, p 240.
[61] *Osborn's Concise Law Dictionary*, above n 43, p 285.

Observe the definition of *manslaughter* in *Osborn*:

manslaughter. A crime of unlawful homicide. Manslaughter may be divided into two categories:

(1) Voluntary manslaughter where the defendant killed with malice aforethought but the presence of a mitigating factor at the time of the killing, namely provocation (*q.v.*), diminished responsibility (*q.v.*) or killing in pursuance of a suicide pact (*q.v.*) reduced the defendant's liability to manslaughter.

(2) Involuntary manslaughter where the defendant killed without malice aforethought but with a certain required fault element. The fault element required is that the defendant caused the death whilst committing an unlawful and dangerous act or that his act or omission which caused the death was grossly negligent or reckless. See CORPORATE MANSLAUGHTER.[62]

To understand the category of *voluntary manslaughter*, we need to examine the various *defences*, and take into account recent changes in the law: see 7.6 below.

7.5.3 US Law Compared

The law of homicide in the United States is similar in many respects to the modern English system. *Black's Law Dictionary*[63] gives a series of compound terms, including *justifiable homicide*, *vehicular homicide* and *felonious homicide*, this last subdivided into two categories: murder and manslaughter. The adjective *felonious* is related to the noun *felony*. *Felonies* and *misdemeanours* are the two traditional classes of crime in the common law, and this terminology is still used today in the USA.[64]

In English law, these two classes of crime have been replaced by *indictable offences* (serious crimes, formerly *felonies*) and *summary offences* (minor crimes, formerly *misdemeanours*). The distinction is significant in relation to the *mode of trial*: indictable offences are *tried on indictment* in the Crown Court before a judge and jury, while summary offences are tried *summarily* by magistrates. Some offences are *triable either way*, that is, either by jury in the Crown Court or summarily in the magistrates' courts.

If you are interested in knowing more about the US system, you are advised to consult *Black's Law Dictionary*, a recognised American authority in the field of the language of law.[65] In the United States, most states subdivide *murder* into two degrees (and some into three degrees): for example, *murder of the first degree* involves *premeditation* or is committed in the course of another serious crime, while all other kinds of murder are classed as *murder of the second degree*. The

---

[62] *Ibid*, p 271.
[63] *Black's Law Dictionary*, 5th edn, above n 47.
[64] With a US spelling variation: *misdemeanor*.
[65] *Black's Law Dictionary*, 11th edn (2011), B Garner (ed), St Paul, Minn: West Publishing Co.

distinction allows for different levels of punishment, depending on the seriousness of the murder.[66] Less serious forms of homicide fall in the category of
manslaughter.

It is interesting to note that the Law Commission of England and Wales recommended reform of the categories of homicide, proposing to introduce *first and
second degree murder*, as in the USA. If the proposals were adopted by the British
legislature, a three-tier structure[67] would replace the current two-tier structure
(*murder* and *manslaughter*), introducing a new middle tier, between first degree
murder and manslaughter, that would include some killings previously regarded
as murder and some killings previously regarded as manslaughter. The Report
examines problems and proposes solutions relating to the structure of homicide
and to defences in English law.[68]

7.6 Defences to Murder: Crime and Punishment—Advanced

In criminal trials, a case must be proved '*beyond all reasonable doubt*'. By contrast, a civil court must decide '*on the balance of probabilities*', a lower *standard of
proof*; for this reason, a civil claim is sometimes successful even when the same
defendant is found not guilty in a corresponding criminal prosecution. In a
murder trial, *the burden of proof*—that is, the duty of a party to prove the facts in
issue before the court—lies on the prosecution. The prosecution must produce
convincing *evidence* to prove not only that the defendant caused the death of
the victim (the *actus reus*), but also that the accused had the necessary *mens rea*
for murder: *malice aforethought*, examined in 7.4.1 above. But even when malice
aforethought is proved, or admitted by the defendant, there are some defences
that may be available to him. Such defences may be either *partial* or *full*. Some
such defences are considered below.

7.6.1 Partial Defences

In the law of homicide, where a *partial defence* to a charge of murder is successful,
the defendant's conviction is *reduced from murder to manslaughter* because of an
extenuating factor at the time of the killing: the accused is convicted of *voluntary
manslaughter*, a less serious category of homicide. He thus avoids the terrible
stigma of being labelled a murderer, but also avoids the *mandatory sentence* of life
imprisonment: the effect is therefore *mitigation of sentence*.

---

[66] *Black's Law Dictionary*, 5th edn, above n 47, p 919.
[67] *A three-tier structure* = a structure with three levels.
[68] Law Com No 304, *Murder, Manslaughter and Infanticide*, published November 2006 and available
at <http://lawcom.gov.uk>. For Recommendations on a new Homicide Act to replace the 1957 Act,
including the three-tier system discussed, see Part 9; for evaluation and comment, A Ashworth and
J Horder (2013), *Principles of Criminal Law*, 7th edn, Oxford: Oxford Univesity Press, pp 282–85.

In one case,[69] a defendant who killed an intruder in the home, inflicting 12 stab wounds in the victim's back, was *found not guilty of murder* even though he had used disproportionate force. The court accepted that it was not surprising that the man had armed himself with a weapon, when he believed his estranged wife and daughter were in the house and in danger. The defendant had not used *reasonable force*, and therefore could not *rely on* the full defence of self-defence (discussed in 7.6.2 below); however, it was accepted that the partial defence of *provocation* was available to him, reducing his conviction from murder to manslaughter; he was *sentenced to five years' imprisonment* for the homicide, a *sentence* reduced to three years *on appeal*.

Provocation was a historical common law defence,[70] consisting of words or conduct that would temporarily deprive a reasonable person of his self-control, and where the defendant in fact lost his self-control: it therefore involved an objective and a subjective test, decided by the jury, taking into account all the circumstances of the case. A more recent law—the Coroners and Justice Act 2009—abolished the defence of provocation,[71] introducing a new *statutory partial defence*: 'loss of control'.[72] This now operates where there is a '*qualifying trigger*', for example where a defendant, in fear of serious violence from the victim, killed as a result of losing self-control.[73] The new legislation is complex and 'may well result in lengthy trials and many appeals' as the courts seek to *construe* (interpret) the meaning of some new terms introduced by the Act.[74]

Two other partial defences mentioned in the definitions examined above are *diminished responsibility* and *suicide pact*.

Diminished responsibility is another *statutory partial defence*;[75] it was amended by the 2009 Act and is available where the defendant was suffering from an '*abnormality of mental functioning*' that arose from 'a recognised mental condition' and had an impact on the defendant's ability to understand the nature of his conduct, or form a rational judgement, or exercise self-control, causing him to act as he did, or being a significant contributory factor.[76] *The burden of proving diminished responsibility lies on the defendant.*[77]

The partial defence of *suicide pact* is available where two or more people have formed an agreement to end their lives.[78] However, while still intending to die

---

[69] House of Commons Research Paper, above n 56, p 17, case 'o.', Barry-Lee Hastings.

[70] Supplemented by the Homicide Act 1957, s 3: N Padfield (2012), *Criminal Law*, 8th edn, Oxford: Oxford University Press, p 205.

[71] Coroners and Justice Act 2009, s 56(1).

[72] Coroners and Justice Act 2009, s 54(1).

[73] Coroners and Justice Act 2009, s 55.

[74] Padfield, above n 70, p 213, citing the first example of such a case.

[75] Introduced by the Homicide Act 1957, s 2.

[76] Coroners and Justice Act 2009, s 52.

[77] Homicide Act 1957, s 2(2).

[78] The term 'suicide pact' is defined in s 4(3) of the Homicide Act 1957.

in pursuance of the pact, one party kills another party to the pact but in the end remains alive himself:

Homicide Act 1957 s 4(1)

> It shall be manslaughter, and shall not be murder, for a person acting in pursuance of a suicide pact between him and another to kill the other ...

Once charged with murder, the burden of proof lies on the survivor—in the words of the Act, '*it shall be for the defence to prove* that the person charged was acting *in pursuance of a suicide pact* between him and the other' (emphasis added); but if the defendant *satisfies* the burden of proof, he is guilty of manslaughter, not murder.

7.6.2 Self-defence: a Full Defence

Self-defence is the right to use *reasonable force* to defend oneself or another person against attack. It is *a common law defence* to criminal charges of *offences against the person*, including homicide. There is also a *statutory right* to use self-defence *in the prevention of crime*, introduced by the Criminal Law Act 1967.[79] The statutory and the common law defences *overlap*, that is, many cases fall within both the common law and statutory right to self-defence; in fact, the same principles and standards are applied by the courts. However, the statutory defence would not be available where the apparent *assailant* (the attacker) is not in fact committing a crime.[80] Some of the common law rules have recently been confirmed in legislative form, an approach that has made the defence more complex.[81]

Self-defence is a *full defence*: if this defence is successful, the defendant is *acquitted*—he is not guilty of any crime, even if the use of force has caused serious injury or the death of the assailant. But if the defence fails, the defendant is convicted of the full crime charged, not of *a lesser crime* (a less serious offence). Therefore, if self-defence is used as a defence to a charge of murder but fails, the defendant is convicted of murder, not of the less serious class of homicide, voluntary manslaughter.

Self-defence is a defence that is also available to a defendant in a civil case. If successful, a claim for damages against a *civil defendant* who has *exercised his right to self-defence* will fail.

Case study: *Revill v Newbery*
In the case of *Revill v Newbery*,[82] Mark Revill was a criminal who, with another man, attempted to steal from William Newbery. Mr Newbery, who was 76 years

---

[79] Criminal Law Act 1967, s 3.

[80] For example, he could be a plain clothes police officer effecting a lawful arrest.

[81] Criminal Justice and Immigration Act 2008, s 76, reproduced with comment in Padfield, above n 70, pp 128–30.

[82] *Revill v Newbery* [1996] QB 567, [1996] 1 All ER 291.

old, was inside his garden shed, where he slept to protect his property from *vandals and thieves*.[83] Although he could not see the two intruders, he could hear them trying to break in and he felt frightened. He put his gun through a hole in the door and shot, intending to scare the men away, but unintentionally *wounding*[84] Mr Revill. These events had both civil and criminal repercussions, as Lord Justice Neill described, in the civil judgment pronounced by the Court of Appeal:

> Mr Revill was subsequently prosecuted for the various offences which he had committed that night and pleaded guilty. Mr Newbery also was prosecuted on charges of wounding but he was acquitted.

> Mr Revill then brought the present proceedings. ... To these claims Mr Newbery raised the defences of ex turpi causa [non oritur actio], accident, self-defence and contributory negligence.[85]

The Court of Appeal generally sits in a panel of three judges, each of whom expresses an individual judgment. In the same case, Lord Justice Millett, below, explained *self-defence* in the common law.

What degree of force is permissible? Was Mr Newbery's defence successful? Why or why not?

> For centuries the common law has permitted reasonable force to be used in defence of the person or property. Violence may be returned with necessary violence. But the force used must not exceed the limits of what is reasonable in the circumstances. Changes in society and in social perceptions have meant that what might have been considered reasonable at one time would no longer be so regarded; but the principle remains the same. The assailant or intruder may be met with reasonable force but no more; the use of excessive violence against him is an actionable wrong. ...

> ... Mr Newbery's conduct was not reasonable. It was clearly dangerous and bordered on reckless.[86]

The common law permits the use of *reasonable force*. The force used must be '*reasonable in the circumstances*'. Mr Newbery's defence failed in this civil case because he did not use *reasonable force*: the use of excessive violence is '*an actionable wrong*', that is, a tort for which a person may *take legal action, suing for damages*. In fact, Mr Newbery was almost '*reckless*', a state of mind where a person is (or should be) aware of the risk he is creating with his act, but persists in his dangerous behaviour. It is stronger than *negligence*. In a criminal case, the jury, composed of 12 ordinary men and women, will imagine the position the defendant believed he was in and decide whether he acted with reasonable force in the circumstances. In a civil case such as this, the judge will make this evaluation. The *circumstances*

---

[83] *Thieves*, irregular pl of *thief*, n, a person who commits *theft*, who steals.

[84] '*Malicious wounding*' is an offence against the person: causing injury with intent.

[85] *Revill v Newbery* [1996] QB 567, [1996] 1 All ER 291, per Neill LJ at 291. The defence of *ex turpi causa non oritur actio* is based on the principle that an action cannot be based on a claimant's own wrong.

[86] *Ibid*, per Millett LJ at 300.

are not measured by an objective test but according to the subjective belief of the defendant at the time, even if he was mistaken about the facts. For example, the defendant may believe the assailant was armed, when he was not. In this civil judgment, the Court of Appeal confirmed that Mr Newbery's conduct was *unreasonable*. On the contrary, it was dangerous, almost *reckless*. Mr Newbery's *appeal* was thus *dismissed* and he was therefore ordered to pay *damages for personal injuries* to Mark Revill. However, the sum of damages was reduced because 'Mr Revill was found two-thirds to blame for the injuries he suffered'.[87] In conclusion, although Mr Newbery's civil defence of self-defence had failed, his *defence of contributory negligence* was successful, leading to a reduction in *civil damages*.

Case study: *R v Martin*

In the case of *R v Martin*,[88] a farmer, Tony Martin, shot dead a young *burglar*[89] in his home and wounded another. Martin *raised the defence* of self-defence to murder, but the jury decided he had used an *unreasonable amount of force* in the circumstances: his defence was therefore unsuccessful and he was convicted of murder. The verdict caused public outcry, and there was also a possibility that the jury in the high security trial had been intimidated by the victim's supporters.[90] The case attracted much publicity and sympathy from the public, also because Mr Martin, like Mr Newbery in the case considered above, *was sued for damages* in a civil claim by the intruder who survived. Eventually, on appeal, the consequences for Mr Martin, who had used excessive force defending his home against criminal intruders, were softened.

What partial defence was successful? Was Martin convicted of voluntary or involuntary manslaughter?

> However, the court admitted fresh psychiatric evidence, that Martin was suffering from a long-term personality disorder. While this was found not relevant to the issue of self-defence, the court substituted a verdict of guilty of manslaughter by reason of diminished responsibility. The new sentences were five and three years imprisonment.[91]

Martin's *conviction* for murder *was quashed* (annulled) on appeal, and a conviction for *voluntary manslaughter* was substituted. He killed with malice aforethought, but the presence of *mitigating circumstances* at the time reduced his liability from murder to manslaughter: he succeeded in the partial defence of *diminished responsibility*.

---

[87] *Revill v Newbery* [1996] QB 567, [1996] 1 All ER 291, per Neill LJ at p 291.

[88] *R v Martin* [2001] EWCA Crim 2245, [2003] QB 1, also reviewed in the House of Commons Research Paper, above n 56, pp 14–16, case 'k.', Anthony Martin.

[89] *Burglary* is a crime related to *theft*, where a person enters the property of another as a *trespasser* (intentionally and without consent or the right to enter) and steals or commits certain other offences there. A *burglar* is a person who commits this crime, verb *to burgle*.

[90] 'Inquiry to be held into claims that jurors were intimidated', in *Guardian Weekly Newspaper*, 27 April–3 May 2000.

[91] House of Commons Research Paper, above n 56, case 'k.', Anthony Martin.

A discussion arose in the Court of Appeal in *Martin*, about the need for reform of the law.

What change in the law was discussed? What impact would this have for a defendant?

> What has been the subject of debate is whether a defendant to a murder charge should be convicted of murder if he was acting in self-defence but used excessive force in self-defence. It is suggested that such a defendant should be regarded as being guilty of manslaughter and not murder. He would not then have to be sentenced to life imprisonment but usually instead to a determinate sentence the length of which would be decided upon by the judge, having regard to the circumstances of the offence.[92]

Where self-defence fails as a defence to murder, in the present state of the law, the defendant is convicted of *murder*. Would it not be better to convict the defendant of *manslaughter*, instead? Importantly, conviction for this less serious class of homicide would give the judge *discretion to pass an appropriate sentence*, taking into account the circumstances of the case. Lord Chief Justice Woolf, in the *Martin* appeal, clearly stated that 'the change would have to be made by Parliament', not by judicial decision.[93] No such change has been made. (See 7.6.4 below.)

Compare and Discuss

Consider the two cases discussed above. How would a person in the position of William Newbery or Tony Martin be treated in your legal system? Consider both criminal and civil consequences. Compare and discuss, contributing your personal views on finding a just and balanced solution in cases of this kind.

7.6.3 The Degree of Force in Self-defence: a Proposal for Law Reform

In the UK, debate has focused on a possible reform to the law of self-defence. In this section, we examine one proposal, a Bill that was introduced in the 2004–05 Parliamentary session, with the purpose of amending the law on self-defence. The document you will read in this section is a *House of Commons Library Research Paper*, compiled for the benefit of Members of Parliament and their personal staff. The Paper contains an analysis of pre-existing law, a series of case studies illustrating the need to reform the law and discussion of the proposed change in the law.[94]

---

[92] *R v Martin* [2001] EWCA Crim 2245 (CA), per Lord Woolf CJ, [9].
[93] *Ibid.*
[94] Research Papers are available as PDF files to members of the general public on the Parliamentary website at <http://www.parliament.uk>.

Task 8 Reading a report: reform proposal and case studies on self-defence

Part One: Summary

Consult the summary of the proposal for reform of self-defence in the House of Commons Report and read the discussion of the proposed change to the law on self-defence under consideration in the 2004–05 session.

First, read the text for global understanding. What is each paragraph of the text about in general? How is the text organised? What main points are discussed? Then, read the report in detail to answer the following questions:

1. Who presented the Bill? What political problems does it face?
2. If passed, what would be the effect of the proposed law?
3. What are the arguments in favour of this proposed change in the law?
4. What arguments are there against adopting the proposed change?
5. Could this legislative change lead to a 'gun society'?

Part Two: Illustrations

Read 'Section B. Illustrations' from the House of Commons Report, which presents a series of recent case studies in self-defence. Prepare a brief profile of each case in answer to the following questions. As you work, focus on the use of legal language in context. Use a general English dictionary as necessary:

What are the facts of each case?

6. What were the consequences for the criminal assailant (the intruder, mugger, etc)?
7. What were the consequences for the citizen who used force in self-defence?
8. What is your view of the legal outcome (result) of each case?
9. Prepare to discuss the cases and explain your views.

House of Commons
RESEARCH PAPER
05/10 31 January 2005

Criminal Law (Amendment)
(Householder Protection) Bill
Bill 20 of 2004-05

Criminal Law (Amendment) (Householder Protection) Bill
Bill 20 of 2004–05

Summary of main points[95]
The *Criminal Law (Amendment) (Householder Protection) Bill* would make a new defence available to a person who had used force in the prevention of crime, or in self-defence, or defence of another or of property, against an intruder in a building. It would provide an absolute defence unless the force used was grossly disproportionate, and that had been apparent.

---

[95] This is an initial summary, to introduce the Research Paper, starting p 3.

The Bill was introduced in the House of Commons on 12 January 2005 by Patrick Mercer, Shadow Minister for Homeland Security, who came first in the ballot for Private Members' Bills.

During the last 20 years, cases in which intruders have been injured or killed have fuelled debate about whether the existing law strikes the right balance between the intruder and the householder. The law allows a person to use reasonable force in self-defence, or the prevention of crime, but it has been suggested that it is not clear to people what this means. There have also been suggestions that the law does not give enough protection to a person who finds intruders in his home.

The case of Tony Martin, who shot an escaping burglar in the back and was convicted of manslaughter, was an extreme case which has attracted a great deal of publicity, but there have been other cases in which decisions to charge or prosecute householders have been criticised. A press campaign to change the law was launched last year after a man was killed at his home by a burglar he had disturbed.

Mr Mercer has said that the intention of his Bill is to shift the balance so that the fear of imprisonment or physical harm should lie with the intruder, not the householder. The Bill would not affect cases like Tony Martin's, where the degree of force used had been grossly disproportionate. The Government has recognised public concern over these issues. Its view is that the existing law is sound, and that the key issue is to ensure that householders understand it.

Private Members' Bills are not subject to the requirement of section 19 of the *Human Rights Act 1998* that the Minister in charge of a Bill should make a statement on its compatibility with the European Convention on Human Rights before second reading.

Patrick Mercer has said that he wishes to rebalance the law in favour of the victim rather than the aggressor. He told *The Sunday Telegraph*:

> My Private Member's Bill will abolish the present statute's requirement that a home owner act with 'reasonable force' when tackling an intruder. It will replace it with the requirement that the home owner's use of force be 'not grossly disproportionate' to the circumstances in which he finds himself. Although it came top of the ballot for Parliamentary time, my Bill will almost certainly fail unless the Prime Minister explicitly supports it.

> There has already been media comment to the effect that my Bill will not provide the clarity in the law that home owners and others so desperately need: that 'not grossly disproportionate' is no better than 'reasonable force' as a definition of what you are allowed to do.

> Let me settle that issue now. The term 'not grossly disproportionate' will allow home owners a much greater degree of latitude in tackling burglars. They will be able to do whatever they think is necessary to defend themselves when confronted by an intruder. What they will not be entitled to do

is chase a burglar down the street and plunge a knife into his back once he is off their property. My Bill is not a licence to commit murder—it is not an English version of the Oklahoma law that indemnifies home-owners from prosecution no matter what they do to an intruder.

II Background

B. Illustrations[96]

The case of Tony Martin, who killed one intruder and injured another, was by no means the first case where a person prosecuted for harming an intruder has attracted much publicity and some sympathy. But it has been a particular focus, with continuing publicity, partly because of the surviving intruder's claim for damages, and issues raised in Mr Martin's appeal against conviction for murder. Some cases in which the issue of self-defence has arisen in the last 20 years are summarised below.

a.

Eric Butler

In May 1987, a retired clerk had a charge of malicious wounding withdrawn by the Crown Prosecution Service after he stabbed a mugger on the London Underground with a swordstick. However, he was later convicted of carrying an offensive weapon. He was fined £200, given a 28-day suspended sentence and had the swordstick confiscated. Lord Lane, the Lord Chief Justice, said Mr Butler 'quite properly' used the stick in self-defence, but upheld his conviction for carrying an offensive weapon and increased his fine from £200 to £300. The sentence and forfeiture order were quashed on appeal the following year.

b.

Kenneth Carrera

In May 1991, a disabled middle-aged man was charged with murder after he was attacked with a knife by a drunken, drugged mugger but succeeded in turning the weapon on his assailant. His counsel said: 'All he wanted to do was to walk the streets peacefully, a basic human right to which we are all entitled.' Mr Carrera was acquitted, but had spent eight months in prison awaiting trial.

> 'I realise there are some gung-ho people around but I don't consider myself one of those. Lots of people sympathised with me. Some said no jury would convict me of any charge. But it was still a terrible anguish for me waiting to hear what was going to happen to me. I really feared going to jail.'

...

---

[96] Starting on p 12 of the Research Paper.

d.
Hugh Williamson

In August 1994, a retired businessman disturbed a burglar he found in his home, and inflicted a deep wound on his neck with a kitchen knife. The case was studied by police for two months. Mr Williamson was then told that he would not face charges.

...

f.
Ben Lyon

In January 1995 a 73 year old man was cleared of attempted murder and wounding with intent after firing his shotgun at a man he believed was about to burgle his allotment shed. He had acted after repeated raids on his allotment. He was convicted of a lesser charge of unlawful wounding and given an 18-month suspended sentence.

Lyon said after the hearing:

'All I want to do now is to go home, look after my sister and feed my pigeons. I am relieved this is all over. I am grateful to the jury for their careful consideration of my case. I think the verdict was fair.

'I also thank the judge for his fair sentence and, as he said, I shall not be in trouble again ...

'I don't think I should have been treated as I was by the police, and I have no confidence in the law and order system.' He said he would 'do it again if my life was in danger. It is my biggest regret that I now have a stain on my character.'

...

© House of Commons Library
Source: <http://www.parliament.uk>
Parliamentary material is reproduced with the permission
of the Controller of HMSO on behalf of Parliament.

Key and commentary to Task 8 Reading a report: reform proposal and case studies on self-defence

1. The Bill was presented by *a member of the Opposition*, Mr Patrick Mercer, *Shadow Minister* for Homeland Security (a member of the *Shadow Cabinet*). It is a type of Bill called *a Private Member's Bill*, which is not part of the Government's political programme; in fact, if it is not supported by the Government, and specifically the Prime Minister, Mr Mercer believes the Bill will fail (as, in fact, happened).

2. The effect of the Bill would be to provide greater protection to people in their homes, with a new defence, wider than the existing right of self-defence, in prevention of crime, or in defence of person or property and specifically, in a building; it would be *a full defence*, unless the force used was '*grossly disproportionate*', permitting a more drastic reaction than the standard of *reasonable force*.

3. The main argument in favour is *to redress the balance* between a private, *law-abiding citizen* in his home and a criminal intruder. A person could do 'whatever they think is necessary' in self-defence.

4. Against the proposal is the accusation that '*grossly disproportionate*' is not defined any better than *reasonable force*: people would still not know how much force is permissible, say the media.

5. In Mr Mercer's view, there is no danger of a 'gun society' as a consequence of this reform: it is not a licence to commit murder, and a person cannot follow and chase an intruder down the street in order to assault him.

6.–8. Below, case by case:

— **Eric Butler** used self-defence against a mugger who attacked him on the London Tube: he was not prosecuted for this (the '*charge* of malicious wounding' was '*withdrawn by the CPS*', presumably *on grounds of public interest* discussed in Task 2 above). However, he was prosecuted and convicted for a less serious offence: 'carrying an offensive weapon', his 'swordstick'. He was sentenced to various punishments, which were all '*quashed on appeal*' (annulled): a fine of £200, raised to £300; a '28-day *suspended sentence*'; a '*forfeiture order*' to confiscate his weapon. We are not told about the consequences for the mugger, except that he was wounded.

— **Kenneth Carrera** was '*charged with murder*' after killing his attacker in self-defence. He was *held in custody* ('prison') for eight months '*awaiting trial*' and describes his anguish, as he feared conviction and life imprisonment. We understand that the jury found him not guilty: he '*was acquitted*'. The attacker in this case died.

— **Hugh Williamson** was not prosecuted for any crime (he did not '*face charges*'), after the police had studied his case for two months. The *burglar* was seriously injured.

— **Ben Lyon** was charged with '*attempted murder* and *wounding with intent*' after he fired a gun in protection of his property. He was convicted, but a *less serious offence* was substituted, carrying a lighter penalty: '*unlawful wounding*'/'an 18-month suspended sentence'. He accepts the verdict and thanks both judge and jury for their work, but feels he was badly treated by the police, and has lost confidence in 'the *law and order* system'. The intruder was wounded.

Comment

It is clear from these cases that the citizens who used force in self-defence against an intruder in their home or an attacker, suffered psychologically from their treatment as criminals or criminal suspects by the authorities. Many were also convicted of crimes that would become 'a stain' on their characters. The criminals against whom they used force were either hurt or killed: thus, a legal response from the criminal justice system became necessary.

7.6.4 Murder: Crime and Punishment

Life imprisonment

In the past, the punishment for murder was *capital punishment (execution)*. The *death sentence* was carried out in England by *hanging*. The *death penalty* was *abolished* for this crime by the Murder (Abolition of Death Penalty) Act 1965, which introduced instead a *mandatory life sentence*: this means that after a defendant has been convicted of murder, the judge *must* sentence him or her to *life imprisonment*, making a recommendation of a minimum *term* (period) of *detention*, for example, 15 or 30 years, during which the prisoner cannot be considered for *release*. Even after release from prison—once he is no longer considered a danger to public safety—a convicted *murderer* remains '*on licence*' for the rest of his life and therefore 'under the state's control'.[97]

As we saw in the *Martin* case, considered in 7.6.2 above, the *imposition* of the *mandatory life sentence for murder* is an integral part of the ongoing debate and criticism of the current *classes of homicide* in English law.

Lord Bingham expresses the view, below, that an offender should get his *just deserts*—the appropriate punishment that he or she *deserves* for the crime.

What factors should be taken into account in determining that punishment?

> It is a cardinal principle of morality, justice, and democratic government that an offender guilty of crime should be sentenced by the court to such penalty as his crime merits, taking account of all the circumstances including the nature of the crime, the circumstances of the offender, the effect of the crime on the victim and the victim's family, the need to prevent the offender from re-offending and deter others from offending in the same way, and the need to protect the public.[98]

Relevant factors that a judge must take into account in *sentencing an offender* include not only the circumstances and *nature of the crime* itself, but also 'the circumstances of the offender' and 'the effect of the crime' suffered by the victim and his or her family; *prevention*, *deterrence* and *protection* of the public are all to be taken into account. Lord Bingham goes on to state strongly that this '*cardinal*

---

[97] Ashworth, above n 48, at p 242.
[98] Bingham, above n 35, Part VIII Crime and Punishment, Paper 3, 'The Mandatory Life Sentence for Murder', at p 329.

principle of morality, justice, and democratic government' has been deliberately abandoned by the British legislature in the case of *murder*, since by statute a single specific *sentence* must be *handed down by the judge*: life imprisonment.[99]

The death penalty
What is your personal opinion on the use of the death penalty? Justify your views.

If you support the death penalty, for what crimes would you propose it? And what methods of execution do you consider humane?

Compare your views to Amnesty International's position, expressed below:

> The death penalty is the ultimate denial of human rights. It is the premeditated and cold-blooded killing of a human being by the state in the name of justice. It violates the right to life as proclaimed in the Universal Declaration of Human Rights. It is the ultimate cruel, inhuman and degrading punishment, whatever form it takes— electrocution, hanging, gassing, beheading, stoning, shooting or lethal injection.[100]

Year by year, Amnesty International's annual reports on the death penalty show a growing trend in the world towards *abolitionism*; in its report on the year 2010, the organisation concluded that countries that continue *to use the death penalty* are 'increasingly isolated following a decade of progress towards *abolition*' as a total of 31 countries had *abolished the death penalty in law or practice* during a 10-year period.[101]

Of the many convincing arguments against the use of the death penalty in a system of justice, perhaps the most impossible to refute is that it is an *irreversible penalty*. The English case of Derek Bentley provides a bitter illustration:

> On the evening of 2 November 1952 Police Constable Sidney Miles was shot dead in the execution of his duty on the roof of a warehouse in Croydon. Two men were charged with his murder: Christopher Craig, who was then aged 16; and Derek William Bentley, who was 19. On 17th November 1952 they were committed to stand trial on 9th December at the Central Criminal Court, where they were tried before Lord Goddard CJ and a jury. They were convicted on 11th December, in Bentley's case with a recommendation to mercy. The trial judge passed on each the only sentence permitted by law: on Craig, because of his age, that he be detained during Her Majesty's Pleasure; on Bentley, sentence of death. An appeal by Bentley against conviction was dismissed by the Court of Criminal Appeal (Croom-Johnson, Ormerod and Pearson JJ) on 13th January 1953. He was executed on 28th January.[102]

---

[99] *Ibid*, the statute in question being the Murder (Abolition of Death Penalty) Act 1965, s 1(1).

[100] 'Facts on the Death Penalty', available on the Amnesty International website at <www.amnesty.org>, visited 12 September 2013.

[101] Amnesty International Report, *Death Sentences and Executions in 2010*, published 28 March 2011, London: Amnesty International Ltd.

[102] *R v Derek William Bentley (Deceased)* [1998] EWCA Crim 2516, summary of the facts given by Lord Bingham CJ in the opening paragraph of the appeal judgment.

Forty-five years later, pronouncing judgment in an appeal against conviction heard in 1998, the Lord Chief Justice, President of the Criminal Division of the Court of Appeal, expressed regret for the *miscarriage of justice*:

> For all the reasons given in this section of the judgment we think that the conviction of the appellant [Bentley] was unsafe. We accordingly allow the appeal and quash his conviction. It must be a matter of profound and continuing regret that this mistrial occurred and that the defects we have found were not recognised at the time.[103]

There had been a *mistrial*: it was found that the judge in the murder trial had *misdirected the jury* (the prefix *mis-* indicates something done wrongly or badly). In addition, *fresh evidence* was assessed by the court, including medical and school reports, casting doubt on Bentley's *mens rea*. The case was conducted *on behalf of* the appellant by a family member, his niece.[104]

Task 9 Consulting legal sources—the death penalty

To learn about the evolution of human rights law in Europe in relation to the death penalty, consult the following legal sources.

Discuss your findings and consider the situation in your country and, if outside these European organisations, in your region of the world, introducing any relevant treaty provisions or national legislation.

Council of Europe, 47 signatories today, including all EU countries:
1. European Convention for the Protection of Human Rights and Fundamental Freedoms (ECHR), signed in Rome, 4 November 1950, Articles 1, 2, 3, 15.
2. Protocol No 6 to the ECHR, signed in Strasbourg, 28 April 1983.
3. Protocol No 13 to the ECHR, signed in Vilnius, 3 May 2002.

Note: In the case of signatories to the ECHR that have signed and ratified a Protocol, the Convention text is adapted accordingly; for parties that have not signed and also ratified a Protocol, the original Convention text remains in force.[105]

European Union, 28 Member States today, itself a signatory to the ECHR:
4. Charter of Fundamental Rights of the European Union (Charter of Nice) signed in Nice, 7 December 2000:[106] Preamble, Chapter I Dignity, Chapter VII General Provisions.

United Kingdom, belonging to both the Council of Europe and the EU:
5. Murder (Abolition of Death Penalty) Act 1965.
6. Human Rights Act 1998 (examined above in 5.4.3).

---

[103] *Ibid.*

[104] The full text of the judgment may be viewed online at <http://www.bailii.org>.

[105] A table showing dates of signatures and ratifications for the Convention and its protocols may be viewed on the Council of Europe website <http://www.coe.int>.

[106] Charter of Nice [2000] OJ C364/01.

Comment

As the European Court of Human Rights in Strasbourg has stated, the text of the ECHR is *a living instrument*, which 'must be interpreted in the light of present-day conditions'.[107] In its interpretation, where a case involves punishment for crime, the Court is influenced by 'developments and commonly accepted standards in the *penal policy* of the member States of the Council of Europe'.[108]

In a 1989 case before the Court in Strasbourg, involving a requested *extradition* of a German national from Britain to the United States on charges of murder,[109] *the Court held that* the '*death row*' phenomenon—with the extreme conditions and anguish of prisoners awaiting execution—would *constitute a violation of Article 3 of the Convention*. The United States itself is naturally beyond the reach of the ECHR. However, a party to the Convention (in this case, the UK) that became responsible for *extraditing a prisoner* to a country where he would face being *condemned to death* would be acting *in breach of its obligations* under Article 3.[110]

European Convention on Human Rights

Article 1 – Obligation to respect human rights
The High Contracting Parties shall secure to everyone within their jurisdiction the rights and freedoms defined in Section I of this Convention.

Article 3 – Prohibition of torture
No one shall be subjected to torture or to inhuman or degrading treatment or punishment.

In a further development, in a 2010 judgment of the Strasbourg Court[111] involving two Iraqi nationals held in a military detention centre by the British authorities in Iraq, but *within the jurisdiction* of the UK, *the Court held that* the death penalty itself, involving 'the deliberate and premeditated destruction of a human being by State authorities',[112] causing physical pain and intense psychological suffering as a result of the foreknowledge of death, *constitutes 'inhuman and degrading treatment'*, and is therefore a violation of Article 3 ECHR; the Court further stated that the protocols and '*State practice* in observing the *moratorium* on capital punishment are strongly indicative that Article 2 has been amended so as to prohibit the death penalty in all circumstances'.[113] It will be recalled that the original text of Article 2(1) ECHR (examined in Chapter one, Text 3) protects the right to life, but *envisaged* the death penalty as a possible exception. '*State practice*' refers to the practice of the States Parties to the Convention, almost all of which have in their practice abolished the death penalty, and have signed and ratified Protocol 13.

---

[107] *Tyrer v The United Kingdom* (App no 5856/72) Series A no 26 (1978) 2 EHRR 1, para 31.
[108] *Ibid.*
[109] *Soering v The United Kingdom* (App no 14038/88) [1989] ECHR 14, (1989) 11 EHRR 439.
[110] *Ibid*, para 111.
[111] *Al-Saadoon and Mufdhi v The United Kingdom* (App no 61498/08) [2010] ECHR 285, (2010) 51 EHRR 9.
[112] *Ibid*, para 115.
[113] *Ibid*, para 120.

Among Western democracies, the question remains when—or whether—the Constitution of the United States, which prohibits '*cruel and unusual punishments*' in its Eighth Amendment, will be definitively interpreted in line with modern European thinking.

Further Reading

Ashworth, Andrew and Horder, Jeremy (2013), *Principles of Criminal Law*, 7th edn, Oxford: Oxford University Press. This authoritative text provides in-depth critical analysis of the principles, policies and doctrines of English criminal law. Chapter 1 introduces criminal justice and the criminal law (pp 1–21); homicide is analysed in Chapter 7 (pp 236–306); Chapters 4 and 5 cover *actus reus* and *mens rea*, respectively, in a wider discussion of criminal conduct (pp 83–136) and criminal capacity (pp 137–92). Advanced level reading.

Bingham, Tom (2000), *The Business of Judging. Selected Essays and Speeches 1985–1999*, Oxford: Oxford University Press. A fascinating insight into the role of English judges by Senior Law Lord, Lord Bingham. From Part I The Business of Judging, Paper 1, 'The Judge as Juror: The Judicial Determination of Factual Issues' (pp 3–24); from Part VIII Crime and Punishment, Paper 1, 'The English Criminal Trial: The Credits and the Debits' (pp 253–68); and Paper 3, 'The Mandatory Life Sentence for Murder' (pp 329–43). Advanced level reading.

Bingham, Tom (2010), *The Rule of Law*, London: Penguin Books. In Chapter 9 of this enjoyable paperback, Lord Bingham analyses the right to a fair trial in both criminal and civil actions, commenting on a number of significant cases that illustrate how the English judiciary protect this fundamental human right (pp 90–109).

Cownie, Fiona, Bradney, Anthony and Burton, Mandy (2013), *English Legal System in Context*, 6th edn, Oxford: Oxford University Press. For a detailed critical analysis of trial by jury in the Crown Court and the role of the jury in the English legal system: from Chapter 17 'The Crown Court', 'Jury trial' (pp 335–47).

Fletcher, George P and Sheppard, Steve (2005), *American Law in a Global Context*, Oxford: Oxford University Press. Examines the concepts and techniques of the common law from an American perspective. Chapter 11, 'The Jury' (pp 243–58) looks at the history and development of the jury in common law jurisdictions, comparing civil law countries; Chapter 29, 'Self-Defense: Domestic and International' (pp 568–90) discusses proportionality and analyses the difference between self-defence in the fields of criminal law and international law.

Mandela, Nelson R (1994), *Long Walk to Freedom*, 1995 Abacus edn, London: Little, Brown and Company. A literary masterpiece that reveals in striking legal and human terms the evils of institutional racism and the power of principles. The full autobiography is recommended reading. Related to our studies in 7.2.2 are Part Five: Treason (Chapters 23–39); Part Seven: Rivonia (Chapters 49–58).

Padfield, Nicola (2012), *Criminal Law*, 8th edn, Oxford: Oxford University Press. Provides a clear explanation of English criminal law, with concise case summaries of the leading cases to illustrate each point. Chapter 1, 'Introduction', including the relation between law and morals, sentencing and the role of the jury (pp 1–21); Chapter 2, 'The conduct element of a crime' (pp 22–42); Chapter 3, 'Criminal states of mind, including intention, recklessness and negligence' (pp 43–69).

Chapter 8

LEGAL GRAMMAR

Verb Forms

Overview of verb tenses – Grammar review: active and passive voice –
Pronouns – Present simple – Modality – Present perfect – The passive

If the law be regarded while it remains in force as constantly speaking …

George Coode, barrister, 1842

This chapter focuses on the most frequently used verb tenses in legal documents: the present simple and the present perfect. Verb tenses introduce the concept of time (past, present and future) and duration of time (progressive and perfect). Other frequently used verbal constructions will also be discussed: for example, the relationship between the subject and object of a verb in a clause which determines voice (active or passive); and the use of modality (modal auxiliary verbs which express certain meanings such as obligation, capacity, permission, necessity, etc). Since historically the modal verbs *shall* and *may* have been a distinctive feature of legal discourse, their usage will be given close attention. The chapter begins with a general overview of verb tenses in various legal contexts, followed by a focus on the most frequently used verb forms.

8.1 OVERVIEW OF VERB TENSES

By examining a complete verb phrase in a clause, the main verb and its auxiliaries, and identifying its grammatical subject, we can understand why certain grammatical choices are made when writing legal documents. So, if the law is 'constantly speaking' as Coode says[1] in the epigraph that introduces this chapter, what grammatical constructions create this situation? Williams[2] clarifies this concept further:

> The idea that words are continually speaking, an expression which uses the present progressive construction, implies a situation that is permanently in progress … another way of saying that the law has constant validity.

---

[1] This expression used by George Coode in 1942 was cited by C Williams (2007), *Tradition and Change in Legal English: Verbal Constructions in Prescriptive Texts*, Bern: Peter Lang, p 85.
[2] *Ibid.*

For example, treaties and Acts have this quality of something that is permanently in progress and with constant validity, yet the verb form frequently chosen is the present simple. In chapter one, legal texts are described as 'performative' in that they *perform* legal actions that produce legal effect. Yet this legal effect is constant and could be said to have a prescriptive[3] force that projects into future. Observe the present simple in the following texts. The use of the present simple assigns power or legal authority to executive bodies, e.g.:

> States Parties undertake to ensure the child such protection and care as is necessary for his or her well-being,[4]

or states the law, e.g.:

> It is unlawful for a public authority to act in a way which is incompatible with a Convention right.[5]

According to Williams,[6] the present simple constitutes 'well over 40 per cent of all verbal constructions' in prescriptive legal texts. It is used in explanations, clarifications or definitions of terminology in a legal document:

> For the purposes of this Declaration, the term 'violence against women' means any act of gender-based violence that results in, … physical, sexual or psychological harm or suffering to women, …[7]

Modals with simple aspect,[8] such as the auxiliary *shall*,[9] combine with the infinitive verb form (without *to*) to impose a duty or an obligation, e.g.:

> Each State Party shall take effective legislative, administrative, judicial or other measures to prevent acts of torture in any territory under its jurisdiction.[10]

or to prohibit actions, such as:

> This Article shall not prejudice the trial and punishment of any person for any act or omission which, at the time when it was committed, was criminal according to the general principles of law recognised by civilised nations.[11]

---

[3] Telling people what they should or should not do, an obligation.

[4] Convention on the Rights of the Child (adopted 20 November 1989, entered into force 2 September 1990), UNGA Res 44/25, Part I, Art 3(2).

[5] Human Rights Act 1998, s 6(1) ('Acts of public authorities').

[6] Williams , above n 1, p 150.

[7] Declaration on the Elimination of Violence against Women (plenary meeting 20 December 1993), UNGA Res 48/04, Art 1.

[8] *Aspect* refers to how verbs are understood in relation to *duration* of time: continuous time (progressive and perfect tenses) and non-continuous time (present simple and past simple).

[9] The modal auxiliary *shall* is the most frequently used modal in legal texts.

[10] Convention against Torture and Other Cruel Inhumane or Degrading Treatment or Punishment (adopted 10 December 1984, entered into force 26 June 1987), UNGA Res 39/46 Art 2(1).

[11] Convention for the Protection of Rights and Fundamental Freedoms as amended by Protocol No 14 CET No 194 (adopted 4 December 1950 entered into force 1 June 2010), ETS I, Art 7(2).

The use of the modal *may* instead of *shall* indicates a discretionary power, e.g.:

> The Times, Places and Manner of holding Elections for Senators and Representatives, shall be prescribed in each State by the Legislature thereof; but the Congress may at any time by Law make or alter such Regulations, except as to the Place of Chusing Senators.[12]

or granting permission, e.g.:

> The holding of a meeting, a demonstration or a vigil on the highway, however peaceable, has nothing to do with the right of passage. Such activities may, if they do not cause an obstruction, be tolerated, but there is no legal right to pursue them.[13]

The present perfect, claimed as the second most common verbal construction in prescriptive texts,[14] often appears at the end of preambles to treaties after the recitals, e.g.:

> HAVE DECIDED to establish a European Union and to this end have designated as their Plenipotentiaries:
>
> [List of plenipotentiaries not reproduced]
>
> WHO, having exchanged their full powers, found in good and due form, have agreed as follows:[15]

or is used to express an action which began in the past but has repercussions in the present, e.g.:

> Furthermore, the Commission has already rebutted Microsoft's arguments relating to the scope of Sun's request and has already stated that the possibility that the products …[16]

or in a subordinate clause that expresses a contingency, e.g.:

> When a State, pursuant to this article, has taken a person into custody, it shall immediately notify the States referred to in Article 5, …[17]

While in the language of the courts, in particular judgments, past simple describes the facts of a case, e.g.:

> By an action brought in the Court of Session the appellant, who was a shop assistant, sought to recover damages from the respondent, …[18]

The passive, which is frequently used in legal texts,[19] reorganises information in a clause so that the 'agent', the person who actively performs the action, is not

---

[12] The United States Constitution, Art I § 4, Elections, Meetings.

[13] *Director of Public Prosecutions v Jones and Another* [1999] UKHL 5.

[14] Williams, above n 1, p 155.

[15] Consolidated Version of Treaty on European Union [2012] OJ C326/13, recitals in Preamble.

[16] *Microsoft Corp v Commission of the European Communities* [2007] ECR Page II-03601, in Judgment of the Court of First Instance (Grand Chamber), Case No: T-201/04, para 1314.

[17] Convention against Torture, etc, above n 10, Art 6(4).

[18] *M'Alister (or Donoghue) (Pauper) Appellant and Stevenson Respondent* [1932] AC 562 (HL).

[19] Williams, above n 1, p 35, claims that 25% of all verbal constructions in prescriptive Legal English are passives.

identified. In the example below, it is impossible to identify the agent since a condition is being expressed:

> The institution or institutions whose act *has been declared* void or whose failure to act *has been declared* contrary to this Treaty *shall be required* to take the necessary measures to comply with the judgment of the Court of Justice.[20]

In the first two passive forms (in *italics*), there is no detectable agent. In the third passive form 'shall be required', it seems that one could easily insert 'by the Treaty' after 'shall be required'. It is omitted because it is obvious. In the first two cases, it is omitted because it is not obvious but also not relevant.

In other uses of the passive, the actor may be obvious, as in this Directive, e.g.:

> Official Journal of the European Communities 22.6.2001 L 167/19
> Article 11
> Technical adaptations
> 1.   Directive 92/100/EEC *is hereby amended* as follows:
> (a)   Article 7 shall be deleted; ...

8.2 QUICK GRAMMAR REVIEW

Before analysing verb forms in a legal context, Table 8.1 below provides a brief overview of active and passive voice. The infinitive *to repeal* has been used to illustrate both the *active* and the *passive* voice.

Table 8.1: Verb tenses: active and passive voice

VERB TENSES: ACTIVE AND PASSIVE VOICE

Active voice: *Parliament repealed the law.*
Parliament is the *actor* or *performer* of the action.

infinitive	*to repeal*
present simple	*repeal*
modal	*must repeal**
present simple continuous	*am/is/are repealing*
past simple	*repealed*
past continuous	*was/were repealing*
present perfect	*have/has repealed*
present perfect continuous	*have/has been repealing*
past perfect	*had repealed*

(Continued)

---

[20] Treaty on European Union [1992] OJ C191/01, Art 176.

Passive voice: *The law was repealed by Parliament.*
The agent (the actor or performer of the action) is not the grammatical subject.

The passive voice contains a form of the auxiliary *be* + the past participle of the main verb, e.g. (*–ed*) for the verb *to repeal.*

infinitive	*to repeal*
simple present	*am/is/are repealed*
present progressive	*am/is/are being repealed*
simple past	*was/were repealed*
past progressive	*was/were being repealed*
perfect infinitive	*have been repealed*
present perfect	*have/has been repealed*
past perfect	*had been repealed*
future *will*	*will be repealed**
future *going to*	*am/is/are going to be repealed*
modal form	*should be repealed*

*The modal forms used in this table may be substituted with other modals (or semi-modals), dependent on the meaning that is intended by the speaker (see 8.5 below), e.g.: It *might* be repealed. It *has to* be repealed. It *may* be repealed.

Task 1 Read, scan and observe—verb tenses

Quickly scan the following texts: a judgment, a convention, an Act and a scholarly opinion by a jurist. Underline the complete verbal phrases in all four texts. Write the complete verbal phrase (include any auxiliaries) next to the appropriate verb tense in the table provided. Do not include incomplete verb phrases, such as formulated in Text 1 below. The first verb in Text 1 has been underlined and inserted into table as an example.

Text 1 Judgment

1123   The Commission first of all <u>rejects</u> the factual observations formulated by Microsoft. It claims, in particular, that the applicant's general assertions concerning the benefits of the integration of new functionalities unrelated to Windows Media Player into client PC operating systems are irrelevant.

1124   Next, the Commission, supported by SIIA, submits that Microsoft has failed to show that the impugned conduct is objectively justified.[21]

---

[21] *Microsoft Corp v Commission of the European Communities*, above n 16, Judgment of the Court of First Instance.

Text 2 Convention

PART I GENERAL PROVISIONS

Article 1

The High Contracting Parties undertake to respect and to ensure respect for the present Convention in all circumstances.

Article 2

In addition to the provisions which shall be implemented in peace time, the present Convention shall apply to all cases of declared war or of any other armed conflict ...[22]

Text 3 Act

3(1)   So far as it is possible to do so, primary legislation and subordinate legislation must be read and given effect in a way which is compatible with the Convention rights.

...

6(1)   It is unlawful for a public authority to act in a way which is incompatible with a Convention right.

...

8(1)   In relation to any act (or proposed act) of a public authority ...

the court or tribunal may grant such relief or remedy, or make such order, within its powers as it considers just and appropriate.[23]

...

Text 4 Scholarly opinion—Lord Denning

May not the Judges themselves sometimes abuse or misuse their power? It is their duty to administer and apply the law of the land. If they should divert it or depart from it − and do so knowingly − they themselves would be guilty of a misuse of power. So, we come up with Juvenal's[24] question, '*Sed quis custodiet ipsos custodies?*' (But who is to guard the guards themselves?) ... You need have no fear. The Judges of England have always in the past − and always will − be vigilant in guarding our freedoms. Someone must be trusted. Let it be the Judges.[25]

Verb tenses

present simple *rejects* ....

....

....

....

present simple continuous ....

---

[22] Geneva Convention relative to the Treatment of Prisoners of War (adopted 12 August 1949, entered into force 21 October 1950), 75 UNTS 135, Pt I, Arts 1 and 2.

[23] Human Rights Act 1998, artt 3(1), 6(1), 8(1).

[24] Juvenal was a Roman satirist and poet.

[25] Lord Denning, 'Misuse of Power' (The Richard Dimbleby Lecture 1980) in *What Next in the Law* (1982), Virginia: Lexis Law Publishing, p 380.

present simple (passive voice)..

....

present perfect ....

imperative ....

past simple ....

passive ....

modal + infinitive ....

....

....

....

....

modal passive voice ....

Answer these questions:
1. Which verb form is used the most frequently?
2. In which of the four texts are there personalised references (e.g. I, you, or we)?
3. Why do prescriptive legal texts (treaties, Acts, etc) avoid using these personalised references?

8.3 PRONOUNS

Legal texts are concerned with exactness of reference. If referential pronouns are substituted for previously mentioned lexical items, there is the risk of ambiguity. As a consequence, reference pronouns are rarely used and are generally avoided as subjects. For this reason, lexical words are continually repeated in order to avoid possible misinterpretation.

8.3.1 Referential Pronouns

In contemporary English, referential pronouns (*he, she, it,* or *they*) refer back to a lexical item that was mentioned previously (an anaphoric reference). In legal texts this back reference is scrupulously avoided. Crystal and Davy[26] explain why:

> The trouble with substitutes of this kind however, is that they can often look back as though they were referring back to an item other than that which the writer had in

---

[26] D Crystal and D Davy (1969), 'The Language of Legal Documents', *Investigating English Style,* Harlow: Longman, p 202.

mind, producing ambiguities and confusions which would be of very little consequence in conversation – or even in a good deal of written language – but quite intolerable in a legal document.

In a humorous tone, Garner[27] says that lawyers have been excessive in their avoidance of referential pronouns by using endless repetition of nouns. He quotes Fred Rodell:

> '... many legal sentences read as if they have been translated from the German by someone who barely knows English.'

To illustrate this endless repetition, observe how the noun 'Commission' is continually repeated for precision of reference instead of a pronoun as an anaphoric reference in this text:

> The Commission, as a body, shall be responsible to the European Parliament. In accordance with Article 234 of the Treaty on the Functioning of the European Union, the European Parliament may vote on a motion of censure of the Commission. If such a motion is carried, the members of the Commission shall resign as a body and the High Representative of the Union for Foreign Affairs and Security Policy shall resign from the duties that he carries out in the Commission.[28]

8.3.2 Referential Pronouns as Subjects

Another peculiarity of legal texts is the avoidance of the personal pronoun (such as *I*, *we*, *you*, *etc*) as subject. For example in legislative provisions, the third person is referred to in a general sense with such words such as 'a person', 'no one', 'everyone', to ensure impartiality and all-inclusiveness. In other cases, reference in a provision may make a specific reference, such as to 'a secure tenant' or 'householder', or even naming the referent such as a 'Native American'.

There are, of course, exceptions to this type of 'depersonalisation'. For example, even though the first person singular *I* or the second person singular and plural *you* are not common in most legal texts, in Text 4 (see 8.2 above), a scholarly opinion, it was used quite freely, e.g.:

You need have no fear.

or

So, *we* come up with Juvenal's question ...

---

[27] BA Garner (1995), *A Dictionary of Modern Legal Usage*, 2nd edn, New York: Oxford University Press, p 702.
[28] Consolidated Version of the Treaty on European Union [2010] OJ C83/13, Art 17(8).

The first person plural *we* is also rarely found in prescriptive texts. However, there are exceptions, such as the following two examples taken from the United States Constitution:

> We the People of the United States, in Order to form a more perfect Union, establish Justice, insure domestic Tranquility, ... (Preamble)

> In Witness whereof We have hereunto subscribed our Names.
> (Article VII. – Ratification Documents Article)

Then again with case law, it is quite common to find *we*:

> The Crown Court stated its conclusion as follows:
> 'We considered ourselves bound by the decision in *Waite v Taylor* (1985) 149 JP 551 ...'[29]

8.3.3 Relative Pronouns as Subject of Clause

Relative clauses (also called adjectival clauses) follow (*post-modify*) noun phrases and provide further information. They are introduced by relative pronouns such as *who* (used for people) and *which* or *that* (used for objects or concepts), as subjects of a clause.

Task 2 STOP and CHECK—relative pronouns
Scan the following legal extracts (1.–4.). <u>Underline</u> the relative pronouns and circle the nouns that precede them:

1. States Parties shall take all appropriate measures:
   (a) To modify the social and cultural patterns of conduct of men and women, with a view to achieving the elimination of prejudices and customary and all other practices which are based on the idea of the inferiority or the superiority of either of the sexes or on stereotyped roles for men and women ...[30]
2. No prisoner of war may be tried or sentenced for an act which is not forbidden by the law of the Detaining Power or by international law, in force at the time the said act was committed.[31]

---

[29] *Director of Public Prosecutions v Jones and Another* [1999] UKHL 5, p 149.
[30] Convention on the Elimination of All Forms of Discrimination Against Women (adopted in 18 December 1979 entered into force 3 September 1981), UNGA Res 34/180, Art 5(a).
[31] Geneva Convention Treatment of Prisoners of War, above n 22, Art 99.

3. States Parties recognize the right of the child to be protected from economic exploitation and from performing any work that is likely to be hazardous or to interfere with the child's education, ...[32]
4. States Parties shall prohibit and condemn all forms of harmful practices ... including:
    (d)   protection of women who are at risk of being subjected to harmful practices or all other forms of violence, abuse and intolerance.[33]

The clauses[34] 1.–4. in Task 2 illustrate examples of *restrictive* clauses. Each clause gives indispensable information about the preceding noun which is essential to the meaning of the sentence. In a *non-restrictive* clause (framed by commas), the meaning of the sentence is not necessarily modified or less clear by omission. Review sections 6.7.3 and 6.7.4 above for an explanation of restrictive and non-restrictive clauses.

NOTE: Grammar—The relative pronoun *that* can replace *which* or *who* in *restrictive* clauses, e.g.:
—   Tort is a body of law *which/that* deals with a vast array of 'civil wrongs'.
—   The purpose of torts is to compensate an injured party *who/that* was wronged by awarding damages.

8.4 PRESENT SIMPLE

The present simple constitutes 'well over 40 per cent of all verbal constructions'[35] and is the most frequently chosen verb tense used for treaties and Acts, particularly in combination with the modal auxiliaries *shall* and *may*.[36] Quickly scan any of the legal texts in this book for the present simple. Does this statistic confirm this statement?

---

[32] Convention on the Rights of the Child (adopted 20 November1989, entered into force 2 September 1990) UNGA Res 44/25, Art 32(1).

[33] Protocol to the African Charter on Human and Peoples' Rights on the Rights of Women in Africa (adopted by the 2nd Ordinary Session of the Assembly of the Union, Maputo, CAB/LEG/66.6 13 September 2000, entered into force 25 November 2005), Art 5(d).

[34] Remember a 'clause' has a subject and a verb.

[35] Williams, above n 1, p 150.

[36] The modal auxiliary typically appears in the main clause, while the subordinate clause uses the present simple.

Task 3 Read, scan and observe—subject identification
Identify the subjects of the clauses and the verb phrases (including any auxiliaries and modal auxiliaries) in sections 8.4.1 (1., 2., 3.) and 8.4.2 (4., 5., 6.) by <u>underlining</u> the subjects and <u>double underlining</u> the verbs. In 8.4.1 the subject and verb phrase have been underlined in 1. as an example.

8.4.1 The Legal Authority as the Subject

In the first example (a Convention) the subject, *States Parties*, is underlined. States Parties are the legal authority that has been assigned the power and legal authority to fulfil this obligation of Article 31. The present simple verb *recognize* is double underlined. Continue to underline the subjects and double underline the verb phrases in (2), a Convention, and (3), an agency agreement.

1. *Article 31*

    1. <u>States Parties</u> <u>recognize</u> the right of the child to rest and leisure, to engage in play …[37]

2. States Parties condemn discrimination against women in all its forms …[38]

3. The Principal hereby appoints the Agent as its sole agent to promote and negotiate the sale of the Products … and the Agent hereby accepts the appointment on those terms.

    Agent's obligations
    The Agent undertakes and agrees with the Principal at all times during the term of this Agreement: …[39]

8.4.2 Present Simple in Subordinate Clauses

Legal texts are characteristically long, containing complex sentences that are both subordinated and coordinated. Yet, regardless of sentence length, the verbal constructions have a minimal variation of verb tense. For example, the present simple is still the preferred verbal construction for subordinate clauses. In prescriptive texts, the main clause typically contains the modal *shall* or *may* + infinitive, while the subordinate clause uses the present simple.

Underline the subject and double underline the verb phrase in the following clauses. The subordinate clauses are in italics. The first clause has been done for you.

---

[37] Convention on the Rights of the Child, above n 32, Art 31(1).
[38] Convention on the Elimination of All Forms of Discrimination against Women, above n 30, Pt 1, Art 2.
[39] Agency agreement (clause 2.1, Appointment) used courtesy of Withers LLP – see <http://www.withersworldwide.com>.

4. *If a* <u>*Member State*</u> <u>*persists*</u> *in failing to put into practice the recommendations of the Council*, the Council may decide to give notice to the Member State ...

5. *Where a Member State is in difficulties or is seriously threatened with difficulties as regards its balance of payments* ... the Commission shall immediately investigate the position of the State in question.[40]

6. *Whenever it deems it necessary*, the Council shall define a common position.[41]

8.4.3 Present Simple in *that*-Clauses

In 8.3.3 above we discussed relative pronouns. Observe how the relative pronoun *that* is often found as the *subject* in a subordinate defining relative clause with the present simple, e.g.:

The Parliament may make a law fixing an age *that is less than seventy years as the maximum age for Justices of a court* ...[42]

or the *that*-clause is placed after the main verb and is the direct object of the sentence, e.g.:

The Conference affirms *that the President of the European Council shall invite the Economic and Finance Ministers to participate in European Council* ...[43]

The subordinate *that*-clause may also be coordinated (*and, or, but*) with other subordinate clauses, once again with the present simple. This was taken from a preamble/recital:

RECALLING *that* Article 2 of the Treaty establishing the European Community includes the task of promoting economic and social cohesion and solidarity between Member States <u>and</u> *that* the strengthening of economic and social cohesion figures among the activities of the Community listed in Article 3; ...[44]

8.5 MODALITY

Modal auxiliaries combine with the base form (infinitive) of the main verb (without *to*) and modify the meaning of a sentence. For example, modal auxiliaries can express obligation (*should*), capacity/permission (*can*), necessity (*need/needn't*), advice/suggestion (*must*), prohibition (*mustn't*), and possibility/probability (*may,*

---

[40] Treaty Establishing the European Community as Amended by Subsequent Treaties 1957, Pt 3, Title VI, Ch 1, Art 104c(9) and Ch 4, Art 109h(1).

[41] Treaty on European Union [1992] OJ C191/01, Art J.2(2).

[42] Commonwealth of Australia Constitution Act 1900, Art 7(iii).

[43] TEU, above n 41, Declaration on Pt 3, Title VI.

[44] *Ibid*, Protocol on economic and social cohesion, recital.

might).[45] Another category of words called semi-modals also express modal mean-ings such as capacity (*be able to*), and obligation (*be bound to, have to, or suppose to*), however, these semi-modals must include the *to*-infinitive with the main verb.

Observe the modal auxiliaries:

> If it had been before the Court of Appeal it *might* well *have affected* their decision, ...[46]

> The level of fair compensation *should take* full account of the degree of use of techno-logical protection measures referred to in this Directive.[47]

Modals exist in both non-legal and legal texts, yet there are two modal auxiliaries which play a central role in legal texts, particularly in contexts that express a contrac-tual obligation: *shall* and *may*. They are often called *words of authority*.[48] As you have noted in previous examples, these two modals play a crucial role in legal discourse.

NOTE: In Standard English grammar rules, the modal *will* expresses futurity, either by making a prediction, e.g. I will pass the Bar this spring; volition[49] or intention, e.g. They will stand up for my rights if they are violated. The modal *will* is not very common in prescriptive texts since the modal *shall* implies present and future obligations.

Task 4 Read, scan and observe—distinguishing the modals *shall* and *may* in a treaty: English and Spanish texts

Read the following extracts taken from the Consolidated Version of the Treaty on European Union.[50] Scan the English version and highlight/under-line the modal auxiliaries *shall* and *may* + the following verb phrase. Article 1 has been done for you. Scan the Spanish version and highlight/underline any verbal constructions that convey authority or obligation.

Observe: What verb tense is used for *authority* in Spanish? What *words of authority* are used for legal texts in your mother tongue?

---

[45] Refer to a grammar book as needed for a more complete list of modal auxiliaries.

[46] *Mandla (Sewa Singh) v Dowell Lee* [1982] UKHL 7, p 5.

[47] Directive on the harmonisation of certain aspects of copyright and related rights in the informa-tion society [2001] OJ LI67/29.

[48] For a comprehensive discussion on *words of authority*, see B Garner (1995), *A Dictionary of Modern Legal Usage*, 2nd edn, New York: Oxford University Press, pp 939–42.

[49] Volition = deciding on your own.

[50] Consolidated Version of the Treaty on European Union [2010] OJ C83/01, Arts 1, 2 and 3(1), (2), (3) and compare your mother-tongue version with the English version. Go to the EU website at <http://www.europa.eu>.

TREATY ON EUROPEAN UNION	TRATADO DE LA UNIÓN EUROPEA
Article 1	*Artículo 1*
By this Treaty, the HIGH CONTRACTING PARTIES establish among themselves a EUROPEAN UNION, hereinafter called 'the Union', on which the Member States confer competences to attain objectives they have in common.	Por el presente Tratado, las ALTAS PARTES CONTRATANTES constituyen entre sí una UNIÓN EUROPEA, en lo sucesivo denominada «Unión», a la que los Estados miembros atribuyen competencias para alcanzar sus objetivos comunes.
This Treaty marks a new stage in the process of creating an ever closer union among the peoples of Europe, in which decisions are taken as openly as possible and as closely as possible to the citizen.	El presente Tratado constituye una nueva etapa en el proceso creador de una unión cada vez más estrecha entre los pueblos de Europa, en la cual las decisiones serán tomadas de la forma más abierta y próxima a los ciudadanos que sea posible.
The Union <u>shall be founded</u> on the present Treaty and on the Treaty on the Functioning of the European Union (hereinafter referred to as 'the Treaties'). Those two Treaties <u>shall</u> <u>have</u> the same legal value. The Union <u>shall replace and succeed</u> the European Community.	La Unión se fundamenta en el presente Tratado y en el Tratado de Funcionamiento de la Unión Europea (en lo sucesivo denominados «los Tratados»). Ambos Tratados tienen el mismo valor jurí dico. La Unión sustituirá y sucederá a la Comunidad Europea.
Article 2	*Artículo 2*
The Union is founded on the values of respect for human dignity, freedom, democracy, equality, the rule of law and respect for human rights, including the rights of persons belonging to minorities. These values are common to the Member States in a society in which pluralism, non-discrimination, tolerance, justice, solidarity and equality between women and men prevail.	La Unión se fundamenta en los valores de respeto de la dignidad humana, libertad, democracia, igualdad, Estado de Derecho y respeto de los derechos humanos, incluidos los derechos de las personas pertenecientes a minorías. Estos valores son comunes a los Estados miembros en una sociedad caracterizada por el pluralismo, la no discriminación, la tolerancia, la justicia, la solidaridad y la igualdad entre mujeres y hombres.
Article 3	*Artículo 3*
1. The Union's aim is to promote peace, its values and the well-being of its peoples.	1. La Unión tiene como finalidad promover la paz, sus valores y el bienestar de sus pueblos.
2. The Union shall offer its citizens an area of freedom, security and justice without internal frontiers, in which the free movement of persons is ensured in conjunction with appropriate measures with respect to external border controls, asylum, immigration and the prevention and combating of crime.	2. La Unión ofrecerá a sus ciudadanos un espacio de libertad, seguridad y justicia sin fronteras interiores, en el que esté garantizada la libre circulación de personas conjuntamente con medidas adecuadas en materia de control de las fronteras exteriores, asilo, inmigración y de prevención y lucha contra la delincuencia.

3. The Union shall establish an internal market. It shall work for the sustainable development of Europe based on balanced economic growth and price stability, a highly competitive social market economy, aiming at full employment and social progress, and a high level of protection and improvement of the quality of the environment. It shall promote scientific and technological advance.	3. La Unión establecerá un mercado interior. Obrará en pro del desarrollo sostenible de Europa basado en un crecimiento económico equilibrado y en la estabilidad de los precios, en una economía social de mercado altamente competitiva, tendente al pleno empleo y al progreso social, y en un nivel elevado de protección y mejora de la calidad del medio ambiente. Asimismo, promoverá el progreso científico y técnico.
It shall combat social exclusion and discrimination, and shall promote social justice and protection, equality between women and men, solidarity between generations and protection of the rights of the child.	La Unión combatirá la exclusión social y la discriminación y fomentará la justicia y la protección sociales, la igualdad entre mujeres y hombres, la solidaridad entre las generaciones y la protección de los derechos del niño.
It shall promote economic, social and territorial cohesion, and solidarity among Member States.	La Unión fomentará la cohesión económica, social y territorial y la solidaridad entre los Estados miembros.
It shall respect its rich cultural and linguistic diversity, and shall ensure that Europe's cultural heritage is safeguarded and enhanced.	La Unión respetará la riqueza de su diversidad cultural y lingüística y velará por la conservación y el desarrollo del patrimonio cultural europeo.

Summing up, the English version of the Treaty predictably uses *shall* to express an obligation followed by a verb (the infinitive form without *to*). In the Spanish version of the EU Treaty, the future tense – *will* – imposes authority. Contrast the English with the Italian version below.

TREATY ON EUROPEAN UNION	TRATTATO SULL'UNIONE EUROPEA
Article 3	*Articolo 3*
1. The Union's aim is to promote peace, its values and the well-being of its peoples.	1. L'Unione si prefigge di promuovere la pace, i suoi valori e il benessere dei suoi popoli.
2. The Union shall offer its citizens an area of freedom, security and justice without internal frontiers, in which the free movement of persons is ensured in conjunction with appropriate measures with respect to external border controls, asylum, immigration and the prevention and combating of crime.	2. L'Unione offre ai suoi cittadini uno spazio di libertà, sicurezza e giustizia senza frontiere interne, in cui sia assicurata la libera circolazione delle persone insieme a misure appropriate per quanto concerne i controlli alle frontiere esterne, l'asilo, l'immigrazione, la prevenzione della criminalità e la lotta contro quest'ultima.
3. The Union shall establish an internal market. ...	3. L'Unione instaura un mercato interno. ...

In Italian two-thirds of verbal constructions in prescriptive texts use the indicative form of the present simple, not the future tense; Williams further explains similarities with other languages in the EU:

> [I]t is a general feature in many European countries that the language of law is written predominantly in the tense that is also most widely used in everyday communication: ... Neither is it particularly projected towards the future or overtly modal in the way the shall has become in English. And neither would there appear to be widespread calls for it to be replaced by, say, modal auxiliary verbs expressing obligation, prohibition or discretionary choice such as *dovere* or *potere* [in Italian].[51]

Other phrases can also express authority and obligation in a legal context, such as *has the power, is obliged, will be empowered, will require, binding, bound*. For example:

— *The monarch has the power to sign international agreements.*
— *The Queen is obliged to act on her ministers' advice.*
— *The Secretary of State of Wales will be empowered to ...*
— *Royal Assent to Ireland Bills will require the intervention of ...*
— *The opinions of the Advocates-General are not binding on the Court.*
— *Signatories to the treaty will be bound for a period of ...*

Task 5 STOP and CHECK—general use of modals

Meanings can change simply by adding a different modal auxiliary. The following modals are found less frequently in prescriptive texts. Fill in the gaps below with the modal that reflects the meaning in the parentheses. Use each modal once only: *should, must, has to, can, needs to, must be, might, ought to*.

The judge dismisses the case. (no modal)

1. *The judge .... dismiss the case.* (possibility)
2. *The judge .... dismiss the case.* (modal of capacity)
3. *The judge .... dismiss the case.* (obligation – personal authority)
4. *The judge .... dismiss the case.* (obligation – outside authority)
5. *The judge .... dismiss the case.* (advice – more personal)
6. *The judge .... dismiss the case.* (obligation – it is the 'right thing to do')
7. *The judge .... dismiss the case.* (necessity)
8. *He .... the judge who dismissed the case.* (logical deduction).

---

[51] Williams, above n 1, pp 152–53.

NOTES ON GRAMMAR: *The modal verbs* need to, have to, be supposed to, *and* ought to *are semi-modals and the* to *must be retained. In modals it is not required*:
I am supposed to pay the fee in June. ~~I am suppose pay the fine in June.~~ (*incorrect*)
I should pay my parking fine. ~~I should to pay my parking fine.~~ (*incorrect*)

Modal verbs do not have an [s] in the third person singular (he/she/it) *and do not use infinitives or participles, e.g.*:
She might be the next president. ~~She mights be the next president.~~ (*incorrect*)
~~He's musting to pass the Legal English exam.~~ (*incorrect*)
Modal questions are formed without do:
Can you help me? ~~Do you can help me?~~ (*incorrect*)

8.6 PRESENT PERFECT

As noted earlier in the overview of this chapter in 8.1 above, the present perfect is commonly used in legal texts. It expresses a duration of time that began in the past yet connects to the present. Present perfect can be used in different ways:

a) situations that have continued up to the present time;
    I have struggled with passing the Bar exam for the last two years.
b) repeated actions that have gone on up to now;
    The Government has initiated many new programs with successful results.
c) the present result or relevance of past actions; and
    The EU still has not found a formula that would solve Europe's spiralling migration crisis.
d) news of immediacy ('breaking news').
    A thousand boat people have just arrived in Lampedusa, Italy.

The present perfect is one of the most frequently used tenses in subordinate clauses and often reflects the condition reflected in example (c) above. As will be noted in some of the extracts in Task 6 below, the present perfect in the subordinate clause includes not only a time reference from the past to present, but also a projection into the future. Observe these examples:

If, within three months of such communication, the European Parliament approves this common position or *has not taken* a decision within that period, the Councils shall definitely adopt …[52]

If, two years after the signature of a treaty amending the Treaties, four fifths of the Member States *have ratified* it and one or more Member States have encountered

---

[52] Treaty Establishing the European Community [Treaty of Rome 1957], Pt 6, Art 214.

difficulties in proceeding with ratification, the matter shall be referred to the European Council.[53]

Task 6 Read, scan and observe—present perfect in subordinate clauses

Read the following extracts. Highlight the subordinate clauses and underline the present perfect:

1.   The members of the institutions of the Union, the members of committees, and the officials and other servants of the Union shall be required, even after their duties have ceased, not to disclose information of the kind covered by the obligation of professional secrecy, ...[54]
2.   As I have already said, the first main question is whether the Sikhs are a racial group. ...[55]
3.   If the Commission has not delivered an opinion within three months of the date on which the matter was brought before it, the absence of such opinion shall not prevent the matter from being brought before the Court ...[56]
4.   Every power of the Parliament of a Colony which has become or becomes a State, shall, unless it is by this Constitution exclusively vested in the Parliament of the Commonwealth or withdrawn from the Parliament of the State, ...[57]

8.7 THE PASSIVE

The passive voice reorganises information in a sentence such that *who* or *what* performed the action is not necessarily identified. The performer or agent of the action is not the focus of the information. Although in the active and passive voice the information is essentially the same, the emphasis changes. Observe these two sentences:

active voice   *The Government committed grave errors.*
passive voice   *Grave errors were committed by the Government.*

In the first sentence, the verb *committed* is active: the Government (the agent) performs the action as the subject of the sentence. In the second sentence, the verb phrase *were committed* is acted upon *by* the Government which has an end-focus. The decision to identify the agent at the end of the sentence is optional in the passive voice (the agent can be named with *by*). Sometimes the decision

---

[53] Consolidated Versions of the Treaty on European Union and the Treaty on the Functioning of the European Union [2008] OJ C115/01, Art 48(5).
[54] *Ibid*, Art 339.
[55] *Mandla (Sewa Singh) v Dowell Lee* [1982] UKHL 7.
[56] [2008] OJ C115/01, above n 53, Art 259.
[57] Commonwealth of Australia Constitution Act 1900, Art 107.

not to include the agent is deliberate. For example, Garner[58] cites the following passive phrase that President Reagan often used while interrogated during the Iran-Contra scandal in order to avoid calling attention to himself or his administration:

Mistakes were made.

At other times, the agent is either unknown, e.g.:

The evidence from the case was stolen.
(We do not know who stole the evidence.)

unimportant for the context, e.g.:

The Treaty on European Union (TEU) was signed in 1992 at Maastricht.
(We are interested in *when* it was signed, not who signed it.)

or so obvious it need not be stated, e.g.:

Until the budget for the first financial year has been established, Member States ...
(It is obvious which body establishes the budget in the EU.)

Task 7 Read, scan and observe – the passive
Read the following texts and scan (highlight or underline) any form of the passive. If necessary, return to the 'Grammar Review' in 8.2 above:

1. The fact that former assistants were awarded pay increases with effect from a certain date does not, of itself, mean that discrimination based on nationality has been removed.[59]
2. First, the commissions qualify as courts. Second, the commissions were appointed, set up, and established pursuant to an order of the President, ...[60]
3. Last, the Commission rejects Microsoft's assertion that the theory applied in the present case does not take account of certain relevant factors and is based on predictions that are contradicted by the facts.[61]
4. The admission of any such state to membership in the United Nations will be effected by a decision of the General Assembly upon the recommendation of the Security Council.[62]
5. This Treaty shall enter into force on 1 January 1993, provided that all the instruments of ratification have been deposited, ...[63]

---

[58] Garner , above n 27, p 643.
[59] *Commission of the European Communities v Italian Republic* [2006] ECR 1-6885 C-119/04, concerning recognition of acquired rights of former foreign-language assistants.
[60] *Hamdan v Rumsfeld* (No 05-184) IIIA, 415 F 3d 33, reversed and remanded, 2006.
[61] *Microsoft Corp v Commission of the European Communities* [2007] ECR Page II-03601, in Judgment of the Court of First Instance (Grand Chamber), Case No: T-201/04.
[62] Charter of the United Nations 1945, Ch 2, Art 4(2).
[63] TEU, above n 41, Art R(2).

6. Change the passive to active:
    In 1993, the Vienna Declaration was adopted by over 171 States.

    ....
    ....

7. Change the active to passive:
    Somalia and the United States have not ratified the Convention on the Rights of the Child.

    ....
    ....

KEY AND COMMENTARY

Key

Task 1 Read, scan and observe—verb tenses

present simple	rejects, claims, are, submits, undertake, considers, come up with (phrasal verb), is
present simple continuous	none
present simple passive	is justified
present perfect	has failed, have [always] been
imperative	Let it be (directive to third person subject) meaning 'Judges must be the ones …'. This usage is a bit archaic and formal.
past simple	none
modal + infinitive	shall apply, may grant or [may] make, [may not] abuse or [may not] misuse, should divert, would be, need have, will be
modal (passive voice)	shall be implemented, must be read and [must be] given, must be trusted

Answers to questions:
1. The present simple was used the most frequently, followed by the modal + verb.
2. Text 4, the scholarly opinion by Lord Denning, uses personal pronouns references such as *you* and *we.*
3. Prescriptive legal texts use the third person rather than the first and second person in order to remain impersonal (thus formal) and all-inclusive, in other words applicable to everyone. The third person tends to be more authoritative.

Task 2 STOP and CHECK—relative pronouns

1. practices <u>which</u>
2. act <u>which</u>
3. work <u>that</u>
4. women <u>who</u>

Task 3 Read, scan and observe—subject identification

8.4.1 The Legal Authority as the Subject
1. <u>State Parties</u> <u>recognize</u>
2. <u>State Parties</u> <u>condemn</u>
3. <u>Principal</u> <u>appoints</u>, <u>agent</u> <u>accepts</u>, <u>Agent</u> <u>undertakes</u> and <u>agrees</u>

8.4.2 Present Simple in Subordinate Clauses
4. <u>Member State</u> <u>persists</u>, <u>Council</u> <u>may decide</u>
5. <u>Member State</u> <u>is</u>, or [<u>Member State</u>] <u>is threatened</u>, <u>Commission</u> <u>shall investigate</u>
6. <u>it</u> <u>deems</u>, <u>Council</u> <u>shall define</u>

Task 4 Read, scan and observe—distinguishing the modals *shall* and *may* in a treaty: English and Spanish texts

Consolidated version of the Treaty on European Union (English)
Article 1   shall be founded, shall have, shall replace
Article 2   none
Article 3(1)   none
Article 3(2)   shall offer
Article 3(3)   shall establish, shall work, shall promote (× 3), shall combat, shall respect, shall ensure.
Tratado de la Unión Europea (Spanish)
Spanish uses the modal future *will* for this treaty.

What have you observed about *word of authority* in the Consolidated Version of the Treaty on European Union in your own language?

Task 5 STOP and CHECK—general use of modals
1. The judge *might* dismiss the case. (possibility)
2. The judge *can* dismiss the case. (modal of capacity)
3. The judge *must* dismiss the case. (obligation – personal authority)
4. The judge *has to* dismiss the case. (obligation – outside authority)
5. The judge *should* dismiss the case. (advice – more personal)
6. The judge *ought to* dismiss the case. (obligation – it is the 'right thing to do')
7. The judge *needs to* dismiss the case. (necessity)
8. He *must be* the judge who dismissed the case. (logical deduction)

Task 6 Read, scan and observe—present perfect in subordinate clauses

1. *even after their duties have ceased,*
2. *As I have already said,*
3. *If the Commission has not delivered an opinion within three months ...*
4. *Every power of the Parliament of a Colony which has become ...*

Task 7 Read, scan and observe—the passive

1. were awarded, has been removed
2. were appointed, [were] established
3. is based, are contradicted
4. will be effected
5. have been deposited
6. Passive to active voice: *In 1993, over 171 States adopted the Vienna Declaration.*
7. Active to passive: *The Convention on the Rights of the Child has not been ratified by Somalia and the United States.*

Commentary

In the overview of verb forms in 8.1 above, most of the examples were taken from treaties, constitutions, contracts and Acts. As prescriptive texts (which impose an obligation or confer a right), they represent the more formal type of legal discourse, and the verb forms selected by legal draftsmen reflect this linguistic conservatism. As we have observed in this chapter, the most frequently used verb constructions in prescriptive texts are respectively: the present simple, the present perfect and the passive.

The present simple in prescriptive texts conveys an idea of constancy in the present yet with a prescriptive force in the future, such as: 'It is unlawful ...' or 'State Parties undertake to ensure ...'. It is further enhanced by the frequent use of modal auxiliaries *shall* or *may*, thus rendering them more authoritative in specific contexts, e.g.: 'The Union shall respect fundamental rights, as guaranteed by the European Convention for the Protection of Human Rights ...'

The present perfect connects the past to the present and, as such, expresses the idea of completion of a situation. This was observed at the end of the recitals in the preamble to a Convention, e.g. 'High Contracting Parties, Have agreed ...'. Since the very nature of the progressive form of a verb implies incompleteness or the temporariness of a situation in which they are used, lawmakers generally avoid using it, particularly in prescriptive texts.

In the passive voice, the person or agent who actively performs an action is not identified. In fact, as we noted in the examples, the omission is often deliberate since the agent is obvious or unknown. By choosing this verbal construction, the emphasis is on the impersonal and, as such, it is more authoritative. Time references are also vague. The Plain Language Movement suggests that an active rather than passive voice would be easy to use without any loss of meaning, nonetheless, it still remains one of the three most frequently used verbal constructions in legal documents.

As with the progressive, the past simple is rarely used in prescriptive texts. Yet in the language of the courts, it is used quite frequently to describe in detail the facts of a case, such as in this excerpt from *Microsoft Corp v Commission*: 'The data gathered by Synovate on behalf of Microsoft and mentioned at 918 to 920 to the contested decision also clearly show a tendency towards …'.

Returning to the theme of depersonalisation, prescriptive texts generally do not use personal references such as *I, you* or *we*, preferring the third person singular such as 'no one' or a more specific reference such as 'secure tenant' in a contract. On the contrary, a jurist's opinion, or the individually pronounced judgment, including a description of the facts of the case, uses personal referential pronouns.

Crystal and Davy[64] say that that 'complexities of legal English are so unlike normal discourse that they are not easily generated, even by experts'. As a consequence, a legal draftsman relies on forms that have worked in the past 'having been subjected to long and thorough testing before the courts'. Therefore, reducing the use of *shall* or *may* will be slow, as will the request to use more active instead of passive voice. Conservatism and formality will continue to be a distinct feature of legal documents, and it will be hard to relinquish linguistic formulae that have characterised verbal constructions of the past.

---

[64] Crystal and Davy, above n 26, p 154.

CONSOLIDATION PART IV – LANGUAGE FOCUS TASKS

Task A – Which One Word or Phrase is Out of Context?

0	*violenti non fit injuria*	*nullum crimen sine lege*	principle of non-retroactivity	*nulla poena sine lege*
1	excessive force	reasonable force	unreasonable force	actionable wrong
2	acquitted	found not guilty	convicted	discharged
3	provocation	murder	diminished responsibility	suicide pact
4	*mens rea*	malice afore-thought	without intention to kill	premeditation
5	misdemeanours	indictable offences	summary offences	minor crimes

Task B – Match the Words with the Definitions[1]

mens rea	coroner	malice aforethought	*actus reus*
involuntary manslaughter	manslaughter	voluntary manslaughter	recklessness

[1] Task B references used to create definitions: BA Garner (1995), *A Dictionary of Modern Legal Usage*, 2nd edn, Oxford: Oxford University Press; *Black's Law Dictionary, Pocket Edition* (1996), BA Garner (ed), Eagan, Minn: West Publishing Co; *Oxford Dictionary of Law* (2009), J Law and E Martin (eds), 7th edn, Oxford: Oxford University Press.

1	....	the *mens rea* in the crime of murder, an intention to kill or to commit grievous bodily harm
2	....	a crime of unlawful homicide but without malice aforethought (voluntary and involuntary)
3	....	a public official who inquires into the circumstances of any deaths that are suspected of being violent or unnatural
4	....	often called the 'guilty mind', the state of mind of the accused that the prosecution must determine in order to secure a conviction when a crime is committed
5	....	murder which is reduced to manslaughter due to mitigating factors/circumstances such as: provocation, diminished responsibility/capacity, or pursuance of a suicide pact
6	....	taking an unjustifiable risk, even if aware of the risk/consequences of one's actions
7	....	killing without malice aforethought but with a certain required fault element such as gross negligence or recklessness while committing a dangerous or unlawful act
8	....	often called the 'guilty act'—concerns the concrete elements and aspects of the crime other than the *mens rea*

TASK C – WORD FORMATION

a)   Fill in the spaces below [.........] with the appropriate word form.

Words that are not necessarily used in a legal context, or a variant no longer in use, have not been included in the table. The [x] in the table indicates that the form does not exist or that it is uncommon in a legal context. If necessary, read chapter 10 before doing this task or consult a dictionary.

	verb	**noun** (concept)	**noun** (person)	**adjective**
1	to convict	conviction	....	convicted
2	to comply	....	x	compliant
3	....	acquittal [criminal law], acquittance [commercial meaning]	x	acquitted
4	to accuse to stand accused [verb phrase]	....	accuser/[the] accused	accusatory [= accusing]/ accusatorial/ accusative
5	to punish	punishment	x	punitive/ .... (2)
6	to prosecute	prosecution	....	prosecutorial/ prosecuting
7	to supervise	....	supervisor	supervisory
8	....	indictment	x	indicted/ indictable

b) Using the table above, insert the appropriate word in the spaces: verb, noun (concept), noun (person), or adjective:

9   Inspectors were sent to visit nuclear power plants and verify ....
     .... with the treaty.

10   .... is alleged to be a member of
     a well-known terrorist group.

11   The defendant is .... and is not guilty of
     any criminal offence.

12   Treason in many countries is ....
     by death.

13   A typical feature of common law is the .... or
     adversarial system of trial in both criminal and civil cases.

14   The Director of Public Prosecutions is the head of the independent
     Crown Prosecution Service, under the .... of
     the Attorney-General.

15   The Court of Appeal held that the appellants' ....
     did not rest on the evidence of Miss Miles 'to a decisive extent'.

16   Attorneys for the .... police
     officers tried to delay the trial.

Task D – Prefixes and Suffixes

Fill in the missing suffixes or prefixes to the following words. Identify the appropriate word form.

The [x] indicates that the form does not exist or that it is uncommon in a legal context.

	Prefixes	adjective	noun concept
1	meditation	x	
2	reasonable		x
3	proportionate		x
4	intentional		x
	Suffixes		
5	provoke	x	
6	neglect		
7	mitigate	(2)	(1)
8	reckless	reckless	

Task E – Verb–noun Collocation

Match the words 1–10 with the appropriate words a–j, and write the matching identifiers in the first column of the table. Think about the meaning of each term or phrase.

...1g...	1	to charge	a	acts as gatekeeper in a jury trial
......	2	to confront	b	over by a judge
......	3	The judge	c	the lawful order of a court
......	4	to be guilty beyond	d	and cross-examine the witness
......	5	in compliance with	e	out by the police
......	6	conviction	f	against conviction
......	7	presided	g	with an offence/crime
......	8	right to a	h	a reasonable doubt
......	9	an appeal	i	quashed by the Court of Appeal
......	10	investigation is carried	j	fair trial

Part V

Understanding the Common Law System
through Civil Law and Language

Chapter 9

LANGUAGE AND LAW

Judicial Precedent and the Law of Torts

Introduction to civil law – Language and concepts of the law of torts – Common law method I: binding precedent and the hierarchy of the courts – Understanding case law: reading a civil judgment – A leading case in the tort of negligence: Donoghue v Stevenson – Common law method II: the ratio decidendi and the development of principles in the common law

On one occasion an expert in the law stood up to test Jesus. 'Teacher,' he asked, 'what must I do to inherit eternal life?'
'What is written in the law?' he replied. 'How do you read it?'
He answered: '"Love the Lord your God with all your heart and with all your soul and with all your strength and with all your mind"'; and, '"Love your neighbour as yourself."'
'You have answered correctly,' Jesus replied. 'Do this and you will live.'
But he wanted to justify himself, so he asked Jesus, 'And who is my neighbour?'
In reply Jesus said: 'A man was going down from Jerusalem to Jericho, when he fell into the hands of robbers …
[The parable of the good Samaritan follows]

Gospel according to Saint Luke, 10:25–30[1]

The liability for negligence, whether you style it such or treat it as in other systems as a species of 'culpa' is no doubt based upon a general public sentiment of moral wrongdoing for which the offender must pay. But acts or omissions which any moral code would censure cannot in a practical world be treated so as to give a right to every person injured by them to demand relief. In this way rules of law arise which limit the range of complainants and the extent of their remedy. The rule that you are to love your neighbour becomes in law you must not injure your neighbour; and the lawyer's question 'Who is my neighbour?' receives a restricted reply. You must take reasonable care to avoid acts

---

[1] *The Holy Bible*, New International Version, 1998.

or omissions which you can reasonably foresee would be likely to injure your neighbour. Who then in law is my neighbour? The answer seems to be persons who are so closely and directly affected by my act that I ought reasonably to have them in contemplation as being so affected when I am directing my mind to the acts or omissions which are called in question.

Lord Atkin (1867–1944), Lord of Appeal in Ordinary, in *Donoghue v Stevenson*[2]

9.1 INTRODUCTION TO CIVIL LAW

9.1.1 Introduction

Lord Atkin, in the famous passage from the civil case of *Donoghue v Stevenson*,[3] cited above, reflects on the nature of the relation between law and morals. He pronounces a grand principle of the common law in eloquent terms, inspired by the Bible.[4] *The neighbour principle* pronounced by Lord Atkin, is a basic tenet of the modern law of *negligence*, the most important tort in the common law world today.

In the law of torts we meet the basic language of private law and civil proceedings as well as the language and concepts specific to tort—the branch of law concerning *civil wrongs*. It is a complex field of the law, and is very much a *common law area*: an area of law where the rules and principles have been developed by the judges case by case in judicial precedents. In this chapter we therefore focus not only on the language and concepts of civil law and proceedings, but also on understanding the English judgment, with an introduction to the distinctive legal method of common law legal systems.

In Section One of the chapter, some key concepts and terminology of civil law are introduced; we examine the torts of *negligence* and *trespass*, and learn about the different remedies of *damages* and *injunctions* (9.2). In Section Two, we consider *stare decisis*, or the *doctrine of binding precedent*: the central feature of common law legal systems. Both English and American viewpoints are discussed (9.3). A structured approach to reading and understanding an English judgment is presented, and we read extracts from a judgment of the Court of Appeal, identifying and focusing on the key elements of a case; the approach of the common law courts to solving disputes is illustrated (9.4).

In the Advanced part of the chapter (Section Three), we examine in greater depth the distinctive judicial approach recognisable as *common law reasoning*.

---

[2] *Donoghue v Stevenson* [1932] UKHL 3, [1932] AC 562 (HL Sc).

[3] *Ibid.*

[4] At the time of the judgment, the biblical text echoed in Lord Atkin's pronunciation was the original translation of The Bible into the English language, the Authorised Version (King James), 1611.

What is the importance attached to the *facts of the case*? How can we read the text of a judgment to understand the *ratio decidendi*—the legal principle on which it is based? This process requires us to interpret the judgment as law. And how do principles develop from case to case in the common law system?

The case of *Donoghue v Stevenson*, examined in 9.5 and 9.6, is memorable not only for its importance in the development of the tort of negligence, but also for its curious facts, revolving around the appearance of an unfortunate snail in some ginger beer. The legal question disputed in this case concerns a fundamental component of the tort of negligence: the *duty of care*. Specifically, this precedent, for the first time, recognised legal rights to consumers of manufactured products independent of contract; it is a precursor of modern consumer protection law.

However, the decision of the House of Lords was also fundamental in initiating the expansion of the *tort of negligence*, making it possible for English civil law to keep pace with developments in modern society. Lord Atkin's pronunciation of the neighbour principle, cited above, was particularly significant in the later development of the law.

9.1.2 Terminology Focus: Civil and Criminal Proceedings

Consider and Discuss

— *Can you explain the difference between a* civil wrong *(a tort) and a crime?*
— *What are the different functions of these two major branches—tort law and criminal law—in a legal system?*
— *The same set of facts can constitute both a crime and a tort: can you think of some examples? In what ways are the consequences different for the parties involved in a crime or a tort?*

Task 1 Terminology focus—civil and criminal proceedings

Consider the following set of facts:

In response to an insult, D attacks V, punching him and breaking his nose.

As a crime
D has committed the crime of *assault*, specifically *assault occasioning actual bodily harm* as V suffered physical injury but was not seriously hurt.

As a tort
D has committed the tort of *trespass to the person*, specifically *assault and battery* since V was put in fear of immediate and unlawful physical force (*assault*) and was subjected to immediate physical force (*battery*); he suffered *personal injuries* (the broken nose) caused by the battery.

Answer the questions and fill in the blank spaces in the box below.

Questions	As a crime	As a tort
What will happen to D?	He will be *prosecuted*, becoming the *defendant* in a criminal *trial*.	If V *sues* D, D will be the *defendant* in a *civil proceeding*.
What role will V play?	V is the *victim* of a crime. He could be called to *testify* as the chief *witness for the prosecution*.	
What public authorities will be involved?	The police The CPS The criminal courts	
What will the consequences be for D?		
What will the consequences be for V?		He may *recover* a sum of *damages* from D, to compensate him for the *injury* suffered.

Comment

In the two branches of civil and criminal law, there are distinct aims, procedures, rules and authorities involved; and the consequences of *civil proceedings* and *criminal prosecution* are quite different. Correspondingly, different language and terminology are generally used in each field of the law.[5] Some terms, such as *defendant*, are found in both criminal and civil law: however, the consequences of being *sued* as a civil defendant are quite different from the consequences of being *prosecuted* as a criminal defendant. If a civil court pronounces *judgment for the claimant* (and therefore against the defendant), the court will order a remedy to satisfy the claimant, e.g. the defendant will have to pay *damages* to the claimant to compensate him for the injury suffered. If the defendant is found guilty by a criminal court, he will be sentenced to a suitable penalty, such as a fine or imprisonment, *to punish him for committing the crime* and deter him from committing further offences in the future.[6] In a civil case, the victim is an active participant (one of the *parties to the case*), while in a criminal case it is generally the public authorities that are responsible for prosecuting offenders and the purpose of a criminal action is not to compensate a victim for the wrong suffered—at most, the victim may participate in proceedings as a witness during the trial.

---

[5] Examples were examined in 7.1.2, Task 1, above.
[6] For the various functions of criminal law, see 7.1 above.

SECTION ONE

9.2 LANGUAGE AND CONCEPTS OF THE LAW OF TORTS

In this section, we meet the language of civil proceedings, and the terminology of tort is introduced, through a discussion of some basic aspects of the law. Extracts from the writings of legal scholars and relevant case law provide the context for vocabulary focus. In this way, it is intended to provide a basic introduction to the key terms and concepts of tort, making this difficult area of the common law more accessible to the civil lawyer, or to those from different legal traditions.

9.2.1 The Law of Tort or the Law of Torts?

Two of the major branches of private law are the law of contract (also called *contract* or *contract law*) and the law of torts (also called *tort, tort law* or *the law of tort*). Tort law is concerned with *non-contractual liability*: that is, legal responsibility (*liability*) based on a *legal duty* towards another person that does not derive from a *contractual obligation*. Instead, the obligation is imposed by the law independently of the will of the parties, in order to protect certain *legitimate interests* of individuals in society. Experts agree that it is difficult to give a satisfactory definition of *tort*:

> Perhaps the best explanation we can offer is this. Tort is that branch of the civil law relating to obligations imposed by operation of law on all natural and artificial persons. It concerns the basic duties one person owes to another whether he likes it or not.[7]

When a person has *a duty* (an obligation) in tort, we say that he or she *owes a duty* to another. Not only *natural persons* (human beings), but also *juristic persons* ('*artificial persons*') are subject to the law of torts: they are capable of *enjoying rights* and *owing duties*.

Some lawyers prefer to speak about the *law of torts* in the plural, because there is no single figure of *liability in tort* (or, *civil liability*) in the common law legal system. Instead, there is a series of different *categories of tort*, each of which is composed of different elements and protects specific interests. In the historical development of the law, *trespass* was the most important tort; today the dominant tort in the common law system is *the tort of negligence*. Trespass, negligence and some other torts are introduced below.

---

[7] M Brazier and J Murphy (1999), *The Law of Torts*, 10th edn, London: Butterworths, p 3.

Discuss

— *Which branch of law does 'tort' correspond to in your legal system?*
— *Are there different categories of tort, as in the common law, or is there a single class of liability based on fault?*
— *What is the source of civil liability in your legal system?*
— *Is this branch of the law codified?*

9.2.2 Tort, Contract and the Protection of Interests

The law of torts is concerned with the protection of fundamental human interests. In society, one person's *conduct* (behaviour, consisting of *acts and omissions*) may cause *harm* (*damage* or *injury*) to another person's *interests*. The interests significant in the law of torts are *legally protected interests*.

In the extract below, the author contrasts the law of torts with the law of contract and discusses the interests protected by these branches of private law.

Before reading, reflect on the differences between tort and contract in a civil law legal system, or in your legal system. What different interests are protected by tort and contract? What are the different functions of tort and contract?

> The law of contract exists, at least in its most immediate reach, for the purpose of vindicating a single interest, that of having promises of others performed. ... Thus while contract law as a rule assures the promisee the benefit of the bargain, tort law has the different function of primarily compensating injuries or losses. Moreover, by comparison the interests vindicated by the law of torts are much more numerous. They may be interests in personal security, reputation or dignity, as in actions for assault, personal injuries and defamation. They may be interests in property, as in actions for trespass and conversion; or interests in unimpaired relations with others, as in causing injury or death to relatives. Hence the field covered by the law of torts is much broader, and certainly more diverse, than that of contract.[8]

The author lists many different *interests* protected by tort law: interests in personal security, reputation, dignity, property and relations with family members. A major distinction is that tort law *vindicates* (reaffirms, gives force to) many interests, while contract law vindicates just one interest: 'having *promises* of others *performed*'.

The primary function of the law of torts is *to compensate victims for damage* ('*injuries or losses*') *suffered*. On the other hand, the function of contract law is to make sure that a person who receives a promise (*the promisee*) enjoys the *benefit of the bargain*.[9]

---

[8] Extract from J Fleming (1998), *The Law of Torts*, 9th edn, North Ryde, NSW: LBC, pp 3–5, quoted in M Lunney and K Oliphant (2000), *Tort Law. Text and Materials*, Oxford: Oxford University Press, p 23.

[9] The noun *bargain* (often used as a synonym for *contract* or *agreement*) indicates an agreement that is mutually beneficial, the essence of a binding contract; verb *to bargain* (to negotiate or deal); see 11.3.4 below.

In the passage above, the following *actions in tort* are mentioned: *assault, personal injuries, defamation, trespass* and *conversion*. Each *action* corresponds to a category of tort, with the exception of *personal injuries*. This term refers to damage in the form of physical *injury* to the person, rather than damage to property. *A claim for damages for personal injuries* may be *in the tort of negligence* or *in trespass*, or it may be founded on *breach of a statutory duty*, that is to say, the violation (*breach*) of a duty imposed by statute, for example on a public authority, an employer, a shop or a restaurant. Statutory duties often impose *strict liability*, also known as *objective liability*: that is, *liability without fault*. Some actions in tort are examined in 9.2.4 below.

From the point of view of *sources of law*, both tort and contract were created and developed by the English courts over the centuries, and still today the law of torts is predominantly *a common law area*, with *rules and principles* deriving mainly from judicial precedent. Naturally, in both tort and contract, the obligations of European Union membership have contributed to changes in the law. Further, the passage of the Human Rights Act 1998, examined in chapter five, has had a profound impact on the law of torts (see 9.2.5 below).[10]

Tort and contract are classified and treated as separate branches in legal systems generally; however, in a practical world, cases often involve elements of both. In English law, it is possible to make a claim in both tort and contract on the basis of the same facts, although the claimant cannot *recover damages* twice. There may be 'a considerable overlap in any factual situation between the law of contract and the law of tort'.[11]

In the case of *Wade v Poppleton & Appleby*,[12] below, the defendants were a firm of insolvency practitioners[13] engaged to give Mr Wade advice about insolvency, since his family business was in serious difficulties.

Examine the outline of the case below. What claims were made by Mr and Mrs Wade against the firm? Identify and check that you understand all the law terms (claimants, case, seek damages, etc).

> RICHARDS, J: The claimants in this case seek damages against the defendant firm for alleged negligence in the course of giving advice. The claim is made both for breach of contract and for breach of a common law duty of care.[14]

Mr and Mrs Wade, the claimants, claimed damages for professional negligence, basing their claim both on contract ('*breach of contract*')[15] and tort ('*breach of a*

---

[10] See S Deakin, A Johnston and B Markesinis (2003), *Markesinis and Deakin's Tort Law*, 5th edn, Oxford: Clarendon Press, pp 68–71: chapter section entitled 'The language of rights is set to play a growing role in tort law, but its influence is likely to be gradual and indirect', pp 68–71.

[11] W Rogers (2006), *Winfield and Jolowicz on Tort*, 17th edn, London: Sweet & Maxwell, p 6.

[12] *Wade v Poppleton & Appleby* [2003] EWHC 3159 (Ch).

[13] A *firm* is a business enterprise; *practitioners* are professional people.

[14] *Wade v Poppleton & Appleby*, above n 12, [1] (High Court).

[15] When a party does not fulfil its duties under a contract: see ch 11 for more on contract.

common law duty of care'). A duty of care, and its breach, are elements of the tort of negligence, examined in more detail in 9.2.4 below.

In reality, cases may involve a complex set of sources of legal obligation. For example, in the field of *product liability*, where *a consumer* suffers damage caused by *a defective product*, the relevant sources may include legislation and common law rules in both tort and contract, as well as *contractual clauses* between various participants in the transaction, including the retailer, middleman and manufacturer.[16]

9.2.3 Functions and Remedies in the Law of Torts

An important aim of tort law is to redistribute *loss* in society in a fair way. This is done by granting a *remedy* to *the injured party*—the party who *suffered damage* as a consequence of the tort. This *relief* or *redress* (remedy) is granted to the injured party by the court, and must be paid or performed by *the tortfeasor*—the party who *committed the tort*. Generally speaking, English law provides the same remedies in tort and contract.

Which two remedies are mentioned in the passage below and what are their primary functions?

> In the great majority of tort actions coming before the courts the claimant is seeking monetary compensation (damages) for the injury he has suffered, and this fact strongly emphasises the function of tort in allocating or redistributing loss. In many cases, however, the claimant is seeking an injunction to prevent the occurrence of harm in the future and in this area the direct 'preventive' function of tort predominates.[17]

In most tort actions, the claimant *seeks damages*: the function is primarily *compensatory* or *reparatory*, that is, to compensate the claimant for the injury suffered. The *purpose of damages* in tort is to put the injured party in the position he would have been in, if the tort had not been committed; in contract, the purpose is to put the innocent party in the position he would have been in if the contract had been performed.

Where the claimant *seeks an injunction* (a court order to do or not to do a particular thing), the *preventive function* of tort law is apparent. An injunction is a particularly effective remedy because *a party who fails to comply with it* is guilty of a criminal offence: *contempt of court*.[18] Injunctions, too, are available in both tort and contract.[19] See 9.2.6 below, for more on damages and injunctions.

---

[16] Rogers, above n 11, p 6.

[17] *Ibid*, p 2.

[18] *Contempt of court* is conduct that 'interferes with the administration of justice or impedes or perverts the course of justice'; for more, see *Osborn's Concise Law Dictionary*, 12th edn (2013), M Woodley (ed), London: Sweet & Maxwell, pp 111–12.

[19] For more about the various functions of tort, consult a textbook on tort (several references are given in this chapter).

9.2.4 Actions in Tort: Trespass and Negligence

A civil case: *Letang v Cooper*

The passage from the case of *Letang v Cooper*,[20] examined in Task 2 below, illustrates the typical elements and language of an action in tort, and introduces the torts of trespass and negligence. In this case, and in some other cases examined in this chapter, the term *'plaintiff'* is used to indicate the *claimant* in the action. In England and Wales, since the Civil Procedure Rules 1998 came into force, the term *'claimant'* has replaced the old term *'plaintiff'* as part of a trend to simplify legal terminology for the general public. In other common law jurisdictions, such as the USA and Ireland, *'plaintiff'* is still in use, and *'plaintiff'* continues to be found in the body of older English case law.

Task 2 Terminology of tort in context—*Letang v Cooper*

Read the first paragraph of the judgment in the civil case of *Letang v Cooper*, below, for general understanding. Answer questions 1 to 3:
1. Identify *the injured party* and *the tortfeasor*.
2. What are the facts of the case? What procedural aspect is also relevant?
3. Which two torts are the basis of the plaintiff's claim?

Read the paragraph in detail to answer the following questions. Focus on both meaning and language:
4. What is the nature of the damage suffered?
5. What is the legal question in dispute before the Court of Appeal?
6. What was the outcome (the result) of the case at first instance? ('*The judge*' refers to the judge who decided the case at first instance.)

COURT OF APPEAL
Letang v Cooper

LORD DENNING, MR:[21] On July 10, 1957, Mrs Letang, the Plaintiff, was on holiday in Cornwall. She was staying at a hotel and thought she would sunbathe on a piece of grass where cars were parked. While she was lying there, Mr Cooper, the Defendant, came into the car park driving his Jaguar motor car. He did not see her. The car went over her legs and she was injured. On Feb. 2, 1961, more than three years after the accident, the Plaintiff brought this action against the Defendant for damages for loss and injury caused by (1) the negligence of the Defendant in driving a motor car and (2) the commission by the Defendant of a trespass to the person. The sole question is whether the action is statute barred. The Plaintiff admits that the action

---

[20] *Letang v Cooper* [1964] EWCA Civ 5, [1965] 1 QB 232, [1964] 2 All ER 929.
[21] MR = the Master of the Rolls, President of the Civil Division of the Court of Appeal.

for negligence is barred after three years, but she claims that the action for trespass to the person is not barred until six years have elapsed. The judge has so held and awarded her £575 damages for trespass to the person.

Under the Limitation Act 1939, the period of limitation was six years in all actions founded 'on tort'; but in 1954 Parliament reduced it to three years in actions for damages for personal injuries …[22]

© **Crown Copyright**
Source: BAILII

Key and comment to Task 2 Terminology of tort in context—
Letang v Cooper

1. *The injured party* is the plaintiff, Mrs Letang. *The tortfeasor* is the defendant, Mr Cooper.
2. The material facts are that the plaintiff was lying on the grass outside a hotel, in a place where cars parked; the defendant, who was driving his car, ran over her legs, causing injury; the defendant's act was not intentional as he did not see the plaintiff. The important procedural aspect is that the plaintiff sued the defendant more than three years after the accident.
3. The plaintiff's claim is based on (i) the tort of negligence; and (ii) the tort of trespass, specifically *trespass to the person*.
4. The damage is physical injury to the person; this is therefore a common type of civil case: a *claim for damages for personal injuries.*
5. The legal question in dispute before the Court of Appeal (*the issue* in this appeal) is clearly stated by Lord Denning: '*The sole question is whether the action is statute barred.*' He then refers to the relevant statute law (the Limitation Acts 1939 and 1954). An action is *barred* when it is too late to commence proceedings, because the maximum period of time permitted by law has passed. If Mrs Letang's action is statute barred, this means that she has lost her right to seek a remedy for the injury she suffered, because she commenced proceedings too late.
6. At first instance, Mrs Letang won the case. The judge *held* (decided) that the action for trespass was not statute barred, and he ordered the defendant to compensate the plaintiff by payment of a sum of damages: '*The judge has so held and awarded her £575 damages for trespass to the person*'.

---

[22] *Letang v Cooper* [1964] 2 All ER 929, 931.

A cause of action

In *Letang v Cooper*, the Court of Appeal considers two different torts in relation to the same set of facts: *trespass* and *negligence*. The same facts constitute the plaintiff's *cause of action* in both torts. Lord Justice Diplock[23] was one of the panel of three judges who heard the appeal; below, he explains the notion of *a cause of action*:

> DIPLOCK LJ: A cause of action is simply a factual situation the existence of which entitles one person to obtain from the court a remedy against another person. ... If A, by failing to exercise reasonable care, inflicts direct personal injury on B, those facts constitute a cause of action on the part of B against A for damages in respect of such personal injuries.[24]

Lord Justice Diplock explains that in the modern law, a single cause of action may have more than one legal description: in this case, it could constitute the basis of *an action for negligence* or *an action for trespass to the person*. Notice the key element: that A injures B '*by failing to exercise reasonable care*'. In his judgment, Diplock LJ explains the transition from the historic *forms of action*, no longer a problem today, to the modern *cause of action*; this judgment is interesting also for its discussion of the development of the law of torts to its modern form.

The tort of negligence

Lord Justice Diplock then transposes the facts of *Letang v Cooper* into the terms of the tort of negligence:

> [T]he defendant, by failing to exercise reasonable care (of which failure particulars were given), drove his motor car over the plaintiff's legs and so inflicted on her direct personal injuries in respect of which the plaintiff claimed damages.[25]

In the above analysis of the case, we can see the elements of the tort of negligence:

— the existence of a legal duty to take care (*a duty of care*);
— *breach* of the duty (consisting of '*failing to exercise reasonable care*');
— *damage* suffered by the injured party and *caused* by the breach of the duty ('*and so inflicted on her ... personal injuries*').

On this basis, the plaintiff takes legal action to seek a remedy *to repair* or *redress the harm* ('*the plaintiff claimed damages*').

In the tort of negligence, the duty of care was originally established as a principle by Lord Atkin's *neighbour test* from *Donoghue v Stevenson*, cited at the beginning of this chapter:

> You must take reasonable care to avoid acts or omissions which you can reasonably foresee would be likely to injure your neighbour.[26]

---

[23] Later, Lord Diplock, one of the most eminent English judges of the 20th century.
[24] *Letang v Cooper* [1964] 2 All ER 929, 934.
[25] *Ibid*, 935.
[26] *Donoghue v Stevenson* [1932] UKHL 3, [1932] AC 562 (HL Sc).

Everybody is under a legal duty to '*take reasonable care*' not to injure others. The question 'Who owes a duty of care and to whom?' can be determined by applying Lord Atkin's answer to his question 'Who then in law is my neighbour?' to the parties, in all the circumstances of the case.[27] The *standard of care* imposed by the law is '*reasonable care*', that is, the typical common law standard of *the reasonable man* (or doctor, teacher, lawyer, driver, etc), considered *in all the circumstances of the case*. Sometimes the *reasonable man* has been called *the man on the Clapham omnibus*, meant to indicate the typical ordinary person, found on a London bus. This figure can be compared to the *bonus pater familiae* of Roman law systems, in that it introduces an objective element into the standard of conduct that the law requires.[28]

Many cases in negligence today involve the question of whether the defendant *owed a duty of care* to the claimant. Other litigation involves the aspect of *causation* (also called *nexus*, or *the causal link*). Was the *damage caused by* the breach of the duty? And was it damage for which the defendant should pay, or was it too *remote* to impose liability? Was the damage, or the type of damage, *foreseeable*[29] by the defendant? Many cases concern these aspects of *causation*, *remoteness of damage* and *foreseeability*.

All the terms highlighted in *italics* in the paragraph above are key terms in the tort of negligence.

The tort of trespass

The tort of trespass may be defined as

> [a] wrongful direct interference with another person or with his possession of land or goods ... The distinguishing feature of trespass in modern law is that it is a direct and immediate interference with person or property, such as striking a person, entering his land, or taking away his goods without his consent.[30]

There are three classes of trespass: *trespass to the person*, *trespass to goods* and *trespass to land*. As we have seen above, the same factual situation may correspond to more than one different tort; and of course, in another perspective, the same facts may constitute a criminal offence in addition to a tort.[31]

---

[27] For later developments, see 9.6.4 below.

[28] V Zeno-Zencovich (2004), 'La responsabilità civile' in G Alpa, M Bonell, D Corapi, L Moccia, V Zeno-Zencovich, A Zoppini (2004), *Diritto privato comparato. Istituti e problemi*, Roma-Bari: Laterza, pp 271–313; the author notes, however, that the division between objective and subjective elements typical of a civil law system is not used in the common law (at p 284).

[29] *Foreseeable* belongs to an important *word family* in tort law: adj, *foreseeable*; verb, *to foresee*; noun, *foresight* (in the sense of the possibility or act of seeing or realising in advance, not *something* seen in advance); noun, *foreseeability* (indicating the possibility to foresee the consequences of one's conduct).

[30] *A Dictionary of Law*, 7th edn (2009, updated reissue 2013) E Martin and J Law (eds), Oxford: Oxford University Press, p 599.

[31] But if so, the criminal prosecution proceeds quite separately from the civil proceeding.

An action in *trespass* may be brought for 'any unlawful injury to the plaintiff's person, property, or rights, involving immediate force or violence'.[32] *Trespass* may be to property, and 'in modern parlance, the term most often connotes a wrongful interference with or disturbance of the possession of property'.[33] Or, as in this case, it may be to the person: *trespass to the person* includes *battery* (involving actual physical contact) and *assault* (where the fear of physical contact is induced in the claimant), and also *false imprisonment*. A trespass is a class of tort that is *actionable* even without *proof of damage*: this means that the courts will provide a remedy purely for interference with the right, in order *to vindicate* (reaffirm) *the claimant's right*.

Both negligence and trespass are considered in *Letang v Cooper* (Task 2 above). The plaintiff admits that she has waited too long, so her action in negligence is *time barred*; she bases her claim on the tort of trespass, winning her case at first instance. The Court of Appeal, however, *rejects her claim*: the defendant's *appeal is allowed* and the *action is dismissed*.[34] In *Letang v Cooper*, Master of the Rolls, Lord Denning explained the modern distinction between trespass and negligence:

> If one man intentionally applies force directly to another, the plaintiff has a cause of action in assault and battery, or, if you so please to describe it, in trespass to the person. 'The least touching of another in anger is a battery.' If he does not inflict injury intentionally, but only unintentionally, the plaintiff has no cause of action today in trespass. His only cause of action is in negligence, and then only on proof of want [lack] of reasonable care. If the plaintiff cannot prove want of reasonable care he may have no cause of action at all.[35]

Trespass involves a *direct interference* and the case of *Letang v Cooper*, above, is authority for the proposition that the interference must be intentional.[36]

9.2.5 Tort Law and Convention Rights

The Human Rights Act 1998, transposing the rights protected by the European Convention on Human Rights (ECHR) into the national legal system, has a major impact on tort law. It will be recalled that under section 6 of the Act, public authorities in the UK must not act in a way which is incompatible with the Convention rights of individuals: under the Act, it is *unlawful* to do so.[37] Many of the *Convention rights* were already protected by the common law, quite independently of the ECHR. This means that the British legal system now has two

---

[32] S Gifis (1991), *Barron's Law Dictionary*, 3rd edn, New York: Barrons Educational Series, Inc, p 499.
[33] *Ibid.*
[34] The decision depends on the court's interpretation of the two Limitation Acts in relation to the law of torts.
[35] *Letang v Cooper* [1964] 2 All ER 929, 932.
[36] *Osborn's Concise Law Dictionary*, above n 18, p 429.
[37] This was explored in 5.4.4 above.

separate, but also interrelated, sets of rights: *common law rights* and *Convention rights*. Further, since the UK courts are *public authorities* themselves subject to the duty imposed by section 6 HRA 1998, they must now interpret common law rights compatibly with the Convention rights.

Examine the passage below. Which Convention right corresponds to which common law tort? Do the authors suggest the victim should take action in tort or directly under the Human Rights Act 1998?

> In many cases, the self-same rights conferred by the Convention are already recognised by the law of torts. For example, Article 5 provides for a right to liberty and security and protects the citizen against arbitrary detention. The ancient tort of false imprisonment protects that same fundamental interest. A person alleging unlawful arrest by the police will not need to resort to claiming a breach of Article 5. He can perfectly well sue in false imprisonment. In determining whether that arrest was lawful, the court will be mindful of the provisions of Article 5 and the jurisprudence of the European Court of Human Rights.[38]

The Convention right mentioned is the right to liberty and security, guaranteed by Article 5 ECHR (protecting individuals against arbitrary detention); the corresponding common law right is protected by the tort of *false imprisonment*, a form of *trespass to the person*. The tort involves unlawful restriction of a person's freedom of movement. It must be total restriction, but not necessarily in a prison; for example, it could be in a shop or even a bus, as in the 'Jubilee mystery bus tour' case examined in chapter seven, where a group of protesters was detained by the police and transported on a London bus, thus restricting the protesters' liberty.[39] False imprisonment is both a crime and a tort; the ancient *writ* of *habeas corpus* can be used to challenge the validity of the detention (this remedy for a violation of personal liberty requires a person who detains another in custody to produce 'the body' before a judge and justify the lawfulness of the detention). In the extract above, the authors suggest that the victim make a claim directly in the tort of false imprisonment (*'He can perfectly well sue in false imprisonment'*); the alternative procedure would be to issue a claim for judicial review directly under the Human Rights Act 1998.[40]

9.2.6 Focus on Remedies: Damages and Injunctions

The common law has traditionally focused on remedies. The old saying *no right without a remedy* shows the close link seen between rights and remedies: the existence of a remedy indicates that there is a corresponding right. In this section we examine aspects and language of two *judicial remedies*: damages and injunctions.

---

[38] Brazier and Murphy, above n 7, p 5.
[39] See 7.1.2, Task 1.
[40] The procedure used in the *Denbigh High School* case, examined in 5.5 above.

The origin of the two remedies in English law is different: one is a *common law remedy*, the other an *equitable remedy*. The common law remedy of damages is *available as of right*: this means that a *successful claimant* (a claimant who wins the case) will always be granted an *award of damages*, even if the *quantum of damages* (the sum of money) may be very small where no real loss has been caused (for example, in one case, the Court of Appeal awarded *nominal damages* of just £2).[41]

By contrast, an injunction is *an equitable remedy* and is available *at the discretion* of the judges (it is *a discretionary remedy*). Its historical origins belong with the Lord Chancellor and the Court of Chancery, which developed the body of law known as *Equity* on a case by case basis, to provide justice in individual cases where the common law was too rigid to provide a remedy. In the passage below, Lord Denning looks back to the time when Sir Thomas More was Lord High Chancellor of England during the reign of Henry VIII:[42]

> I find much interest in the way in which Thomas More, as Lord Chancellor, granted injunctions—just as Thomas Wolsey had done—whenever it was just and convenient to do so. The common law judges objected to it. ... He invited all the judges to dinner ... Then he told them to do likewise and mitigate the rigour of the law by doing equity themselves ... But the judges refused to follow his advice, so he told them he must continue to grant injunctions: ...[43]

More, as Lord Chancellor, granted injunctions 'whenever it was just and convenient', so as to dispense justice and '*mitigate* the rigour of *the law* by doing equity'. 'The law' means *the common law* as contrasted with Equity. But the common law judges refused to administer injunctions, and as a consequence, the injunction remained a remedy *available* only in Equity, not under the common law. We shall see the implications of this when we examine the case of *Miller v Jackson*, below.[44]

Task 3 Consultation and research—investigating torts
In this section we have examined the torts of *negligence* and *trespass*.
There are many different torts in the common law; some are mentioned above and some are mentioned by Lord Denning in the extract below. Read the extract and select one or more torts to investigate, using your law dictionary:

— What are the elements of the tort?
— What interests does it protect?

---

[41] *Surrey County Council v Bredero Homes Ltd* [1993] EWCA Civ 7, [1993] 1 WLR 1361.
[42] Thomas More's refusal to recognise the King as head of the Church of England, and renounce obedience to 'the Bishop of Rome' (the Pope), in connection with the annulment of Henry's first marriage to Catherine of Aragon, ultimately led to his execution for high treason in 1535. Politician and writer, More was author of *Utopia*.
[43] A Denning (1984), *Landmarks in the Law*, London: Butterworths, pp 70–71.
[44] In 9.4.3.

— What damage, if any, is required for action? What remedies may be granted?

Consider whether the torts you have researched correspond in the civil law system, or in your legal system. What factors do you need to take into account? If possible, check your ideas in an appropriate bilingual law dictionary or in a comparative law book.

> Our whole law of tort today proceeds on the footing [basis] that there is a duty owed by every man not to injure his neighbour in a way forbidden by law. Negligence is a breach of such a duty. So is nuisance. So is trespass to the person. So is false imprisonment, malicious prosecution or defamation of character.[45]

---

[45] *Letang v Cooper* [1964] 2 All ER 929, 933.

SECTION TWO

9.3 Common Law Method I: Binding Precedent and the Hierarchy of the Courts

9.3.1 The Law Reports and Judicial Precedent

Judicial precedent is a primary source of English law, also known by the names *case law*, *common law* and *judicial decision*. Precedent is the body of legal principles formulated and developed by the English superior courts over the centuries as they have resolved disputes case by case. In the common law system, it is not possible for a lawyer to argue and win a case in court without reference to precedent; this is true even where the case involves legislation, the other primary source of law, since the *doctrine of binding precedent* also applies to statutory interpretation.[46]

Where must lawyers look to find precedent?

> In order to find a legal principle contained in precedent—and the same is true both for precedent as a direct, primary source of law, and for precedent in relation to the interpretation of statute law—the judge, lawyer, or student of law, must turn directly to the source: the text of the individual judgment itself, reproduced in full and verbatim in the published volumes containing collections of cases, called the *law reports*. For the legal principle decided in a case is to be found in the pronouncement of the judge or judges.[47]

For hundreds of years, the texts of judgments in significant cases have been published in the collected volumes of the law reports.[48] Even Geoffrey Chaucer's *Sergeant of the Lawe* (Serjeant at Law) in the *Canterbury Tales* cited cases and judgments ('*caas and doomes*') dating back to the time of King William I:

> Nowher so busy a man as he there nas,
> And yet he semed bisier than he was.
> In termes hadde he caas and doomes alle
> That from the tyme of king William were falle.[49]

---

[46] See ch 3, Task 2.

[47] A Riley in F Scarpa and A Riley (2000), 'La fisionomia della sentenza in Inghilterra e in Italia: un'analisi orientata alla traduzione' in *Traduttori e giuristi a confronto*, L Schena and D Snel Trampus (eds), Bologna: CLUEB, 227, p 232.

[48] A Simpson (1996), *Leading Cases in the Common Law*, Oxford: Clarendon Press, p 2, notes that already during the second half of the 13th century, 'a different form of text evolved, hand in hand with the evolution of the learned legal profession which it helped to make possible. This was the law report, which principally records things which were said by judges and counsel in the course of court proceedings.' A tradition of private English law reports published in recognisable form dates back to at least 1513, according to the *All England Law Reports. A User's Guide* (1983).

[49] G Chaucer (c 1387–92), *The Canterbury Tales, General Prologue* in F Robinson (ed), *The Complete Works of Geoffrey Chaucer*, 2nd edn (1974), Oxford: Oxford University Press, lines 321–24.

The Norman Duke, later known as William the Conqueror, invaded England in 1066 and became King: the centralised system of justice he developed, with *royal justices* administering general rules *common* to the whole of England, as opposed to *local custom*, gave origin to the common law.

Today, law reports are also available in electronic form and may be accessed directly on the Internet.[50] As well as private series of reports, there are official Law Reports published by the Incorporated Council of Law Reporting for England and Wales, and these must be cited as the source, where available.

It is agreed that without the accurate reporting of judgments, published in the law reports, a legal system based on precedent could not work.

Task 4   Reflection and discussion—the importance of precedent
Do you agree with the statement below?

> It is a basic principle of the administration of justice that like cases [similar cases] should be decided alike. This is enough to account for the fact that, in almost every jurisdiction, a judge tends to decide a case in the same way as that in which a similar case has been decided by another judge.[51]

Is this assertion true of the courts in your legal system? Which courts in particular pronounce influential judgments? Is it appropriate to talk about 'precedent' in civil law systems? Can you distinguish between 'binding' and 'persuasive' precedent? In your view, what is the most important characteristic of precedent in common law legal systems?

9.3.2   *Stare Decisis:* the Doctrine of Binding Precedent

The characteristic that distinguishes the common law legal system is that *judges are under a legal obligation to follow precedent*. This basic principle of the common law system is called the *doctrine of binding precedent*, or *stare decisis*. It is the status of precedent as a primary source of law that is the keystone of the English legal system, and by derivation of the common law family of legal systems operating throughout the world today.

A judge deciding a *later, similar case* (one with similar facts to the precedent) *must* apply the same principles previously established by the courts, depending on the relative position of each court in the hierarchy. A judicial precedent is not merely *persuasive* in a later similar case, it is *binding*. We say that the later court *is bound to follow precedent*, or the later court *is bound by* the earlier court.

The judge therefore enjoys a central role in the common law legal system, not only as arbiter, but also as a type of *law-maker*. The English judge is not usually

---

[50] The British and Irish Legal Information Institute provides a free public service for leading cases, with a rapidly growing selection: <http://www.bailii.org>.

[51] R Cross (1977), *Precedent in English Law*, 3rd edn, Oxford: Clarendon Press, p 4.

described as a *legislator*: this term implies a general power to make law. The judge's power is specific: to decide the issue before the court.[52] If no legislation exists to regulate the dispute and there is no precedent for the case, because it presents new or different facts (such a case is called *a case of first impression*), the judge has power *to make law* by pronouncing a new rule in resolving the dispute. The new rule will become part of the body of precedent, to be applied by the courts in later, similar cases.

Courts do not exercise their power arbitrarily, however; the judges operate within a controlled framework of established rules and practices: key elements are the *hierarchically organised* courts, the network of *general common law principles*, and the distinctive style and approach which typify *English legal reasoning*.

The advanced section of this chapter introduces readers to the distinctive style and approach of English legal reasoning and examines the operation of precedent in greater depth. Next, we examine the *hierarchy of the English courts*.

9.3.3 Following Precedent: the *Ratio Decidendi* and the Hierarchy of the English Courts

In common law legal systems the courts are organised in a strictly hierarchical structure. In the English legal system, only *the superior courts* can create binding precedent. Binding precedent is created in appeal cases, not cases heard *at first instance*. In the English system, cases are heard either *at first instance* or *on appeal*. There may be more than one appeal, always to a higher court in the hierarchy. Each court must *follow precedent* according to its position in the hierarchy. The general rule is that a court *is bound to follow any precedent* decided by a court above it in the hierarchy: in this case, precedent has *vertical* effect on the courts below. What is more, *appellate courts* (except the Supreme Court, or previously, the House of Lords) *are bound by* their own previous decisions: in this case, precedent has *horizontal* effect.

What precisely do we mean when we say that a court 'is bound to follow precedent' or 'is bound by a decision'?

Rupert Cross, renowned authority on English precedent, explains:

> When it is said that a court is bound to follow a case or bound by a decision, what is meant is that the judge is under an obligation to apply a particular *ratio decidendi* to the facts before him in the absence of a reasonable legal distinction between those facts and the facts to which it was applied in the previous case.[53]

---

[52] For a detailed discussion of the most appropriate terminology for judicial law-making, see N MacCormick (1978), *Legal Reasoning and Legal Theory*, Oxford: Clarendon Press, p 188. He suggests a return to 'declaring the law', used in the 18th century.

[53] Cross, above n 51, p 104.

The part of the case which operates as binding precedent is the *ratio decidendi*. We may think of the *ratio* as the principle on which the case was decided: the reason or grounds on which the judge based his decision in the case. That is, the decision on the *legal question* in dispute before the court (*the issue*). Any other statement of law by the judge is not part of the *ratio* but is an *obiter dictum*,[54] something said 'by the way' (*obiter*).

We can see from Cross's explanation, above, that there is a close link between the *ratio decidendi* and the *facts of the case*. Precedent is binding only in later similar cases (*like* cases). For this reason, common law judges analyse the facts of the case carefully, usually at the beginning of their judgments; they elaborate their discussion of the law in relation to the facts. The *ratio decidendi* is investigated in depth in 9.6 below.

Comparative lawyers Zweigert and Kötz note that Continental judgments give little attention to the facts of the case. They also question the validity of using headnotes as 'independent polished formulas' detached from any analysis of the case itself, with the result that it becomes 'practically impossible to go back to the facts of the case and discover the real scope of the headnote'.[55] By contrast, common law judgments are published in full and the headnote, if it exists, is only a useful indicator of the content of the judgment. There is no substitute for reading the judges' judgments to discover the *ratio decidendi* of the case. The judges' judgments are the full, reasoned opinions pronounced individually by each judge in a case. Collectively, they form the judgment of the court.

The typical approach of the common law judge is to extract rules and principles in the process of finding a solution to the case. In the passage below, this process is explained from the viewpoint of the civil lawyer.

What differences do you notice, compared with the approach of the civil law judge? What advantages can you see in the common law approach? What disadvantages?

> The Common Law judge's technique of approaching the case-law and extracting its rules and principles is the product of a mature and workmanlike tradition of 'reasoning from case to case'. The Anglo-American judge starts his process of decision with the individual precedents which counsel for the parties before him have adduced as being most in point. In these precedents, he recognizes certain 'rules', that is, solutions of particular concrete living problems. He observes how these 'rules' have been limited, extended, and refined by other 'precedents' and then, constantly keeping the practical problems in the forefront of his mind, gradually draws out of them high-level 'principles' and 'standards' which he uses to make a tentative resolution of the case before him; his solution he then tests for its appropriateness against the background of similar cases and finally arrives at the decision itself. All these steps

---

[54]   Plural: *obiter dicta*. *Obiter* is adverbial; we may say 'the judge said *obiter* that …'.
[55]   K Zweigert and H Kötz (1998), *An Introduction to Comparative Law*, 3rd edn (tr T Weir), Oxford: Clarendon Press, p 265; they refer here specifically to decisions of the Italian Court of Cassation, when published only in the form of headnotes.

take place in open discourse: arguments for and against are presented in speeches and rebuttals between actual or imaginary opponents. *Ambulando solvitur.*[56]

The *inductive* approach to judicial decision-making in the common law is apparent: the judge proceeds from the facts of the the concrete case to the general rule. By contrast, civil law method is *deductive* in approach, moving from the general rule to its application in the individual case. The common law approach is less abstract and more closely linked to real facts.

Task 5　Consultation—the hierarchy of the English courts

Examine the chart below, showing the hierarchy and jurisdiction of the English courts. Focus on both meaning and language. Consult the chart to answer the following questions:

1. Which are the appeal courts?
2. Which courts can create binding precedent?
3. Which courts have civil jurisdiction? Which have criminal jurisdiction?
4. How can existing legal principles be changed?

Notice the important constitutional reform establishing a new highest court at the top of the hierarchy from October 2009: the Supreme Court of the United Kingdom.

THE HIERARCHY OF THE ENGLISH COURTS (ENGLAND AND WALES) AND THE EFFECT OF PRECEDENT

SUPREME COURT OF THE UNITED KINGDOM (*formerly* HOUSE OF LORDS)

The Supreme Court of the United Kingdom is the final court of appeal for all cases except Scottish criminal appeals.

Until 2009, the highest court in the UK was the House of Lords: the Appellate Committee of the House of Lords exercised the judicial function of the House. Judges were the Lords of Appeal in Ordinary or *Law Lords*, life peers in the House of Lords.

The House of Lords in its judicial function was replaced by the Supreme Court of the United Kingdom as from October 2009, under section 23(1) of the Constitutional Reform Act 2005. Judges are called 'Justices of the Supreme Court' (s 23(6)). The existing Law Lords became the first Justices of the new court (s 24).[57]

---

[56] *Ibid*, p 263.
[57] Visit the website of the Supreme Court of the United Kingdom at <http;//www.supremecourt.gov.uk>.

Vertical effect *of precedents: Supreme Court/House of Lords precedents are binding on all other UK courts.*

Horizontal effect: *the Supreme Court/House of Lords considers its own precedents as 'normally binding' but will 'depart from a previous decision when it appears right to do so', to prevent injustice or restricting 'the proper development of the law'.*[58]

COURT OF APPEAL
Civil Division and Criminal Division

Judges: the Lords Justices of Appeal.

Civil Division: appeals from the High Court, tribunals and, sometimes, county courts. Criminal Division: appeals from the Crown Court.

Most appeal cases reach final judgment in the Court of Appeal. Only a small number of appeals a year go right up to the Supreme Court.

Vertical effect: *the Court of Appeal is bound to follow the Supreme Court/House of Lords; all courts below the Court of Appeal are bound to follow the Court of Appeal.*

Horizontal effect: *the Court of Appeal is bound by its own previous decisions (with very few technical exceptions).*

HIGH COURT (*also called* THE HIGH COURT OF JUSTICE)
Chancery Division, Family Division, Queen's Bench Division (QBD)

Judges: High Court judges.

Divisional Courts of the three Divisions of the High Court have limited appellate jurisdiction.

The **QBD** exercises the criminal and administrative jurisdiction of the High Court. The Administrative Court is the specialist court within the QBD with jurisdiction over judicial review. During the reign of a king, the QBD is named the King's Bench Division (KBD).

---

[58] House of Lords Practice Statement 26 July 1966, [1966] 3 All ER 77; the full text is reproduced with comprehension exercises in A Riley (1991), *English for Law*, Harlow; Pearson Education Ltd, p 109.

All three Divisions have civil jurisdiction and hear different types of cases:
QBD: contract, tort, Commercial Court, Administrative Court, some appeals from the Crown Court and magistrates' courts.
Chancery Division: Equity and trusts, tax partnerships, Companies Court, Patents Court,[59] contentious probate,[60] bankruptcy.
Family Division: matrimonial proceedings, children, probate. Appeals from county courts and magistrates' courts.

Vertical effect: the High Court is bound by the Court of Appeal and by the Supreme Court/House of Lords; Divisional Court decisions of the High Court (heard on appeal) are binding on judges of first instance (High Court, Crown Court, county courts, magistrates' courts, tribunals except the Employment Appeal Tribunal).

Horizontal effect: Divisional Courts of the High Court are bound by their own previous decisions (with very few technical exceptions).

NB: The High Court exercises both appellate jurisdiction and *original jurisdiction* (hearing cases *at first instance*). *Binding* precedent is created only in appeal cases: for this reason only the Divisional Courts of the three Divisions of the High Court create binding precedent. Decisions of single judges are *persuasive*, but not binding.

CROWN COURT	COUNTY COURTS
High Court judges, circuit judges and recorders. The Crown Court is a superior court with criminal jurisdiction; trial is by jury where the defendant pleads not guilty to charges on indictment. The main Crown Court for London is the Central Criminal Court, known as the Old Bailey.	Circuit judges and district judges. County courts are inferior, local courts with limited civil jurisdiction; they hear cases in tort and contract, for example.
MAGISTRATES' COURTS	**TRIBUNALS**
Judicial function exercised by lay magistrates (*Justices of the Peace*) and stipendiary magistrates. Local courts exercising limited civil and criminal jurisdiction; *youth courts* for minors.	Various tribunals hear claims relating to specific matters, for example: employment tribunals for labour law matters, Lands Tribunal for disputes about the value of land.

---

[59] *Patents* are a form of intellectual property.
[60] *Probate* involves determining the validity of a will (*proving a will*); where there is a dispute about the validity of the will, probate is *contentious*.

Key and commentary to Task 5 Consultation—the hierarchy of the English courts

1. The appeal courts are the Supreme Court/House of Lords (*the final court of appeal*, from 2009, the Supreme Court of the United Kingdom), the Court of Appeal and the High Court, sitting in Divisional Courts of the three Divisions of the High Court.

2. Binding precedent can be created by the Supreme Court/House of Lords, Court of Appeal and Divisional Courts of the High Court, the same as the appeal courts.

3. Civil jurisdiction is exercised by the Supreme Court/House of Lords, Court of Appeal Civil Division, High Court (all Divisions), county courts and magistrates' courts. Criminal jurisdiction is exercised by the Supreme Court/House of Lords, Court of Appeal Criminal Division, High Court (QBD), Crown Court and magistrates' courts.

4. Existing principles can be changed by a higher court in the hierarchy or, in the case of the Supreme Court/House of Lords, by the court itself, a power exercised in rare cases.[61] Also remember that at any time, Parliament can legislate to change, abolish or supplement common law rules.[62]

Comment: the European dimension

Even the Supreme Court of the United Kingdom is bound by decisions of the European Court of Justice; also, under section 2 of the Human Rights Act 1998, all courts and tribunals in the UK must '*take into account*' the case law of the European Court of Human Rights and other ECHR bodies.[63]

Note that there is no separate constitutional jurisdiction in the English legal system: criminal cases are tried by courts with criminal jurisdiction; all other cases are heard by the courts exercising civil jurisdiction. An example of an interesting constitutional case heard by the Court of Appeal Civil Division is *Blackburn v Attorney-General*.[64]

9.3.4 Precedent from the American Perspective

The United States is a federal State: it therefore has different levels of judicial organisation. Each state has its own court structure, organised hierarchically, and

---

[61] E.g., in the case of *Pepper v Hart* [1992] UKHL 3, [1993] AC 593, examined in ch 1, Text 9.

[62] E.g., the abolition of the common law doctrine of *privity of contract* by the Contracts (Rights of Third Parties) Act 1999, examined in ch 3, Task 10.

[63] Discussed respectively in 3.6.2 and 5.4.4 above.

[64] *Blackburn v Attorney-General* [1971] EWCA Civ 7, [1971] 2 All ER 1380, referred to in 3.5.2 above.

in addition there are the federal courts, with the Supreme Court of the United States at the top of the hierarchy. It is the highest appellate court in *the federal court system*. The judges of the Court, called *Justices of the Supreme Court*, are nominated by the President of the United States and appointed 'by and with the advice and consent' of the Senate.[65]

In most US states, the *highest appellate court* is called the *supreme court*. It is also described as the *court of last resort*, another term for the *final court of appeal*. The Supreme Court of Florida, for example, adjudicated on the election result that was instrumental in George W Bush's election to a second term as President in 2004. In other states, such as New York, 'the supreme court is a court of general *original jurisdiction* possessing also (in New York) some *appellate jurisdiction*, but not the court of last resort'.[66]

Task 6   Reading and reflection—*stare decisis* in the United States
Read the following text written by an eminent American jurist, explaining the application of the doctrine of binding precedent in the United States legal system. As you answer the questions below, focus on both language and meaning:

1. Describe the two functions of judicial decision in a common law system.
2. What is the status of *stare decisis* in the United States legal system?
3. Identify the four qualities of precedent that justify the principle of *stare decisis*. Evaluate their importance in a legal system.
4. How does the author compare the use of precedent in England and in the United States?

Do you find that the concepts and terminology of precedent are similar in American and English law? Give examples. What do you learn from this passage about the common law world?

The Judicial Function
A judicial decision has two functions in a common-law system: The first, which is not, to be sure, peculiar to the common law, is to define and to dispose of the controversy before the court. ... This determination is the responsibility of the court. It cannot abdicate its duty even should the case be a novel one for which there is no controlling authority. An old view was that the court in such a contingency was to discover the law among the principles of the common law, much as a scientist discovers a natural law, and then declare it. Today, it is more usual to admit that the court creates the law somewhat as a legislature creates law but within the narrower bounds set by the facts of the case before it and the analogous legal principles from distantly related doctrines.

---

[65] Constitution of the United States, Art II, § 2, cl 2.
[66] H Black (1979), *Black's Law Dictionary*, 5th edn, St Paul, Minn: West Publishing Co, p 1292.

Whether the court discovers or creates the law that it applies, its resolution of the controversy has an impact that extends beyond the parties before it. This is because the second function of a judicial decision, and one that is characteristic of the common law, is that it establishes a precedent so that a similar case arising in the future will probably be decided in the same way. This doctrine is often called by its Latin name, *stare decisis*—from *stare decisis et non quieta movere* (to stand by the decisions and not disturb settled points).[1] Reliance on precedent developed early in English law, and the practice was received in the United States as part of the tradition of the common law, though it was much developed in the nineteenth century as a means of restricting the powers of the appellate courts. As a tradition, the doctrine has not been reduced to a written rule and is not to be found in constitution, statute, or oath of office. The justification commonly given for the *stare decisis* may be summarized in four words: equality, predictability, economy, and respect. The first argument is that the application of the same rule to successive similar cases results in equality of treatment for all who come before the courts. The second is that consistent following of precedents contributes to predictability in future disputes. The third is that the use of established criteria to settle new cases saves time and energy. The fourth is that adherence to earlier decisions shows due respect for the wisdom and experience of prior generations of judges.

For several reasons, the doctrine of precedent has never enjoyed in the United States the absolute authority that it is said to have attained in England. The great volume of decisions, with conflicting precedents in different jurisdictions, has detracted from the authority of individual decisions. The rapidity of change has often weakened the applicability of precedents to later cases that have arisen after social and economic conditions have altered with the passage of years. Nevertheless, the doctrine of precedent, though less rigidly applied than in England, is still firmly entrenched in the United States.[67]

[1] The doctrine of *stare decisis* is used here as synonymous with the doctrine of precedent, and the latter term will generally be employed.

E Farnsworth (2010), *An Introduction to the Legal System of the United States*, 4th edn, S Sheppard (ed)
Copyright © 2010 by Oxford University Press, Inc

[67]   E Farnsworth (2010), *An Introduction to the Legal System of the United States*, 4th edn, S Sheppard (ed), New York: Oxford University Press, Inc, pp 58–59.

Key and commentary to Task 6 Reading and reflection—*stare decisis* in the United States

1. The first function of a judicial decision is to *resolve the dispute* before the court ('to *dispose of* the *controversy*'); secondly, the decision '*establishes a precedent*'—it creates a rule that may be applied in a later, similar case. This second function is 'characteristic of the common law'.

2. *Stare decisis* was 'received' as part of the 'tradition of the common law' and was 'much developed' in the United States during the nineteenth century: if judges must follow precedent, 'the *powers of the appellate courts*' are restricted. Professor Farnsworth notes that *stare decisis* is a 'tradition', an *unwritten rule*, with no formal legal source such as the Constitution, statute law or the '*oath of office*' that a judge *swears* when he is appointed.

3. First, '*equality of treatment* for all who *come before the courts*' is an essential requirement of justice. Secondly, 'predictability' in future disputes guarantees the *certainty of the law* (making it possible for individuals to know their legal position and for lawyers to advise their clients effectively). The third quality is a more practical requirement of a legal system: it 'saves time and energy' to use '*established* criteria' to decide ('*settle*') new cases (but the *reasonable length* of proceedings is also a requirement of a fair trial).[68] Fourthly, 'due respect' to the 'wisdom and experience' of earlier judges is a quality based on prudence and good sense.

4. Precedent is applied more 'rigidly' in England than in the US, where individual decisions, in particular, do not have the same absolute authority. Professor Farnsworth explains two reasons for this: '*conflicting precedents in different jurisdictions*', as each state has its own court system and jurisdiction, in addition to the federal court system; and the rapid changes in social and economic conditions. However ('nevertheless'), he concludes by saying that *stare decisis* is 'still firmly entrenched in the United States': it remains, therefore, a foundation of the legal system.

Comment

We can observe from the passage that the concepts and terminology of precedent are very similar in English and American law. Examples are: *the doctrine of stare decisis, to establish a precedent, a similar case, adherence to precedent* and so on. The dual judicial function described belongs to all common law systems. However, it is clear from Professor Farnsworth's discussion that—as we may expect—the common law system in the United States has in time developed distinctively: while sharing its origins in English law, with *stare decisis* a foundation of the legal system, it possesses its own distinct national features.

---

[68] E.g., under Art 6(1) ECHR.

Task 7 Oral presentations—describing a judicial system
Prepare to describe the organisation of a judicial system of your choice: for
example, the English or American system, or the system in your country.
Prepare an outline of points and use examples from this section of the book
for appropriate terminology and expression. Research further information
during your preparations as required. If working online, prefer official
institutional websites to validate your information.

Points to include

— The court structure in the legal system you have chosen. What are the
   main areas of jurisdiction? Which courts have original jurisdiction?
   And appellate jurisdiction? Who are the judges and what is their role?
— Explain the hierarchy of the courts and consider the use of precedent
   in this system; examine the application of *stare decisis* if appropriate.
   Include comparisons with other legal systems.
— Give your evaluation of this legal system: does it ensure justice and
   certainty in the application of the law?

9.4 Understanding Case Law: Reading a Civil Judgment

9.4.1 The Key Elements of a Case

What is the point of reading *a judgment*, the legal text pronouncing a judicial
decision? In a common law system, judicial decisions are the source of the legal
principles which make up the body of law called *judicial precedent*, or *the common
law*, also known as *case law*. From the lawyer's angle, the point of reading judgments is therefore to discover and understand the law: what are the legal rules
and principles that the judges apply, create or develop in the case, in relation to
the facts and the question for resolution in the dispute, and how does this decision fit into the pre-existing body of the common law? Beyond their purely legal
relevance, judgments often tell fascinating human stories, and the high quality of
linguistic expression of the English judiciary also makes them a literary genre in
their own right.[69]

To understand the importance of a case from the legal point of view (and
not just as a story, or a collection of facts plus a decision)[70] there are certain key

---

[69] See Riley, above n 47, 'The language of the judge's judgment', pp 238–39. Of great interest on
the style of the English judgment is Lord Wilberforce's contribution (1988), 'Intervento alla Tavola
rotonda dei Presidenti delle Corti Supremi' in *La sentenza in Europa. Metodo, tecnica e stile*, Padua:
Cedam, pp 360–65.

[70] A mistake that could be made by language teachers with insufficient legal background, as J Swales
amusingly recounts: only when he attended classes given by a criminal law professor did he realise the

elements that are central. These are: the parties, the facts, the dispute, the issue, the law, the reasoning and the decision, explained in more detail below. In this section, we learn to identify and focus on these key elements, adopting a structured approach to reading a common law judgment. The 'case log' approach presented below should provide a firm legal basis for reading cases.[71]

The judgments reported in the law reports are generally *appeal cases*. They may be significant in the development of the law, for example because they make new law or extend the application of existing common law principles; or they may be significant for the interpretation of legislation or of clauses in documents such as contracts, wills etc.[72] Some important cases, however, are not appeals *on the merits* but concern a point of law that must be decided before a trial on the merits at first instance can proceed; *Donoghue v Stevenson*, one of the most important civil judgments in the common law, is a case of this kind.

It is important to realise that appeals in the English legal system are generally *on the law*, not *on the facts* of the case. In both civil and criminal actions, the facts are *established* (determined by the court) at first instance and are not normally the subject of appeal. If there is a disputed question of law, the losing party may appeal to a higher court, requesting it *to reverse* (or *set aside*) the judgment of the lower court.

In a criminal case heard in the Crown Court on indictment, the facts are decided by the jury, which pronounces a verdict of *guilty* or *not guilty*. The jury bases its deliberations on the legal *directions* given by the judge in his *summing-up*. In an appeal, the appellant may claim that the judge has *misdirected* the jury on a matter of law, by giving it wrong directions; in an appeal, the Court of Appeal may *quash* (invalidate) the conviction.

Every judgment centres on one or more specific legal questions—the *issue(s)* which the court must resolve in order to reach its decision in the case. The process of reasoning which the court uses in order to decide the issue in the case is the most important part of the judgment. From this, we can extract the principle on which the decision is based: the *ratio decidendi* (see 9.3.3 above). This constitutes judicial precedent and may have *persuasive* or *binding* effect in *later similar cases*.

Key elements in the judgment

— THE PARTIES: the identity of *the parties to the case.*
— THE FACTS: *the material facts* on which the dispute is based.
— THE DISPUTE: the legal basis for the claim or trial, e.g., breach of contract, tort of negligence; in a criminal case, the charges.

---

need for a problem-solving approach, developing the analytical skill of identifying 'the crucial fact on which the decision ... rested'. The story illustrates how 'the danger of ignoring genre is the danger of ignoring communicative purpose'. J Swales (1990), *Genre Analysis*, Cambridge: Cambridge University Press, pp 72–73.

[71] A photocopiable blank case log is provided for all users at the end of this chapter.
[72] *All England Law Reports. A User's Guide*, above n 48, p 8.

— THE ISSUE(S): the legal question(s) that the court must resolve in order to decide the dispute.
— THE LAW: the applicable provisions of national and/or EU legislation; the relevant common law rules and principles, based on the precedents.
— THE REASONING: the judge's elaboration of legal principle in relation to the facts of the case, involving a reasoned discussion of the relevant legal sources (legislation and precedent).
— THE DECISION: what decision did the court reach on each issue in the case? Consequently, which party won?

9.4.2 Framework for Reading an English Judgment: the Case Log Approach

You can approach an English judgment (or a judgment from another common law jurisdiction) using a *case log*, like the one set out below, to structure your reading of this important text type.[73] By using the case log to provide a focus for your reading, you will identify the key legal aspects of the judgment, and create a useful record of the case.

Examine the case log framework for reading an English judgment, below. Check that you understand the list of key elements in the first column, and read the specifications and examples in the second column to understand the type of information you will look for as you read a judgment.

The completed case log is always an individual analysis of the case: there is no one 'correct' version, but you must be able to justify your version by reference to the language of the judges in the text of the judgment itself.

CASE LOG: Framework for reading a common law judgment	
LIST OF KEY ELEMENTS	**KEY INFORMATION** *Take brief notes while reading the case. Use a notebook to record other details and quotations of interest.*
Name of case	The names of the parties (given in the title, cases are cited by name and number in the law reports).
Citation in law reports	The series of law reports, year, volume, page numbers (indicated on <http://www.bailii.org> with the words 'Cite as …').

(Continued)

---

[73] The case log, created by A Riley, appeared in various collections of course materials at the University of Padua Law Faculty and was first published in A Riley and F Scarpa (1999), 'La Traduzione della sentenza di common law in italiano' in F Scarpa (ed), (1999) 9 *Traduzione, Società e Cultura*, 3, at pp 85–87.

CASE LOG: Framework for reading a common law judgment	
Parties: *claimant/plaintiff*	Name of claimant(s). Appellant(s) or respondent(s) in this appeal?
Parties: defendant	Name of defendant(s). Appellant(s) or respondent(s)? Relationship to claimant (e.g. contracting party, neighbour, employee/employer, etc)?
Court	E.g. Supreme Court of the United Kingdom, Court of Appeal (Civil Division), High Court (Chancery Division)
Stage of action	E.g. First instance, first or second appeal, *interim proceedings*,[74] etc.
Branch of law	Contract, tort, intellectual property, criminal law, etc.
Specific grounds for *legal action*	Breach of contract, tort of negligence, etc. In criminal law: theft, homicide (murder), etc.
Facts of the case	The material facts and circumstances in outline.
Legal history of the case	What happened in previous phases of the proceeding? E.g., who won at first instance? Which party appealed?
Legal sources	Which sources are applicable? E.g. Acts of Parliament, precedents, EU law, etc. Cite each specific source.
Issue(s) for *decision*	What legal question(s) must the court decide in order to resolve the case? Identify the issue(s) in this appeal.
Decision on each issue	What did the court decide in relation to each issue, above?
Reasons for the decision *(on each issue)*	For what reason(s) (or *grounds*) did the court reach the above decision on each issue? In identifying the judges' reasons, try to arrive at the principle of the case (the *ratio* *decidendi*).
Judgment	Which party won the case? Civil: judgment for the claimant or the defendant? Criminal: conviction upheld, defendant discharged, etc.
Award or *criminal sentence*	Civil: what order or remedy did the court grant? Criminal: what sentence was passed?

9.4.3 Reading an English Civil Judgment: *Miller v Jackson*

In Task 8 below we will read an English judgment, using the analytical case log
approach introduced in 9.4.2 above.

The judgment of the Court of Appeal in the case of *Miller v Jackson*[75] shows the
approach of the English courts to *judicial decision-making*. The dispute concerns
two different torts, and also illustrates the task of the court in deciding whether
to grant the discretionary remedy of an injunction. The decision is not easy, since

[74] In the preliminary stages of civil proceedings, for example to determine the evidence admitted.
[75] *Miller v Jackson* [1977] EWCA Civ 6, [1977] QB 966, [1977] 3 All ER 338.

it involves a balance between conflicting interests; in fact, the three judges in this appeal do not agree on their decision. In such a case, the majority decision constitutes the judgment of the court. A member of the court who disagrees with the majority is said *to dissent from the decision.* You may indicate this in your case log by noting, for example: *Lord Denning dissenting.*

In this judgment, the facts of the case explained by the judges are long and detailed. For reasons of space, you will therefore find a summary of the facts (see 'Task 8: *Miller v Jackson*—Introduction' below) before the extracts from the judgment itself.

Task 8 Reading an English civil judgment—*Miller v Jackson*

Use the blank case log, below, to provide a framework for understanding the legal content of the judgment. Note information in the case log as you read.

First, read the 'Introduction' and the text of the judgment, below the case log, for general understanding. Try to understand the 'story' of the case (Who are the people involved? What did they do? What is the nature of the dispute? What important questions are before the court?) before you focus on the central legal elements of the judgment in detail.

When reading for detail, consult your dictionaries as necessary (legal and general), but be selective: which words do you really need to research?

Note: You will find the elements for the case log in mixed order in the different judges' judgments; the text provided contains only short extracts from the full judgment.

KEY ELEMENTS	CASE LOG
Name of case	*Miller v Jackson*
Citation in law reports	[1977] EWCA Civ 6, [1977] QB 966, [1977] 3 All ER 338 [information from BAILII]
Parties: claimants/ plaintiffs	
Parties: defendants	
Court	
Stage of action	
Branch of law	

Specific grounds for legal action	
Facts of the case	
Legal history of the case	
Legal sources	
Issue(s) for decision	(i) (tort) (ii) (tort) (iii) (remedy)
Decision on each issue	
Reasons (or grounds) for the decision on each issue	
Judgment	
Award	

Task 8 *Miller v Jackson*—Introduction

In the case of *Miller v Jackson*,[76] the plaintiffs (claimants), Mr and Mrs Miller, had bought a new house, built by developers right next to the traditional village *cricket* pitch, where the local cricket club had played for 70 years.[77] During cricket matches, balls from the land occupied by the club sometimes went onto the Millers' property, causing damage and a risk of personal injury and interfering with their *enjoyment of the property*, an interest protected by the tort of *nuisance*. Mrs Miller, in particular, became quite obsessive about the risk. Mr and Mrs Miller took legal action, *seeking damages and an injunction* to stop the club from playing there. The case was heard in the High Court at first instance. The judgment below is the appeal.

Task 8 *Miller v Jackson*—text of the judgment

COURT OF APPEAL

Miller v Jackson[78]

MASTER OF THE ROLLS [LORD DENNING]: In summer time village cricket is the delight of everyone. … [*He describes the facts in detail before considering past and present law.*]

It is the very essence of a private nuisance that it is the unreasonable use by a man of his land to the detriment of his neighbour. He must have been guilty of the fault, not necessarily of negligence, but of the unreasonable use of the land: see *The Wagon Mound* (1967) 1 Appeal Cases at page 639 by Lord Reid. …

I would, therefore, adopt this test: Is the use by the cricket club of this ground for playing cricket a reasonable use of it? To my mind it is a most reasonable use. Just consider the circumstances. …

It was said, however, that the case of the physician's consulting room was to the contrary [*Sturges v Bridgman* (1879)]. But that turned on the old law about easements and prescriptions. … It was in the days when rights of property were in the ascendant. … But nowadays it is a matter of balancing the conflicting interests of the two neighbours. That was made clear by Lord Wright in *Sedleigh-Denfield v O'Callaghan* [1940] AC 880, at page 903, when he said:

> 'A balance has to be maintained between the right of the occupier to do what he likes with his own, and the right of his neighbour not to be interfered with'.

---

[76] *Ibid.*

[77] The English game of cricket is similar to baseball; players in two teams must hit a small, hard ball with a bat as far as possible, and run to score points.

[78] *Miller v Jackson*, above n 75.

In this case it is our task to balance the right of the cricket club to continue playing cricket on their cricket ground, as against the right of the householder not to be interfered with. Upon taking the balance, I would give priority to the right of the cricket club to continue playing cricket on the ground, as they have done for the last seventy years. It takes precedence over the right of the newcomer to sit in his garden undisturbed. ... This case ... should be approached on principles applicable to modern conditions. There is a contest here between the interest of the public at large; and the interest of a private individual. The public interest lies in protecting the environment by preserving our playing fields in the face of mounting development, and by enabling our youth to enjoy all the benefits of outdoor games, such as cricket and football. The private interest lies in securing the privacy of his home and garden without intrusion or interference by anyone. In deciding between these two conflicting interests, it must be remembered that it is not a question of damages. ... No, it is a question of an injunction. And in our law you will find it repeatedly affirmed that an injunction is a discretionary remedy. In a new situation like this, we have to think afresh as to how discretion should be exercised. ... As between their conflicting interests, I am of opinion that the public interest should prevail over the private interest. The cricket club should not be driven out. In my opinion the right exercise of discretion is to refuse an injunction. ... The club were entitled to use this ground for cricket in the accustomed way. It was not a nuisance, nor was it negligence of them so to run it. ... But as the club very fairly say that they are willing to pay for any damage, I am content that there should be an award of £400 to cover any past or future damage.

I would allow the appeal, accordingly.

GEOFFREY LANE LJ: [*The facts in detail*]
The plaintiffs claimed damages and an injunction on the grounds of negligence and nuisance. The Judge upheld their claim. He granted an injunction, the effect of which in practical terms will be to stop cricket from being played on the ground. The defendants now appeal.

Negligence
The evidence of Mr Nevins makes it clear that the risk of injury to property at least was both foreseeable and foreseen. It is obvious that such injury is going to take place so long as cricket is being played on this field. It is the duty of the cricketers so to conduct their operations as not to harm people they can or ought reasonably to foresee may be affected. ...

Nuisance
... Was there here a use by the Defendants of their land involving an unreasonable interference with the plaintiffs' enjoyment of *their* land? ...

A balance has to be maintained between on the one hand the rights of the individual to enjoy his house and garden without the threat of damage and on the other hand the rights of the public in general or a neighbour to engage in lawful pastimes. ...

There is here a real risk of serious injury ... There is, however, one obviously strong point in the Defendants' favour. They ... have been playing cricket on this ground ... for 70 years or so. ... It does not seem just that a long-established activity, in itself innocuous, should be brought to an end because someone chooses to build a house nearby and so turn an innocent pastime into an actionable nuisance. Unfortunately, however, the question is not open. In *Sturges v Bridgman* (1879) 11 Ch D 852 this very problem arose. ... [He examines that precedent in detail.] It may be that this rule works injustice, it may be that one would decide the matter differently in the absence of authority. But we are bound by the decision in *Sturges v Bridgman* and it is not for this court as I see it to alter a rule which has stood for so long. ...

Injunction
Given that the Defendants are guilty of both negligence and nuisance, is it a case where the Court should in its discretion give relief, or should the Plaintiffs be left to their remedy in damages? There is no doubt that if cricket is played, damage will be done to the Plaintiffs' tiles or windows or both. There is a ... danger that if they or their son or their guests spend any time in the garden during the weekend afternoons in the summer they may be hit by a cricket ball. So long as this situation exists it seems to me that damages cannot be said to provide an adequate form of relief. ... I would accordingly uphold the grant of the injunction to restrain the Defendants from committing nuisance. However, I would postpone the operation of the injunction for 12 months to enable the Defendants to look elsewhere for an alternative pitch.

CUMMING-BRUCE LJ: I agree with all that Lord Justice Lane has said in his recital of the relevant facts and his reasoning and conclusion upon the liability of the Defendants in negligence and nuisance, including his observation about the decision in *Sturges v Bridgman*. ...

The only problem that arises is whether the learned Judge is shown to be wrong in deciding to grant the equitable remedy of an injunction ... There is authority that in considering whether to exercise a judicial discretion to grant an injunction the court is under a duty to consider the interests of the public. So said Lord Romilly, Master of the Rolls, over 100 years ago ...

So on the facts of this case a court of equity must seek to strike a fair balance between the right of the Plaintiffs to have quiet enjoyment of their house and garden without exposure to cricket balls occasionally falling like thunderbolts from the heavens, and the opportunity of the inhabitants of the village in which they live to continue to enjoy … summer recreation for adults and young persons. … It is a relevant circumstance which a court of equity should take into account that the plaintiffs decided to buy a house which in June 1972 when completion took place was obviously on the boundary of a quite small cricket ground where cricket was played at weekends and sometimes on evenings during the working week. They selected a house with the benefit of the open space beside it. … It is reasonable to decide that during matches the family must keep out of the garden. The risk of damage to the house can be dealt with in other ways …

With all respect, in my view the learned Judge did not have regard sufficiently to these considerations. He does not appear to have had regard to the interest of the inhabitants of the village as a whole. Had he done so he would in my view have been led to the conclusion that the plaintiffs having accepted the benefit of the open space marching with their land should accept the restrictions upon enjoyment of their garden which they may reasonably think necessary. … There are here special circumstances which should inhibit a court of equity from granting the injunction claimed. …

Order: Appeal allowed. Past and future damages at £400.

The case log key, below, is available for your consultation only after you have completed your own case log.

Task 8 Case log key—*Miller v Jackson*
Compare your version of the case log to the case log key below. Your work should contain similar basic content, but will not be identical.

Note: Information given in brackets (…) is secondary. Information in square brackets […] is not contained in the text above.

KEY ELEMENTS	CASE LOG KEY
Name of case	*Miller v Jackson*
Citation in law reports	[1977] EWCA Civ 6, [1977] QB 966, [1977] 3 All ER 338
Parties: claimants (plaintiffs)	Mr and Mrs Miller—respondents in the appeal. (They own a house on the edge of the cricket ground.)

Parties: defendants	Mr Jackson and another—appellants in the appeal. Members of the cricket club [they were sued personally and on behalf of the club].
Court	Court of Appeal (Civil Division). Lord Denning, Cumming-Bruce and Geoffrey Lane LJJ.
Stage of action	Appeal against the decision at first instance.
Branch of law	Law of torts, and civil law remedies.
Specific grounds for legal action	Tort of negligence (claim for damages); tort of nuisance (claim for damages and an injunction).
Facts of the case	The plaintiffs bought a house, recently built by developers, on the edge of a village cricket ground (70 years); balls from the ground repeatedly landed in plaintiffs' property, causing damage to property and risk of damage to persons. This interfered with their enjoyment of their property; there was a continuing risk, not possible to eliminate if cricket was played there.
Legal history of the case	At first instance (High Court), the plaintiffs won their claim and recovered damages for the torts of negligence and nuisance. The judge granted an injunction to stop the cricket. The club (Jackson and another) appealed.
Legal sources	Judicial precedent: common law rules (for the torts of nuisance and negligence) and equity (for the injunction). [15 cases are cited in the judgments, and 9 others during the hearings]
Issues	(i) whether the club was liable in negligence; (ii) whether the club was liable in nuisance; (iii) whether an injunction was an appropriate remedy. (Had the High Court judge decided correctly on these issues, or should the appeal be allowed?)
Decision on each issue	(i) the club was guilty of negligence; (ii) the club was guilty of nuisance; (iii) an injunction was not an appropriate remedy in the circumstances. Lord Denning dissenting on points (i) and (ii). Lord Justice Lane dissenting on point (iii).
Reasons (or grounds) for the decision on each issue	(i) The defendants could foresee the risk of injury to plaintiffs' property as long as they played cricket; they were in breach of their duty not to harm the plaintiffs and by playing they had caused damage (and risked doing so in future): they were therefore guilty of negligence (Lord Denning dissenting).

	(ii) There was an unreasonable interference with the plaintiffs' right to enjoy their property. Even if the plaintiffs had arrived later and the defendants' activity was not previously a nuisance, this was no defence, applying the precedent of *Sturges v Bridgman*, which bound the court (Lord Denning dissenting).
	(iii) In exercising its discretion, the court's task involves a balance of conflicting interests: should the rights of individuals or of the public prevail? Precedent has established that the public interest *must* be taken into account and the High Court judge failed to consider the village as a whole. Relevant factors in favour of the defendants were: that cricket was an innocuous activity, with many benefits for the public (the environment, sport for young people, etc); the club had played there for 70 years, while the plaintiffs had recently arrived; the plaintiffs realised when they bought the property that the cricket ground was there—they knew of the risk: they should accept the restriction, together with the benefit of the open space marching with their land. The case therefore involved special circumstances inhibiting a court of equity from granting an injunction (Lane LJ dissenting).
Judgment	Appeal allowed. For the defendants: injunction not granted. But for the plaintiffs on the issues of nuisance and negligence.
Award	Damages of £400 for past and future damage [an increase in the quantum awarded at first instance].

Comment—*Miller v Jackson*

The three judges of the Court of Appeal in *Miller v Jackson*[79] do not agree on the issues before the court: have the defendants committed the torts of negligence and nuisance? And if they are guilty of nuisance, should the Court of Appeal grant an injunction to restrain the club from playing cricket, the activity interfering with the plaintiffs' enjoyment of their land?

---

[79] *Miller v Jackson*, above n 75.

In Lord Denning's view, the club has not committed the torts of nuisance or negligence, because its use of the land is *reasonable*. Lord Denning takes a modern view of the law, and states that the case of *Sturges v Bridgman*[80] does not bind the Court, since it depended on the old law of property, while the modern approach to nuisance involves balancing the conflicting interests of the two neighbours (this view is supported by precedent).

But the majority of the Court (Cumming-Bruce and Geoffrey Lane, LJJ) consider themselves bound by a specific *authority*, *Sturges v Bridgman*, decided by the Court of Appeal in 1879: this precedent *is applied*. The judges expressly state that they would have decided differently without that precedent to bind them. They underline the importance of not disturbing precedent, whereas Lord Denning (a progressive judge who contributed to many changes in the law in the twentieth century) stresses that the case 'should be approached on principles applicable to modern conditions'.

On the question of granting an injunction, only Lord Justice Lane (dissenting on this issue) is in favour: he believes that damages do not provide adequate relief for the Millers, because the risk of injury to the plaintiffs' property and person cannot be eliminated as long as cricket is played next to their house and garden. By contrast, Lord Denning and Lord Justice Cumming-Bruce, after balancing the different private and public interests involved, decide that the *public interest should prevail*. They agree that in this particular case an injunction should not be granted; the decision of the High Court judge on this question is therefore *reversed*. In the first place, the judge had failed to consider the public interest, and according to precedent ('*There is authority …*' Cumming-Bruce LJ), a court is *under a duty* to consider the interests of the public when exercising judicial discretion to grant an injunction. Then, considering all the facts of the case, reviewed in detail by the judges, this was not an appropriate case for granting an injunction, which would stop the village cricket club from using its pitch ever again, to the detriment of the environment and the villagers.

The Millers' right to enjoy their property, specifically the use of their garden during cricket matches, must be restricted in order to protect the interest of the inhabitants of the village as a whole (an injunction in this case would affect not only the defendants, but also the rights of third persons not before the Court). Some significant factors are underlined and form part of the grounds for the decision: the innocuous activity carried on by the cricket club had existed long before the plaintiffs arrived; by buying land obviously near the cricket ground, they accepted the benefit of the open space next to their property and must therefore accept the restrictions that go with it.

---

[80] *Sturges v Bridgman* (1879) 11 Ch D 852.

To complete Section Two, choose one or both Tasks below.

Task 9 Vocabulary focus—terminology and expression in civil law

To improve your knowledge of legal expression in the context of civil law, select and highlight example phrases and useful collocations in the judgment in *Miller v Jackson* (including the case log key). The following ideas are just examples. Personalise your vocabulary focus and add full examples to your terminology system.

Example phrases
The defendants were in breach of their duty not to harm the plaintiffs (case log key); It is a matter of balancing the conflicting interests of the two neighbours (Lord Denning); The evidence makes it clear that the risk of injury to property was both foreseeable and foreseen (Lane LJ).

Example collocations
(Focusing on the terms *plaintiff* and *defendant*) *The plaintiffs claimed damages/ The defendants now appeal* (Lane LJ); *an injunction to restrain the defendants from committing* nuisance (Lane LJ); *the right of the plaintiffs to have* quiet enjoyment of their house and garden (Cumming-Bruce LJ).

Task 10 Oral presentation and discussion of a case—*Miller v Jackson*

Prepare to present the case of *Miller v Jackson* orally. Use your case log to help you focus on the key elements of the case and illustrate the most important points with citations from the judgment. Give your own evaluation of the importance of the judgment as precedent and comment on the approach of the three English judges to deciding the case. Do you agree with their decision in the case? How would such a case be decided in your legal system?

Suggestion: work in a group of three and each prepare to present one judge's judgment in the case.

9.4.4 References in Judgments: the Proceedings and the Parties

Examine the table, below, showing terms and phrases used in appeal court judgments to refer to the proceedings and parties.

REFERENCES IN JUDGMENTS: THE PROCEEDINGS
When judges pronounce judgment in an appeal, they refer to the proceedings at first instance as *the trial* and to the judge presiding at first instance as *the judge* or *the trial judge*, sometimes, *the learned judge*.

<u>Underline</u> the examples below:
'In the course of his judgment, the judge considered whether the action should be regarded as a claim for trespass to the person or a claim in negligence. He preferred to treat it as a case of neligence.' (*Revill v Newbery*,[81] Court of Appeal, per Neill LJ)

'The trial judge made the following findings which are relevant to this appeal ...' (*Ruxley v Forsyth*,[82] House of Lords, per Lord Jauncey)

REFERENCES IN JUDGMENTS: THE PARTIES
In appeal judgments, the parties may be indicated:

— by name

— by their original roles in the dispute: in a civil case, *the claimant* or *plaintiff* against *the defendant*; in a criminal case, *the prosecution* against *the defendant*. In certain civil proceedings, the party instituting the action is called *the applicant* or *the petitioner*; the party defending a suit initiated by petition is *the respondent*

— by their roles in this appeal: the party making the appeal is *the appellant*, the party defending the appeal is *the respondent*

— by other descriptive terms, e.g.: *the injured party/the tortfeasor* in a tort case; *the seller* or *the vendor/purchaser* in a case involving the sale of land; *the contractor, the builder, the hospital, the company, the agent, the employee*, etc.

<u>Underline</u> the examples below:

'The facts of the case are set out with admirable clarity by the judge ... : "... Wakened by the noise of the plaintiff and Grainger trying to break open the shed, the defendant took the shotgun, loaded it, poked the barrel through a small hole in the door, ... and fired." ... Mr Revill then brought the present proceedings. The claim was based on ... assault, that is, trespass to the person; ...' (*Revill v Newbery*, above, Court of Appeal, per Neill LJ)

'The respondent entered into a contract with the appellants for the construction by them of a swimming pool at his house in Kent. ... The respondents sought to recover as damages for breach of contract the cost of demolition of the existing pool and construction of a new one of the required depth.' (*Ruxley v Forsyth*, above, House of Lords, per Lord Jauncey)

---

[81] *Revill v Newbery* [1996] QB 567, [1996] 1 All ER 291.
[82] *Ruxley Electronics and Construction Limited v Forsyth* [1996] AC 344.

SECTION THREE

9.5 A Leading Case in the Tort of Negligence: *Donoghue v Stevenson*—Advanced

9.5.1 Reading an English Civil Judgment: *Donoghue v Stevenson*

In this section, we will read an English judgment, using the analytical case log approach introduced in 9.4.2 above.

The judgment of the House of Lords in the case of *Donoghue v Stevenson*[83] is one of the most important civil cases in the English common law. The case is highly significant in the modern development of the law of torts; it concerns in particular the tort of negligence, the *duty of care* and the rights of *consumers of manufactured products*.

It is also an important example of the approach of English courts to the development of the common law. In 9.6 below, we use the judgment in *Donoghue* as our basis for exploring the common law in depth, examining the typical style of judicial reasoning and the techniques by which judicial precedent develops as a source of law.

The full text of the judgment is about 60 pages long. The text reproduced on the following pages contains selected extracts from each of the opinions pronounced by the five *Law Lords*, some of whom dissented from the decision of the court. *The leading judgments* are those of Lord Atkin and Lord Macmillan. You may use the indicators in the column to the right of the text to support your reading of this long, but fascinating case.

> **Task 12 Reading an English civil judgment—*Donoghue v Stevenson***
> Use the blank case log, below, to provide a framework for understanding the legal content of the judgment. Note information in the case log as you read.
>
> First try to understand the 'story' of the case (Who are the people involved? What happened? What is the nature of the dispute? What important questions are before the court?) before you focus on the central legal elements of the judgment in detail. You may not understand everything: focus on your task of completing your case log and highlight important passages in the text as you work.
>
> When reading for detail, consult legal and general English dictionaries as necessary, but be selective: which words do you really need to research?

---

[83] *Donoghue v Stevenson* [1932] UKHL 3, [1932] AC 562 (HL Sc).

KEY ELEMENTS	CASE LOG
Name of case	*Donoghue v Stevenson*
Citation in law reports	[1932] UKHL 3, [1932] AC 562 (HL Sc)
Parties: claimant/plaintiff	*(Scottish terminology: pursuer)*
Parties: defendant	*(Scottish terminology: defender)*
Court	
Stage of action	
Branch of law	
Specific grounds for legal action	
Facts of the case	
Legal history of the case	
Legal sources	

Issue(s) for decision	
Decision on the issues	
Reasons for the decision	
Judgment	
Award	

Die Jovis, 26° Maii, 1932. Parliamentary Archives, HL/PO/JU/4/3/873	
<div align="center">**M'ALISTER or DONOGHUE** **v** **STEVENSON**</div>	*Generally cited as Donoghue v Stevenson*
Lord Buckmaster Lord Atkin Lord Tomlin Lord Thankerton Lord Macmillan	*The five Law Lords hearing the case*
Lord Buckmaster. MY LORDS, The facts of this case are simple.	**Lord Buckmaster's opinion**
On August 26th, 1928, the Appellant drank a bottle of ginger beer, manufactured by the Respondent, which a friend had bought from a retailer and given to her. The bottle contained the decomposed remains of a snail which were not and could not be detected until the greater part of the contents of the bottle had been consumed. As a result she alleged and, at this stage her allegations must be accepted as true, that she suffered from shock and severe gastroenteritis. She accordingly instituted the proceedings against the manufacturers which have given rise to this appeal.	THE PARTIES/ THE FACTS OF THE CASE
The foundation of her case is that the Respondent, as the manufacturers of an article intended for consumption and contained in a receptacle which prevented inspection owed a duty to her as consumer of the article to take care that there was no noxious element in the goods, that they neglected such duty and are consequently liable for any damage caused by such neglect. ... [Lord Buckmaster reviews the case law]	THE PARTIES/ THE DISPUTE
In my view, therefore, the authorities are against the Appellant's contention, and apart from authority it is difficult to see how any common law proposition can be formulated to support her claim. ... [8] I am of opinion that this Appeal should be dismissed, and I beg to move your Lordships accordingly.	DECISION

Lord Atkin.	Lord Atkin's
MY LORDS,	opinion
The sole question for determination in this case is legal: do the averments made by the pursuer in her pleading if true disclose a cause of action? I need not restate the particular facts. The question is whether the manufacturer of an article of drink sold by him to a distributor in circumstances which prevent the distributor or the ultimate purchaser or consumer from discovering by inspection any defect is under any legal duty to the ultimate purchaser or consumer to take reasonable care that the article is free from defect likely to cause injury to health. I do not think a more important problem has occupied your Lordships in your judicial capacity: important both because of its bearing on public health and because of the practical test which it applies to the system of law under which it arises. The case has to be determined in accordance with Scots Law: but it has been a matter of agreement between the experienced counsel who argued this case, and it appears to be the basis of the judgments of the learned judges of the Court of Session that for the purposes of determining this problem the law of Scotland and of England are the same. I speak with little authority on this point, but my own research such as it is satisfies me that the principles of the law of Scotland on such a question as the present are identical with those of English law: and I discuss the issue on that footing. The law of both countries appears to be that in order to support an action for damages for negligence the complainant has to show that he has been injured by the breach of a duty owed to him in the circumstances by the defendant to take reasonable care to avoid such injury. In the present case we are not concerned with the breach of the duty; if a duty exists that would be a question of fact which is sufficiently averred and for present purposes must be assumed. We are solely concerned with the question whether as a matter of law in the circumstances alleged the defender owed any duty to the pursuer to take care.	THE ISSUE *averments = statements of facts pleaded in a civil claim* *Importance of the case* *English law and Scots law—the same?* *Negligence and the duty of care* *This HL judgment is only on the legal issue* *ISSUE restated*
It is remarkable how difficult it is to find in the English authorities statements of general application defining the relations between parties that give rise to the duty. The courts are concerned with the particular relations which come before them in actual litigation, and it is sufficient to say whether the duty exists in those circumstances. The result is that the courts have been engaged upon an elaborate classification of duties as they exist in respect of property whether real or personal with further divisions as to ownership, occupation or control, and distinctions based on the particular relations of the one side or the other whether manufacturer, salesman or landlord,	*Duty of care: lack of a general principle in the case law* *Specific duties decided case by case*

customer, tenant, stranger and so on. In this way it can be ascertained at any time whether the law recognises a duty, but only where the case can be referred to some particular species which has been examined and classified. And yet the duty which is common to all the cases where liability is established must logically be based upon some element common to the cases where it is found to exist. To seek a complete logical definition of the general principle is probably to	*What is the general principle?*
[9]	
go beyond the function of the judge, for the more general the definition the more likely it is to omit essentials or introduce non-essentials. The attempt was made by Lord Esher in *Heaven v Pender* in a definition to which I will later refer.	*Is it the judge's function?*
As framed it was demonstrably too wide, though it appears to me if properly limited to be capable of affording a valuable practical guide. At present I content myself with pointing out that in English law there must be and is some general conception of relations, giving rise to a duty of care, of which the particular cases found in the books are but instances. The liability for negligence, whether you style it such or treat it as in other systems as a species of 'culpa' is no doubt based upon a general public sentiment of moral wrongdoing for which the offender must pay. But acts or omissions which any moral code would censure cannot in a practical world be treated so as to give a right to every person injured by them to demand relief. In this way rules of law arise which limit the range of complainants and the extent of their remedy. The rule that you are to love your neighbour becomes in law you must not injure your neighbour; and the lawyer's question 'Who is my neighbour?' receives a restricted reply. You must take reasonable care to avoid acts or omissions which you can reasonably foresee would be likely to injure your neighbour. Who then in law is my neighbour? The answer seems to be persons who are so closely and directly affected by my act that I ought reasonably to have them in contemplation as being so affected when I am directing my mind to the acts or omissions which are called in question. This appears to me to be the doctrine of *Heaven v Pender* as laid down by Lord Esher when it is limited by the notion of proximity introduced by Lord Esher himself and AL Smith LJ in *Le Lievre v Gould*, 1893,1 QB 497. Lord Esher at p 497 says: 'That case established that under certain circumstances one man may owe a duty to another even though there is no contract between them. If one man is near to another	*Liability for negligence and 'culpa'—the moral dimension*
	Relation between morals and law
	'Who is my neighbour?' Lord Atkin pronounces the 'neighbour principle'
	He formulates the principle based on precedent
	The duty is independent of contract

or is near to the property of another a duty lies upon him not to do that which may cause a personal injury to that other or may injure his property.' ... I venture to say that in the branch of the law which deals with civil wrongs, dependent in England at any rate entirely upon the application by judges of general principles also formulated by judges, it is of particular importance to guard against the danger of stating propositions of law in wider terms than is necessary, lest essential factors be omitted in the wider survey, and the inherent adaptability of English law be unduly restricted. For this reason it is very necessary in considering reported cases in the law of torts that the actual decision alone should carry authority, proper weight of course being given to the dicta of the judges. In my opinion several decided cases support the view that in such a case as the present the manufacturer owes a duty to the consumer to be careful. A direct authority is *George v Skivington* LR 5 Ex 1. ...

The principles of tort law have been developed by the judges

lest (archaic) = in case

Reference to the case law

[Lord Atkin reviews a long series of cases in detail]

[19]

My Lords if your Lordships accept the view that this pleading discloses a relevant cause of action you will be affirming the proposition that by Scots and English law alike a manufacturer of products which he sells in such a form as to show that he intends them to reach the ultimate consumer in the form in which they left him with no reasonable possibility of intermediate examination, and with the knowledge that the absence of reasonable care in the preparation or putting up of the products is likely to result in injury to the consumer's life or property owes a duty to the consumer to take that reasonable care. It is a proposition that I venture to say no one in Scotland or England who was not a lawyer would for one moment doubt. It will be an advantage to make it clear that the law in this matter as in most others is in accordance with sound common sense. I think that this appeal should be allowed.

Lord Atkin concludes with a proposition of law

Common sense and the law

DECISION

[20]

Lord Tomlin.
MY LORDS,
I have had an opportunity of considering the opinion prepared by my noble and learned friend Lord Buckmaster which I have already read. As the reasoning of that opinion and the conclusions reached therein accord in every respect with my own views, I propose to say only a few words. ...

Lord Tomlin's opinion

He concurs with Lord Buckmaster's reasoning and decision

[21] **Lord Thankerton.** MY LORDS, …	**Lord Thankerton's opinion**
[22] In my opinion the existence of a legal duty under such circumstances is in conformity with the principles of both the Law of Scotland and of the Law of England. The English cases demonstrate how impossible it is to finally catalogue, amid the ever-varying types of human relationships, those relationships in which a duty to exercise care arises apart from contract, and each of these cases relates to its own set of circumstances, out of which it was claimed that the duty had arisen. In none of these cases were the circumstances identical with the present case as regards that which I regard as the essential element in this case, viz., the manufacturer's own action in bringing himself into direct relationship with the party injured. I have had the privilege of considering the discussion of these authorities by my noble and learned friend Lord Atkin in the judgment which he has just delivered, and I so entirely agree with it that I cannot usefully add anything to it. …	DECISION

Specificity of the case law. No exact precedent

He concurs with Lord Atkin's reasoning |
| [24] **Lord Macmillan.** MY LORDS, The incident which in its legal bearings your Lordships are called upon to consider in this appeal was in itself of a trivial character, though the consequences to the appellant, as she describes them, were serious enough. It appears from the appellant's allegations that on an evening in August, 1928, she and a friend visited a café in Paisley, where her friend ordered for her some ice cream and a bottle of ginger beer. These were supplied by the Shopkeeper, who opened the ginger beer bottle and poured some of the contents over the ice cream which was contained in a tumbler. The appellant drank part of the mixture and her friend then proceeded to pour the remaining contents of the bottle into the tumbler. As she was doing so a decomposed snail floated out with the ginger beer. | **Lord Macmillan's opinion**

FACTS OF THE CASE/THE PARTIES |
| In consequence of her having drunk part of the contaminated contents of the bottle the appellant alleges that she contracted a serious illness. The bottle is stated to have been of dark opaque glass, so that the condition of the contents could not be ascertained by inspection, and to have been closed with a metal cap, while on the side was a label bearing the name of the respondent, who was the manufacturer of the ginger beer of which the shopkeeper was merely the retailer. | *Causal link: appellant's injury caused by defect in the product* |

The allegations of negligence on which the appellant founds her action against the respondent may be shortly summarised. She says that the ginger beer was manufactured by the respondent for sale as an article of drink to members of the public, including herself; that the presence of a decomposing snail in ginger beer renders the ginger beer harmful and dangerous to those consuming it; and that it was the duty of the respondent to exercise his process of manufacture with sufficient care to prevent snails getting into or remaining in the bottles which he filled with ginger beer. The appellant attacks the respondent's system of conducting his business, alleging that he kept his bottles in premises to which snails had access and that he failed to have his bottles properly inspected for the presence of foreign matter before he filled them.

THE DISPUTE

Appellant's case against the manufacturer

The respondent challenged the relevancy of the appellant's averments and, taking them pro veritate, as for this purpose he was bound to do, pleaded that they disclosed no ground of legal liability on his part to the appellant. ...

The manufacturer's defence: no cause of action

I propose therefore to address myself at once to an examination of the relevant English precedents.

Examination of the precedents

I observe in the first place that there is no decision of this House upon the point at issue, for I agree with Lord Hunter that such cases as *Cavalier v Pope* [1906] AC 428 and *Cameron v Young* [1909] AC 640 ... are in a different chapter of the law. ...   [26]

The fact that there is a contractual relationship between the parties which may give rise to an action for breach of contract does not exclude the co-existence of a right of action founded on negligence as between the same parties independently of the contract though arising out of the relationship in fact brought about by the contract. Of this the best illustration is the right of the injured railway passenger to sue the railway company either for breach of the contract of safe carriage or for negligence in carrying him. And there is no reason why the same set of facts should not give one person a right of action in contract and another person a right of action in tort. ...

Coexistence of rights in contract and tort

[30]

In the American Courts the law has advanced considerably in the development of the principle exemplified in *Thomas v Winchester*. In one of the latest cases in the United States, *Macpherson v Buick Motor Co*, 1916, 217 NY 382, the plaintiff who had purchased

Development of negligence in American case law

from a retailer a motor car manufactured by the defendant company was injured in consequence of a defect in the construction of the car and was held entitled to recover damages from the manufacturer. Cardozo, J, the very eminent Chief Judge of the New York Court of Appeals, and now an Associate Justice of the United States Supreme Court, thus stated the law : 'There is no claim that the defendant knew of the defect and wilfully concealed it. … The charge is one, not of fraud, but of negligence. The question to be determined is whether the defendant owed a duty of care and vigilance to anyone but the immediate purchaser. …'	*US Duty of care*
Having regard to the inconclusive state of the authorities in the courts below and to the fact that the important question involved is now before your Lordships for the first time I think it desirable to consider the matter from the point of view of the principles applicable to this branch of law which are admittedly common to both English and Scottish jurisprudence.	*Need for House of Lords to declare principles*
The law takes no cognisance of carelessness in the abstract. It concerns itself with carelessness only where there is a duty to take care and where failure in that duty has caused damage. In such circumstances carelessness assumes the legal quality of negligence and entails the consequences in law of negligence. What then are the circumstances which give rise to this duty to take care?	*Carelessness and negligence contrasted*
	When does the duty of care exist?
In the daily contacts of social and business life human beings are thrown into or place themselves in an infinite variety of relationships with their fellows and the law can refer only to the standards of the reasonable man in order to determine whether any particular relationship gives rise to a duty to take care as between those who stand in that relationship to each other. The grounds of action may be as various and manifold as human errancy and the conception of legal responsibility may develop in adaptation to altering social conditions and standards. The criterion of judgment must adjust and adapt itself to the changing circumstances of life. The categories of negligence are never closed. The cardinal principle of liability is that the party complained of should owe to the party complaining a duty to take care and that the party complaining should be able to prove that he has suffered damage in consequence of a breach of that duty.	*The standards of the reasonable man*
	Evolving standard of legal responsibility
	The principle of liability for negligence

... To descend from these generalities to the circumstances of the present case I do not think that any reasonable man or any twelve reasonable men would hesitate to hold that if the appellant establishes her allegations the respondent has exhibited carelessness in the conduct of his business. For a manufacturer of aerated water to store his empty bottles in a place where snails can get access to them and to fill his bottles without taking any adequate precautions by inspection or otherwise to ensure that they contain no deleterious foreign matter may reasonably be characterised as carelessness without applying too exacting a standard. But, as I have pointed out, it is not enough to prove the respondent to be careless in his process of manufacture. The question is, does he owe a duty to take care, and to whom does he owe that duty? Now I have no hesitation in affirming that a person who for gain engages in the business of

[32]

manufacturing articles of food and drink intended for consumption by members of the public in the form in which he issues them is under a duty to take care in the manufacture of these articles. That duty, in my opinion, he owes to those whom he intends to consume his products. He manufactures his commodities for human consumption; he intends and contemplates that they shall be consumed. By reason of that very fact he places himself in a relationship with all the potential consumers of his commodities and that relationship which he assumes and desires for his own ends imposes upon him a duty to take care to avoid injuring them. He owes them a duty not to convert by his own carelessness an article which he issues to them as wholesome and innocent into an article which is dangerous to life and health. It is sometimes said that liability can only arise where a reasonable man would have foreseen and could have avoided the consequences of his act or omission. In the present case the respondent, when he manufactured his ginger beer, had directly in contemplation that it would be consumed by members of the public; can it be said that he could not be expected as a reasonable man to foresee that if he conducted his process of manufacture carelessly he might injure those whom he expected and desired to consume his ginger beer? The possibility of injury so arising seems to me in no sense so remote as to excuse him from foreseeing it. Suppose that a baker through carelessness allows a large quantity of arsenic to be mixed with a batch of his

12 reasonable men (a jury)

Application of the principle to the facts of the present case

Question: who does the manufacturer owe a duty of care to?

Answer

The test of foreseeability Application to the present case

Suppose that ... (a hypothetical example)

bread, with the result that those who subsequently eat it are poisoned, could he be heard to say that he owed no duty to the consumers of his bread to take care that it was free from poison, and that, as he did not know that any poison had got into it, his only liability was for breach of warranty under his contract of sale to those who actually bought the poisoned bread from him? Observe that I have said 'through carelessness' and thus excluded the case of a pure accident such as may happen where every care is taken. I cannot believe, and I do not believe, that neither in the law of England nor in the law of Scotland is there redress for such a case. The state of facts I have figured might well give rise to a criminal charge and the civil consequence of such carelessness can scarcely be less wide than its criminal consequences. ...	*Carelessness, not pure accident*
	Not only civil, but also criminal liability
[33]	
The burden of proof must always be upon the injured party to establish that the defect which caused the injury was present in the article when it left the hands of the party whom he sues, that the defect was occasioned by the carelessness of that party and that the circumstances are such as to cast upon the defender a duty to take care not to injure the pursuer. There is no presumption of negligence in such a case as the present, nor is there any justification for applying the maxim res ipsa loquitur. Negligence must be both averred and proved. The appellant accepts this burden of proof and in my opinion she is entitled to have an opportunity of discharging it if she can. I am accordingly of opinion that this appeal should be allowed ...	*The burden of proof in negligence*
	Latin maxim: 'the thing speaks for itself'
	DECISION

Task 12 Case log key—*Donoghue v Stevenson*
The case log key, below, is available for your consultation only after you have completed your own case log. Compare your version with this case log key. Your work should contain the same basic points, but will not be identical.

Note: Information given in brackets (...) is secondary.

KEY ELEMENTS	CASE LOG
Name of case	*Donoghue v Stevenson*
Citation in law reports	[1932] UKHL 3, [1932] AC 562 (HL Sc)
Parties: claimant (Scottish: pursuer)	Donoghue. In Scottish terminology, the *pursuer*. Also the appellant in this appeal. A consumer.
Parties: defendant (Scottish: defender)	Stevenson. In Scottish terminology, the *defender*. Also the respondent in this appeal. A manufacturer.
Court	House of Lords (the final court of appeal also for Scottish civil cases).
Stage of action	Appeal. (This is the final appeal on a matter of law only, the merits of the case, depending on proof of the facts, are not in question here.)
Branch of law	Tort.
Specific grounds for legal action	Tort of negligence (personal injury; in particular, the duty of care in the tort of negligence). The question before the lower courts and the House of Lords is whether the appellant has a cause of action in the tort of negligence, not whether, on the facts of the case, the respondents were actually guilty of negligence. If the plaintiff succeeds, the case on the merits can then proceed at first instance.
Facts of the case	The appellant became ill as a consequence of drinking some ginger beer poured from an opaque bottle, which contained the remains of a decomposed snail. As a consequence of the defect in the product, she suffered personal injury (shock and gastroenteritis). The injured party alleged that the drink had been manufactured negligently by the respondent. She had no contractual relationship with the manufacturer or seller of the product: she was simply the ultimate consumer, as her friend had bought the drink for her from a retail seller in a café.
Legal history of the case	Appeal from the decision of the highest Scottish civil court, the Court of Session, which dismissed the action, finding for the defendant (who had claimed that the facts alleged by the plaintiff disclosed no ground of legal liability). At an earlier stage, the Lord Ordinary had 'allowed a proof'—ie the hearing of evidence before a judge—in favour of the pursuer.
Legal sources	Common law: judicial precedent. (Many cases are cited in the judgment, but there is no direct precedent; the judges must therefore develop the common law in one way or another, to decide the dispute.) The judges agree that the law of Scotland and England is the same on the point disputed.

Issue(s)	Whether the appellant, on the facts stated, has a cause of action in the tort of negligence. Specifically, whether a manufacturer owes a legal duty (a duty of care) to the ultimate consumer to take care that an article he produces, sold in such a form that it cannot reasonably be inspected before reaching the consumer, is free from any defect likely to cause injury to the consumer's health.
Decision	The appellant has a cause of action in negligence against the respondent, who owes a duty of care to the appellant. Specifically, the manufacturer of products owes a duty of care to the ultimate consumer to take reasonable care to ensure that the articles he produces are free from defect likely to cause injury to the consumer's health, in circumstances where there is no possibility of intermediate inspection so that the defect may be discovered. Lord Buckmaster and Lord Tomlin dissenting.
Reasons for the decision	(From Lord Macmillan's opinion.) To determine whether a particular relation gives rise to a legal duty to take care, we must apply the standard of the reasonable man. A person engaging in the business of manufacturing food and drink must contemplate that these articles are for human consumption. 'He intends and contemplates that they shall be consumed. By reason of that very fact he places himself in a relationship with all the potential consumers' of his products, and that relationship imposes upon him a duty to take care to avoid injuring them. Applying the test of whether a reasonable man would foresee the damage, it is clearly satisfied in this case. Lord Macmillan refers to articles of food and drink, Lord Atkin more generally to 'products' and injury to 'life or property' in his proposition of the law (p 19). Lord Atkin also formulates a general test for deciding whether a duty of care is owed by one person to another, giving the person injured the right to demand legal relief: 'You must take reasonable care to avoid acts or omissions which you can reasonably foresee would be likely to injure your neighbour. ... [That is,] persons so closely and directly affected by my act that I ought reasonably to have them in contemplation as being so affected when I am directing my mind to the acts or omissions which are called in question.' (Known as the 'Neighbour' test.)
Judgment	For the appellant (the pursuer, Donoghue). (Two of the five Law Lords dissented.)
Award	None. (The decision is on the disputed point of law only; the appellant can now proceed at first instance. To win damages she will need to prove the facts alleged in her claim).

For comment and discussion of *Donoghue v Stevenson* and evaluation of its legal importance, proceed to 9.6 below.

9.6 Common Law Method II: the *Ratio Decidendi* and the Development of Principles in the Common Law—Advanced

We now examine the legal rules decided in the case of *Donoghue v Stevenson* and consider their importance in the development of the common law. During this process, we investigate common law method in greater depth. We shall aim to answer the following questions:

— By reading a judgment, how can we discover the rule or principle decided in the case?
— For what principle(s) is *Donoghue v Stevenson* a precedent?
— How do legal rules develop in the common law system?

To answer these questions, we shall use the work of the great English jurist, Rupert Cross, renowned author of *Precedent in English Law*,[84] considered the basic text-book on the subject for both students and lawyers.[85]

The discussion of precedent naturally focuses on the House of Lords. The creation of the new Supreme Court of the United Kingdom, which now exercises the jurisdiction previously exercised by the Appellate Committee of the House of Lords, is not designed to disturb the rules of precedent or interrupt the continuity of the common law in the British legal system.

9.6.1 The Rules of Precedent

Cross notes the following three constant features of the English system of precedent:

> These are the respect paid to a single decision of a superior court, the fact that the decision of such a court is a persuasive precedent even so far as courts above that from which it emanates are concerned, and the fact that a single decision is always a binding precedent as regards courts below that from which it emanated.[86]

---

[84] Written by Rupert Cross and originally published in 1960, citations given in this section are respectively from R Cross (1977), *Precedent in English Law*, 3rd edn, Oxford: Clarendon Press; and R Cross and J Harris (1991), *Precedent in English Law*, 4th edn, Oxford: Clarendon Press.

[85] Cross and Harris, above n 84, Preface by JW Harris.

[86] *Ibid*, p 5.

He provides the following 'preliminary statement of the rules of precedent', explored in depth later in the book:

> Every court is bound to follow any case decided by a court above it in the hierarchy and the appellate courts (other than the House of Lords) are bound by their previous decisions.[87]

Cross reminds the reader that the rules of precedent are dependent on the practice of the courts and can be changed. In fact, in 1966, a major innovation was announced: the Law Lords, while recognising the indispensable role of precedent in the law and the need for certainty of the law, announced that the House of Lords would no longer be rigidly bound in all cases by its own precedents.[88]

Read the extract from the 1966 Practice Statement, below. What were the reasons for this change?

> Their Lordships … recognise that too rigid adherence to precedent may lead to injustice in a particular case and also unduly restrict the proper development of the law. They propose therefore to modify their present practice and, while treating former decisions of this House as normally binding, to depart from a previous decision when it appears right to do so.[89]

The rule was changed in the interests of justice and to permit 'the proper development of the law'; this introduced greater flexibility into the system (but only for the supreme court itself). It is important to realise that the House of Lords—or today, the Supreme Court of the United Kingdom—considers its own precedents 'normally binding' and the power to change previously decided rules of the common law is very rarely used.[90]

With this limited exception, the system of precedent in English law has both vertical and horizontal effect: *a precedent is binding in later similar cases* both vertically on the courts below and horizontally on courts of the same level (since 1966, with the exception of the House of Lords/Supreme Court since 2009). Refer to 9.3.3, above, for further details of precedent in relation to other courts in the English hierarchy.

Persuasive precedents

Even when a precedent is not binding, it may be persuasive and therefore still influential for later courts. A *persuasive precedent* may originate from a lower court in the hierarchy, or even from another common law jurisdiction. In *Donoghue*, Lord Atkin referred to an American precedent in the following passage. Remember that in this judgment, two of the five Law Lords dissented.

---

[87] *Ibid*, p 6. For the meaning of '*bound to follow*', refer to 9.3.3 above, if necessary.

[88] The statement was read by the Lord Chancellor, Lord Gardiner, on behalf of himself and the Lords of Appeal in Ordinary, before judgments were delivered on 26 July 1966; reported in House of Lords Practice Statement [1966] 3 All ER 77.

[89] House of Lords Practice Statement [1966] 3 All ER 77.

[90] See, e.g., *Pepper v Hart* [1992] UKHL 3, [1993] AC 593: Text 9 in ch 1.

Which view of the law does the American precedent support?

> It is always a satisfaction for an English lawyer to be able to test his application of fundamental principles of the common law by the development of the same doctrines by the lawyers of the Courts of the United States. In that country I find that the law appears to be well established in the sense in which I have indicated. The mouse had emerged from the ginger-beer bottle in the United States before it appeared in Scotland, but there it brought a liability upon the manufacturer. I must not in this long judgment do more than refer to the illuminating judgment of Cardozo J in *MacPherson v Buick Motor Co* in the New York Court of Appeals (217 NY 382), in which he states the principles of the law as I should desire to state them, and reviews the authorities in other States than his own. ... [T]he American decision would undoubtedly lead to a decision in favour of the pursuer in the present case.[91]

Lord Atkin is pleased to remark that the question had already been decided in American law, in line with his own view: *liability for negligence* had been imposed on the manufacturer in a case against Buick Motor Company. References to precedents from another common law jurisdiction are particularly important when the courts must decide *a case of first impression*, for which there is no precedent in the jurisdiction. A persuasive precedent from another common law jurisdiction can be used as a guide to elaborating the legal principle in the case. It is not binding, but it is considered desirable by the judges for common law principles on important matters to develop in harmony.

9.6.2 Interpreting the Judgment as Law: the *Ratio Decidendi*

To interpret a judgment as law in the common law legal system, it is necessary to determine which part of the judgment is binding in later similar cases. As explained in 9.3.3 above, this is not the whole decision, or every element in the court's judgment, but only the part or aspect of the judgment known as the *ratio decidendi*, that is, the reasons or grounds for the judge's decision on the issue before the court (loosely, the principle of the case).

Because English law has never been codified, we do not have a single, authoritative definition of our key terms. Three authoritative definitions that help to understand the concept of *ratio decidendi* are examined below.

Rupert Cross gives this definition of the *ratio*:

> The *ratio decidendi* of a case is any rule of law expressly or impliedly treated by the judge as a necessary step in reaching his conclusion, having regard to the line of reasoning adopted by him, or a necessary part of his direction to the jury.[92]

---

[91] *Donoghue v Stevenson* [1932] UKHL 3, [1932] AC 562 (HL Sc), Lord Atkin.
[92] Cross, above n 84, p 76.

He also notes that more than one '*line of reasoning*' may be used, so a case may have more than one *ratio*.[93] The plural is *rationes decidendi* or *ratios*.

The authoritative legal reference work *Halsbury's Laws of England* provides the following definition:

> **573. Ratio decidendi.** The enunciation of the reason or principle upon which a question before a court has been decided is alone binding as a precedent. This underlying principle is called the ratio decidendi, namely the general reasons given for the decision or the general grounds upon which it is based, detached or abstracted from the specific peculiarities of the particular case which gives rise to the decision. What constitutes binding precedent is the ratio decidendi.[94]

Renowned scholar Neil MacCormick says: 'The trouble is that there is no generally agreed statement either of what a *ratio* is or of how you find the *ratio* in any given case.'[95] Fortunately, he then provides an approach:

> When a Court gives a ruling on a point of law which it conceives to be necessary to its justification of its particular decision, it would seem not unreasonable to regard that ruling as the *ratio* of the case.[96]

The *ratio* is a ruling on a *point of law* and that point of law, or *issue*, must be the one that the court is called on to decide in order to resolve the dispute before it. Judicial comments on any other points of law are not necessary to the decision and are not *ratio* but *dicta*, which do not bind later courts.

Determining the *ratio decidendi*

Determining the *ratio decidendi* of a case requires a process of reading and interpretation of the language used by the judges in pronouncing their judgment in the case. There is no precise formula that we can use,[97] and no part of the judgment text is specifically identified as containing the *ratio*, so it is not an easy task: an analytical skill, rather than a mechanical process. When we talk about *common law skills*, we are thinking of this ability of the common lawyer to use and interpret case law effectively, and to comprehend and adopt the distinctive approach recognisable as *English legal reasoning*.[98]

We suggest that a helpful approach for arriving at the *ratio* of a case when you consult a judgment is to focus clearly on the question, or *issue*, before the court. Helpfully, the issue is often clearly specified by the judge at the beginning of his judgment. In *Donoghue*, for example, Lord Atkin begins his opinion by stating the

---

[93] *Ibid.*
[94] Lord Hailsham (1979), *Halsbury's Laws of England*, 4th edn, London: Butterworths.
[95] MacCormick, above n 52, p 82.
[96] *Ibid*, p 83.
[97] *Ibid*, p 72.
[98] For a full discussion, see F Cownie, A Bradney and M Burton (2013), *English Legal System in Context*, 6th edn, Oxford: Oxford University Press, ch 5 'English legal reasoning: the use of case law', pp 81–100.

issue before the Court (*italics* are inserted in the text, below, to highlight linguistic indicators of the issue):

> My Lords, *the sole question for determination in this case is legal: Do* the averments made by the pursuer in her pleading, if true, *disclose a cause of action?* I need not restate the particular facts. *The question is whether* the manufacturer of an article of drink sold by him to a distributor, in circumstances which prevent the distributor or the ultimate purchaser or consumer from discovering by inspection any defect, is under any legal duty to the ultimate purchaser or consumer to take reasonable care that the article is free from defect likely to cause injury to health. I do not think a more important problem has occupied your Lordships in your judicial capacity...[99]

Keep the issue in mind as we consider the *ratio* of *Donoghue*, below.

9.6.3 The *Ratio* of *Donoghue v Stevenson*

The aim of Task 13 below is to illustrate the nature of a *ratio decidendi* and for you to learn to determine the *ratio* as or after you read a case.

Task 13 Legal reasoning skills—the *ratio* of *Donoghue v Stevenson*[100]
Examine the three options below and choose the proposition you believe to be the ratio of *Donoghue v Stevenson*. As you work, consider the definitions of the *ratio decidendi* given in 9.6.2 above. You may refer to the text of the judgment again during this activity if you wish. Prepare to justify your choice and consider the questions below, as you work.

    Why do you think this proposition (A, B or C) is the *ratio* of *Donoghue v Stevenson*? Why have you excluded the other solutions?

    Compare and discuss your choices.

Proposition A: A manufacturer of ginger beer owes a duty to Scotswomen by whom that drink is lawfully consumed in the cafés of Paisley, to take care that snails do not get into the opaque bottles in which it is contained.
A: Your ideas (Yes/No. Why/Why not?)
Proposition B: A party must take reasonable care to avoid acts or omissions which he can reasonably foresee would be likely to injure persons who are so closely and directly affected by his act that he ought reasonably to have them in contemplation as being so affected when he is directing his mind to the acts or omissions which are called in question.
B: Your ideas

---

[99] *Donoghue v Stevenson* [1932] UKHL 3, [1932] AC 562 (HL Sc).
[100] The idea for this task was suggested by Rupert Cross's approach to the *ratio* in Cross, above n 51. The phrasing of the three propositions is taken from pp 48 and 54.

Proposition C: A manufacturer of products, which he sells in such a form as to show that he intends them to reach the ultimate consumer in the form in which they left him with no reasonable possibility of intermediate examination, and with the knowledge that the absence of reasonable care in the preparation or putting up of the products will result in an injury to the consumer's life or property, owes a duty to the consumer to take that reasonable care.

C: Your ideas

Comment on Task 13   Legal reasoning skills—the *ratio* of *Donoghue v Stevenson*

Proposition A

If you chose proposition A ... are you sure you want to become a lawyer?! Seriously, observing carefully the elements of this '*ratio*', is it likely, or even *possible*, that such precise facts will ever be repeated?

In order to be useful or effective, a legal principle must be capable of application not only in one, unique case, but also in a class or type of case. In fact, a binding precedent must be followed only in later, similar cases. By contrast, the 'rule' expressed in A depends entirely on the particular facts of the specific case (the Scotswoman, the ginger beer, the snail).

When formulating a *ratio*, we need to extract the relevant factual elements in the case which are *material* to the judge's decision (*the material facts*) and transpose them to a broader or higher level or class by a process of detachment or abstraction from 'the specific peculiarities of the particular case'.[101]

To practise this approach, complete the table below by transposing the elements from proposition A to a higher level. Note that there may be more than one possible range of solutions.

Example: ginger beer is a soft drink, it belongs in the class *drinks*. It is also a member of the broader category *food and drink*. Above that, it is an item for human consumption, a category including medicines too. At a more general level it is a product for human use; but so is a car, a pen, a newspaper or a hat, each of which has quite different uses and characteristics. The question for the lawyer therefore becomes: What is the appropriate level of abstraction when formulating the *ratio decidendi*?

---

[101] See the definition of *ratio decidendi* in *Halsbury's Laws of England*, cited in 9.6.2 above.

Specific fact	Class	Broader class	Broader class	Broader class
Ginger beer	Drinks	Food and drink	Any item for human consumption including medicines, etc	Any products for human use [or broader?]
Scotswomen	Scots OR females	All adults	All people, including children	All living beings, including animals
Paisley	Towns in Scotland OR Cafés in Scotland	Anywhere in Scotland? OR Anywhere in the UK?	*Continue …*	[Is it a material fact?]
Snails	Molluscs	Small animals	*Continue …*	
Opaque bottles	Bottles? OR opaque containers?	*Continue …*		

Proposition B

If you chose proposition B, you correctly identified the eloquent expression of a grand legal principle. The words of Lord Atkin are familiar to every British lawyer and are considered to be the foundation of the modern law of negligence; all law students must learn these words by heart and must be able to apply them to a variety of hypothetical fact situations. This important legal principle is known as *the neighbour principle* or *the broad principle in Donoghue*. It is the test used to determine the existence of a duty of care, and applies in all cases unless there is some justification for its exclusion. For the development of the modern three-stage *duty of care test*, see 'Conclusion', at the end of this section, below.

However, proposition B is not the *ratio decidendi* of *Donoghue v Stevenson*. The fact that the principle can be applied to any set of facts in life means that it is too general to be a *ratio*: it is not sufficiently closely connected to the facts of the case. As a general principle, or test, it marked the turning point in the development of the law of negligence into the dominant tort of modern times, but:

> No judge is required by the ruling in that case to hold that a defendant is liable in damages merely because he could reasonably foresee that an act or omission of his might cause loss to some other person.[102]

---

[102] Cross and Harris, above n 84, p 45.

Proposition C

This is considered to be the *ratio decidendi* of *Donoghue v Stevenson*. The words are taken from Lord Atkin's opinion, and the principle stated is based directly on the facts of the case, but has been generalised sufficiently to be capable of application in similar cases. The elements have been abstracted to the level of representative categories (e.g. not a manufacturer of ginger beer, but a manufacturer of products). *Donoghue* establishes the rule of law that in the specific circumstances stated, a duty of care is owed by the manufacturer to the ultimate consumer to take reasonable care not to injure the consumer.

No part of the judgment in the precedent itself identifies the *ratio* by its name. In fact, it is the task of *later courts* to determine the *ratio* of a precedent, in the course of their judgments, when they are taking into consideration the earlier precedent. As Cross explains, in the case of *Donoghue*:

> Elaborate judgments were delivered, but there has been a high degree of unanimity among subsequent judges and writers in regarding the following passage with which Lord Atkin concluded his speech as containing the *ratio decidendi* of the case:
>
>> If your Lordships accept the view that this pleading discloses a relevant cause of action you will be affirming the proposition that by Scots and English law alike a manufacturer of products, which he sells in such a form as to show that he intends them to reach the ultimate consumer in the form in which they left him with no reasonable possibility of intermediate examination, and with the knowledge that the absence of reasonable care in the preparation or putting up of the products will result in an injury to the consumer's life or property, owes a duty to the consumer to take that reasonable care.[103]

In your opinion, was this the only possible determination of the ratio in *Donoghue*?

9.6.4 The Influence of *Donoghue* in the Development of Tort Law

Why was the House of Lords decision in *Donoghue v Stevenson* so significant for the development of the English law of torts? The case had a dual impact on the law, as Carol Harlow explains, below.

What was the dual impact of Donoghue *on the law of torts?*

> By holding the manufacturer and not the retailer primarily responsible for the safety of products, the House of Lords produced a doctrine in tune with twentieth century commercial practices and laid the foundation of what today we call 'products liability'.

---

[103] *Ibid*, citing Lord Atkin in *Donoghue v Stevenson*, p 44.

In deciding that the manufacturer was liable outside the terms of his contracts to people with whom he had no direct relationship, the House greatly extended the range of people who could sue. ... But the case was to have a much wider effect on tort law. Lord Atkin's judgment does not speak of manufacturers, producers or consumers; it is couched in general terms and can be read as a general statement of the circumstances in which one person will incur legal liability to another. Something about the directness and simplicity of the famous 'neighbour' passage gave it a wide appeal which caused it to be read in precisely this fashion.

The neighbour test of Lord Atkin is today used to measure civil liability for negligence. When broken down, it is found to consist of three elements: duty, breach and damage.[104]

First, the decision in *Donoghue* was the origin of modern *products liability*: that is, the liability of manufacturers and other persons for damage caused by defective products.[105] This decision brought the law in line with modern commercial practices. The rule in *Donoghue* gave the ultimate consumer, who suffered injury due to a defective product, a cause of action against the manufacturer, independently of any contractual relationship; the 'narrow rule in *Donoghue*' (as its *ratio* is sometimes called) therefore *extended* legal protection to a wider range of people.

The second, and even greater, impact of *Donoghue* was produced by the application of the neighbour principle in later case law: it has been treated as a general test, applicable in any circumstances, of when one person owes a legal duty in the tort of negligence to another: it is used '*to measure civil liability for negligence*'.

Lord Atkin's neighbour principle introduced a moral dimension into the question of whether a legal duty exists:

[I]t does not form part of the ratio of the case, but the decision has nevertheless been regarded as introducing into the law a general moral principle of 'good neighbourliness'. To answer the question whether A owes B a duty of care necessarily requires a consideration of whether A *ought* to take care to look after B's interests ...[106]

It is interesting to note that the modal verb *ought to*, used by Lord Atkin, tends to indicate a duty which could be of a social or moral nature, rather than a strict obligation. Obligation is more usually expressed with the modal verbs *must* and, in performative legal texts, *shall*.

Murphy and Witting state that the dual importance of *Donoghue* was, first, to firmly establish a new category of duty (the manufacturer's duty towards the ultimate consumer); and, secondly, to 'finally set at rest any possible doubts about whether the tort of negligence was capable of further expansion'.[107]

---

[104]   C Harlow (1987), *Understanding Tort Law*, London: Fontana Press, p 41.

[105]   Products liability expanded significantly from the 1970s, thanks to national legislation and EU obligations: see *A Dictionary of Law*, above n 30, pp 428–29.

[106]   Deakin *et al*, above n 10, p 92; the authors note Lord Atkin's strong Christian conviction that we all have a duty to take care of our 'neighbours', no doubt reflected in the content and language of his opinion.

[107]   J Murphy and C Whitting (2012), *Street on Torts*, 12th edn, Oxford: Oxford University Press, p 27.

The modern three-stage duty of care test

Naturally, since *Donoghue*, the law has continued to develop and change. However, the neighbour principle, with its objective standard of *reasonable foreseeability* of injury, remains at the base of establishing the duty of care. Since the leading case of *Caparo Industries v Dickman*,[108] the courts now consider three separate steps or *issues* in establishing the existence of a duty of care, as explained below:

> First, of course, it must be reasonably foreseeable that the conduct of the defendant will cause damage to the claimant. ... Secondly, there must be sufficient 'proximity' between the parties. And thirdly, 'the situation must be one in which the court considers it fair, just and reasonable that the law should impose a duty of care of a given scope on the one party for the benefit of the other' [Lord Bridge in *Caparo* at [1990] 2 AC 617].[109]

The three steps are clearly examined in the case of *Mulcahy v Ministry of Defence*.[110] The plaintiff was a British soldier, injured during battle when his gun commander negligently fired a Howitzer gun while he was at the front of it. Applying the three-stage test (above) for the duty of care, the first step (involving the neighbour test) and the second step (*proximity*) were satisfied. But the plaintiff's case failed the third step in the test. The Court of Appeal decided that it would not be '*just, fair and reasonable*' to impose a duty of care in such circumstances, taking into account the role and position of the *tortfeasor* and all the circumstances. This precedent establishes that *no duty of care in the tort of negligence is owed by one soldier to another when engaging the enemy in battle conditions.* The Court considered, on the basis of *common sense and sound policy*, that it would not be *fair, just and reasonable* to impose such a duty.

The judgment in *Mulcahy* provides an interesting illustration of common law reasoning. Although there was no direct precedent for the issue before the Court, the judges arrived at their conclusion basing their reasoning on the principles established in the case law, supported also by practical considerations. Sir Iain Glidewell stated in the judgment that:

> Like Neill LJ, it is in my judgment clear that public policy does require that, when two or more members of the armed forces of the Crown are engaged in the course of hostilities, one is under no duty of care in tort to another. Indeed, it could be highly detrimental to the conduct of military operations if each soldier had to be conscious that, even in the heat of battle, he owed such a duty to his comrade.[111]

We may also note that under the rules of *vicarious liability* (where one party is *liable* for the torts of another), the State, in this case the Ministry of Defence, as *employer of the tortfeasor*, would have been liable to pay damages, so *bearing the financial burden* for compensating the plaintiff's injury.

---

[108] *Caparo Industries v Dickman* [1990] UKHL 2, [1990] 2 AC 605.
[109] Rogers, above n 11, p 143.
[110] *Mulcahy v Ministry of Defence* [1996] EWCA Civ 1323, [1996] QB 732, [1996] 2 All ER 758.
[111] *Ibid*, 772.

To conclude, there has been a rapid expansion of the tort of negligence on the basis of *Donoghue*. In particular, where a private individual causes physical injury to another by a positive act (an *act*, not an *omission*), 'it is now safe as a general rule to assume the existence of a duty of care'.[112] But the courts have adopted a more restrictive approach in 'problematic' cases, for example where the claimant has suffered *pure economic loss* or psychiatric damage, where the defendant is a public body, or the negligence consists of an omission: 'In such cases the courts have limited the circumstances in which a duty of care will arise for a variety of reasons'.[113]

These scholars note that the tendency of the courts today, for example in *Caparo Industries v Dickman* above, is to favour a 'cautious, case-by-case approach' similar to Lord Macmillan's pragmatic approach in *Donoghue*, dependent on the specific facts of the case, rather than the broad moral principle advocated by Lord Atkin.[114]

> NOTE: *You can read the case of* Mulcahy v Ministry of Defence, *or another case of your choice, by consulting the website* <http://www.bailii.org>. *To support your reading, copy and complete a blank case log (at end of chapter). To find a case, choose the legal system and court: eg United Kingdom for the Supreme Court or House of Lords; but England and Wales for the Court of Appeal or High Court. Case names or key terms can be used to search for cases of interest.*

9.6.5 English Judicial Reasoning: Developing Common Law Principles

We now consider how the common law is applied and develops from case to case.

Reasoning by analogy

The use of analogy is a significant aspect of English judicial reasoning. It is possible to identify three stages in *judicial reasoning by analogy* used when the English courts are deciding *whether to apply a precedent*: analogy is used in Stages 1 and 3 of this process:[115]

— *Stage 1*: The perception of relevant *likenesses* (similarities) between the previous case and *the instant case* (the case now before the court, the present case).
— *Stage 2*: The determination of the *ratio decidendi* of the previous case.
— *Stage 3*: The decision to apply that *ratio* to the instant case:
  i) the facts may be so close as to require application of the ratio;
  ii) the facts may be sufficiently close as to justify application of the *ratio* if the judge so wishes.

---

[112] Deakin *et al*, above n 10, p 97.
[113] *Ibid*.
[114] *Ibid*, p 93. Also see 9.6.5 below, concluding comments.
[115] This section is based on the analysis of judicial reasoning by analogy given by Cross, above n 51, pp 182–83.

Stage 1. This involves careful examination of *the facts of the case.* 'Like cases must be decided alike.' It is this basic principle of justice, connected with the need for *certainty of the law,* which the common law legal system aims to satisfy through the doctrine of binding precedent. Judicial precedent is only binding in later, *similar* cases. When faced with a dispute, the courts must decide whether the case before them is similar to the precedent under consideration.

English judgments therefore contain a detailed description of the facts of the case and an evaluation of which facts are *material* (legally relevant). The judge in *the instant case* will also outline the facts of the precedent, and explain which facts he believes the earlier judge treated as material in reaching that decision. Where the instant case contains some, but not all, similar facts, this will be underlined and taken into account.

Stage 2. Stage 2 does not involve analogy.

Stage 3. This consists of alternatives, depending on the conclusions of the judge regarding Stages 1 and 2. Where, as in i), the facts of the later case are so close as to *require* application of the *ratio,* the precedent is binding on the later court, and the judge cannot choose to disregard it. Even if the later court is not bound by the precedent (because of its position in the hierarchy), it will depart from the precedent only if there are serious reasons that justify doing so, since the decision of a superior court is a persuasive precedent even for a court above it in the hierarchy.[116]

Where, as in ii), the facts are only sufficiently close as to *justify* application of the *ratio, the judge exercises discretion*: if he decides to apply the same principle, the rule in the precedent will be *extended* to cover a different fact situation; if he decides to apply a different rule, this choice will be explicitly justified by the judge, based on the distinction between the two sets of facts in the cases. This process is called *distinguishing.*

Task 14 Following precedent—a later similar case

First, examine the summary of the facts of the case *Daniels and Daniels v White and Tarbard,*[117] below, a case decided soon after *Donoghue v Stevenson.* Answer questions 1. to 3. below, before reading the editorial note which follows, to check your answers:

1. What likenesses can you see between this case and *Donoghue?*
2. *Daniels and Daniels* was heard by the King's Bench Division of the High Court. Was that court bound by *Donoghue?*
3. Given your answers to 1. and 2. above, do you think the court followed precedent and applied *Donoghue* in this case?

---

[116] Cross and Harris, above n 84, p 5.
[117] *Daniels and Daniels v R White & Sons Ltd and Tarbard* [1938] 4 All ER 258 (annotated).

Daniels and Daniels v White and Tarbard: summary of the facts

Mr Daniels bought a bottle of lemonade at the Falcon Arms Pub in London from Mrs Tarbard, the retail seller. He took the lemonade home, poured some into a glass and both he and his wife drank; they suffered injury as a consequence of the fact that the lemonade contained carbolic acid. When purchasing the bottle from Mrs Tarbard, Mr Daniels had requested R White's lemonade, specifying the brand name.

EDITORIAL NOTE: … We have herein the consideration of the application of this doctrine [the rule in *Donoghue*] to the facts of a modern factory and it is held that, where a manufacturer adopts a fool-proof process carried out under efficient supervision, his duty under the doctrine is fulfilled. It would seem that the plaintiff is ultimately forced to show that there is some possibility that the danger to himself was caused by some error or omission on the part of the manufacturer.[118]

Comment to Task 14 Following precedent—a later, similar case

Although the facts of the case are very similar to those in *Donoghue*, and the High Court was naturally bound by the House of Lords precedent, the plaintiffs lost their claim in tort against the manufacturer of the lemonade. The judge heard detailed evidence which proved to his satisfaction that the manufacturer of the lemonade had in fact taken reasonable care to prevent injury to consumers during the manufacturing process (work methods, inspections, etc). The standard imposed in *Donoghue* is one of *reasonable care*, not of *strict liability*. The judge said:

'I have to remember that the duty owed to the consumer, or the ultimate purchaser, is not to ensure that his goods are perfect. … [the manufacturer's] duty is to take reasonable care to see that no injury is done to the consumer or ultimate purchaser'.[119]

Donoghue was *applied*, but the plaintiff still lost, because the manufacturer was *not in breach of the duty of care*: in fact, the defendant demonstrated that he had taken reasonable care in the manufacturing process; instead, the tort of negligence requires the injury to be *caused by breach of the duty of care*. In negligence actions, the *burden of proof* is on the claimant to prove negligence; it is shifted to the defendant only where, as in *Mulcahy*[120] above, the claimant pleads *res ipsa loquitur*, because 'the thing speaks for itself'.

The case shows that in the system of binding precedent, applying a *precedent* does not mean applying a *decision*. Even if the injured party in the precedent won his or her claim, the claimant in a later, similar case may lose, if, on the facts of the case, the necessary elements of negligence are not satisfied or proved.

---

[118] *Ibid.*

[119] *Ibid*, Lewis J, 261.

[120] *Mulcahy v Ministry of Defence*, above n 110; also see the final paragraph of Lord Macmillan's opinion in *Donoghue*, 9.5.1 above.

Developing common law principles: four cases after *Donoghue*

The final Task in this chapter provides an opportunity to test your powers of legal reasoning and compare your own solutions to those of the common law courts. In Task 15 below, you will need to apply the three stages of judicial reasoning by analogy, presented above.

> **Task 15 Developing common law principles—four cases after *Donoghue***
> Examine the facts of the four cases below, which were decided soon after *Donoghue v Stevenson*.[121] For each case, which elements of the tort of negligence can you identify? What are the material facts?
>
> 1. In which cases do you think *the later court was bound to follow Donoghue?*
> 2. In which cases do you think *the later court could distinguish Donoghue?* On what grounds?
> 3. Where *distinguishing* is possible, do you think that, adopting an approach of *reasoning by analogy*, the court should *apply Donoghue*, thus extending the rule to a new class of case, in the interests of justice?

---

1. *Farr v Butters* [1932] 2 KB 606. The manufacturers of a defective crane sold it in parts to the employers of a workman. The workman was killed as a result of the defects in the crane. He was in fact aware of the defects as he was the man who assembled the crane.

Your notes

---

2. *Grant v The Australian Knitting Mills* [1936] AC 85. The plaintiff contracted dermatitis as a result of wearing underpants which contained an excess of sulphites. The presence of the chemical was due to the negligence of the defendant manufacturers.

Your notes

---

[121] The idea for this task was suggested by Rupert Cross's analysis of these cases in Cross, above n 51, pp 184–88.

---

3. *Otto and Otto v Bolton & Norris* [1936] 2 KB 46. A man (*the purchaser*) bought a house. The mother of the purchaser was injured as a consequence of the collapse of a defective ceiling. The mother and son sued the builders of the house for negligence.

Your notes

---

4. *Haseldine v Daw* [1941] 2 KB 343. The plaintiff was injured as a result of the collapse of a lift (elevator) which he was using to go to the flat (apartment) of one of *the tenants* of a large block; a firm of engineers employed by *the landlord*[122] had repaired the lift, which collapsed as a consequence of the engineers' negligence.

Your notes

Discuss and compare your answers and observations before consulting the key to this task, below.

Key to Task 15 Developing common law principles—four cases after *Donoghue*
Check the courts' decisions (below) against your own ideas, critically. Note that even where your solutions are not the same, your process of reasoning may be a possible alternative.

---

[122] The landlord (or *lessor*) grants the exclusive possession of property to the tenant (or *lessee*) for a specified period, usually on payment of a rent. Such a grant, which embodies a contract, is called a *lease*; it creates a *tenancy*.

1. *Farr v Butters*

In this case, the Court of Appeal did not apply the rule in *Donoghue*, since *the terms of the rule were not met* (not all the conditions of the rule were satisfied). Unlike *Donoghue*, where there was no possibility of intermediate inspection, the workman had had every opportunity to examine the crane and discover the defects; in fact, he had been aware that the crane was defective.

2. *Grant v The Australian Knitting Mills*

In this Australian appeal heard by the Judicial Committee of the Privy Council (bound by the House of Lords and itself composed of Law Lords), the defendant manufacturer argued that *Donoghue* should be distinguished, on the grounds that the *ratio* in *Donoghue* was confined to cases involving food or drink, packaged in such a way that the product could not be interfered with before being opened for use by the consumer. The Court rejected this line of reasoning and applied *Donoghue*:

> Their Lordships do not accept that contention. The decision in *Donoghue's* case did not depend on the bottle being stoppered and sealed. The essential point in this regard was that the article should reach the consumer or user subject to the same defect as it had when it left the manufacturer.[123]

By refusing *to distinguish* this case from *Donoghue*, a possibility of limiting the application of the rule in *Donoghue* only to products for human consumption (food, drink, medicines) was rejected. Lord Atkin, in his opinion, referred to 'products' in general terms, while Lord Macmillan focused on articles of food and drink dangerous to life and health.

3. *Otto and Otto v Bolton & Norris*

This case was distinguished from *Donoghue* because two different classes of property were involved: in *Donoghue*, a *chattel* (*personal property*); in *Otto and Otto*, a building (*real property*). In fact, the Court was bound by a previous decision of the House of Lords (*Cavalier v Pope*, 1906) which involved building a house, as opposed to manufacturing a chattel. However, the rule in *Donoghue* would be applied to these facts today.[124]

4. *Haseldine v Daw*

In this case, the Court of Appeal applied *Donoghue* by analogy. The effect of this was to extend the legal protection *Donoghue* gave to consumers of manufactured goods, to users of repaired goods.

The Court could have distinguished *Donoghue* on two grounds: first, the defendants were not manufacturers but repairers (Lord Atkin refers to a manufacturer of products, a point emphasised in the dissenting judgment

---

[123] Per Lord Wright, cited in Cross and Harris, above n 84, p 193.
[124] Cross and Harris, above n 84, p 194.

in *Haseldine v Daw*); secondly, it would have been possible to inspect the lift (unlike the ginger beer in the stoppered, opaque bottle). Lord Atkin's reference in *Donoghue* to 'no reasonable possibility of intermediate examination' was held in *Haseldine* to mean not merely a possibility of examination, but that the defendant might reasonably have anticipated examination.[125] Lord Justice Goddard stated that:

> Where the facts show that no intermediate inspection is practicable or is con-templated, a repairer of a chattel stands in no different position than that of a manufacturer and owes such a duty of care to a person who, in the ordinary course, may be expected to make use of the thing repaired.[126]

Concluding comment

The cases above are a small demonstration of the way in which the law progresses in the case-law system. The principles of the common law can only develop in relation to the facts of actual cases brought before the courts for decision. The law develops piece by piece (we say, *on a piecemeal basis*) within the framework of the hierarchy of the courts and the doctrine of binding precedent. In some cases, courts have no choice, but:

> On other occasions there is undoubtedly room for choice because lawyers might well take different views concerning the legal significance of some distinctions between the previous case and the one before the court. In that event, everything will depend on whether the judge considers that the rule by which the previous case was decided is one that should be extended or restricted.[127]

The role of the judge is thus central in every respect. The tendency after *Donoghue v Stevenson* was to enlarge and not restrict the ambit of the duty of care *laid down* by the House of Lords, since, in the words of Lord Justice Goddard: 'The common law must expand to keep abreast of modern life'.[128]

The ability of the common law to develop in response to changing needs, illus-trated by *Donoghue*, may be considered one of its strengths. In this case, the House of Lords took into account 'the new conditions of mass production and complex marketing of goods' in order to provide protection to the ultimate consumer, given the chain of intermediaries between the producer and the consumer,[129] and the absence of a contractual relationship between them. In the words of Lord Macmillan in *Donoghue v Stevenson*:

> [T]he conception of legal responsibility may develop in adaptation to altering social conditions and standards. The criterion of judgment must adjust and adapt itself to

---

[125] *Ibid.*
[126] *Ibid*, p 193.
[127] *Ibid*, p 195.
[128] In *Hanson v Wearmouth Coal Co Ltd & Sunderland Gas Co* [1939] 3 All ER 47, 54, in Cross and Harris, above n 84, p 196.
[129] Murphy and Whitting, above n 107, p 27.

the changing circumstances of life. The categories of negligence are never closed. The cardinal principle of liability is that the party complained of should owe to the party complaining a duty to take care and that the party complaining should be able to prove that he has suffered damage in consequence of a breach of that duty.[130]

Commentators today, however, note the trend of 'modern judicial conservatism': this has not led to a closed set of *duty categories* but still 'constrains the future growth of tort', as it is very hard to establish a new *duty-situation* if, considering cases by analogy, precedents have been decided to the contrary.[131] It is likely that the 'frontiers of negligence' will expand gradually, through the application of the three-part *Caparo* test, considered above,[132] which provides the mechanism for establishing a duty of care in new situations.[133] In conclusion, if the courts find that *no duty of care is owed* by a defendant who has caused damage to the injured party, the claimant's claim in negligence will fail, as the duty of care is an essential element of the tort of negligence.

Ideas for Further Reading

Bingham, Tom (2000), *The Business of Judging. Selected Essays and Speeches 1985–1999*, Oxford: Oxford University Press. From Part I The Business of Judging, Paper 2, 'The Judge as Lawmaker: An English Perspective', pp 25–34; from Part IV Human Rights, Paper 4, 'Tort and Human Rights', pp 169–79, giving clear analysis of common law torts that protect human rights enshrined in the Convention; from Part IX Miscellaneous, Paper 2, 'Who then in Law is my Neighbour?', pp 363–73. Advanced level reading.

Lord Browne-Wilkinson (1998), 'The Impact on Judicial Reasoning' in Markesinis, Basil S (ed), *The Impact of the Human Rights Bill on English Law* (The Clifford Chance Lectures, vol 3), Oxford: Oxford University Press, ch 4, pp 21–23. Discusses the impact the Human Rights Act 1998 will have on English judicial reasoning as moral questions come directly before the courts for decision. Advanced level reading.

Cownie, Fiona, Bradney, Anthony and Burton, Mandy (2013), *English Legal System in Context*, 6th edn, Oxford: Oxford University Press. Provides a detailed analysis, including sociological perspectives and discussions of legal theory. Particularly relevant are: Chapter 5, 'English legal reasoning: the use of case law' (pp 81–100); Chapter 9, 'Judges and judging' (pp 155–68).

Cross, R and Harris, JW (1991), *Precedent in English Law*, 4th edn, Oxford: Clarendon Press. The book examines the sources of law, legal reasoning and legal theory, the jurisprudential problems connected with case law in general and especially the English doctrine of precedent. Select a chapter, for example: Chapter 1, 'The English Doctrine of Precedent' (pp 3–38); Chapter 2, '*Ratio Decidendi* and *Obiter Dictum*' (pp 39–98); Chapter 6, 'Precedent and Judicial Reasoning' (pp 186–207).

---

[130] *Donoghue v Stevenson* [1932] UKHL 3, [1932] AC 562 (HL Sc).
[131] Murphy and Whitting, above n 107, p 35.
[132] See 9.6.4 above.
[133] Murphy and Whitting, above n 107, pp 35–36.

Zweigert, Konrad and Kötz, Hein (1998), *An Introduction to Comparative Law*, 3rd edn (tr Weir, Tony), Oxford: Clarendon Press. Chapter 18, 'Law-Finding and Procedure in Common Law and Civil Law' (pp 256–75), provides an interesting evaluation of statute law and precedent in common law and civil law jurisdictions, analysing changing trends and comparing techniques of judicial reasoning and extracting legal rules.

Fiction: The work of American tort lawyers can be seen in John Grisham's legal thrillers, such as *The King of Torts*, or *The Runaway Jury*, fast-paced and fun to read if you like this genre, good for the language and procedures of American civil law in a fictionalised context. Grisham began his professional life as a practising lawyer; many of his bestsellers have become successful films, such as *The Firm* (1993), directed by Sydney Pollack, starring Tom Cruise and Gene Hackman.

*CASE LOG: FRAMEWORK FOR READING A COMMON LAW JUDGMENT—FOR COPYING

KEY ELEMENTS	CASE LOG
Name of case	
Citation in law reports	
Parties: claimant/plaintiff	
Parties: defendant	
Court	
Stage of action	
Branch of law	
Specific grounds for legal action	
Facts of the case	
Legal history of the case	
Legal sources	

Issue(s)	
Decision on each issue	
Reasons for the decision	
Judgment	
Award or criminal sentence	

Comment on the case

Chapter 10

LEGAL GRAMMAR

Word Formation

Root words and roots – Affixes: prefixes and suffixes – Word groups –
Word maps – Collocation

'*When I use a word,*' *Humpty Dumpty said in rather a scornful tone,* '*it means*
just what I choose it to mean—neither more nor less.'

Lewis Carroll, English writer (1832–98)
From *Through the Looking-Glass*

Identifying the morphology of a given language—the form and structure of its
words—enables us to distinguish how meanings are constructed from the simplest
minimal lexical units of language to the more complex. This chapter will thus con-
centrate on the formation of words, challenging readers to draw on their linguistic
knowledge of Latin or Greek through comprehension of the root of a word, or to
just recall common meanings from root words encountered in Standard English.
Understanding the roots of words is the starting point for constructing new meanings when affixes are attached at the beginning or at the end of a word. Usage can
then be further transformed by a word's syntactical relationship with other words
in a sentence. The chapter progresses in this way, building on minimal meanings to
more complex usage of the form of a legal word in legal contexts.

The last part of the chapter is dedicated to introducing strategies for the
organisation of legal terminology, stressing that thumbing through a dictionary
for single meanings is counterproductive. It is suggested that collecting clusters or
chunks of words and placing them into semantic categories within a specific legal
context could be a more efficient approach to learning, referencing and expanding
on legal terminology.

10.1 ROOT WORDS AND ROOTS

A *root word* (often called the base word) has a meaning when standing alone. We
say it is freestanding because it can be understood without adding other word

parts. New words and meanings may be created by adding lexical item(s) either at the beginning of the root word (*prefix*) or at the end (*suffix*), e.g.:

valid (root word)   *in*valid (an adjective prefix)

judge (root word)   judg*ment* (a noun suffix)

A *root* can be distinguished from a root word in that it indicates the origin of the word (etymology), yet it does not typically stand alone. Familiarising yourself with Latin and Greek roots of words could prove useful when you are trying to understand the meaning of words, e.g.:

Latin: *iūs/iūre* – essentially means law, right, duty[1] – *ius*tice, *juris*prudence[2]

Latin: *vōx/vōcis* – meaning voice; call – *voca*lise, ad*voca*te

Greek: *phobos/phobia* – meaning fear – xeno*phobic*, claustro*phobic*

Greek: *onuma/onym* – meaning name – syn*onym*, ant*onym*

Sometimes there are two or more root words attached but they have a single identity or meaning. These are called compound words. Some are written as separate words (*global warming*), while others are hyphenated (*mother-in-law*) or a single word (*copyright*). Usage varies over time. For example, a word usually enters the language as two words (*micro credit*). As it becomes more familiar, a hyphen is placed between the two words (*micro-credit*), while when it becomes quite common, the hyphen is dropped (*microcredit*). Check the newest version in a recent dictionary for its present acceptable form (sometimes the English and American versions may vary). Although the individual meanings of the separate words may help you understand the meaning of the compound word, it is not always the case. Can you work out the meanings of the following compound words from their component parts?

cross-examination	manslaughter	head-hunter
milestone	self-defence	watchdog

Task 1 Root words and affixes
Recognising the root word and the meaning of the prefixes or suffixes can aid comprehension. Circle the root words below. Underline the compound words. What do the prefixes or suffixes mean?

irregularity	distributorship	liability	mistrial
manslaughter	mediation	paralegal	taskforce
unconstitutional	whistleblower	streetwalker	refugee

---

[1] See *Oxford Latin Dictionary* (1982 reprinted 2002), PGW Glare (ed), Oxford: Oxford University Press: 'that which is sanctioned or ordained, law'; 'what one is entitled to (esp by law); one's right, due, prerogative, etc'. See also *iūre* which means 'according to the law, with legal sanction', p 984.

[2] In Latin, the 'i' (as in *iūs/ iūre*) is often substituted with a 'j'; J Morwood (1998), *A Dictionary of Latin Words and Phrases*, Oxford: Oxford University Press, p 99.

> *NOTE:* A hyphen [-] is used when one or more words function together to modify a noun (similar to an adjective), such as: *non-binding texts, non-contractual liability, English-speaking country, three-judge panel.* NB: We say a ten-week trial, not a ten-weeks trial.

10.2 Affixes: Prefixes and Suffixes

More than half of English words are derived from Greek and Latin roots. Becoming familiar with the roots of commonly used prefixes and suffixes is a useful strategy to exploit while determining the meaning of words *before* opening a dictionary.

10.2.1 Prefixes

Prefixes are placed at the beginning of a word. Some common examples are set out in Table 10.1 below (the list is not exhaustive).

Table 10.1: Common prefixes

NEGATION	Examples	DIRECTION OR POSITION	Examples
without, no, not	asexual, anonymous, illegal, immoral, invalid, irreverent, unacceptable	above, over	supervise, supersede
not, absence of, opposing, against	non-negotiable, antipathy, contradict, contravene	across, over	transfer, transferral
opposite to, complement to	counterclaim, counteroffer	below, under	infrastructure, subjugate
do the opposite of, remove, reduce	devitalize, devalue, devolve	in front of	precede, preliminary prerequisite
do the opposite of, deprive of	disadvantage, disapprove	between	intervention interpolate
wrongly, bad	misjudge, misdeed, misdemeanour	out of	exception, explicit,
		into	interdict, enclosed, empower
		around	circumlocution

10.2.2 Suffixes

Suffixes can modify the meaning of a word and can frequently determine its function within a sentence (whether it is a noun, verb, adjective or an adverb). Suffixes are placed at the *end of a word*. Some common examples are set out in Table 10.2 (the list is not exhaustive).

Table 10.2: Common suffixes

Common noun suffixes	noun concept: -ence, -ance, -ment, -ism, -ship, -ency, -sion, -tion, -ness, -hood, -dom, -ty noun person: -ent, -ist, -er, -ee, -or
meaning	*a condition, quality, an act or state of*
noun (concept) noun (person)	enact + ment – enactment = the result of a process (state of being enacted, sometimes the process of enacting) pursue + ance – pursuance = to take action (to pursue, to carry out a suicide pact) terror + ism – terrorism = condition of creating terror reckless + ness – recklessness = state of being reckless respond + ent – respondent = to take action (a person who responds to a court petition) lobby + ist – lobbyist = a person that performs the action (to lobby) teach + er – teacher = a person who is defined by the object of their profession (to teach) trust + ee – trustee = a person who is entrusted with the responsibility of managing the trust properly offer + ee – offeree = a person who receives benefits from a specific action (from the offeror) arbitrate + or – arbitrator = to take action (a person who conducts arbitration)

Common verb suffixes	-en, -ify, -ise (BrE), –ize (AmE), -iate, -ate
meaning	*to have or be characterised by; to cause to become or to make*
examples	strength + en – strengthen = to make stronger different + iate – differentiate = to make or show a difference simple + ify – simplify = to make simple or simpler

Common adjective suffixes	-able, -ible, -al, -tial, -tic, -ly, -ful, -ous, -tive, -less, -ish, -ulent, -ed, -ive, -ic
meaning	*tending towards doing some action, relating to, being, characteristic of, like, having, or without* [less]
examples	select + ive – selective = tending to select fraud + ulent – fraudulent = characterised/done by fraud politic + al – political = relating to politics power + less – powerless = without power

Common adverb suffixes:*	-ly, -wise, -ward, -where
meaning	*tending to be, tending towards a direction*
examples	extreme + ly – extremely = tending to be extreme after + ward(s) – afterwards = at the end
*NB	Not all words that end in *-ly* are adverbs, some are adjectives.

10.2.3 Word Charts

Table 10.3 below contains different *root words* to which suffixes are attached.[3] Words can have many forms depending on where they are placed in a sentence. Table 10.3 gives you an idea of how suffixes change *depending on which part of speech is appropriate*: verb, noun, adjective, adverb. The 'x' indicates that the form does not exist in that particular part of speech in a legal context (although it may exist in Standard English).

Table 10.3: Word formation chart[4]

verb	noun (concept)	noun (person)	adjective	adverb
to 'unionise (BrE) to 'unionize (AmE)	'union unioni'sation (BrE) unioni'zation (AmE)	'unionist	'unionised (BrE) 'unionized (AmE)	x
en'force	en'forcement	x	en'forceable	x
a'buse	a'buse	a'buser	a'busive	a'busively (rare)
'prosecute	prose'cution	'prosecutor	x	x
po'liticise[5] po'liticize	'politic/s politici'zation	poli'tician	'politic po'litical po'liticised po'liticized	po'liticly po'litically
'authorise 'authorize	authori'sation authori'zation authori'tarianism	au'thority	authori'tarian au'thoritative	au'thoritatively (BrE) authori'tatively (AmE)
'constitute	consti'tution constitution'ality	x	consti'tutional	consti'tutionally

---

[3] It is used here to indicate a part of a word that has a common meaning when affixes (inflectional variants) are attached.

[4] The mark ['] before each syllable (for example, en'force) indicates that the stress is on that next syllable.

[5] If you *politicise* someone or something, you tend to make it more political, more involved with politics.

Task 2 Word formation practice chart

Fill in the appropriate word suffix where there is an empty space in the chart below. Please note that '(2)' indicates that two examples are needed. The 'x' indicates that that form of the word is not common in a legal context. You may need to use a legal dictionary.[6] Refer to 10.2.2 as needed.

	verb	noun (concept)	noun (person)	adjective	adverb
1	legalise (BrE) legalize (AmE)	legality legalism/s legalitarianism	legalist	legalistic legalitarian	....
2	ratify	....	x	x	x
3	tolerate	(2)	x	tolerant tolerable	tolerantly
4	rebut	rebuttal	x	....	x
5	....	minimum minima (pl)	x	minimal minimum	x
6	discriminate	....	x	discriminating discriminatory	x
7	....	conveyance conveyancing	conveyee conveyor conveyancer	x	x
8	criminalise (BrE) criminalize (AmE)	(2)	criminal	criminal	criminally
9	allege	allegation	allegator (rare)[7]	allegeable alleged	....
10	x	....	adulterer adulteress (less used today)	adulterous	x

[6] Consult BA Garner (1995), *A Dictionary of Modern Legal Usage*, 2nd edn, Oxford: Oxford University Press, for interesting insights into the modern interpretation of legal terminology: words that are considered archaic, less common in legal contexts, or needless variants.

[7] *Ibid.* Not frequently used. It means one who alleges.

10.3 Word Groups

While you are reading, a good strategy could be to organise your legal terminology into categories so that you have clusters of words that share some semantic meaning/association in that particular legal context.

10.3.1 Grouping Word(s) into Categories Based on a Shared Association

In Table 10.4 below, words are grouped into categories based on their shared association.

Table 10.4: Words grouped according to shared association

Group 1 – contract	Group 2 – treaty (recitals)	Group 3 – human rights
offer and acceptance	reaffirming	European Convention on Human Rights
manufacture and sells	recognising	Universal Declaration of Human Rights
undertakes and agrees	considering	fundamental rights
negotiate and enter	affirming	the right to a fair trial
promote and sell	determined to	safeguards freedom of thought, conscience, and religion
conclude and enter	being resolved to	guarantees freedom from torture

Task 3 Practice word groups

Place the following words into 'word groups' (words that have some association or something in common). Put them into three groups. Share your word groups with the person next to you and discuss your choices.

offeror	verdict	promise	treaty	contractual clause
pact	jury	agent	defendant	terms and conditions
presumed innocent		breach of contract		High Contracting Party
sentence	Convention	accord	nation/State	conviction

10.4 WORD MAPS

Word maps are often referred to as mind maps, spider maps, or bubble maps. By creating word maps, chunks of language are graphically displayed in order to create connections visually between words or concepts that have something in common. This can be useful as an organising strategy for both written and oral exercises.[8]

Task 4 Criminal law word map
Add more bubbles to the word map below using the following terminology: involuntary, voluntary, malice aforethought, without malice aforethought, mitigating factors/circumstances, self-defence, provocation, diminished responsibility, suicide pact, reasonable force, unreasonable force, life imprisonment/capital punishment

---

[8] Another strategy could be to organize collaborative study groups of 3, 4, or 5 students within the classroom to enhance motivation and autonomy. See A Riley and P Sours (2006), 'Sharing a Journey Towards Success: the Impact of Collaborative Study Groups and CALL in a Legal Context in S Borg (ed)', *Language Teacher Resource in Europe*, Alexandria, VI: TESOL, pp 109–123.

10.5 COLLOCATION

A collocation is the habitual co-occurrence of words. By collecting groups of words that collocate, it is easier to enlarge your legal terminology instead of keeping lengthy single word lists. Notice that the core word remains the same:

—	consideration	*without* consideration, *remove* consideration, *no longer require* consideration, *valuable* consideration
—	binding	*binding* precedent, *binding* force, *binding* case, to be *binding* on, to be *bound* by
—	code	criminal *code*, *code* of honour, United States *Code*, administrative *code*
—	copyright	*copyright* licence, *copyright* registration, *copyright* infringement
—	trial	*trial* by jury, *trial* lawyer, criminal *trial*, adversarial *trial*, fair *trial*, civil *trial*
—	contract	commercial *contract*, breach of *contract*, discharge of *contract*, party to a *contract*
—	person	natural *person*, juristic *person*, legal *person*, artificial *person*
—	judgment	previous *judgment*, final *judgment*, pronouncing *judgment*, Strasbourg *judgment*

Task 5 Word formation practice in sentences (a) and in context (b)
In the sentences in (a) below, fill in the empty space with the appropriate form of the word. The base word is in brackets [ ]. You will need to observe carefully *the position* of the words in the following sentences to determine which part of speech is needed (noun concept, noun person, adjective, verb or adverb).[9] Does it describe a noun? Is it the subject of the sentence? Does it add more information about the verb? The first sentence has been done for you.

---

[9] The difference between an adverb an adjective: **Adverbs** provide more information about the verb phrase that they modify and can tell us *how* or *how often* (manner), *where* (place) or *when* (time) something was done, eg: The amendment <u>was ratified</u> *yesterday*. (time – When was it ratified?); The international convention <u>was signed</u> *at the Hague*. (Where was it signed?); The defendant *frequently* <u>refused</u> to answer the prosecutor's question. (manner – How often did he refuse to answer?); Sam <u>called</u> the police *immediately* after he was robbed. (time – When did Sam call the police?). **Adjectives** are words that describe or modify another person or thing in the sentence, eg: 'Save the Children' is an *international* organization; The *crucial* question in the case was whether acts of torture were committed.

(a) Single sentences

0. All the judges in the legal system are known collectively as the ....
   judiciary. [judge]
1. The British monarch continues to perform an important
   .... role today. [constitution]
2. The .... is the party accused of a crime or civil
   wrong. [defend]
3. .... legislation is enacted by bodies using power
   conferred by Parliament. [delegate]
4. .... crime is the duty of the police in the UK.
   [investigate]
5. An .... who pleads guilty will generally receive
   a lighter sentence. [offend]
6. The Supreme Court cannot .... laws that are
   incompatible with Convention rights. [valid]
7. The accused was .... found not guilty and
   discharged. [accord]
8. The .... Parliament has its seat in Edinburgh.
   [Scotland]
9. Under section 4 of the Human Rights Act 1998 the superior courts may
   make a declaration of .... [not compatible]
10. The CPS is responsible for criminal .... in
    England and Wales. [prosecute]

(b) Context

Are you familiar with the controversial rulings in different jurisdictions
concerning patent[10] violations (both for design and utility) in the smart-
phone industry? Here are two excerpts from judgments in the USA (*Apple
Inc v Samsung*) and the UK (*Samsung v Apple Inc*). Fill in the numbered
empty spaces with the appropriate form of the word. The base word is in
brackets [ ].

---

[10] A patent protects the intellectual property rights of the inventor of a product or process capable
of industrial application.

[11] *Apple Inc v Samsung Electronics Co Ltd,* Selected Case Documents (C 11-1846 LHK), Docket No
2197 [2012], Order Denying Motion for Permanent Injunction, United States District Court, Northern
District of California, San Jose Division, p 2 at para 10-22.

[12] Apple's motion for a permanent injunction against Samsung was denied. For further details
consult the judgment.

1. The US judgment – *Apple Inc v Samsung Electronics Co Ltd Inc*[11]

The Patent Act provides that in cases of patent ....
1 [infringe] a court 'may grant injunctions in accordance with the principles of equity to prevent the violation of any right secured by patent, on such terms as the court deems ....2 [reason].' 35 USC § 283. Though injunctions were once issued in patent cases as a matter of course, the Supreme Court ruled in 2006 that 'broad classifications' and '................................ 3 [category] rule[s]' were .... 4 [not appropriate] in analysing whether to grant a permanent injunction. *eBay v MercExchange, LLC*, 547 US 388, 393 (2006). Instead, a .... 5 [patent] seeking a permanent injunction must make a four-part showing:

(1) That it has suffered an irreparable injury; (2) that remedies available at law, such as................................ 6 [money] damages, are... ....7 [not adequate] to compensate for that injury; (3) that, considering the balance of hardships between the plaintiff and defendant, a remedy in equity is warranted; and (4) that the public interest would not be .... 8 [not served] by a permanent injunction.

Id. at 391. In considering Apple's motion, the Court will consider each of these four factors in turn, and will then consider whether, on balance, the principles of equity support the .... 9 [issue] of a permanent injunction in this case.[12]

2. The UK judgment – *Samsung Electronics (UK) Limited v Apple Inc*[13]

189.   This case illustrates the importance of .... 10 [proper] taking into account the informed user's knowledge and experience of the design corpus. When I first saw the Samsung products in this case I was struck by how similar they look to the Apple design when they are resting on a table. They look similar because they both have the same front screen. It stands out. However to the informed user (which at that stage I was not) these screens do not stand out to anything like the same extent. The front view of the Apple design takes its place amongst its kindred prior art. There is a clear family .... 11 [resemble] between the front of the Apple design and other members of that family

---

[13] *Samsung Electronics (UK) Limited v Apple Inc* [2012] EWHC 1882 (Pat), Case No: HC 11 C 03050.

(Flatron, Bloomberg 1 and 2, Ozolins, Showbox, Wacom). They are not ....12 [identify] to each other but they form a family. There are differences all over these products but the biggest differences between these various family members are at the back and sides. The user who is particularly ....13 [observe] and is informed about the design corpus reacts to the Apple design by recognising the front view as one of a familiar type. From the front both the Apple design and the Samsung tablets look like members of the same, pre-existing family. As a result, the significance of that ....14 [similar] overall is much reduced and the informed user's attention to the differences at the back and sides will be enhanced ....15 [consider].

190. The informed user's overall impression of each of the Samsung Galaxy Tablets is the following. From the front they belong to the family which includes the Apple design; but the Samsung products are very thin, almost .... 16 [not substantial] members of that family with ....17 [not usual] details on the back. They do not have the same understated and extreme ....18 [simple] which is possessed by the Apple design. They are not as cool. The overall impression produced is different.

191. The Samsung tablets do not infringe Apple's registered design No. 000181607-0001.[14]

© Crown Copyright
Source: BAILII

---

[14] Apple appealed against this judgment, yet the previous ruling was maintained, ie Apple was required to publish a disclaimer on the Apple website and in the media stating that Samsung did not copy the iPad. Consult judgment for further details.

KEY AND COMMENTARY

Key

Task 1 Root words and affixes

Root words: regular, constitute, mediate, liable, legal, trial, refuge
Check the meanings of prefixes and suffixes in 10.2.1 and 10.2.2.
Compound words: manslaughter, distributorship, whistleblower,
streetwalker, taskforce. Check the meanings in a dictionary.

Task 2 Word formation practice chart

1. adverb – legally
2. noun (concept) – ratification
3. noun (concept) – toleration/tolerance
4. adjective – rebuttable
5. verb – to minimise/minimize
6. noun (concept) – discrimination
7. verb – to convey
8. noun (concept) – criminality/crime
9. adverb – allegedly
10. noun (concept) – adultery

Task 3 Practice word groups

contract	offeror, promise, contractual clause, agent, breach of contract, terms and conditions
agreement	treaty, pact, convention, High Contracting Party, accord, nation/State
criminal law	verdict, jury, presumed innocent, sentence, defendant, conviction

Task 4 Criminal law word map

A possible word map driven by judicial precedents is set out in the figure below.

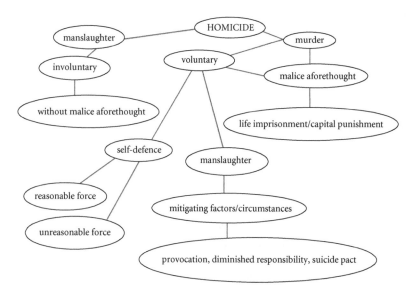

Task 5 Word formation practice in sentences (a) and in context (b)

(a) Single sentences
1. constitutional
2. defendant
3. delegated/delegable
4. investigating
5. offender
6. invalidate
7. accordingly
8. Scottish
9. incompatibility
10. prosecution(s)

(b) Context
1. infringement
2. reasonable
3. categorical
4. inappropriate

5. patentee
6. monetary
7. inadequate
8. disserved
9. issuance
10. properly
11. resemblance
12. identical
13. observant
14. similarity
15. considerably
16. insubstantial
17. unusual
18. simplicity

Commentary

This chapter concentrates on the morphology of words specific to the English language: the root and the root words that express meaning and aid comprehension without always resorting to a dictionary, general or legal. Drawing on previous knowledge of Greek or Latin, or just from personal experience of common meanings of base words, reading becomes less laborious. Having a working knowledge of the prefixes and suffixes of words further facilitates comprehension, such as *il*legal, *de*volve, enact*ment*, arbitrat*or*. This does not mean that reading legal texts will be any less difficult or that consulting a legal dictionary is less necessary, yet having a practical awareness of morphology does accelerate the process of global comprehension at the sentence level, so that reading becomes less tedious and interpretation and usage of legal terms can be given priority.

Using strategies for the collection of legal terminology is essential, such as compiling lists of words that are associated with each other in a specific legal context, e.g. for a contract: *intention, offer and acceptance, consideration.* Another strategy is keeping lists of words that collocate, that habitually co-occur, such as: *binding* precedent, *binding* force, *binding* case, to be *binding* on, to be *bound* by. In this way, you can organise semantic categories that allow for practical application of more than one word, which are then easier to recall and to use either orally or in writing.[15]

Actively observing legal terminology in context is one step towards better understanding of its usage. As you have noticed, this book reinforces this contextual approach; however, in order to expand on this suggestion, use the Internet. Take advantage of the wealth of authentic legal documents that are at your fingertips.

---

[15] Remember to include these aspects as you build your Personal Terminology System, introduced in 1.2.5.

CONSOLIDATION PART V – LANGUAGE FOCUS TASKS

TASK A – WHICH ONE WORD OR PHRASE IS OUT OF CONTEXT?

0	defamation	breach	assault	trespass
1	first instance	appellate court	binding precedent	superior court
2	binding precedent	*ratio decidendi*	*obiter dictum*	material facts of the case
3	common law remedy	granted case by case	equitable remedy	discretionary remedy
4	benefit of the bargain	promisee	injuries and losses	consideration
5	assault	defamation	trespass	*force majeure*
6	duty of care	negligence	breach of duty	injunction

TASK B – MATCH THE TERMS WITH THE DEFINITIONS[1]

claimant	duty of care	product liability	tortfeasor
negligence	injunction	trespass	redress
action	damages	vindicate	battery

---

[1] Task B references used to create definitions: BA Garner (1995), *A Dictionary of Modern Legal Usage*, 2nd edn, Oxford: Oxford University Press; *Black's Law Dictionary, Pocket Edition* (1996), BA Garner (ed), Eagan, Minn: West Publishing Co; *Oxford Dictionary of Law* (2009), J Law and E Martin (eds), 7th edn, Oxford: Oxford University Press.

1	....	a tort liability of a manufacturer or seller to be responsible for any damage or injury suffered by the buyer as the result of a defective product(s)
2	....	to reaffirm, to give force to
3	....	a civil or criminal judicial proceeding
4	....	the party who committed a tort, the 'wrongdoer' (the defendant)
5	....	a standard of conduct for human activity; the legal duty to conduct oneself in a reasonable manner
6	....	the injured party, the person who seeks a remedy against the tortfeasor
7	....	to set 'right' a 'wrong'; to gain satisfaction or compensation for a wrong suffered; also called relief, remedy
8	....	failure to exercise the required duty of care, thereby causing damage to another
9	....	the money the defendant is ordered by the court to pay the claimant (plaintiff) for the loss or injury suffered
10	....	an unlawful act committed against a person, or property of another
11	....	physical force to or offensive contact without consent
12	....	an order of the court prohibiting or commanding a particular act

Task C – Word Formation

a)   Fill in the spaces below [...] with the appropriate word form.

Words that are not necessarily used in a legal context, or a variant no longer in use, have not been included in the table. The [x] in the table indicates that the form does not exist or that it is uncommon in a legal context. If necessary, read chapter 10 before doing this task or consult a dictionary.

	verb	noun (concept)	noun (person)	adjective
1	to vindicate	....	x	vindicable [less used vindicatable]/ vindicatory/ vindictive
2	to act	action	actor	....
3	x	....	x	contingent
4	deduce	deduction	x	deducible/ .... (2)

b)   Using the table above, insert the appropriate word in the spaces: verb, noun (concept), noun (person), or adjective:

5   Growth in the EU is .... on all countries in the Eurozone complying with budget cuts.

6   The civil law method is ....…..... in approach, moving from the general rule to its application in the individual case.

7   If something that you do or say to someone is ...., it gives them a valid reason for bringing a legal case against you.

8   One of the objectives in the law of tort is that it seeks to ....….. legal rights and interests that have been compromised.

TASK D – PREFIXES AND SUFFIXES

Fill in the missing suffixes or prefixes to the following words. Identify the appropriate word form.

The [x] indicates that the form does not exist or that it is uncommon in a legal context.

	Prefixes	*adjective*	*noun concept*
1	solvency	x	
2	dominant		x
	Suffixes		
3	oblige [obligate]	(2)	
4	omit		
5	compensate	(2)	

TASK E – VERB–NOUN COLLOCATION

Match the words 1–6 with the appropriate words a–f, and write the matching identifiers in the first column of the table. Think about the meaning of each term or phrase.

..1d....	1	to grant a remedy	a	reasonable care
......	2	to confer	b	the claimant's right
......	3	to be in breach of	c	a right
......	4	failing to exercise	d	to an injured party
......	5	to compensate	e	contract
......	6	to vindicate (reaffirms, gives force to)	f	victims for damage (injuries or losses)

Part VI

A Contextual Approach to Contract Law and Commercial Agreements

Chapter 11

LANGUAGE AND LAW

Contract and Commercial Agreements

*Introduction to the language of contract law – Terms, parties, discharge, disputes –
Formation of contract and key elements: intention, agreement, consideration –
Commercial agreements: structure, content, clauses, language and legal effects*

	Enter Portia, *dressed like a doctor of laws. …*
Portia:	*I am informèd thoroughly of the cause. –*
	Which is the merchant here, and which the Jew?
Duke:	*Antonio and old Shylock, both stand forth.*
Portia:	*Is your name Shylock?*
Shylock:	*Shylock is my name.*
Portia:	*Of a strange nature is the suit you follow; …*
	[to Antonio] *You stand within his danger, do you not?*
Antonio:	*Ay, so he says.*
Portia:	*Do you confess the bond?*
Antonio:	*I do.*
Portia:	*Then must the Jew be merciful.*
Shylock:	*On what compulsion must I? tell me that.*
Portia:	*The quality of mercy is not strain'd,*
	It droppeth as the gentle rain from heaven
	…
Shylock:	*I pray thee, pursue sentence.*
Portia:	*A pound of that same merchant's flesh is thine:*
	The court awards it, and the law doth give it.
Shylock:	*Most rightful judge! …*
Portia:	*And you must cut this flesh from off his breast:*
	The law allows it, and the court awards it.
Shylock:	*Most learnèd judge! – A sentence! Come prepare!*
Portia:	*Tarry a little: – there is something else. –*
	This bond doth give thee here no jot of blood;
	The words expressly are, a pound of flesh:
	Then take thy bond, take thou thy pound of flesh;
	But, in the cutting it, if thou dost shed

> *One drop of Christian blood, thy lands and goods*
> *Are, by the laws of Venice, confiscate*
> *Unto the state of Venice.*

Gratiano: *O upright judge! – Mark, Jew: - O learnèd judge!*
Shylock: *Is that the law?*
Portia: *Thyself shall see the act:*
            For, as thou urgest justice, be assur'd
            Thou shalt have justice, more than thou desir'st.

William Shakespeare, *The Merchant of Venice, Act IV, Scene I.*

11.1 INTRODUCTION TO CONTRACT

11.1.1 Introduction

Shakespeare's *Merchant of Venice*, in the quotation above, brings us to the theme of the law of contract, in this chapter devoted to the language of contract law and of international commercial agreements.

In the scene above, set in a court of Venice, Portia must convince the court, presided over by the Duke of Venice, not to enforce the cruel terms of Shylock's *bond* against Antonio, the merchant. Antonio and Shylock had entered into *a legally binding agreement* in the form of a *bond*, for the loan of a sum of 3,000 ducats to Antonio, borrowed to help his friend Bassanio. According to the terms of the bond, if Antonio does not repay his debt within three months, Shylock has the right to cut a pound of flesh from his body, causing Antonio's certain death.[1] This strange term was proposed by Shylock and accepted by Antonio, confident that he would be able to repay: In Act I, Scene III, their agreement is decided in the streets of Venice (the moment of *offer and acceptance*) and they arrange to meet at the notary's office. Their agreement constituted an *obligation* enforceable in a court of law, that is, a contract; it was formalised in a solemn legal document, *a deed*, called a *bond*.[2]

Portia appeals to Shylock to show mercy, but he says, 'On what compulsion must I?' Portia replies that the quality of mercy does not have its origin in an obligation, it is freely given, like the rain from heaven; but Shylock is vindictive and demands performance of the legal obligation. He demands justice, in the sense of the strict application of the letter of the law; not justice based on principles of fairness and equity. In the end, Shylock is defeated by his own technique.

---

[1] Shakespeare's phrase *to exact one's pound of flesh* is still used figuratively today, meaning 'something one is strictly or legally entitled to, but which it is ruthless or inhuman to demand', *The New Oxford Dictionary of English* (1998), J Pearsall (ed), Oxford: Clarendon Press, p 1453.

[2] 'A formal deed whereby one person binds himself to do some thing to or for another, normally to pay a specified sum of money immediately or at a future date.' D Walker (1980), *The Oxford Companion to Law*, Oxford: Clarendon Press, p 140.

Inspired by principles of mercy and justice, the court interprets the words of the agreement literally: Shylock may cut his pound of flesh, but if, in doing so, he sheds a single drop of Antonio's blood, all his property (both *'lands and goods'*)[3] will be confiscated by the state of Venice. Ultimately, as Portia warns in the last line quoted above, Shylock obtains *more* justice than he desired … but you are invited to read or see the *Merchant of Venice* to discover the final legal twist in Shakespeare's story.[4]

Section One of this chapter provides a basic introduction to the language of English contract law (11.2). The first aspect is to arrive at a definition of *contract* and understand the relationship between *contract* and *agreement*. We also consider the language connected with the *terms of the contract*, the *parties* and the different modalities of termination of contract, called *discharge*. Extracts from judgments provide examples of disputes.

In Section Two (11.3), the key elements of an English contract are outlined in relation to *formation of contract*. We focus on the notions and language of *intention, consideration* and *agreement*, including *offer and acceptance*, constituent elements in the formation of a valid contract. Some individual contractual clauses are examined. Section Two closes with a selection of reading passages relating to questions of contract law, and readers are invited to analyse the different texts from the legal point of view.

Section Three (11.4) is devoted to the language of written commercial agreements. We analyse the typical structure and organisation of content in an international commercial contract, and examine a series of clauses to learn about their content, language and legal effects.

The main type of text examined in this chapter is the commercial agreement; in addition, some tasks require you to consult legal texts, including judgments and textbooks, in the field of contract law. As you near completion of this course in common law, legal English and grammar, you are encouraged to apply your knowledge of the case-law system and skills of legal analysis to a variety of texts and tasks.

11.1.2 Terminology in Context: Case Study—a Celebrity Wedding

To focus first on the vocabulary of contract law in context, in Task 1 we read extracts from a House of Lords judgment in a dispute concerning two film stars. Their celebrity wedding at the Plaza Hotel, New York, led to lawsuits and appeals in the English courts, involving aspects of both tort and contract.

---

[3] *Land* (usually singular) and *goods* are the two categories of property in English law.
[4] The 2004 film of the play, directed by Michael Radford, was filmed on location in Venice and stars Al Pacino (as Shylock), Jeremy Irons and Joseph Fiennes.

Task 1 Vocabulary in context: case study—a celebrity wedding
Read the extracts from the judgment, below, for general understanding. Who were the famous couple and what happened at their wedding? Then, read the text for detail to answer the questions below. Focus on both language and meaning as you work.

1. The facts of the case involve the film stars and two magazines, *OK!* and *Hello!* Of these three parties, which two are *the contracting parties*? Which two are *the litigants* disputing this appeal?
2. Are the contracting parties *natural persons* or *juristic persons*?
3. What is the subject matter of the contract?
4. What duties did the Douglases *agree to perform* under the contract?
5. What was *the consideration* for the Douglases' *commitment*? That is, what did the Douglases receive in return for their promise?
6. Did the contracting parties *perform* their side of the contract?
7. What *remedy* did *OK!* obtain and why?
8. Did the magazine *sue in tort* or *in contract*? What was the nature of the *damage*?

HOUSE OF LORDS [2007] UKHL 21	LANGUAGE FOCUS
Douglas and another and others v **Hello! Ltd and others** Lord Hoffmann 1. These three appeals are principally concerned with claims in tort for economic loss caused by intentional acts. … (b) In *Douglas v Hello! Ltd* the magazine *OK!* [2006] QB 125 contracted for the exclusive right to publish photographs of a celebrity wedding at which all other photography would be forbidden. The rival magazine *Hello!* published photographs which it knew to have been surreptitiously taken by an unauthorised photographer pretending to be a waiter or guest. *OK!* says that this was interference by unlawful means with its contractual or business relations or a breach of its equitable right to confidentiality in photographic images of the wedding. … 108. Northern & Shell plc publishes *OK!* Magazine and I shall refer to it as *OK!*. In November 2000 *OK!* entered into a contract with Michael Douglas and Catherine Zeta-Jones,	v = versus (say *and* or *against*) Ltd = a limited liability company *Three appeals are considered in the same judgment* *To contract for the right to do sth.* *To be forbidden (forbid, forbad, forbidden)* *Interference by unlawful means with contractual relations* plc = *public limited company* *to enter into a contract with sb.*

whom I shall call 'the Douglases', for the exclusive right to publish photographs of their forthcoming wedding on 18 November 2000 at the Plaza Hotel, New York. The Douglases dealt with *OK!*, who paid them £1m for the rights, in preference to the rival magazine *Hello!*, published by the respondent. The Douglases agreed to engage a photographer and to supply *OK!* with pictures they had chosen. By clause 6 of the agreement they agreed to use their best efforts to ensure that no one else would take any photographs.	*To deal with sb.* *To pay £Xm for the rights* *To agree to do sth* *To supply sb. with sth.* *To use one's best efforts*
109. The Douglases went to some lengths to comply with this obligation and no criticism is made of their security precautions, but a freelance photographer named Rupert Thorpe infiltrated the wedding and took photographs which he sold to *Hello!*. *OK!* obtained an *ex parte* injunction restraining publication by *Hello!* but on 23 November 2000 the injunction was discharged by the Court of Appeal and the photographs were published on the following day. A few hours earlier on the same day *OK!* published its own photographs, having brought forward its date of publication on account of what it knew to be the imminent publication by *Hello!* ...	*To comply with an obligation* *Ex parte*[5] *To obtain an injunction restraining sth.* *To discharge an injunction (to terminate it)*
110. *OK!* sued *Hello!* for breach of confidence and for the tort of causing loss by unlawful means. (The Douglases brought separate proceedings against *Hello!* and recovered modest damages, but these are not in issue in this appeal, to which the Douglases are not parties.)	*To sue for + unlawful act* *A tort: causing loss by unlawful means* *To bring proceedings against sb.* *To recover damages* *To be in issue in an appeal/parties to an appeal*

---

[5] *Ex parte* followed by a name refers to an application in a judicial proceeding made on the part of that side only.

**Key and comment to Task 1 Vocabulary in context: case study—
a celebrity wedding**

1. *The contracting parties* are Michael Douglas and Catherine Zeta-Jones ('the Douglases'), and Northern & Shell plc, publishers of *OK!* (referred to in the judgment as '*OK!*'). The *litigants* in this final appeal to the House of Lords are *OK!* and *Hello!*, the rival magazine. In the dispute between the Douglases and *Hello!*, not considered in this House of Lords appeal, the Douglases had won 'a modest sum of *damages for the invasion of their privacy*' ([110]).

2. The Douglases are natural persons. *OK!* (Northern & Shell plc) is a juristic person, that is, *a corporation*; it is a *public limited company*, that is, a company limited by shares available on the stock market.

3. The subject matter of the contract is the exclusive right to publish photographs of the Douglases' wedding.

4. The Douglases agreed to perform several duties: *to engage*[6] a photographer, to supply *OK!* with selected photographs and *to use their best efforts* to make sure no other photographs were taken at the wedding. The standard of *best efforts* (or *best endeavours*) is often used in commercial contracts; it indicates that a party must try very hard *to fulfil a contractual obligation.*[7] In case of dispute, the courts will decide if the party has reached this standard in the context of the contract.[8]

5. The *consideration* for the Douglases' commitment under the contract is the sum of £1 million; this is the *benefit* they receive in return for their *promises*. The English doctrine of *consideration* is explained in more detail in 11.3.4 below.

6. Yes, the Douglases performed their side of the contract, this point is not disputed: specifically, they engaged a photographer, supplied *OK!* with selected photographs for publication and took adequate security precautions (even though these were not sufficient, in the event). Similarly, there is no dispute about *OK!*'s performance of the contract.

7. *OK!* obtained an injunction *to restrain* (prevent) *Hello! from publishing the photographs* taken by a freelance photographer who infiltrated the wedding, pretending to be a waiter or guest.

8. The damage suffered by *OK!* was *economic loss*; *OK!* sued *Hello!* in tort: 'the tort of causing loss by unlawful means'. The other two cases considered together by the House of Lords in this appeal also concern 'economic loss caused by intentional acts' ([1]).[9]

---

[6] *To engage* or *to hire* somebody to do a job.

[7] Synonymous verbs *to fulfil* and *to perform*; nouns *fulfilment* and *performance*.

[8] For an example of *best endeavours* in a written contract, see Text 4 in ch 1 (clause 3.4), or 11.4.3 below for more detailed comment (Task 7: clause 4 and key).

[9] The other two cases are: *OBG Limited v Allan* and *Mainstream Properties Limited v Young* [2007] UKHL 21.

Vocabulary focus: collocations

The text in Task 1 contains many examples of useful noun + verb collocations typical of the language of civil proceedings and contract law. For example, at [110]: the claimants *'recovered damages'* (*to recover damages*), or, observing the fuller context, *'The Douglases brought separate proceedings against* Hello! *and recovered modest damages'* (*to bring proceedings against the defendant and recover damages*).

Where *phrasal verbs*[10] are used, a particular preposition or adverb follows the verb and accompanies the specific use and meaning. For example, *to comply with an obligation, to enter into a contract* ([109] and [108] respectively).

Note that in legal English, the collocation of verbs and nouns may be more specific than in general English; there is a more limited range of acceptable combinations of words, and synonyms cannot usually be substituted for the precise combination.

Example
A court *awards damages*; a party *is awarded damages* or *recovers damages*.
But not: a court supplies damages; a party earns damages. These verbs make sense in the context, but are not used. They are not collocations and do not communicate the legal message.

Continue to expand your vocabulary by observing examples in original legal contexts. Keep a good record of collocations that you notice in your terminology system, and continue to add new collocations and examples when you meet them. You will be able to improve your comprehension of text and the accuracy and appropriateness of your expression.

To expand your vocabulary, observe the combinations of verbs and nouns in the text in Task 1, and the structural pattern used with each verb, including phrasal verbs; for support, refer to the *Language Focus* column on the right-hand side of the table.

Select some good examples to add to your personal terminology system.

For a useful glossary of phrasal verbs used in legal English, consult Rupert Haigh's *Legal English*.[11] For example:

Enter into means: (1) to begin or become involved in a formal agreement. For example, 'the parties entered into an agreement relating to a share sale'; (2) to begin to discuss or deal with something. For example, 'the company agreed to enter into negotiations'.

In the text ([108]), *to enter into* means *to conclude a contract*: 'In November 2000 *OK!* entered into a contract with Michael Douglas and Catherine Zeta-Jones'.

---

[10] Used here not only to indicate verb + adverb, but in the wider sense of a 'multi-word verb plus one or more particles and operating syntactically as a single unit', S Chalker and E Weiner (1994), *The Oxford Dictionary of English Grammar* (1998 reissue), Oxford: Oxford University Press, p 297.

[11] R Haigh (2004), *Legal English*, London: Cavendish Publishing Ltd, pp 217–26.

NOTE: If you have not yet studied chapter nine, you may find it useful to read 9.2.2 Tort, Contract and the Protection of Interests, and 9.2.3 Functions and Remedies in the Law of Torts, in connection with the case of Douglas v Hello!, *above.*

Select terms and examples from the section above to expand your personal terminology system in the field of contract law and, in general, private law. Continue to expand your system as you work through this chapter.

SECTION ONE

11.2 Introduction to the Language of Contract Law

Can you define a contract in your legal system? What is the source of your definition?

11.2.1 A Definition of Contract—Contract and Agreement

In the common law system, scholars agree that it is difficult to give a definitive or comprehensive definition of a *contract*; this is typical of the English common law approach, where the law has not been created on the basis of a coherent, abstract theory but has developed case by case. 'English law has no formal definition of a contract. In the absence of a Code, it has not needed one.'[12]

In chapter one (see Text 4), we gave this basic definition of a contract: 'A contract is *a legally binding agreement* between two or more *parties*.' What is the relation between *contract* and *agreement*? A contract in itself constitutes a type of agreement: it is a *legally binding* agreement; in addition, a contract is *based on* the phenomenon of *agreement between the parties*.

Sometimes, the term *agreement* is used as a synonym for *contract*; for example, in 11.4.3, we examine a *Distributorship Agreement*.[13] This is a commercial contract in writing, and the term 'Agreement' is typically used in such contracts.

We have noted that every contract is an agreement, and is based on agreement; but the opposite is not true: not every *agreement* is a *contract*.

'Agreement' is also used as a more general word, to indicate a decision or arrangement between people or organisations, relating to business, politics, family or social life, but without *legal force*.

A contract, specifically, is a *legally binding agreement*: that is, an agreement *enforceable in a court of law*. This means that if one party does not *perform its obligations under the contract*, the other party can make a claim to the civil courts, requesting a remedy. In English law, a remedy such as *rescission* (where a contract is treated as having no legal effect) is also available to an *innocent party* even without court action.

A renowned authority on the English law of contract, Professor Sir Guenter Treitel, has provided this basic definition:

> A contract is an agreement giving rise to obligations which are enforced or recognised by law. The factor which distinguishes contractual from other legal obligations is that they are based on the agreement of the contracting parties.[14]

---

[12] E McKendrick (2012), *Contract Law. Text, Cases, and Materials*, 5th edn, Oxford: Oxford University Press, p 3; he explains the historical reason: contract developed around a form of action called *assumpsit* and the procedure, not the substance of the claim, was important.

[13] This type of contract may also be called a *distribution agreement*.

[14] G Treitel (1999), *The Law of Contract*, 10th edn, London: Sweet & Maxwell, p 1.

However, the definition of a *contract* is then qualified in a number of ways.[15] For example, some *contractual terms*, called *implied terms*, are not agreed by *the contracting parties* but are imposed by law. A contract consists of express terms and implied terms. Terms agreed by the parties are called *express terms*; they 'primarily depend on the words used by the parties in entering into the contract'.[16] The author gives three groups of *implied terms*:

a)   terms implied in fact (not expressly stated, but the parties must have intended to include them);
b)   terms implied in law (imported by operation of law);
c)   terms implied by custom or usage.

The terms of the contract are examined further in 11.2.2 below.

See Treitel's explanation, below, on the subject of agreement. When is agreement between the parties reached?

> The first requisite of a contract is that the parties should have reached agreement. Generally speaking, an agreement is made when one party accepts an offer made by the other. Further requirements are that the agreement must be certain and final; and special problems arise from conditional agreements.[17]

A '*requisite*' or '*requirement*' is a necessary element. The time of agreement is 'when one party accepts an offer made by the other': a contract is generally *formed* (also, *concluded*) at the moment of *acceptance*. For more on *offer and acceptance*, see 11.3.3 below.

11.2.2 The Terms of the Contract

The *rights and duties* of the parties *under the contract* are defined by *the terms of the contract* (also, *contract terms*, *contractual terms*). A *term* is a provision that is part of the contract.

Ewan McKendrick clearly explains the importance of *terms*, below:

> A contract is composed of a number of terms. The number of terms will obviously depend on the importance of the transaction. Large-scale transactions often produce contracts of considerable length and complexity and some of the standard form clauses, such as exclusion and limitation clauses, are likely to have been the subject of protracted negotiation between the parties (or at least between their lawyers). The terms of the contract are obviously of great significance to the parties because they define their rights and liabilities. English law gives the parties considerable freedom to define for themselves the terms of the contract: freedom of contract remains a fundamental part of English law. Many commercial parties have their own standard

---

[15]   *Ibid*, pp 1–5.
[16]   *Ibid*, p 183.
[17]   *Ibid*, p 8.

terms of business which they seek to incorporate into the contracts they conclude (hence, the so-called 'battle of the forms' …). However, the freedom of the parties is not unlimited. Parliament has in recent years intervened to regulate the use of certain types of contract terms.[18]

The terms of the contract are the substance of the agreement, defining the 'rights and *liabilities*' (obligations) of each party. The traditional doctrine of '*freedom of contract*' (the freedom of parties to decide the terms of their contract themselves) is subject to certain limits imposed by statute law. In addition, as discussed above (11.2.1), some terms are not expressly agreed by the parties but are implied by law. Commercial parties may try to impose their 'standard terms of business' on the other party.

Vocabulary focus

Compare the word *terms* with:

— *clauses* or *contractual clauses*—most frequently used to refer to the specific numbered provisions of a written contract. For example, in the Agency Agreement examined in chapter one,[19] *clause* 3 establishes the agent's obligations; jurisdiction and governing law are stipulated in *clause 23*;

— *representations*—these are *pre-contractual statements*, which are not part of the contract itself (they are not *terms*), but they may have induced a party to enter into a contract. If a person makes a *false statement* which induces the other to enter into a contract, this is called *misrepresentation* and the innocent party can *sue for* damages and may even *have a right of rescission* of the contract itself;[20]

— *terms and conditions*—this is a phrase often used in documents to indicate all the provisions (*terms*) of the agreement.

Observe the use of *terms and conditions* in the clause below:

> The Principal hereby appoints the Agent as its agent for the promotion of the Products in the Territory, and the Agent hereby agrees to act in that capacity, subject to the terms and conditions of this Agreement. (from an Agency Agreement, clause 2.1)

The relationship of *principal* and *agent* is created by this clause: the Principal *appoints* the Agent and the Agent accepts. Their agreement is *subject to* (regulated by, on the basis of) the *terms and conditions* contained in the contract itself ('this Agreement'). The adverb *hereby* means *by this clause, by these words* and is typically inserted in contractual clauses.

---

[18] E McKendrick (2012), *Contract Law. Text, Cases, and Materials,* above n 12, p 294.

[19] Text 4, 1.3, above.

[20] The remedy of *rescission* can be taken directly by the injured party without court action and the contract is annulled retroactively *ab initio; rescission* may not have a direct equivalent in other legal systems, but it is used in European Union legal texts to indicate *termination:* in the multilingual EU context, the meaning of terms is not peculiar to one legal system.

Conditions and warranties

There is a basic distinction in English contract law between two classes of terms: *conditions* and *warranties*. Both implied and express terms may be either conditions or warranties:

— The fundamental terms of the contract are called *conditions*: these are *the essential terms*.
— The minor terms of the contract are called *warranties*: these are *the non-essential terms*.

The distinction is very important in case of *breach of contract*. If one party *breaks the contract* (that is, *fails to perform* some of its obligations under the contract, called *breach* or *non-performance*), different remedies are available to *the innocent party*, depending on whether *the term broken* is a *condition* or a *warranty*:

— If *the party in breach* has broken *a warranty*, the innocent party may claim damages.
— But if *the party in breach* has broken *a condition*, this is called *fundamental breach of contract* and gives the right to the innocent party *to rescind the contract*, that is, to treat the contract as terminated. The remedy of *rescission* is in addition to damages. Alternatively, the innocent party may decide *to affirm the contract* (in this case it will continue in force) and *recover damages* for the breach.

Every contract consists of both *conditions* and *warranties*, but the distinction is not necessarily clear; it is possible that the parties did not classify each term of the contract when they reached agreement; perhaps they did not consider the relative importance of the agreed terms, especially where the contract is concluded orally. Or, they may have called a term *a warranty* (a minor term) when really it is *essential* to the contract and is therefore *a condition*. If there is a dispute, it will be the task of the judge to decide whether a term is a condition or a warranty, in the context of the entire agreement and evaluating the consequences of breach of that term. Problems may be caused to other operators in the European Union by the subtleties of the common law distinction between *conditions* and *warranties*.[21]

Comparative law scholars Zweigert and Kötz note the confusion, for European lawyers from a different legal tradition, of the use of *condition* for an essential term of the contract:

> Continental lawyers find the use of the word 'condition' in this context very peculiar. ... English lawyers use the word 'condition' to denote an essential term of a contract whose non-performance gives the innocent party the right to declare the contract discharged and claim damages for non-performance.[22]

---

[21] G Alpa (2004), 'Lineamenti di diritto contrattuale' in G Alpa, MJ Bonell, D Corapi *et al*, *Diritto privato comparato Istituti e problemi*, 5th edn, Roma-Bari: Laterza, p 225.
[22] K Zweigert and H Kötz (1998), *An Introduction to Comparative Law*, 3rd edn (tr T Weir), Oxford: Clarendon Press, p 505.

A contract is *discharged* when it is terminated: the contractual obligations are extinguished (see 11.2.4 below for more on *discharge of contract*).

Another possible source of confusion is that the words *condition* and *warranty* both have more than one meaning in English contract law. Examine Table 11.1 below.

Table 11.1: Meanings of condition and warranty in English contract law

CONDITION	WARRANTY
Basic meaning in contract law As explained above, a condition is a fundamental term of the contract, an essential term, a major term. We say that *a condition goes to the root of the contract*; it is *of the essence* of the contract. For example, in a supply contract, the time of delivery of goods or services may be an essential term of the contract. Use of the term '*Time is of the essence*' in the contract could specifically indicate this. But on other occasions, a provision regarding time of delivery may be of only minor importance.	**Basic meaning in contract law** As explained above, a warranty is a minor or subsidiary term of the contract, a non-essential term. A warranty does not go to the substance of a contract. Breach of a warranty can be compensated for adequately by payment of damages. The contract remains in force.
Other meanings A condition may be an uncertain future event: *if X* (condition), *then Y* (legal consequence). Where the event is preliminary to forming a contractual obligation, it is *a condition precedent*: e.g. 'I will enter into a contract with you, if I can borrow €10,000 from the bank'. Where the condition, if fulfilled, brings the contract to an end, it is *a condition subsequent*.	**Other meanings** A warranty is *a guarantee*. In fact, the word *warranty* is generally used in manufacturers' guarantees: e.g. 'Euro *warranty* information. The manufacturer *warrants that* this product *is guaranteed against defects* in material and workmanship at the time of its original purchase and for the further *warranty period* calculated from the date of purchase …'.[23] Notice also the use of the verbs *to warrant* and *to guarantee*.

11.2.3 The Parties to the Contract

The *parties to the contract*, also called the *contracting parties*, may be:

a)   *natural persons*; or
b)   *juristic persons*, that is, entities possessing *legal personality*: in common law systems, they are called *corporations*.

---

[23] From a manufacturer's guarantee: AIWA warranty information (English), AIWA Co Ltd.

Both natural persons and juristic persons are *legal persons*,[24] although sometimes the term *legal person* is used to indicate *artificial persons*, as opposed to natural persons.[25]

Corporations

Read the definition of a *corporation* from *Osborn's Concise Law Dictionary*, below.

In what different ways can a corporation be created? What can a corporation do?

> **Corporation.** A legal person created by Royal Charter, Act of Parliament, international treaty, or registration under a statutory procedure, e.g. under the Companies Acts (the commonest type). A corporation is a distinct legal entity, separate from such persons as may be members of it, and having legal rights and duties and perpetual succession. It may enter into contracts, own property, employ people and be liable for torts and crimes. See *Salomon v Salomon & Co Ltd* [1897] AC 22.[26]

The definition explains that in English law a corporation can be created in a variety of ways, including by international treaty, but the most common means of *incorporation* (creating a corporation) is by registration: *incorporated companies* are registered following a procedure regulated by legislation. Corporations have full legal powers, as the list above shows. They also have *legal liability* for both torts and crimes. For example, under the Corporate Manslaughter and Corporate Homicide Act 2007, a corporation may be guilty of the offence of *corporate manslaughter*, where a gross failure in the way activities were managed or organised results in a person's death.[27]

A *corporation sole* consists only of one member at a time, the holder of a particular office, such as a bishop, or the British Sovereign. The advantage of this is that the office continues without interruption even when the individual holder changes (for example, on the death of a monarch), since corporations have '*perpetual succession*'. By contrast, a *corporation aggregate* consists of a number of persons, as is the case for incorporated companies.

Companies and other corporations may enter into contracts, through authorised persons, in the same way as an individual. No special formalities are required when a contracting party is a corporation.

British and American terminology

If we also consult a specialised American dictionary, we can compare the meaning of terminology in English and American law.

---

[24] *A Dictionary of Law*, 7th edn (2009, updated reissue 2013), E Martin and J Law (eds), Oxford: Oxford University Press, p 321.

[25] See, e.g., in ch 1: Text 10, Art 13(2) of Directive 2002/58/EC.

[26] *Osborn's Concise Law Dictionary*, 12th edn (2013), M Woodley (ed), London: Sweet & Maxwell, p 117.

[27] Ministry of Justice document, October 2007: 'Understanding the Corporate Manslaughter and Corporate Homicide Act 2007', discussed in 7.3.1 above.

Examine the extracts below from an excellent American work of reference, Black's Law Dictionary. *What similarities or distinctions do you note, compared with the English definition given above? Do you think the term* corporation *has basically the same meaning in both English and American law?*

Corporate entity. The distinct status of a corporation which sets its existence apart from the status of its shareholders; its capacity to have a name of its own, to sue and be sued in its own name as well as the right to buy, sell, lease and mortgage its property in its own name.

Corporation. An artificial person or legal entity created by or under the authority of the laws of a state or nation, composed, in some rare instances, of a single person and his successors, being the incumbents of a particular office, but ordinarily consisting of an association of numerous individuals. ...[28]

This preliminary investigation indicates that a *corporation* in English and American law is basically similar. We can note that in the federal American system, a corporation may be created under the authority of national laws or of state laws (Ohio, California) and, naturally, not by Royal Charter. *Black's Law Dictionary* explains that a corporation formed with the purpose of transacting business for pecuniary profit is known as a *business corporation*, as opposed to *corporations not for profit*, also known as *non-profit corporations*.

The dictionary gives a detailed classification of many different types of corporation and a variety of collocations with the related adjective, *corporate*. Some examples are given below.

Which term is a synonym of corporation?

Corporate. Belonging to a corporation; as a corporate name. Incorporated; as a corporate body.

Corporate body. Term is equivalent to 'body corporate'; ie a corporation.

Corporate charter. Document issued by state agency or authority (commonly Secretary of State) granting corporation legal existence and right to function (ie conduct business) as a corporation. **Corporate domicile.** The domicile of a corporation is the state of its incorporation.[29]

The European Union

If you are an EU citizen, do you know the position of the European Union? Can the EU enter into a contract under national law in the Member States? Observe the Treaty texts, following, to check your answer.[30]

Article 47 TEU
The Union shall have legal personality.

---

[28] H Black (1979), *Black's Law Dictionary*, 5th edn, St Paul, Minn: West Publishing Co, pp 306–07.
[29] *Ibid*, p 306.
[30] Each extract is from the consolidated version of the respective Treaty, [2010] OJ C83/01.

Article 335 TFEU

In each of the Member States, the Union shall enjoy the most extensive legal capacity accorded to legal persons under their laws; it may, in particular, acquire or dispose of movable and immovable property and may be a party to legal proceedings. To this end, the Union shall be represented by the Commission. However, the Union shall be represented by each of the institutions, by virtue of their administrative autonomy, in matters relating to their respective operation.

Article 47 of the Treaty of Maastricht (TEU) provides that the EU is a legal person. Article 335 of the Treaty of Rome (TFEU) lays down that the Union must have the maximum *legal capacity* of a legal person in each national system, clearly including *capacity to contract*. Specifically, the capacity to '*acquire or dispose of movable and immovable property*' is mentioned, and to be a party in proceedings. In an internal legal context, different English terms would generally be used for the two categories of property:

— for *movable property*: *goods, chattels, personalty, personal property*;
— for *immovable property*: *land, real property, realty*; in commercial contexts, *real estate.*

The classification of property in the common law is complex and does not correspond precisely to civil law categories; however, the use of the terms *movable* and *immovable property* (also spelt *moveable* and *immoveable property*) in an international context is a satisfactory solution.

11.2.4 Discharge of Contract

The termination of the contractual obligation is often called *discharge of contract*. In legal language, *discharge* generally means *release from an obligation*, e.g. discharge from a *debt* or a *liability*; in criminal law, *discharge* is the release of a defendant from criminal liability; but *to discharge a duty* means to *perform* a duty; and in general English, *discharge* has other meanings, too.

A *contract* may be *discharged* (terminated) in various ways:

— *discharge by performance*—where the parties perform the contract, fulfilling their contractual obligations: the contract comes to a 'natural' end;
— *discharge by express agreement*—where the parties agree to extinguish remaining obligations: to be legally binding, in English law each party must provide *consideration* for the new promise, that is, something of benefit in return, e.g. I agree to accept less money for the work, but you must pay me at an earlier date;[31]

---

[31] On *consideration*, see 11.3.4 below.

— *discharge by breach*—where one party is in breach of contract, it does not fulfil its side of the contract. A contract may be *discharged by breach* where one party:
  — indicates (by words or actions) that it does not intend to perform its part of the contract (called *anticipatory breach* or *repudiation*), or
  — fails to perform its obligations under the contract (*fundamental breach*);
— *discharge by frustration of contract*—a contract is frustrated where, after the formation of the contract, some event beyond the control of the parties:
  a) makes it impossible to perform the contract (*impossibility of performance*), or
  b) makes it illegal to perform the contract (*illegality*), or
  c) prevents the main purpose from being achieved (*failure of main purpose*).
  In these circumstances, each party is released from its contractual obligations.

Given the different modalities of discharge of contract in English law, how could you translate the term into your own language? You will need to consider equivalent or comparable aspects of contract law in your legal system and look for corresponding terms that may be considered equivalent.[32]

Task 2 Analysing cases—discharge of contract
Read the example case summaries below. Analyse each case to decide how the contract is discharged, using the explanation above to guide your choice.

Identify the legal category of discharge of contract (e.g. discharge by performance) and complete the column on the right, as in the example.

Disscuss and compare your solutions before consulting the key. How would each case be treated in your legal system?

Facts of the hypothetical case	Legal analysis
Example The parties enter into a contract for the hire of a room with a view in a capital city, to watch an important procession, but the procession is cancelled in advance.	*The main purpose of the contract has failed, due to an external event. The contract is frustrated for failure of main purpose.*
1. A (a householder) and B (a freelance gardener) enter into a *contract for services* for the landscaping of A's new garden, for a fee of £1,000. B designs and landscapes the garden; A pays B £1,000.	

---

[32] For more detailed discussion, refer to 3.1.3 above, 'Translating Legal Terminology'.

2.	A, *the seller*, contracts with B, *the buyer*, for the sale of a used car. Before the agreed time of payment and delivery, A sells the car to C.	
3.	Goods specified in a *sale of goods contract* are destroyed by fire. They are unique paintings and cannot be substituted by similar articles.	
4.	One party becomes an *enemy alien* because war breaks out. Contracts with enemy aliens are unlawful. (The law term *alien* means a foreigner, not a Martian.)	

Key and commentary to Task 2 Analysing cases—discharge of contract

1. The case is clear: both parties have performed their side of the contract. It is a case of *discharge by performance*. *A contract for services* is a contract for the performance of work on an independent, freelance basis. In such a case, A is *the principal*, and B (here, the gardener) is *an independent contractor*. Payment for services is called *a fee*. We may contrast a *contract for services* with a *contract of service*, also called *an employment contract*: the parties are *the employer* (or *master*) and *the employee* (or *servant*); it is characterised by the control exercised by the employer over the manner in which the employee performs the work. Payment earned for such work is called *a wage* (generally paid on a weekly basis) or *salary* (monthly). What are the corresponding terms in your legal system?

2. The seller, A, is *in breach of contract*; it is a case of *anticipatory breach*: by selling the car to C (a third party), A has indicated his intention not to perform his side of the contract. B can treat the contract as discharged and immediately sue A for damages.

3. The object of the contract (the goods) no longer exists. It is therefore impossible to perform the contract, since the goods were unique and cannot be substituted. *The contract is frustrated by impossibility of performance.*

4. Because of an external event, the outbreak of war, the contract has become illegal. *It is discharged by frustration for illegality.* These facts are inspired by a precedent dating back to the Second World War: a British company had entered into a contract to sell machinery to a buyer in Poland; when Poland was occupied by Nazi Germany, the contract was frustrated, since it would be illegal for the British firm to trade with the enemy in wartime.[33]

---

[33] *Fibrosa Spolka Akcyjna v Fairbairn Lawson Combe Barbour Ltd* [1943] AC 32, in McKendrick, above n 12, p 723.

Frustration of contract and *force majeure*

The facts in the example case given in Task 2 above are similar to those in the case of *Krell v Henry*,[34] in which the defendant agreed to hire a flat for the sum of £75 in Pall Mall, London, in order to watch Edward VII's coronation procession, an event postponed due to the King's illness: the main purpose of the contract obviously *failed* so the contract was *frustrated*.[35] Frustration of contract, as in the example case and hypothetical cases 3. and 4. above, is a general *doctrine of contract law*, explained by Jill Poole, below.

Does the doctrine of frustration always apply? Why or why not?

> If after the formation of the contract, events occur, without the fault of either party, which render further performance of the contract impossible, illegal, or radically different from what was originally envisaged the contract may be automatically discharged on the grounds of frustration and the parties will be excused further performance of their contractual obligations. ...
>
> However, the frustration doctrine applies only in the absence of an express provision in the contract allocating the risk. If the contract contains a *force majeure* clause covering the event that has occurred, that *force majeure* clause will govern and not the frustration doctrine.[36]

The doctrine of frustration operates only where the parties do not *expressly agree* differently. In fact, to avoid this doctrine, *the parties may expressly provide* in their contract for an external, future event, such as a war or fire, in a *force majeure* clause. In this way, the parties *allocate the risk*, by placing it on one party or the other, or, as in the example clause below, by suspending a party's obligations under the contract in relation to difficulties caused by that event. The French term *force majeure*, used in legal English, indicates an external event, *beyond* (outside) the control of the parties.

Observe the following list of events in a force majeure *clause in a commercial agreement. Use a general English dictionary as required. Is the list exhaustive (all-inclusive)?*

14 Force majeure

14.1 The obligations of each party under this Agreement shall be suspended during the period and to the extent that that party is prevented or hindered from complying with them *by any cause beyond its reasonable control*, including (insofar as beyond such control but without prejudice to the generality of the foregoing expression) strikes, lock-outs, labour disputes, act of God, war, riot, civil commotion, malicious damage, compliance with any law or governmental order, rule, regulation or direction, accident, breakdown of plant or machinery, fire, flood, storm, difficulty or increased expense in obtaining labour, materials, goods or raw materials in connection with the performance of this Agreement. (emphasis added)[37]

---

[34] *Krell v Henry* [1903] 2 KB 740.
[35] J Poole (2006), *Casebook on Contract Law*, 8th edn, Oxford: Oxford University Press, pp 521–23.
[36] *Ibid*, p 509.
[37] Agency Agreement used courtesy of Withers LLP: <http://www.withersworldwide.com>.

The general category of legal event covered in this *force majeure* clause is: '*any cause beyond its* [the party's] *reasonable control*'. '*Any cause*' is completely general, and the use of the word 'including' shows that each event in the list that follows is included, and implies that the list is not *exhaustive*. This point is clearly stipulated by the phrase '*without prejudice to the generality of the foregoing expression*'. '*Without prejudice to*' means *without damaging* or *limiting*. Therefore, the '*foregoing*' (previously stated) expression, that is, '*any cause* beyond its reasonable control', is *not limited* by the list that follows. The defining characteristic is that the event must be *beyond the reasonable control* of the party concerned. The long list of types of event provides a very wide range of possible circumstances constituting *force majeure* in this contract, including, it is interesting to note, economic and market factors, such as the increased cost of labour or materials. Observe that the suspension of obligations under this clause is not absolute but operates 'during the period and to the extent that' the event prevents or *hinders* (interferes with) the party's performance.

11.2.5 An International Dispute in Contract Law: *Apple v Apple*

In Task 3 below, apply what you have learnt about contract law and language in 11.2, to understand some aspects of this dispute between two famous 'Apples'. First, examine the term *service*, below:

> **Service:** 'the steps required by rules of court to bring documents used in court proceedings to a person's attention'.[38]

...

Service (verb, *to serve*) indicates notification to parties of steps in court proceedings. *Service out of the jurisdiction* means notification to a party not in the territory over which the courts have authority. For example, service to a party in Scotland or France is *service out of the jurisdiction* of the English High Court. Service is governed by the *Civil Procedure Rules* (CPR) in the English legal system.

Task 3 Law of contract in action: *Apple v Apple*
Read the questions below, then examine the text of the judgment to find the answers. Focus on both language and meaning as you work.

1. Who are the contracting parties? Are they natural persons or corporations?
2. What is the meaning of '*agreement*' in line 6?
3. What is the subject matter of the contract between the two 'Apples'? What do you suppose is the reason for entering into this contract?
4. Which party is alleged to be *in breach of contract*?
5. Why does the claimant *seek* (ask the court to grant) *an injunction*?
6. What is the relevance of the four questions formulated by the judge?

---

[38] *A Dictionary of Law*, above n 24, p 503.

	LANGUAGE FOCUS
HIGH COURT OF JUSTICE **Chancery Division** **[2004] EWHC 768 (Ch)**	
Apple Corps Ltd v Apple Computer Inc	
Mr Justice Mann 1. ... The defendant is the well-known producer of	*THE PARTIES*
computers and software. The claimant ('Corps') is the well-known record company formed by the Beatles. The basis of the claim made against	*THE DISPUTE*
Computer is that that corporation has broken, and intends to break, an agreement made between the two companies in October 1991 which regu-	
lated the use of their respective marks in respect of various areas of activity or proposed activity.	*Marks = trade marks, a type of* *intellectual property*
On 7th August 2003 Master Moncaster granted permission to serve Computer outside the juris-	*Master = a Master of the* *Supreme Court*
diction under CPR 6.20 on two grounds—that the relevant agreement was governed by English	*CPR = the Civil Procedure* *Rules*
law, and that the contract was made in England. At the hearing before me Corps sought to rely on the additional ground that Computer threatens a	*Sought to rely on = tried to base* *their case on*
breach of contract within the jurisdiction which would entitle Corps to an injunction to restrain it. Computer disputes the propriety of service out	*Propriety = correctness* *Out = outside the jurisdiction*
on those grounds, denying the relevant factual bases, and further maintaining that England is not the appropriate forum for the dispute. In the circumstances the applications before me raise the following questions:	
a. Was the contract made in England? b. Was the contract governed by English law? c. Is there a threatened breach of contract within the jurisdiction?	*Three factual questions*
d. If any of those heads are made out, is England the proper place in which to bring the claim?	*THE ISSUE*

Key and commentary to Task 3 Law of contract in action: *Apple v Apple*

1. The contracting parties are corporations. They are both well-known companies: the computer company, Apple Computer Inc (*Inc* is short for *incorporated*) and the record company created by the Beatles, Apple Corp Ltd (Ltd, short for *limited*, indicates a *limited liability company*).

2. '*Agreement*' is used in line 6 as a synonym of *contract*.

3. The two companies concluded a contract in October 1991 to regulate the use of their *trade marks* in different areas of activity. The need for this is apparent: both companies have 'Apple' in their names and as part of their *trade marks*. The purpose of a *trade mark* (a form of *intellectual property*, belonging to its owner) is to distinguish and identify a trader's products or service to the public. As both companies use the word 'Apple', there could potentially be confusion if they deal in similar products.

4. The Beatles' company ('Corps') claims that Apple Computer Inc is in breach of contract. It alleges that Computer 'has broken, and intends to break,' the contract.

5. The claimant ('Corps') *seeks an injunction to restrain the defendant* ('Computer') *from breaking the contract 'within the jurisdiction'*, that is, within the territory over which the English courts have authority. The *equitable remedy of an injunction* (a court order to do or not to do specified things) is available in both tort and contract.[39]

6. The questions formulated by the judge are relevant to decide whether England is the appropriate *forum* for the dispute (see 'Commentary', below). We cannot answer the judge's questions on the basis of the text. According to the allegations made by *the claimant*, question **c.** will have an affirmative answer: there is a threatened breach of contract within the jurisdiction. But Computer deny the '*factual bases*' and maintain that 'England is not the appropriate forum for the dispute'.

Choice of law, jurisdiction and language in international contracts

The *Apple v Apple* case introduces some of the legal problems that arise in the context of international contracts involving aspects belonging to more than one legal system.

Two aspects relevant in this case are generally regulated by specific clauses in international commercial contracts: *governing law* and *jurisdiction*.

The *governing law* of a contract is the law of the specific legal system that *governs (regulates) the contract*: its rules and interpretation. The parties' *choice of law* in a

---

[39] Refer to 9.2.6, for more on injunctions.

written contract is generally respected. In *Apple v Apple*, the judge asks: 'Was the contract governed by English law?' Synonyms of *governing law* are *applicable law* and *proper* law; *choice of law* may be used to indicate this clause in a contract.

The question of *jurisdiction over disputes* relating to the contract is separate: it determines which courts have *authority* (*jurisdiction*) to decide a dispute. Where a dispute is heard by the courts of a different jurisdiction from the *governing law* (for example, the English courts decide a dispute concerning a contract governed by Spanish law), questions of foreign law will be produced by *expert witnesses* during the proceeding and will be treated by the English courts as matters of fact. It is possible for the courts of more than one legal system to have jurisdiction over a dispute. The question of which is the appropriate *forum* may then arise, as in *Apple v Apple*. It seems that the contract has strong links with England, but the judge asks 'is England the proper place in which to bring the claim?' The defendant claims that England is not the appropriate *forum*. The *forum* is the place or country where a case is heard.[40] Where there is a choice of jurisdiction, parties sometimes practise *forum shopping*: they choose the best forum on the basis of which country's laws are more favourable to their cause.[41]

The branch of *private international law* in each country determines the rules for dealing with cases involving a foreign element; it is also called *conflict of laws*.

Lastly, many international business contracts are written in the English language, even where no English language party, or common law system, is involved. Particular questions of meaning and interpretation may arise when the English language of contract law is used to express terminology and principles of a different legal system, such as a civil law system.[42]

Which part of the following clause stipulates the governing law of the contract? What two aspects does 'governing law' include?

23 Governing law and jurisdiction

This Agreement shall be governed by and construed in accordance with English law and each party hereby irrevocably submits to the jurisdiction of the English Courts.[43]

This is the final clause in an Agency Agreement. '*Governing law*' includes both the application of legal rules (the Agreement 'shall be governed by' English law) and the interpretation of the contract (the Agreement shall be '*construed* in accordance

---

[40] *A Dictionary of Law*, above n 24, p 238.

[41] For example, an action may be *time barred* by shorter *limitation periods* in one legal system but not in another. A complex, but interesting case decided by the House of Lords is *Spiliada Maritime Corp v Cansulex Ltd. The Spiliada* [1986] UKHL 10, [1987] AC 460, regarding the forum in which the case can most suitably be heard for the parties' interests and the ends of justice.

[42] Also see Haigh, above n 11, including a list of countries in the world with common law, or mixed, legal traditions, pp 151–52.

[43] Agency Agreement used courtesy of Withers LLP: <http://www.withersworldwide.com>.

with English law'). *To construe* means *to interpret*; it is used for legal documents, such as a contract, or a statute and the related noun is *construction*.

Lord Denning, below, underlines an additional difficulty for the judge when *construing contracts*, as opposed to other legal texts; observe the use of *construe* and *construction* in the passage.

What is the purpose of the courts when they construe a legal text? Why is the meaning of words central?

> When **construing** a statute or a will, you are considering the intentions of one body only—be it Parliament or a testator. When **construing** a contract, be it in writing or by word of mouth, you are considering the intentions of two parties—who have agreed together on the terms that shall bind them. As the maxim goes, there is *consensus ad idem*. But in discovering that intention, you are not to look into their actual minds. ... You have to go by the outward expression of their intentions—as conveyed by the words set out in writing or by the spoken words they used. So once again we come back to the meaning of the words.[44]

Lord Denning explains that in construing a contract, but also a will or Act of Parliament, the courts are trying to discover *the intention* of the party or parties concerned: in the case of Parliament, the intention of the legislator; for a will, the intention of *the testator* (who made the will); for a contract, the intention of the contracting parties. The extra difficulty for a contract is that the parties are two; they have agreed the terms of their contract together, expressed by the Latin term *consensus ad idem*; this is an essential element of a contract, indicating agreement on the same essential terms.

The words used by the contracting parties are central to the construction of a contract, whether written or oral. According to the so-called *parol evidence* rule, 'evidence cannot be admitted to add to, vary or contradict a written instrument'.[45] There is a *presumption* that where the contract is in writing, the writing was intended to include all the terms of the contract.[46] However, there are exceptions to the presumption, and today a court will tend to admit and evaluate any relevant evidence to decide whether additional terms were intended to be part of the contract, rather than exclude such evidence as inadmissible.[47]

This matter may, in addition, be clearly stipulated by inserting specific provisions in a contract.

What is the effect of the two clauses below, from a commercial agreement?

---

[44] A Denning (1979), *The Discipline of Law*, London: Butterworths, p 32.
[45] Treitel, above n 14, p 175.
[46] *Ibid*, p 176; this presumption is *rebuttable*, ie it may be disproved by evidence; *Gillespie Bros & Co v Cheney, Eggar & Co* [1896] 2 QB 59, 62.
[47] In McKendrick, above n 12, p 312.

15 Entire agreement

This Agreement constitutes the entire understanding between the parties with respect to the subject matter of this Agreement and supersedes all prior agreements, negotiations and discussions between the parties relating to it.

16 Amendments

Save as expressly provided in this Agreement, no amendment or variation of this Agreement shall be effective unless in writing and signed by a duly authorised representative of each of the parties to it.[48]

By clause 15, it is stipulated that this document constitutes the entire agreement between the parties, relating to the subject matter of the contract (*understanding*, here, means what the parties have agreed to). Any '*prior agreements, negotiations and discussions*' are replaced ('*superseded*') by this document. The adjective *prior*, common in legal English, means *earlier, previous*.

According to clause 16, *amendments and variations* to the contract are not valid ('*effective*') except if they are made in a specified way: '*unless* in writing and signed'. But the opening phrase '*Save as expressly provided in this Agreement*' indicates that exceptions to this general rule are possible: this document itself may expressly provide for amendments.

In case of dispute, such a clause (which may be called a *merger* or *integration clause*) will have a very strong persuasive effect that the parties did not intend other additional terms to be part of their agreement.[49]

---

[48] Agency Agreement used courtesy of Withers LLP: <http://www.withersworldwide.com>.

[49] Law Commission No 154, Law of Contract: The Parol Evidence Rule (1986), in E McKendrick (2012), *Contract Law. Text, Cases, and Materials*, above n 12, p 310.

SECTION TWO

11.3 Formation of Contract and Key Elements

Have you entered into any contracts, today? Have you had a cup of coffee at the café, bought a newspaper, used public transport? Or transacted in an agency, bank or shop?

Think about the legal implications of these common actions. What elements must be present for the formation of a valid contract in your legal system?

11.3.1 Form and Formalities

In English law, no particular formalities are generally required to form a contract. Most contracts are *simple contracts*, discussed in this chapter. A *simple contract* may be oral (we also say *verbal* or *parol*) or in writing, or it may be concluded by *conduct*: performing an act, such as getting on a bus. It is standard commercial practice to stipulate written agreements. In *commercial transactions*, this promotes certainty about the existence of the contract and its terms.

Some types of simple contract must, however, be made in a particular *form* to be valid. In the case of a *contract of employment*, an employee must receive written particulars of his or her employment, specified by law, even if the contract itself need not be in writing.[50] This is an example of how statute law has supplemented the basic *common law rules of contract law*, also in response to EU obligations.

It is possible to make a contract in a special written form, called *a deed*. A contract not in the form of a deed is *a simple contract*. By law, certain contracts *must be stipulated* in the form of a deed. When buying real property, such as a house, the document that *transfers a legal estate in land* must be in the form of a deed. The term *conveyance* indicates both the document and the transfer.[51] The noun *conveyancing* indicates the procedures involved, carried out for a fee by a practising solicitor or licensed *conveyancer*; in common law systems there is not a separate professional figure like the *notary* in civil law systems. *Deeds* are also important in legal practice, as parties can use a deed to give legal effect to a unilateral gratuitous promise (a promise where there is no consideration—see 11.3.4 below), not otherwise binding in English law.[52]

---

[50] The Employment Rights Act 1996, s 1, also see ss 2–4; these provisions gave effect to Council Directive 91/533/EEC of 14 October 1991 on an employer's obligation to inform employees of the conditions applicable to the contract or employment relationship.

[51] *A Dictionary of Law*, above n 24, pp 133–34.

[52] McKendrick, above n 12, p 261.

The main elements required to form a contract in English law are explained by scholar Ewan McKendrick, below, introducing the basic principles of the English law of contract.

What elements must be present to conclude a contract?

> To conclude a contract, the parties must reach agreement, the agreement must be supported by consideration and there must be an intention to create legal relations. The courts generally decide whether an agreement has been reached by looking for an offer made by one party to the other, which has been accepted by that other party: the acceptance, if it is to count, must be a mirror image of the offer.[53]

The main elements required to form a contract in English law are *agreement*, *consideration* and *intention to create legal relations*. *Offer and acceptance* are also necessary elements, and these are significant in determining when the contract is formed. In 11.3.2 to 11.3.4 below, we focus on the elements of a contract and the language used in connection with them.

11.3.2 Intention

Intention to create legal relations is a required element to form a contract: the parties must *intend to form a legally binding agreement*, not an agreement or arrangement without legal force.

CASE A   *Could this exchange be a contract? Are you sure?*
At work. Anne and Bill are colleagues in the same law firm.

Anne: 'Meet you in the café for a break. Shall we say about 10?'
Bill: 'Fine. See you there.'

CASE B   *Is this a contract? Are you sure?*
At Alan's home. His pet labrador, Lollipop, has recently had a litter of puppies.

Alan: 'So you've decided? You really want one. You have first choice. Which one will you have?'
Beth: 'You said £300?'
Alan: 'That's right, since we're friends. I'm asking £1,000 for the others.'
Beth. 'Right, it's a deal! I'll have this one. He's so cute. I'll call him Sparkie.'
Alan: 'Great. You can come and get him in 3 weeks' time. He'll be 8 weeks old by then.'

---

[53] *Ibid*, p 4.

In case of dispute over *the existence of a contract*, the courts must determine *the intention of the parties*. The starting point of the English courts is to use two different *presumptions*, one for *domestic* agreements (family and personal) and one for *commercial* agreements.

A *presumption* is a legal supposition, important in *the law of evidence*. For example, in criminal law, the *presumption of innocence* is fundamental to a defendant's rights: 'Everyone charged with a criminal offence shall be presumed innocent until proved guilty according to law.'[54] *The burden of proof* is on the prosecution *to prove* that the accused is guilty of a crime. Most presumptions are *rebuttable*: that is, they can be *rebutted* (*disproved*) by producing evidence to the contrary; such presumptions are called *rebuttable presumptions*.[55]

In contract law, the following presumptions apply:

> There is a presumption in the case of domestic and social agreements that there is no intention to create legal relations.
>
> …
>
> There is a presumption of an intention to create legal relations in commercial agreements.[56]

It is presumed that in domestic agreements, the parties do not intend to create legal relations; but in commercial agreements, it is presumed that they do intend to create legal relations when they make agreements in the course of their transactions.

In the example cases above, both Case A and Case B are *domestic or social* agreements. There is therefore a presumption that the parties do not intend to create legal relations:

— **Case A** – Anne and Bill clearly do not intend to be *legally bound* by their arrangement to meet in the café at 10 o'clock.
— **Case B** – Alan and Beth are clearly friends, and in the context, the presumption is that they do not intend to create legal relations. However, they reach certain agreement on the object of *a sale* (a puppy) for a price (£300). If the owner of the puppy (Alan) in fact sold it to a third party, to gain the higher price of £1,000, could his disappointed friend (Beth) *sue for damages* on the grounds that there was a legally binding agreement between them? Could she even *seek a decree of specific performance* to compel Alan to perform his side of the contract?[57]

---

[54] European Convention on Human Right 1950, ECT No 005, Art 6(2).
[55] Opposite: *irrebuttable presumptions*; infinitive: *to rebut* a presumption.
[56] Poole, above n 35, p 179 and p 185.
[57] This equitable remedy is available only in contract law; alternatively, the English courts could grant an injunction to stop Alan from selling the puppy to a different buyer.

If Beth intended to sue, she would need to see her solicitor for advice on her chances of success. In a case against Alan, *the burden of proof would lie on* Beth *to rebut the presumption* that the parties did not intend to create a legally binding contract.

How do the courts determine the intention of the parties? Which approaches are possible and which one do the English courts use? Read the passage below.

> Many of the rules of contract law are said to rest on the intention of the parties. But how does the court ascertain their intention? Does it seek to examine the actual, subjective state of mind of the parties or does it look to the outward manifestation of their intention (as expressed in the words used, their appearance, conduct, etc)? The general rule is that the existence and content of an agreement are objective questions that must be answered by reference to the intention of the parties, objectively ascertained.[58]

This answer confirms Lord Denning's explanation of judicial construction of contracts, examined above.[59]

Reconsider the facts of Case B, above. Examine the words used. If Beth sues Alan, what objective elements could support her claim that the two friends have concluded a legally binding agreement? What elements, on the other hand, support Alan's case?

11.3.3 Agreement

Offer and acceptance

To decide whether agreement has been reached between the parties, the common law courts analyse the facts of the case in terms of *offer and acceptance*. Under English law, a contract is formed at the moment of *acceptance*: that is, when one party (*the offeree*) accepts a valid *offer* made by the other party (*the offeror*). But the question is: 'At what point in the negotiating process did the parties cross the line from negotiating parties to contracting parties?'[60]

Read Ewan McKendrick's textbook commentary, below. Can you understand and explain the following terms?

offer – acceptance – representation – counter-offer

> A contract is created by an offer made by one party that has been accepted by the party to whom the offer was made. There are two vital ingredients of this definition. The first is the 'offer' and the second is the 'acceptance'. Both of these words require further elaboration. An offer can be defined as a statement, whether written or oral,

---

[58] McKendrick, above n 12, p 20.
[59] In 11.2.5, text to n 44.
[60] McKendrick, above n 12, p 45.

of a willingness to be bound by the terms of the statement. Not every statement made in the course of the negotiation process amounts to an offer. The statement may be no more than a representation made by one party to the other that has induced that other to enter into the contract but which has not been incorporated into the contract itself. ...

Not everything that purports to be an acceptance, is, in fact, an acceptance in the eyes of the law. If the acceptance contains terms which differ from those contained in the offer, it is not treated by the courts as an acceptance but as a counter-offer.[61]

The offeror must be *willing* (disposed, with the intention) to be bound by his oral or written statement. The acceptance must come from the party to whom the offer is made (not someone different). The terms of the offer must be accepted, not varied. If they are varied by the other party (for example, all other terms are agreed, but a variation in price is suggested), this constitutes a *rejection* of the original offer and is a *counter-offer*, which may, in turn, be accepted or rejected.

An interesting rule connected with this, is that displaying objects in a shop window for sale with a price label attached does not constitute a contractual offer. It is merely a preliminary offer of availability, an *invitation to treat* or *tender* (*Fisher v Bell*).[62]

The same is true also in a self-service shop, where the customer picks up an article and takes it to the cash desk for purchase. The question was decided in *Pharmaceutical Society of Great Britain v Boots Cash Chemists (Southern) Ltd.*[63] As in *Fisher v Bell*, it was important to determine the exact status of offer and acceptance in the case, to decide whether the defendant (the shopkeeper) had committed a crime. Lord Chief Justice Goddard said:

I think that it is a well established principle that the mere exposure of goods for sale by a shopkeeper indicates to the public that he is willing to treat but does not amount to an offer to sell. I do not think I ought to hold that this principle is completely reversed merely because there is a self-service scheme, such as this, in operation. In my opinion it comes to no more than that the customer is informed that he may himself pick up an article and bring it to the shopkeeper with a view to buying it, and if, but only if, the shopkeeper then expresses his willingness to sell, the contract for sale is completed.[64]

Given this rule, who is the offeror and who is the offeree when a customer buys an article in a shop? Is the offer an offer to sell, or an offer to buy? Compare the position in your legal system.

The cases above show how the specific rules of offer and acceptance have been refined and developed by the courts in response to the facts of the cases that have come before them for decision. This illustrates the inductive common law approach, with the rules of contract law created and developed by the judges in

---

[61] *Ibid.*
[62] *Fisher v Bell* [1961] 1 QB 394.
[63] *Pharmaceutical Society of Great Britain v Boots Cash Chemists (Southern) Ltd* [1953] 1 QB 401.
[64] *Ibid*, reproduced with explanatory comment in Poole, above n 35, p 27.

precedent, case by case, over the centuries. These rules today are supplemented by statute law. To understand English contract law, in the absence of a systematic code, you need to use a good *textbook*, providing a coherent, complete description of the law, in conjunction with a *cases and materials* book.[65]

Consensus ad idem

The concept expressed by the Latin maxim *consensus ad idem* is another aspect of agreement: the negotiating parties must agree on the essential terms of their bargain. A contract is based on *a meeting of minds*.

If one or both parties make a *mistake* about a matter of fact (*a mistake of fact*), the contract may be *void* (invalid, null) or *voidable* (capable of being declared void).

Illegality

The object of a contract must not be illegal or immoral: even if the parties have reached agreement and the other elements of a valid contract are present, the courts will not enforce such an agreement. In fact, there is a general principle expressed in the Latin maxim *ex turpi causa non oritur actio*: no action can be based on a disreputable cause.[66] For example, *an illegal contract is void*. In both contract and tort *a claim may be defeated* (the claimant may lose) on the ground of illegality.

As Treitel says:

> The law may refuse to give full effect to a contract on the ground of illegality, ie because the contract involves the commission of a legal wrong or is in some other way contrary to public policy.[67]

A gang of criminals who agree in the course of their 'business relations' to rob a bank have certainly not entered into a contract. The criminal case of *R v Hayter*,[68] where a woman arranged 'a contract killing' of her husband, is hardly an example of a legally binding agreement.

In other cases, even if a contract is lawfully made, a claim may fail if the contract is performed illegally, 'and the party knowingly participated in that illegal performance'.[69]

---

[65] Ewan McKendrick's textbook *Contract Law. Text, Cases and Materials*, above n 12, is very clearly organised and expressed, and combines authoritative explanation with illustrations from the case law; Jill Poole's *Casebook on Contract Law*, above n 35, provides a very clear and usable collection of cases with comment and explanation; in addition, articles from law reviews also provide critical, in-depth analysis of developments in the law.

[66] *A Dictionary of Law*, above n 24, p 222.

[67] Treitel, above n 14, p 392.

[68] *R v Hayter* [2005] UKHL 6, examined in 7.3.2 above.

[69] *Ashmore, Benson Ltd v Dawson Ltd* [1973] 1 WLR 828, 828, cited in *Hall v Woolston Hall Leisure Ltd* [2001] 1 WLR 225; see the extract from this second case, for a summary of the principles governing illegality in English law, in Poole, above n 35, p 693.

11.3.4 Consideration

A simple contract cannot be formed if there is no *consideration*. *Consideration* can be described as *the price of the bargain* in English law. A contract is viewed as *a bargain*; this commercial term indicates *a transaction* in which both parties have something to gain.[70] The idea is that in *simple contracts*, something must be given in return for the promise: if not, the English courts will not enforce the promise, and there is no contract. The name we give to *what is given in return for the promise* is *consideration*.

> The essence of consideration is *mutuality*: it is the element which distinguishes gratui-tous promises ('I will give you my watch')—which are only actionable if made by deed or are in the form of declarations of trust—from *contractual ones*. Usually, as where you and I come to an agreement, it consists of a *promise* in return for a promise ... [71]

The *doctrine of consideration* has been developed and refined by the courts, prec-edent by precedent. It is 'a complex and multifarious body of rules'.[72]

Examine the following definition of consideration, *explained by Treitel.*

(The *promisor* is the party who makes the promise to the *promisee*.)

> The traditional definition of consideration concentrates on the requirement that 'something of value' must be given and accordingly states that consideration is either some detriment to the promisee (in that he may give value) or some benefit to the promisor (in that he may receive value).[73] Usually, this detriment and benefit are merely the same thing looked at from different points of view. Thus, payment by a buyer is consideration for the seller's promise to deliver and can be described as a detriment to the buyer or as a benefit to the seller; and conversely delivery by a seller is consideration for the buyer's promise to pay and can be described either as a detri-ment to the seller or as a benefit to the buyer. ...
>
> What the law is concerned with is the consideration *for a promise*—not the consi-deration *for a contract*.[74]

Task 4   Consideration: analysing promises

Try to apply Treitel's definition of consideration, above, to the example cases, below, by analysing each agreement in terms of promises made by the parties. Can you identify the promise made by each party?

What is the consideration for each promise? Can you see a detriment (dis-advantage) to the promisee and/or a benefit (advantage) to the promisor? Discuss your ideas before reading the key and comment below.

---

[70] Sometimes, *bargain* is used as a synonym for *contract*.
[71] P James (1985), *Introduction to English Law*, 11th edn, London: Butterworths, p 281.
[72] Treitel, above n 14, p 63.
[73] *Currie v Misa* (1875) LR 10 Ex 153 at 162; the author also provides a long list of other precedents, with the note 'see also'.
[74] G Treitel (1999), *The Law of Contract*, above n 14, p 64.

CASE A	Promises
Alan agrees to sell Beth his old car. Beth agrees to pay Alan £1,000 for the car.	Alan promises to .... Beth promises to ....

CASE B	Promises
Anne promises to give Bill her bicycle. She does not want any money, but Bill must go and collect the bike from the bicycle park at the station and pay for necessary repairs (a new tyre). Bill agrees, and both he and Anne are pleased with the arrangement.	Anne promises to .... Bill promises to ....

Key and comment to Task 4 Consideration: analysing promises

— **Case A** – Consideration typically takes the form of money, which is one type of *valuable benefit*. In this example, Beth's promise of £1,000 is the *consideration for Alan's promise* of the car. The contract is therefore based on two promises; and consideration can be seen from two angles: *in exchange for Beth's promise* of £1,000, *Alan (the promisee) suffers a detriment*, ie that of renouncing ownership of his car. From each party's point of view, there is a benefit to *the promisor* and a detriment to *the promisee* (although Treitel points out, above, that only one of these two possibilities is required for consideration to exist: *either … or …*).

— **Case B** – No money is promised in this agreement. Anne (as promisor) promises to give Bill her bicycle for free. If it is *a gratuitous promise*, the law will not enforce it as *a simple contract* (it would have to be stipulated in the form of a *deed*). But in exchange for Anne's promise, Bill agrees to do something: he will go and get the bike and pay for repairs; each of these obligations is a detriment to the promisee (Bill). In relation to Anne's promise, there is also a benefit to the promisor (Anne): she is relieved of the need to dispose of her bike (left in a public place), and of paying for eventual repairs.

Naturally, in these examples, the intention to create legal relations must also be present for the formation of a valid contract.

The doctrine of consideration applies to *simple contracts*, the common type of contract examined in this book, requiring no special formalities for its conclusion.[75]

---

[75] Discussed above, 11.3.1.

By contrast, a *deed* may be enforced even where there is no consideration. For this reason, it can be used as an instrument to create a legally binding agreement even in the absence of consideration.

If your legal system is one based on Roman law, can you compare the functions of civil law causa *and common law* consideration?[76]

Ewan McKendrick points out that 'international restatements on contract law find no room for the doctrine', specifying that both the Principles of European Contract Law (an important project for the harmonisation of European private law) and the Unidroit Principles of International Commercial Contracts provide for contracts to be concluded without consideration, on the basis of agreement.[77]

11.3.5 The Elements of a Contract: Reading Selection and Analysis

In this section, you will read independently a selection of three different types of text relating in different ways to the law of contract. Which elements or aspects of contract law, examined in this chapter, are illustrated in each text? Bring the knowledge you have gained of law, language and texts, while using this book, to your understanding of the selected extracts.

If you prefer, you may return to Task 5 when you have completed 11.4, 'Commercial Agreements', below.

Task 5 The elements of a contract—reading and analysis

For each text, first identify the text type and read for general understanding. What is the text about?

Then, read the text in greater detail to understand the most important points and the legal significance of the extract. Which elements or aspects of contract law are illustrated in each text? For example: consideration, the intention of the parties, breach of contract, etc.

As you work, focus on both language and meaning. In this activity, you are asked to read a lot of text. Do not worry if you do not understand every word and detail. Focus on the task.

Finally, choose one text for in-depth study, and prepare to present it and discuss its content, language and legal significance, also commenting on relevant comparative aspects.

---

[76] This question has long been the object of in-depth comparative studies. See, e.g., EG Lorenzon (1919), 'Causa and Consideration in the Law of Contracts', *The Yale Law Journal*, vol 28, no 7, May 1919, pp 621–46, consultable online at <http://www.jstor.org/>.

[77] McKendrick, above n 12, p 252.

Text 1: *Contract Law. Text, Cases and Materials*

The courts frequently declare that they are seeking to give effect to the intention of the parties when applying the rules of offer and acceptance. It is, however, important to understand that the courts do not generally seek to ascertain the subjective intentions of the parties. It is their intention, objectively ascertained, that counts … But there is a problem here and it arises from the fact that the parties may not have had any observable intention, one way or the other. Take the case of a couple going into a restaurant for a meal. They look at the menu outside the restaurant and then decide to go in. When they go in a waiter gives them a copy of the menu and awaits their order. They each order their meals. Nothing is said about who is to pay for the meal. At the end of the meal the waiter presents a bill to one or the other party and payment is made. At what point in time did a contract come into existence between the customers and the restaurant owner? Was it when the customers entered into the restaurant, when they ordered the food or when they paid for the meal? Further, how was the contract created? Who made the offer and who accepted it? What is the status of the menu (either outside or inside the restaurant)? Is it an offer or is it simply an invitation to negotiate (or, as it is more commonly put by lawyers, an invitation to 'treat')? Who has concluded the contract? Is the contract between the restaurant owner and the party who pays the bill, or are both customers party to a contract with the restaurant owner? … The average customer in a restaurant is unlikely to have given much thought to the precise process by which a contract is created. He or she intends to eat a meal and to pay for it but, beyond this, is unlikely to have any discernible intention as to the means by which or the time at which the contract is created. It falls to the courts to devise a presumptive rule that can then be applied to the facts of the case at hand. In this way uncertainty and inconsistency can be reduced, if not eliminated. In devising the presumptive rule the courts attempt to produce a rule which is workable and consistent with what they believe would have been the intention of the parties had they given the matter some thought. Oddly enough, there is in fact no authority on the contractual status of a menu displayed or handed to a customer in a restaurant. The consensus of academic opinion is that a menu amounts to an invitation to negotiate, not an offer.[78]

© Ewan McKendrick 2012
By permission of Oxford University Press

[78] McKendrick, above n 12, extract from pp 50–51.

Text 2: *Agency Agreement*

6. Commission and payments

General

6.1   The Principal shall (subject to the Agent performing its obligations under this Agreement) pay to the Agent a commission equal to the following percentages of the Net Price of all Products for which the Agent concludes a sale contract on behalf of the Principal pursuant to and during the term of this Agreement:

(a) if the Net Price in a Year is less than £[   ], [   ]%;

(b) on the amount of the Net Price between £[   ] and £[   ], [   ]%;

(c) on any excess in the amount of the Net Price over £[   ], [   ]%.

6.2   Commission shall become due to the Agent as soon as and to the extent that the Principal receives for immediate value from or on behalf of the customer the price in respect of the sale of the relevant Products. Where the relevant sale contract provides for payment of the price by instalments, a proportionate part of the commission shall become due to the Agent as soon as such instalments are received for immediate value by the Principal, that proportion being equivalent to the proportion which such instalments bear to the total contract price.

6.3   The Principal shall pay the Agent the commission due under this Agreement by no later than the end of the calendar month following the Quarter in which it became due.

6.4   If any dispute arises as to the amount of commission payable by the Principal to the Agent, the same shall be referred to the Principal's auditors for settlement and their certificate shall be final and binding on both parties.

Agency Agreement used courtesy of Withers LLP[79]

© Withers LLP

Text 3: *Mainstream Properties Ltd v Young*[80]

HOUSE OF LORDS [2007] UKHL 21
Mainstream Properties Limited v Young and others and another
LORD HOFFMANN: …   66. … Mainstream was a development company owned and controlled by Mr Moriarty. He engaged Mr Young as a working director and Mr Broad

---

[79] <http://www.withersworldwide.com>.

[80] *Mainstream Properties Limited v Young and others and another* [2007] UKHL 21.

as a manager and left the business to them. In 2000 they diverted the purchase of development land at Findern in Derbyshire to a joint venture consisting of themselves and the respondent Mr De Winter, who financed the project. Judge Norris QC, in a detailed and lucid judgment, found that this was a breach of their contractual and fiduciary duties to obtain the property for Mainstream.

67. There is no challenge to these findings but the question in this appeal is whether Mr De Winter is liable in tort for inducing Mr Young and Mr Broad to break their contracts. The cause of action is therefore the original *Lumley v Gye* tort, based on accessory liability.[81] The judge found that Mr Young and Mr Broad could not have acquired the property without Mr De Winter's financial assistance. His participation was therefore causative. He also knew that they were employed by Mainstream and that there was an obvious potential conflict between their duties to Mainstream and their participation in the joint venture. But the judge found that Mr De Winter was a cautious man who had raised the question of conflict of interest with Mr Young and Mr Broad and had received an assurance that there was no conflict because Mainstream had been offered the site but refused it. This was untrue but Mr Winter genuinely believed it. ...

68. On these findings of fact the judge found that Mr De Winter did not intend to procure a breach of the contracts of employment or otherwise interfere with their performance. The claim against him was therefore dismissed. The finding was upheld by the Court of Appeal (Sedley and Arden LJJ and Aikens J).

69. In my opinion this case comes squarely within *British Industrial Plastics Ltd v Ferguson* [1940] 1 All ER 479. On the finding of the judge, Mr De Winter honestly believed that assisting Mr Young and Mr Broad with the joint venture would not involve them in the commission of breaches of contract.

Read the following comment on the three texts in Task 5 only after you have completed the task, including discussion and comparison.

---

[81] *A Dictionary of Law*, above n 24, p 7: 'If a stranger knowingly and dishonestly assists a trustee in a breach of trust he will be liable as an accessory (*Royal Brunei Airlines Sdn Bhd v Tan*) [1995] 2 AC 378 (PC)).' *Accessory liability* as a tort is analagous to this and was laid down in the case of *Lumley v Gye* (1853) 2 El & Bl 216.

Comment on Task 5 The elements of a contract—reading and analysis

— Text 1 *Contract Law. Text, Cases and Materials*

The extract is from a textbook on the law of contract, by Ewan McKendrick, and illustrates the difficulty of analysing *the intention of the parties* and the moment of *formation of contract* in a common form of human transaction: a couple going for a meal in a restaurant.

The author raises, but does not answer, a series of questions relating to the aspects of intention, and, specifically, *offer and acceptance*. He explains that, in the common law system, the courts must devise '*a presumptive rule*' (ie a rule regarding a legal *presumption*, such as the presumption that parties intend commercial agreements to be binding) in relation to a dispute before them; this provides certainty for future cases, given the operation of the doctrine of binding precedent in later similar cases.

However, the courts can only form rules in the process of resolving disputes that come before them, and there is, in fact, no precedent ('no authority') on the contractual status of a menu. Legal scholars tend to think it is not a contractual offer but only *an invitation to treat*. What is the position in your legal system?

— Text 2 *Agency Agreement*

This clause from an agency contract illustrates the phenomenon of *agreement between the parties*, and sets out certain rights and duties, part of *the terms of the contract*. Also relevant in this clause is the element of *consideration*. Clause 6 stipulates the agent's *commission* for its services, and this is clearly *consideration* for its promises to perform its duties under the contract. The commission represents both *a benefit to the promisor* (in another clause, the agent promises to promote and negotiate the sale of the principal's products in the territory) and *a detriment to the promisee* (the principal must bear the cost of paying the agent's commission). The clause establishes the *amount of payment due* in subclause 6.1, expressed as a graded percentage of the net price of the products. The time when the commission becomes due to the agent is stipulated in subclause 6.2, and the time of payment to the agent in subclause 6.3. The method of resolution of a dispute concerning the amount of commission payable is regulated by subclause 6.4: the principal's *auditors* will give a binding decision. (See 11.4, below, for further analysis of commercial agreements.)

— Text 3 *Mainstream Properties Ltd v Young*[82]

This text illustrates first *the formation of a contract* and then its *breach*. The facts of the case in the appeal before the House of Lords involve a contract of employment between a company (Mainstream) and its working director (Mr Young) and manager (Mr Broad). But Mr Young and Mr Broad set up a joint venture with a third party (Mr De Winter) and carried on business activities *incompatible with their contractual duties*, by 'diverting the purchase of development land' away from Mainstream. Mr De Winter is the respondent in this appeal and Mainstream Properties Ltd is the appellant (and also the claimant in the action). Has Mr De Winter committed *the tort of inducing* Mr Young and Mr Broad *to break their contracts*?

At first instance, the claim was dismissed, because, on the facts, Mr De Winter '*did not intend to procure a breach of the contracts of employment*' or interfere with the two employees' performance of their contractual duties. The Court of Appeal *upheld* (confirmed) that decision. The House of Lords also upheld the decision, because Mr De Winter had behaved cautiously and had 'raised the question of conflict of interest' with Mr Broad and Mr Young. They had been dishonest, because they told Mr De Winter that Mainstream had refused the offer to buy the land ([67]). The Law Lords dismissed the appeal against Mr De Winter (this is not in the extract of text provided). Note the use of judicial precedent in Lord Hoffman's reasoning. This case is one of the three appeals considered together by the House of Lords in the field of claims in tort for economic loss caused by intentional acts; another is *Douglas v Hello!*, examined in 11.1.2 above.

---

[82] *Mainstream Properties Limited v Young and others and another*, above n 80.

SECTION THREE

11.4 Commercial Agreements—Advanced

Section Three of this chapter is devoted to commercial contracts. We examine the textual structure, language and legal effects of a commercial agreement. A document such as the *Distributorship Agreement*, extracts of which are examined in 11.4.3 below, is typical of an international business transaction. It was drafted by English solicitors.[83]

The word *contract* is used in this part of the chapter to denote the written document embodying the parties' agreement, and usually called, on the face of the document: *Agreement*.

11.4.1 The Structure of a Typical Commercial Agreement

The typical structure of a commercial contract is as follows.[84] An example text is examined in Task 6, 11.4.3 below.

Commencement

The *commencement* is the formal opening of the contract. It may state the nature of the agreement (eg *Agency*, *Franchise*, etc), and will always give the date on which the agreement is entered into and the identity of the parties.

Recitals

The commencement may be followed by *recitals* (or *preambles*); these paragraphs provide background information against which the agreement should be read. The recitals may state the purposes for which an agreement is made. Each recital is traditionally introduced by the adverb '*Whereas*'.

---

[83] Withers LLP are gratefully acknowledged.
[84] AGJ Berg (1991), *Drafting Commercial Agreements*, London: Butterworths, was consulted extensively in writing 11.4.1.

Operative part

The operative part of the agreement is the main body of the document. It may be introduced by a conventional phrase, such as:

NOW IT IS HEREBY AGREED as follows:–

It contains provisions agreed by the parties, creating rights and duties for each of them; the provisions are organised in a sequence of *clauses*, divided according to subject matter. Each clause covers a single aspect of the agreement, and may have a descriptive heading (e.g. 'Clause 5. Orders, terms of sale and payments'). For more on clauses, see 11.4.2 below.

The contract may contain an index page at the beginning, listing the themes of each clause and relative page numbers in the document, for ease of reference.

Definitions. The first operative clause is often a *definitions clause*, defining terms which are fundamental to the agreement, and providing rules for interpreting it. The definitions may be absolute, or the definitions clause may specify: 'In this Agreement, *unless the context otherwise requires ...*' to indicate that the particular term may sometimes have a different meaning in the contract, if the context clearly makes that necessary.

Conditions precedent. A contract may contain a clause stipulating a *condition* or *conditions precedent.*[85] The contract, or specified parts of it, will become operative only if the condition is fulfilled. For example, the contract may only come into force provided that certain financial requirements are met.

Other operative provisions. We come to the main body of the contract, stipulating the parties' *rights and duties*. Clauses often include: *representations* (pre-contractual statements, for example concerning the quality of the products) and *warranties*, possibly with a provision specifying and limiting *damages*, in case of breach.[86]

The boiler-plate. This name is given to the final clauses of the contract, typically covering matters such as governing law and jurisdiction, payment of legal fees in connection with the contract, *assignment* of rights (the transfer of rights under the contract to another) and so on.

Closing formula. The final operative clause is followed by a conventional formula, such as the following:

AS WITNESS the hands of the duly authorised representatives of the parties to the Agreement the day and year first before written.

---

[85] Discussed in 11.2.2 above.
[86] See 11.2.2 above for *representations* and *warranties*.

Schedules

The *Schedules*, also called *Annexes*, *Appendices* or *Exhibits*, set out matters of detail, fundamental to the contract, e.g. details of property being conveyed, of products, of intellectual property rights and so on.

Signatures

Traditional English practice is to put the signatures at the end of the contract, after the Schedules.[87]

11.4.2 Clauses and Subclauses: Organisation and Interrelation

When drafting a contract, it is advisable to deal with each particular topic or aspect of the agreement in a separate clause. Some aspects can be expressed briefly in two or three lines, but most are more complex, so that it is necessary to *subdivide the clause*: this means breaking the clause down in a systematic, logical way, into simple component parts called *subclauses* (also written *sub-clauses*).

An example of a brief clause, expressed in a single sentence, without the use of subclauses, is the following, from the Distributorship Agreement examined below.

19 Freedom to contract

The parties declare that they each have the right, power and authority and have taken all action necessary to execute and deliver, and to exercise their rights and perform their obligations under this Agreement.

Note that this clause is only *relatively* simple, compared with more complex clauses. Observe the number of different points each party declares in only three lines. Notice the collocations *'exercise their rights'* and *'perform their obligations'*; compare this last phrase with the verb *'execute'*, meaning *to bring the contract into force*.[88]

The heading of this clause, 'Freedom to contract', refers to each party's capability of entering into and performing the contract; it is not to be confused with the doctrine of *freedom of contract*, the freedom of parties to decide the terms of their contract themselves.

For an example of the subdivision of elements in a clause into subclauses, see Clause 3 in the Distributorship Agreement at 11.4.3 below; and for further subdivision of the subclauses into paragraphs, see Clause 1.

It is interesting to note that each clause in the contract is a self-contained unit; there is generally little interrelation between clauses. Where cross-reference is necessary in one clause to another, the indication is always very clear and precise.

---

[87] Although Berg notes that in American practice the signatures may go before the Schedules: Berg, above n 84, p 4.

[88] Related noun *execution*. Compare: *performance* or *fulfilment* of the contract, where the parties do what they have agreed to do: they *perform* or *fulfil* the contract.

Example: The Principal shall be entitled to terminate this Agreement should the Agent not fulfil its duties under clauses 1.2 (Agency), 2.2 (Orders), ...

In the example above, '*should* the Agent not fulfil' means 'if the Agent does not fulfil' or 'if the Agent fails to fulfil'.

Where cross-references are needed, the precise legal status of one clause or sub-clause in relation to the other must be made explicit. Observe different formulae for doing this in the following examples. In each case, which clause or subclause has priority?

— *Subject to subclause 4, the Agent shall be entitled to an indemnity as a result of the termination of this Agreement.*

Subclause 4 contains a condition qualifying the Agent's right to receive an indemnity for termination.

— *... without prejudice to the general rules of the governing law*

The general rules of the governing law have priority, they remain effective.

— *The Principal shall notwithstanding anything to the contrary in this Agreement, ... enable the Agent to conduct the marketing of the Products in an orderly manner.*

This provision takes priority over any conflicting provision in the contract.

11.4.3 Examining a Commercial Agreement: Content, Language and Effects

In this section, you will carry out two tasks based on long segments from a commercial contract. In Task 6, you will examine extracts from the entire document, to gain a general overview of the contract and understand the structure, organisation and content of the text. In Task 7, you will study the contract in detail, clause by clause, observing the language, content and legal effects of each contractual clause.

Task 6 Examining a contract: general overview
In this task, examine the entire text on the following pages, to understand the textual organisation and general subject matter of the parts of the contract. Do not try to understand the text in detail, or read every word.

As you work, consider what you have learnt about commercial agreements in 11.4.1 and 11.4.2, above:

1. Identify the following parts of the contract and clearly mark them on the text: *the commencement, the recitals, the operative part, any schedules, the parties' signatures.*
2. What do you learn about the Agreement from the commencement and recitals?

3.   Read each clause once for a general overview of its subject matter. What is the subject of each clause?
     Example: Clause 24 provides for the parties' choice of governing law and jurisdiction. It defines which set of legal rules will govern the contract and its interpretation, and which courts will have power to adjudicate, in case of dispute.

Task 7 Examining a contract: clause by clause
In this task, examine specific parts of the contract in detail, in order to answer the following questions. During this activity, use a general or business English dictionary as necessary, monolingual or bilingual.

To understand each clause more easily, make use of its organisation into subclauses and paragraphs. Focus on both meaning and language and identify useful terms and phrases to add to your personal terminology system.

In the questions that follow: D = distributor; S = supplier:

Clause 1 Definitions and interpretation
— What is the purpose of this clause?
— What do you think is the rationale of dividing it into subclauses 1.1 and 1.2?
— Comment on the meaning of 'person' in this contract (subclause 1.2).

Clause 2 Appointment
— Which part of this clause creates the distributorship?
— What duty does the D accept, and what limitation (subclause 2.2)?
— What restriction is imposed on the D and what is the purpose of subclause 2.3?

Clause 3 Distributor's undertakings
— What is the D's first duty under subclause 3.1?
— Who must the D employ and why (subclause 3.2)?
— Under subclause 3.3, what reports and information must the D regularly submit to the S? Can the S request any other information?
— In what circumstances must the D inform the S of a change in its business organisation (subclause 3.5)?

Clause 4 Supply of products
— What mutual promises do the parties make?

Clause 5 Supplier's undertakings
— Examining each subclause, what are the S's duties under clause 5?

DISTRIBUTORSHIP AGREEMENT

[selected clauses, sub-clauses and paragraphs]

DATE   **20 [   ]**

PARTIES

(1) [   ] a company incorporated under the laws of England and
Wales with registered no. [   ] whose registered office is at
[   ] (the **'Supplier'**); and

(2) [   ] a company incorporated in [   ] with registered no.
[   ] whose registered office is at [   ]
(the **'Distributor'**).

RECITALS

The Supplier wishes to appoint the Distributor as its exclusive distributor for
the promotion and sale of *[description of products]* within the Territory, as
defined below.

OPERATIVE PROVISIONS

1. **Definitions and interpretation**

    1.1 In this Agreement including the recitals, the following words and
    expressions shall have the following meanings:

'Commencement Date'	the [ ] day of [ ] 20[ ];
'Products'	the products of the type and specification manufactured and packed under the Trade Marks and listed in Schedule 1;
'Territory'	the areas specified in Schedule 2;
'Trade Marks'	the trade mark registration and applications identified in Schedule 3.

    1.2 In this Agreement:
    (a) any reference to a recital, clause, sub-clause or schedule is to a
    recital, clause, sub-clause or schedule (as the case may be) of
    or to this Agreement;
    (b) the recitals and the headings in this document are inserted
    for convenience only and shall not affect the construction or
    interpretation of this Agreement;
    (c) use of the singular includes the plural and vice versa;
    (d) any reference to a 'person' includes a natural person, firm,
    partnership, company, corporation, association, organisation,
    institution, foundation, trust or agency (in each case whether
    or not having separate legal personality);
    (f) any reference to a party is to a party to this Agreement.

2. Appointment

2.1 The Supplier hereby appoints the Distributor as its exclusive distributor to import and distribute the Products in the Territory on the terms of this Agreement.

2.2 The Distributor shall purchase the Products only from the Supplier, and shall not distribute or manufacture during the duration of this Agreement any goods which compete with the Products.

2.3 The Distributor shall refrain outside the Territory from seeking customers for the Products, and refrain outside the Territory from establishing any branch or maintaining any distribution depot for the sale of the Products.

3. Distributor's undertakings

The Distributor undertakes and agrees with the Supplier at all times during the term of this Agreement:

3.1 to use its best endeavours to promote the distribution and sale of the Products in the Territory;

3.2 to employ a sufficient number of suitably qualified personnel to ensure the proper fulfilment of the Distributor's obligations under this Agreement;

3.3 to submit written reports at regular intervals to the Supplier showing details of sales, service stock, outstanding customer orders and orders placed by the Distributor with the Supplier still outstanding and any other information relating to the performance of its obligations under this Agreement the Supplier may reasonably require from time to time;

3.4 to keep full and proper books of account and records showing clearly all enquiries, quotations, transactions and proceedings relating to the Products;

3.5 to inform the Supplier immediately of any changes in ownership or control of the Distributor and of any change in its organisation or method of doing business which might affect the performance of the Distributor's duties in this Agreement.

4. Supply of products

4.1 The Supplier undertakes to use its best endeavours to meet all orders for the Products forwarded to the Supplier by the Distributor in accordance with the Supplier's terms of delivery and the Distributor agrees to purchase the Products for its own account for resale pursuant to this Agreement.

5. Supplier's undertakings

The Supplier undertakes:

5.1 to supply the Products only to the Distributor for resale in the Territory and not to supply the Products to users in the Territory.

5.2 to provide any information and support as may reasonably be requested by the Distributor to enable it properly and efficiently to discharge its duties under this Agreement;

5.3 to approve or reject any promotional information or material submitted by the Distributor within 28 days of receipt;

5.4 subject to availability, to supply the spare parts requested by the Distributor which are required to enable it to fulfil its repair and service obligations under this Agreement.

24. Governing law and jurisdiction

This Agreement shall be governed by and construed in accordance with English law and each party hereby irrevocably submits to the jurisdiction of the English Courts.

As Witness the hands of the duly authorised representatives of the parties hereto the day and year first above written.

Schedule 1

(The Products)

[List products]   [*Other schedules follow*]

Signed by   )

for and on behalf of   )

[   ]   )

Signed by   )

for and on behalf of   )

[   ]   )

Distribution Agreement used courtesy of Withers LLP © Withers LLP

Key and comment to Task 6 Examining a contract: general overview

1. The commencement is at the beginning of the contract, above the recitals:
    it identifies the parties and gives the date of signature. There is a single
    recital, clearly marked. The operative part begins with clause 1 and ends
    with clause 24. It is followed by the conventional phrase 'As Witness ...',
    the only instance of archaic English in this document, in other respects
    a model of plain English.[89] The phrase introduces the signatures placed
    by '*duly authorised*' representatives of the parties '*for and on behalf of*' the
    parties themselves; the schedules follow, and finally the signatures.

2. From the commencement, we learn the identity of the two contracting
    parties: the distributor and the supplier, and where each party has its
    registered office, since each party is a legal person. The supplier is 'a com-
    pany incorporated in England and Wales'; the distributor is a company
    incorporated, presumably, in another jurisdiction.[90] The single recital
    provides the rationale for the agreement: the supplier wants to appoint
    the distributor as an exclusive distributor, to promote and sell certain
    products in a defined territory.

3. Clause 1 gives definitions, necessary for the meaning and construction of
    the contract. Clause 2 creates the distributorship relationship between the
    parties and sets out some fundamental terms of the contract. The duties
    of the distributor are established by clause 3, and the duties of the supplier
    by clause 5; '*undertakings*' are *obligations assumed* by a party. Clause 4 regu-
    lates *supply* of the products, imposing relative obligations on each party.

Key and comment to Task 7 Examining a contract: clause by clause

Clause 1 Definitions and interpretation
The purpose of the clause is clearly and precisely to define the meaning
of terms used with specific reference in the contract (subclause 1.1), and
to provide rules for the interpretation and construction of the Agreement
(subclause 1.2).

—   *Defined terms* can be recognised every time they occur in the text by the
    use of an initial capital letter (Products, Territory, etc—see subclause
    1.1); this indicates that the products, territory, etc are the precise prod-
    ucts, territory, etc as defined in the contract itself. For some defined
    terms, all or part of the definition is to be found in the Schedules (see,
    e.g., *Trade Marks*). The terms '*Supplier*' and '*Distributor*' also become
    defined terms of the contract. Observe the drafting technique used.

---

[89] The Plain English Movement was discussed in 2.1 above.
[90] For *incorporation*, see 11.2.3 above.

— Subclause 1.2 provides specific parameters for construing the text of the Agreement, in order to avoid any possible confusion or misinterpretation of the parties' intentions. For example:

— by paragraph (a), the words 'recital, clause, etc' refer to these same elements in the Agreement itself; similarly, by paragraph (f), a 'party' is a contracting party;

— under paragraph (b), the recitals and clause headings (e.g. '2. Appointment') do not influence the '*construction or interpretation*' of the Agreement but are simply for convenience;

— in paragraph (d), a 'person' is defined very widely, to include natural and juristic persons, but also a range of businesses, associations and entities (a *firm, partnership, foundation, trust,* etc) that may or may not have legal personality.

Clause 2 Appointment

— Subclause 2.1 creates the distributorship, stipulating that it is *exclusive*, and defining its purpose: '*to import and distribute* the Products in the Territory', as regulated by the terms of this contract.[91]

— Subclause 2.2 places a duty on the distributor *to purchase* (buy) the products only from the supplier, and from no other competitor. The limitation, which is effective for the duration of the contract, is not to distribute or *manufacture* (produce) '*any goods which compete with the Products*'.

— Subclause 2.3 clearly places a territorial limit on the distributor's activity in relation to the products. The distributor *must not seek customers* (try to find or obtain clients), establish a *branch* or maintain a distribution *depot* for the sale of the products outside the defined territory.

Comment. Notice the two verb tenses used to produce legal effects in this clause: 'The Supplier hereby *appoints* …' (present simple); and 'The Distributor *shall purchase* the Products …'. (modal verb *shall* + infinitive).

Clause 3 Distributor's undertakings

— In subclause 3.1, the distributor's first duty reflects the basic reason for the contract, stated in the recital: 'to promote the distribution and sale of the Products in the Territory'. It also sets the standard the distributor must meet: it must *use its best endeavours* in doing so (see comment to clause 4, below).

— Under subclause 3.2, the distributor must employ sufficient qualified staff ('*personnel*') to '*ensure*' (guarantee) the '*proper fulfilment*' (correct performance) of its obligations.

---

[91] See 11.2.2 for the terms of a contract.

— Under subclause 3.3, the distributor must regularly submit to the supplier a range of reports, with details of sales, service stock, orders from customers ('*customer orders*') that have not yet been satisfied (they are '*outstanding*') and similar orders placed by the distributor with the supplier. The supplier may request other information, and the distributor must give it, if the request is reasonable and relates to performance of the distributor's obligations under the contract; '*from time to time*' means at any time.

— According to subclause 3.5, the distributor must inform the supplier of a change in its business organisation, if the change '*might affect* the performance of the distributor's duties' in the agreement, that is, if the change *could have an impact* on the distributor's performance of its duties under the contract.

Comment. Observe from the punctuation and organisation of this clause that each individual subclause must be read in the light of and is introduced by the opening phrase: 'The Distributor *undertakes and agrees* with the Supplier *at all times during the term of this Agreement*: 3.1 ... ; 3.2 ... ; ... etc. This clause sets out the *duties assumed* by the Distributor (the D's '*undertakings*'), in agreement with the Supplier; these duties are effective for the *entire duration* (a different use of the word '*term*') of the agreement.

Clause 4 Supply of products
The supplier promises *to meet all orders forwarded* by the distributor in the specified manner; the distributor promises to buy the products for *resale* '*pursuant to* this Agreement' (on the basis of the agreement).

Comment. The supplier's obligation under clause 4 is not absolute and unqualified: the supplier undertakes *to use its best endeavours* to meet the orders, the same standard agreed by the distributor in subclause 3.1 for promoting the distribution and sale of the products. Where the subject matter of an obligation is outside the full control of the person who undertakes it (it may also depend on external factors, including other people's actions), a variety of phrases can be inserted in the term of the contract, to define an agreed standard.

In descending order, such phrases may be classified as follows; note the position of *best endeavours* in this list:

— A shall do his utmost [the maximum effort]
— A shall use his best endeavours
— A shall use due diligence
— A shall take all reasonable steps
— A shall use reasonable endeavours.[92]

---

[92] Berg, above n 84, p 99.

Where a dispute arises about whether a party has fulfilled a contractual obligation according to the agreed standard, the courts will decide, in the circumstances of the case, also taking into account commercial practice. For example, in one case, it was held

> that an obligation to use 'best endeavours' to promote the sales of a product meant a duty to do what could reasonably be done in the circumstances; the standard of reasonableness was that of 'a reasonable and prudent board of directors acting properly in the interests of their company and applying their minds to their contractual obligations to exploit the inventions'. [93]

In a later case, it seems that a higher standard was set: that of taking all the steps in the party's power 'capable of producing the desired result ... being steps which a prudent, determined and reasonable owner, acting in his own interests and desiring to achieve that result, would take'.[94]

This illustrates how the meaning of terms in a contract may be determined by reference to judicial precedent.

Clause 5 Supplier's undertakings
— Under subclause 5.1, the supplier must not supply the products directly to users in the territory, but must supply them to the distributor for resale in the territory.
— The obligation in subclause 5.2 is to provide '*any* information and support *as may reasonably be requested*'. The purpose of this supporting role is '*to enable* the Distributor *to discharge its duties*' under the contract, that is, to perform its side of the contract 'properly and efficiently'.
— By subclause 5.3, the supplier has 28 days, after receiving promotional information or material from the distributor, to approve or reject it.
— As in 5.2, the supplier's obligation in subclause 5.4 (to supply *spare parts* as requested) is intended to ensure that the distributor is able to fulfil its '*repair and service obligations*'.

On the basis of the selections you have read from this Distributorship Agreement, which would you say is the dominant party in the contractual relationship? Justify your answer by reference to the Agreement.

[93] *Ibid*, p 100, citing Sellers J, in *Terrell v Mabie Todd & Co* [1952] 2 TLR 574.
[94] *Ibid*, p 100, citing Buckley LJ in *IBM United Kingdom Ltd v Rockware Glass Ltd* [1980] FSR 335.

Ideas for Further Reading

Lord Denning (1979), *The Discipline of Law*, London: Butterworths. Chapter 4, 'The construction of contracts' (pp 32–53) provides a fascinating, case-by-case account of the importance and difficulties of interpreting contracts, in cases where the eminent judge played a part.

Haigh, Rupert (2004), *Legal English*, London: Cavendish Ltd. To supplement the work done in Section Three, above, the final part of Haigh's book, 'Contractual Legal English' is a very useful resource, with many examples and helpful explanation of contractual terms and clauses. See, for example: '3 Structure of a Contract' (pp 171–73); 'Content of a Contract' (pp 174–94); '5 Specimen Contract & Analysis' (pp 195–205).

McKendrick, Ewan (2012), *Contract Law: Text, Cases, and Materials*, 5th edn, Oxford: Oxford University Press. This is the textbook most frequently cited in this chapter. It contains a complete guide to the English law of contract in a single volume, with a balance of 40 per cent text to 60 per cent cases and materials. The author gives clear explanations and authoritative analyses of the law, with invaluable extracts from cases and materials to develop essential case-reading skills for students. Closely connected to the work done in this chapter are: Chapter 3, 'Offer and Acceptance' (pp 44–123) and Chapter 8, 'The Terms of the Contract' (pp 293–312).

Riley, Alison (1991), *English for Law*, Harlow: Pearson Education Ltd. The interesting old precedent of *Carlill v Carbolic Smoke Ball Co*, in the field of offer and acceptance, is examined in depth in Unit 7, 'Private Law—Contract' (pp 116–32), text, reading comprehension and vocabulary exercises in the branch of contract law. Unit 8, 'Revision and Consolidation' (pp 133–42) provides further reading and vocabulary activities in the field of contract law.

Zweigert, Konrad and Kötz, Hein (1998), *An Introduction to Comparative Law*, 3rd edn (tr Weir, Tony), Oxford: Clarendon Press. Chapter 26, 'Offer and Acceptance' (pp 356–64) provides interesting comparative analysis of when the contract is formed in common law and civil law systems.

Chapter 12

LEGAL GRAMMAR

Adverbial Clauses and Nominal Structures

Adverbial forms, meaning, and position – Adverbs and adverb phrases – Adverbial clauses – Nominal structures

So unintelligible is the phraseology of some statutes that suggestions have been made that draftsmen, like the Delphic Oracle, sometimes aim deliberately at obscurity …

Carleton K Allen, author of *Law in the Making* (1964)

Despite the complexity of legal discourse—lengthy sentences with multiple patterns of coordination and subordination—the grammatical organisation still follows Standard English sentence structure. One of the ways that this is accomplished is through the use of adverbials. Adverbials have syntactic *mobility*, meaning that they can be placed in various positions in a sentence and are still syntactically acceptable. Legal draftsmen take advantage of this to achieve precision and clarity. This chapter describes how adverbials function in legal discourse.

Another distinct feature of a legal text is that it is highly nominal.[1] For example, in legislative provisions, the qualifications (which dictate the conditions of a provision) immediately follow the word they modify in order to avoid any possible misinterpretation. These additions often create syntactic discontinuity.[2] Sentences taken from a variety of legal texts will illustrate this characteristic in this chapter.

The positioning of adverbials and nominalisations in a sentence is deliberate and calculated. Draftsmen are constantly trying to be as clear and unambiguous as possible, and the use of adverbials and nominal expressions allows them to do so.

---

[1] D Crystal and D Davy (1969), 'The Language of Legal Documents', *Investigating English Style*, Harlow: Longman.
[2] VK Bhatia (1993), 'Legal Discourse in Professional Settings', *Analyzing Genre*, London: Longman; C Williams (2007), *Tradition and Change in Legal English: Verbal Constructions in Prescriptive Texts*, Bern: Peter Lang.

12.1 Adverbial Forms, Meaning and Position

Adverbials have an important role in sentence structure because they provide a link between one part of a text and another. The term *adverbial* refers to any *structure* that functions as a *modifier of a verb* in an independent clause or a whole sentence. By *structure* we mean the way words, phrases and clauses are organised to form larger units.

The *modifier* of the verb may be a single word, a phrase, or a clause containing a subject and a verb. The *form* of modification includes not only adverbs, but also prepositional phrases, nominal phrases and adverbial clauses. Their *forms* remain distinct, even though they may have the same meaning. For example:

> *I did it with my hand. (prepositional phrase)*
> *I did it manually. (adverb)*

Adverbials also have a wide range of *meanings*. If you have problems distinguishing an adverb from another part of speech, ask yourself these questions: 'How?', 'How often?', 'When?', 'Where?' or 'Why?'. Your answer should be the word.

The position of adverbial elements in the sentence structure is flexible: at the beginning, medial or at the end. For example:

> <u>Last year,</u> *national provisions on copyright and related rights varied* <u>considerably</u> <u>from one Member State to the other.</u>

> *National provisions on copyright and related rights* <u>considerably</u> *varied* <u>from one Member State to the other</u> <u>last year.</u>

Most adverbials are optional,[3] which means that if you eliminated them, the sentence would still retain its meaning. For example, the sentence above would become:

> *National provisions on copyright and related rights varied.*

It is also quite common for there to be multiple occurrences of adverbial elements (AE) within a single sentence, such as:

> *Next month (AE1) in Rome (AE2) the proposal by the Council will* *probably (AE3)* be brought *before a national committee for approval (AE4).*

12.2 Adverbs and Adverb Phrases

As a clause element, a simple adverb or adverb phrase provides more information to the verb phrase that they modify. For example:

> A Member of the United Nations which has *persistently* violated the Principles contained in the present Charter may be expelled from the Organization by the General Assembly *upon the recommendation of the Security Council.*[4]

---

[3] However, in obligatory adverbials, the adverbial has to be present in order to complete the sentence, e.g.: 'The witness for the prosecution behaved *inappropriately*.' Without *inappropriately*, the sentence is grammatically incomplete.

[4] Charter of the United Nations (adopted 26 June 1945, entered into force 24 October 1945), Art 6.

Observe the following sentences (the adverbs[5] are in *italics*):

1) The Act was ratified *yesterday.*
     Yesterday answers the question 'When?'

2) Protocols to the Convention are added *frequently.*
     Frequently answers the question 'How often?'

3) The defendant *consistently* refused to answer the prosecutor's question.
     Consistently answers the question 'How?', but also answers 'How often?'
     (meaning 'each time a question was asked')

4) The States Parties shall be advised *accordingly.*
     Accordingly answers two possible questions: 'When?' (at the appropriate
     time), as well as 'How?' (in the appropriate way)

12.2.1 Prepositional Phrases

A prepositional phrase can also function as an adverb phrase. For example:

5) The Treaty on European Union was signed *at Maastricht.*

6) The amendment was not ratified *for many reasons.*

The prepositional phrase *at Maastricht* in the first sentence acts as an adverb
modifying the verb *signed.* It answers the question 'Where?'. The prepositional
phrase *for many reasons* in the second sentence acts as an adverb modifying the
verb *was not ratified* and answers the question 'Why?'.

12.2.2 Noun Phrases

Noun phrases can also act as an adverb. For example:

7) Was the Convention signed *last year?*

8) The senators stayed up *all night* discussing the proposal.

12.3 ADVERBIAL CLAUSES

In 12.2 above, we observed that adverbials exist in many different forms: single
adverbs, adverb phrases, prepositional phrases and noun phrases. Adverbials also
exist in clauses which are dependent (subordinate) to the main clause and modify
the verb of the main clause. Remember, as a *clause*, they must have a subject

---

[5] *Linking* adverbials (however, yet, etc) and *stance* adverbials, which express a comment on the part
of the author (fortunately, frankly, etc), will not be discussed in this chapter.

(either explicit or implied) and a predicate. Adverbial clauses occur in four major types: finite, non-finite, *to*-infinitive clauses and verbless clauses. Observe the various syntactic forms in the sentences below (the adverbial clauses are in *italics* and the semantic *meaning* follows in parentheses):

finite clauses, e.g.:

— 9)   *If States do not act,* cases of violence against women will continue.

The adverbial clause *If States do not act* in this sentence (9) acts as an adverbial and modifies the verb phrase *will continue* in the main (independent) clause. It answers the question of 'Under what conditions?'. (condition)

non-finite[6] clauses: *-ed* and *-ing* forms, e.g.:

— 10)   *Concerned about the welfare of children,* the Declaration of the Rights of the Child declared that every child should have the right to a happy childhood. (purpose)

— 11)   *Desiring to make more effective the struggle against torture and other cruel acts,* a new protocol was added to the Convention. (purpose)

The two examples above (11) and (12) were taken from the recitals of two UN Conventions. The subjects are *implied.*

*to***-infinitive clauses**, e.g.:

— 12)   *To solve this problem,* we resorted to mediation. (purpose)

and verbless[7] clauses, e.g.:

— 13)   *Where appropriate,* a third party will be asked to intervene. (condition)

12.3.1   Coordination with and/or

In legal texts, adverbial elements are often coordinated with *and* or *or.* For example:

Recognising the need to propose a new amendment <u>and</u> *concerned about the continuing discrimination,* an urgent session was planned by the Council.

---

[6] Non-finite forms of a verb do not have tense, person or number (singular or plural).
[7] A 'verbless' clause does not have a verb element.

12.3.2 Adverbial Clauses and Semantic Categories

The basic unit of meaning in a sentence is the subject and predicate (see 6.1). The subject is often a noun phrase, while the predicate consists of a verb phrase and the elements that follow it. Adverbials are part of these elements of sentence structure that follow the verb phrase, although, as mentioned in 12.1 above, adverbials have *mobility* within a sentence structure and may be placed in pre-, mid- or post-positions.[8]

In this section, we focus on the adverbial elements in *clause structure*, and in particular on the *semantic* (meaning) category of *contingency* adverbials, because they are particularly characteristic of legal discourse.

If something is 'contingent', it is dependent on something else. For example, in a legal context, the ratification of a treaty is contingent on its approval at national level (different procedures are used). Contingency adverbials have semantic meanings that are dependent upon one another in a clause. Greenbaum and Quirk[9] go further when they say that 'adverbials can be used to provide a point of reference with respect to which the clause in question derives its truth value'. This truth value is particularly crucial in legal discourse.

12.3.3 Grammar Review—Types of Meaning Expressed by Contingency Adverbials

Table 12.1: Contingency adverbials

Types of clause	Question posed	Some subordinating conjunctions
cause/reason	Why? What caused this?	because, whereas, since, of
purpose	Why? What was the reason?	in order to, for the purpose of
concession	Why? Contrasts with the main clause	if, although it be, despite, whereas, even if, whether, while, however, even if, although
condition	Under what conditions?	if, should there be, unless, whether, whereas, on condition (that), provided (that), unless, even if, where
result	What happened? Describes the results of the main clause	so that, with the result that, to (+ verb)

---

[8] Objects and object complements are also elements of sentence structure that follow the verb phrase. They will not be discussed in this book.

[9] S Greenbaum and R Quirk (1990), *A Student's Grammar of the English Language*, Harlow: Longman, p 159.

The following extract from a Convention exemplifies the interdependency of the sentence elements to create *meaning*:

> When prisoners of war have not the assistance of a retained chaplain or of a prisoner of war minister of their faith, a minister belonging to the prisoners, or a similar denomination, or in his absence a qualified layman, if such a course is feasible from a confessional point of view, shall be appointed, at the request of the prisoners concerned, to fill this office.[10]

Table 12.2 below displays the preceding extract vertically and illustrates how the 'truth value' of the main clause is dependent on all the conditions described by the adverbials (*in italics*) and post-modifying nominal structures.

Table 12.2: Post-modification of nominal structures

Illustration of the extract in linear form	Grammatical structures
When prisoners of war have not the assistance of a retained chaplain or of a prisoner of war minister of their faith,	contingency adverbial clause of condition
a minister	*minister* is the headword[11] of the noun phrase *a minister* which is the subject of the main clause
belonging to the prisoners,	post-modifying prepositional phrase which modifies[12] the noun phrase *a minister*
or a similar denomination,	post-modification coordination (*or*) with noun phrase
or *in his absence* a qualified layman,	post-modification coordination (*or*) with an adverbial phrase with a conditional meaning (= 'if he is not there')
if such a course is feasible from a confessional point of view,	contingency adverbial clause—condition—qualifies the phrase *or in his absence a qualified layman,*
shall be appointed	verb phrase of obligation
at the request of the prisoners concerned,	adverbial prepositional phrase—temporal (= 'when the prisoners request it')
to fill this office.	adverbial prepositional phrase of purpose

The main clause, its modifiers, and the adverbial clauses are often mutually dependent or contingent. Without these contingencies, which limit and qualify the main clause, the rule would have a universal application.

---

[10] Geneva Convention relative to the Treatment of Prisoners of War (adopted 12 August 1949, entered into force 21 October 1950), 75 UNTS 135, Art 37.

[11] A headword is the subject in the noun phrase, in this case, minister.

[12] If something is modified, it is changed in some way. In legal texts, modification limits or qualifies the word, words or clauses that it modifies.

Task 1 Read, scan and observe—contingency adverbials

Read the following texts. Highlight the contingency adverbial clause and underline the subordinating conjunction. What relationship (cause/reason, purpose, concession, condition, or result) is there between the adverbial clause and the independent clause (see Table 12.1)?

In 1. below the adverbial contingency clause is in *italics* and the subordinating conjunction is <u>underlined</u>. Its relationship with the main clause is indicated in parentheses.

1. … Microsoft submits that the present case must be appraised in the light of Magill and IMS Health, paragraph 107 above, <u>*since*</u> *the refusal must be analysed as a refusal to grant third parties a licence relating to intellectual property rights and* <u>*because*</u>, *accordingly, the contested decision implies compulsory licensing.*[13] (cause/reason)

2. Although one of the Powers in conflict may not be a party to the present Convention, the Powers who are parties thereto shall remain bound by it in their mutual relations.[14]

3. No order may be made by the Lord Chancellor or the Secretary of State under section 1(4), 7(11) or 16(2) unless a draft of the order has been laid before, and approved by, each House of Parliament.[15]

4. Section 11 of the Immigration Act 1971 (c. 77) shall have effect for the purpose of the construction of a reference in this section to entering the United Kingdom.[16]

5. Where, in exceptional circumstances, movements of capital to or from third countries cause, or threaten to cause, serious difficulties for the operation of economic and monetary union, the Council … may take safeguard measures with regard to third countries for a period not exceeding six months if such measures are strictly necessary.[17]

12.4 Nominal Structures

A nominal structure is any word, phrase or clause that elaborates the meaning of the headword (which is a noun). In a post-modifying position, it completes the meaning of the noun and its relation to the other components of the sentence. Post-modification of nominal groups is a distinct feature of legal texts. Observe

---

[13] *Microsoft Corp v Commission of the European Communities* [2007] ECR Page II-03601, in Judgment of the Court of First Instance (Grand Chamber), Case No: T-201/04, para 112.

[14] Geneva Convention relative to the Treatment of Prisoners of War, above n 10, Art 2.

[15] Human Rights Act 1998, s 20(4).

[16] Asylum and Immigration (Treatment of Claimants, etc) Act 2004, s 2(14).

[17] Treaty on European Union [1992] OJ C191, Art 73f.

the nominal structure (underlined) after the noun phrase *The provisions* (the subject) in this treaty:

> *The provisions* <u>of the Conventions in force between the Member States governing areas covered by this Article</u> shall remain in force ...[18]

Inserting qualifications immediately after the noun phrase creates what is called a 'syntactic discontinuity'. Sentences become long and rather unusual yet, as Bhatia says, 'never ambiguous'.[19] Verb phrases may also be discontinuous. Typically, the modal auxiliary is usually *not* separated from the main verb, e.g.:

States Parties *shall promote* the right of self-determination ...

However, for precision and clarity, qualifications are intentionally placed *right after the word they modify*. Observe this discontinuous noun phrase where the qualifications are inserted immediately after the noun phrase *The States Party*, while further qualifications are inserted between the modal auxiliary *shall* and the main verb phrase *submit*:

> *The State Party* in the territory under whose jurisdiction a person alleged to have committed any offence referred to in article 4 is found *shall* in the cases contemplated in article 5, if it does not extradite him, *submit* the case ...[20]

If we observe the qualifications of this treaty displayed vertically below, we can perceive its complexity. Qualifications are inserted where needed, and binomials[21] (coordinated with *or*) further generate this quality of all-inclusiveness. For example:

For the purposes of this Convention,
the term 'torture' means any act by which
severe *pain or* suffering,
whether physical *or* mental,
is intentionally inflicted on a person for such purposes as obtaining from
him *or* a third person
information *or* a confession,
punishing him for an act
he *or* a third person
has committed *or* is suspected of having committed,
or intimidating *or* coercing
him *or* a third person,
or for any reason based on discrimination of any kind,
when such pain *or* suffering is inflicted
by *or* at
the instigation of *or* with

---

[18] *Ibid*, Art 100c.
[19] Bhatia, above n 2, p 112.
[20] TEU, above n 17, Art 7(1).
[21] The linking word is [*or*]. See 2.6.3 for further explanations of binomial or multinomial expressions.

the consent or acquiescence
of a public official *or* other person
acting in an official capacity.

As Bhatia[22] suggests, these discontinuities are unavoidable since the qualifications interact with the main clauses 'answering a number of questions that can be legitimately asked in context'.

KEY AND COMMENTARY

Key

Task 1 Read, scan and observe—contingency adverbials
The contingency adverbial clauses are in in italics with subordinating conjunctions underlined. Its relationship with the main clause is in parentheses.

2. _Although_ *one of the Powers in conflict may not be a party to the present Convention,* (condition)
3. _unless_ *a draft of the order has been laid before, and approved by, each House of Parliament.* (condition)
4. _for the purpose of_ *the construction of a reference in this section to entering the United Kingdom.* (purpose)
5. _Where,_ *in exceptional circumstances, movements of capital to or from third countries cause, or threaten to cause, serious difficulties for the operation of economic and monetary union,* (condition) ... _if_ *such measures are strictly necessary.* (condition)

Commentary
Legal texts arrange information with the aim of being as clear and precise as possible, even to the point of creating what have been called 'syntactic discontinuities'. In an effort to avoid ambiguity and to be all-inclusive, complex coordinate and subordinate clauses rearrange sentence patterns to suit these needs. Elaborate binomial and multinomial expressions, noun phrases and adverbials, often placed in a post-modifying position, dictate the conditions or qualifications of a body of rules. Rearranging sentence structure allows draftsmen to render legal documents precise and all-inclusive, thus limiting the possibility of misinterpretation in a court of law.

---

[22] VK Bhatia (2003), *Multilingual and Multicultural Context in Legislation—An International Perspective*, Bern: Peter Lang, p 117.

CONSOLIDATION PART VI – LANGUAGE FOCUS TASKS

Task A – Which One Word or Phrase is Out of Context?

0	offeror	guarantee	acceptance	offeree
1	juristic persons	artificial persons	natural persons	corporations
2	goods	personal property	land	chattels
3	discharge by breach	discharge by performance	discharge by express agreement	discharge by frustration
4	conditions	fundamental terms of a contract	warranty	essential terms
5	breach of warranty	contract remains in force	rescission of contract	payment of damages
6	agreement	terms and conditions	contractual terms	rights and duties
7	consideration	representations	offer and acceptance	intention
8	trademark	limited liability	intellectual property	brand name

Task B – Match the Terms with the Definitions[1]

guarantee	rescission	representations	discharge by express agreement
warranty	breach of warranty	agent	discharge by frustration
legal persons	contractual clauses	conditions	discharge by performance

1	....	a person authorised by the 'Principal' in a contract to act on his/her behalf, such as negotiating a contract with a third party
2	....	essential, fundamental terms of a contract
3	....	annulling or cancelling a contract
4	....	entitles the innocent party to claim damages but does not discharge that party's remaining contractual duties
5	....	a minor term in the contract, non-essential term
6	....	pre-contractual statements
7	....	natural and juristic persons (corporations)
8	....	when parties agree to extinguish remaining obligations
9	....	parties fulfil their obligations and the contract comes to a 'natural end'
10	....	due to some event beyond the control of the contracting parties, it is impossible to fulfill the obligations of the contract
11	....	refers to the specific numbered provisions of written contract
12	....	the act of giving a security against some possible future default or defect

[1] Task B references used to create definitions: BA Garner (1995), *A Dictionary of Modern Legal Usage*, 2nd edn, Oxford: Oxford University Press; *Black's Law Dictionary, Pocket Edition* (1996), BA Garner (ed), Eagan, Minnesota: West Publishing Co; *Oxford Dictionary of Law* (2009), J Law and E Martin (eds), 7th edn, Oxford: Oxford University Press.

Task C – Word Formation

a)   Fill in the spaces below [...] with the appropriate word form.

Words that are not necessarily used in a legal context, or a variant no longer in use, have not been included in the table. The [x] in the table indicates that the form does not exist or that it is uncommon in a legal context. If necessary, read chapter 10 before doing this task or consult a dictionary.

	verb	**noun** (concept)	**noun** (person)	**adjective [adj] adverb [adv]**
1	to enforce	enforcement	enforcer	enforcing/ .... *adj* (2)
2	x	....	x	jurisdictional *adj*
3	....	inference	x	inferable *adj*/ inferentially *adv*
4	to intend	intent/intention	x	intended *adj*/ .... *adj*/ intentionally *adv* (3)
5	to indemnify [often used as a doublet: to indemnify and hold]	indemnity/ .... (2)	indemnitee/ indemnitor [*AmE*]	indemnificatory *adj*
6	to contract	....	x	contractual *adj*/ contracting *adj*/ contractually *adv*
7	to dispute (*to question or challenge*); to be in dispute	dispute	x	disputable *adj*/ disputing *adj* .... *adj* (3)
8	x	....	x	injunctive *adj*

b)   Using the table above, insert the appropriate word in the spaces: verb, noun (concept), noun (person), or adjective:

9   A corporation may enter into ...., own property, employ people and be liable for torts and crimes.

10   The questions formulated by the judge are relevant to decide whether England is the appropriate forum for the ....

11   The court ordered the magazine to ....
     the plaintiffs for the court costs of its defence.

12   The next question before the court is whether the defendant had the
     .... to deceive.

13   It is possible for the courts of more than one legal system to have
     .... over a dispute.

14   My client...from your refusal to negotiate
     that you do not intend to renew the contract with our company.

15   In civil law, rights and claims are ....
     by the courts.

Task D – Prefixes and Suffixes

Fill in the missing suffixes or prefixes to the following words. Identify the appropriate word form.

The [x] indicates that the form does not exist or that it is uncommon in a legal context.

	Prefixes	*adjective*	*noun concept*
1	possibility	x	
2	charge	x	
3	compatible		x
4	moveable		x
	Suffixes		
5	commence	x	
6	void		x
7	intellect		x
8	enforce	(2)	(1)
9	perform	x	
10	transact	x	
11	defame	x	
12	rebut	(2)	(1)

TASK E – COLLOCATION

In the table in a) below, match the verbs 1–7 with the appropriate nouns a–g, and write the matching identifiers in the first column of the table. Think about the meaning of each term or phrase.

a)   Verb–noun

...1f...	1	to seek/to grant	a	impossibility of performance
......	2	to acquire or dispose of	b	a decision
......	3	to enter	c	moveable/immoveable property
......	4	to frustrate by	d	for damages
......	5	to determine	e	into a contract
......	6	to sue	f	an injunction
......	7	to uphold (to confirm)	g	the intention of the parties

In the table in b) below, match words 8–12 with the appropriate words f–j, and write the matching identifiers in the first column of the table. Think about the meaning of each term or phrase.

b)   Words and expressions

...8h...	8	undertakes	f	offer
......	9	conflict	g	appoints
......	10	standard	h	and agrees
......	11	counter	i	of interest
......	12	hereby	j	of best efforts/best endeavors

Consolidation Key to Language Focus Tasks

Consolidation Part I

Task A – Which one word or phrase is out of context?

0   *statute*
1   judgment
2   enact
3   declaration
4   resolution
5   Frankfurt
6   delegated legislation
7   judicial precedent
8   legal codes
9   House of Commons
10 common law
11 minor
12 The Ballad of Reading Gaol

Task B – Match the terms with the definitions

1   High Contracting Parties
2   constitutional convention
3   ratify
4   binding precedent
5   protocols
6   jurisdiction
7   preamble
8   recitals
9   declaration
10 *stare decisis*
11 Royal Prerogative
12 *ratio decidendi*
13 treaty
14 legally binding
15 affidavit

Task C – Word formation

a)   Fill in the spaces with the appropriate word form
1   verb – to obligate
2   adjective – legislative
3   noun (collective) – judiciary (the judicial branch of government)
4   noun (concept) – litigation
5   verb – to approve
6   noun (concept) – ratification
7   verb – to prohibit
8   noun (concept) – enactment

b)   Insert the appropriate word in the spaces below: verb, noun (concept), noun (person) or adjective
9   adjective – judicial
10   noun (concept) – legislation
11   noun (concept) – judgment
12   adjective – enacting
13   verb – prohibited
14   noun (concept) – litigation
15   verb – ratified

Task D – Prefixes and suffixes

Prefixes
0   uncontested
1   illegal (adjective)
2   incompatible (adjective) incompatibility (noun concept)
3   inaccessible (adjective) inaccessibility (noun concept)
4   indirect (adjective)
5   unlawful (adjective)

Suffixes
0   constitutional (adjective) constitutionality (noun concept)
6   implemented (adjective) implementation (noun concept)
7   sovereignty (noun concept)
8   limited (adjective) limitation (noun concept)
9   parliamentary (adjective)
10   violated (adjective) violation (noun concept)

Task E – Collocation

1 d   The Queen in Parliament
2 g   trial by jury

3 h   statutory interpretation
4 i   hereby appoints
5 b   divorce decrees
6 a   legally binding agreement
7 c   collective self-defence
8 j   reach a verdict
9 f   secondary legislation
10 e   producing legal effect

Consolidation Part II

Task A – Which one word or phrase is out of context?

0   *no limitations of legislative competence*
1   written law
2   primary legislation
3   Upper House
4   approve
5   statute

Task B – Match the terms with the definitions

1   exempt
2   come into force
3   invoke
4   outlaw
5   crime
6   contravene
7   fine
8   override

Task C – Word formation

a)   *Fill in the spaces with the appropriate word form*
1   noun (concept) – establishment
2   adjective – constitutional
3   verb – to amend
4   adjective – regulatory
5   adjective – governmental
6   verb – to impeach
7   noun (concept) – implementation

b)   Insert the appropriate word in the spaces below: verb, noun (concept), noun (person), or adjective

8   verb – implement
9   verb – amend
10   adjective – legislative
11   noun (concept) – Regulations
12   adjective – constitutional
13   noun (concept) – establishment
14   adjective – impeachable

Task D – Prefixes and suffixes

1   decentralised (adjective) decentralisation (noun concept)
2   inequity (noun concept)
3   disobedience (noun concept)
4   unelected (adjective)
5   subsection (noun concept)
6   delegated/delegable (adjectives) delegation (noun concept)
7   imprisoned (adjective) imprisonment (noun concept)
8   intended (adjective) intention (noun concept)
9   liability (noun concept)
10   appointed (adjective) appointment (noun concept)

Task E – Collocation

1 d   legislative procedure
2 h   constitutional reforms
3 a   succession to the throne
4 e   Parliamentary sovereignty
5 b   primary legislation
6 i   equitable remedy
7 c   legal rule
8 f   contracting party
9 j   appeal against a conviction
10 g   in accordance with

Task F – Comprehension: True (T) or False (F)?

According to the Scotland Act of 1998 . . .

1   T
2   T
3   F The monarch is the Head of State.
4   T

5   F The UK Parliament still retains sovereignty.
6   T
7   F It can enact legislation only in Scotland.
8   F This is what is referred to as 'reserved matters' in the Act.

Consolidation Part III

Task A – Which one word or phrase is out of context?

0   UDHR
1   European Convention on Human Rights
2   Court of Justice
3   breach
4   implemented
5   observance
6   Great Britain
7   Council of Europe
8   Luxembourg

Task B – Match the terms with the definitions

1   enforce
2   infringe
3   absolute
4   a fair trial
5   rule of law
6   qualified
7   derogation
8   authentic

Task C – Word formation

a)   Fill in the spaces with the appropriate word form
1   adjective – derogable/inderogable (it is usually more common in the negative form)
2   verb - to incorporate
3   noun (concept) – accession
4   noun (concept) – deliberation
5   noun (concept) – draft
6   noun (concept) – entrenchment
7   verb – to validate
8   adjective – persuasive

b)   Insert the appropriate word in the spaces below: verb, noun (concept), noun (person), or adjective

9   verb – incorporate
10   verb – entrenched
11   noun (concept) – accession
12   noun (concept) – deliberations
13   adjective – persuasive
14   noun (concept) – derogations

Task D – Prefixes and suffixes

1   ineffective (adjective)
2   invalidity (noun concept)
3   discrimination (noun concept)
4   accountable (adjective) accountability (noun concept)
5   interference (noun concept)
6   prohibited/prohibitory (adjectives) prohibition (noun concept)
7   controversial (adjective)

Task E – Collocation

1 d   declaration of incompatibility
2 g   persuasive precedent
3 h   to act in accordance with
4 j   remedial order
5 a   discretionary powers
6 b   prescribed by law
7 c   to invoke a right
8 e   entitled to protection
9 f   equally authentic
10 i duly certified

Task F – Comprehension: True (T) or False (F)?

1   F The Charter of the United Nations was established for this reason. The Council of Europe's aim was to achieve a greater unity among its Members, such as human rights, pluralist democracy and the rule of law.
2   T
3   T English and French
4   F
5   T
6   F Only 10 ratifications were needed.
7   T

8   T
9   F Only a Member State of the EU must offer protection.
10   T
11   F It has indirect legal effect.
12   T
13   T

CONSOLIDATION PART IV

Task A – Which one word or phrase is out of context?

0   *violenti non fit injuria*
1   reasonable force
2   convicted
3   murder
4   without intention to kill
5   indictable offences

Task B – Match the terms with the definitions

1   malice aforethought
2   manslaughter
3   coroner
4   *mens rea*
5   voluntary manslaughter
6   recklessness
7   involuntary manslaughter
8   *actus reus*

Task C – Word formation

a)   *Fill in the spaces with the appropriate word form*
1   noun (person) – convict
2   noun (concept) – compliance
3   verb – to acquit
4   noun (concept) – accusation
5   adjective – punishable
6   noun (person) – prosecutor
7   noun (concept) – supervision
8   verb – to indict

b)   *Insert the appropriate word in the spaces below: verb, noun (concept), noun (person), or adjective*
9   noun (concept) – compliance

10   noun (person) – The accused
11   verb – acquitted
12   adjective – punishable
13   adjective – accusatorial
14   noun (concept) – supervision
15   noun (concept – convictions
16   adjective – indicted

Task D – Prefixes and suffixes

1   premeditation (noun concept)
2   unreasonable (adjective)
3   disproportionate (adjective)
4   unintentional (adjective)
5   provocation (noun concept)
6   negligent (adjective)
      negligence (noun concept)
7   mitigated/mitigating (adjectives) mitigation (noun concept)
8   recklessness (noun concept)

Task E – Verb–noun collocation

1 g   to charge with an offence/crime
2 d   to confront and cross-examine the witness
3 a   the judge acts as a gatekeeper in a jury trial
4 h   to be guilty beyond a reasonable doubt
5 c   in compliance with the lawful order of a court
6 i   conviction quashed by the Court of Appeal
7 b   presided over by a judge
8 j   right to a fair trail
9 f   an appeal against conviction
10 e   investigation is carried out by the police

Consolidation Part V

Task A – Which one word or phrase is out of context?

0   *breach*
1   first instance
2   *obiter dictum*
3   common law remedy
4   injuries and loses
5   *force majeure*
6   injunction

Task B – Match the terms with the definitions

1 product liability
2 vindicate
3 action
4 tortfeasor
5 duty of case
6 claimant
7 redress
8 negligence
9 damages
10 trespass
11 battery
12 injunction

Task C – Word formation

a) Fill in the spaces with the appropriate word form
1 noun (concept) – vindication
2 adjective – actionable
3 noun (concept) – contingency
4 adjective – deductive

b) Insert the appropriate word in the spaces below: verb, noun (concept), noun (person), or adjective
7 adjective – contingent
8 adjective – deductive
9 adjective – actionable
10 verb – vindicate

Task D – Prefixes and suffixes

1 insolvency (noun concept)
2 predominant (adjective)
3 obligatory/obligative (adjectives) obligation (noun concept)
4 omissible (adjective) omission (noun concept)
5 compensated/compensatory (adjectives) compensation (noun concept)

Task E – Verb–noun collocation

1 d to grant a remedy to an injured party
2 c to confer a right
3 e to be in breach of contract

4 a   failing to exercise reasonable care
5 f   to compensate victims for damage (injuries or losses)
6 b   to vindicate the claimant's right

Consolidation Part VI

Task A – Which one word or phrase is out of context?

0   *guarantee*
1   natural persons
2   land
3   discharge by performance
4   warranty
5   rescission of contract
6   agreement
7   representations
8   limited liability

Task B – Match the terms with the definitions

1   agent
2   conditions
3   rescission
4   breach of warranty
5   warranty
6   representations
7   legal persons
8   discharge by express agreement
9   discharge by performance
10   discharge by frustration
11   contractual clauses
12   guarantee

Task C – Word formation

a)   *Fill in the spaces below with the appropriate word form*
1   adjective – enforceable
2   noun (concept) – jurisdiction
3   verb – to infer
4   adjective – intentional
5   noun (concept) – indemnification
6   noun (concept) – contract
7   adjective – disputed
8   noun (concept) – injunction

b) *Insert the appropriate word in the spaces below: verb, noun (concept), noun (person), or adjective*

9   noun (concept) – contracts
10 noun (concept) – dispute
11 verb – indemnify
12 noun (concept) – intention
13 noun (concept) – jurisdiction
14 verb – infers
15 verb – enforced; or adjective – enforceable

Task D – Prefixes and suffixes

1   impossibility (noun concept)
2   discharge (noun concept)
3   incompatible (adjective)
4   immoveable (adjective)
5   commencement (noun concept)
6   voidable (adjective)
7   intellectual (adjective)
8   enforceable/enforced (adjectives) enforcement (noun concept)
9   performance (noun concept)
10 transaction (noun concept)
11 defamation (noun concept)
12 rebuttable/rebutted (adjectives) rebuttal (noun concept)

Task E – Collocation

a)   *Verb–noun collocation*
1 f   to seek/to grant an injunction
2 c   to acquire or dispose of moveable/immoveable property
3 e   to enter into a contract
4 a   to frustrate by impossibility of performance
5 g   to determine the intention of the parties
6 d   to sue for damages
7 b   to uphold (to confirm) a decision

b)   *Words and expressions*
8 h   undertakes and agrees
9 i   conflict of interest
10 j   standard of best efforts/best endeavors
11 f   counteroffer
12 g   hereby appoints

Glossary of Grammar Terms

clause is a grammatical unit consisting of a group of words that include a subject and a verb. Sometimes the subject is an *implied* subject, for example, when the *–ing form* and participle *–ed* are used instead of a verb: *Reaffirming the principals of the original treaty ...* The implied subject would be the High Contracting Parties to this treaty.

dependent clause (DC) has a subject and verb, but it cannot exist on its own, e.g.: *When John studied law at Padua*. To complete the thought, the main independent clause is necessary, e.g.: *When John studied law at Padua* (DC), *he lived with his parents*. Dependent clauses are also called subordinating clauses.

independent clause (IC) is a group of words which include a subject and verb and express a complete thought. Every sentence must have at least one independent clause, e.g.: *John studied law at Padua.*

mandative subjunctive is often used in prescriptive legal texts when the main clause contains a strong recommendation or command. It is used in the subordinate *–that* clause without *to*, e.g.: The judge moved *that the court be adjourned* (which is more common in AmE). In BrE, the putative should + infinitive or the indicative are more common, e.g.: *The judge moved that the court should adjourn. The judge moved that the court adjourn.*

modal auxiliaries (*can*, *should*, *etc*) are used to modify the meaning of verbs. They combine with the base form of the main verb (without *to*), to express obligation (*should*), capacity/permission (*can*), necessity (*need/needn't*), advice/suggestion (*must*), prohibition (*mustn't*), and possibility/probability (*may, might*).

modifiers can change the meanings of a word, a phrase or a clause. Adjectives modify nouns and pronouns, while adverbs modify verbs, adjectives and other adverbs.

nominalisation is the process through which a verb is changed into a noun. For example, instead of writing *The contract obligated the two parties ...*, the verb *obligated* is transformed into the noun *obligation* to create this clause, e.g.; *The contract obligation between two parties ...* Nominalisation is a distinct feature of legal discourse.

non-finite *–ed* participle and non-finite *–ing* form in adverbial clauses occur in a subordinate clause and usually lack an explicit reference to time or person. When used in legal texts, they create the sense of an action continuing from the past to the present, e.g.: *Concerned about continuing violence*, a meeting was called.

non-restrictive or non-defining clauses contain words that add information about the preceding subject but do not restrict or limit the possibility of other interpretations (they are framed by commas), e.g.: My cousin, who is a judge, practises law in Boston. In this example, I may have more than one cousin who is a judge.

noun phrases Nouns can combine with other words to form noun phrases. Their main function is to add information to the main noun or subject. They may be placed in a pre- or post-modifying position (before or after the noun). An example of a post-modifying position: The jurors *in the year-long Old Bailey trial* heard of plans to target a shopping centre.

noun phrase (appositive) identifies the same person(s) or thing(s) in a sentence but with different names or words. Word(s) can be easily substituted for the others without changing the meaning, e.g.: The defendant, *a colleague of mine*, has been accused of murder. *or* A colleague of mine, *the defendant*, has been accused of murder.

phrase may be a single word or a group of words, and lacks the subject-predicate structure typical of clauses, e.g.: *Nevertheless*, he was convicted of homicide. *By the way*, the judge is my sister.

predicate consists of the verb and the sentence elements that follow it. A sentence (independent clause) contains a subject and a predicate, e.g.: The professor *walked into the classroom*.

restrictive or defining clauses limit the possible meaning of the preceding subject. If we removed the defining clause, other interpretations of the preceding subject are possible. In the following example, *which* judge is identified? The judge *who walked into the courtroom* is my cousin.

subordinating conjunctions join a dependent clause to an independent clause and express a relationship between the two clauses. Observe the following cause/effect relationship in a clause: *Because* I didn't study, I didn't pass the exam.

syntactic organisation is the grammatical organisation of words in a sentence or paragraph in order to create meaning. Rules of grammar govern this organisation.

verb phrase may be a single verb indicating the past or present tense, or more than one verb, plus its auxiliaries, e.g.: A court *may not substitute* its own reasoning for that of medical experts.

Glossary of Law Terms

KEY The following abbreviations are used:

abbrev = abbreviation	*adj = adjective*	*adv = adverb*
Cf = compare	*eg (exempli gratia) = for example*	*ex = in the past*
f = feminine	*ie (id est) = that is* *m = masculine*	*n = noun*
pl = plural	*prep = preposition* *sb= somebody*	*sing = singular*
sth = something	*usu = usually* *vb = verb*	

Action, *n* An action is a lawsuit, a proceeding in which a party sues for a right before a civil court. If you *take legal action* you proceed against *sb* in a court of law/ *an action in tort*

Act of Parliament, *n + prep + n* An Act of Parliament is a statute: a law enacted by the UK legislature, the Queen in Parliament; it is primary legislation, a principal source of law that has priority over other sources/ *the Constitutional Reform Act 2005*

Actus reus, *Latin n* The *actus reus* is the specific criminal act or conduct and consequences that are the ingredients of a particular crime/ *Actus reus and mens rea*

Arbitration, *n* Arbitration is a form of *alternative dispute resolution* (ADR) in which independent third parties, called **arbitrators**, are appointed by parties to determine a dispute, rather than taking court action/ *vb* **to arbitrate** *adj* **arbitral**/ *an arbitral award*/ *all over the world, arbitrators pronounce decisions in English*

Authentic text, *adj + n* An authentic text is one which is valid in a court of law for interpretation and application by the court/ *The UN Charter is written in five equally authentic texts: Chinese, Russian, English, French and Spanish*

Ban, *n* A ban on *sth* is a prohibition against doing it/ *the smoking ban*/ **to ban,** *vb* When *sth* is banned, it is prohibited by law or other rules; a person may *be banned from doing sth.*

Bill, *n* A Bill is a proposal of law presented to Parliament for discussion and approval. A Bill becomes an **Act** when it receives Royal Assent/ *to introduce a Bill*/ A **bill of rights** is a constitutional charter of human rights/ the **Bill of Rights 1689** is a historic source of the British constitution/ the first 10 Amendments to the US Constitution are known as the **Bill of Rights**

Binding, *adj* **to bind,** *vb* (*irregular:* **bind, bound, bound**) To place a person or entity under legal obligation; to place a court under legal obligation to follow a previous judicial decision (a precedent)/ *a contract is a legally binding agreement*/ *The Court of Appeal is bound to follow judgments of the Supreme Court of the United Kingdom*/ *'We are bound by the decision in Sturges v Bridgman'*/ *binding precedent*

Breach, *n* A breach is a violation of one's legal duty or of another person's rights / *gross breaches of human rights, in breach of a duty of care*

Breach of contract, *n + prep + n* indicates failure by one party to perform its obligations under a contract / *the innocent party took action for breach of contract* / *vb* **to break,** *(also, modern usage)* **to breach**

Case, *n* A legal action or trial; a set of legal circumstances; a precedent or judgment, collectively **case law.** *A case of first impression* presents new facts without a precedent; *a case of first instance* is the original trial in a proceeding, as opposed to an appeal; *the instant case* is the case now under consideration before the court, as opposed to a precedent

Cause of action, *n + prep + n* A cause of action is a factual situation that gives *sb* a right to obtain a remedy in a civil claim / *the only question in this case is whether, on the facts, the claimant has a cause of action*

Charge, *n*, **to charge,** *vb* A charge is a formal accusation of a crime, when a person *is charged*, he is formally accused of a crime / *the defendant was charged with murder* / *he pleaded not guilty to the charges*

Claim, *n* A claim is a demand for a remedy to a civil court; the claim is presented in a document called a **claim form,** *n + n* / *the plaintiff's claim is based on the tort of negligence, a claim for damages for personal injury* / *to make a claim*

Claimant, *n* The claimant (ex **plaintiff** in *English* terminology) is the party who takes legal action against another (the defendant) in civil proceedings / *the claimant sued the defendant for breach of contract*

Common law constitutional statutes A category of particularly important constitutional statutes having an impact on the British Constitution, given special treatment by the courts. *See* **doctrine of implied repeal** / *common law constitutional statutes are not subject to the doctrine of implied repeal*

Common law, *adj + n* The common law is the body of legal rules established in decided cases, created and developed by the English superior courts; a common law legal system is one based on this body of law. See also **judicial precedent** / *general principles of the common law* / *common law rights and remedies* are ones deriving from judicial precedent, as opposed to statute law (*statutory rights*); or, ones deriving from the common law courts as opposed to courts of **Equity** (*equitable rights and remedies*)

Consideration, *n* Consideration is a doctrine of English contract law—the price of the bargain: if a contract is not in a solemn written form (called a deed or specialty) consideration must be present, *ie* something given in return for the promise (an advantage to one party, or a disadvantage to the other), as the courts will not enforce a unilateral promise / *A simple contract cannot be formed without consideration*

Constitution, *n* **constitutional,** *adj* A country's constitution is the system of rules defining the composition, powers and relations of the state organs (the legislature, executive and judiciary); it also regulates relations between the state and individuals / *Britain has a constitution, but it is not embodied in a single written text* / *an unwritten constitution* / *the Constitution of the United States of America*

Constitutional convention, *adj* + *n* A constitutional convention is an obligation that is not imposed by a law or by judicial precedent: it is a recognised political practice, consolidated by usage and considered binding by all the actors in the British Constitution / *by convention the Queen must act on the advice of her ministers*

Contract, *n* A contract is a legally binding agreement between two or more parties. **Contract** or **contract law** is the branch of law regulating **contractual** relations / *The Douglases entered into a contract with OK! The remedy of damages is available in both tort and contract law*

Contractual, *adj* Relating to a contract / *contractual relations, clauses* / But, with *parties,* use: **contracting parties,** *adj* + *n* / *High Contracting Parties*

Convention, *n* A convention is a treaty; **Convention rights** are the rights in Section 1 of the European Convention on Human Rights incorporated into UK law by the Human Rights Act 1998. *Also see:* **constitutional convention** / *to sign, to ratify a convention* / *This Convention shall be open to the signature of the members of the Council of Europe*

Damage, *n (singular)* Damage indicates the loss (harm, injury) suffered as a consequence of a tort or breach of contract / *The primary function of the law of torts is to compensate victims for damage suffered*

Damages, *n (plural)* Damages are monetary compensation that a civil defendant is ordered to pay to the claimant as reparation for damage caused by a tort or breach of contract / *the claimant seeks damages for personal injury*

Defendant, *n* In criminal proceedings, the defendant is the person accused of a crime (also, **the accused**); in civil proceedings, legal action is taken by the claimant against the defendant to obtain a remedy / *the jury convicted the defendant of murder* / *the claimant sued the defendant for damages for breach of contract*

Discharge, *n* **to discharge,** *vb* Discharge of contract is the termination of the contractual obligation; a contract may be discharged in different ways: discharge by performance, by breach, by frustration, etc; in other contexts, **discharge** means release from an obligation (*eg* a debt, a criminal accusation) / *The accused are found not guilty and are discharged*

Doctrine of binding precedent, *n* + *prep* +*adj* + *n* The doctrine of binding precedent (*or,* of the binding case) expresses the fundamental principle in a common law legal system that courts must follow precedent, by applying the same rules in later, similar cases; also called *stare decisis.* See **hierarchy of the courts**

Doctrine of implied repeal, *n* + *prep* + *adj* + *n* The principle applied by the courts that a later law has priority over an earlier one in case of conflict / *common law constitutional statutes are not subject to the doctrine of implied repeal: they can be repealed only by express words*

Doctrine, *n* A basic principle of the legal system / *the doctrine of binding precedent* / *the doctrine of Parliamentary sovereignty*

Duly, *adv* as required / *duly authorised*

Duty, *n* A duty is an obligation to do *sth / the parties' rights and duties are established in the contract /* **duty of care,** an element of the the tort of negligence, a duty to take care not to harm others (my neighbours) by my careless conduct / *does the defendant owe a duty of care to the claimant?*

ECHR, *abbrev* The **European Convention on Human Rights,** full name European Convention for the Protection of Human Rights and Fundamental Freedoms, open for signature in Rome, 4 November 1950

ECtHR, *abbrev* The **European Court of Human Rights,** the Strasbourg Court

Enact, *vb* To enact law means to make law following a recognised legislative procedure / *Parliament enacts laws /* **the enacting words,** after the short and long titles of every Act of Parliament, are the formula indicating the legislative authority of the Queen in Parliament / **enactment,** *n.* an enactment is a piece of primary or subordinate legislation; also, the process of enacting law / **enacted law,** *adj +* *n* enacted law is a collective term for legislation

Enforce, *vb* To enforce means to apply or give effect to a law, rule, obligation, contract / **enforceable,** *adj,* **enforcement,** *n / directly enforceable rights / to enforce the Convention before the national courts / law enforcement*

Entitled, *vb, past participle* You are entitled to *sth* if you have a right to it / *Everyone is entitled to equality before the law / The judge held that the claimant was entitled to equal pay / to be entitled to sth*

Equity, *n* **equitable,** *adj* Equity is a special area of English law, first created by the Lord Chancellor and the Court of Chancery; it consists of rules and remedies that supplement the common law, when this is necessary for justice in a particular case / *equitable remedies are discretionary in nature / the trust is the greatest invention of Equity*

Evidence, *n* (*uncountable, always sing*) Evidence is everything that tends to prove the facts and is produced by parties in court proceedings / *on all the evidence, the accused were found not guilty / documentary evidence, real evidence, the witness gave oral evidence*

Fair trial, *sometimes,* **fair hearing** *adj + n.* The right to a fair trial in civil and criminal proceedings is a human right protected in Article 6 ECHR and includes the right to a **hearing** (*usu* in public) before an impartial tribunal, the right to present argument, evidence and witnesses in one's defence, etc / *can a black man have a fair trial in a white man's court?*

Finding, *n* **to find,** *vb* A finding is a conclusion, a determination of fact or law arrived at by a judge or jury during the decision-making process / *findings of fact, the judge found that the defendant did not intend to … the accused are found not guilty and are discharged*

Follow, to, *vb* In the common law system, a court **follows precedent** when it applies the same principle decided in a previous **case** to the case before it; specifically, it applies the same *ratio decidendi / the High Court is bound to follow decisions of the Court of Appeal*

Franchise, *n* The franchise is the right to vote, suffrage / *British women were granted the franchise in 1918*

Freedom of speech, *n + prep + n* Freedom of speech (*or,* **Freedom of expression**) is one of the fundamental freedoms of the person, a human right: the right to express one's thoughts and opinions freely without unjustified interference / *the Bill of Rights guarantees freedom of speech in Parliament*

Grievous bodily harm, *adj + adj + n* Grievous bodily harm is really serious physical injury and is an element of some crimes / *intention to kill or to cause grievous bodily harm*

Guilty, *adj* opposite, **not guilty** / A person is **guilty** of a crime if he has committed it / *guilty mind, the accused pleaded not guilty, the defendant was found guilty of murder and sentenced to life imprisonment* / **guilt,** *n* / *to establish guilt*

Hearing, *n* **to hear,** *vb* A hearing is a trial; a hearing is an occasion on which a case is examined before a court, tribunal, etc / *judgment was pronounced at the end of the hearings / the Crown Court only hears criminal cases*

Hierarchy of the courts, *n + prep + art + pl n* **hierarchical,** *adj.* The strict hierarchy of the courts in a common law legal system is necessary for the operation of *stare decisis*: a superior court in the hierarchy binds every inferior court and is (generally) bound to follow its own previous decisions / *The Supreme Court of the United Kingdom is at the top of the hierarchy / the hierarchical structure of the courts*

Human rights, *adj +n (pl)* Human rights are rights and freedoms which every human being has a right to enjoy; they may be protected at national and international level / *fundamental human rights, protection of human rights / freedom of expression may be considered the most basic human right / the European Convention on Human Rights: ECHR*

Illegal, *adj* opposite of **legal,** it is illegal to do something that is against the law; criminal / *illegal conduct* / *adv* **illegally** *the two men were illegally hunting with dogs*

Implementation, *n* **to implement,** *vb* Generally: giving effect to (*n*) to give effect to (*vb*) / *The Government must be able to implement its policies through legislation enacted by Parliament* / In EU law: Giving effect to a European directive in the national legal system by enacting legislation. / *The directive must be implemented by January 2015, implementing legislation or measures*

Injunction, *n* An injunction is an equitable remedy: a court order to a party to do or not to do certain specified acts. It is a **remedy** available in private law (tort and contract) / *to grant an injunction*

Injured party, *adj + n* The injured party is the person who suffers damage when a tort, such as negligence, is committed / *the injured party sued the tortfeasor for damages for loss and injury*

Issue, *n* The issue in a case is the legal question that the court must resolve in order to decide the dispute. There may be more than one issue before the court / *the issue in this appeal is whether the defendant owed a duty of care to the claimant*

Judge, *n* A judge is a state official with power to examine and decide disputes in legal proceedings, a member of the **judiciary** / *In the adversarial system the judge is an independent umpire who decides which of the two contesting parties will win*

Judgment, *n* The judgment is the legal reasoning and decision of a court in a case brought before it; the full text of judgments are published in the law reports / *the court pronounced judgment* / *judgment for the defendant* or *for the claimant* / *judgments of superior courts are binding as precedents* / Note this preferred legal spelling

Judicial organisation *or* **order** *or* **system,** *adj + n* Alternative names for the structure of courts in a jurisdiction / *Judicial organisation in England and Wales: the hierarchy and jurisdiction of the courts*

Judicial precedent, *adj + n* Judicial precedent is the body of legal rules established in decided cases, created and developed by the English superior courts: also called common law, case law. A judicial precedent is a single decision that may be binding or persuasive in later, similar cases / *a binding precedent must be followed; a persuasive precedent will influence later courts* / *judicial precedent is a primary source of English law*

Judicial, *adj* Relating to judges or to the activity of the courts / *judicial precedent, a judicial decision, the judicial function*

Judiciary, *n* The judiciary is one of the three state powers, together with the legislature and the executive: it is the collective term for all **judges** / *the independence of the judiciary*

Jurisdiction, *n* The jurisdiction of a court is its power to hear and decide cases; in international law the jurisdiction of a state is the territory over which it exercises authority / *the Court of Appeal has both civil and criminal jurisdiction* / *a State Party to the ECHR must guarantee Convention rights to everyone within its jurisdiction*

Justice, *Uncountable n* Justice is the moral and legal ideal of being right, just / *I never expected justice in court* / **Justice,** *Countable n.* A Justice is a judge / *the Justices of the Supreme Court*

Land, *n* Land is one of the two major classes of property (also called *real property, immoveable property*) consisting in the part of the earth's surface which it is possible to own, including the air above, soil below, trees, buildings etc. *Cf* the other class of property, *goods* (also called *personal property, chattels*) / *land law: the law relating to real property*

Lawful, *adj* If *sth* is lawful, it is permitted by criminal or civil law, not **unlawful** (*opposite*) / *the law of homicide punishes unlawful killing* / *adv.* **lawfully,** *opposite,* **unlawfully**

Law reports, *n + pl n* The law reports are published volumes containing collections of cases: the texts of judgments are reproduced verbatim in full and may be cited as a legal source / *the All England Law Reports*

Lay down, *transitive vb* (**lay, laid, laid**) To provide, to establish by *law*, treaty or judicial decision / *The Vienna Convention on the Law of Treaties lays down rules on the interpretation of treaties*

Legal, *adj* Relating to law, within the law; if *sth* is legal, it is permitted by criminal law; opposite **illegal** / *the English legal system* / **Legality:** the quality or state of being legal, *opposite* **illegality**

Legislation, *n* Legislation is law created by formal enactment, written law, a primary source in the English legal system / *Legislation has priority over judicial precedent in case of conflict* / **to legislate,** *vb* / *Parliament may legislate to create new law or to change pre-existing law* / **legislative,** *adj* / *there is no special legislative procedure for constitutional statutes*

Legislature, *n* The legislature is the body with power to make law in a legal system, it is one of the three state organs: the legislature, the executive, and the judiciary / *The function of the legislature is to enact law*

Liability, *n* **liable,** *adj* Responsibility in law: liability is legal responsibility for one's actions; in civil law it includes an obligation to repair any injury caused / *civil liability* / *criminal liability*

Litigant, *n* A litigant is a party to a legal dispute, one of the sides involved in **litigation,** *n.* Litigation is the process of settling a dispute by court action / *a litigation lawyer*

Malice aforethought, *n + adj* Malice aforethought is the mental element in the crime of murder, consisting of an intention to kill or to cause grievous bodily harm / *the defendant killed with malice aforethought*

Mens rea, *Latin, n* Mens rea, sometimes called **guilty mind,** is the mental element required to commit a particular crime; the *mens rea* for murder is malice aforethought / *Actus reus and mens rea* / *the defendant did not have the necessary mens rea*

Murder, *n* **to murder,** *vb* Murder is the most serious form of unlawful homicide: the crime of killing a person with the intention to kill or cause grievous bodily harm. A person who commits murder is a **murderer** (*m*) or **murderess** (*f*) / *A person convicted of murder must be sentenced to life imprisonment* / *to commit murder* / *the murderer confessed*

Obiter dictum, *Latin, adv + n* Something said 'by the way'; a statement of law made by the judge that was not necessary to resolve the legal question in the case (not the **ratio decidendi**); statements made **obiter** (*used adverbially*) are not part of binding precedent, but may be persuasive. Often abbreviated to **dicta.** Plural, **obiter dicta.** *Cf judicial dicta,* carefully considered pronouncements that are not part of the *ratio*

Offence, *n* An offence is a crime; an **offender** (*n*) is a person who commits an offence / *to commit an offence* / *he was charged with two offences under the Act*

Party, *n* **parties,** *n pl* A party is one of the sides taking part in a legal transaction, such as a contract (*a contracting party*) or a treaty (*a High Contracting Party*); each of the sides involved in a legal dispute is *a party to the case*; a person or entity outside a certain transaction is *a third party*; in politics and government, *a political party* is an organised group representing specific interests and policies, and seeking election

Plaintiff, *n See* **claimant**

Pleadings, *n pl,* **to plead,** *vb* The pleadings (now called *statements of case* in English civil procedure) are oral and written representations made to the court by each party / **to plead guilty** or **not guilty:** to declare at the start of a criminal trial that you have or have not committed the crime accused of / *the defendant pleaded not guilty*

Precedent, *n See* **Judicial precedent, doctrine of binding precedent**

Presumption, *n* **to presume,** *vb* A presumption is a legal supposition, significant in the law of evidence, *eg* the **presumption of innocence**: it is presumed that an accused person is innocent until proved guilty according to law; a **rebuttable presumption** can be disproved by producing evidence to the contrary, an **irrebuttable presumption** cannot be disproved

Primary legislation, *adj + n* In UK law, primary legislation is statute law, Acts of Parliament; in EU law, the Treaties are classified as primary legislation

Provide *vb* To provide + for/that means to regulate by law, to establish a legal **provision** or rule / *the Scotland Act 1998 provides for changes in the constitution*

Provision, *n* A provision is a rule or condition in a statute, contract etc / *the provisions of a law, of a contract / An Act to make provision about terrorism / Under the provisions of the agreement*

Ratification, *n* **to ratify,** *vb* Ratification is the internal constitutional procedure by which a state assumes an international treaty obligation; in national law, confirmation of an act, such as an unauthorised transaction by an agent / *instruments of ratification, to ratify a treaty*

Ratio decidendi, *Latin, n + vb* The *ratio decidendi* is the principle on which a judicial decision is based; the part of a judicial decision that is binding as a precedent in later, similar cases: the reason, or grounds, on which the judge based his decision on the legal question before the court. Often abbreviated to *ratio*. Plural, ***rationes decidendi,*** or ***ratios***

Remedy, *n* A remedy is a means such as **damages**, which the law provides to compensate, repair or prevent a civil wrong / *remedies in tort and contract / an Equitable remedy / a civil claimant seeks a remedy*

Repeal, *n* **to repeal,** *vb* Repeal is the annulment or cancellation of an earlier law or provision by a later law. Repeal may be express or implied. *See* **doctrine of implied repeal** / *According to the doctrine of implied repeal a later law has priority over an earlier law in case of conflict* / When a law or provision is repealed, it is abrogated or cancelled by a later law

Royal Assent, *adj + n* The Royal Assent is the final step in the UK legislative procedure; it indicates the formal assent (agreement) of the British monarch to a proposal of law: the Royal Assent transforms a bill into an Act / *Acts generally come into force on the day of Royal Assent*

Royal Prerogative, *adj + n* The Royal Prerogative is a collective term for the various rights and powers that the king or queen still has at a particular point in history / *Prerogative rights / in the exercise of the Royal Prerogative*

Rule of law, *n + prep + n* A fundamental principle of governance in democratic societies, based on legality: officials must act on a legal basis; justice: the law must be fair and just; *equality*: everyone is equal before the law / *The EU is founded on the principles of liberty, democracy, respect for human rights, and the rule of law*

Schedule, *n* A schedule is an appendix or annex attached to an Act or other legal text, giving important details not included in the main body of the text, which are supplementary to it / *Schedule 5 to the Scotland Act 1998 lists Reserved matters outside the Scottish Parliament's legislative competence*

Secondary legislation, *adj* + *n* In UK law, secondary legislation is **delegated legislation** enacted under the authority delegated by Parliament; in EU law, *EU acts* including regulations and directives are classified as secondary legislation

Sentence, *n* **to sentence,** *vb* The sentence is the judgment of a criminal court stating what punishment is to be given to a convicted criminal / *the judge pronounced sentence / he was sentenced to life imprisonment / the death sentence / he appealed against sentence*

Service, *n* **to serve,** *vb* Service indicates notification to parties in civil actions of steps in court proceedings; a document is served on a party when it is officially notified / *Service on a party abroad is* **service out of the jurisdiction** *of the English High Court*

Source, *n* A source of law gives origin to valid legal rules in a particular legal system / *legislation and judicial precedent are the primary sources of English law / the sources of international law include treaty law and custom*

Specific performance, *adj* + *n* Specific performance is an equitable remedy: it is a court order to a contracting party to perform his/her contractual obligations / *To grant a decree of specific performance*

Stare decisis, *Latin, vb* + *n* This Latin phrase (*lit* to stand by things decided) expresses the **doctrine of binding precedent,** the principle in common law legal systems that judicial precedent operates as a primary source of law and must be followed in later, similar cases / *the doctrine of stare decisis*

Statute, *n* A statute is a law, *ie* a piece of primary **legislation,** an **Act of Parliament** / **statute law,** *n* + *n* Statute law (sometimes **statute**) is a collective term for legislation, Acts of Parliament / *statute is not 'code', statutes are a major source of the modern British Constitution* / See **Common law constitutional statutes**

Sue, *vb* To sue means to take legal action against *sb* in a civil proceeding / *the passenger sued the railway company for damages*

Suffrage, *n* Suffrage is the right to vote, the franchise / *In the UK, women's suffrage was finally introduced at the end of the First World War / Members of the European Parliament are elected by universal adult suffrage*

TEU, *abbrev* The **Treaty on European Union,** also known as the **Treaty of Maastricht.** It established the European Union in 1992

TFEU, *abbrev* The **Treaty on the Functioning of the European Union,** also known as the **Treaty of Rome.** Before the *Treaty of Lisbon,* it was called the Treaty establishing the European Community; originally, the Treaty establishing the European Economic Community

Theft *n* Theft is the crime of stealing; a person who commits theft is a **thief** (*pl* **thieves**) / *the law of theft is regulated by the Theft Act 1968 / the thieves escaped in a getaway car*

Tort *n* A tort is a civil wrong consisting in the breach of a legal duty that causes damage to another; the common law has developed different categories of tort to protect a variety of interests, such as physical integrity, reputation, enjoyment of property, etc: these correspond to different actions in tort / *law of torts, tort of negligence, trespass, nuisance / tort law primarily has the function of compensating injuries or losses*

Tortfeasor, *n* A tortfeasor is a person who has committed a **tort**, such as negligence, causing damage to the injured party / *the tortfeasor's liability*

Tortious, *adj* Relating to tort / *a tortious act or omission*

Treaty, *n* A treaty is an international agreement concluded in writing between two or more states or international organisations; **treaty law,** the law contained in treaties, is a binding source of international law; in the European Union legal order, **the Treaties** are primary legislation / *NATO—North Atlantic Treaty Organisation* / *to ratify a treaty* / *the signatories to a treaty* / *TEU—the Treaty on European Union* / The parties may name their treaty a *pact, alliance, convention, accord, charter, protocol* / *the Charter of the United Nations, the Kyoto Protocol*

Trial, *n* **to try,** *vb* A trial is the process of examining and deciding a civil or criminal case before a court, the judicial examination of a case to determine all questions of law or fact / *The trial took place at the Central Criminal Court* / *Everyone has the right to a **fair trial*** / *to hold a trial* / *to be on trial*

Trust, *n* A trust is a form of property arrangement created in Equity where the *settlor* transfers property to a legal owner (the **trustee(s)**) which he/they must administer for the benefit of one or more *beneficiaries* according to the terms of the trust / *the trust property* / *she set up a trust to provide for her children after her death* / *the trustees hold property on trust for the beneficiaries*

Will, *n* A will is a legal document where a person disposes of his or her property after death / *This is my last will and testament* / *Shakespeare left a bequest of money to his daughter in his will*

Bibliography

A Dictionary of Latin Words and Phrases (1998), Morwood, J (ed), Oxford: Oxford University Press.

A Dictionary of Law, 7th edn (2009, updated reissue 2013). Martin, E and Law, J (eds), Oxford: Oxford University Press.

A Dictionary of Linguistics and Phonetics, 3rd edn (1992), Crystal, D, Oxford: Blackwell.

A Dictionary of Modern Legal Usage, 2nd edn (1995), Garner, BA, New York, NY: Oxford University Press.

All England Law Reports. A User's Guide (1983), London: Butterworths.

Alpa, G (2004), 'Lineamenti di diritto contrattuale' in Alpa, G, Bonell, MJ, Corapi, D, Moccia, L, Zeno-Zencovich, V and Zoppini, A, *Diritto privato comparato Istituti e problemi*, 5th edn October 2004 (from p 147), Roma-Bari: Laterza.

Ashworth, A (2009), *Principles of Criminal Law*, 6th edn, Oxford: Oxford University Press.

Ashworth, A and Horder, J (2013), *Principles of Criminal Law*, 7th edn, Oxford: Oxford University Press.

Barron's Law Dictionary, 3rd edn (1991), Gifis, SH, New York: Barron's Educational Series.

Beatson, J (2001), 'The Role of Statute in the Development of Common Law Doctrine' in 117 *The Law Quarterly Review,* 247.

Berg, AGJ (1991), *Drafting Commercial Agreements*, London: Butterworths.

Bhatia, VK (1983a), *An Applied Discourse Analysis of English Legislative Writing*, Birmingham: University of Aston.

Bhatia, VK (1993), 'Legal Discourse in Professional Settings' in *Analyzing Genre*, London: Longman.

Biber, D, Conrad, S and Leech, G (2002), *Longman Student Grammar of Spoken and Written English*, Harlow: Pearson Education Limited.

Bingham, T (2000), *The Business of Judging. Selected Essays and Speeches 1985–1999*, Oxford: Oxford University Press.

Bingham, T (2010), *The Rule of Law*, London: Penguin Books.

Black's Law Dictionary, 5th edn (1979), St Paul, Minn: West Publishing Co.

Black's Law Dictionary Pocket edition (1996), Garner, BA (ed), St Paul, Minn: West Publishing Co.

Blackstone's Civil Practice 2006, Oxford: Oxford University Press.

Borg, S (ed) (2006), *Language Teacher Research in Europe*, Alexandria, VI: TESOL.

Brayne, H and Grimes, R (1994), *Professional Skills for Lawyers. A Student's Guide*, London: Butterworths.

Brazier, M and Murphy, J (1999), *The Law of Torts*, 10th edn, London: Butterworths.

Brazier, R (1999), 'The Constitution of the United Kingdom' (1999) 58(1) *Cambridge Law Journal* 96.

Browne-Wilkinson, Baron (1998), 'The Impact on Judicial Reasoning' in Markesinis, BS (ed), *The Impact of the Human Rights Bill on English Law. The Clifford Chance Lectures, vol 3*, Oxford: Oxford University Press.

Brownlie, I (2003), *Principles of Public International Law*, 6th edn, Oxford: Oxford University Press.

Chalker, S and Weiner, E (1994, 1998 reissue), *The Oxford Dictionary of English Grammar*, Oxford: Oxford University Press.

Chaucer, G (c 1387–92), *The Canterbury Tales*, General Prologue, in Robinson, F (ed), *The Complete Works of Geoffrey Chaucer*, 2nd edn (1974), Oxford: Oxford University Press.

Cownie, F, Bradney, A and Burton, M (2013), *English Legal System in Context*, 6th edn, Oxford: Oxford University Press.

Cross, R and Harris, JW (1991), *Precedent in English Law*, 4th edn, Oxford: Clarendon Press.

Cross, R (1977), *Precedent in English Law*, 3rd edn, Oxford: Clarendon Press.

Crystal, D (1995), *The Cambridge Encyclopedia of the English Language.* Cambridge: Cambridge University Press.

Crystal, D and Davy, D (1969), 'The Language of Legal Documents' in *Investigating English Style*, Harlow: Longman.

Deakin, S, Johnston, A and Markesinis, BS (2003), *Markesinis and Deakin's Tort Law*, 5th edn, Oxford: Clarendon Press.

Denning, A, Baron (1979), *The Discipline of Law.* London: Butterworths.

Denning A, Baron (1982), 'Misuse of power' (The Richard Dimbleby Lecture 1980) in *What Next in the Law*, Virginia: Lexis Law Publishing.

Denning, A, Baron (1984), *Landmarks in the Law*, London: Butterworths.

Dizionario giuridico, Vol 1 Inglese–Italiano (1984), de Franchis, F, Milano: Giuffrè Editore.

Dictionary of Linguistics and Phonetics (1992), Oxford: Blackwell

Elsmore, MJ and Starup, P (2007), 'Union Citizenship—Background, Jurisprudence, and Perspective: The Past, Present, and Future of Law and Policy' in (2007) 26 *Yearbook of European Law* 57.

European Commission (2004), *Many tongues, one family*, Luxembourg: Office for Official Publications of the European Communities.

Farnsworth, EA (2010), *An Introduction to the Legal System of the United States*, 4th edn (ed S Sheppard), New York: Oxford University Press, Inc.

Farnsworth, EA (1996), *An Introduction to the Legal System of the United States*, 3rd edn, New York: Oceana Publications, Inc.

Fleming, J (1998), *The Law of Torts*, 9th edn, North Ryde, NSW: LBC.

Fletcher, GP and Sheppard, S (2005), *American Law in a Global Context*, Oxford: Oxford University Press.

Fontaine, P (2010), *Europe in 12 lessons*, Luxembourg: Office for Official Publications of the European Communities.

Gardiner, J (ed) (2000), *Who's Who in British History*, London: Collins and Brown.

Garner, BA (2001), *Legal Writing in Plain English*, Chicago, Ill: The University of Chicago Press.

Garner, BA (2009), *Garner's Modern American Usage,* 3rd edn, New York: Oxford University Press.

Gomien, D (2005), *Short Guide to the European Convention on Human Rights*, 3rd edn, Strasbourg: Cedex Council of Europe Publishing.

Greenbaum, S and Quirk, R (1990), *A Student's Grammar of the English Language*, Harlow: Longman.

Greenbaum, S, Leech G, Quirk, R and Svartvik, J (1972), *A Grammar of Contemporary English*, London: Longman.

Haigh, R (2004), *Legal English*, London: Cavendish Publishing Ltd.

Halsbury's Laws of England, 4th edn (1979), Lord Hailsham of St Marylebone (ed), London: Butterworths.

Harlow, C (1987), *Understanding Tort Law*. London: Fontana Press.

Hartley, TC (2004), *European Union Law in a Global Context. Text, Cases and Materials*, Cambridge: Cambridge University Press.

Hegland, K (1983), *Introduction to the Study and Practice of Law*, St Paul, Minn: West Publishing Co.

Higgins, R (1987), 'United Kingdom' in Jacobs, FG and Roberts, S (eds), *The Effect of Treaties in Domestic Law*, London: Sweet & Maxwell.

Hoey, Michael (2000), 'A world beyond collocation: new perspectives on vocabulary teaching' in Lewis, M (ed), *Teaching Collocation. Further developments in the Lexical Approach*, Hove: Language Teaching Publications.

House of Commons Research Paper. Criminal Law (Amendment) (Householder Protection) Bill, Bill 20 of 2004–05, United Kingdom: House of Commons.

Jacobs, FG and Roberts, S (eds) (1987), *The Effect of Treaties in Domestic Law*, London: Sweet & Maxwell.

James, P (1985), *Introduction to English Law*, 11th edn, London: Butterworths.

Kafka, F (1925), *The Trial* (English trans first published Picador 1977), London: Pan Books Ltd.

Krapp, GP (1962), *A Comprehensive Guide to Good English*, New York: Ungar.

Lewis, M (2000), 'Language in the lexical approach; Learning in the lexical approach; Materials and resources for teaching collocation' in Lewis, M (ed), *Teaching Collocation. Further developments in the Lexical Approach* Hove: Language Teaching Publications, pp 126–54; 155–85; 186–204.

Lewis, M (2002), *The Lexical Approach. The State of ELT and a Way Forward*, Boston, Mass: Thomson Heinle.

Leyland, P (2007), *The Constitution of the United Kingdom. A Contextual Analysis*, Oxford: Hart Publishing.

Leyland, P (2012), *The Constitution of the United Kingdom. A Contextual Analysis*, 2nd edn, Oxford: Hart Publishing.

Leyland, P and Anthony, G (2009), *Textbook on Administrative Law*, 6th edn, Oxford: Oxford University Press.

Leyland, P and Anthony, G (2012), *Textbook on Administrative Law*, 7th edn, Oxford: Oxford University Press.

Loveland, I (1999), 'Incorporating the European Convention on Human Rights into UK Law' (1999) 52 *Parliamentary Affairs* 113.

Lunney, M and Oliphant, K (2000), *Tort Law Text and Materials*, Oxford: Oxford University Press.

MacCormick, N (1978), *Legal Reasoning and Legal Theory*, Oxford: Clarendon Press.

Macmillan English Dictionary for Advanced Learners (2002), Oxford: Macmillan Education.

Mandela, NR (1994), *Long Walk to Freedom* (1995 Abacus edn), London: Little, Brown and Company.

Markesinis, BS (ed) (1998), *The Impact of the Human Rights Bill on English Law. The Clifford Chance Lectures, Vol 3*, Oxford: Oxford University Press.

Marshall, G (1998), 'On Constitutional Theory' in Markesinis, BS (ed), *The Impact of the Human Rights Bill on English Law. The Clifford Chance Lectures, Vol 3*, Oxford: Oxford University Press.

McKendrick, E (2005), *Contract Law. Text, Cases and Materials*, 2nd edn, Oxford: Oxford University Press.

McKendrick, E (2012), *Contract Law. Text, Cases and Materials*, 5th edn, Oxford: Oxford University Press.

Mellinkoff, D (1963), *The Language of the Law*, Boston and Toronto: Little, Brown and Company.

Millett, P (ed), (1993 reissue), *The Encyclopaedia of Forms and Precedents*, 5th edn, London: Butterworths.

Morgan, K (1984), *The Oxford Illustrated History of Britain*, Oxford: Oxford University Press.

Osborn's Concise Law Dictionary, 12th edn (2013), Woodley, M (ed), London: Sweet & Maxwell.

Oxford Latin Dictionary (1982, reprinted 2002), Glare, PGW (ed), Oxford: Oxford University Press

Pennycook, A (1994), *The Cultural Politics of English as an International Language*, Harlow: Pearson Education Limited.

Poole, J (2006), *Casebook on Contract Law*, 8th edn, Oxford: Oxford University Press.

Pugh, M (1987), 'Legal Aspects of the Rainbow Warrior Affair' (1987) 36 *International and Comparative Law Quarterly* 655.

Raimes, A (1990), *How English Works: A Grammar Handbook with Readings*. New York, NY: St Martin's Press, Inc.

Riley, A (1991), *English for Law*, Harlow: Longman (Pearson Education Ltd).

Riley, A (1996), 'The Meaning of Words in English Legal Texts: Mastering the Vocabulary of the Law—A Legal Task' in (1996) 30 *The Law Teacher* 68.

Riley, A and Scarpa F (1999), 'La Traduzione della sentenza di common law in italiano' in Scarpa, F (a cura di), *Traduzione, Società e Cultura* n 9, p 3, Trieste: Edizioni Università di Trieste.

Riley, A and Scarpa F (2000), 'La Fisionomia della Sentenza in Inghilterra e in Italia: un'analisi orientata alla traduzione' in Schena, L and Snel Trampus, D (a cura di), *Traduttori e giuristi a confronto. Interpretazione traducente e comparazione del discorso giuridico*, Bologna: CLUEB.

Riley, A and Sours, P (2006), 'Sharing a journey towards success: the impact of collaborative study groups and CALL in a legal context' in Borg, S (ed), *Language Teacher Research in Europe*, Alexandria, VI: TESOL.

Riley, A and Sours, P (2012), *Legal English and the Common Law With Legal Grammar Handbook*, 2nd edn, Padua: Cedam.

Robinson, F (ed) (1974), *The Complete Works of Geoffrey Chaucer*, 2nd edn, Oxford: Oxford University Press.

Rogers, WVH (2006), *Winfield and Jolowicz on Tort*, 17th edn, London: Sweet & Maxwell.

Russell, F and Locke C (1993), *English Law and Language*, Hemel Hempstead: Prentice Hall International (UK) Ltd.

Salmond, J (1947), *Jurisprudence*, 10th edn by Williams, G, London: Sweet & Maxwell.

Scarpa, F (a cura di) (1999), *Traduzione, Società e Cultura* n 9, Trieste: Edizioni Università di Trieste.

Scarpa, F and Riley, A (2000), 'La fisionomia della sentenza in Inghilterra e in Italia: un'analisi orientata alla traduzione' in Schena L and Snel Trampus RD (a cura di), *Traduttori e giuristi a confronto*, Bologna: CLUEB.

Schena, L and Snel Trampus, D (eds) (2000), *Traduttori e giuristi a confronto. Interpretazione traducente e comparazione del discorso giuridico*, Bologna: CLUEB.

Shakespeare, W *The Merchant of Venice*.

Shakspeare, W [*usu* Shakespeare] (no date), *The Works of William Shakspeare*, London and New York: Frederick Warne & Co.

Sharma, R and Yuhong, Z (2003), 'Introduction to the legal system of the People's Republic of China' in Bhatia, VK, Candlin, CN, Engberg, J and Trosberg, A (eds), *Multilingual and Multicultural Contexts of Legislation: An International Perspective*, Frankfurt: Peter Lang.

Simmons KR (1976), *International Encyclopedia of Comparative Law: National Reports: the UK*, under the auspices of the International Association of Legal Science, V Knapp (chief editor), The Hague: Mouton.

Simpson, AWB (1996), *Leading Cases in the Common Law*, Oxford: Clarendon Press.

Steyn, J (2001), '*Pepper v Hart*: A Re-examination' (2001) 21(1) *Oxford Journal of Legal Studies* 59.

Swales, JM (1990), *Genre Analysis*, Cambridge: Cambridge University Press.

Swales, JM (1981) 3 'Definitions in science and law—evidence for subject-specific course components?' in *Fachsprache* 106.

The Chambers Dictionary (1993), Edinburgh: Chambers Harrap Publisher Ltd.

The Holy Bible (1611), Authorized Version (King James).

The Holy Bible (1998), New International Version.

The New Oxford Dictionary of English (1998), Pearsall, J (ed), Oxford: Clarendon Press.

Treitel, G (1999), *The Law of Contract*, 10th edn, London: Sweet & Maxwell.

Understanding the Corporate Manslaughter and Corporate Homicide Act 2007, UK Ministry of Justice document (October 2007).

Walker, DM (1980), *The Oxford Companion to Law*, Oxford: Clarendon Press.

Wilberforce, Baron (1988), 'Intervento alla Tavola rotonda dei Presidenti delle Corti Supremi' in *La sentenza in Europa. Metodo, tecnica e stile*, Padua: CEDAM, pp 360–65, 600–05.

Wilde, O, 'The Ballad of Reading Gaol' in (1973) *De Profundis and Other Writings*, Harmondsworth: Penguin Books Ltd.

Williams, C (2004), 1 'Legal English and Plain Language: An Introduction' in (2004) 1 *ESP Across Cultures* 111.

Williams, C (2007), *Tradition and Change in Legal English: Verbal Constructions in Prescriptive Texts*, Bern: Peter Lang.

Willis, D (2003), *Rules, Patterns and Words: Grammar and Lexis in English Language Teaching*, Cambridge: Cambridge University Press.

Wydick, RC (1998), *Plain English for Lawyers*, 4th edn, Durham, NC: Carolina Academic Press.

Zander, M (1999), *Cases and Materials on the English Legal System*, 8th edn, London: Butterworths.

Zeno-Zencovich, V (2004), 'La responsabilità civile' in Alpa, G, Bonell, MJ, Corapi, D, Moccia, L, Zeno-Zencovich, V and Zoppini, A, *Diritto privato comparato Istituti e problemi*, 5th edn enlarged Oct 2004, Roma-Bari: Laterza.

Zweigert, K and Kötz, H (1998), *An Introduction to Comparative Law*, 3rd edn (tr Weir, T), Oxford: Clarendon Press.

Index